D1288132

Emergency Medicine Risk Management

A COMPREHENSIVE REVIEW

SECOND EDITION

Gregory L. Henry, MD, FACEP, Editor-in-Chief

Daniel J. Sullivan, MD, JD, FACEP, Associate Editor

 American College of
Emergency Physicians®

About the Editors

Gregory L. Henry, MD, FACEP, *Editor-in-Chief*

 Greg Henry has been a practicing emergency physician for more than 20 years and is the Immediate Past President of the American College of Emergency Physicians. Currently, he is Chief Executive Officer of Medical Practice Risk Assessment, Inc., in Ann Arbor, Michigan, and Chief of the Department of Emergency Medicine at Oakwood Hospital, Beyer Center, in Ypsilanti. Dr. Henry is a Clinical Professor in the Section of Emergency Services, Department of Surgery, at the University of Michigan Medical School, and President of American Physicians Assurance Society, Ltd., Bridgetown, Barbados, West Indies.

Dr. Henry is a 1973 graduate of the University of Michigan Medical School. He did residency training in neurology at Mary Hitchcock Hospital, Dartmouth Medical School. Among his academic appointments are faculty positions in the emergency medicine residency program at St. Joseph Mercy Hospital/University of Michigan and the emergency medicine rotation of the family practice residency at the University of Michigan.

In the past 10 years, Dr. Henry has conducted more than 1,500 medical-legal and risk management consultations for emergency physicians. He is a peer reviewer/consultant to *JAMA*, *Annals of Emergency Medicine*, and the *Journal of Academic Emergency Medicine*, and a member of the editorial advisory boards for *Emergency Medicine* magazine and *Emergency Department Management*. Dr. Henry has presented more than 500 lectures and continuing medical education sessions covering a broad range of topics in emergency medicine, and is the author of numerous articles and book chapters.

Dr. Henry and his wife, Margene, live in Ann Arbor. They have three children, Chris, Sara, and Allison.

Daniel J. Sullivan, MD, JD, FACEP, *Associate Editor*

 Dan Sullivan is President of Midwest Emergency Associates in Oak Brook, Illinois, and Chairman of the Department of Emergency Medicine at Ingalls Memorial Hospital in Harvey, Illinois. He also is Assistant Professor of Emergency Medicine and an attending physician at Cook County Hospital/Rush Medical College, Chicago, and Immediate Past President of the Illinois College of Emergency Physicians.

A graduate of Rush Medical College, Dr. Sullivan performed an internship in internal medicine with additional residency training in pediatrics and surgery at Cook County Hospital. He has practiced emergency medicine for more than 15 years and, in 1987, received his Juris Doctorate degree from IIT Chicago Kent College of Law.

Dr. Sullivan is the author of *The Yearbook of Law and Emergency Medicine*, now in its second edition, and the co-author of ACEP's *Before You Sign: Contract Basics for the Emergency Physician*. He is Executive Editor of *Emergency Department Legal Letter* and has written on a variety of emergency medicine and risk management topics. In 1997, Dr. Sullivan was recognized by the Newsletter Publishers Association with a first place award in the category of Best Single Topic Health Newsletter.

Dr. Sullivan lives in Oak Brook, Illinois, with his wife, Andria, and their children Stassia, Gia, and Mari.

About the Authors

Hugh M. Barton, JD

Mr. Barton is Assistant General Counsel for the Texas Medical Association. (Mr. Barton's views as expressed herein do not necessarily represent the positions of the Texas Medical Association.)

Robert A. Bitterman, MD, JD, FACEP

Dr. Bitterman is Director of Risk Management and Managed Care in the Department of Emergency Medicine at Carolinas Medical Center, Charlotte, North Carolina, and Clinical Assistant Professor of Emergency Medicine at the University of North Carolina Medical School, Chapel Hill.

Brooks F. Bock, MD, FACEP

Dr. Bock is Dayanandan Professor and Chair of the Department of Emergency Medicine at Wayne State University, Detroit Receiving Hospital.

Ioliene B. Boenau, MD

Dr. Boenau is Emergency Medicine Residency Director, Department of Emergency Medicine, at Newark Beth Israel Medical Center, Newark, New Jersey, and Assistant Clinical Professor at the New York College of Osteopathic Medicine.

Cathy Bowerman, JD, MPH

Ms. Bowerman is a Principal in the law firm of Siemion, Huckabay, Bodary, Padilla, Morganti, and Bowerman, PC, in Southfield, Michigan. She has practiced full-time medical malpractice defense for the past 20 years, representing physicians, hospitals, and other health care facilities. Her subspecialty focus is emergency medicine.

Marilyn Bromley, RN

Ms. Bromley is Director of the Emergency Medicine Practice Department of the American College of Emergency Physicians, Irving, Texas.

Paul K. Bronston, MD, FACMQ, FACEP

Dr. Bronston is Chairman of the Ethics Committee, Treasurer and member of the Board of Trustees of the American College of Medical Quality. He also is a staff physician in the emergency departments at Brotman Medical Center, Century City Hospital, and Huntington Beach Hospital, and a physician reviewer for California Medical Review, Inc. Dr. Bronston is a member of the National Council Against Health Fraud, and a Diplomat of the American Board of Quality Assurance and Utilization Review Physicians. He is Special Consultant on HMOs for the Department of Corporations, State of California, and Expert Medical Reviewer for the Medical Board of California.

W. Richard Bukata, MD

Dr. Bukata is Assistant Clinical Professor of Emergency Medicine at Los Angeles County/University of Southern California Medical Center, and Medical Director of the emergency department at San Gabriel Valley Medical Center, San Gabriel, California.

Joseph J. Calabro, DO, FACOEP

Dr. Calabro is Chairman and Residency Program Director in the Department of Emergency Medicine at Newark Beth Israel Medical Center, Newark, New Jersey, and Associate Clinical Professor at Seton Hall University School of Graduate Medical Education. He also is Associate Clinical Professor at the New York Osteopathic School of Medicine, and Assistant Clinical Professor at the University of Medicine and Dentistry of New Jersey. Dr. Calabro is President of the New Jersey Chapter of ACEP, Secretary of the American College of Osteopathic Emergency Physicians, and President of Physicians' Practice Enhancement, Inc.

Arthur G. Calise, DO

Dr. Calise is Medical Director of the emergency department at West Hudson Hospital, and a faculty member at Newark Beth Israel Medical Center Emergency Medicine Residency Program. He also is Assistant Medical Director of Occupational Medicine at Doctors on Duty, Union, New Jersey, and Clinical Instructor at the New York College of Osteopathic Medicine.

Stephen A. Colucciello, MD, FACEP

Dr. Colucciello is Director of Clinical Services and Trauma Coordinator in the Department of Emergency Medicine at Carolinas Medical Center, Charlotte, North Carolina, and Assistant Clinical Professor of Emergency Medicine at the University of North Carolina School of Medicine, Chapel Hill.

Paul A. Craig, RN, JD

Mr. Craig is a Risk Consultant, Insured Risk Services, at MMI Risk Management Resources, Inc., Deerfield, Illinois.

Arthur R. Derse, MD, JD

Dr. Derse is Associate Director for Medical and Legal Affairs at the Center for the Study of Bioethics, and Associate Clinical Professor of Bioethics and Emergency Medicine at the Medical College of Wisconsin, Milwaukee.

Phyllis T. Doerger, MD, FACEP

Dr. Doerger is Vice Chair of the Emergency and Trauma Center at Miami Valley Hospital, Dayton, Ohio, and Assistant Clinical Professor of Emergency Medicine at Wright State University School of Medicine, Department of Emergency Medicine. She also is a Partner with Premier Health Care Services, Inc.

Michelle Regan Donovan, BSN, RN

Ms. Donovan is a Principal with Ambulatory Care Advisory Group, Inc., Chicago.

Stephen J. Dresnick, MD, FACEP

Dr. Dresnick is Vice Chairman of FPA Medical Management, and President/CEO of Sterling Healthcare Group. He also is Clinical Professor in the Department of Emergency Medicine at the University of North Carolina, Chapel Hill.

Gary W. Eiland, JD

Mr. Eiland is a Partner with Vinson & Elkins L.L.P. in Houston, Texas, and Immediate Past President of the American Academy of Healthcare Attorneys.

Peter M. Fahrney, MD, FACEP

Dr. Fahrney is Staff Physician at Suburban Hospital, Bethesda, Maryland.

David L. Freedman, MD, JD, FACEP

Dr. Freedman is an emergency physician at Chelsea Community Hospital, Chelsea, Michigan, and an Associate, Health Law Practice Group, at Miller, Canfield, Paddock & Stone, PLC in Ann Arbor, Michigan.

James E. George, MD, JD, FACEP

Dr. George is President of Emergency Physician Associates, PA, in Woodbury, New Jersey, and a Partner in the law firm of George, Korin, Quattrone, Blumberg & Chant, also in Woodbury. He is the editor of *Emergency Physician Legal Bulletin, Emergency Nurse Legal Bulletin,* and *EMT Legal Bulletin*, and an attending physician in the Department of Emergency Medicine at Underwood Memorial Hospital. Dr. George is Director of the Department of Professional Liability Control for the Medical Society of New Jersey.

Peggy L. Goldman, MD, FACEP

Dr. Goldman is Clinical Faculty at the University of Washington Medical School, and Staff Physician, Emergency Medical Services, at Swedish Hospital Medical Center, Seattle.

Melvin E. Harris, MD

Dr. Harris is President and CEO of Physicians Geriatric Services, PA, Dallas, and Past President and CEO of Century American Insurance Company and Coastal Emergency Services, Inc., Durham, North Carolina.

Steven M. Harris, JD

Mr. Harris is a Partner in the firm of Harris Kessler & Goldstein, Chicago. He represents single and multispecialty physician organizations and counsels privately and publicly owned corporations, IPAs, MSOs, and regional physician networks. Mr. Harris served as legal counsel to the American Academy of Orthopaedic Surgeons on its publication *Contracting and Negotiating Managed Care Agreements* and contributed to ACEP's *Before You Sign: Contract Basics for the Emergency Physician*. His column, "Contract Language," appears monthly in *AMA News*.

Hugh F. Hill III, MD, JD, FACEP, FCLM

Dr. Hill is an Instructor of Emergency Medicine at Johns Hopkins University and President of the Legal Medicine Center. He also is Medical Director of the Montgomery Hospice Society.

Paul W. Kolodzik, MD, MBA, FACEP

Dr. Kolodzik is Vice President of Premier Health Care Services, Inc., Dayton, Ohio.

Nancy C. LeGros, JD

Ms. LeGros is with Vinson & Elkins L.L.P. in Houston, Texas. Her practice areas include operational issues, Medicare and Medicaid reimbursement, and fraud and abuse.

Neal E. Little, MD, FACEP

Dr. Little is Clinical Assistant Professor of Surgery, Department of Surgery, at the University of Michigan Medical School.

Dan M. Mayer, MD

Dr. Mayer is Associate Professor of Emergency Medicine at Albany Medical College, and Attending Physician in the emergency department at Albany Medical Center, Albany, New York.

Peter J. Mariani, MD, FACEP

Dr. Mariani is Associate Professor of Emergency Medicine and Medical Director of Health Connections telephone triage at SUNY Health Science Center, Syracuse, New York. He also is a member of the Advisory Board for the monthly report *Parameters, Guidelines and Protocols*.

James C. McClay, MS, MD

Dr. McClay is Director of Medical Informatics for Emergency Physicians Medical Group, PC, Ann Arbor, Michigan.

Joseph P. McMenamin, MD, JD, FCLM

Dr. McMenamin is a Partner in the Richmond, Virginia, office of McGuire Woods Battle & Boothe LLP, a firm that represents health care providers in health law and malpractice matters.

David L. Meyers, MD, FACEP

Dr. Meyers is Chief of Emergency Medicine at Sinai Hospital of Baltimore.

Karen Iezzi Michael, Esquire

Ms. Michael is an attorney specializing in tort defense, medical malpractice, and commercial litigation at McGuire Woods Battle & Boothe LLP, Richmond, Virginia.

Mark M. Moy, MD, MJ, FAAFP, FACEP

Dr. Moy is an emergency physician in the Department of Emergency Medicine at Hinsdale Hospital, Hinsdale, Illinois, and Associate Clinical Professor in the Department of Emergency Medicine at the University of Chicago.

William D. O'Riordan, MD, FACEP

Dr. O'Riordan is an emergency physician at Paradise Valley Hospital, National City, California, and President of Crisis Communication Corporation.

Marc L. Pollack, MD, PhD, FACEP

Dr. Pollack is Attending Physician at York Hospital, York, Pennsylvania, and Assistant Clinical Professor of Medicine at Penn State University College of Medicine.

Michael T. Rapp, MD, JD, FACEP

Dr. Rapp is Chairman of the Department of Emergency Medicine at Columbia Arlington Hospital, Arlington, Virginia, and a member of the Bar in the District of Columbia, Virginia, Illinois, and Maryland. He is a member of Board of Directors and Secretary-Treasurer of the American College of Emergency Physicians.

Mark E. Reagan, Esq.

Mr. Reagan is a Partner at Foley Lardner Weissburg & Aronson in San Francisco.

M. Elizabeth Sassano, MSN, JD

Ms. Sassano is Vice President and Assistant General Counsel for MMI Companies, Inc., Deerfield, Illinois, an international risk management insurance and consulting company serving clients in the health care industry.

Norman Schneiderman, MD, FACEP

Dr. Schneiderman is Director of the Emergency and Trauma Center at Miami Valley Hospital, Dayton, Ohio, and Associate Clinical Professor of Emergency Medicine at Wright State School of Medicine.

Barbara C. Sexton, RN, MSN, CNS

Ms. Sexton is Clinical Nurse Specialist in the emergency department at Illinois Masonic Medical Center, Chicago.

David M. Siegel, MD, JD, FACEP, FACP, FCLM

Dr. Siegel is Associate Clinical Professor of Medicine in the Department of Medicine, University of South Florida School of Medicine, Tampa.

Earl Silverstein

Mr. Silverstein is President of Alliance Risk Management Services, and Director of Risk Management and Legal Affairs for Healix Infusion Therapy, Inc. He also is Director of Operations for Darius Health Group, Houston, Texas.

Vicky A. Trompler, MD, JD

Dr. Trompler is an attorney, of counsel, with the firm of Fowler, Wiles & Keith, L.L.P., Dallas. Her practice is medical malpractice defense with an emphasis on emergency medicine.

Marcus S. Villarreal, MD

Dr. Villarreal is with Occupational Health Centers, Houston, Texas, and a physician adviser on utilization management for Intracorp, Inc. He also practices emergency medicine with InPhyNet and STAT Emergency Physicians.

Ellen F. Wodika, MA, MM

Ms. Wodika is a Consultant with MMI Risk Management Resources, Health Care Consulting Services, Deerfield, Illinois.

Charles L. Zeller, Jr., MD, FACEP

Dr. Zeller is President of Southwestern Michigan Emergency Services, PC, and Director of Continuing Medical Education, MSU/KCMS. He also is a faculty member in the Emergency Medicine Residency, MSU/KCMS, and Associate Clinical Professor at Michigan State University, College of Human Medicine, Division of Emergency Medicine.

Leslie S. Zun, MD, MBA, FACEP

Dr. Zun is Associate Professor of Emergency Medicine at Finch University/Chicago Medical School, and Chairman of the Department of Emergency Medicine at Mount Sinai Hospital Medical Center, Chicago. He also is a Principal of Emergency Resources Group.

ACEP Development and Publishing Staff

Rebecca Garcia, PhD, Education Director

Susan Magee, Managing Editor

Beth Paul, Editorial Assistant

Marta Foster, Publishing Director

Mike C. Goodwin, Publishing Manager

Jody Hundley, Publishing Coordinator

Table of Contents

Preface

"Justice without force is powerless: force without justice is tyrannical." — Blaise Pascal, *Pensées*.

The effect of the law throughout the 20th century cannot be underestimated. Physicians are wont to criticize anything to do with the legal system as somehow being unjust, unfair, and not understanding the medical world. Although all professions have practitioners of questionable reputation, and there have long been some natural tensions between physicians and lawyers, it should be pointed out that all societies require some type of legal system to adjudicate the social contract. No profession can expect to function in a vacuum that ignores the rest of society. It is the duty and obligation of the legal system to see that our relationship between the medical world and the interests of the public is properly served.

Physicians also tend to believe that malpractice and societal governance of medical behavior are somehow recent phenomena. Upon ascending the throne in 1750 BC, Hammurabi, the sixth ruler of the first dynasty of Babylon, memorialized his famous code of legal cases as a guide to jurists throughout his land. It is interesting to note that there was a malpractice case involved, and the paraphrased summary of that case indicated that a surgeon whose patient died during the draining of an abscess was punished by having both his hands cut off. To some extent, practice in this the 20th century AD is somewhat less harsh in its retribution against physicians. The law proceeds to be both exasperating and necessary. To think that it will in any way change during our practice life would be folly.

The function of this book, as it was in the first edition, is to guide physicians in decision-making. It is impossible to avoid medical-legal situations in the emergency department. We are essentially the centerpiece of both societal shortcomings and the pit where human emotions, tragedy, and devastation of lives all combine to form all the elements necessary for legal action. The intelligent physician, however, can learn from others. As philosopher and poet George Santayana is quoted as saying: "Those who do not study the past are condemned to repeat it." I hope that the readers of this book will not be forced to learn from their mistakes, but from the mistakes of others.

I had immense satisfaction and pleasure in editing the first edition of *Emergency Medicine Risk Management: A Comprehensive Review*. I can truthfully say, however, that this second edition was not only needed, but has surpassed our expectations. The authors have scrutinized their previous chapters and have added new works. Areas in the law that have become more and more complex and provide us with greater depth in case coverage have been reexamined and included in this work. The first edition was a landmark for the College. We were able to pull together experts throughout emergency medicine, the legal community, and the insurance world to provide true direction. An interesting progression takes place with this book. More of our authors are emergency physicians who have legal training. As we mature as a specialty, not only the legal decisions concerning emergency medicine and various state laws concerning our practice become further delineated, but also the expertise of our own members has increased dramatically. This combination of the savvy of a practicing emergency physician with a clear understanding of the law has produced, I believe, a work of unique quality.

It is fair to answer the question of the discerning purchaser as to what has changed since the first edition in 1991. The answer to such a question is straightforward: a tremendous amount. In the past seven years, whole new vistas have opened in the law. EMTALA, or "COBRA," which has had time to mature, now has a tremendous body of case law and legal interpretations that have greatly clarified our current positions. State laws, the duties and responsibilities of hospitals, attending physicians, and EMS have become clearer and clearer. The penalties and the number of investigations have risen dramatically. With the fall of eastern Europe and the ability of the federal government to put more of its investigatory personnel in health care, the legal situation surrounding fraud and abuse has skyrocketed. The famous decision against the University of Pennsylvania for $30 million with regard to the charging of resident supervision has now become landmark. Physicians are now starting to realize that they do not exist in any type of protective vacuum. They have an ethical and moral responsibility to make certain that their documentation and coding practices meet the highest of ethical standards. This society has little tolerance for its citizens who are as educated as physicians not to know and understand the law.

The only constant in the emergency department is change. It is still evolving at a rapid pace, and as new mechanisms of payment become available, ethical and moral questions with regard to the workup of various diseases and the location for such evaluations will be a constant struggle. It is good to remember that the legal system still views the patient as the center of such health care decision-making. It is still the obligation of physicians to ask the ultimate question: what type of medical care would I want for myself or my family? The legal relationship of the parties involved is that the physician has been retained by the patient, and only the patient, to act in that patient's best interest. To start viewing medicine as any more or less than a physician-patient relationship experience is to flirt with medical-legal disaster.

The new management systems on the horizon, particularly managed care, have put the societal decision-making directly on the line. Physicians do not practice in the abstract. The human condition is only human because it is unique. Each person presents to the physician with a sui-generic set of problems and conditions that require judgment. It is this physician judgment and the intelligent utilization of resources that are placing physicians between the proverbial rock and a hard place. The physician must safeguard the society's resources while doing what is best for the individual patient. No small task in this era of rethinking the goals and aspirations of medicine.

The rights and responsibilities of individual patients are also coming to the forefront. Patients are more and more being asked to shoulder larger amounts of health care costs, and yet it is expected that, as emergency physicians, we will do what is right and not what is economically convenient. This balance between access, quality, and affordability will not go away. The emergency department is a centerpiece of such decisions as we become the hub of clinical decision-making. More and more the emergency department will be asked to determine which patients truly need expensive inpatient care for improvement in their overall health and which ones can be handled on a less expensive outpatient basis. This difficult decision-making will require more than just science and physician discussion. These are societal issues, which need broad input in defining what the general public views as its overall rights with regard to health care. Recent congressional debates on such issues as "drive-through deliveries" and minimum hospital time after cancer therapy are only a symptom of a larger malaise in the country. These are the attempt of legislators to deal in areas where they are ill-prepared to make decisions. They do so because they feel the crunch of change, and the threat of financial motivations controlling patient care as opposed to quality and outcome measures. This is a natural reaction to a society that is concerned but lacks direction.

Larger and larger entities are upon us. Health care organizations are consolidating from both the hospital side and the third-party payer side. More and more layers of bureaucracy will mean more and more potential areas for medical-legal conflict. More and more entities will be forced to take responsibility, and such entities, which have believed that they could have authority without responsibility, will be sadly mistaken. People will be called on to step up the bar of justice for their actions.

This second edition also marks some significant changes with regard to authorship and editorship. The new authors in the book are welcomed with open arms. The quality and enthusiasm they bring to this project have been absolutely uplifting. I particularly wish to welcome as the associate editor, Dan Sullivan, MD, JD, FACEP. Dr. Sullivan represents the coming of the new era. He is both an attorney and an emergency physician. He brings a new level of sophistication to the work, and his legal and medical knowledge, combined with his down-to-earth street sense, makes him an ideal editorial partner. His contributions have been Herculean, as he has figuratively cleaned out the legal "Aegean stables" of shepherding a multiauthored text. This work is much better for his efforts. In truth, it could not have been done without him. I am indeed pleased with Dan as a colleague and friend, and the College is much in his debt.

In closing, I would like to reiterate advice from the preface of the first book: do not put this work on the shelf or just keep it within the emergency physician community. It needs broad distribution and debate. Get one for your risk manager, your hospital attorney, and the administrator in charge of your department. This book should be consulted whenever policy is to be made or behavior examined. I firmly believe it represents the accumulated factual knowledge and best opinions of the most talented and experienced medical-legal personnel in the field of emergency medicine and will serve as a reasonable basis for discussion in emergency departments throughout the country. Emergency physicians who on a day-to-day basis have been practicing for many years will look at many of these chapters and suggestions and merely dismiss them as common knowledge. They are common only to those who have been baptized by fire and have made the mistakes. I hope that those less experienced will use this work to set the course of their practice so as to make risk management not a add-on, but a true cornerstone of the way they practice medicine every day. It is always good to remember that the only person who has real risk is the patient. Protection of the patient is the beginning and end of what we do as physicians. In the final analysis, juries do not judge the standard of care — they judge the standard of caring. To do less is to insult the ancient and honorable traditions of medicine.

Gregory L. Henry, MD, FACEP
Editor-in-Chief
September 1997

Most acts of negligence do not result in litigation. Most patient complaints to plaintiffs' attorneys do not result in lawsuits. Most lawsuits result in defense judgments or verdicts. Despite this good news, emergency medicine remains one of the high-risk medical specialties. Emergency physicians can manage and minimize this risk. You can empower yourself by reading the lessons in this text and modifying certain behaviors to reduce risk. The practice of emergency medicine, more than any other specialty, requires an awareness of the medical-legal environment. It is critical that emergency physicians be aware of particular state and federal laws and regulations, the fundamentals of malpractice litigation, the risk associated with certain clinical presentations, the essentials of documentation, and several other important medical-legal issues and principles.

What risks do we need to reduce or eliminate? Risk management is loss prevention, both economic and noneconomic. Loss comes in many forms. The most obvious focus is avoiding missed diagnoses and other causes of malpractice lawsuits. Many chapters, such as those on communication, high-risk clinical entities, information systems, staff orientation, and several others, squarely address malpractice issues. However, it is just as important to know how to evaluate a malpractice policy in order to be certain that the insurance carrier is healthy and reserves are sufficient. It is equally important to understand basic contract analysis to make sure that your malpractice risk is covered and your rights and responsibilities are properly addressed.

In the new managed care medical marketplace, emergency physicians must avoid strategies that result in exposure to antitrust litigation, with its huge expense in both dollars and time. Managed care organizations may cause delays in patient evaluation and admission, ultimately increasing the emergency physician's exposure to liability. Improper management of patients who refuse care may lead to patient injury, or the patient may leave and injure someone outside of the patient-emergency physician relationship. That third party may sue for damages, alleging negligent conduct. These potential causes of dollar loss, and how to avoid them, are not immediately apparent to the busy clinician.

Noneconomic loss is just as real but more difficult to measure. Missing a diagnosis and becoming the subject of a malpractice lawsuit is a trying ordeal. The deposition and trial experience can be frightening. As a result, some emergency physicians question whether it is worth continuing practice in this high-risk environment. Having your name in the National Practitioner Data Bank may present hurdles to future employment. Managed care organizations may refuse to work with emergency physicians known to overutilize laboratory tests or imaging studies. Perhaps most difficult is living with the knowledge that your action or inaction resulted in an unnecessary injury to an individual, whether the final result is damage to a patient's myocardium, the death of an intoxicated patient who left the department too soon, or harm to an abused child who should have been admitted under protective custody. These issues, and many others, are addressed by our outstanding group of authors.

One striking change in emergency medical practice since the first edition of this book is the impact of the Emergency Medical Treatment and Active Labor Act (EMTALA) and its regulations and administrative guidelines. Concern over this law is pervasive. You will find an excellent chapter directly on the subject. Although historically the emergency physician's actual out-of-pocket expense related to EMTALA violations is minimal, hospitals are justifiably very concerned that emergency physicians help keep them in compliance. This text provides a thorough treatment of the subject.

Another important change in emergency practice is the increasing influence of managed care organizations. As we prepared the outline for this text, it was apparent that we needed an analysis of managed care and a complete explanation of the risks associated with practice in this new environment. The text contains an outstanding chapter on managed care and many references to risk in the managed care environment in other related chapters.

It has been a privilege and a pleasure participating in the preparation of this text. My sincere thanks to Dr. Greg Henry for the opportunity. I would like to thank all the authors for their hard work and contribution to our specialty. My wish for you the reader is practice without loss, personal or economic, and finally — *Good Reading.*

Daniel J. Sullivan, MD, JD, FACEP
Associate Editor
September 1997

Dedication

"To the family — that dear octopus from whose tentacles we never quite escape, nor, in our innermost hearts ever quite wish to." — Dodie Smith, in *Dear Octopus.*

This modest effort is dedicated to my wife, my children, and my mother, all of whom have reluctantly paid for yet another addition to my curriculum vitae with patience, understanding, and tears.

GLH

To Andria, Stassia, Gia, Mari, Cathy, and Nora: Thank you for your undying love and support. You inspire me, and make every day a delight.

DJS

Chapter 1

Philosophy of Risk Management

Gregory L. Henry, MD, FACEP

The term "risk management," like "quality assurance" and "corporate communication," has become one of the buzzwords of our generation. But it seems that, when speaking to hospital administrators, risk management is a term more often bandied about than actually understood at the fundamental level of emergency medicine practice. It is often said that the function of quality assurance is to design the ideal medical care experience for a patient, while the function of risk management is to protect the health care providers from the wrath of the patients they serve. This distinction does not do justice to the true role of risk management.

One of the principal functions of this book is to erase the unnecessary line that has been drawn between risk management and quality assurance. Although this book focuses on risk in emergency medicine, it is good to remember that quality management is the only real basis for true risk insurance.

Using conventional terminology, risk management focuses on identifying those situations that place the provider of service in jeopardy. In a traditional approach to risk management, incident reports, patient complaints, and identified poor outcomes are the criteria for the need to manage risk, and protecting the assets of the institution the ultimate goal. The problem inherent in such an approach is that it deals with relatively rare occurrences the delivery of emergency medical care. A reactive posture based solely on the institution's identified problems is not enough to provide reliable protection, either to the patient or to health care providers. Here's why: an emergency department in the United States may be sued, on average, once every 20,000 visits. At this rate, a medium-sized emergency department may have only one or two occurrences per year on which to judge the effectiveness of its risk management program. Clearly, with the vast array of statutes under which a department can be sued, such a limited frequency basis does not provide adequate stimulus for risk identification.

The new trends in risk management are obvious. Over the past 10 years, a number of journals have sprung up in the field of risk management, directed at both physicians and hospitals, which allow one hospital's risk management personnel to learn from the predicaments of others. Only through a broader understanding of what is happening in the medical-legal arena throughout the country can reasonable risk management policies be constructed. The vital step in completing the marriage between risk management and quality assurance occurs when knowledgeable risk managers channel this national information back into their own quality assurance programs so that proper adjustments can be made to protect patients. These corrective actions to prevent patient injury or unacceptable patient outcomes are essential if risk management is to have any influence in preventing the "next" lawsuit.

Health care professionals must understand that legal interpretations of what constitutes negligence are constantly changing and vary from state to state and between state and federal systems of law. However, there are general trends in a particular direction. With regard to emergency medicine, there is a tendency to break down or try to isolate responsibility whenever a negative patient outcome occurs. Within the scope of an institution, various groups tend to argue as to who is at fault. What we in the medical community must understand is that society in general views health care as a single, coordinated entity. People are reluctant to assess separate blame. As medicine has become more corporate in its structure, recent court decisions concerning hospital liability have tended to lump all health care providers together.[1,2]

Another important trend in risk management is the movement away from "absolute harm" to the concept of "percentage chance" of an improved outcome or survival. Such doctrines, if carried to the extreme, can place emergency health care staff in jeopardy from dissatisfied patients for whom a poor outcome was not only predicted but expected.[3-5]

A third trend in risk management is the redefinition of fault within contractual relationships so as to shift the burden for financial loss from one entity to another whenever combined verdicts are reached. The concept of indemnifying a physician for the hospital's error — or vice versa, the hospital for the physician's error — is now a well-recognized concept in contract law that has been supported in the courts.[6]

In addition, new pressures, both legal and ethical, have been applied to hospital emergency departments based on the concept of right to care. A growing series of decisions across the United States has essentially established the concept that the hospital emergency department — and by logical extension the emergency physician — is obligated to admit patients into the health care system regardless of their ability to pay.[7] The old concept of managing risk by transferring a potential problem to another institution is gone. Both state statutes and the actions of the federal government are making health care institutions and their agent physicians responsible for properly attending to the needs of all patients who present to emergency departments.[8]

The cost to the health care community and to the patients it serves for compensating actual or perceived losses has escalated even faster than the cost of health care itself.[9,10] But the true dollar costs of malpractice actions in this country are considerably higher. The expense of ordering extra laboratory tests and x-rays and admitting patients for the purpose of "defensive medicine" are conservatively estimated at $52 billion per year. Others have estimated these costs at $180 billion a year, or one third of the nation's total health care expenditures.

Growing evidence suggests that an aggressive approach to risk management — that is, identifying potential problem areas and investigating reported incidents thoroughly and early — can lower the lawsuit rate and better protect health care institutions.[11] What is often overlooked is that a vital element — the human element — should also be protected by risk management efforts. The negative effects of lawsuits on physicians who are caught in the current adversarial, fault-based legal system are significant.[12] Well-documented studies have shown that physicians who are being sued experience a higher incidence of depression, anxiety, and physical illness, including myocardial infarction. An aggressive risk management system can provide not only insight into protecting patients and prompt management of incidents, but also positive reassurance to health care providers caught in the web of maloccurrence as opposed to malpractice.

Properly performed risk management requires the commitment of adequate resources. The hospital must pay attention to high-volume events, high-risk events, and problem-prone areas then feed this information into the quality assurance system so that each patient interaction can be managed properly. The hospital or health care institution that does not want to commit sufficient dollars into providing adequate staff, proper training, and proper follow-up systems will pay the added cost of legal judgments such inattention brings. Risk management really begins "on line." All members of the health care team must understand their relationship to the well-being of the patient and must be alert to identify any high-risk situations that develop. Responsibility for risk management does not belong solely to the risk management department: it belongs to every individual on the health care team.

A good test of an institution's commitment to risk management is to evaluate its overall presence and power in the hospital's operation. Currently, risk management is an area of expertise without official portfolio. In many institutions, an administrator who was running the laundry yesterday is in charge of risk management today. These generic management techniques are to be condemned. True risk management is specific to each area and site. The emergency department has a completely different set of risks than does obstetrics or surgery. The person in charge of emergency medicine risk management must understand the specifics of each type of risk and the specific medical actions, modes of medical documentation, and proper entry into the health care system that are required to achieve excellence in patient care and the least harmful exposure for the institution.

Physicians are also guilty of being less than committed to risk management. True leadership comes from the top. Responsibility for integration of the quality assurance program and risk management lies with the director of the department. If such duties are relegated to an inexperienced physician, the message is then sent to the entire health care team that risk management activities are a low priority.

The purpose of this book is to move beyond simple platitudes and general statements to the specific risk situations encountered in the emergency department. This book provides succinct chapters on specific issues that are applicable to everyday emergency situations. Each chapter stands on its own and presents a problem, a typical case or cases illustrating the problem, an analysis, and conclusions. We emergency physicians do not function in an ethereal world. The situation of choosing between the lesser of two evils is common. We must make quick decisions on virtually all patients. In the heat of battle, we must summarize issues rapidly and begin treatments immediately.

Although no single text can address all potential problems, every attempt has been made in this book to look at the most common ones we face as practicing emergency physicians. The case studies, as presented, will remind all of us of patients we have seen and predicaments we have encountered. I hope that the conclusions recommended in each chapter will help reassure you of your options and legal rights should a negative outcome occur. Tragically, poor outcomes in emergency medicine are inevitable: emergency physicians must often make judgments based on incomplete and rapidly changing information. But not to act or to delay action out of fear of a potential lawsuit would be a far greater tragedy resulting from the current medical-legal crisis.

References

1. *Thompson v Nason Hospital*, 535 A2d 1177, Pa Sup Ct, January 11, 1988.
2. *Oehler v Humana Inc.*, No. 18971, Nev Sup Ct, June 22, 1989.
3. *McKillips v Saint Francis Hospital, Inc.*, 741 P2d 467, Oklahoma, 1987.
4. *Jeanes v Milner*, 428 F2d 598, 604 (8th Cir 1970).
5. *Herskovitz v Group Health Coop.*, 664 P2d 474, 475, Washington, 1983.
6. *Ollerich v Rotering*, 419 NW2d 548, SD Sup Ct, February 10, 1988.
7. Curran WJ. Economic and legal considerations in emergency care. *N Engl J Med* 1985;312:374-375.
8. Consolidated Omnibus Budget Reconciliation Act of 1985, Section 9121, Examination and Treatment for Emergency Medical Conditions and Women in Active Labor, Section 1876.
9. Reynolds RA, Rizzo JA, Gonzalez ML. The cost of medical professional liability. *JAMA* 1987;257:2776-2781.
10. Manuel BM. The effects of the professional liability crisis on the quality of health care. *Res Staff Phys* 1989;35(9):128-135.
11. Fetzer BC. Early investigation of incidents important in malpractice defense. *Perspectives Healthcare Risk Management*, Summer 1988.
12. Charles SC, Pyskoty CE, Nelson A. Physicians on trial—self-reported reactions to malpractice trials. *West J Med* 1988;148:358-360.

Chapter 2

Patient Expectations

Gregory L. Henry, MD, FACEP

Health care workers at all levels of the medical system can quickly forget that the system exists to serve the patient. During years of professional indoctrination that borders on initiation rites, we physicians and nurses can easily acquire a cloistered and overly clinical attitude toward the practice of medicine. Medicine, in its purest form, is a service industry, and as with all service industries, its success or failure is measured by the satisfaction level of the people it serves. Thus, medicine can be scientifically correct and humanistically wrong.

Attitude is the dividing line between those of us who have a medical job and those who have a career in the healing professions. The courts have gone so far as to carry the concept of "psychological damage" to the point where even a health care provider's comments or attitude that upset the patient and contribute to a negative outcome may constitute a compensable loss.[1] In general, patients come to the emergency department with realistic expectations. They expect that we will treat them with dignity and will regard their welfare as our principal concern.[2] As one expert in risk management stated, "People just want what is rightfully theirs until you deny them, then they want revenge."[3]

This expectation — that true kindness and caring will be shown by health care workers — is held by people from all strata of society. It is a misconception that the poor sue more aggressively than do the rich.[4-8] The health care system in the United States is essentially measured against higher ethical and moral standards than is any other business. Patients, the general public, and the legal system expect that emergency medical care will be provided without regard to the patient's ability to pay.[9] They also expect that care will be rendered to the maximum ability of our resources and that transfers to other facilities will occur only in the patient's best interests — not for the fiscal well-being of the hospital.[10-12] This belief is so deeply ingrained in the American populace that it has been codified into federal law.[13]

Beyond the physical act of having a condition diagnosed and treated, patients expect to receive care. This is a totally different concept than scientifically correct medicine. Patients want interaction with people who will listen to their problems. Real listening is the highest compliment you can pay another person. Remember: people conduct the business of every company, no matter what product that company produces.[3]

In any health care delivery system, the only "product" is patient satisfaction. Most patients realize that medicine is a practice with an ultimate outcome that is definitive 100% of the time — patients either get better or they don't. How the patient is handled along the way is the hospital's ultimate risk management tool. As consumers, we medical professionals often have no mercy on people who make inferior products. Likewise, why should patients — health care consumers — have mercy on us?[3] When expectations are not met, patients feel they have not gotten their "money's worth."[14] Anger can be expressed in many ways in our culture, and filing a lawsuit is one of them.

Every patient who enters the health care system has a preconceived notion of what that system should be like and what benefits it should deliver. For example, in multiple studies, patients at all socioeconomic levels had strongly preconceived notions about what a doctor should look like.[15-17] These same patients knew how they wanted to be addressed and how the staff should behave. Patients fully expect to be informed of their medical conditions and have input into decisions made about their bodies.[18]

Classic examples of the failed expectations of patients can be found in many common emergency department situations, return visits, for example. Patients return with the expectation that we will be more concerned about their problems because they have been seen once and their problems were not solved. In contrast, emergency department personnel often view such patients as annoyances. Instead of greeting them with an open and receptive attitude, some view them with hostility.[19] Yet in a significant number of cases, the return visit itself is a red flag for a previous misdiagnosis or improper discharge instructions. Considering these findings, we should give return visit patients the same care and attention we would give any first visit patient and properly reevaluate their presenting complaints.

Another issue that creates conflict between patient care and patient expectations is pain relief. Studies indicate that a physician's perception of a patient's pain is invariably lower than that patient's perception of the pain.[20] Irrational fears about the use of pain medication and myths about the long-term effects of drugs have created an atmosphere in which patients with legitimate pain may be denied effective relief.

Waiting time is another issue on which patient expectations and system performance are likely to be different.[21] No one likes to wait a long time for services. The emergency physician who has not suffered the wrath of patients because of time delays is the exception, not the rule.[22] Some authors have suggested that we should apologize to patients for lengthy delays. Such a gesture is not only socially correct, but also useful in diffusing patient anger. Recognizing that the patient has been inconvenienced helps to establish good rapport.

Encounters with the health care system, like all human interactions, have a beginning, a middle, and an end. At the beginning, health care workers should be able to follow a simple system for on-line risk management that will allow them not only to determine a patient's expectations for care, but also to identify the patient's principal reason for coming to the emergency department. Sometimes a patient will have an unreasonable expectation or unobtainable goal. This must be articulated so that both patient and physician can form a treatment "contract" acceptable to both This simple system involves three steps that can help us satisfy the patient's needs. First, after introducing yourself, ask the patient: "What can we do for you today?" An attempt to discover not only the patient's complaint but also what was accomplished during the visit is extremely important. Patients may request particular laboratory tests and x-rays that you may not consider useful.[23] If so, explain to the patient why a particular test is or is not being performed. Such education may be crucial to establishing patient confidence. Then outline briefly what will happen during the course of the visit and give a probable timeline. Do not underestimate how long the patient can expect to wait. These simple steps will help satisfy the patient's concerns and needs.

Another area of significant risk, one that is often overlooked by both physicians and nurses, is the follow-up program and instructions given to the patient after treatment. Between one third and one half of all emergency medicine legal cases are associated with the discharge instructions or the discharge program constructed for the patient.[24] The ultimate professional arrogance is to present patients with discharge instructions they cannot understand.[25] Assure the patient and the family that they have an easily accessible and understandable entry into the health care system. Providing them a safety net through proper instructions and the option of unencumbered return visits not only provides for a high level of patient satisfaction, but also establishes a way to catch diagnosis and treatment errors made during the initial visit. Follow-up systems that include callbacks from the emergency department can result in significantly higher patient satisfaction with the emergency department experience.[26]

At the time of discharge, ask the patient: "Is there anything else we can do for you today?" Many patients have concerns, such as off-work notes, special diets or restrictions, inability to obtain care at home, or financial constraints, that can make carrying out prescribed treatment regimens impossible. Make an effort to understand these impediments and other patient needs immediately. When patients see that you and other department staff are concerned about their general well-being, and not just about the time they are in the emergency department, their confidence in the care you provide increases. Besides, a few minutes spent considering how the patient will function in the outside world and the kind of environment to which the patient is being returned may alter your treatment plan. Take time to explain the details of the discharge program to those who accompany the patient, such as a friend or family member.

Discharge instructions should be time-specific and action-specific. No patient will completely understand the instruction "see your doctor if not better" unless a specific time frame is provided. Have the patient and those who will take charge of the patient repeat the discharge instructions. This precaution can help detect and correct any misconceptions in the way the information has been conveyed.

At the end of the visit, tell the patient to come back to the emergency department if the healing process is not proceeding on the course as outlined. As providers in a service industry, emergency department staff members must adopt the concept that they "service" what they sell. Emergency departments function as the unofficial safety net for the entire health care system. All disease entities change with time, and one emergency department visit may not fully expose a patient's problem or the direction in which the problem is going. By projecting a concerned and supportive attitude about follow-up care, you protect not only the hospital, but also — and most importantly — the patient.

Understanding the elements of risk management and patient expectations alone is not enough to help the practicing emergency physician avoid the risk of liability. Another element lies in how we view ourselves as emergency physicians. The emergency physician, charged with the evaluation and treatment of a patient is, at that moment, the physician of record. We've all heard private attending physicians say: "That's my patient." This is a definitional problem. Physicians do not own patients. Patients are the responsibility of whatever physician they are seeing at that moment. An emergency physician presented with a patient takes on both responsibility and liability. Not to combine this with the proper authority to manage that patient is to invite disaster. Adopting this "intern mentality" in emergency medicine frequently leads an emergency physician to accept advice from other physicians and health care providers that may not be in the best interests of the patient.

From the time that patients enter the emergency department until they have been properly discharged or admitted into the health care system, the emergency physician's duties are clear. Providing scientifically based, compassionate, and timely medical care is often difficult and demanding. The need to consult with outside specialists requires the emergency physician to "inconvenience" other physicians. This interdependency should be combined with a mutual respect, respect based on the fact that health care is an ongoing process in which the system must work if unfortunate outcomes are to be avoided. Good things happen only when planned; bad things happen all by themselves.[3]

References

1. *Seitz v Humana of Kentucky Inc.*, No. 87-CA-2511-S, Kentucky Court of Appeals, November 4, 1988.

2. Merrill JM, Laux L, Thornby JI. Troublesome aspects of the patient-physician relationship: a study of human factors. *South Med J* 1987;80:1211-1215.

3. Crosby PB. *Quality Is Free: The Art of Making Quality Certain*. New York: McGraw-Hill Inc; 1978.

4. Michigan Dept of Social Services. *Medicaid Matters*, February 1989.

5. Rosenbaum S, Hughes D. The medical malpractice crisis and poor women. In: Brown SS, ed. *Prenatal Care: Reaching Mothers. Reaching Infants*. Washington, DC: Institute of Medicine; 1988:229-243.

6. Medical Malpractice. Characteristics of Claims Closed in 1984. Washington, DC: US General Accounting Office, 1987; GAO-HRD-87-55.

7. Stoll K. Don't blame the poor for the malpractice crisis. *Washington Post*. Health Section 6, April 30, 1986.

8. Dept of Health, Education, and Welfare Secretary's Commission on Medical Malpractice. Consumers' Knowledge of the Attitudes Towards Medical Malpractice. Washington, DC: Dept of Health, Education, and Welfare 1973:658-694.

9. Ohsfeldt RL. Uncompensated medical services provided by physicians and hospitals. *Med Care* 1985;23:1338-1344.

10. Annas GJ. Your money or your life: "dumping" uninsured patients from hospital emergency wards. *Am J Public Health* 1986;76:74-77.

11. Kellermann AL, Ackerman TF. Interhospital patient transfer. The case for informed consent. *N Engl J Med* 1989;319:643-647.

12. Schiff RL, Ansell DA, Schlosser JE, et al. Transfers to a public hospital. A prospective study of 467 patients. *N Engl J Med* 1986;314:552-557.

13. Consolidated Omnibus Budget Reconciliation Act of 1985, Section 9121, Examination and Treatment for Emergency Medical Conditions and Women in Active Labor, Section 1876.

14. Schwartz LR, Overton DT. Emergency department complaints: a one-year analysis. *Ann Emerg Med* 1987;16:857-861.

15. Taylor PG. Does dress influence how parents first perceive house staff competence? *Am J Dis Child* 1987;141:426-428.

16. Colt HG, Solot JA. Attitudes of patients and physicians regarding physician dress and demeanor in the emergency department. *Ann Emerg Med* 1989;18:145-151.

17. Dunn JJ, Lee TH, Percelay JM, et al. Patient and house officer attitudes on physician attire and etiquette. *JAMA* 1987;257:65-68.

18. Boisaubin EV, Dresser R. Informed consent in emergency care: illusion and reform. *Ann Emerg Med* 1987;16:62-67.

19. Lerman B, Kobernick MS. Return visits to the emergency department. *J Emerg Med* 1987;5:359-362.

20. Forrest M, Hermann G, Andersen B. Assessment of pain: a comparison between patients and doctors. *Acta Anaesthesiol Scand* 1989;33:255-256.

21. Saunders CE. Time study of patient movement through the emergency department: sources of delay in relation to patient acuity. *Ann Emerg Med* 1987;16:1244-1248.

22. Spendlove DC, Rigdon MA, Jensen WN, et al. Effects of waiting on patient mood and satisfaction. *Fam Pract* 1987;24:200-202.

23. Deyo RA, Diehl AK, Rosenthal M. Reducing roentgenography use. Can patient expectations be altered? *Arch Intern Med* 1987;147:141-145.

24. Henry G, Little N: Personal impressions based on evaluation of 1,300 malpractice cases. Report.

25. Powers RD. Emergency department patient literacy and the readability of patient-directed materials. *Ann Emerg Med* 1988;17:124-126.

26. Shesser R, Smith M, Adams S, et al. The effectiveness of an organized emergency department follow-up system. *Ann Emerg Med* 1986;15:911-915.

Chapter 3

Image of the Emergency Physician

Neal E. Little, MD, FACEP

When patients seek emergency care, they go to a hospital, not a physician. In most cases, they choose the emergency department in closest proximity. The reputation of that hospital, its affiliation with physicians the patients know, and the reputation of the emergency department itself may be factors in this decision, but rarely do patients go to a particular emergency department because they believe they will see a specific physician. In fact, many patients expect to be seen by an "intern."

For these reasons, emergency physicians need to understand that patients respond to the preconception of the emergency department and their experiences there. We need to understand not only what they expect of us, but also what they perceive of us — the common images they have of the emergency department, emergency physicians, and physicians in general. These images may be negative. They may be based on stereotypes of uncaring physicians or institutions. If emergency department personnel or emergency physicians act in ways that reinforce these negative stereotypes, they create obstacles to effective therapeutic relationships.

Fortunately for us, most people understand that physicians are human, and as such, are less than perfect. But it is also a fact that many lawsuits are initiated because patients or family members get angry about a bad outcome or a perceived bad outcome. And when the physician or other personnel anger the patient or family in a more personal way, the lawsuit becomes a way to "get even." In a lawsuit, the plaintiff has the option to name or not to name

certain people or hospitals. Some plaintiffs choose not to name a certain physician or other provider — even though that person may have some potential liability — simply because they liked that person.[1] Perhaps that person demonstrated a caring and concerned attitude when others did not, and the plaintiff genuinely believes that whatever damage occurred can be attributed to other parties. Research has shown that the strongest predictor of patient satisfaction is the patient's perception of the physician's behavior.[2]

Other common denominators in lawsuits against physicians are patients' perceived lack of confidence in a physician and the impression that a physician "doesn't care." Patients often judge the quality of their care based on intangibles, such as caring and concern expressed by the physician.[3-5] The impression of competence and evidence of a caring and concerned attitude have been shown not only to improve actual therapeutic outcome, but also to help alleviate the patient's anxiety about the quality of care.

We physicians need to recognize that patients do not usually rely on "technical" measures of satisfaction, such as what a careful and thorough examination we perform or test we order, or how efficacious the drugs we administer. Instead, patient satisfaction typically is related to nontechnical interventions, such as patient education, stress counseling, and negotiation.[6] One of the secrets of success of the well-run emergency department is that physicians and other personnel do all they can to create a positive image of a caring and concerned department and a feeling of confidence in the skills of all personnel.

High-Risk Behaviors — How to Fix Them and Improve Your Image

Ask physicians about self-image and you'll get, for the most part, uniformly positive responses. We take pride in having undergone an extensive period of high-pressure, intensive learning in the technical, scientific, and rigorous discipline of medicine. We spent years preparing and made enormous personal and financial sacrifices to become physicians. We make all of our medical care decisions with the patient's best interests in mind, and we work constantly to update our knowledge and skills to ensure our patients have the best outcomes.

Ask the public about the image of physicians, however, and the responses might not necessarily be so positive. Most patients will concede that physicians are generally bright individuals who have studied and worked hard to get where they are. However, patients also have negative images of physicians — labels such as overbearing, unconcerned, interested only in money, too busy, uncaring, incompetent. Emergency physicians in particular have image problems. Many patients still think that emergency departments are staffed by interns. What's worse, many attending physicians either still believe this or reinforce this negative stereotype. The image of the itinerant emergency physician as someone who "can't get a real job" is an impediment to the confidence that patient care demands.

What people think about the emergency department itself can be just as negative. For many, it is a place where you have to wait forever, where only critically ill or injured patients get attended to, and where staff members are too busy and do not care about what patients need.[7] As emergency physicians and emergency department staff, we have a responsibility to overcome the negative images that patients bring to our departments.

Get Off on the Right Foot

Overcoming a bad first impression is extremely difficult. A patient's perception of your image is likely to be conditioned by his first interaction with the emergency department.

How do patients initially judge the quality of an emergency department? A major factor is how clean it is. Airline industry studies have concluded that passengers judge the quality of an airline's maintenance program by the cleanliness of their seat trays. They believe that failure to attend to details of cleanliness in one area translates to failure to attend to details in other areas. Our patients are no different. A messy, run-down emergency department creates an image of incompetent patient care. Besides, blood, urine, and other stains on the floor, chart, or side rail are not only unsightly but also unsanitary and may expose patients and staff to infectious organisms.

How do patients judge an emergency physician's competence? Like it or not, how we dress is an important factor in the perception of professional competence. That means it takes about 15 seconds for a patient to decide whether you are competent. When we dress and act like interns, it is no wonder that patients think of us that way. Several studies on patients' attitudes toward physician dress conclude that appropriate dress enhances the physician's professional image.[8] For men, "appropriate" dress includes a clean white coat, a dress shirt and tie, dress slacks, and dress shoes — not running shoes or sneakers — and for women, a clean white coat, blouse, and skirt or slacks. We are expected to look clean and well-groomed but not flashy. Health care personnel who dislike the "official" dress should regard it as necessary "professional camouflage." Remember: emergency department patients are entrusting their medical well-being to you — and you are a total stranger. They have little on which to judge your abilities, so unless you plan to hand out copies of your CV to all your patients, be prepared for them to judge you based on whatever information is at hand.

Another major factor is the attitude of caregivers and other personnel. Patients need to feel that other human beings truly care for them, and the initial greeting is an extremely important aspect of this perception. The first person to see a patient is one who can make that patient feel welcome and cared for and safe. In fact, the hospital should ensure that courteous, caring, and concerned people are the first ones to see the patient. The qualifications for these staff positions should include the ability to welcome patients and visitors.

Call patients by their names. Certainly when you or some other caregiver greets a patient, do so with the attitude that you are genuinely glad to have that patient in the emergency department and that helping him is neither a bother nor an imposition.

Another high-risk behavior to avoid is the

failure to introduce yourself. Patients need to know that you are, in fact, a fully qualified practitioner, not an intern. Tell the patient your name and position in the emergency department. Introduce yourself to the patient's family or friends, too, and listen to their questions or issues. In many cases, the concerns of the persons accompanying the patient need to be addressed first. To fail to address that concern, even if it is not medically legitimate, is a failure to address why the patient came to the emergency department. We all know that it is the mother, father, or other caregiver who must be satisfied when the patient is a child. Likewise, it may be the son or daughter of an elderly patient or a spouse or friend who has important issues to be addressed.

A Failure to Communicate

Physicians often underestimate patients' needs for communication concerning their care. Some studies suggest a direct relationship exists between increased physician communication skills and fewer medical malpractice lawsuits.[9] Use all techniques at hand to enhance the patient's perception of the time you take to communicate effectively.

Medicine is highly technical and has a language of its own. Over time, we begin to think and talk in that language. However, when interacting with patients and their families, we must be careful to use words and expressions our patients understand and refrain from using technical terms that can be confusing and disturbing. Why use such terms as "radical" prostatectomy, when in fact it is a "total" prostatectomy? What do you gain by using the term "radical," which can be frightening? Similarly, "serous otitis" could be interpreted as "serious otitis" or "gastritis" could imply "gas." Remember: some patients are intimidated by physicians, and if so, are less likely to address their real concerns. Specifically, ask for questions.

A common complaint among patients is that physicians do not spend enough time with them. Time spent with the physician is an important determinant of patient satisfaction.[10] The emergency department interaction between physician and patient, by its nature, must be brief, but there are several simple things physicians can do to enhance the patient's perception. For one, sit down to talk to the patient. The act of sitting down not only signals that time is being taken, but also that your full attention is focused on the patient. Anticipate the patient's needs. Offer pain medications or work excuses, if that is an issue. The act of offering may be the most important component. Physicians must show that they are truly concerned about the welfare of each patient. There should be no need for a patient advocate other than the physician.

Perhaps the greatest source of patient dissatisfaction in emergency departments is enduring lengthy waiting times.[11] Physicians can do a great deal to alleviate this dissatisfaction. Begin your interaction with the patient by apologizing for how long he had to wait. Patients value their time as much as anyone else does. Recognizing this and apologizing for the wait sets the tone for the rest of the physician-patient encounter. The apology can include some explanation of the delay, such as a sudden rush of ambulances, as long as it does not minimize the importance of the patient's problem.

Another common complaint among patients is that physicians never explain what their treatment opinions are. Involve the patient in decision-making. Present several options and let the patient help decide which of them is best. Patient outcome and satisfaction are enhanced by participation in health care decisions.[12] Give discharge instructions to the patient, but also to anyone who accompanies the patient. Encourage them to ask questions. This step may seem time-consuming, but it can save a great deal of time later if it prevents a miscommunication and a return visit. A frequent patient complaint is physicians' inadequate attention to questions.[13]

You Are Not the Social Police

As physicians, we do not get to decide who deserves care based on social worth or lifestyle or other conditions. Patients come to the emergency department for help with specific medical problems, not for judgment. Of course, patient education is useful, and it is appropriate for the emergency physician to advise patients to avoid certain types of behavior, but that advice should be dispensed at the end of the visit and in such a way that patients are allowed to make their own decisions. If a patient feels that the physician is genuinely concerned, caring, and competent, then that patient is more likely to follow the medical advice offered. Emergency physicians also are not in a position to berate patients for seeking medical care. Doing so is not only pointless as a patient education issue, but also counterproductive. On the other hand, patients have been known to change their behavior in response to the physician's legitimate caring and concerned approach, which they certainly will not do if the physician belittles their complaints or berates them for their behavior.

Emergency physicians should avoid other specific behaviors that patients may perceive as being judgmental. For example, be careful not to underestimate a patient's anxiety, discomfort, pain, or activity limitations. Studies show that our estimates are typically much lower than what patients are actually experiencing.[14] Minimizing a patient's perceptions in these areas creates a poor therapeutic relationship.

Another high-risk behavior is creating the impression that the patient's decision to seek care in the emergency department is not warranted. For example, do not ask a patient why he did not call his own physician, or follow up as previously instructed, or take prescribed medications. Instead, address the complaint or concern that led the patient to seek care in the emergency department. Surveys note patient dissatisfaction when the professional fails to recognize the validity of patient concerns.[13] Even if the patient's concerns do not appear to be legitimate medical issues, take these issues seriously and discuss them with the patient. The fact is that the patient has presented with a concern and emergency department staff members should put out their best efforts to evaluate and take care of the problem as quickly as possible. The goal is not to get patients out of the emergency department, but on the road to recovery.

Nobody Knows the Trouble You've Seen (or Cares)

Do not use patients as sounding boards for your own complaints. The truth is, patients really do not care how tired you are or how long it has been since you ate, or whether you are having problems with co-workers or other patients, and that is as it should be. Patients come to emergency departments because they need our services. As "customers," they are no different from customers in any other setting. If you have waited for an hour to be seated in a restaurant, do you really care whether the waiter's feet hurt or he has too many other tables to wait on, or that he just got stiffed for his tip?

Other High-Risk Situations and How to Avoid Them

Those of us who work in emergency medicine understand that, in an emergency depart-

ment, waiting is a fact of life. Our patients, however, have different levels of experience and, as a result, different expectations. Do not underestimate how big a factor waiting time is in your patients' perception of the care they receive. Days, weeks, or months after they have been treated in the emergency department, patients generally will not remember the technical details of what you did for them. They have little framework in which to place the technicalities of what happened. As a result, what they are likely to remember about their emergency department experiences will be based on an overall perception of care given. And how long they were there is likely to be one of the most significant factors.

Establish a system to notify patients about waiting times and to explain why they are occurring. The unscheduled nature of patients' arrivals, the unknown severity of their ailments, and many other factors affect patient waiting time. Tell patients why they are waiting and give them some expectation as to when they may be seen. Then, when they are actually seen within that period of time, they are more likely to be satisfied with the emergency care provided.

Give patients some idea of what is going to happen while they are in the emergency department, such as laboratory tests, x-rays, review of previous records, discussion with private physicians, and so on. Tell them whether they can eat or drink or leave the room. Be sure that your time estimates for these steps are generous so the patient can plan to stay occupied during this time. Patients frequently will hold physicians to a specific time period beyond which they are viewed as being slow and incompetent.

Make sure that the emergency department has efficient systems to generate a medical record, obtain previous records, transport the patient to and from x-ray labs, obtain laboratory and other data in a timely and efficient manner, identify the flow of the patient through the department, identify the location of family members, and so on. Take these responsibilities seriously, not only as part of the job of patient care, but also for risk management purposes.

Too frequently in our emergency departments we separate patients from their family or friends, usually in the interest of speed and efficiency. Waiting with a friend or family member decreases the patient's perception of waiting time and provides support and assistance that may be valuable during treatment. The patient may not remember much from the physician-patient interaction, but the family member or friend present is likely to remember in great detail the care — and caring — that was demonstrated toward the patient. We have nothing to hide about what we do. Unless certain procedures are particularly unpleasant or traumatic for family members, make every effort to let them stay with their loved ones. Countless people have described how terrible it is to bring an ill or injured loved one to an unknown emergency department and have to turn that person over completely to the care of strangers, then sit alone in a waiting room wondering what is happening. Keeping a patient's family and friends in the dark by not allowing them to see their loved ones generates unnecessary anxiety.

The hospital also should instill in its personnel that being friendly and showing concern toward patients and family members are essential parts of their jobs. The belief that only technical medicine, nursing care, and clerical procedures are the jobs of the emergency department places that department at high risk, especially if patients have poor outcomes. For this same reason, the perception that the nursing staff is uncaring, unfriendly, or judgmental also creates a negative image.[15] Patients generally spend more time being cared for by nurses than by physicians, and their overall impression of the emergency department is heavily dependent on their interaction with nurses. Like it or not, emergency medicine is a "service industry," even though the service rendered is a professional one.

The use of humor in the emergency care setting is a touchy issue. Many emergency physicians and other medical personnel use humor for a variety of reasons, such as to reduce their own tension, but this type of humor seldom seems appropriate to the ill or injured patient. To belittle a patient's problem or joke about it may alienate the patient or family and create an impression that you are not serious about your work or you do not care about the patient. Humor has its place, but that place is not in front of the patient or anywhere the patient or family can overhear it.

Key Points and Conclusion

This chapter presented the following key points:

- Present a positive first impression. Introduce yourself to the patient and family members, shake hands, and apologize for any lengthy wait.
- Present a positive image for the emergency department. The first person to greet the patient should present a caring attitude. Be sure to keep the department clean.
- Anticipate patients' needs and give generous time estimates to accomplish them.
- Involve family and friends.
- Ask for questions and concerns from the patient and family members.

References

1. University Hospital Building, Inc., dba Memorial Hospital of Jacksonville (FL) v Gooding, August 20, 1983. *Emerg Phys Legal Bull* January 1989:1-8.
2. Blanchard CG, Labrecque MS, Ruckdeschel JC, et al. Physician behaviors, patient perceptions, and patient characteristics as predictors of satisfaction of hospitalized adult cancer patients. *Cancer* 1990;65:186-192.
3. Cherkin DC, MacCornack FA. Patient evaluations of low back pain care from family physicians and chiropractors. *West J Med* 1989;150:351-355.
4. Estabrook B, Zapka J, Lubin H. Consumer perceptions of dental care in the health services program of an educational institution. *J Am Dent Assoc* 1980;100:540-543.
5. Lovdal LT, Pearson R. Wanted: doctors who care. *J Health Care Mark* 1989;9(1):37-41.
6. Brody DS, Miller SM, Lerman CE, et al. The relationship between patients' satisfaction with their physicians and perceptions about interventions they desired and received. *Med Care* 1989;27:1027-1035.
7. Parrish GA, Holdren KS, Skiendzielewski JJ, et al. Emergency department experience with sudden death: a survey of survivors. *Ann Emerg Med* 1987;16:792-796.
8. Gjerdingen DK, Simpson DE, Titus SL. Patients' and physicians' attitudes regarding the physician's professional appearance. *Arch Intern Med* 1987; 147:1209-1212.
9. Adamson TE, Tschann JM, Gullion DS, et al. Physician communication skills and malpractice claims. A complex relationship. *West J Med* 1989;150:356-360.
10. Chesteen SA, Warren SE, Wooley FR. A comparison of family practice clinics and free-standing emergency centers: organizational characteristics, process of care, and patient satisfaction. *J Fam Pract* 1986;23:377-382.
11. McMillan JR, Younger MS, DeWine LC. Satisfaction with hospital emergency department as a function of patient triage. *Health Care Manage Rev* 1986;11(3):21-27.
12. Lerman CE, Brody DS, Caputo GC, et al. Patients' perceived involvement in care scale: relationship to attitudes about illness and medical care. *J Gen Intern Med* 1990;5:29-33.
13. Williamson V. Patients' satisfaction with general practitioner services: a survey by a community health council. *J R Coll Gen Pract* 1989;39:452-455.
14. Wartman SA, Morlock LL, Malitz FE, et al. Impact of divergent evaluations by physicians and patients of patients' complaints. *Public Health Rep* 1983;98:141-145.
15. Keeping the lid on malpractice in the emergency department. *Emerg Phys Legal Bull* January 1989:1-8.

Chapter 4

Conflict Resolution: Attending Physician – Emergency Physician

Neal E. Little, MD, FACEP

Emergency physicians provide immediate, short-term care rather than ongoing care for patients they see in the emergency department. Under such circumstances, the patient's relationship with the emergency physician is necessarily brief. Even so, it has the same characteristics as any other physician-patient relationship, with the exception of follow-up. The emergency physician has an independent duty to each patient, and that duty is not superseded by any other relationship the patient may have with other health care providers.

There is, however, a fundamental difference between attending and emergency physicians once the patient has established a relationship with them. Attending physicians, after giving adequate notice, can terminate the physician-patient relationship. Emergency physicians, however, do not have the option of refusing to care for a patient once the patient arrives in the department. This fact makes their situation unique in the health care facility.

Emergency physicians have an independent body of knowledge and skills in their own right, which forms the basis of their practice. They possess an independent, unrestricted license to practice medicine. Emergency physicians, unlike interns or residents, are not the trainees or apprentices of any other physician on the medical staff. This fact may not be as well recognized by attending physicians as it is by emergency physicians, a discrepancy that can be a source of conflict.

Also, because the practice of medicine is far from an exact science, many opinions concern-ing diagnostic and treatment options exist for virtually every patient problem encountered. If two physicians are involved in the care of the patient, they may have two different opinions about treatment procedures. As the number of physicians involved in a case increases, so will the number of opinions.

This fact does not relieve emergency physicians of the duty to act on their own judgment concerning the best interests of the patient. The emergency physician has an independent duty to see that the patient understands and agrees to whatever care is administered. When an attending physician and an emergency physician substantially disagree about patient care, a potentially major liability problem exists. As a result, there must be some means of resolving these conflicts before the patient leaves the emergency department. At a minimum, the patient should be informed of both physicians' opinions in order to make an informed choice about treatment.

Case Study

A man complaining of severe chest pain comes to the emergency department, where he is seen by an emergency physician previously trained in internal medicine. The emergency physician correctly diagnoses an acute anterior wall myocardial infarction and decides that the patient should be admitted to the hospital.

He calls the patient's attending physician, who asks that the patient be transferred across town to another hospital where he believes he can manage the patient better. The emergency physician objects; he does not believe the transfer is safe based on the patient's condition.

At the request of the emergency physician, the patient's attending physician comes to the emergency department to evaluate the patient himself. The attending physician subsequently has the patient transferred by ambulance to the other hospital. The emergency physician and the attending physician disagree and meet in private to discuss the transfer. During transport, the patient experiences ventricular fibrillation and dies.

The patient's wife files a lawsuit against both physicians. In the action against the emergency physician, she argues that he had an independent duty not only to see and evaluate her husband, but also to render his best medical opinion regarding treatment. Although the emergency physician and the attending physician disagreed with each other, the patient and his wife were never given the benefit of the emergency physician's opinion. She claims that she would have made a different decision about transfer knowing that a different opinion existed. The wife won this lawsuit and continued to win on appeal all the way to the Pennsylvania Supreme Court.[1]

The Medical-Legal Perspective

This case illustrates the fact that, although emergency physicians may not be able to control everything that happens to a patient, patients are entitled to the physician's best opinion about treatment. This is especially true when that opinion conflicts with another physician's opinion.

Attending physicians do not "own" their patients — that is, they cannot dictate the course of patients' medical care against their will. Nor can they direct other practitioners to agree to actions that may be against a patient's will. Patients cannot know what their "will" is in any given circumstance unless they are given all pertinent information by the emergency physician. This includes the physician's opinion about the best course of treatment and care.

Attending physicians do have their own duty to patients, and that duty includes both follow-up[2] and consultation.[3] Likewise, the emergency physician has a duty to consult with attending physicians when appropriate.[4] Clearly, the emergency physician and the attending physician are inextricably intertwined in their respective care of the patient. A smooth working relationship is essential. Both must understand their own independent duties to the patient.

When two physicians disagree about the care rendered to a patient and a poor outcome results, their disagreement often fuels a lawsuit. The plaintiff's counsel will have little difficulty obtaining the opinion that something else should have been done for the patient — one of the two physicians will provide that opinion. With the prospect of physicians pointing fingers at each other in court, it is not difficult to see why conflict between an attending physician and an emergency physician must be resolved satisfactorily.

The emergency physician's duty to the patient includes making sure that acceptable and attainable medical care is rendered to that patient. The emergency physician does not have a duty to the attending physician. The emergency physician's duty to the patient supersedes any consideration of ego; finances; or the schedule, medical practices, or sleep patterns of an attending physician.

Emergency physicians may often be the bearers of bad news, requiring an attending physician to get out of bed in the middle of the night to care for a patient. Emergency care frequently involves difficult decisions that may disrupt an otherwise smooth interaction between two physicians. To avoid the potential for finger-pointing when a poor patient outcome occurs, areas of potential conflict need to be identified and adequate systems to document their resolution put in place. The most common potential conflict is patient admission to the hospital. If the emergency physician believes that a patient should be admitted and the attending physician disagrees, their conflict must be resolved. Another frequent conflict concerns transfer of the patient to another facility. The Pennsylvania Supreme Court case previously discussed illustrates not only the issue of transfer but the responsibility of emergency physicians to voice their opinions about whether a patient should be moved.

The timing of follow-up care can be a third serious conflict. If a patient's medical condition warrants a repeat evaluation within 24 hours and it happens to be Saturday, then follow-up care should occur on Sunday. To change your opinion about the timing of follow-up tests based on traditional office hours may not be in the best interests of the patient. Recommend that the patient have follow-up care regardless of the time of day or the day of the week.

A fourth potential conflict may be the choice of medication used, or the request by attending physicians to be contacted before certain medications or treatments are administered to a patient.

A fifth potential conflict may arise when the "private patient" presents to the emergency department. Patients may come in with the expectation of seeing their own private physicians and may even have made such arrangements. However, the fact that the patient has a private physician may not relieve the emergency physician of the duty to examine that patient.[5] Although the arrival of the patient and the need for care are certain, the arrival of the attending physician is not as certain. If the attending physician is not immediately available for patient evaluation, then the emergency physician becomes the primary caregiver. When the attending physician arrives in the emergency department, he can take responsibility for the patient.

A sixth potential conflict is the recommendation that patients need the personal attention of their attending physicians immediately. That may mean disrupting the attending physician's office hours, sleep, or social commitments, which can create friction between emergency and private physicians.

Finally, writing orders is also a potential source conflict. This subject is addressed more fully in Chapter 43, "Admitting Orders" and in Chapter 47, "Discharge and Follow-up Instructions."

Conflict Resolution Policy

Every health care facility should develop a conflict resolution policy that emergency and attending physicians can rely on when faced with a potential disagreement. This policy must recognize that the emergency physician has an independent duty to the patient and a legitimate interest in patient care. It must state that if, after discussions between the attending and emergency physicians the conflict cannot be resolved, then several steps should take place.

First, the attending physician must evaluate the patient personally to obtain the same knowledge base as the emergency physician has about the patient's immediate condition. Second, if the two physicians still cannot agree on a course of action, the patient must be informed of both opinions in order to make a sound, informed decision about treatment. Third, a neutral third party can be called in to arbitrate the dispute.

This person might be the chief of the department of the attending or emergency physician, or the chief of staff, or a designee. This option should be agreed on in advance of a conflict.

The foundation of any conflict resolution policy is twofold:
- The concerns of the emergency physician must have at least equal weight with those of the attending physician.
- The emergency physician's duty to see that a patient receives appropriate medical care is not relieved by some previous physician-patient relationship. Discussion of such a conflict resolution policy should occur before the conflict is under way.

In some cases, a conflict resolution policy satisfactory to emergency physicians cannot be created. The attending physicians, hospital, or both should then indemnify emergency physicians against malpractice actions alleging a lack of agreement between attending and emergency physicians. Such a binding agreement forces the attending physician and the hospital to back up their opinions with their assets.

Key Points and Conclusion

This chapter covered the following key points regarding attending physician and emergency physician conflict resolution.
- Conflict between emergency physicians and attending physicians is inevitable, given the conditions of emergency care.
- Each physician has an independent duty to the patient that is not superseded by prior physician-patient relationships.
- Physicians do not "own" patients.[2] Patients choose their own physicians.
- An emergency physician who disagrees with treatment ordered by an attending physician should not allow this treatment be performed unless the patient is informed and can make a reasonable choice.
- The hospital should develop a conflict resolution policy that recognizes emergency and attending physicians' independent duties and that resolves conflicts in the patient's best interests.

References

1. *Dohan v C. Stephen Stahlnecker, Riddle Memorial Hospital and Concordville Fire and Protection Association.* Common Pleas of Delaware, Pa, 1971 Term No. 9919, Sup Ct Pa, 1980 Term No. 2349.
2. *Davis v Weiscopf*, F139 NE2d 60 (1982) as reported in *Emerg Phys Legal Bull* 1983;9(4).
3. Medical staff responsibility to the ED and hospital. *Emerg Phys Legal Bull* 1982;7(3).

4. Duty to consult. *Emerg Phys Legal Bull* 1981;7(2).

5. *Lassala v Dreyer Medical Center Clinic*, et al. 4589 NE2d 958 (1983) as reported in *Emerg Phys Legal Bull* 1986;12(1):5-8.

Chapter 5

Conflict Resolution: Physician – Nurse

Neal E. Little, MD, FACEP

Given the stresses and unique demands of emergency medicine, conflicts between emergency physicians and nurses are inevitable. These conflicts may be based on their different perceptions of a patient's medical condition or disposition, or appropriateness of medications or other treatments. Conflicts between physicians and nurses indicate a failure of communication within the department. However, a more serious problem is created when such conflicts send mixed messages to patients and undermine their confidence in the medical care they receive. And if one of these patients files a malpractice lawsuit, the conflicts between the physician and nurse will call their credibility into question.

To manage this area of risk, health care administrators and staff should implement conflict resolution policies to settle disputes when they arise. There are many sources of conflict between physicians and nurses, but few are as common or potentially high risk as those related to charting a patient's history, physical examination, and response to treatment. The most common cause of charting discrepancies is that patients frequently tell their histories in different ways to different caregivers. This phenomenon is documented in the medical literature and well known to all physicians, and is, for the most part, unavoidable.

Why does this happen? The very nature of taking a patient's history is a factor. One patient may develop a better rapport with the physician and tell him things he would not tell the nurse, or vice versa. Some patients will not tell the second caregiver what they told the first. Some patients are "doctor pleasers" — reluctant to complain about their symptoms to the physician. And some patients allow themselves to be led by the physician or nurse through a series of questions for which they are given subtle clues to "appropriate" responses.

Many patients reserve their most serious complaints for the physician, because they believe that the physician has more power to act on them. Other patients describe their most serious complaints to the nurse and expect the physician to "just do something." Add to this the fact that patients' friends and family members provide additional history, and it becomes clear that physicians and nurses must take steps to obtain and chart a coherent picture of the patient presentation and response to treatment.

There are other legitimate reasons that physicians and nurses record patient complaints differently. For example, if the complaint is one that a nurse cannot act on, the nurse may simply take the complaint at face value and not obtain all the details to direct a specific treatment. A physician presented with a similar complaint may ask more probing questions and elicit more details to facilitate specific treatment.

This is not to say that a physician necessarily takes a better history. Rather, physicians and nurses put different emphasis on some aspects of patient care based on their authority or responsibility to act on specific complaints.

The Medical-Legal Perspective

Because charting discrepancies between physicians and nurses are common, the patient's permanent chart may reflect two different perceptions of the history, physical examination, or response to care. And if it does, keep in mind that the patient's chart then becomes a permanent record of conflict between physician and nurse. The charting of a patient's vital signs may represent an area of particularly high risk, especially if abnormal vital signs are noted on the chart but not acted on appropriately.

For these reasons, patient charts created by nurses and physicians must be available to both parties so they can recognize conflicts at the time of documentation and do something to resolve them. If they are not aware that a discrepancy exists and it is reflected in the permanent record, the patient may be at risk — as is everyone else involved in the patient's care.

What You Can Do

There are several ways to prevent conflicts between physicians and nurses. Staff and administrators must give serious consideration to developing conflict resolution policies such as the following:

- The emergency department should have policies to ensure that charting by the physician and the nurse can be seen by both parties before disposition.
- Physicians should have a system for reading completed nursing notes routinely. They must have the opportunity to review these notes before patient disposition.
- Policies should be in place to notify the physician of any significant change in the patient's condition. This change should not have to be communicated exclusively in writing. All significant changes in patient status should immediately be communicated verbally to the emergency physician. Charting a decline in the patient's condition without notifying the physician immediately creates unnecessary conflict and risk.
- There must be a policy and procedure in place so that when a nurse significantly disagrees with a physician on any aspect of patient evaluation or care, the nurse can begin steps to resolve the conflict. Within the nursing staff structure in the emergency department, there should be a system that will help the nurse feel comfortable bringing concerns to the physician's attention before patient disposition. These policies must be developed in advance and agreed on by all parties so that conflict resolution will not be viewed as a violation of anyone's authority or as a question of competence.

- Policies should specify that no significant unexpected or unknown events should be charted after patient disposition or discharge. A nurse's observations written at a time when they cannot be acted on by the physician are not in the patient's best interests and represent an area of high risk to the hospital and its staff.
- Once an area of conflict has been identified and resolved, that resolution should be charted by the appropriate person. If a nurse has charted a finding that contradicts the physician's report and they agree on the version that is correct, the record should be corrected by the person who was in error. The correction should always acknowledge that a conflict arose and was resolved. Existing entries should not be crossed out so that the original observation cannot be read.

Physicians and nurses should recognize that conflicts are inevitable and should take steps to identify and resolve them. Conflict resolution must take place in a timely manner before patient disposition. When other caregivers are involved in the patient's management, they must have similar access to the nurses' and physicians' observations.

Key Points and Conclusion

This chapter covered the following key points about conflict between physicians and nurses:

- Recognize that conflicts are inevitable.
- Develop systems to identify conflicts when they occur.
- Develop policies to resolve conflicts before patient disposition.
- Develop policies to ensure that conflict resolution is documented in the patient's record.

Chapter 6

Patient Confidence in the Health Care Team

Neal E. Little, MD, FACEP

Few tasks in the delivery of health care are as complex as engineering the smooth operation of the emergency department. The medical care rendered to an emergency department patient represents the sum total of a health care team's efforts. In fact, physician care would be impossible without the support of other members of the team — registration, medical records, laboratory, radiology, nursing, pharmacy, housekeeping, maintenance, engineering, administration, and security.

When patients receive medical care, especially in an emergency department, they form an overall impression of their experiences. They may not necessarily distinguish which aspects of care were rendered by which provider, and they may not be aware of the quality of technical care delivered. But they do have an experience they will remember and recall in the future. In a service industry such as emergency medicine, the perception of care is extremely important. Members of the health care team must not undermine a patient's confidence in other team members because, by doing so, they undermine that patient's confidence in themselves.

Sometimes patients will pick up on conflict among members of the health care team. This perception can damage the therapeutic relationship between the team and the patient, raise questions about caregivers' competency, and contribute to patient dissatisfaction. One of the most damaging situations occurs when one caregiver criticizes another's work. For example, a patient who presents to the emergency department may have been treated for the same problem at another hospital or by another physician. His condition may not have responded as he wished, and he may be seeking other medical opinions. The second physician who has the benefit of hindsight may be tempted to criticize care previously rendered. However, he needs to keep in mind that he was not present when care was rendered the first time and cannot know the exact condition of the patient at that time. Patients' conditions change with time, but hindsight is always 20/20.

On the other hand, the patient may be angry that his condition is not improving and, in an attempt to deflect the patient's anger, the second physician may want to point out what the first physician did wrong. Criticizing prior care in this situation can have negative effects. The patient may, in fact, have more confidence in the first physician or the care provided and question the credibility of the second. If a lawsuit is filed, this criticism will be the foundation of a legal action, which will more than likely include both physicians. Lawyers get no credit for leaving a physician out of the action; naming the second physician will provide further justification that the care was substandard. Rest assured that the physician will find some aspects of the second physician's care inadequate.

Criticism can take many forms. The most obvious is overt criticism, which should be avoided at all times. Judging treatment previously provided is not a necessary part of good care. Besides, opinions about proper medical care are diverse and change with time. Today's dogma is tomorrow's heresy. If a physician feels strongly that prior care was inadequate, there are proper forums for resolution. A less obvious form of criticism — covert — is more difficult to recognize and eliminate but equally important to avoid. When taking a clinical history, for example, be careful not to elicit historical facts in a way that suggests some other steps should have been taken. Comments such as: "So he waited five days to give you a prescription?" "They didn't do blood tests?" "So you didn't get an x-ray?" give the impression that those steps should have been taken and call into question the prior care rendered.

Routine interactions in the emergency department also can draw covert criticism of the health care team. If physicians complain about how slow the lab is or how long they have been waiting for a consultant, for example, they give patients the impression that the hospital is inefficient. As a result, when patients leave, their overall impression of the emergency department is one of incompetence. A physician who asks a nurse why certain procedures have not been done yet in front of the patient or family may give the impression that someone is delaying or denying the patient proper care. If timeliness of ancillary services or nursing care is a problem, then it needs to be solved. Open-ended complaining in the patient's presence may vent the physician's frustration but does little to solve the problem.

Physicians should not merely refrain from criticism, however. They should actively praise the health care team for tasks well done. This practice creates an atmosphere of mutual trust that shows the patient that the team is working together and that good care has been provided. Patients typically have nothing on which to judge the quality of care they receive other than their perception of the caregivers' competence. Health care team members who offer a positive comment on the technical aspects of care reinforce a positive image of treatment.

Another practice that can undermine patient confidence in the health care team is correcting medical students, residents, interns, and nurses in front of patients and their families. In an academic setting, public discussions about patients' physical findings or ways to conduct certain procedures are common. However, this teaching tool can be frightening for patients and can undermine confidence if they see emergency physicians criticizing or correcting someone in a student capacity. The patient may not understand that corrections are technical or theoretical. They may feel that someone has made harmful mistakes in their care. As a general rule, do not correct someone in a student capacity in front of patients. If it is necessary to do so, be sure that patients understand the corrections have no negative impact on their care.

What You Can Do

- Good physicians and nurses should be complimented on their work. The emergency physician should compliment patients on their choice of personal physicians or stress the special skills of that physician. Likewise, they should praise nursing personnel for tasks well done. The patient has little frame of reference to judge the technical quality of the care, and a comment from the physician will go a long way in building their confidence. Similarly, nurses can speak positively about components of a physician's care.

- The emergency physician should provide positive background information on the physician the patient will be seeing for follow-up care. This approach communicates to the patient a sense of caring. Right away, the patient feels good about the relationship with the other physician.

- Praise in public and criticize in private. Any criticisms of health care staff should occur in a private setting as part of a quality improvement program.

Key Points and Conclusion

This chapter covered the following key points regarding patient confidence in the care rendered by an emergency department team:

- Patient confidence in the health care team is not only part of quality care, but also a key component of risk management.

- Patients' conditions change over time. Patients have their own perceptions of the care they received from prior and current physicians.

- Legitimate differences of opinion about medical care are a normal, healthy part of patient care.

- Do not overtly or covertly criticize another member or component of the health care team except within the context of a formal quality improvement effort.

- Actively praise and recognize good care by other members of the health care team.

Chapter 7

Patient Complaints

Norman Schneiderman, MD, FACEP
Phyllis T. Doerger, MD, FACEP

Satisfying patients in the emergency department is becoming more challenging. The public now views health care providers much as they view other service providers: as fallible human beings who at times behave rudely and even lose their tempers.

Since patients have taken health care providers off the pedestal, they have become more willing to complain about the care they receive. They are also suing physicians and health care facilities for a wide variety of injuries, both real and imagined. However, there is a positive side to the fact that patients view physicians and staff as human beings. Patients who have had negative outcomes of treatment are more forgiving if they genuinely feel that the physician tried hard to help them, cared about their welfare, and treated them kindly.

Naturally, preventing patient complaints is preferable to "handling" them. Yet, occasionally, everyone in the health care field receives a complaint. Any physician who sees 3,000 to 5,000 patients every year is going to displease a few people along the way. How can we keep these complaints to a minimum? In general, the simplest way is to meet or exceed each patient's expectations for care. Providers know that they cannot and should not always acquiesce to patients' wishes or demands. But, good communication skills can turn a potentially unhappy or disappointed patient into one who leaves the emergency department saying, "That doctor really cared about me!"

Types of Complaints From Patients

Health care institutions must deal with three general types of complaints:

- Completely unfounded complaints
- Complaints based on the patient's lack of knowledge
- Complaints based on provider error

The first type is easy to handle because it is groundless. These are complaints that would make a normal layperson wonder, "Why is this person even bothering to complain?" Periodically, the complaint is lodged by a psychotic or neurotic individual. Try to resolve this complaint, but understand that the conversation may end simply with thanking the person for making an observation. The complainant may threaten to call the news media or write to the medical society. Perhaps expressing the complaint will be enough.

The second most common type of complaint is based on medical ignorance, misconceptions, or miscommunication. Usually, providing the patient with information will resolve these complaints to everyone's satisfaction. Because these are the most frequently expressed, hospitals will find that educating patients solves most of them.

The third type of complaint arises from provider errors. When a patient has a legitimate complaint about the quality of care received, the situation is difficult to resolve. Most health care providers want to be helpful and sensitive to the complaint without admitting their guilt outright. The best advice in these situations is to be honest without ever saying words like "mistake" or "error," especially if these conversations must be put in writing. Show sorrow or regret without implying guilt. Letters to patients must be worded carefully and reviewed by the hospital's malpractice attorney before they are sent, particularly if the letter concerns a potentially serious case.

Case Studies

1

A 22-year-old man with known migraine headaches presents to the emergency department. He has a headache that is a little worse than usual and his neck feels a little stiff. However, he never mentions his neck symptoms because he overhears the emergency physician make a disparaging comment about another patient who is obese. Overweight himself, the patient feels insulted and consequently volunteers little information about his symptoms. The physician performs a superficial examination and offers an analgesic. The patient refuses the medication and leaves the emergency department very displeased.

He presents to another emergency department in the same city. This time, history is elicited carefully. The patient describes an acute onset of his headache. He is evaluated and found to have meningism; a CT scan reveals a small subarachnoid bleed. No surgery is required, and the patient makes an uneventful recovery. There is no true injury, but this patient does find a lawyer willing to file a lawsuit against the first emergency physician. Two years and numerous depositions later, the case is dropped.

2

A 28-year-old man goes to the emergency department for a treatment of a scalp laceration. He admits to being in a bar brawl but claims he was sober at the time. He is not sure how he got cut.

After being treated, he has three complaints against the hospital. First, the physician who sutured him kept leaving to take care of other patients. This delay necessitated a second injection of local anesthetic because the first dose wore off. Second, a piece of glass eventually worked its way out of the wound shortly after the sutures were removed. Third, the nurses did a poor job of cleaning his scalp. When the patient got home, there was still so much dried blood on his face that his mother fainted, fell, cut her head, and had to get sutured — at the

same emergency department. They refused to pay either of the bills.

3

A 32-year-old woman seeks treatment at an emergency department for what is diagnosed as acute salpingitis. She is married and has three young children and is incensed that her husband has apparently given her this infection. She is treated with appropriate antibiotics. The next day, the patient visits her gynecologist, who criticizes the emergency physician for not drawing a CBC. (Appropriate cultures were obtained at the time of the emergency visit.) The gynecologist insinuates that this alleged oversight constitutes poor care. The patient is understandably upset and wants to meet with the hospital's chief executive officer.

Case Discussions

1

In this case, the patient freely admitted that his motivation was revenge for being insulted. Emergency department personnel must be careful about what they say about their patients. Offhand comments and laughter may be misinterpreted by people overhearing them. Even more important, complaints should be viewed in a positive manner — not as a purely negative occurrence. All complaints are legitimate to the complainer and offer a window of opportunity for a hospital to see itself as others see it. Every business needs complaints in order to improve. Without them, a business has little idea how consumers view its product. Although some people will praise a hospital's emergency department, most patient feedback will be negative. These complaints should be regarded as constructive criticism and made to work for the hospital rather than against it.

Complaint management carries with it substantial public relations implications. Research reveals that the average company never hears 96% of the total complaints people have about its products and services. This is a contradiction of the notion that everyone complains about every little thing that goes wrong. So, why bother managing the 4% of complaints that we do hear about? There are two good reasons. First, the 4% probably includes the most unhappy or dissatisfied patients. Second, just an average unhappy patient will tell as many as 10 friends about a bad experience at a hospital. In either case, these patients often provide an excellent profile of the patient most likely to sue.

Second, unhappy patients take their business elsewhere. Consider this interesting statistic: an estimated 54% to 70% of complaining patients never return to the offending institution unless their complaints are resolved to their satisfaction, an excellent argument for the importance of resolving patient complaints in an appropriate and timely manner. Often, adequate complaint resolution gives the patient a good memory of the emergency department experience. As a result, the patient, and the patient's family and friends, continue to patronize the institution.

Although avoiding complaints is a goal that all health care providers strive for, no one succeeds completely. Health care providers' time is limited; even though they often realize the value of attending to complaints, they want to keep them to a manageable number. The best way to manage a complaint is to prevent one from happening. How can health care providers counteract some of the classic and sometimes unavoidable negative aspects of their emergency departments? The answer is surprisingly simple but effective: good eye contact, a smile, a warm and gentle touch, and a sympathetic ear. Despite the constant press of their duties, emergency physicians and nurses need to take a few minutes with their patients to communicate, develop a rapport, and inspire confidence. Do not underestimate the power of these simple remedies. People form their opinions of others within the first few moments of an encounter. Aside from healing the sick and saving lives, emergency physicians face another challenge: developing a rapport with patients in only a few minutes. Other specialists have it much easier in this regard. An emergency physician may see 30 to 40 patients during an 8- to 10-hour shift. When physicians handle this case load or reach the 23rd hour of a 24-hour shift in the emergency department, they may find it difficult to have the time or motivation to make every patient feel important.

Nonetheless, building good physician-patient relationships is the physicians' task. They must be friendly and sincere, attempt to get all personnel in the emergency department to act likewise, and try to behave as if the patient is the only one being treated at that moment. A few guidelines can help physicians establish a rapport quickly with patients. Put a stool at the bedside and sit down, even if you are seeing the patient for only two minutes. The time will seem longer to the patient if you are not standing. After a brief introduction, refer to the patient by name — (Mr. Smith, Mrs. Jones). If in doubt about how to address the patient, ask. The next step may be to touch the patient, either by shaking hands or, if the patient is ill, placing a hand on the patient's hand or arm. The sense of touch conveys a feeling of acceptance. Sensitive hands can be soothing and reassuring to an anxious patient. The beneficial effects of "laying on of hands" have been tested by time.

Most patients take physicians' and nurses' competency for granted. They do not judge health care personnel in terms of their medical ability. They assume that providers must have the basic skills. However, they will judge physicians, nurses, and staff according to their display of genuine interest, thoroughness of approach to patients' problems, understanding, compassion, personal warmth, and the degree of clarity with which they give patients insight into their medical problems.

After greeting the patient, ask about how and what the patient is feeling at that time and what has occurred concerning this particular illness. Remember: the purpose of the medical interview is to collect historical data that can be used to make a diagnosis and to understand the patient's illness. A helpful technique in the interviewing process is to restate periodically what the patient has said. This helps reinforce the patient-physician communication process. Some patients will draw out a story and will need to be guided back to the essential points without feeling rushed. Many patients come to the emergency department just to talk, and they will not be satisfied unless given the chance. Like it or not, this is a fact of life in primary care medicine. Try to take a complete history without prejudice and without leading or rushing the patient.

The physical examination is probably the least criticized part of patients' encounters with physicians. The most common complaint is that the physician or hospital charged too much for the examination. Patients occasionally complain that physicians do not respect their privacy, a problem made worse by the impersonal design of many emergency departments. Rectal and pelvic examinations should be performed where there is little chance of intrusion from outside the cubicle or room. Most patients are already embarrassed enough about these examinations without having to endure an audience.

After the examination, give the patient some

explanation of the clinical impression and treatment plan. If tests are needed, the physician should explain what they are, why they are needed, and how long they will take. This time estimate should be generous to allow for delays. Patients and families particularly resent waiting times in excess of two hours. This time factor seems to be a the magic number.

A patient relations representative can be helpful in preventing or resolving complaints. This person helps facilitate communication among the patient, family, and department staff. More departments are hiring these people to "work" the waiting room. They often catch problems early, and prevent formal complaints, and even potential litigation. Sometimes they discover critical medical information from a patient's family or friends that can change the treatment plan, particularly in the case of elderly patients.

Flexibility is a virtue in emergency medicine. Physicians should try not to be too dogmatic for example, refusing to conduct a test requested by a patient. Everyone wants to reduce costs, but if an explanation fails to convince the patient that a skull x-ray is not necessary, the physician should consider complying with the request. This is particularly true when children are involved. Try stepping into the parents' shoes before denying their requests. If there is a poor outcome and you refused to order an x-ray or blood test, you likely will hear from an attorney for the family.

When all medical data are gathered, review the case with the patient and the family, if they are present. Outline a course of action, including specific follow-up measures. These should include (in writing) when, why, and with whom the patient should continue with follow-up care.

Every patient in every patient-physician encounter should be treated in a kind, considerate, and unhurried manner. Physicians must be good listeners and good communicators. Most important, they should show their human side.

2

This case presented a difficult problem to handle and required a combined effort by nurses and the physician to resolve. Some parts of the bills probably can be eliminated because the patient had legitimate complaints. First, the nurse coordinator should ascertain if the patient's story is true. If it is, the nurses involved should be counseled or educated about proper wound cleansing and dressing. The patient also

deserved an apology, including a reasonable explanation of why the physician needed to tend to other patients. The physician needs to be encouraged to consider using longer-acting local anesthetics in a busy emergency department, and to be more careful when searching for foreign bodies, particularly when the patient cannot clearly recount the mechanism of injury.

3

In this case, the gynecologist's criticism of a colleague's care was inexcusable. Aside from being medically inaccurate, the physician may have prompted a meritless malpractice lawsuit. The patient, still upset about her husband's infidelity, wanted to lash out at the messenger. The emergency department medical director needs to have a frank discussion with the gynecologist about his reckless and unfounded remarks. If the gynecologist does not understand the problem after this discussion, it may be necessary to bring up the matter at the next Ob-Gyn department meeting. This kind of comment must not pass without action. History will repeat itself if such behavior goes unchecked.

Handling Complaints

A single approach to complaint management, usually developed by the department director (or nurse manager for nursing complaints), ensures consistency and conveys the desired message that the complaint is taken seriously. Complaints should be managed by someone other than the providers directly involved, as they may find it difficult to remain objective. Losing your temper will only make the situation more volatile. The complainant usually is more comfortable speaking with a third party, preferably someone of higher authority.

The efficient complaint manager will work with the patient relations representative or other identified staff to field the initial call, thank the caller, put the grievance in writing, and gather all the pertinent records. Armed with such background material, the manager should then contact the patient or family promptly.

Some complaints, such as an obvious billing error, can be resolved by the patient relations representative. Others will require one or more telephone calls, while a few are serious enough to warrant face-to-face meetings. The time factor in responding to complaints depends on the case. One to nine days is readily acceptable to most callers, especially if they are informed of the need for investigation. Complaint managers should allow adequate time for the first meeting or telephone conversation with a patient and/or family.

The key to successful complaint management is listening. The manager's attitude should be one of concern and sincerity. Listen for facts but, perhaps more important, listen for feelings and attempt to clarify the caller's agenda. Explore all concerns prior to any attempt to explain or defend. Sometimes the manager can offer an apology — without blaming anyone — for the perceived poor care the patient received. Reflect back and validate the patient's or family's feelings and offer support: "I can see how long the wait must have seemed when you were so frightened." Avoid medical jargon or imparting any guilt for any action or nonaction of the patient or family. Comments such as, "Well, you knew she had cholelithiasis, why didn't you bring her in sooner?" are counterproductive to complaint resolution. Express gratitude to the caller for bringing attention to a potential problem. Summarize the concerns to be sure there is mutual understanding. This approach to complaint management forges a provider-patient partnership for problem-solving.

The complaint may be resolved at this point because often the caller's goal is simply to vent frustration. Patients are often driven by the desire to prevent a similar occurrence for another person. They are satisfied when their concerns are heard. At times, the matter cannot be easily resolved. In such cases, after the investigation is complete, the manager should call or write the patient or family to explain the facts discovered. This step is important because miscommunication is frequently the foundation of the complaint. Lack of explanations about what was done may leave a patient with the impression that the care was inadequate. Remember: for the patient, the perception is the reality. If the investigation uncovers an actual problem with care, this creates an ideal opportunity to educate the staff.

Such feedback is essential to facilitate staff learning and to foster a positive patient relations attitude. Prompt notification of risk management is important in those few cases where a significant problem is found.

The patient's bill can also be an effective complaint management tool. The manager can approve reducing or eliminating physician charges and, occasionally, hospital charges to help resolve a dispute. The extent to which bills are adjusted varies from one hospital to another. As a general rule, reduced charges should be clearly identified as a customer courtesy and not an admission that a mistake in medical care occurred.

Management must track spontaneously offered complaints and develop valid survey techniques as part a system to identify problems that can lead to a marked decrease in patient satisfaction. Many institutions distribute questionnaires with discharge instructions, use callback sampling, or employ agencies to assess patient satisfaction. Trending analysis techniques are replacing technologies that monitor gaps in patient expectations and satisfaction. Managed care plans also closely monitor their delivery of care. Health care institutions should mimic the models provided by large customer service organizations like the Disney Corporation. One particularly helpful tool is the development of scripts to provide pleasant, standardized responses practiced by all personnel to handle potential problems, such as violations of the visitor policy or the hospital's food and drink regulations.

The last task of complaint management is the critical analysis of carefully collected complaint data. No problem can be solved until it is clearly defined. Institutions should not be completely satisfied until their patients are!

Key Points and Conclusions

Patient complaints can work for the emergency department by making staff and administrators aware of the public's perception of emergency services. The staff should embrace patient criticism, not ignore this valuable source of data. The following guidelines can help health care providers handle complaints successfully:

- Make patients feel as though their criticisms will make a difference.
- Investigate all complaints thoroughly and follow through with all staff and patients involved.
- Try to visualize the complaint from the patient's perspective. Remember: the patient is not medically sophisticated.
- Use common sense when dealing with a patient's complaint concerning services rendered. It is foolish to pursue a small bill at the risk of a malpractice lawsuit.
- Be a good listener. Real listening is the highest form of respect one person can pay to another.

Suggested Reading

Adamson TE, Tschann JM, Gullion DS, et al. Physician communication skills and malpractice claims: a complex relationship. *West J Med* 1989;150:356-360.

Brown S. Capitalizing on customer complaints. *Sky,* September 1987.

Buller MK, Buller DB. Physicians' communication style and patient satisfaction. *J Health Soc Behav* 1987;28: 375-388.

Cameron CT. *Public Relations in the Emergency Department.* Bowie, Md: Robert S. Brady Co; 1980.

Evans BJ, Kellerup FD, Stanley RO, et al. A communication skills programme for increasing patients' satisfaction with general practice consultations. *Br J Med Psychol Soc* 1987;60:373-378.

Hirsh HL. The physician's duty to stop, look, listen, and communicate. *Med Law* 1986;5:449-461.

Korsch BM, Gozzi EK, Francis V. Gaps in doctor-patient communication. Doctor-patient interaction and patient satisfaction. *Pediatrics* 1968;42:855-871.

Ley P. Complaints made by hospital staff and patients. A review of the literature. *Bull Br Psychol Soc* 1972;25:115-120.

Truelove A. On handling complaints. *Hosp Health Serv Rev* 1985;5:229-232.

Chapter 8

Communication Barriers in the Physician-Patient Relationship

Marcus S. Villarreal, MD

Good communication between physicians and patients is an essential component of quality emergency medical care. During each part of a patient's emergency department visit — signing a consent for treatment or a special procedure, history-taking, physical examination, discussing possible diagnoses, explaining treatment, and the need for follow-up — an unimpeded flow of information between the patient and emergency department staff is vital for optimal management of the patient's problem. Good communication is also one of the most important ways the emergency physician can establish a positive relationship with patients. Communication is a critical tool by which the emergency physician can limit malpractice risk.[1]

Certain situations present significant barriers to the flow of information between patients and physicians. The most well known is the barrier created when patients and physicians are not fluent in a common language. Also, patients with hearing impairments and those with limited or no reading ability may not be able to communicate effectively with emergency staff.

Language is a socially shared code or conventional system for representing concepts through the use of arbitrary symbols and rule-governed combinations of those symbols.[2] Communication is the primary function of language and, more important, is the process of exchanging information and ideas between participants.[2] The physician-patient relationship is built through good communication. When the physician and the patient do not share a common language or when the patient is hearing impaired,[1] the usual flow of information is interrupted.

Along with clinical reasoning, observations, and nonverbal cues, the physician's skillful use of language endows the medical history with its clinical power and establishes the medical interview as the clinician's most powerful tool.[3-6] Language is the means by which a physician uncovers a patient's beliefs about health and illness,[7] creating an opportunity to address and reconcile different belief systems. Furthermore, it is through language that physicians and patients achieve an empathetic connection that may be therapeutic in itself.[8] The provision of quality emergency medical care demands the rapid, complete, and accurate understanding of information that can be achieved only through clear communication.[9]

Case Studies

1

A 68-year-old Hispanic woman presents to the emergency department with a chief complaint of abdominal and back pain. She had been transported to the hospital by paramedics after she became ill while waiting for a connecting flight at a local airport. She is a recent Nicaraguan refugee, has no family or friends with her, and does not speak English.

2

A 28-year-old hearing impaired woman presents to the emergency department indicating that she has a severe headache. Neither she nor her boyfriend can lip-read or communicate orally. When the emergency physician enters the room, the patient appears to be in increasing distress secondary to her headache pain.

3

A 2-year-old girl who lives with her mother and maternal grandmother is brought to the emergency department after she fell out of her high chair and hit her head on an uncarpeted floor. According to her 17-year-old mother, the child did not lose consciousness or exhibit neurologic signs or symptoms. Findings of the physical examination, including a complete HEENT, cervical spine x-ray, and neurologic examination, are within normal limits. After the nurse reviews the routine emergency department "Instructions for Observing a Patient Who Has a Head Injury" with the patient's grandmother, who signs the document, the patient is discharged. One hour later, the grandmother calls the emergency department asking for clarification of several terms in the discharge instructions. No one in the house is able to read them.[1]

The Medical-Legal Perspective

Any problem with timely and accurate exchange of information between a patient and the emergency department staff during the course of the patient's visit can lead to misdiagnosis, inappropriate treatment, poor patient compliance, bad outcome, and a claim of negligence.[1] Many states are beginning to take an active role in ensuring that language is not a barrier to the delivery of quality medical care. Several states address particular communication problems, such as ensuring access to an interpreter or the right to speak one's own language.[10,11] This requirement means that emergency departments must have interpreters readily accessible for patients who need them. This type of language legislation is found in Arizona, California, Colorado, the District of Columbia, Florida, Hawaii, Illinois, Indiana, Maryland, Massachusetts, Michigan, Minnesota, New Jersey, New Hampshire, New York, North Dakota, Rhode Island, South Dakota, Texas, Vermont, and Washington.[12-26]

Informed Consent

According to the American College of Legal Medicine Foundation, "The responsibility to obtain the patient's informed consent belongs to the attending or treating physician. Hospitals also have the responsibility to implement appropriate mechanisms with a view toward ensuring that informed consent is properly obtained."[27] Consent obtained from people without the use of competent interpreters is unlikely to be truly informed.[28] The medical record should note that an interpretation service was used, that some oral confirmation was obtained from the patient through the use of an interpreter, and that the patient understood the diagnosis and treatment. If possible, the consent should be written in the patient's native language to ensure the person understood what they were agreeing to and to prevent charges that the consent was truly not informed.

Legal Case Histories

The courts have also addressed the need for clear communication in health care delivery. In Texas, a Laotian patient brought a medical malpractice action against a surgeon for failing to obtain informed consent for a Morrison procedure, which involves removing skin, blood vessels, and bone from the big toe and attempting to use the material to reconstruct a thumb. The interpreter testified that the surgeon never informed the patient that the surgery would involve removal of nerves, blood vessels, tissue, and bone from the big toe. The patient testified that he was told his toe and thumb would be normal after the operation.[29]

Department of Health and Human Services Regulations

The Office for Civil Rights requires DHHS-funded health programs to provide patients with limited English skills access to services equal to those provided to English speakers.[30-34] Programs that do not comply risk losing all federal funds, including Medicare and Medicaid payments.[32]

EMTALA Requirements

The Health Care Finance Administration guidelines state that hospitals must be in compliance with all state and federal laws pertaining to the health and safety of the patient. This includes the Emergency Medical Treatment and Active Labor Active Labor Act (EMTALA) provision regarding informed refusal of treatment (see Chapter 45, "EMTALA"). Again, compliance requires translation for the non–English-speaking patient.[9,34]

Joint Commission on Accreditation of Healthcare Organizations

The Joint Commission (JCAHO) begins its *Accreditation Manual for Hospitals* with a section on "Rights and Responsibilities of Patients." Section RI.1 of the JCAHO guidelines concerns ethical issues in providing patient care. Sections CC.1 and CC.2 deal with patients having access to appropriate types of care within the hospital. Sections PE.5, PE.6, and PE.7 deal with assessments of patients who have special needs due to their age, disability, or condition. None of these guidelines can be complied with unless non–English-speaking patients have the information translated into a language they can understand.[35]

Interpretation Services

The use of an interpreter is probably the most effective method of improving the flow of information between patient and physician. An interpreter not only provides oral communication but may possibly share a common cultural background with the patient. In addition, the interpreter serves as an advocate for the patient by asking questions that the patient may not know how to ask or by taking extra time to address the concerns of the patient or the family.[36,37]

The emergency physician must be aware of the limitations and pitfalls inherent in using an interpreter. Interpreters may unintentionally distort communication in a number of ways. For example, relevant information may not be completely conveyed or it may be embellished. The interpreter may also misinterpret the patient or physician and thus convey false assumptions or conclusions. Even with an experienced interpreter, communication can be impaired. For example, the physician-patient relationship may not fully develop because the patient's sense of privacy is compromised by the presence of a third party. Finally, patient care incorporating the use of an interpreter may require more time than the usual patient encounter. For this reason, it is tempting for both the physician and the patient to cut corners during the encounter by omitting what is thought to be less essential or less relevant information. Unfortunately, such omissions can undermine appropriate treatment.[38]

With the growth of managed care, hospitals to have instituted cost containment measures to remain competitive. Institutions are making adjustments by reducing staffing and by consolidating positions. This trend may make it increasingly difficult for hospitals to afford interpreter services. Professional interpreter salaries vary with level of experience and training. In the federal court system, salaries range from \$31,888 to \$76,733.[9,39]

When interpreters are unavailable, many hospitals use telephone interpretation services. The cost of such a services versus hiring multilingual personnel may be justified as long as a proper interpreter can be found on a timely basis. The following is a list of some of the telephone translation services currently in use:

- Interpret, Inc. (Houston, Tex., 800-892-9959, www.mitsi.com/interpret) offers an archival recording for all interpretation sessions linked to a digital audio tape. Written transcripts of the interpretations are also available. Interpret, Inc., charges a per minute rate regardless of the language and can interpret 25 different languages. Interpret, Inc., offers a patented, portable, hands-free, speakerphone that can be placed at the patient's bedside to allow off-site teleconferencing between the provider, patient, and the interpreter. The connection to the translator is made within minutes by a speed-dialing mechanism designed for the speakerphone.

- Pacific Interpreters (Portland, Ore., 503-223-8899, www.pacinterp.com) charges a per minute rate according to the language and can interpret more than 100 languages. Pacific Interpreters offers on-site interpretation, off-site teleconferencing, or video conferencing and file-sharing.

- AT&T Language Line Service (Monterey, Calif., 800-752-6096) is a 24-hour communications center that provides hospitals and other health care providers with telephone-based access to more than 140 languages. AT&T charges a per minute rate according to the language. Written translation services are also available.

A number of other simple interventions can improve access to quality care for patients with limited English skills. These include the use of signage printed in the community's languages and bilingual phrase sheets with common expressions, words, and questions. Translation cards are another tool designed to circumvent communication problems with non–English-speaking individuals.[40-42] These cards list written phrases in both English and the language of the patient; some cards display pictures. Use of these cards can facilitate medical evaluation and communication relating to treatment. Unfortunately, communication achieved by this method often is not detailed enough to ensure a good understanding of a complex problem by either the patient or the physician.[9]

Written emergency department discharge instructions are currently a JCAHO requirement.[35] The emergency physician should make every effort to ensure that foreign language discharge instructions sheets are available in any emergency department that serves a significant percentage of non–English-speaking patients. If such preprinted, same-language instructions are not available, an interpreter can help the emergency physician and staff prepare written discharge instructions in the patient's native language.[1]

Communicating With Hearing Impaired Patients

In the United States, there are approximately 1.8 million hearing impaired people. Many of these people often need to obtain medical care in the emergency department.[43]

The problems encountered in creating an adequate exchange of information with these patients are similar to those in caring for non–English-speaking individuals, but without most of the cultural barriers. Community resources, such as skilled sign language interpreters, are usually more available than are foreign language interpreters. Nevertheless, the communication barriers that exist in the emergency treatment of hearing impaired patients pose significant challenges and medical-legal risks.

A variety of techniques and options exist to facilitate communication with hearing impaired patients. All emergency department staff — physicians, nurses, technicians, clerical staff — must understand that they are involved in the management of a hearing impaired patient. This can be achieved by placing a note or symbol on the patient's chart and orally communicating this fact to the involved hospital personnel.[44]

Writing and reading messages may be enough to ensure an adequate flow of information between the patient and the emergency department staff. Translation cards may also be a viable option to achieve an appropriate level of communication. A hearing impaired patient skilled in lip-reading may not require an interpreter.[45] The emergency physician and staff should determine which method of communication is best to address the patient's problems.

The use of sign language is the most common way to communicate among the hearing impaired. Although various sign languages are commonly used in the United States, American Sign Language is the most common.[46] Information flow with this technique depends on the skills and experience of both the patient and the interpreter. Although some large hospitals have individuals on staff to provide signing interpretation services, more often, this is not the case. Fortunately, most communities, through a municipally supported or United Way supported organization, provide signing interpretation.

Patient Illiteracy

Illiteracy is a well-recognized national crisis. Functional literacy is defined as the ability to use reading, writing, and computational skills at a level adequate to meet the needs of everyday situations.[47,48] However, functional literacy varies according to the context and setting. The literacy skills of a patient may be adequate at home or work but marginal or inadequate in the health care setting. Adequate functional health care literacy means being able to apply literacy skills to health-related materials, such as prescriptions, appointment cards, medicine labels, and directions for home health care. The prevalence of low literacy is supported by data from the U.S. Census, which defines illiteracy as the inability to read at an eighth-grade level or lower. Using that definition of illiteracy, 27 million Americans are illiterate. Another 45 million are only marginally literate, which means that up to one of every three adult Americans is functionally illiterate.[47,49,50] One fourth of those in the lowest reading level are immigrants whose native language is not English.

There is no easy way to identify patients with inadequate literacy skills. Screening questions and self-reported reading difficulty are unreliable indicators of true reading ability. In addition, patients with low literacy levels harbor a tremendous amount of shame and may not have disclosed their reading problems even to family or friends.[51-54] It is unrealistic to expect these patients to volunteer this information to health care providers. To correctly identify patients with inadequate literacy skills, screening tests for reading ability may be necessary. The appropriate tool for measuring functional health literacy should use real and relevant medical texts from hospitals or clinics. In addition to measuring prose-reading skills, tests should measure numeracy skills, which are an essential component of functional health literacy. The Test of Functional Health Literacy in Adults (TOFHLA) is a valid, reliable indicator of a patient's ability to read health-related materials. The TOFHLA measures the ability of both English- and Spanish-speaking patients to perform health-related tasks that require reading and computational skills.[47]

Wingert et al documented the poor reading ability of emergency department patients and pointed out that a patient's inability to understand written material is a potential source of medical-legal problems for the emergency physician.[1,55] Several studies have shown health education materials and consent forms are written at levels exceeding many patients' reading skills.[56-67] For example, if a patient cannot understand the meaning of the "against medical advice" form or the terms of an informed consent for a medical procedure, the documents do not serve their intended legal purpose. Patients who are unable to read the contents of prepared discharge instructions have a higher risk of poor medical outcomes, thus increasing the physician's risk of liability.

If patient-directed materials are to serve their purpose, they must be written at a level that the majority of emergency department patients can read and understand. This approach may mean writing materials at lower reading levels for a significant number of emergency department patients. If such materials can improve overall patient understanding and compliance, they will also reduce malpractice risks for emergency physicians.

Emergency physicians can further reduce the risk of liability by asking patients if they understand the written materials or have any questions regarding them. Typically, patients will not volunteer that they have reading deficiencies. The emergency physician must encourage patients to ask questions and to discuss any written materials they are given. It may be appropriate to make sure patients comprehend the items in question by asking them to repeat the contents.

Case Discussions

1

An adequate history could not be obtained from this patient, nor could an appropriate physical examination be performed without establishing effective communication between physician and patient. Because a myriad of serious medical problems were associated with this presentation, the use of an interpreter was essential. The interpreter should be fluent in Spanish, preferably of the same sex as the patient, and of the patient's age or older. Such an interpreter should be selected from a previously prepared list of interpreters. The patient's acceptance of the interpreter should be documented in the medical record. The physician can use the interpreter in any informed consent process, including rewriting an informed consent document in Spanish. The possible diagnoses, treatments, and discharge instructions or reason for admission should be explained carefully through the interpreter. The patient's acknowledgment that she understands these discussions should also be documented.

2

Both federal law and generally accepted standards of quality emergency medical care dictate that a signing interpreter be obtained to facilitate communication during the management of a hearing impaired patient. As in the first case, interpreters should be made available through a previously arranged call list. Providers can use written messages, or translation cards may be used prior to the interpreter's arrival or in the place of an interpreter if the patient feels these alternatives are acceptable.

3

This case illustrated a problem often encountered by emergency physicians. The physician was at increased risk when treating a patient with poor reading skills. Patients whose reading ability is insufficient to understand written documents often do not tell the emergency staff that they do not read well. Consequently, emergency physicians and staff should consider the following suggestions:

- Develop against medical advice forms, informed consent documents, and discharge instructions that are written simply and clearly at a eighth-grade reading level or lower.
- Ask patients if they have any questions about these materials and if they understand the contents fully.
- Document the patient's statement in the medical record.[1]

Key Points and Conclusion

Information exchange is essential to quality medical care and is an integral part of limiting the risk of liability. Emergency physicians are responsible for ensuring effective communication. Patients who speak a foreign language, those who hearing impaired, and those with limited reading ability must be approached cautiously. In these situations, quality medical care can be ensured and medical-legal risk reduced by adhering to the following tenets:

- A means of communication between patient and physician that is acceptable to the patient should always be used to overcome communication barriers.

- Qualified, trained interpreters should be readily available to the emergency physician.

- Any critical issue in the management of a patient should be discussed fully with the patient. The patient should then be asked for any questions regarding these issues. Once patients say they understand the issues, their statements should be documented in the medical record.

References

1. Kolodzik P. Communication barriers in the patient-physician relationship. In: Henry GL, ed. *Emergency Medicine Risk Management.* Dallas: American College of Emergency Physicians; 1991.

2. Owens R. *Language Development.* Columbus, Ohio: Merril Publishing Company; 1988.

3. Lipkin M Jr. The medical interview and related skills. In: Branch WT, ed. *Office Practice of Medicine, Third Edition.* Philadelphia: WB Saunders Co; 1994.

4. Hampton JR, Harrison MJG, Mitchell JRH, et al. Relative contributions of history-taking, physical examination, and laboratory investigation to diagnosis and management of medical outpatients. *Br Med J* 1975;2:486-489.

5. Lipkin M Jr, Quill TE, Napodano RJ. The medical interview: a core curriculum for residencies in internal medicine. *Ann Intern Med* 1984;100:277-284.

6. Sandler G. The importance of the history in the medical clinic and the cost of unnecessary tests. *Am Heart J* 1980;100:928-931.

7. Kleinman A, Eisenberg L, Good B. Culture, illness, and care: clinical lessons from anthropologic and cross-cultural research. *Ann Intern Med* 1978;88:251-258.

8. Suchman AL, Matthews DA. What makes the patient-doctor relationship therapeutic? Exploring the connexional dimension of medical care. *Ann Intern Med* 1988;108:125-130.

9. Woloshin S, Bickell NA, Schwartz LM, et al. Language barriers in medicine in the United States. *JAMA* 1995;273:724-727.

10. Accreditation Manual, at xiii; VT. Stat Ann tit 18, §1852 (Supp1989); Minn Stat Ann §144.651 (West 1989) (promising "reasonable accommodations"); Md Health-Gen Code Ann §19-344(e) (1990) requires that treatment information be "in language that the resident reasonably can be expected to understand."

11. Dellinger A. *Healthcare Facilities Law.* Boston: Little, Brown and Co; 1991.

12. Cal Civ Code §56 to §56.37 (West 1982, Supp 1990); Cal Welf Inst Code §5510 to §5550, §9700 to §9741 (West 1984, Supp 1989).

13. Colo Rev Stat §25-1-120 to §25-1-121 (1989).

14. DC Code Ann §32-1301 to §32-1309 (1988, Supp 1989).

15. Ill Ann Stat ch 111 1/2, 4152-101 to 4153-215 (extended care facilities); id ch 111 1/2, 5403 (medical patients) (Smith-Hurd 1988).

16. Ind Code §16-14-1.6-1 to §16-14-1.6-11 (1983, Supp 1988).

17. Md Health-Gen Code Ann §19-301 (1990), §19-342 to §19-350, §19-370 to §19-374 (1990). See also Md Regs Code tit 10, §10.07.10.13 (Supp 1988).

18. Mass Ann Laws ch 111, §70E to §70F (Law Co-op 1985, Supp 1989).

19. Mich Comp Laws Ann §333.20201 to §333.202~3 (West 1980, Supp 1989).

20. Minn Stat Ann §144.651 to §144.652 (West 1989).

21. NH Rev Stat Ann §151:19 to §151:29 (1989).

22. ND Cent Code §5-10.2-01 to §50-10.2-04 (Supp 1989).

23. RI Gen Laws §23-17-19.1 to §23-17.5-24 (1985, Supp 1988).

24. SD Cod Laws Ann §36-2-16 (1986).

25. Tex Health Safety Code Ann §311.022 (Vernon 1990).

26. Vt Stat Ann tit 18, §1851, §1852 (Supp 1989) (hospital patients); §2101-06 (Supp 1989) (nursing home patients).

27. *Medicolegal Primer.* Pittsburgh: American College of Legal Medicine Foundation; 1991.

28. President's Commission for the Study of Ethical Problems in Medicine and Biomedical Research. The law of informed consent. In: *Making Health Care Decisions: The Ethical and Legal Implications of Informed Consent in the Patient Practitioner Relationship, III.* Washington, DC: President's Commission for the Study of Ethical Problems in Medicine and Biomedical Research; 1982.

29. *Melissinos v Phamanivong.* 823 SW2d 339.

30. Application of Title VI in health and welfare programs: effect on agency employment practices (national origin). *Title VI Compendium* 1971;1:193-194.

31. Community mental health services to Hispanics. *Title VI Compendium.* 1980;1:66-68.

32. Crivella BJ. *Policy Guidance Applicable to Foster Home Placements of LEP Children.* Washington, DC: US Dept of Health and Human Services, Office for Civil Rights, Office of Management and Policy; 1982.

33. Establishment of a separate hospital ward and services for Vietnamese patients. *Title VI Compendium.* 1980;1:72-73.

34. CFR §80.8(a) (1989).

35. *1996 Accreditation Manual for Hospitals, Volume I, Standards.* Chicago: The Joint Commission on Accreditation of Healthcare Organizations; 1996.

36. Faust S, Drickey R. Working with interpreters. *J Fam Pract* 1986;22:131-139.

37. Radar GS. Management decisions: do we really need interpreters? *Nurs Manage* 1988;19:46-48.

38. Holden P, Serrano AC. Language barriers in pediatric care. *Clin Pediatr* 1989;28:193-194.

39. New York State Unified Court System. *Classification Plan.* New York: New York State Unified Court System; 1994.

40. Haigh N. Communication across language barrier. *Nat News* 1988;25:11-13.

41. Linney B, Ryan TJ. Visual communication for health and development. *Int J Dermatol* 1988;27:299.

42. Dollinger R. *Pocket Medical Spanish, An Instant Self Use Interpreting Aid for Medical Professionals.* Reseda, Calif: JDV Publishing Company; 1992.

43. McEwen E, Anton-Culver H. The medical communication of deaf patients. *J Fam Pract* 1988;26:289-291.

44. Jones L, Wolf MA. Regulation promulgated pursuant to section 504 of the Rehabilitation Act of 1973: a brief history in presence status. *Congressional Research Service* 1985; Report number 86-53a:1-14.

45. Carbary LJ. "What did you say?" Caring for the patient who has a hearing impairment. *J Pract Nurs* 1988;38:36-39.

46. Vonberg DW. Emergency police, fire, and medical services for the deaf. *Emerg Med Tech J* 1981;5:106-107.

47. Parker RM, Baker DW, Williams MV, et al. The Test of Functional Health Literacy in Adults (TOFHLA): a new instrument for measuring patients' literacy skills. *J Gen Intern Med* 1995;10:537-541.

48. Kirsch IS, Jungeblut A, Jenkins L, et al. *Adult Literacy in America: A First Look at the Results of the National Adult Literacy Survey.* Washington, DC: National Center for Education Statistics, US Dept of Education; 1993.

49. General Accounting Office. Report to Congress. *The Adult Basic Education Program: Progress in Reducing Illiteracy and Improvement Needs.* Washington, DC: US Office of Education; 1975.

50. US Dept of Commerce Bureau of the Census. *English Language Proficiency Study.* Washington, DC: Government Printing Office; 1982.

51. Williams MV, Parker RM, Baker DW, et al. Inadequate functional health literacy among patients at two public hospitals. *JAMA* 1995;274:1677-1682.

52. Samways MC. Functionally illiterate worker also has right-to-understand. *Occup Health Saf* 1988;57:49-53.

53. Beder H. The stigma of illiteracy. *Adult Basic Educ* 1991;1:67-78.

54. Parikh NS, Parker RM, Nurss JR, et al. Shame and health literacy the unspoken connection. *Patient Educ Couns.* In press.

55. Wingert WA, Grubbs JP, Friedman DB. Why Johnny's parents don't read. An analysis of indigent parents' comprehension of health education materials.*Clin Pediatr* 1969;8:655-660.

56. Doak L, Doak C. Patient comprehension profiles: recent findings and strategies. *Patient Couns Health Educ* 1980;2:101-106.

57. Grundner TM. On the readability of surgical consent forms. *N Engl J Med* 1980;302:900-902.

58. Leichter SB, Nieman JA, Moore RW, et al. Readability of self-care instructional pamphlets for diabetic patients. *Diabetes Care* 1981;4:627-630.

59. Holcomb C. Reading difficulty of informational materials from a health maintenance organization. *J Reading* 1981;25:130-132.

60. Boyd M, Citro K. Cardiac patient education literature: can patients read what we give them? *J Card Rehab* 1983;3:513-516.

61. McNeal B, Salisbury Z, Baumgardner P, et al. Comprehension assessment of diabetes education program participants. *Diabetes Care* 1984;7:232-235.

62. Powers RD. Emergency department patient literacy and the readability of patient-directed materials. *Ann Emerg Med* 1988;17:124-126.

63. Jaycox S. Smoking literature and literacy levels (lett). *Am J Public Health* 1989;79:1058.

64. Meade CD, Byrd JC. Patient literacy and the readability of smoking education literature. *Am J Public Health* 1989;79:204-206.

65. Davis TC, Crouch MA, Wills G, et al. The gap between patient reading comprehension and the readability of patient education materials. *J Fam Pract* 1990;31:533-538.

66. Jackson RH, Davis TC, Bairnsfather LE, et al. Patient reading ability: an overlooked problem in health care. *South Med J* 1991;84:1172-1175.

67. Davis TC, Mayeaux EJ, Fredrickson D, et al. Reading ability of parents compared with reading level of pediatric patient education materials. *Pediatrics* 1994;93:460-468.

Chapter 9

Orientation

David L. Meyers, MD, FACEP

The emergency department is a busy, complex interface between the hospital and the community. The department must be able to marshall and coordinate the many resources and services offered by the hospital, the medical staff, and the community to care for the variety of patients and their families who pass through its doors. From the most complex medical and trauma cases to the "worried well" and everything between, the needs of emergency department patients and accompanying family and friends can challenge the most organized and effective providers.

To bring order to the potential chaos of the typical emergency department, the staff must function as a patient care team. The physician serves as the leader of that team. All team members must clearly know their roles in the patient care process and have the ability to carry those roles out. Beyond possessing a special skill set and knowing the duties of the job, each staff member must also understand the mission of the institution and the role of the emergency department in fulfilling that mission.

The care of emergency department patients requires many services, some not routinely available in the department. As a result, one of the primary roles of the emergency department staff is to recruit and coordinate resources for patient care. This responsibility may include contacting attending physicians and consultants, assignee or "on-call" physicians, rotating residents and other trainees, laboratory and imaging services, social and other ancillary services, operating rooms, clinics, rehabilitation resources, and many others. External resources may include private physicians, managed care organizations, hospitals and other acute care facilities, nursing homes and other nonacute facilities, emergency medical services, police and fire departments, housing agencies, child protective agencies, and domestic violence and other victim support services. As patient needs and expectations grow more sophisticated and government and other regulatory bodies establish more stringent requirements for care and documentation, the staff must be able to perform to these exacting levels.

To fulfill their roles effectively, staff members must have some basic information about the available health care and support resources and how to access and use them. Proper care of patients can be delayed or impaired by staff who lack such knowledge. The failure of management to provide staff with basic information regarding department function, flow, and resources will ultimately result in a variety of patient care and other problems, some of which could lead to claims of negligence.

Consider these examples: the newly hired emergency physician does not know clinical protocols or the patient flow process of the department. The triage nurse does not know how to expedite the management of a patient with chest pain. The clerk is unfamiliar with the procedure for notifying consultant physicians. The resident performs a procedure independently and incorrectly, unaware of the requirement for supervision. The paramedic does not follow prehospital protocols for patients who refuse service. The unit secretary does not alert the charge nurse regarding a physician calling in to arrange a transfer. The volunteer gives incorrect information about a patient's medical condition to the patient's family. At the very least, mistakes such as these can lead to delays, inconvenience, or misunderstanding on the part of patients and families. At worst, serious patient harm may result. Often, when harm occurs, litigation follows.

Any new staff member should be guided by a knowledge of policies, procedures, and protocols. This goal can be accomplished by a well-planned, comprehensive orientation process that improves performance and ultimately reduces risk. The Joint Commission on Accreditation of Healthcare Organizations (JCAHO) has long required that members of a hospital's board of trustees receive orientation regarding their duties and responsibilities. According to the *1996 Comprehensive Accreditation Manual for Hospitals* (CAMH), where the standards of the JCAHO are delineated, hospital personnel are required to undergo an orientation process that is used to assess the individual's ability to fulfill specific responsibilities and to familiarize the worker with the job and work environment.[1,2] Hospital leaders and department directors, including physician department leaders, are responsible for "the orientation and continuing education for all persons in the department or service"[3,4]

Because of the great diversity in training, skills, and experience of the members of the emergency department staff, proper orientation can help them to develop an understanding of the institution and its mission and a strong sense of belonging to a team. A comprehensive orientation is an important first step in enabling new department staff members to see how their performance fits into the overall scheme of patient care. It also provides staff an opportunity to learn about the policies and procedures governing the work environment and patient care.

During orientation, each staff member becomes familiar with how to perform specific duties under the existing conditions of the emergency department while being closely supervised. Nurses and other staff traditionally undergo extensive orientation. A large body of literature describes the philosophy and most effective methods to integrate these individuals into the institutional culture and to ensure they have adequate knowledge of their duties and responsibilities.[4-6]

The value of in-depth orientation for physicians, including emergency physicians, is increasingly recognized as an important step in the effective integration of new providers. Even though the physicians' time is expensive and time spent in orientation may not be reimbursed, the contribution of the process to the physicians' and organization's productivity should be apparent. Simply knowing how to perform the necessary history and physical examination and which diagnostic tests to use does not ensure that the physician can perform effectively within the organization and as a member of the care team. This goal can be achieved by orienting the emergency physician to all elements of the department's operations. Just as no medical student or resident should be given patient care responsibilities without preparation, neither should the new emergency physician begin patient care duties until an orientation has been provided.

To be most effective, the orientation process should be well-planned and organized, permitting the new physician to take on clinical duties as soon as practicable. All the relevant policies and important duties of the job or role must be presented clearly and comprehensively during orientation. At the end of the process, the physician should be able to function as an effective member of the team.

Case Study

A 6-month-old child is brought to the emergency department in status epilepticus, which began two hours earlier at her home. While in the department, the patient's condition deteriorates, and she suffers severe brain damage. The parents file a lawsuit against the hospital because of the delay in treatment. Some of the nurses' notes had been recorded using a 12-hour clock (AM/PM), others a 24-hour clock (military time). The plaintiff's attorney, by focusing on the different methods used to designate times of events in the care of the child, is able to cast doubt on the accuracy of the recorded times and information.

The hospital had recently changed its policy regarding the method to be used by nurses when charting times in nurses' notes. Management had directed the 12-hour method and adopted the 24-hour military notation. Unfortunately, not all nurses had modified their practices to conform to the new policy.[6]

Case Discussion

Although this case focused on nursing practices, there are several legal doctrines under which hospitals have been held responsible for the acts of its professional staff, including physician employees, physician contractors (individuals and groups), and physician members of its medical staff. Failure to provide appropriate orientation may expose the hospital or contracting entity to claims of negligence based on these or other theories.

The Orientation Process

Orientation is often best accomplished in stages. First, present an administrative orientation to the external community and hospital-wide matters, such as mission, history, policies, and so on. Second, orient the physician to general emergency department procedures and guidelines. Third, orient the physician to each department with which the individual will interface in caring for emergency department patients.

Management must allow adequate time for new staff to complete the orientation process, with specific responsibilities added as soon as individuals are capable of assuming them. The process must also take into consideration the institution's need to get people working without needless delay. An orientation process should also be conducted whenever new duties or policies are introduced or as the need is identified.

Each individual's orientation must be tailored to the duties to be performed although there will often be elements common to more than one job. The portion devoted to institutional mission and culture is generally best presented by administrative staff. Within the emergency department, supervision during orientation may be performed by designated peers or by special training staff, depending on the size or complexity of the department and the organization's resources.

Orientation should provide information appropriate to the individual's position and duties. An information manual is helpful both during orientation and later for reference. The orientation manual should include an outline and schedule of the process, important policies, rules, procedures, and other essential information, such as location of equipment and supplies.

A typical administrative orientation process for physicians and other staff contains the following:

[handwritten: Admin]

- A statement of orientation objectives.
- Personal introductions, which should include meeting the administrative staff.
- Descriptions of meals, dress codes, vacation, sick time, and other personnel policies, as appropriate.
- Review of basic safety, employee health, infection control, biohazards, and other policies, with special attention to procedures for preventing exposure to potentially infectious blood and body fluids (such as Universal Precautions), and the handling of such an exposure, should it occur.
- Identification of individuals or departments that may serve as resources for further information and assistance (e.g., nursing supervisors, risk management and legal staff, credentials staff).
- A tour of the facility.

An orientation process for the emergency department should include:

[handwritten: ESD]

- A statement of orientation objectives.
- An introduction to the department staff.
- A tour of the department and a description of its location relative to frequently used services, such as imaging, laboratory, electrocardiography, operating room, coronary and intensive/critical care units, cafeteria, parking, and others, as appropriate.
- Capabilities of the facility, such as the level of trauma care, special imaging equipment, hyperbaric chamber, special perinatal facilities, and cardiac catheterization labs.
- The role of the emergency department staff in making these services available to patients (either on- or off-site) who require them.
- Capabilities or services specifically lacking, for which transfer of patients or other alternatives must be sought, and how to gain access to them (e.g., pediatric intensive care, burn unit).
- Description of the typical flow of patients, both ambulatory and ambulance borne, through the department.
- Location and description of all department equipment and supplies, with particular attention to how similar equipment from different manufacturers may operate differently (e.g., cardiac defibrillators, pacemakers, autotransfusion devices).

Figure 1

Sample form for use in physician orientation

PHYSICIAN ORIENTATION PROGRAM

Hospital .... Physician _____
Medical Director...

I. Physical Plant of Health Care Facility
    A. Tour of hospital .... Interviewer _____ Date _____
    B. Oriented to hospital floor plan .... Interviewer _____ Date _____
    C. Location of conferences, ICUs, X-rays, lab, administration .... Interviewer _____ Date _____

II. Physical Plant of Emergency Health Care Unit
    A. Waiting areas .... Interviewer _____ Date _____
    B. Nursing station .... Interviewer _____ Date _____
    C. Physician offices, including uses....................... Interviewer _____ Date _____
    E. Cupboard and drawers in each room..................... Interviewer _____ Date _____
    F. Exits .... Interviewer _____ Date _____
    G. Location of security.................................. Interviewer _____ Date _____

III. Medical Equipment and Drugs
    A. Slit lamp and eye equipment........................... Interviewer _____ Date _____
    B. ENT equipment .... Interviewer _____ Date _____
    C. Intubation material and cricothyroid instrument .... Interviewer _____ Date _____
    D. Suction .... Interviewer _____ Date _____
    E. Oxygen system....................................... Interviewer _____ Date _____
    F. Central line.. Interviewer _____ Date _____
    G. Chest tray .... Interviewer _____ Date _____
    H. Abdominal tray .... Interviewer _____ Date _____
    I. Cutdown tray .... Interviewer _____ Date _____
    J. Zoll pacemaker .... Interviewer _____ Date _____
    K. Monitor defibrillator.................................. Interviewer _____ Date _____
    L. Doppler... Interviewer _____ Date _____
    M. IVACs .... Interviewer _____ Date _____
    N. Chest tubes.. Interviewer _____ Date _____
    O. Drainage systems..................................... Interviewer _____ Date _____
    P. Locked instruments .... Interviewer _____ Date _____
    Q. Pelvic equipment..................................... Interviewer _____ Date _____
    R. Location of medications............................... Interviewer _____ Date _____
    S. Drug list/facility formulary .... Interviewer _____ Date _____
    T. Obtaining nonstandard equipment .... Interviewer _____ Date _____
    U. MAST .... Interviewer _____ Date _____
    V. Suture trays and materials .... Interviewer _____ Date _____

IV. Quality Assurance Program
    A. Material given – facility program .... Interviewer _____ Date _____
    B. Enrolled in Practice Science School .... Interviewer _____ Date _____
    C. Medical Ethics Policy given and explained .... Interviewer _____ Date _____
    D. Given example copy of previous Quality Assurance Reports ... Interviewer _____ Date _____

V. Working Environment
    A. Observed shifts .... Interviewer _____ Date _____
    B. Putting patients through the system and admitting .... Interviewer _____ Date _____
    C. Contact attendings .... Interviewer _____ Date _____
    D. Discharge policies.................................... Interviewer _____ Date _____
    E. ALS system and law enforcement intention .... Interviewer _____ Date _____

VI. Introduction to Policies and Procedures
 A. Billing policy . . . . Interviewer _____ Date _____
 B. Department policy manual. . . . . Interviewer _____ Date _____
 C. Call schedule/specialists backup . . . . Interviewer _____ Date _____
 D. Industrial medicine work excuses . . . . Interviewer _____ Date _____
 E. Return visit policies . . . . Interviewer _____ Date _____
 F. Facility back-up policies . . . . Interviewer _____ Date _____
 G. Health insurance forms . . . . Interviewer _____ Date _____
 H. Referral procedures and idiosyncrasies . . . . Interviewer _____ Date _____
 I. Rape examination. . . . . Interviewer _____ Date _____
 J. Transfer procedures . . . . Interviewer _____ Date _____

VII. Social/Political Orientation
 A. Head nurse . . . . Interviewer _____ Date _____
 B. Administrator or assistant. . . . . Interviewer _____ Date _____
 C. Chief of staff . . . . Interviewer _____ Date _____
 D. Synopsis of political problems at facility . . . . Interviewer _____ Date _____
 E. Medical staff – special considerations. . . . . Interviewer _____ Date _____
 F. Physicians-patient interactions . . . . Interviewer _____ Date _____

VIII. Paper Systems
 A. How and when to fill out chart. . . . . Interviewer _____ Date _____
 B. Dictation system. . . . . Interviewer _____ Date _____
 C. Access Medical Examiner System. . . . . Interviewer _____ Date _____
 D. Civil commitment. . . . . Interviewer _____ Date _____
 E. Medical documentation: billing, coding, and confidentiality . Interviewer _____ Date _____

IX. Staff Responsibilities
 A. Committees . . . . Interviewer _____ Date _____
 B. Department meetings . . . . Interviewer _____ Date _____
 C. Compliance with quality assurance program . . . . Interviewer _____ Date _____
 D. In-house emergencies . . . . Interviewer _____ Date _____
 E. Specifics of job description. . . . . Interviewer _____ Date _____
 F. Meeting attendance . . . . Interviewer _____ Date _____
 G. Medical records. . . . . Interviewer _____ Date _____
 H. Disaster plan responsibilities . . . . Interviewer _____ Date _____
 I. Order writing. . . . . Interviewer _____ Date _____

X. Ancillary Services
 A. ECG. . . . . Interviewer _____ Date _____
 B. Blood gas . . . . Interviewer _____ Date _____
 C. X-ray . . . . Interviewer _____ Date _____
 D. CT . . . . Interviewer _____ Date _____
 E. Ultrasound. . . . . Interviewer _____ Date _____
 F. Angiography . . . . Interviewer _____ Date _____
 G. PT . . . . Interviewer _____ Date _____
 H. OHS program . . . . Interviewer _____ Date _____
 I. Laboratory tests and special testing . . . . Interviewer _____ Date _____
 J. Nursing role and technical support. Interviewer _____ Date _____
 K. Secretarial support . . . . Interviewer _____ Date _____
 L. Library . . . . Interviewer _____ Date _____
 M. Transportation for patients. . . . . Interviewer _____ Date _____
 N. Social services, indigent care, and child abuse . . . . Interviewer _____ Date _____
 O. Chemical dependency services . . . . Interviewer _____ Date _____
 P. Community mental health . . . . Interviewer _____ Date _____
 Q. Poison center. . . . . Interviewer _____ Date _____

- Description of patient care protocols, including the emergency screening evaluation for compliance with the provisions of the Emergency Medical Treatment and Active Labor Act (EMTALA).
- Nursing policies and procedures, including those that nurses may carry out using "standing" orders, drugs that may be administered by IV "push," and conditions that require immediate physician notification and the expected physician response.
- Policies for resolving physician-nurse conflicts over questions regarding appropriate orders or other patient care matters.
- The chain of command for resolving disputes among department staff at any time of the day or night.
- Emergency department policies governing safety, infection control, and handling of biohazardous and other dangerous or hazardous materials.
- Policies governing consent and treatment of minors or others lacking decision-making capacity.
- Specific duties of the emergency physician, including responsibilities for patients outside the department (e.g., response to "codes"), administrative activities (quality assurance, supervision of physician assistants and other staff), teaching, and participation in medical staff committees and other activities.
- Relationship of emergency staff to the attending physicians and specific policies for admission of patients, transfer of responsibility to the attending physician, and resolution of disputes over patient disposition.
- Policies for handling managed care patients.
- Policies and procedures for preliminary and final interpretations of radiographs, ECGs, and other tests.
- Policies relating to on-call and consulting physicians.
- Policies, procedures, and standards for record keeping and documentation, including an introduction to forms used in the department.
- Protocols for patient care, with standards, when defined.
- Policies and procedures for special situations, such as interhospital transfer of patients, patients who refuse care or wish to

sign out against medical advice, patients who abscond, the care of minors, and "do not resuscitate" orders.
- Responsibilities for oversight of prehospital patient care, including EMS policies, procedures, and protocols.
- Billing, coding, reimbursement, and compensation policies, as appropriate.
- Special considerations for practices governed by institutional, local, regional, or other factors (e.g., the signing of death certificates, access to pastoral care services, interhospital transfer agreements).
- Statutory requirements affecting care of patients, such as laws related to certification and petitions for psychiatric patients, transfers of patients, and notification of civil authorities.
- Procedures for ordering diagnostic tests and gaining access to medical records, social services, and other resources.
- Disaster and evacuation plans.
- Operation of equipment typically used during patient evaluation or management, including defibrillators, pacemakers, monitors, slit lamp.
- Resources available to repair, adjust, or replace all important equipment and supplies and how to access these services when needed.
- Resources for obtaining unusual and seldom-used equipment.
- Resources for problem solving, day or night.

Certain details of the orientation process may vary, depending on the physician's relationship with the hospital (i.e., whether the physician is an employee, a contractor, or subcontractor), on the complexity of the institution, and on other factors. The time allotted to the orientation and the timetable for the staff member assuming full responsibilities may vary. In addition, orientation to the contracting group and its policies and procedures may be needed, separate and distinct from the hospital. In any case, the basic principles for creating an orientation process remain the same.

A record of the orientation process should be maintained as part of the physician's personnel file. A common method of tracking a physician's progress during this time is to use a checklist to mark off the required elements when they have been addressed (Figure 1). Physicians may assume clinical and other duties as they complete the appropriate portions of the orientation.

The time required for the orientation process will depend in part on physicians' and staff members' individual abilities and needs. Furthermore, as emergency medicine practice becomes more complex, the orientation process is likely to require more time and effort to be effective.

Key Points and Conclusion

The benefits of a comprehensive orientation process will justify the time spent on and by new staff. Properly done, the process will enhance new physicians' understanding of their duties and roles in the organization and provide essential information about institution and department culture and practices. This information will help newcomers adapt to the facility's environment and assume their responsibilities in a timely, professional manner.

- The physician group and the hospital, through the chief or director of emergency services, have an obligation to orient new personnel to the department, and all personnel to new equipment, policies, and procedures.
- A comprehensive orientation is essential for the physician new to the emergency department.
- Portions of this process should take place before the physician assumes clinical duties in the department.
- The process should be sufficiently detailed to enable the physician to function effectively and knowledgeably in the department.
- A record documenting the orientation should be kept as part of the physician's personnel file.
- The policy and procedures manual should be familiar to everyone, including the physicians.

References

1. *1996 Comprehensive Accreditation Manual for Hospitals*, Standard LD.2.8. Chicago: Joint Commission for the Accreditation of Healthcare Organizations; 1995:280-299.

2. *1996 Comprehensive Accreditation Manual for Hospitals*, Standard HR.4. Chicago: Joint Commission for the Accreditation of Healthcare Organizations; 1995:393.

3. *1996 Comprehensive Accreditation Manual for Hospitals*, Standard MS.4.2.1.14. Chicago: Joint Commission for the Accreditation of Healthcare Organizations; 1995:488.

4. Rowland RS, Rowland BL, eds. *Nursing Administration Handbook*, 3rd ed. Gaithersberg, Md: Aspen Publications; 1992.

5. O'Connor A. *Nursing Staff Development and Continuing Education*. Boston: Little, Brown & Co; 1986.

6. Brooten D. *Leadership in Nursing*. Philadelphia: JB Lippincott; 1984.

Chapter 10

The Impaired Physician

Marc L. Pollack, MD, PhD, FACEP

Physician impairment is defined as the inability to practice medicine with reasonable skill and patient safety, by reason of physical or mental illness, including alcoholism or drug dependence, or the aging process.[1] There are many reasons that a physician's clinical skills can become compromised, but substance abuse is the most common.

In fact, approximately three fourths (and perhaps more) of physician impairment cases are the result of substance abuse or addiction.[2] Physician skills, conduct, and responsibilities are also compromised because of unremitting situational crises, such as marital or financial stress.

Chemical dependency impairment is currently viewed as a disease rather than a manifestation of psychopathology. The core symptoms of this disease include denial of the problem, compulsion to use a substance despite its obvious negative consequences, progression of the problem, and relapse. Relapse is common and is generally brought on by resurfacing of denial.

The exact number of practicing physicians who are impaired at some time during their careers is unknown, but estimates have been as high as 16%.[3] Failure to recognize and treat physician impairment can result in patient injury and malpractice litigation. The potential consequences to the physician are enormous, both in terms of clinical failures and financial loss.

Case Study

A 45-year-old man is brought to the emergency department because he is having chest pain. Within 30 minutes, acute myocardial infarction is diagnosed and t-PA administered. The patient develops ventricular fibrillation and resuscitation efforts are not successful. The emergency physician pronounces the patient dead. The patient's wife files a malpractice lawsuit against the emergency physician, the hospital, and the medical staff alleging physician impairment. She claims she smelled alcohol on the emergency physician's breath. The emergency physician had been treated for alcoholism one year earlier, but did not receive follow-up treatment or monitoring.

Identifying the Impaired Physician

The most difficult aspect of helping an impaired physician is making the diagnosis. A pattern of events is more likely to indicate a problem than a single precipitating incident. For example, a physician seeks credentialing at a hospital in a new area, perhaps in an attempt to find a "geographic cure." Ambiguous letters of reference, a history of frequent job changes, prolonged periods of time between jobs, and over qualification for the position may be clues to chronic chemical dependency. A chemically dependent physician may refuse to take a pre-employment drug screen or attempt to delay it for several days in hopes of producing a negative urine specimen. Successfully recovering physicians do not object to drug screens.

In many cases, the symptoms of impairment appear first in the nonwork situation. Eventually, problems begin to arise in the medical practice setting, problems that are, at first, subtle and difficult to detect. The usual medical staff screening tools, such as quality assurance or morbidity and mortality, may not pick up on an impairment problem until its later stages.

Many physicians who are impaired by drugs or alcohol exhibit personality changes, such as changes in demeanor, intolerance of differing opinions, increasing argumentativeness, and loss of empathy. These behaviors will lead to a significant deterioration in the physicians' relationships with patients. These situations will not appear on quality assurance filters, but they will certainly increase the risk of litigation for poor outcomes. If action is not taken at this point, the quality of an impaired physician's care will deteriorate and lead to a higher risk of poor outcomes and malpractice liability.

Physicians typically are reluctant to pass judgment on a colleague's behavior. However, they have an ethical and legal responsibility to protect patients from inadequate medical care delivered by an impaired physician. Although a professional colleague should be given the benefit of the doubt, there comes a time when action is necessary to protect both physician and patients.

The Medical-Legal Perspective

The Health Care Quality Improvement Act of 1986 (HCQIA)[4] requires hospitals to report to the state medical licensing board, and ultimately the National Practitioner Data Bank (NPDB), any "professional review action," including physician impairment, that adversely affects the clinical privileges of a physician for longer than 30 days. HCQIA was intended to protect the public from poor quality physician services. Thus, if a physician is "peer reviewed" following an allegation of practicing under the influence of drugs of alcohol, resulting in a decrease in, or loss of privileges, that adverse action is reportable to the NPDB.

The penalty for a hospital's failure to report adverse privilege actions is significant. It results in loss of the qualified immunity of HCQIA that protects the hospital and physicians from lawsuits related to peer review.[4] This immunity from liability for good faith peer review has been a very effective defense to antitrust claims brought by physicians who are subject to discipline or privilege limitations. Hospitals are also obligated to query the NPDB during the process of physician application to the medical staff, and every two years during the recredentialing process. A physician's entry into a drug rehabilitation program, in itself, is not a reportable action.[5]

When addressing the issue of medical malpractice tort reform, some experts have advanced the theory that impaired and incompetent physicians may be responsible for a significant number of injuries, lawsuits, and damage awards. There are little data to support or refute this claim. However, physicians who have numerous malpractice cases may be more likely to be impaired or incompetent.

Under the doctrine of hospital corporate liability, the hospital owes a legal duty to its patients to monitor the quality of medical care provided by its independent staff physicians. This duty is nondelegable and is separate from the physician's individual duty of care. Juries tend to come down hard on hospitals named in lawsuits involving physicians who were impaired. In a case against a Houston hospital, a $52 million judgment was awarded to the family of a 39-year-old woman who died following elective surgery. The case focused on the defendant anesthesiologist, who had a history of drug and alcohol abuse, and the hospital's inadequate credentialing and monitoring.[6] The threat of litigation gives hospitals an incentive to implement effective credentialing processes and systems that will detect problems and monitor physician performance. The courts have clearly demonstrated a hospital's obligation to protect its patients from the acts of physicians that it knows are incompetent, including those whose incompetence results from abuse of alcohol or drugs.[3]

Also, many physician employment contracts now include provisions for mandatory pre-employment drug screens and random screening for cause. The consequences of a positive drug screen should be clearly delineated in the employment contract.

Taking Action to Help the Impaired Physician

The emergency physician suffering from chemical dependency must be confronted and entered into a comprehensive treatment program. This process is called intervention. Intervention is a preplanned event — a group confrontation by colleagues, friends, family members, and other members of the physician's support system.[7] In this confrontation, each person should take a turn to express concern and support and provide indisputable evidence of the physician's impairment problem. The consequences of not seeking treatment should be clearly delineated, such as job loss or loss of medical license. The goal is to break down the shield of denial long enough to get the physician into a treatment program. Preintervention planning should involve people who are knowledgeable and experienced in the process. Because desired outcome is likely to be inpatient treatment, arrangements should already have been made to have a treatment bed available. This will prevent the rapid resurfacing of the denial response and possible suicide risk.

Following treatment, aftercare and monitoring are essential to prevent and detect relapse, which is common with chemical dependency. These programs are individualized but should include a written agreement that delineates the consequences if relapse occurs and provide for random drug screening and continued counseling. The monitoring period is extensive, with a minimum of three years.

An important resource for physicians who are concerned about a colleague is the medical staff well-being committee. If none exists, most state medical societies have impaired professional programs. These programs can provide information about physician impairment and assistance with intervention, treatment, and monitoring. They usually function with the cooperation of the states' licensing boards, as the goal is to protect the consumer as well as to help the impaired professional. In general, the licensing board will not take disciplinary action as long as the physician is in compliance with the treatment program.

Can It Be Prevented?

Emergency medicine is an exciting and challenging specialty, but it also places unique stresses on emergency physicians' bodies, relationships, and minds.[8,9] It is fundamentally different from all other medical specialties in several ways — rotating shifts with altered circadian rhythms, unpredictable patient volumes, no prior relationship with patients, and working many weekends and holidays. Failure to acknowledge and adjust to these realities contributes substantially to burnout and attrition in the specialty.

How can an emergency physician avoid the pathway to impairment? Can an emergency physician stay well enough to practice in the emergency department for an entire career? Absolutely! There are many physicians who have practiced emergency medicine for many years without signs or symptoms of burnout. The emergency physician can "stay well" and practice emergency medicine by paying careful attention to career planning and to personal health, family, friends, and finances. Physicians frequently take a narrow view of their careers, mistakenly defining success by income or prestige rather than by personal fulfillment.

A successful and healthy lifestyle for an emergency physician should integrate the professional side of life with the personal side. Develop a life plan and establish personal and professional goals, both short-term and long-term. Planning and evaluation are essential to ensuring that time and energy spent reflect priorities. Goal-setting facilitates achievement of desires without getting sidetracked and having time consumed by unimportant projects. Setting unrealistic goals and impossible standards is common among physicians. This often leads to failure, burnout, and depression. It is OK not to be perfect.

Money cannot ensure happiness or professional satisfaction, but a physician who is beset by financial insecurity cannot devote full attention to professional endeavors or other needs. Financial planning is an important requirement for well-being because it allows for a predictable standard of living despite life's inevitable surprises.

Maintaining physical and mental health is critical to emergency physician longevity. The demands of a busy shift can be physically and emotionally exhausting. Optimal performance requires physical and mental fitness. Rotating shifts, especially night shifts, are associated with decreased alertness and decreased performance.

Families and friends are often the most essential components of the physician's support system. Relationships require personal presence in order to survive, so "sacred" time should be allotted to them. Families and friends provide a most effective antidote to the stress of emergency medicine.

Case Discussion

This case illustrates how appropriate medical care and a bad clinical outcome can result in malpractice litigation when an impaired physician is involved.

A family member who perceives the use of drugs or alcohol will automatically assume that the clinical care is less than adequate. Any bad outcome, even if it is unavoidable, will be questioned.

The hospital medical staff is held responsible for the appropriate monitoring of recovering physicians. Treatment of the impaired physician is only the initial step in the recovery process. Monitoring for several years is usually required. The medical staff should have regulations and guidelines for credentialing of impaired physicians.

Key Points and Conclusion

Emergency physician impairment by drugs, alcohol, physical or mental illness, or the aging process is a problem for the profession and the health care delivery system. Impairment affects the quality of patient care and, as a result, presents a risk management problem. Chemical dependence is a treatable disease. Fortunately, the recovery rate among physicians is very high. Think of the impaired physician as a patient who needs care and compassion. Identifying the impaired physician early in the disease progression is of great benefit to the hospital, the community, patients, and the physician.

References

1. American Medical Association, Council on Mental Health. The sick physician. Impairment by psychiatric disorders, including alcoholism and drug dependence. *JAMA* 1973;223:684-687.

2. Department of Health and Human Services. *Report of the Inspector General on Medical Malpractice and Impairment*, 1986.

3. Walzer RS. Impaired physicians. An overview and update of the legal issues. *J Leg Med* 1990;11(2):131-198.

4. 42 USC §11101-11152.

5. US Dept of Health and Human Services. *National Practitioner Data Bank Guidebook*. Rockville, Md: Health Resources and Services Association; 1990.

6. Verdict forces RMs to focus on physician monitoring. *Hospital Risk Management,* August 1989.

7. Whitehead D: Substance abuse in emergency physicians. *ACEP News*, July 1993.

8. Andrew LB, Pollack ML, eds. *Wellness for Emergency Physicians*. Dallas: American College of Emergency Physicians; 1995.

9. Gallery ME, Whitley TW, Klonis LK, et al. A study of occupational stress and depression among emergency physicians. *Ann Emerg Med* 1992;21:58-64.

Chapter 11

Privileges and Credentials

Stephen A. Colucciello, MD, FACEP

Balancing the complex issues of credentialing can be a medical-legal highwire act. These decisions involve potential liability for both the hospital and members of the credentialing committee, entanglement with federal antitrust law, and most recently, pressures from managed care organizations (MCOs). Physicians correctly perceive refusal of credentials as a career-threatening event, and aggrieved parties often seek legal redress. Credentialing committees also face difficult issues, such as how to grant privileges for new procedures, how to credential members of different departments in the same or similar procedures, and how legally to deny reappointment. Although medical staff bylaws should describe in detail the processes that guide credentialing, ultimately, it is the hospital's board of trustees or directors that grants privileges — the right to perform certain procedures or admissions — and credentials — the right to practice at the hospital.

Even though the ultimate goal of the credentialing process is excellence in clinical care, the process can become a battle in which departments or individuals jockey for power and bridle at perceived invasions of "turf." To aggrieved parties, the proceedings may appear capricious or discriminatory. Some credentialing committees rely heavily on instinct, self-preservation, friendships, and allegiances to make their decisions.[1] However, to ensure quality care and to withstand judicial scrutiny, the process must be dispassionate and scientific, relying on objective evidence, such as peer review, performance reports, and disciplinary records.

General Principles

The hospital has three charges with respect to credentialing[2]:
- Evaluate new applicants.
- Evaluate existing staff members for reappointment.
- Monitor and discipline staff physicians.

Physicians either join a particular hospital department or may receive a joint appointment to several departments.

In most hospitals, the chief of the medical staff appoints members of a privileges and credentials committee, which reviews applications for hospital credentials, determines the scope of privileges, and votes on staff reappointment. The committee can recommend a variety of membership levels, including courtesy, provisional, assistant, or full.[3] These levels of membership vary among institutions but usually reflect seniority. New applicants typically receive provisional status, and physicians who are semi-retired or do not admit patients serve as courtesy staff. Once the committee evaluates an applicant or reviews a request for reappointment, its recommendations go to the medical staff executive board and then on to the hospital's board of trustees for final approval.

The credentialing committee has significant authority, and it is here that departments may vie for power. Through the committee process, a particular department may attempt to usurp an entire class of procedures, such as conscious sedation, as their exclusive domain. To protect patients' interests, the department of emer-

49

gency medicine must secure representation on this committee.

Hospital credentialing does not authorize a physician to participate in a particular managed care plan. MCOs often insist on conducting their own credentialing, a process that may lack the usual guarantes of due process, and may jeopardize the physician-patient relationship and endanger a physician's ability to practice at a particular hospital.

The Medical-Legal Perspective

When a hospital-based physician is sued, the hospital may also be named as a defendant, based on the fact that it granted privileges to the defendant physician. This principle is known as corporate liability. If the physician named in a lawsuit is a hospital employee, the plaintiff usually invokes the doctrine of *respondeat superior*. This means that the "master" (the hospital) is legally responsible for the actions of its "servant" (the physician).

Health care facilities are liable in malpractice lawsuits if incompetent physicians are granted hospital privileges and allowed to maintain them. In the case of *Darling v Charleston Community Hospital*, the hospital was liable for failure to properly credential a physician in orthopedics.[4] In a similar case, another hospital was found liable when it did not restrict the privileges of an incompetent physician.[5]

The hospital medical staff has clear authority to grant or deny clinical privileges and to take disciplinary and corrective action, but such decisions must be based on concerns for patient safety.[6] In *Walsky v Pascack Valley Hospital*, the court held that any denial of medical privileges must be related to goals of high-quality patient care.[5] In recent years, the courts have supported physicians who proved discrimination when denied hospital privileges.[7] Such physicians successfully argued that the credentialing or peer review process was either discriminatory, lacked due process, or was based on factors other than clinical care. For this reason, members of credentialing committees incur legal risks and are often anxious regarding possible liability.[8] However, they are protected by the Health Care Quality Improvement Act (HCQIA) from exposure to liability if they adhere to its precepts.[3] This legal shield is not absolute, however, and immunity is jeopardized if credentials are denied because of improper motives.

The medical staff should refuse to credential physicians who practice substandard medicine

as demonstrated by objective means, such as multiple patient complaints, persistently high complication rates, and frequent warning letters from quality assurance committees. However, some unscrupulous physicians have used the credentialing process to eliminate competition by refusing credentials to financial rivals. In the landmark case of *Patrick v Burget*, physicians on a credentialing committee denied privileges to an economic competitor. The judge likened it to a scheme that allowed "General Motors, Chrysler, and Ford to review the safety of Toyotas to determine if the public should be allowed to drive them."[9]

The Sherman Antitrust Act

Physicians who have been denied hospital privileges have used the Sherman Act, a law that allows courts to rule on restraint of trade, as a legal remedy to gain credentials.[10] Violation of this law carries substantial penalties, including jail sentences, fines of up to $1 million, and treble damages and attorney's fees in successful civil lawsuits.[9]

The U.S. Supreme Court case of *Summit Health, Ltd v Pinhas* liberalized the jurisdiction of the Sherman Act to include cases of hospital credentialing.[11,12] Since Pinhas, decisions by credentialing committees are coming under increasing federal scrutiny.[13] If a hospital denies privileges to a physician, the reasoning should clearly reflect patient care issues. Hospital lawyers should review all denials of privileges in the light of federal regulations.[14] Pursuit of excellence in the medical staff is a legitimate goal,[9] but antitrust problems will arise if the medical staff acts to exclude potential competitors.[15] To complicate matters, almost every decision made by a credentialing committee affects the economic interests of some member of the medical staff.[9]

Exclusive Contracts

Hospitals may have exclusive contracts with hospital-based physician groups, such as emergency physicians, radiologists, pathologists, and anesthesiologists. Specialists who do not belong to the contracted groups, therefore, are excluded from the medical staff. These contracts are now being challenged in court.[16] To date, hospitals have successfully defended such contracts against conspiracy claims in the name of operating efficiency.[9] For example, in the case of *Dos Santos v Columbus-Cuneo-Cabrini Medical Center*, the court upheld an exclusive contract with an anesthesiology group based on the legitimate business interests of the hospital.

The Health Care Quality Improvement Act

In *Patrick v Burget*, the court held physicians and a hospital liable under federal antitrust law because of bad faith peer review. The multimillion dollar award in this case had a sobering effect on many credentialing committees, who began to worry that physicians who were refused credentials would routinely sue in federal court, thus stifling quality improvement efforts. These and other concerns gave rise to the passage of HCQIA in 1986.[17] This law provides limited immunity to medical staffs in the course of peer review, credentialing, and reappointment decisions.[18] HCQIA deals with antitrust, defamation claims, and other forms of litigation arising from peer review and credentialing. Subsequent court decisions have demonstrated that conditional immunities provided by HCQIA do indeed protect the process of credentialing and peer review.[17]

To ensure protection under HCQIA when refusing or removing a physician's privileges, credentialing committees must adhere to the following precepts[3,13,18,19]:

- The action of the committee is intended to promote quality care.
- The credentialing committee made a reasonable effort to obtain the facts.
- Adequate notice and hearing were provided to the physician involved.
- The committee believed the action was warranted by the facts of the case.

The protection granted by HCQIA does not extend automatically to all peer review activities. To qualify for immunity, the credentialing committee must comply with the details of the law[20]; and hospital attorneys should review credentialing procedures in this light.[21] As a general rule, credentialing criteria based on considerations of patient care and hospital operations will almost certainly withstand judicial review.[22]

The National Practitioner Data Bank

One of the provisions of HCQIA was the creation of a national reporting system, the National Practitioner Data Bank (NPDB).[23] Hospitals, other care facilities, and malpractice insurers are required to report to NPDB adverse actions taken against physicians.[6] These reporting requirements are complex and sometimes conflicting.[24] In 1992, the U.S. Department of Health and Human Services issued a supplement to its 1990 guidebook, which some authorities believe caused even more confusion.[24]

Hospitals are required to use this information clearinghouse in their credentialing processes.[6] They must also query NPDB at least every two years to update information on medical staff members.[5] Failure to query NPDB as mandated by law carries penalties of up to $10,000 per violation and poses additional corporate liability in cases of physician malpractice. Reports from NPDB are essential to acquire staff privileges, reappointment, professional credentials, and licenses throughout a physician's career. Unfortunately, most physicians have a poor understanding of this process.[25] NPDB information is accessible only to hospitals, medical societies, and MCOs and to physicians who want to obtain their own information. However, state medical boards maintain data banks containing similar, if not identical, information regarding malpractice and disciplinary actions. In Massachusetts and Florida, the public now has access to these files, and other states are likely to follow.[26]

Economic Credentialing

Through the use of computers, hospitals and MCOs amass vast quantities of information on physicians: what tests they order, procedures they perform, and the frequency with which they admit patients. This information is now being used to grant privileges and reappointment.[27,28]

Data collection is routine. When the emergency department secretary enters an order for a particular radiologic or diagnostic test, a computer code automatically "credits" a particular physician for the test. These data, coupled with other information such as admission rates, form a practice profile. With a simple spreadsheet program, a hospital administrator or credentialing committee can distinguish "expensive" physicians from those they believe are cost-effective. Hospitals may elect to share such data with MCOs, or the MCOs can generate their own profiles based on hospital bills. More than half of all hospital executives are generating practice profiles on medical staff members, but barely half are sharing the data with the physicians.[29] Many physicians being profiled are unaware of the practice.

Some hospitals pressure credentialing committees to use economic data in appointment and reappointment decisions. When physicians are employees, the hospital may not renew the contracts of those who over-test or over-admit. Proponents of this practice argue that these utilization and economic guidelines simply reflect good performance[16] and that health care entities must ensure efficiency.[30] One third of hospital CEOs at major academic health centers see nothing wrong with economic credentialing and review practice profiles when deciding whether to deny or terminate a physician's hospital privileges.[31] Some administrators believe that the threat of losing clinical privileges is the best way to ensure compliance with cost-saving standards.[32] Physicians terminated because of economic credentialing have sought redress in the courts. However, some tribunals have supported hospitals that deny credentials based on economic criteria.[33]

Economic credentialing has created tension between physicians and administrators.[34] The American Medical Association (AMA) opposes this practice as a sole criteria for appointment or reappointment to the medical staff.[35] The AMA also believes that hospital administrators should share measures of cost performance with the physicians involved.

The managed care industry is increasingly using financial data when credentialing health care providers.[36] More worrisome, reappointment to a hospital's medical staff may be influenced by pressure from MCOs.[37] These organizations have credentialing processes for physicians that are separate and distinct from the hospitals'. These two credentialing bodies, hospital and MCO, may be at odds, which creates significant turmoil. Consider the following example: a hospital that has a contract with a particular MCO grants hospital credentials to an emergency physician. The MCO may refuse credentials to the same emergency physician. As such, the MCO will not pay for services rendered by that physician, leaving the hospital to pay the bill. This gives the hospital a strong economic incentive to dismiss or not renew that emergency physician's contract.

Despite the growing influence of MCOs, a variety of factors may limit their power to credential physicians on economic grounds. A number of states have developed "any willing provider" rules that restrict MCOs from picking and choosing among physicians. These laws require an MCO to establish written criteria for credentialing. In these states, any willing provider who meets the criteria may participate in the MCO. MCOs have challenged these statutes, but the U.S. Supreme Court has allowed any willing provider laws to stand.[38]

Credentialing

Because the credentialing process requires an extensive system to collect and maintain data on physicians, a medical staff coordinator is essential for the smooth operation of the program. This coordinator must supervise data collection and assemble supporting information, such as medical licenses, DEA certificates, and residency and fellowship diplomas (Figure 1). Much of this information requires the applicant's written consent. Original or notarized copies of medical school and other diplomas are essential, as up to 5% of physicians falsify their credentials on hospital applications.[39] To detect fraud, the medical staff office must independently verify information regarding residency training, board certification, and work history. In the case of *Johnson v Misericordia Community Hospital*, the hospital was found liable because it failed to discover an applicant's false credentials.[5] The medical staff coordinator must also ensure that the applicant answers all questions on the hospital application or reappointment form.[2] This exhaustive process may take several months.

In addition to verifying documents such as licenses and diplomas, the credentialing committee must evaluate a physician's performance. To provide a comprehensive assessment of the applicant or reapplicant, risk managers must share data with the credentialing committee.[21] Unfortunately, hospitals commonly fail to use in-house data in the reappointment process.[2] Letters of reference, reports from quality assurance committees, malpractice history, and reports from NPDB are essential. The staff coordinator must collect a wide variety of peer-review information that includes incident reports, verified patient complaints, problems with drug and blood utilization, violation of medical record requirements, medical audits, morbidity and mortality review, and infection control.[40,41] Other performance data include chart documentation, attendance at meetings, and interpersonal behavior problems.[42] In some hospitals, physician proctors evaluate the performance of the applicant by directly observing clinical practice.

Issues concerning interpersonal relations, physician impairment, and incompetence are problematic. Courts have upheld that the inability to work with others is a sufficient basis for denying or terminating privileges, provided the hospital demonstrates that the behavior poses a "real and substantial danger" to patient care.[2] Hospitals must be sure that adverse actions taken against a physician because of personality conflicts are not a subterfuge to dismiss a vexing but otherwise qualified physician.[2] The committee must also investigate reports of physician impairment caused by drug or alcohol abuse.

Some hospitals require board certification or board eligibility as a prerequisite for privileges. Specialty boards define qualifications and issue certificates in hopes of ensuring the physician's preparation and skill.[43] Physicians who do not maintain their board certification put their hospital privileges at risk. There is a growing consensus that to improve quality, hospitals must hire and retain high-quality emergency physicians.[44] However, the issue of credentialing only board-certified emergency physicians remains contentious.

Computerization is becoming essential to the credentialing process. Computer databases provide access to large amounts of information.[45] Software applications can automate the process and allow the committee to meet its changing needs.[46] The best programs can be modified to meet the demands of an individual institution.[47]

Although each hospital has its own system, credentialing procedures tend to be similar across the country. This suggests that a uniform, even nationwide credentialing system is possible. Because a number of states are currently developing uniform programs for quality assurance and peer review,[48] similar programs could standardize the credentialing process. The U.S. Navy and the Joint Commission on Accreditation of Healthcare Organizations (JCAHO) have undertaken a three-year, multi-institutional privileging project. The concept involves granting privileges in one facility that are recognized throughout the system. It entails the following:

- Use of specialty-specific standardized privilege lists.
- Designation of a single authority to grant privileges.
- Use of a single credentials file.
- Medical staff bylaws applicable to the entire system.

This credentialing concept could be expanded to the civilian hospital system.[49]

Figure 1

Credentialing information [5,65]

State medical license

Diplomas and certificates from training programs, including college, medical school, residency, fellowships, board certification

Drug Enforcement Agency certificate

Professional references

Professional societies

Publications

Work history, including affiliations with other hospitals, past and present, explanation of any career gaps

Disciplinary actions taken against the physician, including NPDB, criminal convictions, peer review actions

Proof of medical malpractice coverage

Review of malpractice history (mandatory query to NPDB)

Physical and mental health status

Evaluation of moral and ethical character

Evaluation of ability to work with others

Figure 2

Clinical privileges of emergency physicians

Anesthesia

Anoscopy

Arthrocentesis

Bladder catheterization

Cesarean section-perimortem

Cannulation, vascular

Cardiac defibrillation

Cardiac massage

Cardiac pacing

Cardiorrhaphy

Cricothyrotomy

Culdocentesis

Delivery of newborn

Diagnostic tests interpretation

Endotracheal intubation

Escharotomy

Esophageal airway intubation

Foreign body removal

Fracture/dislocation immobilization/reduction

Gastric lavage

Heimlich maneuver

Incision-drainage

Laryngoscopy

Lumbar puncture

Nasal packing/cautery

Nasogastric intubation

Ocular tonometry

Pericardiocentesis

Pericardiotomy

Peritoneal lavage

Respirators

Skin grafts

Skull trephination-perimortem

Slit lamp examination

Spinal immobilization

Thoracentesis

Tube thoracostomy

Thoracotomy

Wound debridement/repair

A patchwork of credentialing procedures characterizes MCOs. A single hospital may have 30 or more contracts with different MCOs. To obtain credentials from each group, an emergency physician may have to complete dozens of separate applications. A uniform document used statewide or nationwide would greatly simplify the process.[50] Several states are developing such forms.

Due Process

In any credentialing process, some physician will be denied hospital credentials. To protect the rights of the physician and to limit liability for the credentials committee and the hospital, decision-making must proceed in a standard manner. In addition, the hospital must provide a structured process for appeal.[51] This uniform, nondiscriminatory approach is known as due process and serves to resolve conflicts among the hospital, medical staff committees, and individual practitioners.[52] Credentialing committees must provide a fair review and permit the physician to respond to unfavorable allegations.[53] In addition to damaging a physician's reputation, unfair review practices lead to liability exposure and expensive and prolonged litigation.[54] Ultimately, the hospital's board of directors is responsible for due process by protecting the physician's right to fair treatment.[55]

When an MCO denies credentials to an emergency physician, the implications are profound. Adversely affected physicians should receive the same procedural protection currently afforded by hospitals, including a fair hearing that provides a notice of charges and an opportunity to respond.[56] However, some MCOs do not provide the traditional protections of notice, peer review, due process, or right to appeal.[35]

Privileging

The term privileges refers to a variety of activities, including general practice privileges such as history-taking and physical examinations, ordering and interpreting diagnostic tests, administering medication, and requesting consultation. It also refers to specific procedure privileges, such as permission to perform a particular procedure within the hospital. Admitting privileges allow the physician to admit patients to the hospital or to a particular ward, such as the ICU. Emergency physicians should be privileged in techniques or procedures that are necessary for rapid patient care (Figure 2). Privileges are granted based on training and experience, usually as a result of residency training.

Emergency physicians must be privileged in the same manner as the rest of the medical staff. If an emergency physician is competent to perform a procedure by value of either training or prior clinical experience, that physician should receive hospital privileges. Competence in a procedure may be certified by the residency director, department chairman, specialty board, or designated proctor. The raw number of procedures performed should not be the sole criterion for competence. Other concerns, such as cognitive skills, technical skills, and quality of training, must be considered. The complication rate associated with an individual's performance is important in regard to the annual or biannual reprivileging process.

The JCAHO maintains that clinical privileges are subject to the authority of the department chairman. Thus, the chairman of emergency medicine may grant different clinical privileges to different members of the department.[57] Some large emergency departments have separate areas, such as a fast track or "quick care" area. At times, the department may employ physicians who may be privileged to work exclusively in that area.

Although a specific list of privileges is standard, the emergency physician must have broad latitude to intervene in life- or limb-threatening situations. For this reason, privileging documents may include such language as: "The emergency physician may perform any other procedure in the emergency department that is potentially lifesaving, especially when there are no reasonable alternatives." The JCAHO states: "In the case of an emergency, any individual who is a member of the medical staff or who has been granted delineated clinical privileges is permitted to do everything possible, within the scope of his license, to save a patient's life or to save a patient from serious harm, regardless of the individual's staff status or clinical privileges."[58]

Some privileges, such as conscious sedation, rapid sequence intubation, and diagnostic ultrasound, cross department lines. In the past, emergency physicians were forced to seek permission from other departments to perform these procedures.[57] Radiologists may object to emergency physicians performing diagnostic ultrasound, and anesthesiologists may be threatened by the use of conscious sedation in the emergency department. Although these departments may protest such emergency department procedures, claiming patient advocacy, these arguments often mask underlying financial concerns.[59] All too frequently, issues of ego, turf, and economics restrict clinical procedures.[57,60]

With respect to cross-department privileging, the credentialing committee should generate a specific list of privileges and apply the written criteria uniformly to the medical staff. Language that defines the scope of the particular procedure is often helpful. For example, an emergency physician performing diagnostic ultrasound is more focused than a radiologist performing the same procedure. In other words, instead of performing a general survey of the abdomen, the emergency physician seeks to answer a particular question, such as: "Does this 75-year-old hypotensive man have an abdominal aortic aneurysm?" Defining the scope of procedures that overlap different departments may decrease political tensions.

Privileging that involves a new technology or new application, such as emergency department ultrasound, is problematic. To advance medical care, credentialing committees must recognize alternative pathways to competence once residency training is over — old hands must be allowed to acquire new skills.[1] Continuing medical education (CME) courses can be used to teach physicians new procedures. The hospital or the clinical department may initiate a preceptor program to demonstrate new techniques and to incorporate a quality assurance review.[61] Such programs promote new skills while at the same time ensuring competence. Specialty societies occasionally provide recommendations for the number of proctored or reviewed procedures that should be documented prior to granting full privileges.

As privileging becomes more rigorous, documentation of procedural experience becomes essential. In the near future, emergency physicians might need to keep a procedure log to demonstrate competence in of a variety of procedures. This log would provide patient information, procedure, technique, immediate and delayed complications, and final patient outcome.[57]

The HIV-Positive Physician and Privileges

The past several years have seen vigorous debate over the rights and responsibilities of physicians and other health care professionals infected with the human immunodeficiency virus (HIV).[62] The Americans with Disabilities Act protects the rights of HIV-infected health care workers from certain types of job discrimination. On the other hand, hospitals have the right and duty to protect the public from transmission of a lethal disease. The credentialing committee should address the scope of practice for infected physicians and under what circumstances patients should be informed of a physician's HIV status. In general, only invasive procedures are curtailed.

Key Points and Conclusion

A medical license does not confer the right to practice at a particular hospital. Instead, physicians must undergo rigorous credentialing processes that involve initial appointment to the medical staff, granting of clinical privileges, and reappraisal and/or reappointment. Granting privileges and credentials is a legal balancing act. Patients sue hospitals when there are allegations of malpractice, claiming that hospitals fail to screen or monitor physicians adequately. Physicians denied credentialing sue under federal antitrust law.[63]

To avoid these legal entanglements, criteria for credentials and privileges must be uniform throughout the medical staff. With the growth of MCOs, credentialing has taken on new significance with associated problems. Prejudice, ignorance, and economics are the greatest roadblocks to emergency physician credentialing.[59] The goal of the credentialing and privileging process is high-quality patient care. Therefore, the gold standard must remain training, experience, ability, and competence.[64]

- Credentialing and privileging decisions must be based primarily on issues of patient care.
- The credentialing process is regulated by medical staff bylaws and federal law.
- Hospital lawyers must ensure that the credentialing process conforms to standards of the Sherman Act and HCQIA.
- Credentialing committees must ensure due process and allow the physician denied credentials an opportunity for appeal.

References

1. Achord J. The credentialing process: rational decisions of hospital committees for granting of privileges in gastrointestinal endoscopic procedures. *Am J Gastroenterol* 1987;82:1064-1065.
2. Baker CH. Taking care of the doctors: the hospital's duty to evaluate, monitor, and discipline its medical staff. *QRB* 1994;88-93.
3. Packard D. Physician credentialling. In: Salluzzo RF, Mayer TA, Strauss RW, et al, eds. *Emergency Department Management: Principles and Applications.* St Louis: Mosby–Year Book, Inc; 1997.
4. Dunn JD. Credentialing. In: Mayer TA, Salluzzo RF, Strauss RW, et al (eds). *Emergency Department Management: Principles and Applications.* St Louis: Mosby–Year Book Inc; 1997.
5. Hagg-Rickert S. Medical staff credentialing and privileging determinations: the emerging role of the risk manager. *Perspec Healthcare Risk Manage* 1991;11:2-4.
6. Blaes SM, Knight GE. Effective physician credentialing. Properly monitoring medical staffs can protect hospitals from liability. *Health Progress* 1990;71:60-65.
7. Firestone MH, Schur R. Malicious deprivation of hospital staff privileges. *Leg Med* 1986:199-215.
8. Koska MT. Peer review, privileges: MDs fear legal tangles. *Hospitals* 1989;63(23):28-29.
9. Piche G. Dodging the bullet: avoiding conspiracy claims in professional staff disputes. *Hosp Health Service Admin* 1988;33:531-542.
10. Timmons G, Ridenour N. Restraint of trade implications for nurse practitioners: denial of hospital admitting or staff privileges. *J Am Acad Nurse Pract* 1993;5:175-178.
11. Trentalance AE. A case of wrongful use of quality management: *Summit Health, Ltd v Pinhas. Phys Exec* 1994;20:28-29.
12. Devlin MM. Federal laws govern the conduct of peer review. *Am J Med Qual* 1992;7:88-90.
13. Busey RC. Federal antitrust jurisdiction in peer review cases: the *Pinhas* decision. *Hospital Law Newslett* 1991;9:1-7.
14. Jacobsen RA Jr, Wiggins RB. Denials of staff privileges face increased antitrust scrutiny. *Health Care Manage Rev* 1992;17(4):7-15.
15. Horoschak MJ. Medical staff privileges and the antitrust laws: a view from the Federal Trade Commission. *Med Staff Counselor* 1992;6:17-24.
16. Koska MT. Review exclusive contracts in light of recent challenges. *Hospitals* 1992;66(8):38-42.
17. Snelson E. Quality assurance implications of federal peer review laws. The Health Care Quality Improvement Act and the National Practitioner Data Bank. *Qual Assur Util Rev* 1992;7(1):2-11.
18. Trostorff DL. Medical staff privileging: how to avoid pitfalls in the administrative process. *QRB* 1994; Quality:198-204.
19. Penner I. Special report on medical staff relationships: Ninth Circuit buttresses peer review immunities. *Health Care Law Newslett* 1994;9:15-20.
20. Valiant C. New peer review law provides immunity with obligations. *Phys Exec* 1987;13:26-27.
21. Purtell DL. Data bank has operational impact. Proper peer review can protect hospitals from antitrust and defamation suits. *Health Progress* 1990;71:66-71.
22. Searcy VL. The role of medical staff credentialing in a risk management program. *Top Health Rec Manage* 1991;12:34-39.
23. Puryear MA, Politzer RM, Anderson J, et al. The National Practitioner Data Bank: the first 18 months. *Phys Exec* 1993;19:13-17.
24. Snelson EA. National Practitioner Data Bank: more guidelines, more problems. *Med Staff Counselor* 1993;7:1-9.
25. Ankney RN, Coil JA, Kolff J, et al. Physician understanding of the National Practitioner Data Bank. *South Med J* 1995;88:200-203.
26. Troia PJ. Consumers and organizations demand physician profiling in Massachusetts. *Common Sense,* Winter 1997.

27. Blum JD. Evaluation of medical staff using fiscal factors: economic credentialing. *J Health Hosp Law* 1993;26:65-72.

28. Gramling A. Piecing together your profile: what plans know about you, and how they use it. *Managed Care* 1994;3:17-18.

29. Koska MT. Physician practices go under the microscope. *Hospitals* 1990;64(4):32-37.

30. Baxter MJ, Hornback M. The evolution of medical staff credentialing. *Med Staff Counselor* 1993;7:33-39.

31. Riley D. Economic credentialing survey of university teaching hospitals. *Healthcare Finan Manage* 1993;47:42-48.

32. Greene J. Hospitals eyeing physicians' practice patterns: economic credentialing is being tested to reduce expenses and improve quality. *Mod Healthcare* 1991;21:30-31.

33. Benesch K. Economic credentialing and the fraud and abuse caveat. *Med Staff Counselor* 1992;6:27-35.

34. Wilcox DP. Recognizing physicians' rights under exclusive contracts. *Tex Med* 1993;89(4):29-32.

35. Schafermeyer R. Economic credentialling — a perspective for emergency medicine. *ACEP News*, February 1997.

36. Bloom A. Physician credentialing in managed care. *Ann Health Law* 1992;1:93-106.

37. Blum JD. Economic credentialing moves from the hospital to managed care. *J Health Care Finance* 1995;22(1):60-71.

38. Leone PR. New developments in 'any willing provider' laws. *Healthcare Finan Manage* 1994;48:32-35.

39. Schaffer WA, Rollo FD, Holt CA. Falsification of clinical credentials by physicians applying for ambulatory-staff privileges. *N Engl J Med* 1988;318:356-358.

40. LaCova F. A second look at medical staff privileges. *Trustee* 1985;36:22-23.

41. Burkhalter E. The credentialing process. *Mil Med* 1987;152:509-511.

42. Haun JP. A process for objective review of physician performance. *Phys Exec* 1992;18:51-55.

43. Langsley DG. Medical specialty credentialing in the United States. *Clin Orthop* 1990; August 22-28.

44. Hagland MM. ED overcrowding spurs interest in quality and credentialing issues. *Hospitals* 1991;65(14):33-36.

45. Roth LG. The physician's practice profile: a piece of the quality puzzle. *Phys Exec* 1991;17:16-214.

46. King JP, McKeeby J, Bayless J. Evolution of sacred (staff authority credentialing): an automated credentialing system. *Top Health Information Manage* 1995;15:55-69.

47. Walker J, Perry WF. A system to manage records for credentialed providers. *J Healthcare Qual* 1992;14:12-15.

48. Gabel RA. Quality assurance/peer review for recredentialing/relicensure in New York State. *Int Anesthesiol Clin* 1992;30:93-101.

49. Peterson JL. Multi-institutional privileging: a pilot demonstration project of the United States Navy and the Joint Commission on Accreditation of Healthcare Organizations. *Mil Med* 1992;157:604-608.

50. Pelberg AL. Credentialing: a current perspective and legal background. *Qual Assur Util Rev* 1989;4(1):8-13.

51. Wilson FC. Credentialing in medicine. *Ann Thorac Surg* 1993;55:1345-1348.

52. Guthrie MB. Due process key element of physician grievance. *Phys Exec* 1987;13:11-13.

53. Liswood J, McClure AE. Revoking hospital privileges: new directions in Ontario: Dr. N. v Brantford General Hospital. *Leadership Health Serv* 1993;2:16-18.

54. Rozovsky FA, Rozovsky LE. Strategies for eliminating unfairness in peer review. *Med Staff Counselor* 1992;6:27-32.

55. Appointments and clinical privileges: role and responsibilities of the board of trustees. *QRB* 1994;5-9.

56. Curtis T. Fair hearings for physicians denied participation in managed care plans. *Med Staff Counselor* 1990;4:45-48.

57. Ramoska EA, Sacchetti AD, Warden TM. Credentialing of emergency physicians: support for delineation of privileges in invasive procedures. *Am J Emerg Med* 1988;6:278-281.

58. Joint Commission on Accreditation of Healthcare Organizations. *Comprehensive Accreditation Manual for Hospitals — The Official Handbook* (CAMH). Chicago: JCAHO; 1995.

59. Hedges JR, Singal BM. Credentialing of emergency physicians. *Am J Emerg Med* 1988;6:314.

60. Jessee WF. Delineating clinical privileges. *QRB* 1994;209-214.

61. Sequeira R, Weinbaum F, Satterfield J, et al. Credentialing physicians for new technology: the physician's learning curve must not harm the patient. *Am Surg* 1994;60:821-823.

62. Tamborlane TA. AIDS and the health care professional: 1993 update. *Med Staff Counselor* 1993;7:17-22.

63. Meghrigian AG. Medical staff privileges and the antitrust laws: does the intracorporate conspiracy doctrine apply? *Med Staff Counselor* 1992;6:9-16.

64. Tobin M. Fair hearing testimony. *Fam Med* 1993;25:566-567.

65. Hamilton GC, Lumpkin JR, Tomlanovich MC, et al. Emergency medicine core content. Special committee on the core content revision. *Ann Emerg Med* 1986;15:853-862.

Chapter 12

National Practitioner Data Bank

Joseph P. McMenamin, MD, JD, FCLM
Karen Iezzi Michael, Esquire

In 1986, Congress passed the Health Care Quality Improvement Act (HCQIA).[1] There were two purported purposes of the Act, as follows[2]:

- To encourage good faith peer review activities by providing peer review participants with immunity from certain kinds of liability, notably private antitrust claims, with their substantial risk of enormous damage awards.
- To restrict the ability of allegedly incompetent physicians to move to new jurisdictions without disclosing their prior performance elsewhere.

As a *quid pro quo* for the guaranty of immunity and as a means to track allegedly incompetent physicians nationwide, the Act created the National Practitioner Data Bank (NPDB). This data bank contains a wide array of sensitive and potentially highly damaging information about individual physicians, dentists, and other health care professionals. Its application to emergency physicians does not appear to be materially different from its application to other practitioners. The data accumulated in the NPDB, although generated and collected to improve the quality of health care in the United States, also can be used to the detriment of health care institutions and practitioners.

A five-year, $15.9 million contract was awarded to UNISYS Corporation to establish and operate the NPDB.[3] Legislation set forth the criteria and procedures for the collection and release of information, in accordance with the requirements of Title IV, Part B, of HCQIA. No information was to be reported to the NPDB until it opened in late summer 1990. No retroactive reporting was required.

The provisions of the NPDB do not apply to federal health care entities nor to physicians, dentists, or other health care practitioners employed by the federal government. Coverage under HCQIA is intended to be broad, however.[4]

The Medical-Legal Perspective

The constitutionality of the NPDB was challenged in *Doe v United States Department of Health and Human Services*[5] (DHHS) by a physician who was reported to the NPDB. The physician claimed that the NPDB report injured his reputation and violated the Fifth Amendment's guaranty of due process. The court held that the NPDB does not violate due process guaranties. In the court's opinion, damage to reputation does not implicate any liberty or property interests.

Immunity in Peer Review

The Sherman Act[6] forbids contracts, combinations, or conspiracies in restraint of trade. Professionals, including physicians, are indisputably subject to the Sherman Act.[7] Physicians who have participated in peer review actions or voted to terminate physicians' privileges have been sued and held liable for antitrust violations.[8] In private antitrust claims, actual damages must be trebled. Medical malpractice insurance seldom covers such liability.

Congress became concerned about physicians' natural reluctance to get embroiled in professional disputes that could result in the award of heavy damages for which they could be personally liable. Allegations that there was "an increasing occurrence of medical malpractice," a "need to improve the quality of medical care," and a "national need to restrict the ability of incompetent physicians to move from state to state" were the impetus for passing HCQIA.

The Act establishes a cloak of immunity from certain types of liability for peer review activity if the activity is conducted in accordance with the Act's guidelines. A peer review action taken in accordance with the following five tests warrants immunity from liability:

- The peer review must be taken in the reasonable belief that it was done to promote the quality of health care[9];
- After a reasonable investigation of the facts[10];
- With adequate due process and procedural safeguards afforded to the accused physician;
- In the reasonable belief that the action taken to discipline the physician was warranted by the evidence; and
- The reviewing entity [see Glossary] must comply with the reporting requirements of the NPDB.[11]

There is a rebuttal presumption that all review actions meet the standards for immunity.[12] A physician challenging the validity of a review action must prove by a preponderance of the evidence that the immunity requirements were not met.[13] If a health care facility fails to report as required, it may lose three years of immunities and protections provided for in the Act and is subject to a civil penalty of up to $10,000.[14]

Austin v McNamara[15] is the first reported case applying the Act to peer review activity. In *Austin*, a neurosurgeon, following the suspension of his hospital privileges, brought a Sherman Act claim against a hospital and five individual physicians. The court dismissed the case. In doing so, the court relied on the "ten months' worth of evaluations and monitoring of the plaintiff's work [by in-house reviewers and] a comprehensive external review of the plaintiff's work by independent neurosurgeons appointed by the California Medical Association . . ." which showed a "reasonable effort to obtain the facts"[16] as required by HCQIA. The neurosurgeon's suspension was ultimately found to be unreasonable, but the antitrust immunity nevertheless applied.

Immunity for Review Bodies

HCQIA was designed, in part, to protect the professional review body. The professional review body includes the hospital, the governing body of the hospital and its committees, and medical staff committees assisting the governing body, as well as group practices, HMOs, and medical societies that perform peer review. It also protects individuals, including members of the professional review body and its staff, those under contract to that body, and those who participate in or assist in deliberations of the body, such as witnesses and informants.[17] A person who provides information to the review body regarding the competence or professional conduct of a physician is given immunity against libel or slander lawsuits, unless knowingly providing false information, and against lawsuits for tortious interference with the plaintiff physician's ability to earn a living.[12] Failure to report substandard performance will cost the facility its immunity but will not affect the immunity of individuals participating in peer review.[18]

Protection of the reviewers and health care facility extends to a physician's initial application for privileges, to reappointment and reappraisal of clinical privileges, and to all disciplinary actions. Protection is limited, however, to damages in private actions and to proper peer review as defined in the Act. If the challenged professional review activity fails to meet the standards of the Act, no immunity is provided. A lawsuit against the review participants then can be tried without regard to provisions of the Act.[19] The Act also leaves entirely intact the jurisdiction of the Federal Trade Commission, the Department of Justice, and state attorneys general to bring antitrust actions. These actions may entail civil monetary penalties, injunctions, disgorgement of profits, and, as with private antitrust lawsuits, awards or damages several times those actually proved in court. However, HCQIA does not restrict the right of a disciplined physician to bring a private action for injunctive or declaratory relief.

On the other hand, HCQIA does not provide immunity for professional review activities involving nonphysician, nondentist providers, such as chiropractors, podiatrists, psychologists, or nurse anesthetists. These practitioners may still bring private antitrust claims against reviewers. HCQIA does not provide immunity for a hospital against claims of negligent credentialing. In fact, such claims may actually be encouraged by the Act. Also excluded from immunity are actions brought under the statutes of state or federal civil rights laws.[18]

Other Theories of Liability

Other theories of liability may possibly remain viable after the Act. Depending on the jurisdiction, these may include defamation,[20] harmful interference with professional or business relationships,[21] conspiracy,[22] breach of contract,[23] intentional infliction of emotional distress,[24] or even claims of racketeering or organized crime.[25] Despite these possibilities, however, no such claims have been brought since the NPDB became operational.

If a practitioner brings an antitrust claim against those who have immunity under the Act, the defendants may be able to recover their costs and reasonable attorneys' fees. Such an award will be made if the defendants subsequently win the lawsuit, and if the plaintiff's claim or conduct was frivolous, unreasonable, without foundation, or in bad faith.[26] Courts may have difficulty dismissing a case on such pleadings "because the plaintiff is entitled to attempt to prove that the hearing was unfair despite procedural compliance with [the Act]. Thus, those who participate in the peer review process may still be subject to depositions and other discovery requests . . ."[18]

Due Process

Immunity is granted under the Act for those peer review proceedings in which the following safeguards are provided:
- Notice to the practitioner,[27]
- A hearing before individuals not in direct economic competition with the practitioner under scrutiny,[28]
- The right to counsel,[29]
- The right to cross-examine witnesses and to present evidence,[29] and
- The right to receive a written decision, including a statement of the basis of the decision.[30]

As stated in *Austin v McNamara*, "[w]hile the legislative history indicates that the Due Process requirements can always be met by the procedures specified in §11112(b)(1986) U.S. Code Cong. and Admin. News at 6293, both the text of §11112(b) and the legislative history agree that these procedures need not be followed to the letter in order to satisfy the Due Process requirements."[31] The Act does not create a private right of action to enforce procedural rights.

Because the Act permits a suspension proce-dure to avert substantial risk to patients,[32] the *Austin* court was satisfied that the plaintiff neurosurgeon had been given due process, even though his hearing followed his suspension. Relying on 42 USC §11112, the court also ruled that the hospital need not provide for appellate review of decisions reached as a result of every hearing.

Due process issues may be implicated in clinical privilege denials and terminations that do not involve peer review proceedings. Such summary terminations often occur when a hospital terminates a contract with a provider or grants an exclusive contract to another provider, effectively stranding the physician or practitioner without hospital privileges. State courts' rulings have differed on whether physicians who lose privileges when contracts with providers are terminated have due process rights to hearings.

In *Lewisburg Community Hospital v Alfredson*,[33] a radiologist sued the defendant hospital when his corporation lost its exclusive contract with the hospital. The Tennessee Supreme Court held that the physician had a right to a hearing because the medical staff bylaws provided for a fair hearing for physicians before the hospital could take any action that would significantly reduce a physician's clinical privileges. The court held that the bylaws constituted a contract with the radiologist. Thus, the radiologist's lawsuit was actually for a breach of contract, citing the hospital's failure to provide a hearing as required in the bylaws.

A slightly different result was reached by the Maine Supreme Court in *Bartley v Eastern Maine Medical Center*.[34] This lawsuit was brought by four emergency physicians whose contracts were terminated without a hearing. The court held that the notice and hearing requirements in the hospital bylaws were not relevant to the hospital's action. The court agreed with the physicians that the hospital's bylaws may constitute an enforceable contract; however, the court also agreed with the hospital that the termination of the emergency physicians' contract resulted from a more favorable contractual arrangement with another group. As the termination did not result from the hospital taking "major corrective action," as outlined in the bylaws, the bylaws' hearing requirements did not apply.

In *Babcock v Saint Francis Medical Center*,[35] the plaintiff sought injunctive relief, reinstatement of privileges, and damages against the hospital and its medical staff after her staff privileges were suspended following concern about her drinking. Granting summary judgment in favor of the hospital and its staff, the court made several significant rulings regarding due process and the peer review process.

First, the court upheld the immunity granted through the Act on the issue of damages. Because the decision to terminate privileges was clearly made "in the reasonable belief that the action was in furtherance of quality health care" and because the remaining suggestions of §11112(a)(1)-(4) were met, immunity was necessary.[36]

Second, the court would not enjoin, that is, prohibit, the hospital from reporting the physician to the NPDB because, it noted, the report had already been made. The court added, however, that it would grant equitable relief from the report made to the NPDB if the court found that the privileges were wrongfully revoked, a finding the court did not make.

Finally, the court reasoned that it could not substitute its judgment for that of the hospital's. In other words, even if the court would have not suspended under the facts, the question was whether the hospital acted properly in the process, and not whether the result was justified.

What Is Reported to the NPDB?

A medical practitioner's name can become part of the NPDB in three ways, as follows:

- Medical malpractice judgments or settlements.
- Adverse actions by medical boards.
- Professional review actions and other reportable conduct.

Once the information is entered into the NPDB, it remains on permanent record, even after the physician dies. Although it is possible to correct erroneous information, no provision in the NPDB allows for the removal of information.

Medical Malpractice Judgments or Settlements

Any time a payment is made on behalf of a licensed health care practitioner as a result of a claim or judgment for medical malpractice, the payment must be reported to the NPDB and to the relevant state licensing board. In addition, the original claim for payment must have been in writing and money must have changed hands. Under these regulations, a waiver of fees or cancellation of debt does not need to be reported, nor does a refund of fees unless the refund was made by an insurance company in response to a written refund request. In cases of periodic payments, reporting is required only at the time of the first periodic payment; however, the report should indicate an expectation of subsequent payments. When more than one defendant is involved, the total payment must be reported and details concerning each health care practitioner provided on separate reporting forms. Payments made solely on behalf of a hospital, clinic, or physician's professional corporation need not be reported. If a practitioner's name is added to the terms of a settlement to obtain release from further threat of litigation but the practitioner is not named in the original claim, no report is required.

Any payment, regardless of its size, must be reported. The DHHS has acknowledged that a payment does not create a presumption of malpractice. Congress has refused to adopt a minimum payment level for reporting.

Payments from both judgments and settlements are reportable. When an insurance company or a hospital settles a case, with or without the physician's consent, that physician's name will be entered in the NPDB. There is a legal presumption that a hospital or insurance company has a right to settle within the limits of the policy unless a consent to settle clause is included in the physician's contract. In *Melendez v Hospital for Joint Diseases Orthopedic Institute*,[37] a hospital settled a wrongful death claim on behalf of one of its surgeons. The surgeon sued the hospital, claiming that it violated his due process rights by failing to ask for his consent. He also sued the insurance company for breach of fiduciary duty. The court held that, without a consent to settle clause in either contract, the physician had no cognizable claim in protesting the settlement.

The actual report submitted to the NPDB by the payer of the malpractice claim must contain the following information about the practitioner: name and work address, date of birth, professional school and year of graduation, license number, field of licensure, the state or territory awarding the license, and, if known, the practitioner's DEA number, Social Security number, home address, and hospital affiliations. The reporting entity must furnish its own name and address, the name, title, and telephone number of the responsible official submitting the report on behalf of the entity, and the relationship of the reporter to the defendant. With respect to a judgment or settlement, the adjudicative body and the case number must be reported, as well as the date of the act or omission giving rise to the claim, the date of judgment or settlement, the amount paid, the date of payment, and whether payment was made as the result of a judgment or a settlement. The reporter must also describe any settlement conditions, including terms of payment, and the facts of the case. The actual act or omission on which the claim is based must be classified into one of 90 codes developed by the DHHS. Because it is sometimes difficult to fit the action into one of the codes, up to two codes are permitted to describe the act. The report must be made within 30 days of the date of the payment check, even if the case is still on appeal and even when the court records have been sealed.[38]

Adverse Actions by Medical Boards

A state licensing agency must report to the NPDB any action it takes based on a physician's or dentist's lack of professional competence or professional conduct that revokes, suspends, or otherwise restricts the physician's or dentist's license, or which results in the physician's censure, reprimand, or probation. The Board of Medical Examiners in each state must also report any action under which a physician or dentist surrenders a license.[39] The information is reported on an "Adverse Action Report," which includes the physician's or dentist's name and work address, date of birth, professional school, year of graduation, license number, field of licensure, licensing jurisdiction; the actual omissions or commissions complained of and their classification, and the board action taken, the date taken, and the effective date. The report must also include, if known, the physician's or dentist's home address, Social Security number, and DEA number. The DHHS Secretary may supplement the data contained in the report.[40]

Section 5 of the Medicare and Medicaid Protection Act of 1987[41] amended the Act by broadening reporting requirements in accordance with the state's Medicaid plan. Adverse actions taken by a state or any political subdivision of a state against any licensed health care provider must be reported if such authority closed formal proceedings then pending against the provider or caused any other loss of licensure by a practitioner. Any revision of the original action must be reported. For example, the reporting entity must update the report when a physician's license has been reinstated or a professional review action reversed or modified.

The procedure is the same as for reporting the original event.

Information relating to professional competence or conduct must be reported. Actions that do not need to be reported include retirement, relocation, failure to pay fees, and advertising, even though an entity may impose some licensure limitation or sanction on the dentist or physician.[40]

Professional Review Actions and Other Reportable Conduct

Professional review actions fall into two general categories: clinical privileges and society memberships. If a hospital or another health care facility, such as an HMO or a medical or dental group practice, imposes any disciplinary actions on a practitioner lasting 30 days or longer based on professional competence or conduct, such actions must be reported to the NPDB. If, because of a formal peer review process, any professional society of physicians or dentists takes adverse action against a practitioner based on the competence or professional conduct of that practitioner, that action also must be reported.

A health care entity must report adverse actions regarding a physician's clinical privileges. These actions include the following:

- Any professional review action of 30 days' duration or longer that adversely affects the clinical privileges of a physician or dentist.
- Surrender of clinical privileges or any restriction of such privileges by a physician or dentist while under investigation regarding incompetent or improper professional conduct, or in return for not conducting such investigation or proceeding.
- A professional review action by a professional society.[42]

A loss of clinical privileges lasting less than 30 days need not be reported.[43] Reports must be made to the Board 15 days after the action taken; the Board then has another 15 days to relay the information to the NPDB.

Any negative action or finding against a practitioner made as a result of a peer review must be reported. What constitutes such a review or action, however, is a gray area. Whether an action is a peer review depends on the hospital's bylaws and the practitioner's possible right to a hearing.

A hospital's denial of a practitioner's application for a staff position or privileges is reportable in certain circumstances but not in others. The denial is not reportable if the physician simply failed to meet the hospital's threshold requirements, such as insufficient experience. In some cases, a physician may withdraw an application before the hospital makes its final decision. Such a withdrawal is not reportable unless, owing to the manner in which a physician exercised his temporary privileges, a denial was likely.

If a practitioner is suspended for failure to attend staff meetings, or is reprimanded or censured for nonclinical conduct, no report is required. Investigations that do not end in a negative action are not reportable. The voluntary surrender of privileges before an investigation is begun is not reportable as long as such a surrender is not undertaken "in return for not conducting such an investigation."[44]

Entry into a drug, alcohol, or psychiatric rehabilitation program is not reportable unless the practitioner has done so because of a professional review action. Voluntary reductions in clinical privileges are not reportable, for example, if a family practitioner decides not to provide obstetrical services any longer. Neither a change in staff status to courtesy or honorary nor a denial of privilege for want of board certification is reportable.

Whenever a physician's or other practitioner's registration to dispense controlled substances is revoked or suspended, the DEA must notify the NPDB. State drug enforcement agencies, where they exist, need not report this information. The following information must be supplied with the report: the practitioner's name and work address, Social Security number, date of birth, professional school and year of graduation, license number, field of licensure, and issuing state or territory; the actual omissions or other reasons for the loss of privileges or, if known, for the surrender of privileges; the action taken, the date taken, and the effective date; and, if known, the practitioner's DEA number.[45] If the Board discovers that a health care entity has failed to report the required data, it must inform the NPDB of the oversight.

There is some uncertainty about which actions by a physician are adverse enough to be reported. This confusion can lead to varied reporting standards among states and to possible abusive or selective reporting. For example, restrictions requiring a physician to obtain further training, to allow patients to be co-managed with another physician, or to be assisted in operations by another surgeon are on the bor-

derline. Whether these restrictions need to be reported often depends on hospital bylaws. If the bylaws allow a physician to request a hearing for any such action, this may indicate that the restriction is significant and, thus, reportable. If by co-management a physician loses the right to make independent treatment decisions, the DHHS takes the position that this is probably significant enough to be reported.[46]

Summary suspensions that last for more than 30 days are reportable unless the bylaws say otherwise and indicate that such a suspension is merely an administrative precaution rather than a final action.

A hospital may not always take individual action, but instead terminate a group provider contract, which results in an individual practitioner's revocation of privileges. Such a loss may be reportable, depending on whether the hospital considered the revocation a peer review action based on the quality of clinical services.

Under the Act, professional societies of physicians or dentists engaging in formal peer review must report decisions adverse to their members to the State Medical or Dental Board 15 days of the action. The Board then has 15 days to relay the information to the NPDB. The Board is obligated to report any professional society's failure to submit such information.

Time Limits

The information to be reported to the NPDB must be submitted within 30 days after the action to be reported takes place. Specifically, medical malpractice payments must be reported within 30 days after the date of the check. Adverse licensure decisions must be reported within 30 days after the action is taken. Adverse privileges decisions must be reported by the health care entity to the relevant licensing board in the jurisdiction within 15 days after the action is taken. The board then has 15 days from the date it gets the information to report it to the NPDB. For licensure and clinical privileges actions, the date of formal approval of the adverse action by the board's or entity's authorized official is the triggering event.[47]

Who Is Reported?

Physicians and dentists must be reported for any medical malpractice payments, license revocations, and adverse actions taken by hospitals or professional societies. All other health care practitioners are reported for malpractice payments only. The state medical board is not required to report all other health care practitioners for adverse license decisions, but may do so. Even if a practitioner has died, any malpractice payments made on that practitioner's behalf postmortem must be reported. In group settlements, a report must be submitted for each physician settling. The same reporting requirements apply to residents and interns, but students are not reportable.

Although hospitals and entities (see Glossary) are not reportable, a corporation or entity consisting of only one physician must be reported under the physician's name. Of practitioners reported to the NPDB for malpractice, 75% have been physicians, 15% have been dentists, and 10% have been other health care providers.[48] Studies have purported to show that 72% of all medical malpractice claims are brought against 20% of all physicians.[49]

Who Reports?

In malpractice actions, insurance companies or any entity that makes a malpractice payment on behalf of any practitioner licensed, certified, or registered by a state must report such payment directly to the NPDB. This applies to primary and excess carriers, although not to reinsurers. Physicians who pay a portion of their malpractice insurance deductibles must report their payments. Physicians who pay on their own behalf, however, need not report. In *American Dental Association v Shalala*,[50] the court held that DHHS regulations requiring individuals to report such payments contradicted the legislative intent to limit reporting requirements to entities. If a practitioner owns the corporation or business, however, that practitioner is regarded as an entity and not an individual; thus, the payment is reportable. State medical boards, hospitals, HMOs, PPOs, professional societies, and any peer review organizations must report adverse actions.

If an entity fails to report or does not comply with the reporting requirements, it may be fined up to $10,000, have its name printed in the Federal Register, and lose its immunity for up to three years from antitrust lawsuits and civil damages. If a state board of medicine fails to report adverse licensure decisions, it will be given an opportunity to correct this deficiency. On further failure, the DHHS Secretary will simply designate another reporter to provide the missing information.[51]

Who Has Access to the NPDB?

The NPDB receives about 3,000 queries per day, the vast majority of which are submitted by hospitals.[52] Before reports are released, the identity of the inquirer is verified by checking the requester's ID number and password and matching the new information submitted about the requester against information previously provided.[46] DHHS maintains a list of all requests for information. The individual health care professional has access to that list on request but is not routinely notified when the NPDB releases a report in response to an inquiry. Individual practitioners have a right to access their reports free of charge.

Although medical malpractice carriers do not have a right to access the reports in the NPDB, they may require a practitioner to disclose such a file as a condition of insurance coverage. DHHS has not prohibited this practice, leaving it as "a matter between the insurer and the insured." The same type of pressure to disclose has been applied by employers, requiring HMOs and PPOs to report periodically on their physicians. The regulations state that information may be disclosed only for the purpose for which it was authorized or as provided by state law. Any other disclosure is a breach of confidence, punishable by a fine of up to $10,000.[53] The employer disclosure practice may violate this provision. DHHS has rejected a suggestion "to forbid further disclosure of information coming from a requesting party because this is contrary to the intent of the Act. An individual or entity who receives information from the NPDB is permitted to disclose it further in the course of carrying out the activity for which it was sought."[54] Also, medical professional societies may query NPDB when screening applicants for membership or affiliation and in support of a professional review activity.

There have been occasional accidental breaches of confidence. Hospitals have received reports on physicians other than those they requested. Also, several disclosures have allegedly occurred to parties unauthorized to make requests, such as insurance companies.[55]

Disputing or Updating Data

Any health care practitioner may dispute the NPDB's information concerning personal records. About 10% of physicians reported dispute the information reported, although only about 1% actually appeal it to the Secretary.[56] Over two thirds of all disputes involve reports of medical malpractice payments.[56] The Secretary will routinely mail a copy of any report filed in the NPDB to the individual who is a subject of the report. The practitioner then has 60 days after the date of mailing to dispute the information. However, the information is released to inquirers only 30 days after the report is filed. Disputing an action reported to the NPDB has been held to be a question of state law.[57]

In *Bigman v Medical Liability Mutual Insurance Co.*,[58] the court addressed whether the plaintiff could force his insurance company to revise what he believed was inaccurate information previously reported to the NPDB. He claimed that his former insurance company settled a matter and reported it to the NPDB after advising him that the action against him was going to be "discontinued without payment and without prejudice" and that the case would be settled on behalf of other defendants.[59] After the case "settled," the physician signed a consent to settle form sent to him by the defendant insurance company, which then made a report to the NPDB. The report stated that, owing to the physician's "alleged" failure to diagnose meningitis in a 3-month-old boy, a $1 million settlement was "paid in behalf of Dr. Bigman."[59] The physician took initial administrative steps through DHHS, which had not reached a decision when the case was heard in federal court. The court held that there is an administrative procedure clearly set forth in 45 CFR §60.14 providing that DHHS will act as an arbitrator if the dispute is unresolved. The court concluded that the administrative procedure was valid and that the physician had to exhaust all administrative procedures before pursuing court action. This was true even though he was suing a private party and not DHHS.

What May Be Disputed

The practitioner may dispute the following:
- The factual accuracy of the report submitted.
- Whether the entity was eligible to submit the report.
- Whether the report was submitted in accordance with the rules.

The practitioner may not use the dispute process to do the following:
- Protest a decision to settle without the practitioner's consent.
- Appeal the underlying reasons for the adverse action taken against the practitioner.

In some cases, a statement is submitted disputing a report on the basis that due process was denied in the adverse action taken. The DHHS Secretary will not void the report unless one of these two conditions applies:
- The original submitter of the report files another report stating that the original proceedings or report was a mistake.
- A court rules that due process was denied and orders a new peer review action or reinstatement.

Finding, Disputing, and Correcting Errors

After receiving a copy of the NPDB report, the practitioner should scrutinize it, in particular, Section C, which discloses the terms and amounts of any settlement and assignment of liability. This step is especially important when multiple physicians are involved in the dispute. Because the malpractice or acts or omissions must be classified into up to two of 90 codes, there is significant danger of misclassification. The encoding should be checked carefully. If a practitioner is reported as the result of a subordinate's acts or omissions, the same codes of classification will be used in the practitioner's report as in the subordinate's. It is important that the written portion explains that the superior did not commit the act or omission and is being reported for the acts of the subordinate.

If the practitioner is dismissed prior to settlement, that practitioner's name should not appear in the report.

To dispute or correct information in a report, the physician should follow established procedure. Discuss the error with the entity that reported it. If that entity agrees that the report is in error, it should be corrected within the first 60 days.

If the reporting entity denies any error, the physician can dispute the accuracy of the report directly by returning the notification document attached to the copy of the report mailed to the practitioner. The practitioner should certify attempts to resolve the issue directly with the reporting entity. When this document is returned to the NPDB, a notation of "disputed" will be made to the entry.

The practitioner may also ask the DHHS Secretary to review the accuracy of the report. On investigation, the Secretary may correct or void the report. If he finds that it is sufficiently accurate, the physician may attach to the report a statement of up to 600 characters disputing or explaining any item in the report. A copy of the statement will be included with the report and sent to all requesters for as long as the report exists.

Practical Effects of the NPDB

One positive effect that opening the NPDB has had on medical practitioners is the decline in both licensure and disciplinary actions by state medical boards. When the NPDB first opened in 1990, there was a 10% decrease in license revocations and probations and a 15% increase in other nonreportable licensure actions.[60] Hospitals have found ways to shield their staff and physicians with privileges by decreasing formal actions and increasing informal, unreportable actions.[60] Some hospitals require physicians to sign a waiver of right to peer review in their employment contracts. If they do, a termination need not be reported if it occurs without a hearing or peer review.[46] The "corporate shield" practice has been used by group practices, HMOs, and hospitals to avoid the reporting of medical malpractice payments. The hospital drops the physician's name from the controversy prior to reaching a settlement; thus, the physician's name is not submitted because no payment was made on his behalf.

Other hospitals handle the reporting issue by refusing to grant temporary privileges except in exceptional circumstances. Although this action may leave a physician in limbo for a time, it also prevents the need to report a surrender of privileges should the physician's application ultimately be denied or withdrawn.[61]

On the negative side, the establishment of the NPDB has increased tension and conflicts between medical practitioners and hospitals. As a result of settlement reporting, physicians have become more reluctant to settle medical malpractice lawsuits, including frivolous ones that, in the past, could be settled for nuisance value. A California study revealed that, in the first year after the NPDB opened, 13% more medical malpractice cases went to trial than in the year immediately preceding the NPDB.[62] Because hospitals and group practices are exempt from reporting requirements, they have less to lose from settling and often do so without the physician's permission, as the *Melendez* case illustrates. Some hospitals have begun requiring practitioners to sign "waiver of consent" clauses as part of their employment contracts, granting the hospital authority to settle on the physician's behalf.[63]

How to Avoid Being Reported

Practitioners need to know how to avoid having their names included in reports submitted to the NPDB. The following are suggestions:

- The practitioner who senses that a malpractice claim is imminent should consider having his attorney encourage the plaintiff's attorney to negotiate orally and to avoid putting the complaint in writing. If there is no written complaint on which a settlement is reached, the settlement is not reportable.
- If a practitioner is being sued along with a hospital, HMO, PPO, or group provider, the practitioner can negotiate to have his name dropped from the claim prior to settlement. However, the dismissal cannot be part of the consideration for settlement, or reporting may be required. If the practitioner is dismissed prior to settlement, the action will not be reported, and an entity's subsequent settlement is not reportable to the NPDB. This tactic, however, works only for practitioners in multimember entities. If the practice is a corporation or entity composed solely of one physician and that practice settles, the practitioner's name must be reported.
- To prevent being forced to settle by an insurance carrier and the attendant reporting, the practitioner should make sure a consent to settle clause is provided in his employment contract and professional liability policy.
- If a practitioner is summarily suspended or quietly dismissed, these actions are not necessarily reportable. As a result, the practitioner should think twice before requesting review. A loss of privileges or a dismissal without peer review may not be reportable. However, when the practitioner requests a hearing, he may turn what the hospital has deemed an "administrative action" into a reportable review proceeding.
- If the hospital has lost its immunity from antitrust lawsuits for prior violations of HCQIA, the threat of a lawsuit may induce the hospital to drop its investigation or peer review action, thus allowing a practitioner to quit before any reportable action occurs. However, the hospital cannot drop its investigation in exchange for a practitioner's resignation.
- If a practitioner has been reported by a hospital for a loss of privileges or a

disciplinary action and that practitioner feels he has been deprived of due process, the practitioner may want to bring a claim against the hospital. A court's ruling that due process was denied may not only cancel the hospital's immunity under the HCQIA, allowing the practitioner to bring an antitrust lawsuit, but also may give grounds for the DHHS Secretary to void the report in the NPDB, as it was based on a faulty peer review action. If the court rules that the practitioner was not denied due process and that the claim is frivolous, the practitioner is at risk for court-imposed sanctions.

Key Points and Conclusion

Although HCQIA does afford a measure of protection from liability for good faith peer review, it appears to offer relatively little new protection beyond that already provided under state law in many jurisdictions. It does not ensure protection from antitrust laws and other liability risks where the review is carried out by physicians who are in direct economic competition with the physician under review. Particularly in smaller communities, it may be difficult or impossible to find individuals with sufficient expertise in the relevant specialty to perform an intelligent review other than those in direct economic competition with the physician being reviewed.

In malpractice litigation, the statute and the existence of the NPDB may well increase the already substantial control that insurance carriers have over the decision whether to settle or to litigate a case. Insured practitioners may be more inclined to try cases than to settle them, as under this legislation nuisance payments are reported to the NPDB just as major judgments are. Malpractice lawsuits are often settled, of course, for reasons utterly unrelated to the merits. These cases are costly to try in terms of time, money, and psychological strain. To the price of settlement, previously measured in dollars, the Act adds the extra cost of entry of data into the NPDB. The data may cause some requesters to make unwarranted judgments about the quality of a practitioner's care.

This risk is particularly troublesome given the Secretary's refusal to purge old data, a decision that could damage the practitioner's interests for many years following a payment, unrelated to the size of the settlement or judgment and unrelated to its rationale. On the other hand, if plaintiffs' counsel anticipate that the

reporting requirements will make practitioners more willing to try cases and less willing to settle, they may be less likely to file questionable lawsuits in the first place.

Moreover, the mechanism by which plaintiff's counsel or a plaintiff acting for himself can query the NPDB about an individual practitioner may actually encourage the current unfortunate tendency of plaintiffs to sue multiple parties. Because a plaintiff gains access to the NPDB information only by suing the physician's hospital, HCQIA provides plaintiffs with an incentive to do so. However, this practice also facilitates the use of the corporate shield, enabling physicians to have their names erased from settlements between the hospital and plaintiff, thus avoiding being reported to the NPDB.

In sum, HCQIA may have taken away from health professionals and institutions more than it has given them. Although the *Austin* case shows the potential value of the Act's immunity provisions, the NPDB has the potential to be a playground for plaintiff's counsel and a minefield for defendants. Practitioners and institutions must do all they can to avoid conduct that would have to be reported to the NPDB. Providers should strive to understand the requirements of existing law and comply with them as best they can to take advantage of the immunity the law does provide.

Glossary

The following definitions are provided by federal regulations existing before passage of HCQIA. They are important to understand the meaning of the Act and of the NPDB (see 54 *Federal Register* 42730 and 42731 (1989), 45 CFR §60.3).

Adversely affecting. Reducing, restricting, suspending, revoking, or denying clinical privileges or membership in a health care entity.

Clinical privileges. The authorization by a health care entity to a physician, dentist, or other health care practitioner for the provision of health care services, including privileges and membership on the medical staff.

Formal peer review process. The conduct of professional review activities through formally adopted written procedures that provide for adequate notice and an opportunity for a hearing.

Health care entity. a) a hospital; b) an entity that provides health care services and engages in professional peer review activity through a formal peer review process for the purpose of furthering quality health care, or a committee of that entity; or c) a professional society or a committee or agent thereof, including those at the national, state, or local level, of physicians, dentists, or other health care practitioners that engages in professional review activity through a formal peer review process, for the purpose of furthering quality health care. Section b) includes an HMO or a group or prepaid medical or dental practice that meets the other criteria set forth therein.

Entity. a) provides health care services; and b) engages in professional review activity through a formal peer review process to further quality health care. Includes any group or prepaid medical practice that fits these criteria.

Health care practitioner. An individual who is licensed or otherwise authorized by a state to provide health care services. The phrase "otherwise authorized" is used because some states grant authority to provide health care services by mechanisms other than licensure, such as registration or certification. All health care practitioners authorized by states to provide health care services by whatever formal mechanism the state employs are included.

Medical malpractice action or claim. A written complaint or claim demanding payment based on the health care practitioner's provision of or failure to provide health care services and including the filing of a cause of action based on the law of tort brought in any state or federal court or other adjudicative body. This includes the filing of judicial claims or actions as well as malpractice claims filed on an administrative level, such as before arbitration boards or other dispute resolution mechanisms.

Professional review action. An action or recommendation of a health care entity: a) taken in the course of a professional review activity; b) based on the professional competence or professional conduct of an individual physician, dentist, or other health care practitioner that affects or could adversely affect the health or welfare of patients; and c) that adversely affects or may adversely affect the clinical privileges or membership in a professional society of the physician, dentist, or other health care practitioner. Excludes actions based primarily on: a) the physician's, dentist's or other health care practitioner's association or lack of association with a professional society or association; b) the physician's, dentist's, or other health care practitioner's fees, advertisements, or other acts to get or keep business; c) the physician's, dentist's, or other health care practitioner's participation in

prepaid group health plans, salaried employment, or other manner of delivering health services whether on a fee-for-service or other basis; d) a physician's, dentist's, or other health care practitioner's association with, supervision of, delegation of authority to, support for, training of, or participation in a private group practice with a member or members of a particular class of health care practitioner or professional; e) any other matter that does not relate to the competence or professional conduct of the physician, dentist, or other health care practitioner. Hence, technical or administrative failings unrelated to the health or welfare of the patient, such as failure to attend staff meetings or failure to complete medical records or billing forms, are not included.

Professional review activity. An activity of the health care entity with respect to an individual physician, dentist, or other health care practitioner: a) to determine whether the physician, dentist, or other health care practitioner may have privileges or membership in the entity; b) to determine the scope or conditions of such privileges or memberships, or to change or modify such privileges or membership. "Professional review activity" relates only to various types of actions that may or may not lead to modification or curtailment of clinical privileges and membership. Only professional review actions, not professional review activities, are reportable. Hence, if the hospital denies privileges to an anesthesiologist because it already has enough anesthesiologists, that is not a reportable event.

References

1. Title IV of Public Law No. 99-660, 100 Stat 3784, Nov 14, 1986 (codified at 42 USC §§ 11101-11152 (Supp 1987). The statute was later amended by Title IV of Public Law No. 100-177 §402, 101 Stat 1007, Dec. 1, 1987 (codified at 42 USC §11101-11152 (Supp 1987) known as the Medicare and Medicaid Patient and Program Protection Act. It was further amended by additions to the Public Health Service Amendments of 1987, Omnibus Budget Reconciliation Act of 1989, Title VI, §6103(6) of Public Law No. 101-239.
2. See 42 USC §11101 (4); HR Rep No. 903, 99th Cong 2d Sess 9, reprinted in US Code Cong. and Admin. News 6384, 6391-92.
3. 45 CFR Part 60.
4. A "Memorandum of Understanding" is an agreement similar to a contract setting forth the understanding of rights and obligations.
5. 871 F Supp 808 (ED Pa 1994).
6. Sherman Act, 15 USC §1 et seq (1983).
7. *Goldfarb v Virginia State Bar Association*, 421 US 773, 787 (1975); *Arizona v Maricopa County Medical Society*, 457 US 332 (1972).
8. See, *Patrick v Burget*, 486 US 94 (1988).

9. The requirement that action be taken in the reasonable belief that it furthered quality health care was not intended "to test the subjective state of mind of the physician conducting the professional review." The reviewers, with the information available to them at the time of the professional review activity, need but reasonably conclude "that their action would restrict incompetent behavior or would protect patients." 42 USC §11112(a)(1).

10. 42 USC §11112(a)(2).

11. 42 USC §§11111 (a)(1), 11131(c)(1), and 11151(2).

12. 42 USC §11111(a)(2).

13. *Bryan v James E. Holmes Regional Medical Center*, 33 F3d 1318 (11th Cir 1994).

14. 42 USC §11111(b).

15. *Austin v McNamara*, 731 F Supp 934 (CD Cal 1990).

16. For similarly strict construction of the immunity provision, see *Matthews v Lancaster General Hosp.*, 883 Supp 1016 (ED Pa 1996), aff'd, 87 F3d 624 (3rd Cir 1996) (affirming lower court's order granting immunity from antitrust action).

17. 42 USC 11111(a)(1).

18. "Immunity for Peer Review Participants in Hospitals," Peer Review Immunity Task Group, American Academy of Hospital Attorneys, American Hospital Association (1989) hereinafter cited as "Peer Review Participants."

19. HR Rep No. 903, 99th Cong, 2d Sess 6, reprinted in 1986 US Code Cong and Admin News 6384, 6392-3.

20. See, for example, *Dorn v Mendelzon*, 196 Cal App 3d 933, 242 Cal Rptr 259 (1987) and *Auld v Holly*, 418 S2d 1020 (Fla App 1982), quashed in part, 450 So2d 217 (Fla 1984).

21. *Nanavati v Burdette Tomlin Memorial Hospital*, 857 F2d 96 (3d Cir 1988), cert denied, 109 S Ct 1528 (1989); *Hospital Corp of Lake Worth v Romguera*, 511 So2d 559 (Fla App 1986).

22. *Zoneraich v Overlook Hospital*, 212 NJ Super 83 514 A2d 53 (AD 1986), cert denied, 107 NJ 32, 526 A2d 126 (1986).

23. *St. John's Hospital Medical Staff v St. John's Regional Medical Center*, 242 NW2d 482 (SD 1976) (But see *Weary v Baylor University Hospital*, 360 SW2d 895 [Tex Civ App 1962]).

24. *Greenfield v Kanwit*, 546 F Supp 220 (SDNY 1982) aff'd 714 F2d 113 (2d Cir 1982).

25. *Sigmond v Brown*, 645 F Supp 243 (CD Cal 1986), aff'd, 828 F2d 8 (9th Cir 1987); also Racketeer Influenced and Corrupt Organization (RICO) claims, at 18 USCA §1961 et seq.

26. 42 USC §11113.

27. 42 USC §11112(a)(3), (b).

28. 42 USC §11112(b)(3)(A).

29. 42 USC §11112(b)(3)(C).

30. 42 USC §11112(b).

31. 731 F Supp at 934.

32. 42 USC §11112 (c)(3).

33. 805 SW2d 756 (Tenn 1991).

34. 617 A2d 1029 (Me 1992).

35. 4 Neb App 362, 543 NW2d 749 (1996).

36. Id at 373, 543 NW2d 757.

37. 179 AD2d 610 (NY 1992).

38. 42 USC §11131, codified by 45 CFR §60.5.

39. 42 USC §11131 codified at 45 CFR §60.8.

40. 45 CFR 60.8.

41. Public Law No 100-93, 101 Stat 680-99.

42. 42 USC §11131; 45 CFR §60.9.

43. 45 CFR §60.9(a)(I).

44. 42 USC §1113(a)(1)(B).

45. 45 CFR §60.9(c).

46. NPDB Guidebook, 1994, e-22.

47. 45 CFR §60.5.

48. Elisabeth Ryzen, The National Practitioner Data Bank: Problems and Proposed Reforms, 13 *J Leg Med* 409 (1992).

49. Scott Stephens Thomas, An Insurer's Right to Settle Versus Its Duty to Defend Nonmeritorious Medical Malpractice Claims, 16 *J Leg Med* 545, 583 n 100 (1995).

50. 3 F3d 444 (DC Cir 1993).

51. 45 CFR §60.8(c).

52. Goffen, Dube, et al: The National Practitioner Data Bank: Bane or Benefit?, 268 *JAMA* 3429 (Dec. 23, 1992).

53. 42 USC §11135 – 11137; 45 CFR 60.13(a)-(b).

54. 45 CFR §60.13.

55. Ryzen, supra note 25 at 427.

56. Fitzhugh Mullan, The National Practitioner Data Bank: Report from the First Year. *JAMA*, July 1, 1992, available in Westlaw, 1992 WL 11637570.

57. See *Janes v Centegra Health System*, 1996 WL 210018 (ND Ill.) (holding that plaintiff's complaint seeking, among other things, an injunction from a reporting to the NPDB was not a question of federal law since interpretation of HCQIA was not required).

58. 1996 WL 79330 (SDN. 1996).

59. Id at 1.

60. Ryzen, supra note 25 at 423.

61. Barbara A. Blackmond, Current Issues — The National Practitioner Data Bank and Hospital Peer Review. *Health Law* 1993;Fall:1,6.

62. Ryzen, supra note 25 at 435.

63. Id at 441.

Chapter 13

Staffing in the Emergency Department

Leslie S. Zun, MD, MBA, FACEP

In an era of cost reductions and downsizing, managers must ensure optimal staffing for the emergency department. Determining the proper staff is difficult because there are so many factors to consider — type and training level of emergency department personnel, number of physicians, nurses, and other health care providers, patient volume, acuity, and many more. Nonetheless, it is commonly accepted that a hospital is legally responsible for staffing its emergency department adequately.[1] Not only is the hospital responsible for the staffing, but so are the hospital's board, its chief executive officer, and medical staff. They must ensure that the hospital has appropriately trained and experienced people providing care in the emergency department.[2]

Hospitals typically are staffed by physicians and nurses, but emergency departments today also rely on the services provided by physician assistants (PAs), nurse practitioners (NPs), orderlies, nurses' assistants, radiology technicians, and phlebotomists, and support personnel, such as clerks and other noncertified providers.

Staff and the level of training directly affect the degree of risk involved in providing patient care in the emergency department. This chapter addresses many of these difficult questions — Who should staff the emergency department? What is the appropriate staffing ratio? What qualifications should the staff possess? Are there any other staffing options available to reduce costs while maintaining quality?

Case Study

A 3-month-old child experiences cardiac arrest at home and is taken to a moderate-volume suburban emergency department. The department is very busy; two nurses are out on lunch break, and another is caring for an intubated patient. A staff member takes the child to a resuscitation room immediately and calls the emergency physician. The emergency physician and one nurse respond.

In an attempt to save the child, the physician begins giving orders in rapid succession. The nurse assisting him has considerable trouble carrying out his orders. She has difficulty intubating the patient and starting an IV line. The physician becomes irate and says, "There are never enough people here when something serious happens."

Who Should Staff the Emergency Department?

We all know that emergency departments should be staffed by appropriately trained and certified personnel, including physicians and nurses. However, the Libby Zion case brought the issue of appropriate staffing of emergency departments to the forefront. This case, although specific to New York, changed the manner in which emergency department staffing is viewed. In retrospect, this case will be viewed as a major landmark in establishing emergency medicine as a specialty that every hospital should have.

In 1986, the Fourth Grand Jury for the 1986 April/May term in and for the County of New York submitted a report and recommendations regarding its investigation into the death of an 18-year-woman, Libby Zion, at a New York County hospital. She had been admitted through the hospital's emergency department with fever and agitation and subsequently died after experiencing cardiac arrest.

Although this case did not result in an indictment, the court's ruling noted serious deficiencies in the staffing and supervision of emergency departments. The State of New York grand jury recommended that the state's Department of Health establish regulations to cover staffing and supervision of emergency departments.[3] After lengthy hearings, new regulations were adopted by the New York State Hospital Review and Planning Council in 1988 and became effective in late 1988 and early 1989. These regulations ranged from recommendations on the necessary qualifications for directors of emergency departments to the credentialing of emergency physicians, supervision of residents, resident workloads, and ancillary support staff.

Two recommendations of the grand jury specifically applied to the emergency department[4]:

- The State Department of Health should promulgate regulations that mandate all level one hospitals to staff their emergency rooms with physicians who have completed at least three years of postgraduate training and who are specifically trained to evaluate and care for patients on an emergency basis.
- The State Department of Health should promulgate regulations to ensure that interns and residents in level one hospitals are supervised contemporaneously and in person by attending physicians or those members of the house staff who have completed a three-year postgraduate residency program.

The Joint Commission on Accreditation of Healthcare Organizations (JCAHO) has new guidelines, found in various standards. These standards are less specific than in past years about the appropriate staffing of the emergency department. The criteria are found in the following standards[5]:

- CC.1 states that patients have access to the appropriate type of care.
- L.D.1.3 states that the plan(s) includes patient care services based on identified patient needs and is consistent with the hospital's mission.
- L.D.1.3.2 states that the design of the hospital-wide patient care services is appropriate to the scope and level of care required by the patients served.
- HR.2 states that the hospital provides an adequate number of staff members whose qualifications are consistent with job responsibilities.

JCAHO leaves interpretation and application of these standards to the hospital.

What Are the Staffing Ratios for Personnel in Emergency Departments?

When determining the number of personnel necessary for an emergency department, staff members are categorized into four groups: nurses, nurse extenders, physicians, and mid-level providers. Making decisions about number and type of personnel is difficult and is compounded by the duties and responsibilities, training and experience, and interaction of these providers with other personnel.

Staffing ratios for nurses have been studied using various patient classification systems.[6,7] Mason[8] presented a formula for using a typical classification system to determine the number of nurses needed depending on the number and types of illnesses. Helmer et al[9] performed a computer simulation of nurse staffing to provide quality, cost-effective care. Piper[10] presented a budgeting formula for the emergency department using visits, nursing hours, productivity, hours required, staff mix, peak activity, and staff distribution. The Emergency Nurses Association (ENA) believes that staffing ratios based on nurse-to-patient ratios or medical diagnoses are not reliable or practical.[11] ENA recommends that each setting consider factors that include staffing issues, patient mix, emergency department setup, organizational structure, and regulatory agencies.[12]

The administrator or medical director of the emergency department should investigate local laws and rules that affect staffing requirements. Some states have legislation concerning the credentials of nurses who staff emergency departments. In Illinois, for example, a trauma center must have at least one registered nurse in the emergency department who has completed a trauma nurse specialist course.[13]

The number of nurses needed depends on the number of nurse extenders available in the emergency department. Nurse extenders are clinical support staff, such as paramedics, emergency department technicians, nurses' aides, stock clerks, patient liaisons, secretaries, and clerks. ENA states that nurses should supervise and train, manage and administrate, orient and review, monitor, and evaluate these nurse extenders.[14] The impact of ancillary personnel on staffing needs depends on their numbers, shift length, duties and responsibilities, training, and experience.[14] Furthermore, there should be one registered nurse available and a ratio of one nurse extender to each professional nurse to ensure quality care.[14] There is an absence of literature on the effect of these nurse extenders on reducing the number of nursing staff needed to work in the department.

Staffing ratios for emergency physicians vary from 1.8 to 5.0 patients per physician per hour.[15] The Health Care Financing Administration (HCFA) did a survey that found emergency physicians saw 2.8 patients per hour.[16] Rosenbach et al[16] profiled emergency physicians and found that the average number of patients seen per hour worked was 3.1. van de Leuv[17] used approximately 2.4 patients per hour in his calculation of optimal staffing. Goff[18] interpreted the JCAHO as having a standard of 2.5 to 2.8 patients per physician per hour. Graff et al[19] indicated that staffing ratios needed to account for not only the number of patients seen per hour, but also the length of stay. He proposed a formula for emergency physician staffing that included length of stay, intensity of service, service type, volume of patients, and physician efficiency.[20] The number of patients seen per hour depends on additional duties and responsibilities of the emergency physician (e.g., cardiac arrests, other emergencies outside the emergency department). In smaller hospitals, the emergency physician may be the only physician. ACEP discourages emergency physicians providing patient care outside of the emergency department unless the emergency department and its patients' medical needs can be safely provided for at all times.[21]

Staffing ratios for physicians are tied to emergency physician manpower needs. Various authors and groups have looked at emergency physician manpower; there is no easy answer. Currently, the most reasonable conclusion is that there is a shortage of properly trained and qualified emergency physicians. A study published in 1990 by Salluzzo et al[22] found that, in Connecticut in the mid-1980s, 31% of physician staffing was provided by board-certified emergency physicians, and 20% of all positions in the state were unfilled. Future projections are difficult to make because how these factors will influence future need is unknown.

In general practice, there is reasonable information as to how the number of PAs and NPs will affect the number of physicians to staff clinic sites. One study of outpatient visits[23] indicated that PAs could be substituted at a ratio of 0.5:1 to 0.75:1 when the number of patients was used as an outpatient measure. The mid-level provider's effect on the staffing ratios of physicians and nurses has not been well studied. In 1992, PAs and NPs saw 4% of the total number of patients in the emergency department.[24] A study of public teaching hospitals[25] found that NPs and PAs were used in 33% of the hospitals. How the number of PAs and NPs will alter the number of physicians or nursing staff needed is unknown. However, the role for PAs in rural hospitals is different because there are fewer emergency physicians.[26] In some hospitals, PAs provide the care in the emergency department with the emergency physician providing telephone backup.

What Qualifications Are Needed by Emergency Department Personnel?

Emergency Physicians

The training and qualifications of emergency physicians will affect the risk of exposure to malpractice liability. Various emergency medicine organizations view the qualifications of emergency physicians differently. ACEP policy states that a qualified emergency physician is defined as one who possesses the training and experience in emergency medicine sufficient to evaluate and initially manage and treat all patients who seek emergency care.[27] ACEP has also stated that certification of knowledge and skill in emergency medicine can result only from successful completion of examinations administered by a recognized board in emergency medicine.[28] ACEP also strongly discourages the use of certificates of completion of courses to be used for credentialing or employment.[28]

On a state level, as an example, the Illinois administrative code for Level I trauma center designation criteria states the qualifications for and minimum number of nurses and physicians. A physician needs board certification by ABEM, residency training in emergency medicine, or completion of an internship followed by

Figure 1

Sample policy for scope of PA practice in the emergency department

Policy: Patients presenting in the emergency department with the following complaints may be evaluated and referred by the examining PA without being seen by an attending physician:

1. All venereal diseases in men; the following venereal disease in women: moniliasis, trichomoniasis, scabies, and lice
2. Allergic reactions not accompanied by shortness of breath, wheezing, or hypotension
3. Animal bites
4. Bleeding from any orifice that is minor (determined after objective examination)
5. Cerumen removal
6. Chronic peripheral vascular disease
7. Conjunctivitis
8. Constipation
9. Fatigue or dizziness without associated findings
10. Foreign body removal (uncomplicated)
11. Headache not associated with acute neurologic findings
12. Hemorrhoids
13. Hepatitis (uncomplicated) or exposure to hepatitis
14. Hypertension that is asymptomatic and accompanied by a diastolic blood pressure of less than 110 mm Hg
15. Incision and drainage of simple abscesses
16. Low back pain that is chronic and not associated with neurologic findings
17. Medical clearance for psychiatric patients
18. Minor burns
19. Minor febrile illnesses
20. Minor gynecologic disorders, such as vaginitis, and insignificant abnormalities of menstruation
21. Minor laceration
22. Minor psychiatric disorders
23. Minor symptoms of alcohol or drug withdrawal
24. Normal pregnancy without accompanying medical problems
25. Otitis media and otitis externa
26. Prescription refills
27. Referral to specialty service (e.g., detoxification, follow-up on wound check, cast check, suture removal, abortion, social service)
28. Shortness of breath not accompanied by upper airway obstruction, or acute distress
29. Skin rashes
30. Upper respiratory infections
31. Urinary tract infection

Policy: All patients presenting in the emergency department with the following complaints must be evaluated by the attending physician on duty before discharge by the physician assistant:

1. Abdominal pain: all patients

2. Alcohol or drug withdrawal: associated with confusion, hallucinations, fever, seizures, or delirium

3. Allergic reaction: accompanied by shortness of breath, wheezing, or hypotension

4. Arrhythmias: recent onset or associated with unstable hemodynamics

5. Bleeding: significant bleeding from any orifice confirmed by objective examination

6. Burns: any third-degree burns; second-degree burns of more than 10% of the total body surface; burns of the eyes, ears, face, hands, feet, and perineum; electrical injury; inhalation injury

7. Chest pain that is not typical of ischemic chest pain; is not accompanied by syncope, shortness of breath, arrhythmias; and for which an etiology is clear (e.g., costochondritis)

8. Chest pain: typical of ischemic chest pain or accompanied by syncope, shortness of breath, or arrhythmias

9. Coma or acute change in mental status: all patients

10. Head trauma: accompanied by loss of consciousness, neurologic findings, or other associated injuries

11. Heat injury: hypothermia (temperature less than 35°C [95°F]) or hyperthermia (temperature more than 40.5°C [104.9°F])

12. Headache: associated with acute neurologic findings

13. Hypertension: diastolic blood pressure of 110 mm Hg or more; with or without symptoms

14. Neurologic deficits: all patients with acute onset

15. Shock of any etiology

16. Sickle cell crisis: all patients

From Sturmann KM, Ehrenberg K, Salzberg MR. Physician assistants in emergency medicine. *Ann Emerg Med* 1990;19:304-308. Adapted with permission.

at least 7,000 hours of emergency department experience and 50 hours annually of continuing medical education. The Illinois law also requires that the emergency department director be an ABEM-certified physician.[11] Other states also may have laws governing the staffing of emergency and trauma units.

Debate about the proper supervision of emergency medicine residents in the teaching setting continues. Rosen and Markovchick[29] debated the issue and concluded that it is a 24-hour responsibility. In 1989, Henneman et al[30] found that 72.2% of the emergency medicine residencies had 24-hour attending coverage. Press et al[31] found that programs with residents experienced a 18.5% decrease in malpractice claims and a 70.1% decrease in disbursements when they initiated full-time attending coverage of residents. Medicare regulations significantly restrict the ability of attending physicians to bill for residents' activities that are not directly supervised. According to HCFA, the teaching physician must be physically present during the portion of the service that determines the level of service billed.[32]

Nurses

According to ENA, the professional nurse is an essential element in the provision of safe, effective care.[11] However, ENA does not specify any additional training or coursework that emergency nurses should possess. Emergency nurses are strongly encouraged to obtain additional certifications in advanced cardiac life support, trauma nurse core curriculum, and certified emergency nurse.[33]

Mid-Level Providers

The term mid-level providers refers to PAs and NPs. According to ACEP, PAs in the emergency department should be directly supervised by the emergency physician, and their scope of practice should be clearly delineated.[34] The emergency department director should carefully delineate the scope of the PAs privileges[35] (Figure 1). Physician supervision and backup should also be well defined for NPs. Again, according to ACEP, the scope of practice of NPs should be clearly delineated, and the NPs should have specific experience or specialty training in emergency care.[36] Packard[15] believes that PAs and NPs are better suited for a fast track environment. In one recent study,[37] NPs were found to care for approximately 21% of the patients presenting to an adult emergency department.

Maxfield et al[38] found that mid-level providers can handle the initial management of 62% of all presenting complaints. Meyer et al[39] stated that 80% to 90% of emergency department cases can be managed initially by PAs.

Emergency physicians are responsible for the work done by PAs and NPs, and any legal action against a mid-level provider is likely to involve the emergency physician as codefendant.[40] The AMA states that the physician is ultimately responsible for coordinating and managing the care of patients.[41] The AMA's "Guidelines for Physicians Nurse Practitioner Integrated Practice" states that physicians are responsible for managing the patient's health care.[41] PAs are certified by the National Commission on Certification of Physicians Assistants with the board of medical examiners. PAs must recertify every six years. NPs are credentialed by four certifying bodies: the American Nurses Credentialing Center, the National Certification Board of Pediatric Nurse Practitioners, the American Academy of Nurse Practitioners, and the National Certification Corporation for Obstetric, Gynecologic and Neonatal Nursing Specialties. PAs are required to perform a preceptorship in primary care or emergency medicine before graduation from a PA program.[42,43] NPs do not have a similar requirement.

What Are Other Options to Reduce Staff and Costs While Maintaining Quality?

Many emergency departments are looking for ways to reduce costs while maintaining quality. Two options are an on-call and back-up system and reengineering the emergency department.

Emergency departments are typically staffed at the high end of the volume curve. If they staffed for the lower end of the patient volume and acuity scale, they could rely on additional physicians and nurses on an on-call system to provide backup when volume increased or the acuity changed substantially. Ratzan[44] proposed that emergency departments have back-up policies and procedures for patient overload. He did not address the issue of the optimal staffing arrangement based on the maximum or minimum number of patients.

Reengineering emergency departments is a technique to modify the roles and responsibilities of personnel. Many emergency departments are also expanding the role of support personnel, such as nursing assistants, and decreasing the number of registered nurses. Clerks could also expand their role to reduce the work of the nurses, such as doing order entry or setting up tests. Tzirides[45] found a significant cost savings in cross-orientation and cross-coverage of the nursing staff. She proposed using emergency department nurses and outpatient nurses in outpatient and emergency departments.

Case Discussion

The child could not be resuscitated and died in the emergency department. The parents filed a lawsuit, in which one of the allegations against the hospital referred to an inadequate number of nurses on duty to deal with actual or expected emergencies. Another allegation stated that the staff member assisting the physician had received inadequate training and had not been properly oriented in pediatric cardiac arrest.

During the deposition phase of this legal action, the emergency physician stated that he had been critical of the hospital's policy regarding nurse coverage during breaks and lunch time. The plaintiff provided further documentation by gathering staffing patterns and levels of training in emergency departments of similar size in the same area.

Key Points and Conclusion

Hospital and emergency department administrators must address the risk exposure related to emergency department staffing. The number of physicians and nurses working in the emergency department, their level of training and expertise, and the use of mid-level providers must be carefully considered. Although common sense dictates the higher the number of staff, the less the risk, this philosophy is cost prohibitive. Determining the level of physician and nurse staffing should be specific to the hospital's needs, accounting for patient acuity, services provided, and personnel.

Mid-level providers can reduce the number of physicians needed, but the physicians must have the time and desire to supervise them appropriately. Most authorities agree that the best-trained and best-qualified emergency physicians and nurses will reduce the risk exposure. Alternative staffing arrangements may reduce costs but need to be well planned with an appropriate evaluation process.

References

1. Morrison T, Segar G, DiCostanzo C. The patient with behavior disorders in the emergency department. *Communiqué*, November 1989.

2. Trautlein JJ, Lambert RL, Muiller J. Malpractice in the emergency department—review of 200 cases. *Ann Emerg Med* 1984;13:709-711.

3. New York State Department of Health. *Final Report of the New York State Ad Hoc Advisory Committee on Emergency Services*, 1987.

4. Asch DA, Parker RM. The Libby Zion case. One step forward or two steps backward. *N Engl J Med* 1988;318:771-775.

5. *1996 Comprehensive Accreditation Manual for Hospitals.* Oakbrook Terrace, Ill: Joint Commission on Accreditation of Healthcare Organizations; 1996.

6. Kromash EJ. Patient classification and required nursing time in a pediatric emergency department. *J Emerg Nurs* 1984;10:69-73.

7. Schulmerich SC. Converting patient classification data into staffing requirements for the emergency department. *J Emerg Nurs* 1986;12:286-290.

8. Mason JD. Nursing and support staff planning. In: Hellstern RA, ed: *Managing the Emergency Department: A Team Approach.* Dallas: American College of Emergency Physicians; 1992.

9. Helmer FT, Freitas CA, Onaha B. Determining the required nurse staffing of an emergency department. *J Emerg Nurs* 1988;14:352-358.

10. Piper LR. Basic budgeting for ED nursing personnel. *J Emerg Nurs* 1982;8:285-287.

11. Position Statement, Staffing and productivity in the emergency care setting. Emergency Nurses Association, Park Ridge, Ill, Approved by the Board; 1995.

12. Illinois Administrative code chapter I, 540.70 Subchapter f Section 540.70.

13. Addendum, Staffing model determination factors. Emergency Nurses Association, Park Ridge, Illinois, Approved by the Board; 1995.

14. The use of non-registered nurse (Non-RN) caregivers in emergency care. Emergency Nurses Association, Park Ridge, Ill, Approved by the Board; 1995.

15. Packard DC: Physician staffing of the emergency department. In: Hellstern RA, Auerbach BS, Geist M, et al, eds. *Managing the Emergency Department: A Team Approach.* Dallas: American College of Emergency Physicians; 1992.

16. Rosenbach ML, Harrow B, Cromwell J. A profile of emergency physicians 1984-1985: demographic characteristics, patterns, and income. *Ann Emerg Med* 1986;15:1261-1267.

17. van de Leuv JH. Physician staffing. In: van de Leuv JH, ed. *Management of Emergency Services.* Rockville, Md: Aspen Publishers; 1987.

18. Goff R: Managers ask and answer. *J Emerg Nurs* 1991;17:168.

19. Graff LG, Wolk S, Dinwoodie R, et al. Emergency physician workload: a time study. *Ann Emerg Med* 1993;22:1156-1163.

20. Graff LG, Radford MJ: Formula for emergency physician staffing. *Am J Emerg Med* 1990;8:194-199.

21. Emergency Physicians' Patient Care Responsibilities Outside of the Emergency Department. ACEP Policy Statement, approved August 1992, reaffirmed March 1997. To obtain a copy, call (800) 798-1822, touch 6, or go to www.acep.org.

22. Salluzzo R, Terranova G, Gemmell W, et al. Connecticut emergency department physicians survey. Implications for graduate medical education. *Conn Med* 1990;54:3-4.

23. US Dept of Health and Human Services, Public Health Service, Health Resources Administration. *Report of the Graduate Medical Education National Advisory Committee* (GMENAC) to the Secretary, Department of Health and Human Services, Non-Physicians Health Care Provider Technical Panel. Washington, DC: US Government Printing Office, 1980:6:9.

24. McCraig LF. National Hospital Ambulatory Medical Care Survey: 1992 emergency department summary. Advance data from vital and health statistics, No. 2(45), Hyattsville, Md: National Center for Health Statistics, *Vital Health Statistics*; 1992.

25. Holley JE, Kellermann AL, Andrulis DP. Physician staffing in the emergency departments of public teaching hospitals: a national survey. *Ann Emerg Med* 1992;21:53-57.

26. Physician assistants can complement ED team with lower-cost practitioners. *ED Management* 1990;2:169-174.

27. Physician Credentialing and Delineation of Clinical Privileges in Emergency Medicine. ACEP Policy Statement, approved September 1995. To obtain a copy, call (800) 798-1822, touch 6, or go to www.acep.org.

28. Certification in Emergency Medicine. ACEP Policy Statement, approved August 1992. To obtain a copy, call (800) 798-1822, touch 6, or go to www.acep.org.

29. Rosen P, Markovchick V. Attending coverage. *Ann Emerg Med* 1985;14:897-899.

30. Henneman PL, Hockberger RS, Chiu CY. Attending coverage in academic emergency medicine: a national survey. *Ann Emerg Med* 1989;18:34-41.

31. Press S, Russell SA, Cannor JC, et al. Attending physician coverage in a teaching hospital's emergency department: effect on malpractice. *J Emerg Med* 1994;12:89-93.

32. Health Care Financing Administration, Carrier Manual Instructions, Medicare Final Ruling for Teaching Physicians, May 30, 1996.

33. Koran Z. Emergency. *Graduate Nurse* 1992;Spring:20-24.

34. Guidelines on the Role of Physician Assistants in Emergency Departments. ACEP Policy Statement, approved September 1996. To obtain a copy, call (800) 798-1822, touch 6, or go to www.acep.org.

35. Sturmann KM, Ehrenberg K, Salzberg MR. Physician assistants in emergency medicine. *Ann Emerg Med* 1990;19:304-308.

36. Guidelines on the Role of Nurse Practitioners in Emergency Departments. ACEP Policy Statement, approved July 1995. To obtain a copy, call (800) 798-1822, touch 6, or go to www.acep.org.

37. Buchanan L, Powers RD. Establishing an NP-staffed minor emergency area. *Nurs Manage* 1996;27(2):25, 28,30-31.

38. Maxfield RG, Lemire MD, Thomas M, et al. Utilization of supervised physician's assistants in emergency room coverage in a small rural community hospital. *J Trauma* 1975;15:759-799.

39. Meyer RJ, Beckett GA, Conrad JP. Emergency department and the physician assistant. In: Carter RD, Perry HB, eds. *Alternatives in Health Care Delivery: Emerging Role For Physician Assistants*. St Louis: Warren H. Green; 1984.

40. Wolman D, Madden JF. Mid-level providers in the emergency department. *foresight*, April 1996.

41. Seward PJ. Physician Assistants and Nurse Practitioners, American Medical Association, Report to the Board of Trustees, 1995.

42. Oliver DR. *Eleventh annual report on physicians assistants educational programs in the United States, 1994-1995*. Alexandria, Va. Association of Physicians Assistants Program.

43. Barzansky B, Jonas HS, Etzel SI. Educational programs in US medical schools, 1994-1995. *JAMA* 1995;274:716-722.

44. Ratzan RM. Defining a rational back-up policy for emergency departments. *J Emerg Med* 1987;5:49-52.

45. Tzirides EC: Cross orientation/cross coverage: one approach to cost containment. *Nurs Manage* 1988;19:80B,80D-80F, 80H.

Chapter 14

Facility Design

Peter M. Fahrney, MD, FACEP

Very few aspects of life in emergency medicine are without risk, and the physical "plant" of the emergency department is no exception. And why not? It is extremely accessible — open 24 hours a day, seven days a week to all comers, in most cases. It is the embodiment of the health care system's open door policy. The stress level within is very high, not just for physicians and staff, but also for patients and family members. Patient volume and acuity vary from shift to shift, as do staffing levels and number of available security personnel. So, any measures that can be taken in the design and construction or reconstruction of the emergency department to minimize risk should be.

The hospital's responsibility to provide a safe environment may be as important as its responsibility to provide high-quality care. Most of us still believe that a hospital should be a "safe haven," much in the same way that a church is, even though this may seem impossible in today's society. Perhaps more than any other part of the hospital, the emergency department's physical design affects a patient's sense of well-being, comfort, protection, and satisfaction. For a hospital to have as many as 80% of its inpatient beds occupied by patients who were admitted through the emergency department is not uncommon. Do not minimize the importance of the patient's initial impression. The department's design should be equally reassuring to physicians and staff and enable them to provide patient care effectively and efficiently, and should also allow other hospital staff to conduct business in the emergency department effectively and with as few barriers as possible.

Getting Started

The process of planning an efficient and safe emergency department and seeing that plan through to completion is a long and arduous one. The design requirements are complex — how can we improve patient flow? Will we be able to increase our capacity? How can we build in security measures that don't become obstacles to patient care? The opportunity to design an emergency department as a new facility is rare. Most "improvements" occur during a renovation and are encumbered with the existing space and structural limitations of the old department. Even with a new design, it is not common to work with an architectural firm or general contractor that specializes in emergency departments and understands the requirements of such a specialized unit. When redesign and construction are concurrent with the actual delivery of patient care, as is the case with many renovation projects, design and planning are even more complicated, and intense and precise planning even more important.

Regardless of whether the design is being planned for new construction or remodeling, one of the secrets to success is to use a long-range multidisciplinary team approach. To begin, bring together physicians and staff from the emergency department itself — those people who have first-hand knowledge of how the department works and what its needs are — then add other experienced professionals from other areas of the hospital. By necessity, specialists and other interested persons should be

Figure 1

Members of the planning and design group

Emergency Department Personnel

    Physician Director

    Administrative Nurse-Director

    Chief Technician/Nurse Extender

    Chief Receptionist/Registrar

    Staff Emergency Physician

    Staff Emergency Nurse

Hospital Representatives

    Administrative Director

    Risk Manager

    Security Director

    Representatives from Ancillary
    Departments (permanent or as needed):

        Admitting

        Laboratory

        Radiology

        Operating Room

        Public Relations/Marketing

Community Agency Representatives

    Fire Department Representative

    Police Department Representative

    Rescue Squad Representative

    Community/Patient Advocate

Architectural Firm Representative

involved to incorporate different perspectives of patient care and safety (Figure 1). All team members must have the time, dedication, and consistent energy to follow through with planning, design, and implementation.

General Design Considerations

The design of the department must take into consideration demographic information, such as patient volume, type of patient (trauma, pediatrics, elderly, psychiatric, obstetric), the anticipated acuity level of both common and specific patient conditions, methods of patient arrival, admission rate, and how much usable space is actually available. Many design decisions must be made in conjunction with overall hospital decision-making conducted by hospital administration and the board of trustees. The design should be conducive to reducing risk in several areas — treatment delays, injury from accidents, violent acts against patients, visitors, and staff.

The best design for optimal patient care, flow, safety, and security is a well-integrated plan that incorporates the essential needs of a department with acuity and patient flow. One such planning approach is the "bubble design" (Figure 2).[1] Fitting the "bubble components" together in the most effective way requires the knowledge and expertise of experienced architects.

Ideally, essential ancillary units, such as laboratory and radiology, should be next to — if not in — the emergency department. Taking patients away from the careful monitoring performed in the emergency department creates a greater risk of an untoward event. Imaging tests make up the majority of procedures performed outside the department. This area is not always staffed or supplied to handle the types of conditions that are common in the emergency department. Options to minimize this risk are as follows: perform procedures in the emergency department, when indicated; design the radiology support unit close to or within the emergency department; assign a nurse or other appropriate staff to stay with patients who are sent out of the emergency department for testing.

Laboratory testing usually does not necessitate the patient's leaving the department. Specimens are usually obtained in the emergency department by laboratory personnel or department staff and then delivered to the laboratory. Results are usually returned electronically, except for the return of crossmatched blood.

Figure 2
"Bubble" design

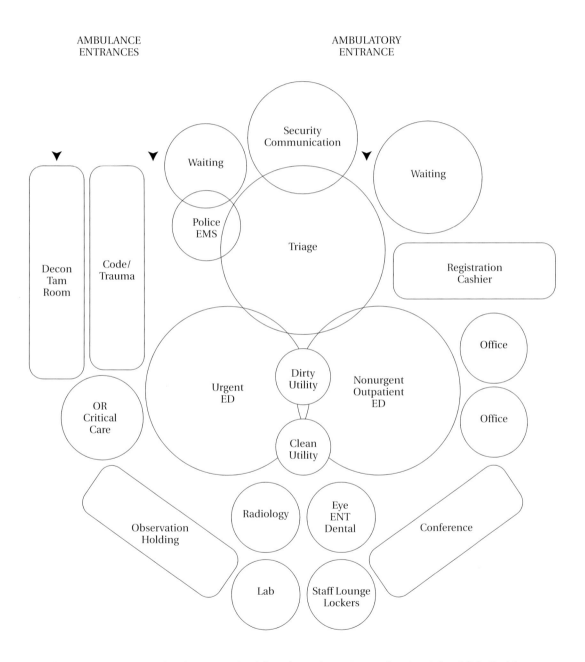

From Porter D. *Hospital Architecture – Guidelines for Design or Renovation*. Ann Arbor, Mich: Health Administration Press; 1982. Adapted with permission.

External Design and Entrances

Signs that are easy to find and easy to read are critical for directing people to the hospital and the emergency department. This information will speed up access to emergency care and decrease the level of frustration of patients and family.

Separate entrances for ambulances and walk-in patients should be well marked and easily differentiated, even for someone who cannot read. Well-lighted parking with easy access to the emergency department is important; parking reserved for emergency department patients is even better. Entrances must be at street level and should be protected from the elements as much as possible.

The ambulance entrance should be well ventilated to prevent vehicle exhaust fumes from building up and circulating inside. Intake air vents should be placed far away from this and other loading areas. In colder climates, make provisions for protection against the hazards of snow and ice at the entrances. If the design plans anticipate that helicopters will land adjacent to the entrance, be sure that there is adequate protection from direct hazard and blown objects.

For safety reasons, shrubbery and other possible concealing structures or hiding places should be eliminated. A closed-circuit television camera is a simple and expedient safety addition for every emergency department entrance. Ideally, all entrances should have automatic sliding doors made of shatterproof glass. At a minimum, the doors must have windows to prevent collisions and to discourage people from attempting to conceal and bring in weapons. Doors should be positioned to prevent a direct line of sight (or gunfire) from the street.

The ambulance entrance should be physically separated from the walk-in entrance to prevent accidents and protect patients' privacy. It must have easy vehicular access. This entrance also should have automatic sliding doors, but access should be controlled by key, swipe card, or a code used by ambulance and security personnel. The ambulance entrance is a special purpose entrance and should be designed or indicated as such so that walk-in patients are not frustrated in their attempts to enter through this controlled and limited access point.

The emergency department may, indeed, be the "open door" to the health care system, but for safety reasons, all entrances should be monitored by security personnel. In areas where violence, gang activity, and other crimes are more prominent, metal detectors, hand-held or portable, should be used to detect weapons.

Security Office

The hospital security officers and office should be located in the front of the emergency department. Security officers should have direct line of sight to the entrances in the department and the waiting area. Closed-circuit television monitoring may be helpful, but remote monitoring is not as effective in crime deterrence as the physical presence of an officer.

Triage

The patient triage area should be designed to handle both normal and unexpected patient flow and acuity. As such, it should be planned to be two to three times larger than the anticipated usual need. This extra space is not likely to be wasted, as it can accommodate temporary clerical or clinical functions. The triage area should be staffed at all times with an adequate number of well-trained health care professionals who function in accordance with EMTALA and JCAHO requirements.

Triage should not be a barrier to rapid patient care and flow. Registrars should not be expected to triage patients, and triage nurses should not act as registrars. The area should be designed to protect the patient's privacy and provide security for patients and staff. If glass partitions are used, one-way glass or curtains should be installed for privacy. Doors should be positioned to enhance traffic flow and protect the triage staff and patients.

Of all areas in the emergency department, triage is the most vulnerable and likely site for violent acts. The triage area should be equipped with a "panic button" that is wired directly to the security office and hospital switchboard.

Registration

Registration of ambulatory, noncritical patients should take place in a safe, private booth to protect the patient from visual or auditory incursion. It must be designed for ease and access for patients requiring a wheelchair or crutches.

As added protection for staff, thick Plexiglas, even bulletproof glass partitions, should at least be considered. Panic buttons also should be incorporated into the design.

Waiting Room

A well-lit, cheerfully decorated waiting room designed to maximize comfort and minimize stress creates a good impression of the hospital and decreases the possibility of violent acts. A television set in the area or a partitioned TV viewing area helps distract visitors from necessary delays. Likewise, a separate area equipped for children to play is helpful. The waiting area and people in it should not be visible from the street. However, it should be visible from the triage and security areas, possibly through the use of one-way glass. Furniture should be immovable, or at least heavy enough that it cannot be lifted easily or used in a violent manner. Divided waiting areas will separate visitors into smaller, perhaps more agreeable groups and minimize the risk of conflicts. As opposed to Greyhound bus terminal type seating, small pods or areas where families may have some degree of privacy is preferred.

Waiting patients and visitors should have access to water, other refreshments, telephones, and rest rooms. Smoking is not allowed in most hospitals, but a nearby designated smoking area, outside perhaps, is still a good idea.

A family consultation room also should be available, but with limited access. Ideally, a second access to the "back" treatment area is preferable for consultations with family members in crisis or bereavement. This room, like other closed rooms in the department, should have two controlled access doors and a panic button.

General Treatment Area

The treatment area should be designed to facilitate patient flow, keeping in mind the special requirements of the patient. Inherently, maximal efficiency for staff usually translates to some loss of privacy for the patient. Special areas dedicated to behavioral emergencies, multiple trauma, cardiac resuscitation, pelvic examinations, eye examinations, pediatric care, and other anticipated special needs should be considered individually and designed for incorporation into the smoothly functioning emergency department.

The main nurses' station should be in the "core" of the treatment area. Ideally, the treatment units and observation beds should "fan out" and be visible from the core, but not from each other. In hospitals where acts of violence are a common threat, it may be advisable to enclose the nurses' station with Plexiglas or bulletproof glass. The main nurses' station should be equipped with multiple types of communication systems that are linked to the emergency department as well as other hospital departments.

Panic buttons should be placed at the nurses' station and strategically throughout the treatment area. Special treatment areas located away from the core, such as those designated for resuscitation or observation, may need dedicated staff. Ideally, there should be no "blind spots" in the core treatment area. If this is not possible, having staff dedicated to these areas reduces the risk of an untoward event. Staff assigned to these remote areas of the department should be equipped with hand-held alarms, private channel telephones, or wireless panic buttons.

Reducing the number of entrances to and exits from the treatment area also reduces the threat of incursion by curious visitors or those intent on doing harm. All entrances and exits should have limited access and be controlled by staff or security officers. Hospital staff should not be allowed to use outside department entrances as a general entrance to the emergency departments.

Closed-circuit television observation of entrances is an inexpensive way to monitor activity but may give the staff a false sense of security. Blind spots at intersections of hallways should have curved mirrors placed strategically to eliminate the possibility of collisions and hidden perpetrators of violence.

Access to the central medication area should be clearly visible from and protected by the main nurses' station. Medications that are on the controlled substances list must be handled according to the guidelines promulgated by the JCAHO and other regulatory agencies. Panic buttons or silent alarms should be located in this area.

All treatment areas should be designed to include standard equipment, monitoring, oxygen, suction, electrical, and wash facilities. To the extent possible, the layout of these patient care areas should be the same so that they will be more versatile for differing patient acuity demands. In mass casualty situations, all areas become potential treatment areas. In addition, patients who have a sudden and unexpected status change do not have to be moved into another area that may already be occupied. Electrical outlets should be connected directly to the emergency power source.

Most treatment areas are separated by curtains, but some treatment rooms should have doors. These must be designed to allow gurneys and equipment to be moved easily and quickly. A patient with a behavioral emergency probably should be treated in a secluded room that has special features, such as doors that conceal service utilities (e.g., oxygen, suction, water, electrical outlets), no protruding surfaces or equipment, surfaces that are easy to clean, access doors that lock, and recessed closed-circuit television camera. Patients who occupy this room frequently require sedation, restraints, or both. The risk of untoward events in this high-risk area should be minimized by designing in some feature for direct vision (e.g., one-way shatter-resistant glass) or video or audio monitoring. Sedated and restrained patients must be monitored closely and frequently.

Treatment rooms designated for pelvic examinations should be equipped to maximize the patient's comfort and privacy but should also allow for rapid clinical intervention in unexpected conditions, such as precipitous birth, hemorrhage, or some other physiologic deterioration.

Another treatment room should be equipped for eye-ear-nose-throat emergencies. Risk to the patient can be reduced by having equipment and supplies readily available to treat hemorrhage, shock, or cardiac emergencies. An examination chair must have the capability of being converted into the Trendelenburg position.

Treatment of children is a high-risk area in emergency medicine. Emergency departments that expect to care for a large number of young children should dedicate an area to this patient group. Not only is special-sized equipment necessary, but also existing examination furniture must be designed to prevent injury to the child. Electrical, oxygen, and vacuum outlets should be placed high enough to be out of reach of children. Protruding edges must be rounded. In general, the area should be "childproofed."

Environmental Hazards

One specific issue that must be addressed when planning the design of an emergency department is how to deal with environmental hazards and protect patients, staff, and visitors from harmful exposures.

External Sources

The risk of exposure to environmental hazards brought into the department from external sources is a growing concern. Not only are more chemical materials being transported by surface carriers, but also the public has greater access to these materials than ever before. The design of the emergency department should include, at a minimum, at least one decontamination room. If possible, one or more additional similar rooms should be planned in the treatment area. Emergency department staff must be able to recognize conditions of general threat quickly to protect themselves and isolate patients and visitors from contamination.

The design and construction of a decontamination area is simple, but expensive. It should be separated from the general treatment area, near the ambulance entrance, and of adequate size to accommodate several gurneys and several staff members. The walls should be lined with an impervious material. Adequate heating and cooling for expected climatic conditions are as important here as elsewhere in the hospital. The department's design plan should allow for a negative air flow ventilation system that is chemically filtered and exhausted to the outside, away from air intake vents. An adequate, copious supply of warm water is necessary. Most important (and expensive) in the design is the treatment of waste water(runoff). The waste rinse water should not be allowed to contaminate the general waste water. It should be collected and held in appropriate tanks until it can be treated by toxic material management specialists.

The decontamination room must be equipped to protect health care workers from exposure to the toxin that has affected the patient. When radiation exposure is a possibility, the necessary monitoring and protective equipment should be readily available. Chemical exposure, which is a more likely concern, should be prevented with adequate impervious barrier suits, gloves, masks, respirators, and other protective equipment. This equipment should be stored in the decontamination room in supply adequate for the planned number of workers. The plan also should address the need to have a spray hose and shower area in the decontamination room. In some communities, the fire department may be able to provide decontamination equipment. This is an excellent resource, especially if a dedicated "decon" room is not feasible and the local EMS system has a HazMat team.

Internal Sources

Significant environmental hazards also exist within the emergency department itself — exposure to a contagious disease, a "slip and fall," physical injury to staff caused by a patient, exposure to contaminated body fluids, skin breaks from improperly handled needles, knives, and other sharps.

The design of the facility and provisions for placing protective equipment in each treatment area should precede construction. Particular attention should be given to areas that are designed to handle contaminated linens and equipment. The risk of a health care worker contracting a serious infection should be minimized from the planning stage through the daily execution of protective policies and procedures.

Premises Safety Standards

The emergency department is a dangerous area in which to work, visit, or be a patient. Increasingly, violence from the street has extended into the hospital through the department. Hundreds of emergency physicians, nurses, and other staff members are assaulted every year, some fatally. Although some of this violence is unpredictable, much of it can be anticipated. In addition to designing a facility to maximize protection and safety, training, recognition of potentially violent situations, and preventive measures are extremely important.

The high-stress, fast-moving, variable patterns and varying patient, staff, and visitor needs require careful scrutiny, not only in the design phase, but also in the day-to-day monitoring of general operations. The staff must plan for and minimize the possibility of accidents involving patients who may be disoriented or have visual, hearing, or speech impairments, or are unable to read or follow instructions, or have specific mental or physical impairments. The combination of all the necessities of medical care, stress, excitement, potential for violence, accidents, and simple miscommunication makes the emergency department an extremely high-risk environment.

Although planning for all contingencies is impossible, careful thought about high-volume and high-risk areas is mandatory. A carefully constructed but realistic plan for the routine operations and the exceptional contingency should be written, reviewed by all concerned, published, and kept in an accessible place in the department. Patient protective safety standards are found in the publications of the JCAHO.[2] Premises fire and safety standards are recorded in information from the International Association for Healthcare Security and Safety.[3] Universal precautions information for the prevention of contagious diseases also can be obtained from the Centers for Disease Control and Prevention and the U.S. Department of Health.[4]

Security and Law Enforcement Agencies

The two areas of the hospital most likely to experience an act of violence are the psychiatric unit and the emergency department.[3,4] The hospital's security director must be involved in the planning and design of any new or renovated emergency department. Personality disorders and simple personal stress come to the surface quickly among patients, family members, and visitors when faced with the frustration of sudden and unexpected injury or illness, the loss of personal directive control, lengthy waiting times, complications or withdrawal from alcohol or drugs, and poor communications between staff and patients or visitors.

Sometimes, the same stressors affect emergency department staff. These high-stress factors, combined with the accessibility of the emergency department, the prevalence of drug and alcohol abuse, and the easy availability of guns and other weapons produce a volatile mix that sometimes culminates in the emergency department.

The type and number of hospital security staff vary and depend on the type and number of problems the hospital expects to encounter. The use of uniforms and equipment, including weapons, also depends on what is anticipated for patient and crowd control. Generally, the "softer" look of identifiable uniforms without weapons carries less risk exposure than the "hard" appearance of a uniformed police officer equipped with Mace, handcuffs, and handguns. However, in some hospitals, this show of authority is necessary.

The approach that the security staff takes varies depending on the community and the hospital, but these staff members should always be prepared to manage problems of a far greater magnitude than usual. The protection of staff, patients, and visitors is mandatory to avoid disruption to patient care, injury, and litigation. This should be taken into consideration when planning all areas of the emergency department.

In addition to panic buttons, silent alarms, wireless personal alarms, personal communicators, and other devices, the design should also address the use of controlled access doors, metal detectors, convex mirrors, shatterproof (or even bulletproof) glass, and "safe areas."

The parking lot is hospital property, and patients and visitors expect to be safe from physical hazards and violence. Direct observation of the parking area and entrances should be possible, at least by remote closed-circuit television surveillance.

One of the most important steps in designing an emergency department is to develop a security plan that is a collaborative effort of emergency department personnel, the hospital's security department, and local law enforcement agencies. Having such a plan that is well thought-out and allows for staff training can reduce the possibility of injury. For example, this security plan should stipulate that evaluation of a potentially violent patient must be conducted in a seclusion room, and that the patient should be assigned to this room at the beginning of the visit. The security plan should be based on the anticipation of violence so that routine preventive measures can be taken before a situation becomes a crisis.

Key Points and Conclusion

A multidisciplinary planning approach to designing an emergency department is the best way to ensure an appropriate facility for emergency medicine professionals to care for the sick and injured. The design team must analyze present and future needs and formulate realistic requirements for medical care, consider the needs of staff professionals, and thoroughly evaluate the community's "violence content" to create a design that is efficient and safe for patients, visitors, and staff. The design team also must anticipate areas of potential injury or liability before construction in order to provide a safe environment through the lifetime of the new facility.

References

1. Porter D. *Hospital Architecture – Guidelines for Design or Renovation*. Ann Arbor, Mich: Health Administration Press; 1982.

2. Joint Commission on Accreditation of Healthcare Organizations. *1996 Comprehensive Accreditation Manual for Hospitals*. Oakbrook Terrace, Ill: JCAHO; 1996.

3. International Association for Healthcare Security and Safety. *Annual Survey of Crime in Hospitals*. Lombard, Ill: IAHSS; 1989.

4. Occupational Safety and Health Administration, US Dept of Labor. *Guidelines for Preventing Workplace Violence for Health Care and Social Services Workers – OSHA 3148-1996*. May 1996 (with appendixes: SHARP-Staff Assault Study (Staff Survey); Workplace Violence Checklist; Assaulted and/or Battered Employee Policy; Violence Incident Report Forms.)

Additional Reading

Alspach G. Nurses as victims of violence. *Crit Care Nurse* 1993;13(5):13-14,17.

American Medical Association, Young Physicians Section. *Violence in the Medical Workplace: Prevention Strategies*. Chicago: AMA; 1995.

Blumenreich P, Lippmann S, Bacani-Oropilla T. Violent patients. Are you prepared to deal with them? *Postgrad Med* 1991; 90:201-206.

Brayley J, Lange R, Baggoley C, et al. The violence management team. An approach to aggressive behaviour in a general hospital. *Med J Aust* 1994;161:254-258.

DiBenedetto D. Occupational hazards of the healthcare industry. Protecting healthcare workers. *AAOHN J* 1992;43(3):131-137.

Goetz RR, Bloom JD, Chenell SL, et al. Weapons possession by patients in a university emergency department. *Ann Emerg Med* 1991;20:8-10.

Gosnold JK. Violence in the general hospital: the violent patient in the accident and emergency department. *R Soc Health J* 1978;98:189-190,198.

Healthcare security's role: redefined for the year 2000. *J Healthcare Protect Manage* 1994;10(2,Summer).

Hutson HR, Anglin D, Mallon W. Minimizing gang violence in the emergency department. *Ann Emerg Med* 1992;21:1291-1293.

Keep N, Glibert P, and the 1990-91 California ENA Government Affairs Committee. California Emergency Nurses Association's informal survey of violence in California emergency departments. *J Emerg Nurs* 1992;18:433-442.

Kinkle SL. Violence in the ED: how to stop it before it starts. *Am J Nurs* 1993;93:22-24.

Lavoie FW, Carter GL, Danzl DF, et al. Emergency department violence in United States teaching hospitals. *Ann Emerg Med* 1988;17:1227-1233.

Lundberg GD, Young RK, Flanagin A, et al, eds. *Violence – A Compendium from JAMA, American Medical News, and the Specialty Journals of the American Medical Association*. Chicago: AMA; 1992.

Mahoney B Sr. The extent, nature, and response to victimization of emergency nurses in Pennsylvania. *J Emerg Nurs* 1991;17:282-294.

Pallarito K. Security forces in battle against dangerous threats. In: *Modern Healthcare's Facilities Operations and Management*. 1990; Aug 6:4-8.

Protection from Physical Violence in the Emergency Department. ACEP Policy Statement, approved January 1993. To obtain a copy, call (800) 798-1822, touch 6, or go to www.acep.org.

Riccio J, Meade D, eds. Violence in the emergency department. *Top Emerg Med* 1994;16(3).

Riggs L, ed. *Emergency Department Design*. Dallas: American College of Emergency Physicians; 1993.

Taylor KS. Defensive medicine; physicians fight the 'violence epidemic.' *Hospitals and Health Networks* 1994;July:42-43.

Turner JT, ed. *Violence in the Medical Care Setting: A Survival Guide*. Rockville, Md: Aspen Publishers; 1984.

van de Leuv J. *Management of Emergency Services*. Rockville, Md: Aspen Systems Corp; 1987.

Violence in the ED is a concern across nation, Parts 1,2,3. *ACEP News*, May-July 1993.

Wasserberger J, Ordog GJ, Harden E, et al. Violence in the emergency department. *Top Emerg Med* 1992;14(2):71-78.

Chapter 15

Hospital Environmental Risks: Drugs, Products, and Equipment

Michelle Regan Donovan, BSN, RN

Safety is a "people problem." According to Dan Petersen, author, lecturer, and renowned safety management expert, the answer to managing safety and risk is to get rid of statistics and listen to the real experts on safety — the employees. "Behind every unsafe condition," Petersen says, "there is a management system that . . . allowed that hazard to exist."[1]

There are five basic theories central to environmental safety:

- Accidents are caused by unsafe acts and conditions.
- There are certain essential elements to any safety program.
- Accident statistics tell us something.
- Audits predict results in a survey.
- Regulatory compliance ensures safety results.

In Petersen's view, and despite the Occupational Health Safety Act of 1971, the two keys to a "world class" environmental safety program are to make the line organization accountable for safety performance and to have employee involvement.[1] Such views are seldom more valid than in the emergency department, where an atmosphere of "organized chaos" is more often the rule than an exception.

Environmental Risk Issues

Growing public interest, increasing federal government controls, and media portrayals of accidents and carelessness in the health care industry have created an increased awareness and concern for the safety and control of all patient-related technology, procedural equipment, and medicinal products prescribed by practitioners. Although medical and nursing personnel may be held responsible for exhausting the lion's share of emergency medicine malpractice dollars, there is increasing evidence of hospital or vendor liability relative to faulty or malfunctioning equipment and product construction.

Even recent health care controls, such as universal precautions for infection control and prevention, have created new occupational hazards for patients and health care workers. For example, since 1987, the Centers for Disease Control and Prevention (CDC) has mandated that health care workers wear latex gloves when in contact with all patients. However, no one could have predicted the escalating numbers of serious and often fatal latex allergies generated by using latex gloves. Issues surrounding latex sensitivity and the reported escalating incidence remain a growing concern for health care workers and patients.

Sophisticated automation and physiologic monitoring capabilities are the standard of care in patient management. They also present concerns related to patient and staff safety. These concerns include whether there is a sufficient supply of these items to meet demand and whether federal regulatory monitors are available to maintain proper safety levels.

In fact, in many instances, risk and liability related to quality and regulatory compliance pale compared with a greater concern of obtaining sufficient and appropriate equipment and supplies for the increasing numbers and types of patients treated. Legal entities and the media thrive on discovering physician or hospital failure to comply with standards of care or state-of-the-art practice. Increasingly, incidents (especially those involving the pediatric population) are related to the unavailability or delayed access to appropriately sized or types of equipment required for basic resuscitation or diagnostic procedures. Immediate availability of appropriate therapeutic and emergency drugs, along with sufficient supplies and procedural equipment for different patient types, is essential to safe, quality care management. Tighter cost controls, declining budgets, and more stringent purchasing guidelines in response to managed care should not overshadow the significance of these components in emergency care delivery. Each component is essential to patient care and cost, as well as to physician and nursing practice quality and potential liability.

Accessibility of Equipment, Supplies, and Waste Disposal

As the concepts of cost awareness and productivity are introduced to caregiver staff, management places an increasing emphasis on the availability of supplies, equipment, and pharmaceuticals and the importance of their location in the emergency department. From a risk management perspective, the convenient location of these items and their organized and uniform distribution in individual rooms or care areas is beneficial to patients and staff.[2] Similarly, organized and labeled drawers, cabinets, or appropriately stocked and labeled supply exchange carts facilitate ease of use for various patient presentations. Physicians, residents, seasoned emergency and hospital personnel, and agency personnel who may be unfamiliar with emergency department resources and supply locations benefit from an organized system for storing supplies and equipment.

Organization can help prevent and reduce risk of staff injuries. For example, accidental needlesticks from contaminated needles or instruments remain a high-risk problem for all health care workers, especially emergency department staff. Preventive measures include a designated location for the closed foot-operated contaminated-trash containers, and sharps containers placed on both sides of the patient cubicle or at the headwall for convenient disposal. These simple efforts will reduce the risk to those staff who clean or transport contaminated equipment and supplies to another location.

Furthermore, assigned parking or storage space for larger equipment makes it easier for staff to locate and access these items quickly and reduces the time required for patient intervention and treatment. It also encourages staff to return the equipment to its assigned space when the room is cleaned up or when the item is no longer needed. Likewise, specific storage spaces for unused gurneys or wheelchairs reduce the potential for mishap and enhance their rapid acquisition.

The Patient-Focused Environment and Liability

The emergency department environment is only as safe as the staff makes it! Chair-height gurneys have reduced the potential liability associated with patient falls and subsequent injury; however, these incidents still occur because someone forgets to set the brakes or leaves an elderly or mentally unstable patient unattended. These and other general patient safety issues related to equipment should be outlined in a written patient safety policy for the emergency department and communicated to all physician, nursing, and technician staff.

The nurse call system is a second hazard. It is perhaps the most patient-focused item found in the patient care area, but its actual use is encumbered by the distance of the gurney to its location on the wall and the limited reach of the patient's arm. Unless otherwise configured, attached, or mandated by policy, the nurse call system presents more of a liability than an asset, especially for the elderly or confused patient who is detained with side rails.

Department policy should outline the components for dealing with high-risk patients while allowing flexibility in areas of lesser liability and hazard. The emergency department must find ways to manage risk in the face of changing standards of care, new patient categories, higher public expectations, and the need for classifying risk-prone groups (e.g., the elderly, patients with behavioral disorders, substance abusers).

Latex Allergies — A Growing Occupational Hazard

Exact estimates of the scope of latex sensitivity are difficult to ascertain. The American Nurses Association and the American Dental Association report escalating incidents. Some workers have left the health care profession because of latex sensitivity. Even more serious, the medical literature illustrates numerous examples of death due to anaphylactic shock attributable to latex products.[3] Health care workers have a higher incidence of adverse reactions to latex gloves, ranging from mild irritation to anaphylactic shock. In either case, affected individuals must often drastically alter their lifestyles, as many environmental and household products are also latex based. According to a medical epidemiologist at the CDC, various studies indicate that 4.5% to 21% of health care workers are affected by this hazard.[3]

Hospital policy should reflect up-to-date research and medical professional group recommendations that health care workers use powder-free gloves whenever possible. Protein levels of the latex products should be obtained from the manufacturer, and only those with the lower levels should be selected for use. To avoid liability from latex sensitivity, hospitals may need to designate "latex-free" procedure areas for staff and patients who are sensitive to these products. As the risk for patient sensitivity to latex escalates, yet another question may be added to routine triage screening —"Are you aware of any latex sensitivity?"

Drug-Related Policy, Procedure, and Acquisition

The use of specific pharmaceutical agents and the development of the floor stock drug list for the emergency department should be guided by policy formulated by emergency physicians and nursing staff in conjunction with the hospital pharmacist, then approved by the hospital's executive committee. Only drugs approved for use by the hospital formulary and Federal Drug Administration (FDA) and dispensed by the hospital pharmacy should be administered, and then only by licensed emergency personnel. Still, there is inherent risk when emergency department staff dispense pharmaceuticals from department stock or drug company samples, because neither the hospital nor the emergency department providers have a license to dispense outpatient drugs. This restriction can be overcome, to the benefit of patients, if state or local jurisdiction allows a special Class C hospital pharmaceutical license or hospital policy that authorizes the pharmacist to dispense a prescribed drug to an outpatient under special circumstances and duress.

All emergency departments have patients whose financial conditions prohibit timely acquisition of prescription or over-the-counter drugs required to treat an illness or injury. When sample drug dispensation is permitted in the emergency department, these drugs should be secured as inventory drugs are and their use recorded on individual patient records. Official department documentation (i.e., physician's signature, date, patient's name, prescription provided, number of units released) should also be included. Medical staff bylaws and emergency department policy should specify the types of drugs and anesthetics, appropriate or inappropriate, for use in the department. These policies should define the circumstances and professional guidelines or monitoring requirements for selected or restricted drugs and conscious sedation agents as defined by regulatory agencies (i.e., state, pharmaceutical, JCAHO). Nursing care guidelines should address the administration of drug groups relative to the type and frequency of monitoring required. Generally, separately defined policies include the administration of distinct drug groups with the special precautions for each (i.e., intravascular or intramuscular narcotics, vasodilators, paralytics, and thrombolytic agents).

New drugs should not become stock until the nursing staff has been educated about their adverse effects and administration precautions. Administrative policy should also define who (e.g., physician, nurse, anesthesiologist) may administer selected pharmaceuticals and by which route. The policy should also outline physicians' orders and professional documentation (i.e., administration time, route, initials).

To avoid treatment delays, health care facilities should make sure that adequate and convenient supplies of emergency and frequently used drugs are always available. Automated inventory control systems (e.g., Pyxis, Baxter, Lionsville) allow individual dose retrieval, inventory control, direct patient charge applications, redeploying nursing accountability, and optimizing charges. Secured, pharmacy-controlled, and par-level exchange carts are also an efficient method to maintain drug control and avoid an outdated inventory. Although these methods may enhance the management of the department, the responsibility for maintaining adequate supplies and appropriate par levels of pharmaceuticals remains often falls to the nursing staff rather than pharmaceutical staff. Inadequate drug supplies or lack of convenient access translates to costly patient delays, poor quality of care, patient dissatisfaction, and loss of staff productivity.

Emergency department staff often complain that their facilities either have difficulty procuring or fail to stock essential and state-of-the-art drugs (e.g., nitroglycerine , t-PA). The reasons most frequently cited by the hospital pharmacy to explain this situation have to do with drug cost, short shelf-life of drugs, or drug reconstitution requirements. For example, in a patient experiencing a heart attack, treatment delays can translate to vessel occlusion, loss of cardiac muscle and function, and ultimately poor cardiac event outcomes. Department policy should ensure appropriate drugs in sufficient quantities for the types of patients seen. Regardless of an automated or a par-level exchange vehicle, the hospital pharmacy should be ultimately responsible for maintaining the designated quantities of pharmaceutical supplies.

Biomedical Equipment

Proper equipment function and operation in the emergency department are essential to ensure positive patient care outcomes. Although the traditional responsibility and accountability for equipment care and maintenance have been delegated to the nursing staff, the recent alliance between Occupational Safety and Health Administration (OSHA) legislation and JCAHO requires more defined and stringent monitors.[4] Quality assurance activities and department policy must include routine inspection and monthly documentation of designated department equipment by hospital-certified biomedical engineers. Daily and regular inspections and documentation of critical equipment function are mandatory and should be part of an established emergency department policy. Federal and state licensing, as well as JCAHO regulations,[4] require the emergency department to be properly stocked with equipment and supplies to provide adequate emergency services for all patients.

Equipment malfunction and its absence or failure in the department can endanger patients' lives. Policies and procedures should state how often and which equipment should be inspected and maintained by department staff and biomedical engineers. Although the defibrillator is probably the most dangerous of all equipment used in the emergency department, others (e.g., external pacemakers, oxygen flow meters, suction apparatus, ECG machines) also pose potential hazards for patients and staff. All levels of emergency department staff should be trained and certified for all equipment they will manage, monitor, or operate. Emergency department staff should not use unfamiliar equipment until they have attained competency levels for safe operation and monitoring parameters. This ensures staff proficiency, safety, and comfort levels, and reduces treatment delays.

A facility's equipment policy and retained documentation should reflect OSHA and JCAHO guidelines for the monthly equipment checklist, inspection monitors by hospital biomedical engineers, and nursing's recorded completion of equipment and supply inspections, especially resuscitation equipment. Battery-powered equipment (e.g., defibrillators, monitors) enables emergency personnel to use equipment that does not require an immediate power source. However, another risk potential is created for patients when staff neglect to charge the equipment appropriately or fail to notice a disconnected power source. The death of a patient secondary to a malfunctioning defibrillator is a tragic event and may result in costly litigation. Detailed documentation, a valuable risk management tool for nurses assigned to maintain and operate equipment, should contain the location and type of equipment for testing and time frames for chargeable battery replacement. This policy is even more crucial for those departments using significant numbers of outside personnel (e.g., locum tenens or agency) who may be unfamiliar with equipment operation, location, or department policy. Nursing management should embrace accountability and responsibility for this function. According to risk-aversive practice, emergency equipment checks should be assigned to an individual on each shift and conducted a minimum of twice daily and after each use.

Securing Faulty Equipment

The hospital and the emergency department are required to enforce a policy for reporting any incident related to faulty equipment, with or without a bad outcome. If any staff member fails to comply with this standard and a patient has an adverse outcome, the department and hospital may be liable. An important aspect of risk management is establishing and communicating policy and detailed procedures for staff to report missing or malfunctioning equipment or immediately to secure vital equipment replacement. Documented department procedures in the event of equipment malfunction should include emergency telephone numbers and safeguards and steps for equipment removal and security (Figure 1).

Additional procedures for minor equipment inspections and repairs should be included with department protocols. In the event of any equipment deficiency or malfunction, staff using the equipment must submit an incident report to biomedical engineering or to the staff member responsible for equipment maintenance and repair, followed by an OSHA report,[5] as required. The staff member noting the deficiency should remove, replace, and label the faulty equipment, as well as notify biomedical engineering. Similarly, when vendors notify hospitals of potentially dangerous or recalled equipment, the hospital must immediately communicate such information to all user groups. The hospital and the department are responsible for obtaining back-up equipment or duplicate life-support capabilities.

Responsibility for Product Evaluation and Quality Control

Emergency department staff should be represented on the hospital's product evaluation committee. This practice can help reduce risk because certain equipment is often used primarily in the emergency department. If administrative staff other than emergency department staff evaluate or make equipment decisions relative to new or unfamiliar equipment, this will only increase risk factors. Administration and materials management departments should work together with the emergency department to acquire the most appropriate equipment and supplies and to decide on the quantities to be stocked in the emergency department.

New equipment or product purchases for hospital use should be screened by a multidisciplinary product evaluation committee before purchase. If new equipment will be used exclusively in the emergency department, the emergency department staff should participate either in an on-site trial evaluation or a beta-site visit to become familiar with its use and operation. Equipment or product purchases should be delayed until the committee designates the item safe for use. Staff evaluation of a product's effectiveness, efficiency, safety, and cost should be included in the process for all capital expenditure purchases. Any short-term cost may yield long-term savings in efficiency, productivity, and user satisfaction. Purchasing decisions should not be made by one staff person. Major

investment items, such as physiologic monitoring modules, and smaller budget items, including endotracheal tubes, suction adapters, bulb syringes for infant airway clearance, disposable laceration trays, and suture materials, should be evaluated by the users before large quantities are purchased. Conversely, items requested by physicians or other staff should be reviewed by the hospital product evaluation committee and the user group for overall cost and liability.

The committee alone cannot realistically evaluate items such as preassembled syringes whose needles may often come loose while in patient tissue or generic suture sets whose needle holders will not grasp fine suture needles. From a risk and efficacy perspective, purchase price, vendor applications, and marketing ploys should not be the only determinants for purchasing department-specific equipment and supplies. Quality controls must ensure that items are user-friendly, easily operated for timely intervention, and safe and efficient to produce good patient outcomes. Items subject to infection control standards, such as disposable versus resterilized equipment, should be judged on the advantages relating to cost, patient benefit, and safety. Purchasing decisions should involve members of the hospital infection control committee. All items should be evaluated for their improvement over existing products and whether they meet quality and safety standards. Clearly, the evaluation process should include written comments from staff with specific attention paid to safety, performance, and ease of operation.

Responsibility for Equipment Management

Equipment evaluation is best implemented after training sessions. Although vendors are often the best trainers for emergency department staff, they may not be available to provide a thorough session for each employee once the equipment has been purchased. Management is responsible for ensuring adequate employee training and safety standards. Vendors sometimes will provide short videotapes to assist with the learning process. When appropriate training media are not available, the hospital may videotape a vendor presentation and demonstration to assist with staff training and implementation. Certain equipment requires documented certification for operation.

As more sophisticated equipment is updated or replaced, changes in operation procedure

Figure 1

Algorithm for reporting medical equipment failures

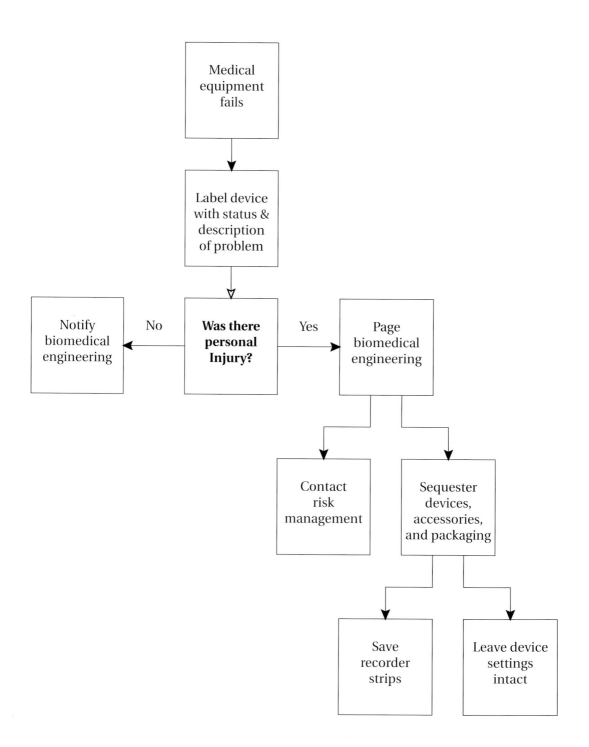

may mandate reeducation or recertification of staff before operation. These processes should be formalized in policy for each level of personnel, included in credentialing or competency records, and documented for state and JCAHO requirements. Orientation and training programs for department physicians, nurses, residents, and other new staff should include the safe operation and proficiency testing for department equipment.

Case Study

A woman calls the local hospital and tells the night nursing supervisor that her husband is having chest pain. The supervisor advises the woman to bring her husband to the hospital to be evaluated by a physician. The couple arrives at the emergency department at 12:15 AM, and the patient continues to experience chest pain. A staff physician interviews and examines the patient and orders an ECG. The hospital technician attempts to perform the ECG but is unable to "get the machine to work." Someone had plugged it into a damaged electrical outlet the day before and it had not worked correctly since.

When the physician is notified of the malfunction, she tells the technician to use another machine. A second ECG machine cannot be located. The patient and his wife are told that no other physicians are available, so they leave the emergency department and drive to a town about four miles away. The patient dies in the second hospital's emergency department of a myocardial infarction while an ECG is being performed.

The Medical-Legal Perspective

Any product or equipment directly involved in an incident, regardless of the reason, should be reported and documented by nursing staff and, if appropriate, removed from use until the problem can be investigated. Failure to recognize and report defective or malfunctioning equipment may be a breach of duty for standard patient care and may involve potential liability for any resulting patient harm. Hospital policy must define the guidelines and protocols for staff to follow when equipment fails or a patient is injured. Faulty or hazardous equipment must be removed from service and reported to biomedical engineering or maintenance staff as soon as possible.

If biomedical engineering staff is unavailable for immediate repair, the product or equipment should be removed from service, removed from the treatment area, and tagged with a label describing the malfunction. Many hospitals facilitate equipment tracking by using an equipment book that tracks individual equipment repairs, routine maintenance, replacement equipment, and loans to other departments. Tracking procedures should also include the acquisition and source of a replacement item for the malfunctioning equipment during the repair interim, as well as returning the equipment to the vendor.

Case Discussion

The case study dealt with the issue of nursing responsibility for clinical deficiencies in the emergency department and illustrated, in part, the fatal outcome of treatment delay caused by equipment malfunctions. This type of litigation can be avoided if the health care facility establishes a routine inspection, backup, and maintenance policy for all equipment and products.

Key Points and Conclusion

Failure to comply with state and federal guidelines (OSHA) and JCAHO standards that require a safe health care environment, written safety-related policies and procedures, and adequate and functional equipment for proper patient care may result in liability risks, in loss of accreditation, licensing, and federal funding for a hospital. Appeal of the case cited in this chapter resulted in a state supreme court decision that stated in part: "A hospital owes to its patients . . . the duty of exercising ordinary care to furnish equipment and facilities reasonably suited to the uses intended and such as are in general use under the same, or similar, circumstances in hospitals in the area."[6,7]

Ultimately, emergency department management must ensure that adequate in-service, safety-related training is available for all staff. The hospital administration must support emergency department staff with sufficient equipment, supplies, and appropriate pharmaceuticals for timely intervention; safe, state-of-the-art patient management; and positive patient outcomes.

References

1. Minter S. Dan Petersen: why safety is a people problem. *Occupational Hazards,* January 1997.

2. Donovan MR. *The Changing Face of Emergency and Trauma Centers: Promoting Efficacy with Design.* Chicago: American Society for Hospital Engineering of the American Hospital Association; 1992.

3. Murphy C. Latex allergy as an occupational hazard. *The Washington Post*, July 16, 1996.

4. Joint Commission on Accreditation of Healthcare Organizations: *Comprehensive Accreditation Manual for Hospitals: The Official Handbook.* Oakbrook Terrace, Ill: JCAHO; 1996.

5. OSHA Standards for General Industry, CCII Business Law, 29 CFR 1011, *OSHA Guide for Health Care Facilities*, November 1996.

6. George J. ED equipment failure. *Emerg Nurs Leg Bull*, Fall 1983.

7. *Hamil v Bashline*, 292 A2d 1280 (1978).

Chapter 16

Infection Control

Michelle Regan Donovan, BSN, RN

The emergency department has a higher risk of contagion and infection for patients, staff, and visitors than any other department within an academic or general community hospital. This situation can be attributed to its 24-hour accessibility to all patient types and its large volume of patients whose conditions who are generally unknown to the emergency physician and nursing staff.

The actual risk levels differ among institutions for various types of contagion and patient susceptibility to infectious disease. Factors depend on urban, semiurban, or rural settings, as well as the medical and socioeconomic status of the general population in these sectors. Secondary factors may include the use of emergency departments by institutions, such as prisons, nursing homes, and community shelters, where continued close contact is unavoidable.

In its escalating role as the principal community access to health and emergency care, the emergency department attracts significantly more risk of exposure to all types of contagion. Regardless of the geographic region and type of institution they work in, however, emergency department personnel are faced with controlling infection from a variety of sources to protect patients, visitors, and themselves.

Education is the primary tool for preventing infection in the emergency department. Hospital administrative staff and department managers must identify the main objectives of infection control for the department and implement the appropriate control mechanisms to achieve these ends. They should consider policies and procedures related to airborne or bloodborne infections, incident prevention and control monitors, reporting mechanisms for communicable disease and exposure to pathogens, and environmental procedures or facility improvements that conform with federal infection control guidelines (Figure 1).

Case Studies

1

A 35-year-old woman had worked as an operating room nurse for five years before being hired by her present employer. Ten months after joining her present employer, she is diagnosed as having chronic persistent hepatitis B. She files for Worker's Compensation benefits. The industrial commission denies compensation, saying that the woman is unable to prove that she was exposed to hepatitis during her employment. The trial court affirms the commission's decision.

2

A 24-year-old man presents to the emergency department with a laceration to the forearm. The wound is washed and sutured, and the patient is discharged. He returns three days later with an acute infection in his forearm. The patient undergoes surgical debridement of the region and grafting. He sues for negligent transmission of the infection.

Figure 1

Primary objectives of infection control in the emergency department

- Identify potential carriers and contacts of communicable disease.

- Provide care for patients afflicted with a suspected or known communicable disease.

- Protect patients, staff, and visitors from the potential for infection within the department.

- Adhere to hospital, state, and accreditation regulatory standards for preventing and reporting communicable disease.

- Comply with OSHA, CDC, and EPA guidelines related to occupational health control measures for workers.

Potential Infection in the Emergency Department

Clearly, the risks of contracting a communicable disease are high for emergency department patients and staff. The busy environment, overcrowding and confined space, and nature of the workload create hazards unique to the practice. Staff is frequently exposed to blood, IV fluid spills, bodily secretions, exposed needles, instruments, sharps, and airborne organisms.

Emergency department personnel must establish protocols and education programs about various areas of infection control. The advent of universal precautions specified handwashing techniques, handling of linen, disposal of sharp instruments, environmental surface cleaning, patient isolation and terminal disinfection of these rooms, and infective waste disposal.[1]

Today, hospital administrators, emergency department managers, and infection control personnel have a myriad of responsibilities. Each must be aware of the latest information and findings on communicable diseases and the related control and prophylaxis recommendations. They are charged with identifying potential occupational hazards and creating and endorsing federal, state, and local policies, procedures, and guidelines that reduce risk to everyone in the department. These measures include identification of personnel risk and exposure to airborne pathogens, needlesticks, bloodborne routes, as well as the reporting, prophylaxis, and treatment modalities relative to these incidents.

Airborne Transmission of Diseases

The focus has recently shifted from the hazards of bloodborne infection to the newer, perhaps greater risks of infections transmitted through the air, especially *Mycobacterium tuberculosis*. The significant morbidity and mortality secondary to multiple–drug-resistant tuberculosis has created increased concern for health care workers and hospitals on the part of the Centers for Disease Control and Prevention (CDC).[2,3]

The alarm that has been sounded once again places emergency department staff in a high-risk group because most patient populations with potentially airborne transmitted diseases are likely to present to this department. Aging facilities, poor ventilation, and a lack of negative airflow areas to isolate a potentially contagious patient are also factors in the transmission. The increased incidence of *Aspergillus* (a fungal spore) and other environmental airborne contaminants is associated with respiratory illness and other difficult-to-treat conditions. The higher incidence of specific airborne pathogens has brought attention to inadequate facility design and poor air filter quality.[3,4] All of these factors combined create a major risk for patients and emergency department personnel.

The incidence of respiratory illness contracted after airline travel or among certain populations (e.g., nursing homes, homeless shelters, or during hospital facility construction) has escalated concerns among medical professionals and the general public about airborne transmission of pathogens. In the emergency department — the primary point of entry for the contagious population, especially in the triage area — there tends to be little direction and few procedures to address the potentially contagious patient.

Media attention has shifted the focus from sexually transmitted and bloodborne diseases to dangers of airborne contaminants. As public awareness increases about the Ebola virus, tuberculosis, and *Aspergillus*, more concerted and focused efforts by hospital administrations, health care workers, architects, and engineers to reduce risk for transmission and exposure to airborne infectious pathogens are necessary.

Today, mandatory tuberculosis screening and annual retesting of PPD-negative health care workers are in place as an infection control program for hospitals. Unprotected individuals who have been exposed after such an evaluation are also screened for tuberculosis. Adherence to these and other procedures recommended by CDC guidelines (e.g., immediate patient isolation, masks, particulate respirators)[3] is important. Guidelines prepared by the Occupational Safety and Health Administration (OSHA), the Environmental Protection Agency (EPA), and the CDC continue to advise the health care industry on products and precautions related to all types of infection control.[3,5-7]

Many of these regulations are published as "guidelines" because the outcome data for specific chemoprophylaxis and exposure prevention are inconclusive and subject to revision. As a result, some organizational policies for management of high-risk openings in the emergency department, such as triage, are left to the discretion of department directors and hospital administrators.

Facility Planning

Recent changes in facility planning have been made to adhere to CDC and OSHA guidelines. In particular, there are standard recommendations for new and renovated facility design, space, and construction requirements; consideration for patient protection during interim construction; and engineering and airflow regulations specific to airborne transmitted infections. These design guidelines reflect the recommended care for general infection control, including airborne infection control, protective isolation, and isolation of the immunosuppressed patient with an infectious disease.

New and specific recommendations for preventing the transmission of airborne infectious pathogens in the emergency department are reflected in new airflow exchange rates and exhaust requirements (e.g., isolation rooms, triage, waiting areas, and public waiting areas, radiology).[8] Rooms with negative airflow configurations that exhaust to the outside are required as a minimum standard for new or renovated emergency departments. Further, in-room switch panels for controlling individual room airflow configurations from positive to negative and vice versa are unacceptable because of the potential for error.

Bloodborne Infection and Needlesticks

Needlesticks are the most common source of exposure to hepatitis B, hepatitis C, HIV, and AIDS in the emergency department. The typical, somewhat chaotic, emergency department and the unknown or undiagnosed patient clientele contribute to this problem. An incident report and a documented medical record of any needlestick injury are essential to protect the health and safety of employees and to reduce liability risk for the hospital. Emergency department policy and procedures should be current with OSHA and CDC regulations that specify the protocols to be followed when an accidental needlestick occurs. Other recommendations for antiretroviral prophylaxis for the three risk groups (i.e., highest risk, increased risk, and no increased risk as they relate to exposure of body fluids) may be included as a directive for physicians. However, periodic updates for these should be the responsibility of infection control committee.

Updated recommendations and guidelines for all CDC-related issues can be accessed

Figure 2
Sample policy and procedure for exposure to blood and body fluids and tissue

Procedure for surveillance, prevention, and control of infection.

1. **General**

   a. During the hours of 7:30 AM and 4:00 PM, Monday through Friday, all employees with potential exposures will report to the Employee Health Service (EHS) with an employee's report of injury or illness form.

   b. At other times, all individuals will contact the needlestick hotline (xxx-xxxx) for direction. If emergent care is required, individuals should report to the emergency department for immediate evaluation and appropriate wound care.

2. **For Hepatitis B Evaluation**

   a. If the source patient is known, the EHS will request a hepatitis B surface antigen test. If the hepatitis B surface antigen is positive, the patient's primary care physician will be notified by the EHS. The employee will be tested for hepatitis B surface antibody. Hepatitis B immunoglobulin or hepatitis B vaccine will be offered as indicated by the test results and according to the recommendation of the CDC. The test results on the source patient will be filed in the employee's medical record.

   b. If the source is unknown, the CDC recommendations will be followed (*MMWR* June 1990).

3. **For Hepatitis C Evaluation**

   a. If the source patient is known, the EHS will request a hepatitis C antibody test. If positive, the patient's primary care physician will be notified by the EHS. The exposed health care worker will be tested for HCV antibody after consent has been obtained.

   b. If the source is unknown, baseline hepatitis C antibody testing will be offered to the employee and performed if the employee agrees to testing and has signed a consent.

4. **For HIV Evaluation and Testing of the Health Care Worker**

   a. The EHS will request the health care worker's informed consent to perform HIV antibody testing. This consent is required before contacting the source patient for HIV testing.

   b. Baseline testing is advised for all potential exposures as defined in this policy.

   c. All samples for HIV testing related to an exposure will be coded to protect confidentiality.

   d. Alternative testing sites, including anonymous testing sites, will be offered to the health care worker if on-site testing is not desired.

   e. If the employee consents to baseline blood collection but does not give consent at that time for HIV serologic testing, the sample will be preserved for at least 90 days. If, within 90 days of the exposure incident, the employee elects to have the baseline sample tested, such testing will be done.

   f. Follow-up HIV testing will be encouraged and offered to all persons who have had an exposure at six weeks, three months, and six months postexposure. Follow-up hepatitis C antibody testing will be encouraged and offered to all persons who have had an exposure at three and six months postexposure.

   g. Employees will be counseled as indicated according to the protocol for managing the health care worker exposed to blood or body fluid, found in the Bloodborne Pathogens Control Plan.

5. For HIV Evaluation and Testing of Source Patient

a. If the source patient is known, the EHS will contact the patient's primary care physician to notify that the EHS will be counseling for HIV testing. Substitute consent may be used if the patient is not competent to consent. If a source patient is discharged before the EHS has the opportunity to seek consent, a physician may counsel and obtain consent on the designated form. If consent is obtained by someone other than the EHS, a sample of blood and the consent form will be held for EHS coding and to avoid patient billing. The EHS will notify the patient of test results.

b. If consent is obtained from the source patient, the EHS will document counseling and test results separately. The patient will sign a form indicating understanding that the test results will not be placed in the medical record, there will be no charge for testing, and the patient may determine who is to be informed of the test results when known. This record will be filed with the exposed employee's record.

c. Patient and health care worker test results will be reported to the EHS, who will notify the patient directly (or individual providing consent if the patient is incompetent) and the health care worker within 48 hours of confirmation of HIV test result. The EHS will provide the employee with the health care professional's written opinion within 15 days of completion of the investigation.

d. The hospital epidemiologist will be notified of all health care workers with positive test results for HCV, hepatitis B surface antigen, or HIV.

online from the CDC's *Morbidity and Mortality Weekly Report* (www.cdc.gov). Policy for pre- and postneedlestick testing for source of the contact and the exposed health care worker are outlined in the sample policy and procedure in Figure 2. All postexposure prophylaxis given to the exposed health care worker should be preceded with counseling and procedure directives according to the most recent organization and government guidelines.[9]

Equipment and Tagging Biological Hazards

Only freshly issued supplies and equipment should be used for each patient. From an infection control perspective, disposable equipment is preferable to reprocessed or sterilized items. Regardless of the type of equipment, all machine components should be cleaned after use according to protocol. Those that are reusable should be clean and dry, and identified and tagged appropriately. Disposable thermometer probes, suction catheters, and other invasive supplies should be used according to procedure and then discarded after use with each patient.

To reduce the risk of infection to other handlers or support workers, emergency department staff should outline a policy for tagging hazardous materials (e.g., red-bagging linen and contaminated waste, and red-boxing sharp object disposal and disposable equipment). Many institutions double-bag and color-code autoclavable bags that contain heavily soiled or infective trash or linen for predisposal decontamination. Although universal precautions always need to be maintained, staff should use special labels identifying high-risk body fluids.

Clearly marked, visible contaminated waste receptacles (e.g., trash or sharps) reduce the risk to patients and health care workers. Preferably, sharps containers should be mounted on the wall and ergonomically located on each side of the patient cubicle. Similarly, trash containers should be readily accessible and secured with a cover that is foot-operated rather than hand-accessed. Ideally, the trash container should be conveniently placed and of an appropriate size to handle large disposable items (e.g., bedpans, basins). All personnel should handle these trash and sharps containers with caution. The environmental control department is responsible for periodic removal of contaminated waste containers. The same precautions should be observed for postmortem handling of bodies as those used for live patients.

Communication and Staff Education

It is the responsibility of hospital management to provide education, training, and appropriate support for all emergency department and hospital employees to help prevent the spread of communicable diseases. The recent resurgence of multiple–drug-resistant organisms, such as *Staphylococcus aureus* and *M. tuberculosis*, introduce new concerns for patients, staff, and visitors, especially those who are immunosuppressed.

The control and transmission of pathogens is primarily an educational process and should be integrated into the annual training and orientation of all employees, including nonhealth care workers (e.g., environmental personnel, volunteers). Emergency personnel should understand and practice universal precautions to ensure individual personal protection and to protect patients, staff, and visitors against accidental exposure. Hospital policy and procedures for the isolation of potentially contagious patients, especially those with symptoms of airborne transmitted disease, should cover all points of entry, but especially the emergency department.

Universal Precautions

Universal precautions, as defined by the CDC, are designed to prevent the spread of microorganisms among patients, staff, and visitors (Figure 3). Their primary purpose is to interrupt the chain of infection by preventing the transmission of pathogens. Department guidelines and policy should outline procedures for properly educating personnel about the use of universal precautions. The increased incidence of AIDS and hepatitis has prompted OSHA and the CDC to develop, recommend, and enforce universal precautions by all health care workers, especially those in high-risk areas, or by any worker who has contact with blood or other body fluids (i.e., environmental personnel, volunteers). Strict enforcement of these precautions is essential to prevent the transmission of bloodborne pathogens and to provide adequate protection for health care workers (e.g., substitutions of gloves for hand-washing procedures is unacceptable; however, observation and evidence indicates that this may be a common practice among some health care workers). Visible reminders of routine and emergency procedures (e.g., signage and coworker enforcement) are recommended.

Hospital management should also provide other sources of information and quick reference for emergency procedures. Few personnel will always refer to the policy and procedure manual or remember each step of appropriate procedures; however, posted quick-reference lists for common emergencies are essential (Figures 4 and 5).

Managing HIV Exposure

The CDC suggests the following protocol for managing HIV exposure[3,10,11]:

- Significant exposure is suspected if a person is inoculated with contaminated blood or body fluid parenterally, is splashed with blood or fluid on the mucous membranes of the eyes or mouth, or has extensive cutaneous exposure to open skin lesions.
- The person considered to be the source of HIV infection should be assessed clinically and epidemiologically to determine the likelihood of HIV infection. If the assessment suggests that the patient is infected, the patient should be informed of the incident and requested to have serologic testing.
- The person possibly exposed to HIV infection should be serologically tested as soon as possible if the source person has AIDS, has evidence of HIV infection, or has declined to be tested.

If the recently exposed person has seronegative test results, that person should be retested in six weeks and subsequently on a periodic basis (i.e., 3, 6, 12 months) to determine whether transmission has occurred. Most infected individuals have seroconversion during the first 6 to 12 weeks. During follow-up, especially the first 6 to 12 weeks, the recently exposed individual and that person's employer or health service should observe the U.S. Public Health Service recommendations for the prevention of transmission of AIDS.[11]

Managing Hepatitis B Exposure

Hepatitis B is the second most common infectious disease reported to the CDC. Similar procedures must be used for hepatitis B exposure or after needlestick injuries. The source patient's blood should be tested for HBsAg. If results are positive, the health care worker should receive hyperimmune serum globulin. If the source patient tests negative, prophylaxis is not required. Testing after needlestick injuries may be required in some institutions to satisfy

Figure 3

Universal precautions

- Wash hands immediately after accidental contamination with blood or body fluids.
- Handle used needles and other sharp instruments with care. They should be considered potentially infective until properly cleaned or disposed of.
- Place intact needles, syringe units, and other sharp objects in designated puncture-resistant containers. Do not recap, break, or bend needles.
- Wear protective clothing when exposure to blood or body fluids is possible.
- Gloves alone may be required when handling contaminated articles. Other protection (e.g., masks, gowns, eye protection) may be necessary when there is risk of extensive contact or splashing.
- A 1 to 10 dilution of household bleach is an effective environmental decontaminant for blood spills.

Figure 4

Sample policy for spills (blood and body fluids) suitable for posting

- Wear gloves when managing blood or body fluid spills. For large spills, additional barrier protection (e.g., impervious apron or gown, mask, eyewear) must be used.
- Decontaminate the area with appropriate disinfectant (e.g., cavicide) sprayed over and around the spill.
- Contain the spill with a disposable towel or pad and discard the item into a trash container with a liner at least 3 mm thick to prevent leakage.
- After the initial cleanup, completely clean the area again with disinfectant.
- Refer to the policy and procedure manual for detailed instructions.

Figure 5

Sample infection control guidelines

- Body substance isolation requires the use of barriers for all contact with body substances (e.g., blood, urine, wound drainage, oral secretions, feces, emesis).
- Barriers consist of gloves, eye protection, mask, and gown.
- All patients' blood and body fluids are considered potentially dangerous.
- Any task that includes exposure or potential exposure to blood or body fluid requires the use of precautions (i.e., secretaries who are labeling blood, transporters who are transporting specimens, volunteers who may assist with procedures or transport).
- Procedure-specific dress codes are located in the emergency department in the Nursing Procedure Manual.
- The categories of isolation are AFB (acid-fast bacilli) isolation, respiratory isolation, and MDRO (multiple–drug-resistant organism) isolation.
- Eating food or drinking beverages in any patient care or work area is prohibited.

the burden of proof requirement for job-related exposure to hepatitis B infection.

Although OSHA is processing standards for occupational exposure to hepatitis B, HIV, and other bloodborne pathogens, health officials estimate there are approximately 300,000 new hepatitis B infections each year in health care workers, with an estimated 300 cases resulting in death. This trend is still occurring even though a vaccine has been available since 1982. A truly contaminated needlestick poses a 30% likelihood of transmitting hepatitis B, while the chance of contracting HIV is estimated at less than 1 in 200.[9,12] Evidence indicates that hepatitis B is still many times more potent and more easily transmitted than the HIV. This fact has prompted health officials to propose a standard that will require all health care workers to receive vaccination against the hepatitis B virus.

The Medical-Legal Perspective

Employment laws regarding AIDS in the workplace have evolved from a medical understanding of the disease and its transmission. Certain laws that pertain to rehabilitation and the physically disabled prohibit employers from discriminating against the employee or patient with a known or suspected communicable disease. Current trends qualify the employee with AIDS as an "individual with handicaps," and therefore offer protection under section 504 of the Rehabilitation Act. In *Arline v School Board*,[13] the U.S. Supreme Court held that persons with a contagious disease may be an "otherwise qualified handicapped person" within the scope of the Rehabilitation Act of 1973.

The legal aspects and ramifications of employer and employee rights, as applied to HIV-positive individuals, require careful scrutiny by management and a health care facility's legal counsel. When the facility develops a written policy on this issue, it should be communicated to the entire workforce. Outlining the rights of management, healthy employees, and employees with AIDS in an easily understood policy and step-by-step procedure should clarify the existing law and help apply it in specific work-related situations. Semiannual monitors and updates should align policy with recent literature and CDC guidelines. These controls should be the responsibility of the hospital infection control committee.

Reporting Communicable Disease

Federal, state, and independent accreditation agencies as well as individual hospitals require standard reporting systems for various diseases or suspected communicable diseases. If the hospital or its staff fail to report communicable diseases to designated health agencies for follow-up, the hospital and physicians may be at risk for legal action. Such responsibilities and penalties are explicitly delineated in each state's reporting statues. A current list of communicable diseases that must be reported to the state, as well as the process for this accountability, should be outlined in department policy.

Case Discussions

1

In the first case, *Sperling v The Industrial Commission,* the Illinois Court of Appeals ruled that the nurse was entitled to Worker's Compensation, even though she was unable to present proof of contact. The court found evidence that showed her work environment to be at increased risk of contraction of the disease and "more likely than not the disease resulted from contact with a carrier in the hospital."[14]

2

The patient brought legal action against the hospital and physicians. In that action, he alleged that several employees who treated his wound were not wearing gloves. He also alleged that his infection was the direct result of personnel violating the standard of universal precautions that were designed to protect the health care worker and the patient. Hospitals need to review their responsibility to protect employees and patients from unnecessary exposure to infectious diseases and pathogens. Developing policies and procedures and enforcing standards for mandatory universal precautions, for incident reporting, needlestick protocols, and employee education should assist in resolving exposure and liability concerns.

Key Points and Conclusion

Prevention is always the best medicine. As the incidence, potential, and concern of environmental and airborne pathogen transmission are increasing, standards for risk control should include an infection control risk assessment plan to identify patients, visitors, and health care workers at risk for infection. As specific organizational risk factors are determined, additional measures for prevention and control may be needed. Emergency departments considering new construction or renovation must consider issues related to airborne contaminants and air filtering systems. Because emergency departments represent the highest occupational exposure to infectious pathogens and patients are the most susceptible in this setting, a high priority status for infection control processes is required. Because the hospital administration must support special programs and facility renovation to control airborne infection, emergency department management must educate, communicate, and monitor universal infection control policies for all personnel and visitors.

Hepatitis B infection and transmission have led federal organizations to require vaccination of high-risk employees. Vaccination procedures, together with an education program for employees who may refuse the vaccine, and signed documentation and release of responsibility may emphasize the importance of such programs.

Hospital and department management must document all educational programs, environmental and personnel compliance, and treatment of exposure to protect all patients, visitors, and health care workers. This type of plan must be mandated to minimize risk and liability related to infection control.

References

1. Centers for Disease Control. Recommendations for prevention of HIV transmission in health-care settings. *MMWR Morb Mortal Wkly Rep* 1987;36(Suppl2F):1-18, (Suppl2S):2S-85.

2. Davidson SH. Multi-drug resistance and other "wildcard" diseases. *Healthcare Forum Journal*, January-February 1996.

3. Centers for Disease Control. *Guidelines for Preventing the Transmission of Mycobacterium Tuberculosis in Health Care Facilities.* Atlanta: Centers for Disease Control; 1994.

4. Streifel AJ. *Aspergillosis and Construction: Architectural Design and Indoor Microbial Pollution.* New York: Oxford University Press; 1988.

5. Burleson S, et al: Fighting TB: a program for air quality management. In: *Health Facilities Management.* Chicago: AHA; 1996.

6. Kuehn T. *Impact of Construction on Indoor Air Quality for Health Care Facilities.* Atlanta: American Society for Heating and Refrigeration Engineers; October 1996.

7. Centers for Disease Control. *Guidelines for Prevention of Nosocomial Pneumonia.* Atlanta: Centers for Disease Control; 1997.

8. American Institute of Architects and the Health Care Financing Administration. *Guidelines for Design and Construction of Hospital and Healthcare Facilities.* Washington, DC: AIA Press; 1996.

9. Centers for Disease Control. *Provisional Public Health Service Recommendations for Chemoprophylaxis after Occupational Exposure to HIV, by Type of Exposure and Source Material.* Atlanta: Centers for Disease Control; June 7, 1996.

10. Halpern J. Precautions to prevent transmission of human immunodeficiency virus infections in emergency settings. *JFN* September-October 1987:299.

11. Centers for Disease Control. Recommendations for preventing transmission of infection with HTLV-III/LAV in the workplace. *MMWR Morb Mortal Wkly Rep* 1985;682-686,691-695.

12. Voellker R. Health workers support proposed OSHA standard. *American Medical News*, October 1989.

13. *Arline v School Board*, Nassau County, Florida, Cit 480 US 273 (1987).

14. Can nurses sue for AIDS? *Patient Care Law*, December 1988/January 1989.

Additional Reading

American Institute of Architects and the Health Care Financing Administration. *Guidelines for the Construction of Hospitals and Healthcare Facilities.* Washington DC: American Institute of Architects; 1996.

Centers for Disease Control and Prevention. Case-control study of HIV seroconversion in health-care workers after percutaneous exposure to HIV-infected blood — France, United Kingdom, and United States, January 1988 – August 1994. *MMWR Morb Mortal Wkly Rep* 1995;44(50):929-933.

Centers for Disease Control and Prevention. Public Health Service statement on management of occupational exposure to human immunodeficiency virus, including considerations regarding zidovudine postexposure use. *MMWR Morb Mortal Wkly Rep* 1990;39(No. RR-1):1-14.

Centers for Disease Control and Prevention: Update: provisional Public Health Service recommendations for chemoprophylaxis after occupational exposure to HIV. *MMWR Morb Mortal Wkly Rep* 1996;45(22):468-472.

Core Curriculum on Tuberculosis: What the Clinician Should Know. 3rd ed. Atlanta: Centers for Disease Control 1994. Provisional Public Health Services Recommendations for chemoprophylaxis after occupational exposure to HIV, by type of exposure and source material, Atlanta, CDC, June 1996.

Morbidity and Mortality Weekly Report. Web page http://www.cdc.gov. Go to "Publications, Products, and Subscription Services," then to "Morbidity and Mortality."

Rehabilitation Act of 1973, 29 USC, Section 504, Public Law 93-1F, "The Rights of Individuals with Handicaps Under Federal Law," Washington, DC. (West 1985 and Supp 1988).

Voellker R. Hepatitis B: planned standard takes aim at confusion, risks. *American Medical News*, October 1989.

Chapter 17

Disaster Preparedness and Response

Ioliene B. Boenau, MD
Arthur G. Calise, DO
Joseph J. Calabro, DO, FACOEP

Disaster medicine principles are an important part of emergency medicine. Often it is the emergency physician who is best aware of the special situations that occur during a disaster and also is best suited to coordinate the medical response to a disaster situation. Disasters also place the emergency physician at increased medical-legal risk during the planning phase as well as during and after the disaster.

Hospital and Physician Preparedness

A disaster is an event that results in injury or loss of life that produces a demand for medical services which exceeds available resources.[1] Disasters include events such as hurricanes, earthquakes, or bombings but may also include events such as motor vehicle collisions involving multiple victims if the capabilities of the local hospital and EMS system are overwhelmed.

All hospitals and emergency departments are required to have policies and procedures governing daily operations.[2] However, whether these policies and procedures establish a standard of care for emergency physicians involved in a disaster situation is an important issue in disaster medicine. Clearly, emergency physicians have a central role in disaster preparedness and response. Although state and federal agencies help to prepare for and respond to disasters, they require time to arrive on the scene. They cannot substitute for a well-planned local response.[3]

Emergency Physician Liability

As one of the key members in the disaster response team, the emergency physician may be asked to participate on or chair the hospital's disaster committee. As a result, this gives the physician a direct administrative responsibility for the development and implementation of the hospital's disaster plan, and raises the issue of individual physician liability for the plan. Arguably, in this capacity, the physician is carrying out duties as directed by the hospital and as an agent of the hospital. Ideally, the individual should not be held personally liable for participating in these activities. At this point, such an argument has not been tested in the courts. Therefore, the physician should obtain contractually guaranteed relief from any liability resulting from participation on hospital or local disaster committees.

The emergency physician also has potential liability exposure related to participation on state committees, such as the State Emergency Response Commissions (SERC). In general, individual physicians who are members of these committees would be considered public employees or agents of the government entity and thus receive immunity or at least limited protection under state law. Much of the uncertainty regarding this issue has to do with the capacity in which the individual has participated on the committee. The law in most states provides immunity for those involved as direct government agents; however, the courts have yet to rule on whether emergency management activities are covered in this area. Many authors warn that the status of these issues is still undetermined in most states, and the emergency physician should be aware that immunity is far from guaranteed.[4]

Before accepting an appointment to a disaster-related committee, the emergency physician should seek counsel to determine whether state law provides any protection from exposure to liability. Local defense attorneys, hospital counsel, or emergency medical colleagues with extensive experience related to disaster medicine may be able to provide valuable information in this regard. State and local governments can be held liable if they fail to use all reasonable available information to plan for, prevent, or respond to a disaster.[4]

Currently, there are no established standards of care related to disaster medicine. Evidence regarding the standard of care comes from many sources. These include hospital policies, procedures, and bylaws, along with standards of care endorsed by the general medical community. The American College of Emergency Physicians has policy statements regarding disaster medicine.[5] However, no policy statement can possibly cover all circumstances that may be encountered during a disaster. Therefore, in civil litigation related to a disaster, the emergency physician will be held to general standards of practice.[6] As of 1990, there were no known cases in which a physician had been successfully sued for decisions made in a disaster situation.[7] The authors are not aware of any published cases since that time.

In general, the physician's legal duty is to provide care that is reasonable "under the circumstances." Therefore, when an actual disaster occurs, the physician and other medical personnel should document the presence and nature of the disaster conditions on all medical records. Should there be subsequent litigation or administrative proceedings, this precaution would support the argument that the physician's conduct must be evaluated in the context of the special circumstances that existed at the time of the disaster.[6]

JCAHO Standards

The Joint Commission on Accreditation of Healthcare Organizations (JCAHO) has also set standards for hospital preparedness in case of a disaster, either within the hospital or from an external source. The JCAHO requires that hospitals "establish and maintain a program to insure effective response to disasters or emergencies affecting the environment of care."[2] This includes implementing specific procedures and adjusting staffing and staff roles to the disaster situation.[2,8] JCAHO standards also dictate the need for physician participation in the execution of the plan on a semiannual basis either in response to an emergency or in planned drills.[2,9]

Emergency physicians participating in disaster preparedness should customize their disaster plans given locations and composition of their communities (e.g., chemical plants, earthquakes, or hurricane risk).[8,10] For chemical disasters, this task is made somewhat easier by the fact that all facilities using, storing, or manufacturing hazardous chemicals are mandated to report their inventory and any release of these chemicals to health care personnel.[11] Protective equipment for the emergency department staff in case of hazardous materials exposure should also be easily accessible and maintained in proper working order.[12]

In preparing a disaster plan, the emergency physician should know what types of additional staff members are available from neighboring institutions. In the past, some authorities have suggested creating in advance special medical/staff credentialing categories for providers from neighboring institutions so their staff will be able to deliver care in an emergency situation.[13] Another method would be to set up, in advance, an informal arrangement for the staffing of neighboring hospitals in an emergency situation.[2,14,15]

The disaster plan should also include provisions for distribution of patients among all area hospitals based on the services available at each institution. These arrangements should be made in advance so that patients may be directed to the appropriate facility directly from the site after triage. The hospital closest to the scene probably will receive the most patients (either as walk-ins or via EMS), thus stretching their resources to the limit. If the appropriate provisions for patient distribution are not in effect, the hospital and physician are placed at significant risk. Under these circumstances, physicians may not be able to provide adequate care because of the extremely high volume of patients.

EMTALA Standards

The standards of patient care and procedures for transfer are further defined by the Emergency Medical Treatment and Active Labor

Act (EMTALA).[16] Under this law, any patient presenting to a hospital emergency department must be evaluated and receive a medical screening examination to determine if an emergency medical condition exists, and the medical facility must generate a medical record.[17-21] This law applies to any patient who is transported by a hospital-operated ambulance, as this is considered to be an extension of the emergency department.[18] The law also applies to any patient who has arrived by any ambulance onto hospital property. Once the ambulance arrives on the hospital property, it may not be diverted without violating the statute.[18] Radio communication and medical direction do not, in itself, create an obligation under EMTALA. Likewise, a "field screening examination" by an EMT or paramedic would not meet the requirements of the EMTALA screening examination.[6]

EMTALA requires either stabilization of the patient's emergency medical condition or an appropriate transfer.[16,17,21-23] This requirement is particularly important as it relates to the disaster situation. Under the law, patients may be transferred to another institution if the benefits of transfer outweigh the risks. In a disaster, many patients may have an emergency medical condition but cannot receive adequate treatment because of the volume of patients presenting to the hospital. These patients may be legally transferred to another facility. The transferring facility is required to complete an affidavit certifying that the benefits of transfer outweigh the risks of transfer.[16] For other issues related to patient transfer, see Chapter 45, "EMTALA."

Neither the statute nor the related regulations contain any provision or exception for disaster situations. EMTALA is clearly applicable in the disaster setting. The best way to manage risk is to provide for optimal patient care through a carefully thought-out and implemented disaster plan.

Good Samaritan Laws

The issue of Good Samaritan laws with respect to disaster situations is extremely controversial. These laws were originally put into effect to provide protection for volunteers who came to the aid of the ill or injured person. Even though most states now have Good Samaritan laws, the protection afforded to health professionals varies from state to state.[24,25] In most cases, these laws cover only unplanned acts and afford little, if any, protection to medical personnel even in a disaster situation, particularly

if there is a preexisting duty to provide care.[24-29] In general, the more formalized the rescue plan, the less likely that physician actions can be defended on the basis of the Good Samaritan laws.[24] Despite the fact that there are cases in which EMS providers[30] and physicians[31] have been successfully defended using the Good Samaritan laws, no cases are reported specifically related to disaster situations. Remember: Good Samaritan laws provide limited protection from liability and do not prevent a plaintiff from filing a lawsuit. In situations where the statute does apply, Good Samaritan laws provide the defendant with protection from liability.[26,28,32]

Key Points and Conclusion

Even though emergency physicians are accustomed to anticipating the unexpected, the disaster response must be planned. Disaster situations place the emergency physician and the entire emergency medical system at increased risk of litigation. State laws provide little specific protection or exceptions for disaster situations. The emergency physician's best means to reduce risk in these situations is to structure, implement, and rehearse appropriate disaster plans and to document thoroughly the hospital course on the medical records.

References

1. Lewis CP, Aghababian R.: Disaster planning, Part I. Overview of hospital and emergency department planning for internal and external disasters. *Emerg Med Clin North Am* 1996;14:439-452.
2. Joint Commission on Accreditation of Healthcare Organizations.*Comprehensive Accreditation Manual for Hospitals: The Official Handbook.* Oakbrook Terrace, Ill: JCAHO; 1996.
3. Witt JL. National disaster plans crucial; local practitioner readiness essential. *Acad Emerg Med* 1995;2:1021-1022.
4. Hunter A: The liability of state and local governments for negligent emergency management. *Information Society* 1985;3(40):313-325.
5. Disaster Medical Services. ACEP Policy Statement, approved June 1985, reaffirmed March 1997. To obtain a copy, call (800) 798-1822, touch 6, or go to www.acep.org.
6. Frew SA. Emergency medical services legal issues for the emergency physician. *Emerg Med Clin North Am* 1990;8:41-55.
7. Bern AI. Disaster planning. In: Henry GL, ed. *Emergency Medicine Risk Management.* Dallas: American College of Emergency Physicians; 1991.
8. Friedman E. Coping with calamity. How well does health care disaster planning work? *JAMA* 1994;272(23):1875-1879.
9. Becker B. Disaster management: problems and solutions. *R I Med J* 1991;74:383-389.
10. Ricci E, Pretto E. Assessment of prehospital and hospital response in disaster. *Crit Care Clin* 1991;7:471-484.

11. Leonard RB, Calabro JJ, Noji EK, et al. SARA (Superfund Amendments and Reauthorization Act), Title III: implications for emergency physicians. *Ann Emerg Med* 1989;18:1212-1216.

12. Occupational Health and Safety Administration. 29 CFR 1910.120.

13. Dinerman N. Disaster preparedness: observations and perspectives. *J Emerg Nurs* 1990;16:252-254.

14. Haines ET, Weidenbach B. Planning for medical support of disasters. *Mil Med* 1993;158:680-683.

15. Gough AR, Markos K. Hazardous materials protections in ED practice: laws and logistics. *J Emerg Nurs* 1989;15:477-480.

16. Emergency Medical Treatment and Active Labor Act. 42 USC 1395dd(c)(1)(A)(2).

17. Frew SA, Roush WR, LaGreca K. COBRA: implications for emergency medicine. *Ann Emerg Med* 1988;17:835-837.

18. Diekema DS. Unwinding the COBRA: new perspectives on EMTALA. *Pediatr Emerg Care* 1995:11:243-248.

19. *Johnson v University of Chicago Hospital*, 982 F2d 230 (7th Cir 1992).

20. Rosenstein DN. Emergency stabilization for a wounded COBRA. *Issues Law Med* 1993;9:255-294.

21. Calderone BJ. COBRA's caveats. *J Health Care Risk Manage* 1996;9(3):251-295.

22. Pepe PE, Kvetan V: Field management and critical care in mass disaster. *Crit Care Clin* 1991;7:401-420.

23. Hall JL, Meyers MR: The COBRA patient anti-dumping law: part two: impact on physician liability. *Med Staff Counselor* 1992;6(3):29-35.

24. Northrop CE. How good samaritan laws do and don't protect you. *Nursing* 1990;20(2):50-51.

25. Shanaberger CJ. The good samaritan placed in jeopardy. *JEMS* 1989:58-60.

26. Curry RD. Why good samaritan laws don't work (and what you can do about it). *JEMS*, August 1985.

27. Regan T, ed: Letters. *JEMS*, October 1985.

28. Shanaberger CJ: So you want to be a good samaritan? *JEMS*, May 1987.

29. Shanaberger CJ. Look before you leap. *JEMS*, July 1988.

30. Ayres RJ Jr. Legal considerations in prehospital care. *Emerg Med Clin North Am* 1993;11:853-867.

31. Tammello AD. Does good samaritan immunity continue after crisis? *The Regan Report on Nursing Law* 1991;32(7).

32. Regan T, ed. Good samaritan laws. *JEMS*, May 1981.

Additional Reading

Auf der Heide E. *Community Medical Disaster Planning and Evaluation Guide*. Dallas: American College of Emergency Physicians; 1995.

Chapter 18

Managing Emergency Department Information

James C. McClay, MS, MD

Emergency medicine is an information-intensive business. Reducing risk in the emergency department requires systematic methods for handling what can be a flood of information. For example, radiographs and ECGs typically are interpreted first in the emergency department, then again later by a radiologist or cardiologist. If there are any discrepancies between these two readings, they must be accounted for. A systematic step-by-step approach to tracking these discrepancies is very important. Laboratory test results that become available after a patient is discharged also must be tracked. There are computerized systems available to track these tasks; however, the introduction of automation into the emergency department carries its own risks and responsibilities.

Case Studies

1

A 75-year-old woman comes to the emergency department complaining of a sore, swollen ankle, which she injured in a fall. She lives alone and is on multiple medications, including digoxin. Her daughter expresses concern that she may not be taking her medications properly, even though she checks on her fairly frequently. The woman does seem a little confused, admits to some nausea and a lack of appetite, and says that she has taken none of her medications that day. Ankle x-rays reveal no fracture. A digitalis level is ordered to address the daughter's expressed concerns. The woman

is discharged in the care of her daughter, who decides to take her mother home for the night. Several hours later, the test results come back and indicate a high digitalis level.

2

A 28-year-old laborer presents to the emergency department complaining of a sore shoulder. The emergency physician interprets the x-ray as negative and treats the patient conservatively for musculoskeletal pain. The next day, the radiologist overreads the x-ray. His report indicates four possible diagnoses, including cancer. This information is never conveyed to the patient. Six weeks later, he is diagnosed with bone cancer and ultimately dies.

Amended X-Ray

Any physician who reads x-rays will have a "miss rate," that is, will misinterpret some films. In published studies, emergency physicians misinterpret x-rays more often than radiologists do.[1] Although studies have shown that there is often disagreement between the readings of radiologists and emergency physicians, the critical factor is how often the difference in readings has any clinical impact. In one study of emergency services benchmarks,[2] emergency physicians ordered x-rays at a rate of 550 for every 1,000 patients seen. The average patient call-back rate for x-ray variances was about 0.5%, or 5 for every 1,000 patients seen. In another study comparing emergency physician and radiologist x-ray interpretations,[3] the incidence of disagreement was approximately 10%. However, the disagreement was clinically relevant in only 3.1% of the cases.

The process for having a radiologist interpret x-rays ordered by an emergency physician depends on a number of factors. X-rays ordered and taken during business hours are often interpreted by the radiologist before the films are returned to the emergency department. When the radiologist is not available, as is typically the case during the night and on weekends, the emergency physician receives the films from the radiology department, makes a preliminary interpretation (called a "wet reading"), and treats the patient based on this interpretation.

Sometimes, an emergency physician will provide a wet reading when the radiologist is busy doing a procedure or some other activity. In these situations, rather than delay patient care, films are sent immediately to the emergency department. The emergency physician reads the film and documents the interpretation on a form or slip of paper included in the x-ray jacket or on an emergency department log. The films are then returned to the radiology department for formal interpretation at a later time. The radiologist, with the emergency physician's wet reading in hand, then provides an "overread" (the final formal interpretation), usually the following morning. In some hospitals, this final reading does not occur until several days after the emergency physician's wet reading.

When the radiologist is available, a formal reading is dictated and later transcribed for inclusion in the patient's record. Because the patient has already been treated and released based on the emergency physician's interpretation of the x-ray, this reading by the radiologist usually does not directly affect patient care. However, the radiologist's reading may differ from the initial interpretation by the emergency physician. Without an amended x-ray system in place, there is no way to recognize this discrepancy.

When an emergency physician misreads an x-ray, the result can be patient injury — and liability. For example, missed fractures compose one of the major categories for dollars spent in emergency medicine-related litigation.[4] A "well-oiled" amended x-ray system can help minimize the potential for exposure to liability by quickly identifying misreads improving patient care. Any method used to compare the initial interpretation of the x-ray with the radiologist's final interpretation is essentially an amended x-ray system, and most hospitals now have some procedure for doing this. Most departments use slips of paper passed back and forth for this communication.

An amended x-ray system should contain the following components:

- An initial wet reading should be done by the emergency physician, documented on the medical record, and communicated in some form to the radiology department or recorded in an emergency department log.
- The radiologist should provide a rapid overread of the x-ray, with the benefit of the emergency physician's wet reading in hand. In general, if the overread function is to influence patient care, it must occur within a matter of hours after the x-ray is taken.
- If there is a significant difference between the emergency physician's and the radiologist's readings, the radiologist should contact the emergency department. This communication should include the results of the wet reading and the formal interpretation. The radiologist may make an immediate telephone call regarding missed readings that can result in patient morbidity or mortality (e.g., widened mediastinum).
- The emergency department staff should present the x-ray discrepancy and the patient's chart to the medical director or to the emergency physician on duty. That person will determine if some type of follow-up is indicated.
- The radiology department should keep track of discrepancies, and the emergency department should keep a log of wet readings. Emergency department staff should perform routine quality review to address and properly manage all amended x-ray interpretations.
- The emergency department staff should use an amended x-ray follow-up form so that any intervention can be documented in the patient's medical record (Figure 1). Some emergency departments document the amended reading directly on the original medical record with the appropriate identifiers (i.e., date and signature).
- Emergency physicians should consider instituting a periodic review of amended x-rays as part of the department's quality improvement program. This represents an outstanding educational opportunity, as well as a way to identify those physicians who need continuing education in this area.

Figure 1

Sample form for x-ray, ECG, and laboratory follow-up

HOSPITAL NAME HERE	Addressograph

Patient name _____ ED chart # _____

Telephone _____ Person notified _____

Date seen in ED _____ Time _____ Physician _____

ED discharge diagnosis _____

Follow-up required: ❏ X-ray ❏ ECG ❏ Laboratory ❏ Other

Results _____

EMERGENCY DEPARTMENT FOLLOW-UP

Date _____ Time _____

Reviewing physician _____

Action

Treatment

Attending physician _____

Nurse _____

X-Ray Follow-up

ED physician reading: ❏ Negative ❏ Positive
Comments

Radiologist reading: ❏ Negative ❏ Positive
Comments

ECG Follow-up

ED physician reading: ❏ Negative ❏ Positive
Comments

Internist reading: ❏ Negative ❏ Positive
Comments

Laboratory Follow-up

If variance identified, notify ED and send to ED immediately.

Reviewing physician, Emergency Department (Signature): _____

Distribution: Pink, Medical Records; White, ED File; Yellow, Attending Physician; Blue, ED Physician

There are computer programs that support these auditing functions electronically. However, the system still requires the emergency physician's input to determine whether the amended reading is significant and whether patient follow-up is necessary. These programs also require that the results be entered into the computer system regularly. Any automated system will require an interface with the radiology department computer system to transmit readings back and forth.

Amended ECG

Similar approaches are used for overreading of ECGs by cardiologists. Recent studies correlating initial and final ECG interpretations have found the incidence of clinically significant differences to be low.[4] In some hospitals, overreading of ECGs by cardiologists is not thought to be clinically helpful. In those hospitals, the emergency physician acts as the final reviewer.

However, malpractice claims associated with missed myocardial infarction continue to account for the largest dollar amount of any single category of emergency medicine-related claims (25.5%).[5] The literature clearly indicates a significant incidence of missed acute myocardial infarction ECG readings by emergency physicians. In addition, it is clear that the computerized ECG interpretations are not sensitive enough to identify myocardial injury in all cases. Therefore, each hospital should work with its emergency physicians to determine, based on the expertise of the emergency physician group, whether an amended ECG system will have a significant clinical impact.

Speed is essential in an amended ECG system. Next-day reviews are completely inadequate. Cardiologists can review emergency department ECGs by fax or by modem transmission. This can be accomplished routinely or whenever the emergency physician needs assistance or has questions regarding the interpretation or in specific clinical situations. Researchers have demonstrated that the time required for the entire process of faxing and interpretation (at times including clinical discussion with the cardiologist) is about five minutes.[6]

Laboratory Follow-Up

Most laboratory tests ordered during an emergency department visit are completed and reviewed by the emergency physician before the patient is discharged. However, with some tests, results are not expected until the following day or even later (e.g., cultures, thyroid testing, certain drug levels). The emergency department must establish a mechanism for reviewing any laboratory test results that are not reviewed by the emergency physician prior to patient discharge.

In general, these laboratory follow-ups are sent to the emergency department by the laboratory and are reviewed by nurses or other members of the staff. The staff will call for the patient's records then either review the case according to department protocol or give the results and the chart to the emergency physician, who will determine whether any follow-up is necessary.

For example, a patient presents with urinary tract symptoms. Urine culture test results typically are returned 24 to 48 hours later. The emergency physician or a person designated by the emergency physician will need to determine whether antibiotics were administered and whether the choice of antibiotic was appropriate based on the antibiotic sensitivity report.

Failure to respond to laboratory follow-ups can result in patient injury and exposure to liability. The hospital and the emergency physicians need an effective laboratory follow-up system to provide optimal patient care and reduce the risk of malpractice. Any time the emergency department staff or emergency physician provides a review of a laboratory test result, that action should be documented in the patient's medical record (Figure 1). At the most basic level in a large-volume emergency department, it may be helpful to computerize the flagging and matching of records and laboratory slips. The department would also benefit from an information system that tracks outstanding laboratory test results and immediately notifies staff when they are available and whether they are abnormal. Such a system can be used for both outstanding laboratory results and for the amended x-ray system but requires a computer interface to the laboratory and radiology systems. The emergency department staff enters the initial interpretation, then abnormal results are flagged and presented directly to the staff in the emergency department. Any outstanding laboratory test results that will be delayed should also be flagged. Again, the medical record and test results should be reviewed to determine whether contacting the patient is necessary.

Automating Emergency Department Information

Emergency medicine is in the information business. Pieces of data from test results and radiology reports need to be combined with the patient record generated in the department to create complete information about a patient encounter. Information needs to be collected and reported to internal and external agencies. When computers and computer communications are used to collect and process these data, a computerized information system is in place. Emergency department computer information systems include automated log books, patient tracking systems, medical record generation systems, and quality assurance databases.[7]

Analysis of errors and adverse events in patient care reveal a number of areas where information systems can contribute. These systems can improve individual physician decision-making, reduce systematic errors, and facilitate communication among parties, with support for the education of both the patient and the physician.

Preventing Adverse Events

Using a computerized drug interaction analysis system, researchers in one study[8] found that 9.7% of patients presenting to the emergency department appeared to be suffering from clinically significant interactions from medications being taken at the time of the visit. Medications initiated in the emergency department created clinically significant interactions about 3% of the time.

Online computerized medical records can reduce the incidence of such adverse events. By monitoring data entered into the medical record, computerized reminder systems can prompt caregivers of abnormal laboratory test results and potential medication errors.[9,10] A recently developed system allows physicians to interact with the order entry system and receive reminders of dosages, preferred medications, and warnings of potential drug interactions. This system has been shown to reduce the incidence of adverse drug events in inpatients.[11]

Discharge Instructions and Prescriptions

The emergency department discharge process is critical in providing optimal patient care. Not only does the patient need to understand treatment instructions, but also prescriptions have to be filled and taken correctly. In an investigation of the accuracy of discharge instructions and prescriptions, Johnson et al[12] found that discrepancies among prescriptions, discharge instructions regarding medication use, and the labels of the dispensed medications existed for 12% of the prescriptions. Half of these errors occurred in the original prescription.

Automated discharge instruction systems and prescription writing systems provide a method of supplying accurate, legible prescriptions and instructions. There has been a dramatic increase in use of computerized discharge instruction programs in emergency departments in the past several years.

Physician Charting and Information

Another major focus of commercial emergency department information systems has been the automated generation of the physician's portion of the patient's medical record. Documentation on the medical record is critically important in patient care and in the defense of subsequent malpractice litigation. A number of commercially available systems have been shown to improve documentation, including voice recognition systems,[13] dictated charts, and the use of structured forms.[14] All of these technologies help create records with better structure and improved legibility.

The use of structured data collection forms may also assist in patient assessment and management. Improved diagnostic accuracy has been attributed to computer-based decision support tools. The interaction between the clinician and the computer appears to encourage objective decision-making.[15]

Reference Systems

Computer systems also provide an effective source of continuing medical education,[16] and online reference systems have been shown to be beneficial to patient care.[17] At the most fundamental level, computerized databases of reference material allow immediate access to all of the textbooks commonly used by emergency physicians. In addition, there are several commercially available sources on nontextbook reference information, which are updated regularly. Used to answer questions and check facts, these reference materials can retrieve more detailed and more up-to-date information than is available in textbooks. The courts support the contention that physicians should check these reference sources if there is doubt about a particular issue.[18]

Risks Associated With Computerized Information Systems

Computer technology and information systems are not perfect. To use an information system, the emergency department staff must have contingency procedures in place to deal with the unavailability of the computer system. These down time procedures are common in all hospitals that use computerized registration systems. Every department will also need procedures to deal with test result reporting when the computer system is unavailable.

When patient records are collected in computer databases, some degree of confidentiality is sacrificed in exchange for the expectation that the data collected will be used to improve the quality of care. There must be controls in place to avoid breaches of patient confidentiality or inaccurate patient records.[19,20] Without controls in place, patient data can be used in improper ways.

Two recent incidents highlight this risk. In Maryland, it was alleged that certain HMO officials bribed state Medicaid officials for confidential patient information prior to bidding for contracts.[21] At a Boston hospital, a convicted child molester gained access to nearly 1,000 patient records with an improperly acquired password then made repeated calls to young children and their families.[22] The physical protection of patient data requires the institution of standard information systems policies and procedures that are beyond the scope of this chapter.[23]

Case Discussions

1

Although the elderly patient in this case came to the emergency department for evaluation of one complaint, she needed to be notified regarding another finding — the high level of digitalis in her blood. Digitalis levels typically are available before patient discharge. If this test is not flagged in some manner before discharge, the staff will not know that the patient and physician need to be notified. A method to contact the patient promptly at home needs to be in place if there is an abnormal test result. If there is a log of outstanding test results, the emergency department can follow up on the test if it is delayed in any way.

2

The patient in the second case study should have received explicit, documented discharge instructions telling him the follow-up procedures, that his x-ray film would be officially reported by the radiologist the following day, and by what methods he would be notified if the official report suggested a need for additional medical intervention.

Key Points and Conclusion

Information systems provide useful risk management tools in the emergency department. Systems for tracking x-ray interpretations help prevent problematic variations in the readings. A system for tracking outstanding laboratory test results simplifies the process of reviewing results and following up with patients. The addition of computerized systems in the emergency department also improves performance by assisting in documentation, monitoring for adverse events, and improving the legibility and completeness of patients' discharge instructions. Computerized reference systems are becoming a more important part of practice; however, computerized patient records must be secured from unwanted intrusion.

- Variances between initial and final x-ray interpretations represent a malpractice risk that needs to be addressed with an adequate amended x-ray system.
- Although ECG interpretations by emergency physicians are adequate in most cases, a system for contemporaneous cardiologist review of ambiguous ECGs should be considered.
- Follow-up systems for x-rays, laboratory test results, and ECGs can be automated with simple computerized log programs.
- The introduction of computerized systems in the emergency department offers a number of opportunities for improved physician and staff performance and risk reduction.
- Computerized information systems can introduce their own risks into the department and must be developed carefully.

References

1. Mayhue FE, Rust DD, Aldag JC, et al. Accuracy of interpretations of emergency department radiographs: effect of confidence levels. *Ann Emerg Med* 1989;18:826-830.
2. Premier Benchmarking Services. *Best Practices in Emergency Services Patient Flow.* Charlotte, NC: Premier, Inc; 1997.

3. Simon HK, Khan NS, Nordenberg DF, et al. Pediatric emergency physician interpretation of plain radiographs: is routine review by a radiologist necessary and cost-effective? *Ann Emerg Med* 1996;27:295-298.

4. Snoey ER, Housset B, Guyon P, et al. Analysis of emergency department interpretation of electrocardiograms. *J Accid Emerg Med* 1994;11(3):149-153.

5. Karcz A, Korn R, Burke MC, et al. Malpractice claims against emergency physicians in Massachusetts: 1975–1993. *Am J Emerg Med* 1996;14:341-345.

6. Bertrand CA, Benda RL, Mercando AD, et al. Effectiveness of the fax electrocardiogram. *Am J Cardiol* 1994;74:294-295.

7. Aghababian RV, Williams KA, Holbrook JA, et al. Computer applications in quality assurance. *Emerg Med Clin North Am* 1992;10:627-647.

8. Herr RD, Caravati EM, Tyler LS, et al. Prospective evaluation of adverse drug interactions in the emergency department. *Ann Emerg Med* 1992;21:1331-1336.

9. McDonald CJ, Hui SL, Smith DM, et al. Reminders to physicians from an introspective computer medical record. A two-year randomized trial. *Ann Intern Med* 1984;100:130-138.

10. Rind DM, Safran C, Phillips RS, et al. Effect of computer-based alerts on the treatment and outcomes of hospitalized patients. *Arch Intern Med* 1994;154:1511-1517.

11. Bates DW, O'Neil AC, Boyle D, et al. Potential identifiability and preventability of adverse events using information systems. *J Am Med Inform Assoc* 1994;1:404-411.

12. Johnson KB, Butta JK, Donohue PK, et al. Discharging patients with prescriptions instead of medications: sequelae in a teaching hospital. *Pediatrics* 1996;97:481-485.

13. Bergeron B, McClay J. Voice recognition: Current status as an enabling tool for clinical data capture. *Healthcare Inform Manage* 1996;10(3):67-72.

14. Wrenn K, Rodewald L, Lumb E, et al. The use of structured, complaint-specific patient encounter forms in the emergency department. *Ann Emerg Med* 1993;22:805-812.

15. de Dombal FT. Computers, diagnoses and patients with acute abdominal pain. *Arch Emerg Med* 1992;9:267-270.

16. Papa FJ, Meyer S. A computer-assisted learning tool designed to improve clinical problem-solving skills. *Ann Emerg Med* 1989;18:269-273.

17. Pugh G, Tan J. Computerized databases for emergency care: what impact on patient care? *Methods Inf Med* 1994;33:507-513.

18. Skolnick M. Expanding physician duties and patients rights in wrongful life: *Habeson v Parke-Davis, Inc. Med Law* 1985;4:283-298.

19. Donaldson M, Lohr K, eds. *Health Data in the Information Age: Use, Disclosure, and Privacy.* Institute of Medicine. Washington, DC: National Academy Press; 1994.

20. Byars W. Legal challenges created by computerized medical records. *Top Health Inform Manage* 1996;16(4):61-65.

21. Valentine P. Medicaid bribery alleged: HMPOs, Md. agency implicated by state. *Washington Post* 1995:B1.

22. Brelis M. Patients' files allegedly used for obscene calls. *Boston Globe* 1995:A1.

23. Bakker A. Security in medical information systems. *Yearbook in Medical Informatics.* 1993:52-60.

Chapter 19

Clinical Practice Guidelines

Marilyn Bromley, RN
Peter J. Mariani, MD, FACEP

Traditionally, physicians have enjoyed a great deal of professional autonomy in practicing the art of medicine. However, the explosion of medical costs has added pressure to improve the practice of medicine by individual physicians and by the systems within which they operate.

Although most health care consumers believe that medical practice is firmly grounded in scientific research, this generally is not the case. According to the former Office of Technology Assessment, only about 10% to 20% of all medical tests and procedures have been proved effective in clinical trials. This leaves a great number of current medical practices of uncertain benefit being provided at substantial costs.[1]

High-quality treatment must not only be done; it will be necessary. When researchers at the RAND Corporation evaluated several common medical procedures for appropriateness, they were surprised to find substantial rates of inappropriate care. Research conducted at Dartmouth College consistently revealed wide regional variations in treatment rates for numerous medical procedures.[2]

In order to place value on health care services, there must be some notion of what is necessary and appropriate with respect to the diagnosis, treatment, or prevention of medical conditions. The use of clinical practice guidelines is intended to bring consistency to the evaluation of the appropriateness of health care services. Additionally, the establishment, dissemination, and enforcement of clinical standards may be relevant for legal purposes, especially as evidence of fault or lack of fault in medical malpractice cases.

Just as it is imperative that a physician become knowledgeable and conversant in medical terminology, it is important that today's emergency physician know and understand the terms associated with clinical policies, how they are developed, the questions that should be asked before implementing a clinical policy, and what risks are associated with clinical policy development and implementation.

Definitions

The emergency physician is faced with a plethora of policies on how to practice medicine. Clinical practice guidelines, practice parameters, critical pathways/protocols, clinical indicators, care maps, utilization guidelines, outcomes management, demand management, case management, and disease management are all terms frequently heard. Some of these are familiar or speak for themselves. Some of the terms associated with clinical policies may be used interchangeably. However, there are some subtle differences.

Clinical policies/practice parameters/clinical guidelines are systematically developed statements to help the practitioner make appropriate health care decisions for specific clinical circumstances. Clinical guidelines should be based on graded, scientific literature review. When such literature is not available, the developing body should reach consensus on issues and must submit the draft to peer and expert review and field testing before completion.

The Institute of Medicine (IOM) committee on clinical practice guidelines outlines five major purposes for guidelines[2]:

- To assist in clinical decision-making by practitioners
- To educate individuals or groups
- To assess and assure the quality of care
- To guide allocation of resources for health care
- To reduce the risk of legal liability for negligent care

The Joint Commission on Accreditation of Healthcare Organizations (JCAHO) defines clinical guidelines as care guidelines that are statements of professionally appropriate care processes that have been derived from either empirical research or professional consensus. They are not outcome indicators but can be used as follows:

- As tools in peer review of individual cases of adverse outcome
- In evaluating the appropriateness of surgery or other invasive procedures
- To assist in developing process indicators of quality
- For monitoring and evaluation activities
- As benchmarks for reviewing the appropriateness of the use of ancillary services

JCAHO drafts standards for care but does not develop clinical policies. The JCAHO publication *Abstracts of Clinical Care Guidelines* is designed to assist in the dissemination of clinical care guidelines.[3]

Critical pathways/clinical pathways are procedurally based, tend to be inpatient focused, and coordinate the activities of multidisciplinary teams. The only decision-making involved in the use of critical pathways/clinical pathways is whether the patient enters the pathway. Once the decision is made to use a particular pathway for a certain patient, management of the patient is clearly delineated and addresses what should be done and in what sequence it should be done.

Clinical protocols are essentially the consensus guide for physicians and nurses to use in treating specific disease problems that may occur relatively often. Clinical protocols are measurement-intensive and follow more closely what might be found in a research protocol. The protocols may change rapidly because they are usually dealing with a cutting-edge treatment.

Disease management is generally defined as a comprehensive, integrated approach to a systematic way of treating patients with similar characteristics. Included in the management of a specific disease may be practice guidelines, treatment algorithms, clinical pathways, or some combination. The use of a guideline is not in and of itself a disease management program. It is an essential element.[1]

Outcomes management aligns with information technology and scientific evidence to produce a rational framework of medical decision-making. David Nash, MD, of the Office of Health Policy Outcomes at Thomas Jefferson University is quoted as saying: "Accurate data analysis is the *sine qua non* of outcomes management. 'If you can't measure it, you can't improve it.' "[4]

Utilization guidelines are guidelines developed to determine the need for certain medical services. These include hospital admission, continued stays, discharge, and outpatient and rehabilitation services. These guidelines are most often used in managed care.

Credentialing guidelines are guidelines or parameters by which a determination is made to allow a physician to be granted privileges at a hospital or to join a managed care organization (MCO). Review of adherence to clinical policies may be a consideration in credentialing or recredentialing. Physicians who are decredentialed or "deselected"[5] by a hospital, physician group, or MCO might also assert causes of actions against the guideline developers if the guideline or its use was instrumental in a decision against the practitioner.

Guidelines for the provision of clinical care have been linked in recent years to almost every major problem and proposed solution on the U.S. health policy agenda. Those who are involved in the development of practice guidelines hope that the use of guidelines will raise the quality of care, improve both the real and perceived value obtained for health care spending, clarify the acceptable and unacceptable variation in medical practice, and reduce the risk of malpractice litigation.

The How and Who of Clinical Policies Development

According to the author of an article in the April 1997 issue of *Journal of Family Practice*,[6] clinical policies have become a constant feature of the health care landscape. They are showing up in all forms and at an alarming rate.

How Should Clinical Practice Guidelines Be Developed and Used?

The IOM has specified the following attributes that the content of a clinical practice guideline should be:

- Substantive
- Valid
- Reliable
- Clinically applicable and flexible

The clinical policy should include the descriptions of the strength of the evidence and expert judgment behind them. The guidelines must be unambiguous. Guidelines must include statements about when they should be reviewed to determine whether revisions are warranted given new clinical evidence or professional consensus.[2]

How a clinical practice guideline is developed can strongly affect its potential for effective use. The guideline must include a statement of what constitutes minimum or required care for particular clinical problems. Guidelines that are based on available scientific evidence and that are clear, specific, and developed by a reputable process should carry greater weight in malpractice decision-making than vague, nonspecific guidelines that lack documentation and careful referencing. Guidelines that underscore their recommendations with reference to a strong foundation of scientific evidence should be particularly helpful.

Physicians should develop and maintain competency at evaluating clinical policies for soundness. Providing student physicians with these skills should be a goal of undergraduate and graduate medical education. Such skills are no less important than the traditional goal of competency in evaluating journal articles and research studies.

Physicians, physician educators, and administrators should be responsible for making trainees and staff cognizant of clinical policies relevant to their practices. Included may be guidelines issued by entities outside a physician's specialty. Staff should consider adapting selected clinical policies for incorporation into department policy and procedures. If administrators are aware of guidelines issued from their own specialties that might have implications for wider hospital practice, the hospital's risk management department, legal counsel, or policies committee should be notified.

Who Develops Clinical Practice Guidelines?

Several organizations have had significant roles in the development, implementation, evaluation, and use of guidelines, from the Agency for Health Care Policy and Research (AHCPR), U.S. Preventive Services Task Force, specialty societies, MCOs, individual hospitals, physicians and physician groups, private utilization management firms, and consulting firms, such as Millman & Robertson, Inc.

Federal health agencies have taken a leading role in fostering the development of guidelines. The Health Care Financing Administration, for example, has sponsored research on the length of hospital stays. It underwrote the RAND Corporation development of appropriateness criteria in the 1980s. The Physician Payment Review Commission urged Congress to create an entity to ensure that taxpayers received their money's worth from rapidly rising Medicare and Medicaid expenditures.

It is not surprising that professional societies are involved in guidelines development. A 1991 General Accounting Office survey revealed that the two primary reasons for specialty society involvement in the development of clinical policies were to improve quality of care and to defend against outside forces.[2] The second objective may enhance efforts to reduce malpractice and its associated costs, to encourage greater uniformity in health care delivery, and to counter conflicting guidelines developed by other specialty societies. Specialty societies view clinical policy development as part of their role in leadership, research, professional education, policy development, and enhancement of standards for medicine. The American Medical Association (AMA) concurs that physician organizations need to be involved in guideline development "to ensure that practice parameters are properly developed and that quality improvement, rather than cost containment, serves as the foundation for their development."[7] The American College of Emergency Physicians (ACEP) began its clinical policies program in 1990. The protocol and process used to develop clinical policies have met all of the criteria set forth by the IOM and the AMA.

How Good Are Efforts to Develop Clinical Practice Guidelines?

Emergency physicians today, faced with a multitude of clinical policies developed by a multitude of organizations, must be able to assess a policy and its development. These two steps are paramount in the risk and legal liability assumed when adapting a clinical policy into practice. Beyond medical malpractice, the more fundamental question remains: which of several applicable guidelines may best help provide quality emergency care?

To begin to address that dilemma, look at the strengths of the current efforts in clinical policy development. The first strength is their pluralism. The commitment of public and private sector resources helps protect guidelines development from real or perceived domination by narrow interests.

The second strength of guideline development is that policymakers have endorsed the undertaking: funding is increasing and "how-to-do-it " conferences and similar products have been multiplying. Recently, the AHCPR, a division of the Department of Health and Human Services, announced that it will collaborate with two private sector organizations to develop a comprehensive Internet-based source for clinical practice guidelines. The new National Guideline Clearinghouse (NGC) will make available a full range of current guidance on treatment for specific medical conditions. Under the plan, AHCPR, the American Association of Health Plans, and the AMA will work jointly to develop the new guideline clearinghouse.[8]

Third, guidelines are gaining credibility. Expectations about the rigor needed to develop sound guidelines are increasing. Recently, the AMA developed a program to review and approve clinical guidelines. The criteria for approval include definitions of what constitutes an appropriate development panel, the level of scientific review of all available literature required, expert review, field testing, and the mechanism that must be in place to review and rewrite clinical policies periodically or as new information becomes available.

The fourth strength is that researchers, clinicians, educators, and managers of health care are being stimulated to consider how guidelines and other efforts to improve the quality and efficiency of health care can support and complement each other. For guidelines to improve the practice of medicine, they must be:

- Based on the best synthesis of scientific evidence and expert judgment
- Clinically specific so that they can be appropriately applied
- Able to improve health by eliminating both underuse and overuse of resources
- Placed in the public domain

ACEP was one of the first associations to develop joint policies with other specialty societies. ACEP's Clinical Policies Committee also reviews clinical policies developed by others to determine if there is a conflict with an ACEP policy or if the clinical policy could be abstracted and used by the emergency physician.

What Are Some of the Limitations of Current Efforts?

The pluralism of clinical policy development has a negative aspect as well. The lack of cohesiveness of the diverse groups developing guidelines can lead to haphazard development and dissemination. A recent article in *Lancet*[9] indicated that guidelines produced by some managed care plans, specialty societies, or proprietary firms are likely to be subject to stringent bottom-line concerns about the cost of producing the guidelines; guidelines paid for by firms that have products to sell probably will devote more effort to addressing how those products can be used as opposed to how they should not be used; guidelines produced by single-specialty societies are likely to emphasize the overuse of services provided by those societies, and guidelines paid for by proprietary firms are not likely to be placed in the public domain.

A reasonable assumption is that government efforts to advance the use of practice guidelines will be concerned foremost with the public good. However, concerns have arisen regarding inappropriate use of guidelines in the private sector (e.g., by MCOs, insurance companies, or utilization management firms). The lack of quality control over the methodology of the procedures is a serious drawback for all organizations involved in policy development. Potential assessors of guidelines may have a difficult time or have no real means to judge the soundness of material produced by different groups with different approaches. The use of guidelines developed by those who would implement them has been called into question in a number of ways. Case law has criticized reliance by insurers on their own guidelines, no matter how carefully they were developed.[10]

Another weakness is that proof is still lacking that these guidelines improve quality of care and cost-effectiveness. Development of definitions for data to measure efficacy is problematic. Many institutions do not have consensus internally about what goes into a certain data field. Trying to look at this issue nationally exacerbates the problem of reviewing data that are not consistent and not clearly defined by all.

Risk Management, Medical Liability, and Practice Guidelines

Given the context in which clinical guidelines are being developed and promoted, the emergency physician is right to be concerned about medical liability. Any strategy to apply clinical guidelines must take into consideration the opportunities and obstacles presented by risk management programs and medical liability reforms. The strategy must also recognize the complexities introduced by continuous quality improvement (CQI) principles and by the existence of multiple and potentially conflicting guidelines.

For risk management programs, clinical practice guidelines offer several potential benefits. Wider application of good guidelines should improve clinical performance and thereby reduce the number of adverse events. Physicians should find that well-developed condition-specific or treatment-specific guidelines help them communicate with their patients and, as a result, reduce their liability risk.

Guidelines that define appropriate care for specific clinical conditions can help determine whether identified adverse events are the result of poor care rather than the unfortunate consequence of medical uncertainty.[2] Sound guidelines should provide a strong basis for distinguishing between negligent and nonnegligent care. This, in turn, should help prevent unjustified malpractice claims, resolve justified claims earlier, and improve decisions for cases that go to trial. Increasing numbers of physicians have confidence in clinical guidelines and expect that their documented compliance will help protect them against unwarranted claims of malpractice.

The legal theory of liability provides a deterrent to wrong behavior as well as a form of redress for such behavior when it occurs. To influence behavior, the liability strategy relies on economic penalties and fear. The role of guidelines is to motivate and assist decision-making prospectively in the case of clinicians and retrospectively in the case of those who evaluate claims of malpractice. In one study of adverse medical events and related litigation,[11] existing guidelines could have provided relevant evidence for an estimated 20% of medical injuries identified. Because the availability of practice guidelines is growing, this percentage is also likely to grow.[2]

In addition, for guidelines to influence legal decision-making, courts would have to accept guidelines as important evidence of the standard of care.

Antitrust Liability

A guideline that would limit the practice of a particular procedure to a particular medical specialist might be alleged to damage physicians or physician groups through restraint of trade. If a clinical policy references training requirements that might actually limit a physician's ability to perform a procedure, this policy might run the risk of being considered in violation of antitrust statutes.

A court may view a particular guideline or guidelines in general as procompetitive and, therefore, of no antitrust concern. The court will also determine whether alleged antitrust repercussions of a guideline are harmful to overall competition or to only a few individual competitors.[12] If the latter is true, the antitrust action will likely fail. Courts have generally approved the good faith efforts by industry to set and maintain standards of quality.[13] The guidelines movement in medicine comes under this rubric. In evaluating potential antitrust violations, a clinical policy guideline will be subject to "rule of reason" analysis rather than the more difficult *per se* test, unless the guideline establishes outright price-fixing or dividing of markets. Additionally, if a medical specialty society or other entity does not have the capacity to force or coerce its members, or anyone else, to conform to the guideline, antitrust liability is negligible.

Antitrust protection can extend to the efforts of medical societies to influence government adoption of certain guidelines. For example, the Noerr-Pennington doctrine, rooted in the First Amendment, holds that concerted efforts to influence government action are protected from antitrust liability. If a medical specialty society or other organization were to petition the government regarding adoption of a guideline, the organization's discussions, meetings, and publications pursuant to this would probably be immune from antitrust claims. Under Noerr-Pennington, "influence" does not include "coercion." Threats of action, however, such as withholding of medical services pending resolution of reimbursement disputes, are not immune. An organization should also be aware that quasi-government entities may not be covered by this doctrine (e.g., a medical specialty society "petitioning" JCAHO on some issue). If an organization assists a state's enactment of guideline legislation, such activity may be immune from antitrust concerns under the state action doctrine. Such immunity may be more likely the more the state oversees the organization's efforts to assist state legislators.[12]

Legislation, Regulation, and Public Policy

The eagerness of state legislatures to use clinical policies parallels that of the medical specialty societies in generating them. More than a dozen states as well as the federal government have guidelines legislation enacted or proposed.[14] Maine's legislation has received much discussion in the medical literature.[15] The experience of that state, however, is not easily applied to others. Compared with other jurisdictions, Maine has been characterized to have the qualities of "smallness," absence of medical "town and gown" animosity, less professional jealousy among physicians, an efficient legislature, and a less litigious population.[16] In Maine, in a medical malpractice lawsuit, only the defense may introduce an approved clinical policy guideline. The defendant must prove by a preponderance of evidence that the guideline was followed. To date, no court cases have involved the specific guidelines. However, the primary point of the Maine effort was not to alter a medical malpractice climate but rather to alter physician practice behavior.[16,17] One effect has been improved communication among physicians and medical societies and, in particular, better information outreach to physicians located in rural regions of the state.[17]

Variations on components of clinical policy guideline legislation have been incorporated by other states' guidelines legislation. Maryland's legislation requires more than 60% of specialists affected by a clinical policy guideline to first approve it before its adoption[18] (compared with Maine's 50% standard). States differ on whether guidelines may be introduced with equal ease by plaintiff or defendant and on the evidentiary weights conferred to guidelines. Such weighting varies from presumption of nonmalfeasance rebuttable by a preponderance of evidence as proposed in New York,[19] or by clear and convincing evidence as proposed in the U.S. Senate,[20] to dispositive evidence and absolute defense, as in Minnesota,[21] where such a provision appears to establish strict or per se immunity.[22]

Malpractice

Medical malpractice has been described as deviation from the accepted medical standard of care that causes injury to a patient for whom a clinician has a duty of care. Medical specialists, including emergency physicians, are required to conform to the standard of care applicable to the particular medical condition involved. A breach of duty occurs when the physician fails to conform to that standard. When a physician breaches the duty owing to the patient, that physician becomes legally responsible for all of the damages that reasonably flow from that breach.[23]

It is the duty of the emergency physician to exercise the degree of skill ordinarily demonstrated under similar circumstance by the members of the specialty in good standing and to use reasonable care and diligence along with the best judgment in the application of skill to the case. The emergency physician is not required to exercise the right degree of skill and care possible.

A physician claiming to be a specialist is bound to exercise not only that degree of skill exercised by the average practitioner, but also the special degree of skill and knowledge possessed by specialists in the same field.[23]

In case law, the accepted medical standard of care has been described as that degree of care delivered by physicians of good standing in the same or similar locality as the defendant physician. More recently, case and statutory law have moved away from geographically delimited standards of care to national standards of care, particularly for specialists. Geographic factors may be considered if they affect the availability of medical facilities and resources. Industry customs may be cited to help juries and courts assess what is reasonable, but evidence of customary practice carries far less weight than it has in the past in medical malpractice.

Assuming that good guidelines can be used in everyday medical practice and as a basis for evaluating performance, what else is necessary to accord guidelines greater weight in determining the legal standard of care? The following are options for recognition of guidelines in medical malpractice law[2]:

Source of Recognition
- Legislation
- Rules of evidence developed within or by the judiciary and promulgated through administrative rule-making
- Judicial precedent

Authoritative Status

- Guidelines developed by a specific entity are authoritative.
- Guidelines developed according to specified criteria are authoritative.
- Judges have case-by-case discretion to determine whether a guideline is authoritative.
- Juries can decide as matter of fact whether a guideline is authoritative.

Right to Use

- Only the defendant can cite and use guidelines as a shield to claim immunity from liability for care delivery in accordance with guidelines.
- Only the plaintiff can cite and use guidelines as a sword to claim malpractice by the defendant.
- Both defendants and plaintiffs can cite guidelines.

Weight

- A guideline provides *per se* or conclusive definition of applicable standard of care.
- A guideline raises a rebuttable presumption; proof to counter this presumption can be offered.
- A guideline can be considered as some evidence of an applicable standard.

A lack of legislative imprimatur does not mean that guidelines cannot and will not be increasingly used to define the standard of care. Judges are in a position to consider the reputation of an organization that develops guidelines. As the development and assessment of guidelines become more firmly grounded and more recognized in practice, judges and juries should eventually give them greater weight.[2]

The state of Massachusetts created a risk management unit in the state's medical licensing and discipline agency and requires physicians to participate in a quality assurance program as a condition of licensure. Guidelines feature prominently in the quality assurance program, and the statute includes certain requirements for their content and for the development process. Physicians who participate in the program are entitled to reductions in malpractice insurance premiums from the state's liability insurers. Emergency medicine is one of the two specialties that have developed guidelines that initially qualified participating physicians for a 20% discount in liability premiums. Also, one of the major malpractice carriers has adopted all of ACEP's clinical policies into its "risk prescription modules."

Emergency physicians must make it a priority to keep abreast of clinical policy development, especially in the field of emergency medicine. Rest assured that plaintiffs' attorneys will. Legal experts in this area have stated that, in most instances, it is not adherence to the policy that is the problem, it is the ignorance that such a policy exists.

Dissemination of information or guidelines is, by itself, insufficient to induce use of the information or to change behavior. In fact, excessive distribution of information to physicians can lead to information overload. Nonetheless, bringing guidelines to their attention and making them available as requested or required are precursors to more direct efforts to influence behavior.

Methods to improve physician compliance with guidelines are being investigated. For example, a computerized charting system that incorporated guidelines as online prompts for appropriate interventions improved treatment of health care workers who were exposed to body fluids.[24] After its discontinuation, many care parameters returned to preintervention baselines, leading investigators to conclude that guidelines work best as "time of care"[25] devices rather than as instruments of more general provider education. A cooperative effort between the New York State Department of Health and the New York Chapter of ACEP also examined the effect of computerized templates in the emergency department.[26]

Physician Developers of Clinical Policy

Developers of guidelines should expect to be treated as being legally accountable for exercising due care in formulating their recommendations and in updating them in light of new knowledge.

Apart from being named individually in lawsuits, guideline committee members might encounter additional problems. When the substance, soundness, or intent of a clinical policy is argued in a trial, the committee members may be subpoenaed to testify. There is, however, legal precedent that where learned treatise evidence is in dispute, it stands or falls on its own merits. Attempts to subpoena the authors or researchers usually fail.[27]

For a developer or third-party user of a guideline to be held liable for medical harm to a patient, four questions must be answered positively, as follows:

- Do the guidelines developers or review

programs applying guidelines have a duty of care to patients?

- Has the duty been breached?
- Was there injury?
- Was the breach of duty a proximate cause of the injury?

Prudent practice dictates that promulgators should assume that they may be held accountable in the future. Under traditional doctrines of negligence, if an entity develops a clinical policy, it should take measures to develop it well. The developers should be aware of existing criteria that determine the appropriateness of the development of a clinical policy. Given the liability risks associated with guideline promulgation, physicians and other professionals who serve on guideline development committees should consider the risk of individual liability if the guideline is later implicated in patient harm. Participants may want to consider requesting indemnification from the sponsoring organization and determining whether their committee activity is covered under their malpractice or other insurance policies.

When possible, guidelines efforts within the hospital should proceed under the auspices of quality assurance, total quality management, or peer review to maximize the possibility that statutory immunity and nondiscoverability might apply. Such guidelines should be deemed clearly advisory, with final adoption and enforcement by entities so empowered within the hospital.

Review programs have more to worry about than independent developers of guidelines, such as medical specialty societies. Case law on this issue is scant, and no specialty societies have been involved in litigation for clinical policy development.

From the Courts

The case of *Martin v Prudential Health Care Plan, et al* arose from the death of the plaintiff's 51-year-old wife, in 1989, as a result of cardiac arrest she suffered during a cardiac catheterization procedure. Mr. Martin alleged that the procedure should not have been carried out in a hospital that was not equipped with an intra-aortic balloon pump or cardiac surgery facility, and that they should have been made aware of that fact. An expert witness for the plaintiff testified that the absence of such facilities was a deviation from good and accepted standards of care, citing a document entitled, "ACC/AHA Guidelines for Cardiac Catheterization and Cardiac Catheterization Laboratories," which was published in 1991. The trial judge barred any use of the published guidelines at the trial, stating that they had not been published until two years after the incident. The trial court's decision was reversed. The appeals court found that there was no question that the guideline document was a "reliable authority" and, despite its publication two years after Mrs. Martin's death, it reflected the standard of care that existed in 1989.[28]

In the case of *Cunningham v Fredonia Regional Hospital* (10th Circuit Court of Appeals), Mrs. Cunningham complained of chest pain to her physician and later in the same day to her physician's partner. The partner recommended that she go to the hospital and ordered a prescription pain shot for her at the hospital. When she arrived at the hospital, she was examined by a nurse, given the shot, and sent home. She died of a heart attack later that evening.

The patient's estate sued the hospital, alleging that the hospital failed to follow its own chest pain policy in assessing the patient's condition. The hospital's chest pain policy required that a physician, rather than a nurse, examine any patient with "life-threatening symptoms of chest pain." The hospital argued that the applicable policy was its emergency illness policy, which required examination by a physician of an emergency patient only if the patient showed symptoms of an emergency illness or injury. The district court agreed and ordered summary judgment for the hospital, noting that the chest pain policy applied only when the patient presented chest pain symptoms that were potentially life-threatening.[29]

Failure to follow established protocols requiring the identification of the type of contrast dye to be used in a myelogram procedure was a significant factor in a recent federal court decision. The case, *Musselman v E.R. Squibb & Sons, Inc dba Bristol Meyers Squibb Pharmaceutical Groups and Bracco Diagnostics, Inc*, was decided in an opinion issued May 5, 1997. This case provides a recent example of the emerging trend in litigation to rely on protocols in establishing negligence in cases of medical misadventure.[30]

In *Conerly v State of Louisiana et al*, decided on March 3, 1997, the plaintiff alleged that the hospital was both vicariously negligent for the actions of its employees and directly negligent because of its alleged failure to provide adequate guidelines and to enforce the existing guidelines. This resulted in the death of their child the day after her fifth birthday. A significant issue on appeal was the validity of the plaintiffs' claims that the hospital and the state were directly negligent because of a failure to provide adequate policies and a failure to enforce its existing policies. The trial court ruled that the nurses and physicians were negligent, but it ruled that the policies and operation of the hospital were reasonable.[31]

A recent class action complaint filed in April 1997 in the Supreme Court of the State of New York questions the use of guidelines in determining the appropriate standard of care. In this pending case, *Batas and Vogel v The Prudential Insurance Company of American and Prudential Health Care Plan of New York, Inc*, the plaintiffs allege several examples of improper guideline use, including some created by a third-party actuarial company, Millman & Robertson, Inc. This third-party developer had created utilization guidelines to determine the necessity for admission to the hospital, as well as for the length of stay. The allegations claim that the determination of which medical care will or will not be provided is sometimes influenced by undisclosed guidelines and decided by personnel who are not properly trained. The complaint also asserts that such guidelines are not reflective of proper clinical standards. The plaintiffs assert that such guidelines must be based on clinical data and must not be used as a substitute for a physician's independent judgment.[32]

The clinical policies developed by ACEP are guidelines to help emergency physicians make critical decisions as to what and how care will be delivered. The very nature of clinical policies merits considerable attention from attorneys. ACEP's Clinical Policies Committee has been cognizant of this fact from the beginning of ACEP's involvement in clinical policy development; therefore, the impact of each word, rule, and guideline is carefully considered with respect to how it would look in court and to how it might bring harm to the emergency physician involved in a malpractice situation.

Guidelines in Credentialing

Guidelines can be worked into credentialing. Guidelines may contribute to the definition of what constitutes acceptable clinical performance for purposes of education, feedback, or evaluation. Conformity to good guidelines may be used in selective and economic credentialing. Many MCOs look to this criteria when determining what physician or group of physicians they may wish to contract with.

Key Points and Conclusion

Current and future uses of clinical practice guidelines in health care delivery raise numerous medical and legal concerns. Physicians and medical educators should support efforts to validate individual clinical policies and to strengthen the role of science in the development and promulgation of clinical policies. Medical specialty society members should be aware of guidelines promulgated by their own societies.

Clinical policies are not "cookbooks" — they are guidelines to permit physicians flexibility in response to individual patient care situations. However, deviations from the guidelines should be explained and justified on the patient's medical record. Physicians should document their actions, thoughts, and plans.

References

1. Todd WE, Nash DB, eds. *Disease Management: A Systems Approach to Improving Patient Outcomes*. Chicago: American Hospital Association; 1994.

2. Field MJ, Lohr KN, eds. *Guidelines for Clinical Practice: From Development to Use*. Washington, DC: National Academy Press; 1992

3. JCAHO. Recognition and initial assessment of Alzheimer's Disease and related dementias. *Abst Clin Care Guidelines* 1997;9(5):2.

4. Outcomes management comes of age. *Business & Health: Special Report* 1996;14:(4,Suppl B):7-10.

5. Lang DA, Kadzielski MA, Liset JR. *Managing Medical Staff Change Through Bylaws and Other Strategies*. Chicago: American Hospital Association; 1995.

6. Nutting PA. Why can't clinical policies be relevant to practice? *J Fam Pract* 1997;44:350-352.

7. American Medical Association. *AMA Policy Compendium*. Chicago: AMA;1997.

8. AHCPR, AAHP, and AMA to develop national clinical guideline clearinghouse. AHCPR Press Release, May 28, 1997.

9. Brook RH. Practice guidelines: to be or not to be. *Lancet* 1996;348:1005-1006.

10. National Health Lawyers Association. *Colloquium Report on Legal Issues Related to Clinical Practice Guidelines*. Washington, DC: National Health Lawyers Association; 1995.

11. Garnick DW, Hendricks AM, Brennan TA. Can practice guidelines reduce the number and costs of malpractice claims? *JAMA* 1991;266:2856-2860.

12. Bierig JR, Raskin RD, Ile ML. Antitrust considerations for medical societies. In: Johnson KB, Hirshfeld EB, Ile ML, eds. *Legal Implications of Practice Parameters*. Chicago: American Medical Association; 1990.

13. Kelly JT, Hirshfeld EB. Introduction. In: Johnson KB, Hirshfeld EB, Ile ML, eds. *Legal Implications of Practice Parameters*. Chicago: American Medical Association; 1990.

14. Schanz SJ. *Parameters Guidelines Protocols*. 1995-1996:1-14.

15. Me Rev Stat Ann tit 24, §2971-2979 (1993).

16. Smith GH. A case study in progress: practice guidelines and the affirmative defense in Maine. *J Qual Improv* 1993; 19:355-362.

17. Schanz SJ, Smith GH. Special interview. *Parameters Guidelines Protocols* 1995;1(10):5-7.

18. Md Health Code Ann §19-1601-06 (1993).

19. Quality Medical Practice Standards Act. New York State Senate, SB 5135, 1995.

20. Access to Affordable Health Care Act. US Senate, S294, 1995.

21. Minn Stat Ann §62J.30-46 (West 1993).

22. Hyams AL, Brandenburg JA, Lipsitz SR, et al. *Report to the Payment Review Commission: Practice Guidelines and Malpractice Litigation.* Boston: Harvard School of Public Health; 1994.

23. Rothenberg MA. *Emergency Medicine Malpractice, Second Edition.* New York: John Wiley & Sons, Inc; 1994.

24. Schriger DL, Abrishami P, Liu AYC, et al. Removal of a computerized guideline charting system from the ED: effect on the quality of care of health care workers exposed to body fluids (abstr). *Acad Emerg Med* 1996;3:466.

25. Schriger DL. Emergency medicine clinical guidelines: we can make them, but will we use them? *Ann Emerg Med* 1996;27:655-657.

26. Kapp MB. The clinical practice parameters movement: the risk manager's role. In: *Colloquium Report on Legal Issues Related to Clinical Practice Guidelines.* Washington, DC: National Health Lawyers Association; 1995.

27. Holder AR. The biomedical researcher and subpoenas: judicial protection of confidential medical data. *Am J Med Law* 1986;12:405-421.

28. Trial court's failure to admit cardiac catheterization standards leads to reversal by appeals court. *Parameters, Guidelines and Protocols* 1996;2(11):3-4.

29. Hospital's adherence to emergency treatment policy overcomes patient anti-dumping act challenge. *Parameters, Guidelines and Protocols* 1996;2(11):4-5.

30. Federal court notes failure to follow protocols in myelogram injury case. *Parameters, Guidelines and Protocols* 1997;3(7):4-5.

31. Hospital's guidelines support court finding of no direct negligence. *Parameters, Guidelines and Protocols* 1997;3(7)5-7.

32. Use of guidelines questioned in class action complaint. *Parameters, Guidelines and Protocols* 1997;3(5)1-3.

Additional Reading

A critical path by any other name: is it the same? *ED Management* 1994;6:123-125.

AHCPR updates CONQUEST database. *Research Activities* 1997;205:17.

AHCPR. *Program Note: Clinical Practice Guideline Development.* Rockville, Md: US Dept of Health and Human Services; 1993.

American Academy of Pediatrics Committee on Drugs Section on Anesthesiology. Guidelines for monitoring and management of pediatric patients during and after sedation for diagnostic and therapeutic procedures. *Pediatrics* 1992;89:1110-1115.

American College of Radiology. ACR Standard for Performing and Interpreting Diagnostic Ultrasound Examinations [Res. 9]. Reston, Va: ACR; 1992.

American College of Radiology. ACR Standard for Use of Intravenous Conscious Sedation [Res. 13]. Reston, Va: ACR; 1995.

American Diabetes Association. Hospital admission guidelines for diabetes mellitus. *Diabetes Care* 1995; 18(Suppl 1):35.

American Fertility Society. Guideline for Practice: Early Diagnosis and Management of Ectopic Pregnancy. Birmingham, Ala: The American Fertility Society; 1992.

American Medical Association Office of Quality Assurance and Medical Review. *Implementing Practice Parameters on the Local/State/Regional Level.* Chicago: American Medical Association; 1994.

American Medical Association. Practice parameters update. *JAMA* 1996;7(Suppl 1):1-62.

American Medical Association Specialty Society Practice Parameters Partnership. *Attributes to Guide the Development of Practice Parameters.* Chicago: American Medical Association; 1994.

American Society of Anesthesiologists Task Force on Management of the Difficult Airway. Practice guidelines for management of the difficult airway. *Anesthesiology* 1993;78:597-602.

American Society of Anesthesiologists. *ASA Standards, Guidelines and Statements.* Park Ridge, Ill: American Society of Anesthesiologists; 1992.

Ayres JD. The use and abuse of medical practice guidelines. *J Leg Med* 1994;15:421-443.

Bierig JR, Raskin RD, Fleisher LD, et al. Tort liability considerations for medical societies. In: Johnson KB, Hirshfeld EB, Ile ML, eds. *Legal Implications of Practice Parameters.* Chicago: American Medical Association; 1990.

Bierig JR, Raskin RD, Hirshfeld EB. Malpractice considerations for physicians. In: Johnson KB, Hirshfeld EB, Ile ML, eds. *Legal Implications of Practice Parameters.* Chicago: American Medical Association; 1990.

Brennan TA. Methods for setting priorities for guidelines development: medical malpractice. In: Field MJ, ed. *Setting Priorities for Clinical Practice Guidelines.* Washington, DC: National Academy Press; 1995.

Brown JG. *Clinical Practice Guidelines Sponsored by the AHCPR: Early Experiences in Clinical Settings.* No. OEI-01-94-00250. Rockville, Md: US Department of Health and Human Services; 1992.

Bukata WR. Practice guidelines: do they really improve outcome? *Emerg Med News* 1995;17:12-13.

Cantrill SV. National clinical policies: how will they affect your practice? Syllabus for American College of Emergency Physicians, Winter Symposium, Tucson, Ariz, 1994.

Carter A. Background to the "guidelines for guidelines" series. *Can Med Assoc J* 1993;148:383-431.

Cascade PN. Setting appropriateness guidelines for radiology. *Radiology* 1994;192:50A-54A.

Cline DM, Welch KJ, Cline LS, et al. Physician compliance with advanced cardiac life support guidelines. *Ann Emerg Med* 1995;25:52-57.

Clinical policy for the initial approach to adolescents and adults presenting to the emergency department with a chief complaint of headache. ACEP Clinical Policy, approved January 1996. To obtain a copy, call (800) 798-1822, touch 6, or go to www.acep.org.

Clinical policy for the initial approach to patients presenting with a chief complaint of nontraumatic acute abdominal pain. ACEP Clinical Policy, approved October 1993. To obtain a copy, call (800) 798-1822, touch 6, or go to www.acep.org.

Clinical policy for the initial approach to adults presenting with a chief complaint of chest pain, with no history of trauma. ACEP Clinical Policy, approved September 1994. To obtain a copy, call (800) 798-1822, touch 6, or go to www.acep.org.

Clinical policy for the initial approach to patients presenting with a chief complaint of seizure, who are not in status epilepticus. ACEP Clinical Policy, approved March 1992. To obtain a copy, call (800) 798-1822, touch 6, or go to www.acep.org.

Clinical policy for the initial approach to children under the age of two years presenting with fever. ACEP Clinical Policy, approved March 1992. To obtain a copy, call (800) 798-1822, touch 6, or go to www.acep.org.

Clinical policy for the initial approach to patients presenting with acute blunt trauma. ACEP Clinical Policy, approved September 1992. To obtain a copy, call (800) 798-1822, touch 6, or go to www.acep.org.

Clinical policy for the initial approach to patients presenting with acute toxic ingestion or dermal or inhalation exposure. ACEP Clinical Policy, approved June 1994. To obtain a copy, call (800) 798-1822, touch 6, or go to www.acep.org.

Clinical policy for the initial approach to patients presenting with penetrating extremity trauma. ACEP Clinical Policy, approved October 1993. To obtain a copy, call (800) 798-1822, touch 6, or go to www.acep.org.

Committee on Drugs, American Academy of Pediatrics. Reappraisal of lytic cocktail/demerol, phenergan, and thorazine (DPT) for the sedation of children. *Pediatrics* 1995;95:598-602.

Computerization of guidelines leads to greater acceptance. *Healthcare Leadership Rev* 1997;16(1):10.

Cotie CJ. Sedation protocols — why so many variations? *Pediatrics* 1994;94:281-283.

Couch JB. *Physician Managers and the Law: Legal Aspects of Medical Quality Management*. Tampa, Fla: Lithocolor; 1989.

Davidson SJ. Practice, malpractice, and practice guidelines. *Ann Emerg Med* 1990;19:943.

Dunn LJ. The legal basis of the physician/patient relationship. In: Mackuaf SH, ed. *Malpractice in the Emergency Room*. New York: Practicing Law Institute; 1988.

Eddy DM. *A Manual for Assessing Health Practices and Designing Practice Policies*. Philadelphia: American College of Physicians; 1992.

Emerman CL, Cydulka RK, Skobeloff E. Survey of asthma practice among emergency physicians. *Chest* 1996;109:708-712.

Evidence-based care: practice guidelines raise pathways to a higher level. *Patient Care Management Abstracts* 1997;4(4):1.

Field MJ, ed. *Setting Priorities for Clinical Practice Guidelines*. Washington, DC: National Academy Press; 1995.

Fisch C, Ryan TJ, Williams SV, et al. ACP/ACC/AHA task force statement: clinical competence in electrocardiography. *J Am Coll Cardiol* 1995;25:1465-1469.

Fish R, Ehrhardt M. The standard of care. *J Emerg Med* 1994;12:545-552.

Flick GM. *Medical Malpractice: Handling Emergency Medicine Cases*. New York: McGraw-Hill, Inc; 1991.

Francis GS, Williams SV, Achord JL, et al. ACP/ACC/AHA task force statement: Clinical competence in insertion of a temporary transvenous ventricular pacemaker. *J Am Coll Cardiol* 1994;23:1254-1257.

Friesinger GC, Williams SV, Achord JL, et al. Clinical competence in hemodynamic monitoring. A statement for physicians from the ACP/ACC/AHA Task Force on Clinical Privileges in Cardiology. *J Am Coll Cardiol* 1990;15:1460-1464.

Georgia case discusses scope of physician/patient relationship. *Parameters, Guidelines and Protocols* 1997;3(6):7.

Gosfield AG. Clinical practice guidelines and the law: applications and implications. In: *Colloquium Report on Legal Issues Related to Clinical Practice Guidelines*. Washington, DC: National Health Lawyers Association; 1995.

Greenes RA. Medical education and decision support using network-based multimedia information resources. *Ann N Y Acad Sci* 1992;670:244-256.

Grisham J. ACEP policy statement on pediatric sedation and analgesia (lett). *Ann Emerg Med* 1994;23:140-141.

Guideline criteria project. *Quality Evaluation News* 1997;9(1):5.

Guideline Committee of the American College of Critical Care Medicine, Society of Critical Care Medicine, and American Association of Critical Care Nurses. Guidelines for the transfer of critically ill patients. *Crit Care Med* 1993;21:931-937.

Guidelines attacked in NY class action lawsuit. *Parameters, Guidelines and Protocols* 1997;3(2):1-3.

Guidelines help plans manage physician practices; improvements needed. *Directions: Looking Ahead in Healthcare* 1997;1(1):10.

Hall KN, Mile ST, Hamilton CA, et al. Effect of an asthma practice guideline on documentation and outcome in an urban ED (abstr). *Acad Emerg Med* 1996;3:472.

Healthcare Standards Directory 1996. Plymouth Meeting, Pa: ECRI Publishers; 1995.

Hirshfeld EB. Tort considerations for medical societies. In: Johnson KB, Hirshfeld EB, Ile ML, eds. *Legal Implications of Practice Parameters*. Chicago: American Medical Association; 1990.

Hirshfeld EB. Should practice parameters be the standard of care in malpractice litigation? *JAMA* 1991;266:2886-2891.

Hirshfeld EB. Should ethical and legal standards for physicians be changed to accommodate new models for rationing health care? In: *Colloquium Report on Legal Issues Related to Clinical Practice Guidelines*. Washington, DC: National Health Lawyers Association; 1995.

Ho S. The evolution of the specialist. *Healthcare Leadership Rev* 1997;16(3):4.

Holzman RS, Cullen DJ, Eichhorn JH, et al. Guidelines for sedation by nonanesthesiologists during diagnostic and therapeutic procedures. *J Clin Anesth* 1994;6:265-276.

How to increase physician adherence to guidelines. *Healthcare Leadership Rev* 1997;16(1):10.

Kapp MB. Cookbook medicine. A legal perspective. *Arch Intern Med* 1990;150:496-500.

Kapp MB. The legal status of clinical practice parameters: an updated annotated bibliography. *Am J Med Qual* 1995;10:107-111.

Knudtson DL, Tobiasz R. Practice guidelines: salvation for the emergency department (lett). *J Emerg Nurs* 1994;20:450.

Montgomery JT, Thompson D. Surviving the stand: the ED physician as expert witness. *ED Legal Letter* 1996;7(3):21-28.

Most watched emerging information technologies identified. *Directions: Looking Ahead in Healthcare* 1997;1(3):3-4.

Nelson MD Jr. Guidelines for the monitoring and care of children during and after sedation for imaging studies. *AJR* 1993;160:581-582.

Noonan WD. Patenting medical technology. *J Leg Med* 1990;11:263-319.

Pierson KA, Portman RM. US court in Vermont declares patent claims on surgical procedure invalid and unenforceable. *Health Law Digest* 1996;24(4):77-78.

Practice guidelines can help providers decipher a tangle of information. *Patient Care Management Abstracts* 1996;4(7):10.

Protocols: Standards of care or guidelines? *Emerg Phys Leg Bull* 1995;6:1-8.

Rosenblum J. Practice parameters/practice guidelines from the operating room to the courtroom. *Newslett Am Bar Assoc Tort Prac Section [Medicine & Law Committee]*. 1991; Spring:16-24.

Rosoff AJ. The role of clinical practice guidelines in health care reform. *Issue Brief Leonard Davis Inst Center Health Policy* 1994;1:1-4.

Sacchetti A, Schafermeyer R, Geradi M, et al. Pediatric analgesia and sedation. *Ann Emerg Med* 1994;23:237-250.

Schachar v American Academy of Ophthalmology, 870 F2d 397, 399 (7th Cir 1989).

Schanz SJ, Mariani PJ. Special interview. *Parameters Guidelines Protocols* 1995;1(7):4-6.

Schanz S. AHCPR launches Internet site. *Parameters Guidelines Protocols* 1996;2(4):4.

Schriger DL, Cantrill SV, Greene CS. The origins, benefits, harms, and implications of emergency medicine clinical policies. *Ann Emerg Med* 1993;22:597-602.

Shandell RE, Smith P. *The Preparation and Trial of Medical Malpractice Cases.* New York: Law Journals Seminars Press; 1990.

Spernak SM, Budetti PP, Zweig F. *Use of Language in Clinical Practice Guidelines.* Washington, DC: George Washington University; 1992.

Stahmer SA, Shofer FS, Furey K. Asthma clinical pathway: Reduction in ED treatment times (abstr). *Acad Emerg Med* 1996;3:472.

Standard LD. 1.6. In: Joint Commission on Accreditation of Healthcare Organizations. *Comprehensive Accreditation Manual for Hospitals.* Oakbrook Terrace, Ill: JCAHO; 1995.

Strassner LF. Evaluating critical pathways. *Continuing Care* 1996;(4):25-35.

Sullivan DJ. *1993-1994 Yearbook of Law & Emergency Medicine.* Physician's Law Review;1993.

The use of pediatric sedation and analgesia. ACEP Policy Statement, approved March 1992. To obtain a copy, call (800) 798-1822, touch 6, or go to www.acep.org.

Toepp MC, Kuznets N, Herrera SP, eds. *Directory of Practice Parameters.* Chicago: American Medical Association; 1996.

Trager GW, Levy R, Janiak BD. Merit badge medicine (lett). *Ann Emerg Med* 1984;13:1167.

Use guidelines as navigation tools but don't let them steer your ED. *ED Management* 1995;8:37-40.

Use of ultrasound imaging by emergency physicians. ACEP Policy Statement, approved June 1997. To obtain a copy, call (800) 798-1822, touch 6, or go to www.acep.org.

Vleck C. Protecting the rights of computer artisans. *Nurs Educator Microworld* 1992;6:35.

Wagner DK. Graduate education for emergency medicine: the choice of yaks and horses or mules and zoes. *Ann Emerg Med* 1984;13:967-971.

White LJ. Clinical uncertainty, medical futility and practice guidelines. *J Am Geriatr Soc* 1994;42:899-901.

Wigder HN, Arai DA, Narasimhan K, et al. ACEP chest pain policy: emergency physician awareness. *Ann Emerg Med* 1996;27:606-609.

Chapter 20

Insurance Coverage

Steven M. Harris, JD
Earl Silverstein

In today's litigious society, physicians must have professional liability insurance to protect their assets. Needless to say, when seeking such coverage, they should secure a policy with adequate limits from a financially stable company. Depending on the company issuing the policy and the nature of the coverage, there could be an element of "risk sharing" associated with the coverage offered. In such instances, the nature of the coverage being offered should be examined carefully.

When purchasing a professional liability policy, physicians must realize that not all policies are created equal. Be cognizant not only of the type of coverage, but also of the terms, conditions, and exclusions set forth in the policy. Failure to educate yourself regarding policy language or failure to understand your rights and duties as specified in the policy can result in financial disaster.

Definitions

The following definitions are provided to help you understand some of the concepts discussed in this and other chapters.

Primary Insurance. The first layer of insurance coverage that will afford a "first-dollar" payment with regard to any loss covered under the policy.

Reinsurer. An insurer, who in consideration of a premium paid by another insurer, assumes all or some of the risks of that insurer. In so doing, the reinsurer agrees to indemnify another insurer for a percentage of the losses sustained under the insurance policy issued by that insurer (e.g., primary insurer).

Off-Shore Insurance. Insurance provided by an insurer whose domicile (place of doing business) is located outside the United States.

Admitted Carrier. An insurer who is licensed to do business in a particular state and is therefore subject to the rules and regulations of the insurance department of that state.

Risk Retention Group. A form of association captive insurance company that allows for persons or organizations engaged in similar businesses or activities to provide liability insurance for the types of liability to which the members are exposed. All the insureds must be owners of the captive, and all the owners must be insureds.

Risk Pool. A group of individuals or organizations who purchase insurance whereby the policy limits (and therefore the risks) are shared by the members comprising the pool.

Channeled Insurance Program (Hospital/ Physician Shared-Risk Program). Consists of the establishment of a captive insurance company or reinsurance company for the purpose of providing insurance to a hospital or group of hospitals and its affiliated (staff) physicians.

Best Ratings. A rating system that indicates the operational condition of insurance companies. The data comprising the rating are developed and published annually by the A.M. Best Company.

Captive. An insurance company that normally insures the risks and exposures of its parent company and affiliates, or it may be owned by a number of companies in the same industry, insuring risks common to the group. Captives can be further identified by type, (e.g., pure captive, association captive, reinsurance captive, etc.).

Types of Coverage

Claims-Made. Policies written on this basis cover claims made during the time the policy is in force for any occurrences transpiring during that year or during any previous period that the policy holder was insured under the claims-made contract. It is important to note that because the claims must be made during the current policy year, the insured would not have coverage on a claim made after the policy holder canceled the insurance coverage or switched to another insurance carrier.

Nose Coverage. Also known as retroactive coverage. Nose coverage is purchased from the new insurance carrier to provide coverage to the insured during the time when the previously held policy expired or was canceled by the policyholder.

Occurrence. Policies written on an occurrence basis cover claims transpiring within the specified policy period regardless of the date a claim was filed.

Tail Coverage. This type of policy is also known as an extended reporting endorsement. Tail coverage provides extended protection to the insured during a time when the previously held policy has expired or was canceled by the policyholder. The insured typically purchases the extended reporting endorsement from the former insurer prior to changing to a subsequent claims-made policy.

The Professional Liability Policy

To avoid ambiguities in policy language that could lead to coverage disputes, it is important to understand common terms in an insurance policy. Definitions of terms can and do differ greatly from one policy to another. As such, the following definitions are meant to serve as examples only.

Schedule of Declarations. The portion of the insurance policy that summarizes the basic information concerning the insurance provided by the policy. This information includes the name and address of the insured, the policy period, the limits of liability, the retroactive date (for claims-made coverage), and the premium amount.

Named Insured. Any person, firm, or corporation, or any of its members specifically desig-

nated by name as insured in the policy. This category distinguishes the named insured from others who are protected by the policy definition. A named insured under the policy has rights and responsibilities not attributed to additional insureds. These include premium payments, premium return, notice of cancellation, and dividend participation.

Endorsement. A form bearing the language necessary to record any change in an insurance policy.

Occurrence. Any incident or event that happens, especially one that is not designed or expected.

Claim. The filing of a lawsuit, notice of intent to file a lawsuit or to arbitrate, a demand for money or service, or an occurrence involving injury or disability of which the insured becomes aware and which in the opinion of the named insured may result in the filing of a lawsuit or the receipt of a demand for money.

Lawsuit. A generic term of comprehensive significance referring to a proceeding by one person or persons against another or others in a court of justice. The plaintiffs pursue the remedy the law affords for the redress of an injury or the enforcement or a right, whether at law or in equity.

Medical Professional Services. The rendering of the usual and customary service directly related to the practice of medicine.

Injury. Bodily injury, sickness, or disease sustained by any person that occurs during the policy period, including pain and suffering, mental anguish, loss of income, or death at any time resulting from the injury.

Damages. All monetary sums that the insured has a legal duty to pay, including defense costs, charges, and expenses incurred in the defense of actions.

Although most professional liability policies differ widely in their format and language, they also contain many common elements. These key policy components may include the following:

- Declarations
- Insuring agreements
- Exclusions
- Conditions
- Endorsements

Declarations

This section of a policy contains basic underwriting information, including the named insured, policy period, limits of liability, and premium amount.

Of particular importance are the policy limits, which on a typical professional liability insurance policy are defined in terms of two numbers: one represents the per occurrence limit, and the second represents the aggregate limit. The occurrence limit indicates the amount of coverage available for each incident occurring and reported during the policy period (if it is a claims-made policy). The aggregate limit, on the other hand, represents the maximum amount of coverage available during any given policy period regardless of the number of claims reported.

For example, in a typical policy, a physician would have coverage for $1 million for each incident but would have a maximum of $3 million available for this particular policy period. Obviously, it is important to obtain sufficiently high limits to protect your assets against a large adverse judgment in a lawsuit. This factor will be balanced by your willingness and ability to pay the high premiums associated with the higher limits. Usually, specific limits are required by a hospital as a condition of staff privilege. They are virtually always required in an emergency department contract.

Given that many emergency physicians are insured through an emergency medicine group, they should have a complete understanding of the coverage available. In our example, the physician is the policyholder, and he understands the $1 million/$3 million in coverage. But what if the named insured is an emergency medicine group that contracts with 50 other physicians, all of whom are additional insureds (see section on insuring agreements) under the policy? If the limits on this policy are as stated above, $1 million/$3 million, how much coverage is now available to the physician?

He could get the full benefit of the limits as noted, but he could also find the policy limits have been exhausted when he is asked to pay a claim. For example, what if the emergency medicine group has the misfortune to pay three $1 million claims relative to the policy period in question? Because the aggregate limit of the policy is $3 million, the physician essentially would have no coverage. Under these circumstances, how would the group respond to his claim? Would this group be financially strong enough to pay his claim out of corporate funds, should the need arise?

The issue of availability of coverage can be further compounded if the group is in a pooled program with other groups. In this case, all the physicians associated with these groups would share the same limits. Although the limits on such an insurance program on the surface may appear quite adequate (i.e., a very large aggregate), those limits should be examined closely to determine what they actually represent in terms of the number of physicians insured and the overall risk exposure their practices represent. Furthermore, be concerned about the financial viability of a commercial insurance carrier when purchasing insurance, as well as the financial viability of a pool's as well as a group's ability to respond to a claim against a contracting physician should the policy limits of the pool be exhausted as a consequence of prior claims paid. Dollars set aside per patient seen is still the most reliable gauge needed to calculate the amount of insurance that actually exists for any pool arrangement.

Insuring Agreements

This section of a policy specifically outlines the nature of the coverage afforded under the policy. Items to look for in this section include:

- Persons insured
- Indemnity
- Defense costs
- Definitions
- Settlements

Because policy language differs greatly from one policy to the next, examine each section of the policy carefully to determine its applicability to your practice and to understand exactly what is covered under the policy.

Persons Insured. If the physician is not a named insured on the policy, that name should be noted as an "additional insured," usually as an endorsement to the policy. In some instances, the physician may be employed with an emergency medicine group and not be listed as an additional insured on the policy. At the very least, there should be specific language stating that all employed or contracted physicians are afforded coverage while providing professional services for the group.

One way to certify that coverage is afforded to a physician is to have a certificate of insurance issued to the physician in question, thereby removing any doubt. Physicians should also consider that as additional insureds under the policy, they may not have all the rights (or responsibilities) as would a named insured.

Indemnity. This section should specify what the policy will cover in terms of damages claimed by an injured party as well as the cost of defense. In a physician's professional liability policy, it is customary to see language suggesting that the physician is covered for damages as a result of injuries suffered by any person arising out of the rendering of or failure to render medical professional services during the policy period. At issue is the following:

- What is included under the term "damages"? Does this include such items as punitive damages, libel, slander, or other penalties?
- What is meant by "medical professional services"? If there are questions whether these or any other activities constitute "medical professional services" in the practice of emergency medicine, then coverage may not be afforded under the policy, or an ambiguity may exist that can open the door to a subsequent lawsuit in order to enforce coverage. One place to look for clarification is in the Definitions section of the policy. If these coverage issues are not clarified via definition, either as an endorsement to the policy or specifically excluded in the policy, the physician must obtain clarification of coverage in writing to avoid future disputes.

Defense. This part of the policy outlines an insurer's responsibility to provide a defense to its insureds. It is customary for the insurer to provide such a defense even if a claim or lawsuit is totally groundless. The cost of the defense is usually borne by the insurer; however, the nature of these costs and the effect they might have on the policy limits differs from policy to policy.

Every physician should understand what is meant by the "cost of defense." Does it include interest after a judgment has been rendered, the cost of appeal bonds, or expenses incurred by the physician in preparing the defense of the case (e.g., loss of earnings)? Perhaps even more significant is the effect defense costs have on the policy limits. For example, if defense costs exhaust the policy limits, the physician could find he has far less coverage than anticipated, given today's cost for defending claims and lawsuits.

Definitions. Each policy should define important terms to clarify the nature and extent of coverage and eliminate, whenever possible, ambiguities that might lead to future coverage disputes. Some of the more commonly defined terms have been included in the preceding pages, such as occurrence, claim, medical professional services, injury, and damages.

Two terms worth special mention are medical professional services and claim, as they often lead to coverage disputes. The practice of emergency medicine can differ from one location to another; therefore, all covered physicians must be certain their activities fall under the policy's definition of medical professional services. Because a broad definition is often used, clarification may be warranted via an endorsement to the policy.

Likewise, a claim is often defined in many different ways. In some policies, it might be considered a written demand; another policy may consider verbal notification of intent to sue as being a claim. In some cases, the filing of an incident report is considered notice of claim, whereas in others, such documentation is not accepted. If claims-made coverage is in effect, then what constitutes a reportable occurrence (i.e., what occurrence is considered a claim) becomes significant in determining whether coverage will be afforded.

Settlements. The insurer's position regarding settlements is stated in this section. By reviewing this section, you can usually determine whether the insured has the right to consent to a settlement, or whether this is left solely to the insurer's discretion. Even if a consent provision exists, this section may contain certain provisos wherein the consent of the insured can be obtained via other means.

Exclusions

The purpose of the Exclusions portion of the policy is to limit the broad coverage provided in the Insuring Agreements portion of the policy. These exclusions are specific and may include particular types of medical treatment, liabilities covered under other types of insurance policies, or punitive damages. The exclusions can significantly affect the coverage provided by a policy. This portion of a policy, therefore, needs to be examined carefully before providers decide which policy to purchase.

When examining exclusions in a policy, carefully consider the sum and substance of the duties to be performed by the emergency physician. For example, if a physician is required by contract to serve on various committees and this activity is excluded in the policy, then that physician could be "bare" if sued for such committee activity. To remedy this situation, purchase a policy that covers the activity, attempt to have an endorsement added to the policy covering this activity (it may mean a higher premium), or make sure the hospital's policy covers this activity.

In summary, it is just as important to know what is not covered under the policy as what is covered. Failure to discover these facts could prove very costly.

Conditions

This section of a policy includes those provisions that must be met by the insured in order to be afforded coverage by the policy once a claim is made. A violation of one or more of the policy conditions could result in an insurer denying coverage.

One of the most common and essential provisions found in a professional liability policy refers to notice. In essence, "notice" means the insured must notify the insurer as soon as practicable of any incident that the insured believes may lead to a claim. Failure to do so could result in "late notice," which, if found to impair the insurer's ability to successfully defend the claim, could result in denial of coverage.

Another common provision is one that explains how coverage may be affected if the insured has another applicable professional liability insurance policy (often referred to as the "other insurance clause"). For example, the hospital's policy may also provide coverage for the emergency physician. The policy may contain a pro rata clause that states the carrier will pay only that portion or percentage of the claim that the limits of coverage bear to the combined limits of both policies. Other policies may contain different provisions in this regard.

Most policies also have a condition stating that agreements, such as "hold harmless" agreements, that provide for the insured to indemnify a third party will not bind the carrier without the carrier's prior written consent. For example, an emergency physician may sign a contract with a hospital stating that in the event the hospital is sued as a result of the physician's acts, the physician will defend and indemnify the hospital. It is important to understand that although the physician personally would be bound by that agreement, an insurance carrier would not unless there is a specific provision in the policy to do so.

One final condition that should be discussed is the one requiring the insured to cooperate in the defense of claims. Such cooperation includes attendance and assistance in trial or trial preparation and is generally required at the insured's own expense. This condition should be strictly observed by all insureds. Violation of this condition is often used by insurers as a reason to deny coverage on a particular claim.

Endorsements

Any change in the policy language of the insuring agreement should be accomplished by means of an endorsement. An endorsement can have unlimited uses. It can expand coverage by adding a named insured, put in force additional coverage for specific medical services being rendered, or extend coverage to additional territories. It can also limit coverage by adding exclusions. Make sure that endorsements are added to meet your specific needs and that you thoroughly understand all restrictive endorsements.

Negligence Versus Responsibility: Implications of Existing Law

A defendant's liability exposure is not always directly related to the actual negligence attributed to that person. Under the doctrine of *respondeat superior*, when the relationship of employer and employee is shown to exist, an employer is liable to third persons for the tortious (wrongful) acts of its employees done in the furtherance of the employer's business, in the discharge of the employment, and for the purpose for which the employee is hired.[1,2] This liability is founded on the contractual agreement vesting the employer with the right to dictate the manner in which work is performed. It is through this doctrine that a hospital is held vicariously liable for the acts of its employees. This doctrine is also applied to render a principal liable to a third person for the wrongful acts of an agent.

This doctrine of ostensible or apparent agency is an emerging vehicle that plaintiffs are using effectively to establish liability against hospitals. The Restatement (2d) of Agency 267 (1968) defined ostensible agency as follows:

> One who represents that another is his servant or other agent and thereby causes a third person justifiably to rely upon the care or skill of such apparent agent is subject to liability to the third person for harm caused by the lack of care or skill of the one appearing to be a servant or other agent as if he were such.

Using this mechanism, plaintiffs in some jurisdictions are increasingly able to establish liability of hospitals for the acts of their independent contractor physicians. The controlling element in establishing apparent or ostensible agency with regard to emergency physicians seems to be the hospital's representations, actual or implied, to the patient regarding the status of the emergency physician. In other words, if the patient has accepted treatment from the physician in reasonable belief that the physician is an employee of the hospital, then the hospital may be held ostensibly liable for that physician's negligence.[3]

A Joint Defense

Once a claim develops into a lawsuit and more than one party is named as a defendant, the question arises whether a joint defense should be used. A joint defense can be defined as either one attorney defending both defendants or two attorneys in a single defense strategy, or "united front." The latter arrangement is more common. A joint defense should be undertaken only if there is no conflict of interest between the defendants (i.e., one defendant is not accusing the other of any negligence).

Advantages

First, there are real economic savings. Both defendants can share information concerning the facts of the case without the need of lengthy and costly discovery. Also, if the case does proceed to trial, the possibility of finger-pointing between the defendants is eliminated. Thus, there would be no surprises to the codefendant, including any behind-the-scenes agreements made between the plaintiff and any one codefendant. This tactic is often referred to as a Mary Carter agreement, named for the seminal case *Booth v Mary Carter Paint Company*.[4]

A joint defense may also impress the jury that the defendants are united. If the jury believes that one defendant should be exonerated, it may be more likely to exonerate the other.

Disadvantages

It may be more difficult for defense counsel to exonerate one less-culpable defendant over another if the defendants are perceived as united. If one defendant is found clearly liable by the jury, the other defendant has an increased chance of also being found liable.

The situation can be compounded in a state where joint and several liability exists in its original form or in some modified form. Where joint and several liability exists, defense counsel may find it in the client's best interests to direct liability toward a more culpable party, hoping that the client will be fully exonerated. Failure to do

so may result in that client bearing exposure to a judgment indicative of his share of the negligence or an even greater share if joint and several liability exists and the more culpable co-defendant is underinsured or insolvent. Before any codefendant agrees to a joint defense for any reason, the economic consequences of such a decision should be fully considered.

Named Insured's Consent-to-Settle Right

Advantages

By having the right to consent to settlement, those named insureds (see difference between named and additional insured) are in control, to a large extent, of their own destiny. That is, the physician who has the right of consent can force an insurer to proceed to trial in an effort to be exonerated via the legal process. Because most physicians are required to report all claims or lawsuits filed against them (as well as any settlements made in their behalf) when applying for professional liability insurance, the existence of any settlements can adversely affect a physician's insurability. Thus, having the right to consent, which allows a physician to be vindicated, could also have a positive effect on the future availability of insurance for that physician.

Disadvantages

On the other hand, having the right to consent to settlement could have serious consequences. A physician who has this right and refuses to consent when asked to do so by an insurer could be viewed as an undesirable risk. This could result in the insurer canceling or not renewing the physician's professional liability policy in those states where such an option is available and where failure to provide consent results in an adverse judgment.

Additionally, by having the right to consent and refusing such consent when requested to do so by an insurer may remove any exposure to the insurer for any judgment subsequently rendered in excess of the policy limits (see Stowers Doctrine). This action would greatly increase the personal risk exposure physicians might face. Finally, in some cases, physicians are the additional insureds and the group they are employed with is the named insured and the only party with the right to consent. The onus may be on the group to consent, with the proviso that the individual physician be dismissed from the lawsuit and settlement entered on behalf of the group. This would, in effect, leave the physician with a clean slate, which would be desirable when the person applies for coverage in the future with some other insurer.

Coverage Outside the Emergency Department

In many instances, physicians purchasing individual professional liability insurance policies in which they are the named insured will be provided coverage for rendering medical professional services outside the emergency department setting. However, this is the case only as long as the services rendered do not place that physician in a higher risk classification or are not specifically excluded by policy language or endorsement. It is important that a physician know what venues of practice are covered by any policy.

In some situations, a physician contracts with a group and the group issues a single policy to cover all its physicians (i.e., a separate policy is not purchased for each physician). There may or may not be coverage for services rendered by the physician outside of the emergency department setting. With some policies, coverage is extended to the physician solely when acting within the scope of any existing contract with such a group or while under the control of or for the direct benefit of the group. Under these conditions, any medical professional services rendered outside of the emergency department setting and not done so for the direct benefit of the group would not be covered.

On the other hand, some group policies are more liberal with regard to coverage. Some contain language that indicates the physician will be covered for activities outside the emergency department as long as the physician works a specified number of hours for the group (e.g., 30 hours) and as long as the physician's activities outside of the emergency department are not specifically excluded by the existing policy.

In summary, before physicians undertake to render services outside the emergency department setting, they must scrutinize their existing policies covering emergency department activities. Where a question of coverage exists or ambiguities in policy language are present, physicians should obtain clarification (preferably in writing) from their insurers.

National Practitioner Data Bank: Effect on Insurance Availability

The Health Care Quality Improvement Act (HCQIA) passed by Congress in 1986 was intended to help improve the quality of health care in the United States. Essentially, the Act encourages the review of physician performance and provides limited immunity from liability to peer review committees, hospitals, medical staff, and the like charged with this process. However, to receive this immunity, peer review committees are required to comply with HCQIA's due process and reporting requirements.

To achieve this goal of improved health care quality, the Act called for the development and establishment of the National Practitioner Data Bank for Adverse Information on Physicians and Other Health Care Practitioners (NPDB) for the purposes of collecting and tracking data on medical malpractice payments made by or on behalf of physicians, dentists, or other licensed health care practitioners. The purpose of the data collection is to detect and prevent physicians from moving from state to state without disclosing previous damages or incompetent performance. (See Chapter 12, "National Practitioner Data Bank.")

The reporting requirements of HCQIA are applicable to hospitals, health care entities, boards of medical examiners, professional societies of physicians, dentists, or other health care practitioners who take adverse licensure or professional review actions, and individuals and entities, such as insurance companies, making payments as a result of medical malpractice actions or claims. The required information must be submitted within 30 days following the action to be reported to the state board of medical examiners (i.e., malpractice payments, licensure actions) and within 15 days for adverse actions.[5]

All medical malpractice payments made by each person or entity — including insurance companies — must be reported to the NPDB and to the appropriate state licensing boards in the state in which the act or omission occurred and on which the medical malpractice claim is based. Those persons or entities reporting such information are responsible for its accuracy and for submitting any revisions of actions originally reported.

The NPDB may be accessed by physicians, or dentists if they are subject to a report, and by state boards, hospitals, HMOs, PPOs, and so on. Attorneys or individuals filing malpractice claims also have access to the NPDB. However, this information is disclosed only on the submission of evidence that a hospital failed to request information as required and may be used solely with respect to litigation resulting from an action or claim against a hospital.

The information contained in the NPDB will not be disclosed except with respect to professional review activities used for furtherance of health care. All persons or entities requesting information other than the physician, dentist, or other health care practitioner are required to pay an access fee. Information reported to the NPDB is considered confidential and must be used solely for the purposes stated in the law. Persons accessing data illegally may be fined up to $10,000 for each violation.[6]

The NPDB has been referred to as the Orwellian nightmare by members of the health care community, and much fear surrounds the potential misuse of the data it contains. In addition to the $10,000 penalty to prevent illegal access, all inquiries made to the NPDB are recorded electronically and supplied to the various persons or entities responsible for data input, should any discrepancies or questions arise.

Ultimately, what effect the HCQIA and the NPDB will have on health care and, in particular, the availability of insurance, is yet to be determined. As the database evolves, its effect on the health care community will be more evident. Currently, it must be used only for identifying or flagging incompetent physicians, dentists, and health care professionals to ensure that acceptable standards of health care and professional conduct are maintained.

Key Points and Conclusion

The insurance policy issued to any physician is a contract between the insured and the insurer. Like any other contract, the language in a professional liability policy is often subject to interpretation. The insured's understanding of what is insured may differ vastly from what the insurer intended to cover. Good risk management dictates that each physician must clearly understand all elements of the insurance policy. Any questions regarding coverage must be clarified prior to the filing of any claims or lawsuits.

Physicians must also closely scrutinize their professional liability policies to determine whether coverage is appropriate for all aspects of their practice. Again, if questions arise concerning coverage for particular activities, physi-

cians should obtain clarification from the insurer in writing as soon as possible.

Also, from a risk management standpoint, because insurance policies are designed to preserve physicians' assets, physicians should determine the adequacy of policy limits in light of their financial position as well as the viability of the company(ies) issuing the policy. Physicians must determine the amount of risk they are willing to accept when deciding what limits are appropriate and when selecting the insurer.

References

1. *J.V. Harrison Truck Line Inc. v Larson,* 663 SW2d 37, 38 (Tex Civ App, El Paso Ref NRE 1983).
2. *London v Texas Power and Light,* 620 SW2d 718, 720 (Tex Civ App, Dallas, no writ 1981).
3. See *Arthur v St. Peter's Hospital,* 169 NJ 575, 405 A2d 443 (1979), *Nicholson v Memorial Hospital System,* 722 SW2d 746 (Tex Civ App, Houston, Ref NRE 1986), *Smith v Baptist Memorial Hospital System,* 720 SW2d 618 (Tex Civ App, San Antonio Ref NRE, 1986).
4. *Booth v Mary Carter Paint Co.,* 202 So2d 241 (Fla Dist Ct App 1967).
5. 45 CFR §60.5 (1995).
6. 42 USCA §1137 (a) (2) 1986.

Chapter 21

Theories of Settlement

Steven M. Harris, JD
Earl Silverstein

Given the physician's right, in many instances, to dictate whether a claim is settled, it is imperative that each physician be well versed in the settlement process. Many variables have to be taken into account when considering a settlement. Defense counsel is, in most instances, the physician's best resource for advice. Physicians must understand that they can have an impact on the management and settlement of a claim or lawsuit and need to be prepared to exercise their legal prerogatives. Failure to do so can have an adverse effect on their finances, their future insurability, and their ability to practice medicine. A physician should realize that both settlements and judgments must be reported, by law, to the National Practitioner Data Bank.

What Is a Settlement?

A settlement is the negotiated conclusion of a claim for injuries or damages before, during, or after litigation has begun and before the rendering of a verdict. In some cases a settlement is made after a verdict has been rendered, and one party is considering an appeal. Thus, rather than being a judgment imposed on the parties to a lawsuit, a settlement is reached by agreement of those parties. In most cases, a settlement is the desired conclusion to any claim or lawsuit — a demand is made and met, and a specific sum of money is paid. This course is particularly desirable when liability is clear and damages are evident; however, there may be other justifications for entering into a settlement.

When settling a claim, each party estimates what amount constitutes the settlement value of the claim. The settlement value, as opposed to the judgment value, takes into account such issues as potential exposure in terms of damages, the degree of liability of the insured, the potential assessment of damages among the parties, the cost to defend a lawsuit through trial and the appeals process, prejudgment and postjudgment interest, available coverage, and any damages that may not be insurable (e.g., punitive damages).

Settlement in Terms of the Insurance Contract

Settlement in terms of the insurance contract or policy refers to the payment of a sum of money on behalf of an insured, a sum the insured is legally obligated to pay as damages. This is often referred to as an indemnity payment. The insurance policy also addresses the extent to which an insured has the right to approve or disapprove of any settlement as well as any conditions that might apply where a consent-to-settle provision is included in the policy.

Consent to Settle

At some point during the course of a claim or lawsuit, an insurer will have to evaluate all aspects of the case to determine whether a settlement can or should be negotiated. Many, although not all, professional liability policies require a physician's consent to settle a claim before settlement can be arranged. Consent to settle can be defined as the voluntary agreement by an insured physician allowing the insurer to resolve a claim or lawsuit by the payment of an unspecified sum of money within the policy limits. An example of a consent-to-settle clause is as follows: "The Company shall not compromise any claim hereunder without the consent of the Insured." Recently, there has been a tendency to remove such clauses from policies because they severely hamper an insurer's ability to have the final word regarding whether a settlement is economically prudent.

When a consent-to-settle clause does exist, it is not unusual for the policy also to include some type of provision for binding arbitration. Should the insurer and insured disagree regarding settlement, arbitration can be invoked to secure the insured's consent. The following are examples of such provisions:

- "The Company will not settle any claim or lawsuit without the written consent of the Insured. Except, however, if the Insured and the Company fail to agree that such claim or lawsuit should be settled, either may request a review and decision by a committee appointed by or with the approval of the [state] Medical Society. The decision of such committee will be final and binding on the Company and the Insured."

- "In the event the Insured refuses to consent to the settlement or compromise by the Company of a claim or lawsuit against the Insured, either the Insured or the Company shall have the right to submit the matter to an Advisory Committee of three physicians or surgeons. The Insured and the Company shall each nominate one member of such committee. The two members so chosen shall select a third member who shall act as umpire in case of disagreement between the two members chosen by the Insured and the Company. The facts of the case shall be presented to the committee, and the decision of a majority of said committee shall be binding upon the Insured and the Company."

If consent to settle is secured in such a manner, it is still incumbent on the insurer to enter into a good faith settlement within the policy limits.

Named Insured Versus Additional Insured

Although a named insured would benefit from a consent-to-settle clause in the insurance policy, an additional insured may not be the beneficiary of such a clause. In most instances, emergency physicians who are under contract to a specific group and are covered by the group's professional liability policy are categorized as "additional insured" and are not given the right to withhold consent to settle. Rather, the named insured may be the only party with the right to make that determination. Thus, if a claim is made against an additional insured who seeks to be exonerated by proceeding to trial, the individual may discover the option does not apply.

Therefore, physicians should have a clear understanding not only of the policy conditions regarding any consent-to-settle clause but also whether as an additional insured they will be a beneficiary of this option.

Other Terms Defined

Several other concepts and common terms are used in any discussion of settlements.

Present Value. The sum of money that, if invested now at a given rate of compound interest, will accumulate exactly to a specified amount at a specified future date. For example, at 12% interest, the present value of $112 due one year from now is $100.

Judgment Value. The sum of money that, in all likelihood, a jury would award to a plaintiff in satisfaction of a judgment against the various defendants.

Settlement Value. The sum of money that a defendant in a claim or lawsuit would consider paying to a claimant/plaintiff based on available information at any given point to bring a claim or lawsuit to conclusion without the necessity of a trial.

Allocated Loss Adjustment. The process of determining the cause and amount of a loss to the insured. It begins upon prompt notification of loss to the insurer or agent. The process includes checking the coverage, investigating the claim, and filing necessary reports. A determination is then made as to the amount of insurance the insured may recover after all allowances and deductions have been made and the amount that each insurer is required to pay under its policy, if there is more than one insurance company involved.

Loss Reserves and Expense Reserves

The establishment of reserves is an integral part of a process by which an insurer estimates its outstanding liabilities, including:

- Claims reported and adjusted but not yet paid.
- Claims reported but not adjusted.
- Claims incurred but not reported.

The reserves represent funds set aside by insurers to pay claims and the expenses associated with the adjustment of those claims.

With regard to the loss reserve (or indemnity reserve), which represents what an insurance company believes it will have to pay on any one claim, the reserve covers several factors in an effort to equate overall exposure. Such factors include the venue, damages, age and sex of the claimant, experience of plaintiff's counsel, applicability of joint and several liability, and caps on damages.

Expense reserves, on the other hand, reflect anticipated expenditures in defense preparation. These expenses include attorneys' fees, investigation fees, court costs, expert witness fees, and so on.

When considering any settlement, the established reserves are an important factor because the reserve represents the potential exposure that an insurer faces (i.e., money expected to be paid in resolving a claim). The insurer must take this fact into consideration when deciding what is appropriate for any settlement. For example, if the reserves on a particular claim total $100,000 and there is an opportunity to settle the claim for $5,000, the insurer is likely to prefer a settlement regardless of how strongly the insured feels about taking the issue to court. On the other hand, if the settlement demand exceeds the established reserves, the insurer is more likely to choose to defend the claim.

The insurer rarely discusses the reserves on a particular claim with an insured. But, if a physician has the right of consent to settle, this information can help the physician understand the insurer's estimate of the potential exposure. It also will help determine whether it is in the best interest of the physician to settle a claim, either from the standpoint of personal exposure (where, for example, there may be inadequate insurance limits in light of the potential judgment value of the case) or from the standpoint of the impact such a settlement might have on the physician's future insurability.

Bad Faith Claims

The term bad faith generally implies actual or constructive fraud, intent to mislead or deceive or neglect, or refusal to fulfill a stated duty or contractual obligation. The term suggests a conscious wrongdoing rather than an honest mistake regarding a person's rights or duties.

In recent years, the insurance industry has seen a proliferation of bad faith claims involving primary insurers, excess insurers, and insureds. In the past, it was not unusual to find an excess insurer suing a primary insurer for bad faith. However, given the potential long-term impact of any settlement on an insured (e.g., reporting such settlements to the National Practitioner Data Bank), more policyholders are likely to file bad faith actions against both primary and excess insurers. Courts are now having to rule on such issues as the following:

- Excess insurers filing bad faith claims against primary insurers for failure to settle a claim within the primary policy limits.
- Policyholders (with significant self-insured retentions) bringing a lawsuit for bad faith against insurers for forcing the policyholders into a settlement.
- Primary insurers bringing claims for bad faith against excess insurers for forcing them to accept a settlement.

In terms of the relationship between a primary insurer and an excess insurer, the courts in the past were quick to recognize that the failure to settle a claim within the primary limits could create needless liability exposure for an excess carrier. Therefore, they were willing to hold the primary insurer liable in such cases. With the complexity of today's insurance relationships, however, and certainly with the greater advent of self-insurance, there appears to be a growing trend to recognize mutual duties owed among the insured, the primary insurer, and the excess insurer to act in good faith.

More than likely in lawsuits alleging bad faith, the key in deciding such disputes will hinge on the courts determining whether the defendant's actions were not simply the result of an honest mistake regarding that person's rights or duties, but the result of an intent to mislead or deceive one of the parties at risk. Thus, it is important for each insured to understand what constitutes bad faith and, more specifically, to understand their appropriate rights and duties to avoid being embroiled in this type of litigation.

Cases With a Potential for Financial Disaster

Most claims and lawsuits are settled well within the limits of the insured physician's professional liability policy and pose no threat to the physician's personal assets. There are cases, however, that if taken through to trial could result in a judgment in excess of the physician's policy limits or beyond damage awards covered by the policy issued. In either case, the physician involved could face financial disaster.

Any claim or lawsuit involving patient loss of life or significant permanent dysfunction can result in large judgments. More specifically, in claims or lawsuits where there is loss of life and the decedent was a relatively young working individual, the future loss of earnings alone can push a judgment into the seven-figure range. In those cases involving brain damage, paraplegia, quadriplegia, or loss of limb, the potential loss of future earnings, past and future medical expenses, continued pain and suffering and mental anguish, as well as the emotional impact these cases have on a jury make them particularly dangerous. Likewise, injuries involving minors, especially those involving obvious disfigurements, can result in a large award against a physician, with serious financial consequences.

Any case involving circumstances that might inflame a jury can create major problems as well. For example, any claim involving alleged malpractice in which a jury might perceive an attempt to destroy, conceal, or alter evidence is likely to result in a large award to the plaintiff.

Also, any lawsuit in which punitive or exemplary damages are claimed can have severe financial consequences. Many insurance policies exclude coverage for punitive damages and, in some states, punitive damages are uninsurable. In these situations, any award of punitive damages will be borne by the physician. Because many states have no cap on the amount of punitive damages that can be awarded, such an award can be substantial. Likewise any claim or lawsuit based on allegations regarding behavior that may not be covered by insurance (e.g., supervision of EMTs, an EMTALA violation) could have a serious financial impact.

Finally, any claim or lawsuit in which the defendants are either underinsured or uninsured and for which the doctrine of joint and several liability applies, carries potential risk. Obviously, the physician at highest risk is the one with the greatest assets. These types of situations are often compounded by a lack of cooperation, by mutual blaming, and by separate agreements with the plaintiff(s), all of which could inflame a jury and increase the size of a judgment.

Under any of these circumstances, it is important for the physician to weigh all options and consider a settlement versus facing personal financial loss. When a settlement is chosen, the physician may be wise to demand that an insurer negotiate the settlement within the policy limits. An insurer's failure to do so could serve to insulate the insured physician against any verdict that may affect the individual's personal assets.

Settlement Due to Negligence Versus Economic Benefit of Settlement

In a professional liability claim or lawsuit where the negligence of the physician is clear and a successful defense is unlikely, an insurer usually will choose to settle if a reasonable settlement can be reached. There are times, however, when the negligence of a physician cannot be established. Would a settlement be considered under such circumstances? Such cases may be considered nuisance claims having nuisance value.

The insurance community is divided philosophically regarding the best approach in dealing with such claims. Some believe that paying unjustified claims will serve only to encourage more of these claims. Others weigh the economic benefit of such settlements. In so doing, some in the industry believe that if costs can be significantly reduced by settling these claims, the end result is justified. For physicians, the real issue is what effect the insurer's decision will have on their future insurability or future practice in medicine.

Cost of Settlement Versus Legal Cost

When determining the cost of settlement, take into account all legal costs and then decide whether a settlement should even be considered. As the average indemnity payment has risen over the years, so, too, has the cost of defense. Today, it is not unusual for an insurer to pay in excess of $20,000 in preparing to defend a lawsuit. If an insurer proceeds to trial, defense costs of $100,000 are not uncommon. Given the dollars spent in defense preparation, the insured and the physician should work to avoid or limit legal costs. It is in both their best interests to determine quickly whether liability exists and to negotiate a settlement, if one is justified, before instigating litigation or extensive discovery proceedings.

Needless to say, in so doing, both sides stand to benefit, which usually results in a more advantageous settlement. When extensive legal costs are incurred by both parties to a lawsuit and factored into the settlement equation, it often makes settlement more difficult and certainly more costly to the insurer. In the absence of liability, potential legal costs must often be weighed against the economic benefit of a settlement.

Stowers Doctrine

In many instances, the insurance company has the exclusive right to settle claims, and its liability is limited to the amount defined in the insurance policy. Many states, however, use the Stowers Doctrine, which creates additional liability in certain instances. For example, an insurer, under the terms of this policy, assumes control of a claim, investigates the claim, and hires an attorney on behalf of the insured. The insurance company, in effect, becomes an agent of the insured, and the attorney becomes the subagent of the insured. As an agent of the insured, the insurer is held to that degree of care and negligence that an ordinary, prudent person would exercise in the management of one's own business.

As a result, the insurer's duty is not limited solely to the narrow boundaries of settlement but extends to the full range of agency relationship. Also included within the insurer's duty is investigation, preparation for defense of the lawsuit, and trial of the case.[1] If an insurer refuses an offer of settlement when it appears that an ordinary person in a similar insured situation would have settled, the insurer may be held liable for any damages the insured sustains that are not covered under the policy.

Thus, if the insurer has an opportunity to settle a case within the policy limits and fails to do so and a judgment is rendered in excess of the policy limits, the insurer may be held liable for the entire amount. Additionally, a breach of an agency relationship constitutes an independent tort (wrongdoing). The insured can bring an action for damages against the insurer and may be awarded exemplary damages as well.

Implications of Refusing to Settle

When a lawsuit is filed, there is a natural tendency for physicians to want a trial to vindicate themselves. Obviously, without a consent-to-settle clause in the policy, the choice to proceed to trial rests solely with the insurer. This fact can prevent the insured from having a day in court. However, there are potentially serious economic consequences when a physician chooses not to consent to settle a claim or lawsuit within the policy limits.

First, the insured may be personally liable for part of the judgment if the case is lost at trial (e.g., if the judgment is in excess of the insured's policy limits). The insured could also be personally liable for costs and/or part of the judgment, depending on certain provisions in the insurance policy. For example, there may be a provision that if the insured does not consent to settle the claim, as recommended by the insurance carrier, the insured will be required to pay the amount of the judgment in excess of the settlement demand, as well as any additional defense costs incurred. The insured may also be required personally to pay damages excluded by the policy (e.g., punitive damages).

Second, there is the consideration of the time and emotional energy required of the insured while participating in the defense of a case. In fact, the process could take several years to resolve. This can be very costly to the physician considering the potential interruption of the physician's practice to attend meetings with defense attorneys, to give depositions, to attend the trial, and so on. It is the physician's duty to give all reasonable aid and participation.

Finally, it is possible that even if an insured is vindicated at trial, the insurance carrier may consider the case lost if it spends a substantial amount to defend it. The insurance policy may be canceled or not renewed by an insurance carrier that is more concerned with managing costs than with the insured's right to vindication.

Structured Settlements

Historically, malpractice settlements have been made via a lump sum payment. Structured settlements to settle catastrophic cases that had large judgment potential came into use in the 1970s. A structured settlement is one in which one or more payments are made to the plaintiff at specific intervals over a specified time.

Many different funding vehicles exist for structured settlements, but the most common is the annuity. An annuity is an insurance contract purchased from a life insurance company, which in turn provides periodic payments in exchange for a single premium paid by the settling defendant as part of the settlement agreement. The payments are predetermined, again as part of

Figure 1

Example of structured settlement

John Doe
Date of Birth: 07/05/84
Normal Life Expectancy: 63.6 Years

Benefits	Guaranteed Payments	Potential Yield	Cost of Benefits
1. $200,000 cash, including attorney fees	$200,000	$200,000	$200,000
2. $2,125 per month for life with	$336,110	$16,272,768	$981,933
10 years guaranteed compounded annually @ 6% — first payment 30 days after settlement.	$536,110	$16,472,768	$1,181,933

$2,125 per month, compounded @ 6% annually will generate:

In Year	Monthly Benefit
1	$ 2,125
5	2,683
10	3,590
15	4,804
20	6,429
25	8,604
30	11,514
35	15,408
40	20,620
45	27,594
50	36,927
55	49,417
60	66,131

Prepared using standard rates of life insurer (actual case).

the settlement agreement. One significant difference is that a life insurance policy normally pays when a person dies, and an annuity usually pays until a person dies. The actual payment period, however, can vary.

Figure 1 illustrates one form of a structured settlement, in which a benefit of $16,472,768 can be realized from a settlement of $1,181,933. This large payout greatly enhances an insurer's ability to negotiate settlements for substantially less cost, particularly in those instances where the damages are severe.

Implications of Delay of Settlement

By delaying a settlement, the expenses associated with the defense of the lawsuit continue to rise. The plaintiff, in preparation for trial, is also continuing to invest money in expert fees, discovery, and court costs. Therefore, as the plaintiff's costs, or investment, in the lawsuit, increase, so can the plaintiff's demands.

The entire time a lawsuit is progressing, prejudgment interest accrues, which also adds to the settlement value of the case. In rare instances, causes of action may be created that expand a party's exposure either through the legislature or the courts. Given inflationary trends, the judgment value of the lawsuit will more than likely increase with time, thereby resulting in a more costly settlement. And in cases where the parties involved are old or infirm, there is always the potential for losing key witnesses because they can no longer be located, are unwilling to cooperate, or have become incapacitated or died.

Considering all the factors, if a settlement is indicated, it is far more advantageous to take this course of action early on in the proceedings to limit costs — both time and money. If a case goes to trial, a physician may stand to lose not only financially but also in terms of his practice and future insurability.

Key Points and Conclusion

The decision to settle a claim or lawsuit can have far-reaching short-term and long-term consequences for a physician. A physician may face uninsured liabilities in any claim or lawsuit (i.e., potential liability for damages not covered under the physician's professional liability insurance policy). These may include exposure based on acts not specifically covered under the policy, damages specifically excluded (e.g., punitive damages), or damages awarded that might be in excess of the policy limits.

Besides the obvious financial considerations, a physician must reflect on the long-term effects of an adverse settlement. It is customary for an insurer to determine what settlements may have been negotiated in the past when considering a physician's application for insurance. If the application reflects a number of adverse settlements, the insurer may deny coverage. Likewise, if coverage is already in place, an adverse settlement could result in policy cancellation or nonrenewal. Needless to say, a physician who is deemed to be an uninsurable risk may find it difficult to continue practicing medicine.

Considering these points, physicians should have a clear understanding of the settlement process, their rights as defined by the insurance policy, and the consequences of their decisions to settle or to pursue a case to trial. Any settlement, like any judgment, must be reported to the National Practitioner Data Bank.

Reference

1. *Range County Mutual Insurance Co. v John Welsy Guin,* 723 SW2d 656 (Tex 1987).

Chapter 22

Joint and Several Liability

Steven M. Harris, JD
Earl Silverstein

In the 1970s, the health care industry began to experience a malpractice crisis, a period of time marked by an escalating number of claims and lawsuits, spiraling legal costs, and unprecedented judgments in favor of plaintiffs. Even now, U.S. tort costs, which include legal and administrative costs as well as jury awards and settlements, routinely exceed those of other industrialized countries as a percentage of gross national output. The tort system cost $152 billion in 1994, or 2.2% of gross domestic product. It has been stable at 2.2% since 1985.[1]

As a consequence, professional liability insurance, especially for physicians, became unavailable or unaffordable. In response to this crisis, the insurance industry spearheaded a movement to bring about tort reform. Many experts in the insurance community believe that one of the primary inequities in the U.S. system of jurisprudence was the application of the common law theory of joint and several liability. As a result, this issue became one of the focal points in the tort reform movement of the 1980s.

Common Law Theory

The common law theory of joint and several liability holds joint tortfeasors (or wrongdoers) equally liable for damages sustained by a plaintiff. Many states have modified their joint and several liability statutes, which means that a health care provider's exposure can vary from state to state, or even county to county, depending on the law in a particular jurisdiction. A state's position on this legal issue can dramatically affect the defense, management, and even settlement of a claim or lawsuit.

Case Study

A 40-year-old man is brought to the emergency department by paramedics at about 10:00 AM. He had been digging up an electrical line when he sustained a shock. A passerby found him lying on the ground, unconscious. In the emergency department, the staff perform an ECG, place him a cardiac monitor, and administer IVs and oxygen but do not record vital signs. The patient regains consciousness. He does not complain of chest pain and has no indication of a burn.

Based on his evaluation, the emergency physician determines that the patient has not sustained an injury and releases him approximately one hour after arrival. Later that evening, the patient's private physician calls the emergency physician to advise him that the man died at home of a cardiac arrest.

The patient's family files a lawsuit against the emergency physician and the hospital. The court awards the plaintiffs economic damages of $1 million and noneconomic damages of an additional $1 million. The court determined the percentages of negligence be as follows:

Plaintiff 0%
Emergency physician 90%
Hospital 10%
Total 100%

The Medical-Legal Perspective

Under the concept of joint and several liability, each wrongdoer may be held wholly liable for the damages sustained by the plaintiff. A plaintiff may elect to sue one or all of the wrongdoers. Each one can be held liable for the entire amount of the damages sustained by the plaintiff.

In other words, each defendant is liable for the whole of the sustained damages, and the injured party may pursue each defendant separately or jointly. The court's reasoning has been that this furthers the "fundamental policy of modern tort law to compensate those who are injured."[2]

The Washington Supreme Court in *Seattle 1st National Bank v Shoreline Concrete Co.* further elucidated the rationale behind joint and several liability,[3] as follows:

> Since the harm caused by both joint and concurrent tortfeasor is indivisible, similar liability attaches. We have long held that such tortfeasors are each liable for the entire harm caused and the injured party may sue one or all to obtain full recovery while such liability at common law applies only to joint tortfeasors, the indivisible nature of the harm caused by both of these tortfeasors, required, at a minimum, that each be wholly responsible for the entire harm caused."

> While the indivisibility of the harm caused warrants imposition of entire liability upon those tortfeasors, sound policy reasons also support application of the procedural, or several, aspects, of the liability rule. The cornerstone of tort law is the assurance of full compensation to the injured party. To attain this goal, the procedural aspect of our rule permits the injured party to seek full recovery from any one or all of such tortfeasors. So long as each tortfeasor's conduct is found to have been a proximate cause of the indivisible harm, we can conceive of no reason for relieving that tortfeasor of his responsibility to make full compensation for all harm he has caused the injured party.

There must be at least two wrongdoers for defendants to be held jointly and severally liable in a case. A person incurs joint and several liability in two instances:

- When acting in concert with another to cause an injury, or

- When the wrongdoer and others act independently in causing an injury, and the responsibility cannot be divided among them.

When addressing the issue of joint and several liability, consider that, in addition to compensation for injuries, parties to a lawsuit routinely request that punitive damages be awarded. Punitive damages are intended to "punish" a defendant for outrageous conduct. Punitive damages, like the compensable damages under strict joint and several liability, may be collected from all negligent parties. Clearly, this acts to punish someone, but in many instances not the intended party.

Case Discussion

In the case study, the jury awarded damages of $2 million. If joint and several liability were strictly applied, the defendant's estate could expect the hospital to pay the entire judgment, even though the hospital was found only 10% negligent. This principle can mean that the defendant who is minimally at fault pays for not only the damages it caused but also the damages caused by the other joint tortfeasor(s). The joint tortfeasor has a right of contribution and hence can look to other joint tortfeasors for restitution. This, however, is a hollow remedy when one is dealing with an insolvent or judgment-proof joint wrongdoer.

State legislatures and courts alike have recognized these inequities involved in the law. In response, many states have attempted to find a compromise between the ideal of compensating those who are wrongfully injured and the inequity of having a nominally liable party pay for damages it did not cause. Some states have abolished joint and several liability and instead have adopted a strict comparative negligence approach that apportions liability based on percentage of responsibility. Still others have attempted to find a compromise between the two opposing views and have limited joint and several liability to instances such as those cases in which a joint tortfeasor has more than a certain percentage of the liability risk. This action is an effort to prevent a party who is only nominally liable from bearing the brunt of the judgment. Instead, the defendant who is more than nominally liable should bear the cost of the damages sustained by the plaintiff.

Contributory negligence refers to conduct on the part of the plaintiff that falls below the standard to which that person or entity should conform for its own protection and that is a legally contributing cause, along with the negligence of the defendant, in bringing about the plaintiff's harm.[4] Contributory negligence is a complete bar to the plaintiff for recovery from the defendant. On the other hand, comparative negligence is a concept that apportions liability for damages in proportion to the contribution of each wrongdoer causing the injury or damage.[5] Comparative negligence does not bar the plaintiff from recovery, but the amount of recovery is reduced by the percentage of fault attributed to the plaintiff.

Some states, while recognizing the inequities involved but wishing to compensate the injured parties for their actual damages, have limited the applicability of joint and several liability strictly to economic losses. Economic losses are pecuniary damages that include, but are not limited to, medical bills and loss of earnings. Excluded from joint and several liability would be such damages commonly known as "pain and suffering."

Finally, many states continue to use the strict joint and several liability statute. The court's rationale, in these instances, is that in the case of an injured plaintiff and a negligent defendant, no matter how small the negligence, it is the defendant(s) who should bear the costs associated with the plaintiff's damages.

The following are examples of different state interpretations of joint and several liability.

California

In 1986, California adopted Proposition 51, The Fair Responsibility Act of 1986. Proposition 51 eliminated joint and several liability for noneconomic damages. Wrongdoers are severally liable only for noneconomic damages, defined as "subjective nonmonetary losses," which include pain and suffering, emotional distress, loss of society and companionship, and loss of consortium.[6] Each defendant shall be liable for only the amount of noneconomic damages that are allocated to that defendant in direct proposition to his percentage of fault. Defendants still remain jointly and severally liable for economic damages.

Applying the California law to the case study, because a joint and several liability is still applicable for economic damages, both the physician and the hospital can be held liable. With regard to noneconomic damages, the hospital is liable for its 10% of fault ($100,000) and the physician liable for 90% of fault ($900,000).

Florida

In 1986, Florida limited the doctrine of joint and several liability by passing the Tort Reform Insurance Act. There are now limited circumstances in which the doctrine is applicable. Joint and several liability is applicable only in those cases where a liable party's percentage of fault equals or exceeds that of a particular claimant. The court will enter judgment with respect to economic damages against that party on the basis of the doctrine of joint and several liability. In cases where the defendant's percentage of fault is less than the plaintiff's, the defendant is liable on the basis of the party's percentage of fault. A defendant is now responsible only for the portion of noneconomic damages that is equivalent to the percentage of fault attributed to that defendant at trial.[7]

In the case study, because both the physician and hospital percentages of fault exceed that of the plaintiff, both defendants can be held jointly and severally liable for the economic damages ($1 million). For noneconomic damages, the hospital is liable for its 10% of fault ($100,000) and the physician liable for 90% of fault ($900,000).

Illinois

In 1995, Illinois eliminated its doctrine of joint and several liability by amending 735 ILCS 5/2-1117. A defendant is severally liable for only the portion of recoverable economic and noneconomic damages that equals the amount of that defendant's fault, if any, bears to the aggregate amount of fault of all wrongdoers, whose fault was approximate cause of the death, bodily injury, economic loss, or physical damage to property. In addition, 735 ILCS 5/2-1115, was amended and now imposes a cap on noneconomic damages. In actions that seek damages on account of death, bodily injury, or physical damage to property based on negligence, the recovery for noneconomic damages is limited to $500,000 per plaintiff. The amended law applies to causes of action filed on or after March 9, 1995. The constitutionality of the statute is being challenged.

Applying this new law to the case study, the hospital is liable for $100,000 in economic damages and $100,000 for noneconomic damages. With regard to the physician, the liability for economic damages is $900,000. In addition, the physician's liability for noneconomic damages is also be $900,000. However, because there is a cap of $500,000 on noneconomic damages, the plaintiff can receive only $400,000 in noneconomic damages from the physician if the plaintiff collects the $100,000 in noneconomic damages from the hospital.

New York

As part of its tort reform, New York adopted new legislation regarding joint and several liability. The new legislation applies only to noneconomic damages. In an action in which two or more wrongdoers are found to be jointly liable and in which the liability of a defendant is found to be 50% or less than the total liability assigned to all persons liable, each defendant's liability for noneconomic loss shall not exceed the defendant's equitable share as determined in accordance with the relative culpability of each defendant who caused or contributed to the total liability for noneconomic loss.[8] All defendants are jointly and severally liable to the plaintiff for economic damages.

With regard to economic damages, both the hospital and physician in the case study can be held jointly and severally liable for $1 million. Because the hospital's percentage of fault is less than 50% of the total liability assigned to all persons liable, the hospital's responsibility for noneconomic damages will not exceed $100,000. However, because the physician's liability does exceed 50% of the total liability assigned, the physician can be liable for the total $1 million in noneconomic damages.

Effects on Case Defense, Management, and Settlement

How joint and several liability is followed in a particular jurisdiction can radically affect the defense, management, and settlement of claims. For example, consider the patient in the case study and assume that the case has not yet gone to trial. The potential judgment value in this case is estimated to be $2 million. Assume that the emergency physician's negligence is assessed at 10%. To complicate the issues further, let us assume that the hospital's negligence is recognized to be 90%, and the hospital is uninsured and essentially insolvent.

In a jurisdiction where strict comparative negligence is applied, the physician's defense counsel, looking at the client's percentage of negligence and the damages sustained by the plaintiff, will value the potential exposure to the physician at $200,000. Defense counsel will then consider this amount in subsequent settlement negotiations. Thus, the settlement value of the

claim will be based on both the overall judgment value and the percentage of liability that defense counsel directly attributes to the physician, plus the costs associated with his defense.

If, on the other hand, the case is tried in a state that recognizes joint and several liability, then the defense counsel will also be required to take into consideration the very real possibility that the client may have to pay $2 million as opposed to $200,000, simply because the primary wrongdoer is insolvent. Clearly, the settlement value of the case in regard to the physician has significantly increased. This increased exposure can serve as additional impetus to settle a claim that counsel might otherwise consider taking to trial.

Impact of Adequate Insurance Limits — Mandating Limit by Hospitals

Every health care provider must be concerned about the applicability of the common law theory and about the insurance coverage of potential codefendants. Where joint and several liability applies, practitioners must make sure not only that they have adequate insurance limits to protect their assets, but also that other parties have adequate coverage. Failure to do so can result in exposure to a judgment far in excess of one party's own degree of culpability, which, in turn, could lead to financial disaster.

In fact, this situation is precisely why hospitals and their insurers today often require their staff physicians and contracting physicians to carry specified limits of liability coverage. In those jurisdictions where joint and several liability exists, the hospital, more often than not, has the most significant assets and thus often becomes the plaintiff's main target. To protect themselves from having to assume all the liabilities of other potentially more culpable parties, hospitals and their insurers have instituted mandatory insurance requirements for their physicians.

Imposing these requirements on the physician population, however, has often created a strained relationship. Needless to say, the cost of carrying higher liability limits can and often does become a financial burden for physicians, a burden they may ill afford or be unwilling to bear.

Nevertheless, a hospital can be held liable for a sum totally disproportionate to its actual negligence in any given case. Thus, failure to have a bylaw imposing minimum mandatory insurance limits for its physicians or failure to enforce such a bylaw can result in a hospital being considered an unacceptable risk to an insurer. In some instances, insurers have canceled or refused to renew a hospital's professional liability insurance policy for this reason.

From the hospital's standpoint, there are economic considerations in setting forth insurance requirements for physicians. To avoid alienating its staff physicians by mandating the purchase of professional liability insurance, many hospitals will forego such a proviso. However, because the hospital generally is more concerned about losing its insurance than about alienating contracting physicians, the rule that adequate professional liability limits be carried by contracting physicians is usually passed and enforced.

The doctrine of joint and several liability does play an important part in a hospital's decision to mandate adequate insurance limits for its physicians. Furthermore, such requirements can influence the ongoing relationship between a hospital and its physicians and between a hospital and its insurer.

Key Points and Conclusion

Where joint and several liability exists in a jurisdiction, it affects not only the settlement value of a case but also the defense and management of the case. In jurisdictions that do not have joint and several liability, but rather strict comparative negligence, it may be advantageous for the defense counsel to help the plaintiff prove its case against the joint defendants. If, for example, strict comparative negligence were applicable, it would be best for defense counsel to move the jury's attention away from the physician and focus it on a more culpable codefendant.

On the other hand, if the case is being tried in a jurisdiction where joint and several liability exists, the physician's defense counsel would not necessarily want to expose the liability of the codefendant. The physician could be held liable for the transgression of the codefendant as well as his own negligence should judgment be rendered against both parties.

Also affected by the doctrine of joint and several liability is the relationship between hospitals and their staff and contracting physicians. As the economic interests of a well-insured party, or one with substantial assets, to a claim or lawsuit can be adversely affected by an under-insured or noninsured party, hospitals have had to impose mandatory insurance requirements on their physicians. In some instances, this action has strained the physician-hospital relationship. Where both the hospital and its physicians are trying to maintain their financial viability, mandated insurance limits will remain an ongoing issue until the doctrine of joint and several liability is either eliminated or effectively modified in all states.

References

1. Sturgis RW. *Tort Cost Trends: An International Perspective.* Tillinghast-Towers (Perrin); 1995.
2. *Duncan v Cessna Aircraft Co.*, 665 SW2d 414, 429 (Tex 1984)
3. *Seattle 1st National Bank v Shoreline Concrete Co.* 588 P2d 1308, 1312-13 (1978).
4. Reinstatement (Second) of Torts §463 (1963).
5. Callaghan CB. *Comparative Negligence Manual.* §1:1 (3rd ed. 1995)
6. CC §1431.2(b)(2).
7. FS 768.31 (3).
8. NY Civ Prac Sec 1601.

Chapter 23

Malpractice and Civil Case Law

Cathy Bowerman, JD, MPH

The legal system has two purposes in our society: to set public policy and to resolve disputes. Some medical malpractice cases do both.

For those who are unfamiliar with the process, a malpractice lawsuit can be a mystifying and frightening experience. Indeed, the details of what happens behind closed doors in any given case will likely never be disclosed. But certain steps are followed, or at least should be, in the initial phases of all malpractice litigation.

Statutes and case law associated with malpractice actions not only vary from state to state, but also change over time. This chapter is written as an introduction to the legal system and how to operate within it. As such, it is not a guide for specific cases or problems because of the wide range of circumstances that affect each case.

How Law Is Made

Traditionally in this country, there have been two main sources of law: statutes and case law. Statutes are laws developed and codified by the elected legislative branch of federal, state, and local governments. These laws are written for all to read. Depending on the nature of the statute or legislation, the executive branch of government will formulate rules and regulations to flesh out the administrative details of the law.

Case law is a term used to refer collectively to rulings on the facts of a lawsuit by a trial court judge, court of appeals, or supreme court. Case law is far more complex and nebulous than statutes because of the larger number of cases,

and because facts vary from one case to another, and opinions coming from different courts are often in conflict.

Case law shapes most of the medical malpractice environment and influences the passage of statutes. One example is the statute of limitations, a law that determines when an action is no longer subject to a claim. Much of the detailed workings of medical malpractice law must be picked out of case law at the state level. Many states have passed legislation known as tort reform to organize and solidify the medical malpractice laws within the state. To varying degrees, these reforms have precluded some lawsuits from being filed. They also have altered the procedures followed in filing lawsuits. Qualifications of expert witnesses have been more clearly defined, and noneconomic damages, for example, for pain and suffering, loss of society and companionship, and loss of consortium, have been limited.

Definitions

A general understanding of the terms and concepts involved in a medical malpractice case is important. Medical malpractice as a cause of legal action has evolved from an entire body of tort law, a tort being a wrongful act. There are two major types of legal actions: criminal and civil.

In the **criminal** lawsuit, the state or government sues an individual for a wrongdoing considered against public interest, such as murder, rape, or theft. Penalties for criminal acts range from fines to imprisonment, and to the death penalty in some states. All crimes are based on *mens rea*, or intent. The consequence or harm is not punished as much as is the act itself, which is considered so heinous to the fabric of society, that the society acts to protect its value structure.

Civil actions are private disputes among one or more persons or entities. The state takes no active role except to provide the forum where such disputes are resolved. One subset of civil law is tort law. A tort is defined simply as a wrongdoing. A tort can be an intentional act, such as one person hitting another, or a negligent act, such as a person picking up a golf club and swinging it without looking to see who or what might be in the path of the swing. **Negligence** is defined as doing something that a reasonably prudent person would not do under the same or similar circumstances.

Within the body of negligence falls **professional negligence** and, more specifically for the purposes of this discussion, medical professional negligence or **malpractice**. The definition of these terms has evolved through case law and statutes. In general, this definition is uniform throughout the country, although specific language may vary. In Michigan, for example, professional negligence or malpractice of a defendant emergency physician is the failure to provide care that an emergency physician of ordinary learning, judgment, or skill in emergency medicine would do, or the commission of an act that an emergency physician of ordinary learning, judgment, or skill would not do under the same or similar circumstances. This is determined by a jury in any given case, or by a judge if both parties waive the right to a jury trial.[1]

Standard of care is the level of care that patients should receive as defined by professional experts. The standard is always determined by testimony at the time of trial. The higher standard of care reflects the fact that the practice of medicine, like all professions, is a monopoly regulated by the state, because medicine is recognized as a learned profession. It is for the jury to decide, based on the evidence, what an emergency physician of ordinary learning, judgment, or skill would or would not do under the same or similar circumstances.[1]

In medical malpractice cases, the plaintiff has the **burden of proof** for each of the following elements:

- **Duty** — That a duty exists to provide a certain level of care. For the emergency physician, this includes providing service in the first instance for any patient coming through the door.
- **Breach** — That the defendant was professionally negligent in one or more of the ways claimed by the plaintiff.
- **Harm** — That the plaintiff sustained injury and damages.
- **Proximate Cause** — That the professional negligence or malpractice of the defendant was a proximate cause of the injury and damages to the plaintiff.

The burden of proof for a civil (medical malpractice) case is far less stringent than it is for a criminal case. In a criminal case, the state must prove a defendant's guilt beyond a reasonable doubt. In a civil case, the plaintiff must establish fault by the **preponderance of evidence**. In simple terms, a jury must conclude there is at least slightly more evidence in favor of the plaintiff than in favor of the defendant to meet the burden of proof criteria.

Historically, plaintiffs were barred from bringing medical malpractice cases or personal injury cases if it could be established that the plaintiff was in any small way negligent as well. Even 1% of the fault assigned to a patient could negate the cause of action. This was known as the law of **contributory negligence**. Today, however, most states have switched over to a system of **comparative negligence**, in which a plaintiff's negligence, no matter how significant, does not prohibit a recovery by the plaintiff against the defendant physician. However, the total amount of damages to which the plaintiff would otherwise be entitled is reduced by the percentage that the jury assigns to the plaintiff's negligence. This is known as the **doctrine of comparative negligence**.[2]

Here's an example: a patient is given follow-up instructions to return to the emergency department within 48 hours to have the progression of an infection evaluated. If, in fact, the patient waits 72 hours before seeking follow-up care, such negligent action may contribute to the damages but not be the sole cause of them. Under the old system of contributory negligence, a plaintiff in this scenario would be unable to pursue a claim for malpractice even if the defendant emergency physician was negligent. Under comparative negligence, however, juries are asked to attribute a percentage of the damages to the plaintiff's delay. They would then be permitted to reduce a plaintiff's damage award by that percentage.

In presenting a medical malpractice case, the plaintiff has the burden of proof, that is, the plaintiff must establish the four elements of proof by testimony from an expert or experts before any monetary award can be recovered. This expert does not have to be an independent witness. The necessary expert testimony often can be obtained from the defendant physician directly or from another treating physician. There must be expert testimony regarding the standard of care, the specific breaches of the case, the extent of injury, and the fact that the defendant physician's actions caused or contributed to the injuries.[3]

This last element — proximate cause — has been commonly defined as follows: first, negligent conduct must have been a cause of the plaintiff's injury, and second, the plaintiff's injury must have been a natural and probable result of the negligent conduct.[4] Here's an example of professional negligence with no proximate cause: a child is brought in with end-stage Reye's Syndrome, which is not diagnosed until autopsy. Even if a timely diagnosis had been made, the fatal outcome would have been the same. In theory, only after the plaintiff has presented all four elements of a malpractice case by evidence must the defense respond to the various allegations by presenting witnesses and submitting exhibits.

The **damages** the plaintiff is entitled to recover vary substantially depending on the case. Elements of damage include past and future lost wages, past and future medical expenses, pain and suffering, and loss of consortium. There are other special damages that may be awarded depending on the case. These include loss due to embarrassment, humiliation, or emotional distress resulting from the injury or disfigurement, or loss of a business because of inability to continue work.

The law in every state requires **expert testimony** be given on the elements of medical malpractice. What varies among the states are the qualifications an expert must have to testify. It has been relatively common (particularly prior to tort reform legislation) for general practitioners, surgeons, and other nonemergency physicians to give testimony on the standard of care. All too often the "expert" merely has to be licensed to practice medicine somewhere and able to attest to being "familiar with the standard of care." No testimony regarding actual experience or hands-on contact with patients in the emergency department setting is required.

Under recent sweeping tort reform acts, more stringent rules have been established to determine who can be an expert in a given case.

Many states have passed new legislation called **tort reform**. The purpose of tort reform is to rectify inappropriate practices that place physicians and other health care providers at distinct disadvantages in the trial court system. First and foremost has been the liberal use of experts. Second, tort reform acts typically have reduced the time patients are given to bring lawsuits after the alleged malpractice has occurred. Third, the acts have placed limits on damages — a cap — on the amount of money that a party can receive.

The **statute of limitations** on malpractice has varied from state to state. By definition, the statute of limitations is the length of time after medical care has been rendered that a lawsuit can be instituted. For example, in Michigan, for years plaintiffs have had to file their claims within two years of the date of last treatment with the defendant or within six months from the time the plaintiff discovered or should have discovered the alleged acts of malpractice, whichever is longer. Also, a minor (person under 18 years of age) could bring a claim beyond the two-year or six-month discovery limit, as long as the claim was brought before the person's 19th birthday. This requirement may vary from state to state.

Now in some states, with tort reform, the two-year time frame does not run from the date of last treatment but from the date of the actual act or omission that serves as the basis of the claim. In addition, instead of allowing a discovery rule which, in theory and often in practice, was unlimited, the majority of states have enacted legislation limiting the discovery period to a given number of years after the alleged act, regardless of when the claim was discovered or should have been discovered. These statutes are called **statutes of respose**.[5]

Exceptions to the statute of limitations include discovery prevented by fraudulent conduct of the health care provider, a foreign body wrongfully left in the patient's body,[6] and an injury involving the reproductive system. The burden is still the plaintiff's, however, to prove that the alleged malpractice was not or could not have been discovered within six months of when the lawsuit was filed.

Each state has a number of other exceptions to these rules. Physicians should ask an experienced local attorney to help them carefully evaluate the statutes and current case law in their states.

Investigation and Workup of a Malpractice Claim

When examining the steps followed in the investigation and workup of a malpractice claim, it is helpful to view the process from both sides. From the plaintiff's side (the patient), the goals of litigation rarely seem so altruistic as to be a search for the truth. Often, the case appears to be a search for monetary gain for the client (and, of course, the lawyer).

The first major consideration is how extensive are the damages, or how extensive can the damages or injury be made to seem. Second, but not far behind, is whether blame can be assigned to a health care professional or institution. Again, the burning question is not the truth of the matter, but what evidence as accepted by the court can be presented to convince a jury that malpractice occurred.

For the purposes of investigating these damage and liability aspects, the plaintiff's attorney uses a number of methods to get information. First, the attorney talks with the patient and family members to find out who the medical caregivers were and the sequence of events. Second, the attorney obtains copies of medical records, which can be accomplished in a variety of ways, as follows:

- The patient can ask for and obtain a copy of the chart by signing an authorization. According to case law and statute in every state, patients are entitled to copies of their medical charts. The only exception would be in a psychiatric setting: access to records that are deemed a danger to a patient's mental health if disclosed may be denied.
- The patient's attorney, acting on behalf of the client, can request a copy of all medical records as long as a properly executed authorization, signed by the patient, accompanies the request.
- Before a physician is named in a lawsuit, it is ethical for an attorney to interview the physician personally or request a written summary of the care and treatment rendered. No physician is obligated or required to attend such a meeting or to write such a report. In fact, in any circumstance, the meeting should occur only after the physician retains an attorney and the attorney attends the meetings. Virtually all malpractice insurance companies will

provide an attorney at this point in an investigation.

Next, the plaintiff's attorney turns the medical records and information from the preliminary review over to a selected panel of physicians or nurses, or both, who scrutinize the data. They study every fact in the case to determine whether there is enough evidence for the jury to find that malpractice has occurred. Then, a Summons and Complaint is drafted and filed with the clerk of the court, and the lawsuit begins.

Keep in mind that there are perhaps as many variations of investigations as there are lawyers and lawsuits. The spectrum goes from extremely scanty to overly thorough. Some plaintiff law firms have full-time physicians and nurses on staff whose function is simply to investigate potential claims. There are opportunities for large profits in this business. Many plaintiff attorneys recognize these potential gains and are prepared to invest considerable funds to screen claims that come their way and weed out those not worth pursuing. Either the damages are negligible or the evidence of liability is too thin against a physician or health care provider, or both.

Many malpractice actions develop in conjunction with automobile collisions, Worker's Compensation claims, and product liability cases, in which the medical care provided is being analyzed to promote the other claims. It is not uncommon for a physician's care to become the new issue in such a case or in a separate malpractice case. Thus, physicians who cooperate in these cases for either the plaintiff or the defendant should not be misled into thinking that the spotlight will not turn toward them. They should assume that any accident resulting in injury will be reviewed by an attorney.

From the defense perspective, a case can be investigated for a variety of reasons. When an emergency physician becomes aware of any one of the events listed below, the investigation process should begin immediately. All of these events are likely to be reviewed by an attorney at some point:

- Some events are instant warning flags of a possible lawsuit: the wrong medication, wrong dose given; a patient dying within hours or days of an emergency department visit; subsequent diagnoses of fracture, meningitis, heart attacks, etc; all cervical spine cases in which the patient develops paralysis; all cases involving motor vehicle collisions; all on-the-job injuries.

- Often, before the actual filing of the lawsuit, a hospital will get a request for records. This should trigger an investigation immediately.
- Occasionally, before filing a lawsuit, a plaintiff attorney will write a letter to the physician or hospital requesting that its malpractice insurance carrier be put on notice.
- The "grapevine" often knows about an angry patient who is threatening to sue before hospital officials do. Sometimes, a patient or family member will contact the emergency physician or hospital administrator to express discontent with the care given.
- The service of the Summons and Complaint on the physician may be the first notice of the lawsuit.

Whenever a lawsuit or potential lawsuit is first suspected, the hospital staff should take a number of investigative safeguards. By now, every hospital has or should have an organized system for quality assurance and risk management. Within the bounds of that framework, all medical records, x-rays, ECGs, laboratory test results, billings, incident reports, indeed, every record having to do with that patient should be gathered and stored in a locked place out of the hands of a microfilmer, or worse still, a paper shredder. The hospital is a large, open place with many people coming and going. Records not separated from the rest are vulnerable to tampering or theft. If the staff do not make a concerted effort as soon as possible to collect all data, this lapse could prove problematic, if not disastrous, later on.

There are many reasons to take such precautions. Years may pass before a case reaches trial. It may not be until the trial itself that a laboratory sample or an x-ray becomes the material issue of the case. If records are not preserved early on, normal hospital policy may dictate microfilming the original x-ray or destroying old laboratory and x-ray worksheets. It cannot be emphasized enough how often seemingly incidental information proves to be crucial for the defense. Remember: a patient's medical record does not contain all of the information about that patient's emergency department visit. Laboratories keep their own records; ECGs and fetal monitor records may be documented more completely in their respective departments. Conceivably, a hospital may be charged with withholding evidence if it is later discovered that key evidence was buried in some other department's file.

The emergency department log of patients seen during the time of the plaintiff's care is a document that should be preserved, as is the monthly schedule of emergency physicians and employees. If laboratory tests were performed or x-rays taken and technicians or other hospital personnel were involved directly or indirectly with the care, a list of all their names may ultimately help the defense.

Another important step in the investigation is to notify all those involved in primary care of the patient that a claim is likely to be filed. They should be advised not to talk about the case with anyone outside of risk management, the hospital, or their personal attorneys. This means no locker room or lunchroom conversation. Even discussions with the hospital's attorney may not necessarily be protected under attorney-client privilege, because the hospital attorney is not the physician's legal counsel.

The investigation and gathering of witnesses' statements should be done with great caution and planning. The concern is to handle an investigation in such a way as to prevent the plaintiff's attorney from discovering and using the fruits of such fact-finding. Every state has its own rules on what information can be discovered. A local attorney can help establish a system of investigation for all cases or potential cases and protect an attorney's work products from discovery by the opposition.

For example, written statements taken from nurses can help preserve their memory of what happened. On the other hand, this information can prove devastating at trial if plaintiff's attorney can force its discovery. Generally speaking, most states provide no discovery for data gathered by or for a health care committee, such as peer review or quality assurance. However, if a witness keeps a copy of the statement at home or in a personnel file, it may be discovered under the assertion that it was not created solely for hospital functions.

As an example, the following is the Florida state statute regarding discovery of witnesses' statements[5]:

(2) A medical review committee of a hospital or ambulatory surgical center or health maintenance organization shall screen, evaluate and review the professional and medical competence of applicants to, and members of, medical staff. As a condition of licensure, each health care provider shall cooperate with a review of professional competence

performed by a medical review committee . . .(5) The investigations, proceedings, and records of a committee as described in the preceding subsections shall not be subject to discovery or introduction into evidence in any civil or administrative action against a provider of professional health services arising out of the matters which are the subject or evaluation and review by such committee, and no person who was in attendance at a meeting of such committee shall be permitted or required to testify in any such civil action as to any evidence or other matters produced or presented during the proceedings of such committee or as to any findings, recommendations, evaluations, opinions, or other actions of such committee or any members thereof. However, information, documents, or records otherwise available from original sources are not to be construed as immune from discovery or use in any such civil action merely because they were presented during proceedings of such committee, nor should any person who testifies before such committee or who is a member of such committee be prevented from testifying as to matters within his knowledge, but the said witness cannot be asked about his testimony before such committee or opinions formed by him as a result of said committee hearings.

Thus, the investigations, proceedings, and records of the review meeting and the disclosures of persons at the review are immune from discovery. However, the information, documents, and records may still be discovered to the extent they are available from original sources. Simply presenting the information at the review does not automatically guarantee immunity and prevent the use of such information in a civil action.

The Importance of the Medical Record

For the emergency physician, the best defense is a well-documented medical record. There is no substitute for a chart that commits to writing the patient's chief complaint and presenting signs and symptoms, as well as a thorough history and physical examination to evaluate those signs and symptoms. The record should document in detail the treatment given and results of such treatment, as well as the diagnosis or impression. The record also should document that clear follow-up instructions specific to the patient's condition were given to the patient or a friend or family member.

Emergency physicians should get into the habit of completing medical charts as if every case might become a lawsuit. They must remember that physician notes are not the only documents scrutinized and dissected by plaintiff's counsel. Nursing notes and any other notations are fair game. Generally speaking, the medical record can be a physician's best defense or biggest problem, depending on its content. Juries, as a rule, are more likely to believe the chart rather than any testimony rendered by the physician or the patient.

Alteration of Records

Once the chart has been completed in the normal course, it is not only inappropriate, but also a potential criminal violation to alter or change it. In the emergency department setting, most records are filled out at least in triplicate. For a plaintiff's attorney, the pearl in the oyster is finding two copies of the same chart with different information recorded on each. No matter how innocent or incidental the differences may be, they will become key elements of the lawsuit. The focus will shift from the true medical issues to the credibility and integrity of the defendant physician.

Even when a case is truly defensible, if a jury believes the physician has been dishonest, it will punish the physician by awarding heavy damages to the plaintiff. Although juries in civil cases generally are instructed to award actual damages as opposed to punitive ones, the monetary value of a given injury is obviously subjective. An angry jury will award a much higher dollar figure if given the chance.

Can a record ever be changed legally? The answer is a carefully qualified "yes." If, in reviewing the chart, a physician or nurse believes that something is incomplete or inaccurate, an addendum can be placed with the chart, along with the date and time the addendum was made. Physicians should develop the habit of dating and timing all entries to the medical records.

If a physician or staff member needs to make a correction on the medical chart itself, a single line should be drawn through the portion to be deleted, and the change dated and initialed by the person making the correction. The same is true when adding data to the chart. Medical staff should make every effort to ensure that the change does not appear to be entered for the purpose of deception.

Dictated charts are a particular problem. It is common practice for the dictated notes to become a permanent part of the chart without ever being read by the physician. This means that the physician is at risk for inaccurate transcription, mistakes in dictation, and inadvertent errors. Any of these is a potential gold mine for the plaintiff's attorney.

How Claims Are Investigated

The investigation process for a lawsuit or claim must be tailored to the specific case. Generally speaking, a defense attorney becomes involved at the claim stage, and certainly by the time a lawsuit is filed. As part of tort reform, some states require prelawsuit notification to potential defendants to allow time for negotiation of a settlement. Insurance carriers and hospitals differ on whether attorneys should become involved in this prelawsuit stage or only if and when the actual lawsuit is filed. Whenever an action is initiated, the lawyer should be the one to orchestrate the entire investigation. Any activities and information obtained by the attorney are protected under the attorney-client privilege or the attorney work product provisions of the law. With rare exceptions, an attorney cannot be forced to divulge any work product or information obtained in interviewing witnesses informally in preparation for a case.

The lawyer's investigation should include a thorough interview with the named physician early in the case. Records and documents are discovered and become available over time. As these materials accumulate, the case must be reevaluated. Follow-up conversations between the attorney and the physician should be routine. A close working relationship between attorney and client can be an essential ingredient in a successful defense. It is not always possible or even necessary for the two to become best friends, but feeling comfortable and confident with an attorney is important. The physician should talk to the lawyer frequently, particularly as a case becomes more involved. The defense of a case is a team effort, and the defendant is the most important expert on the team.

The investigation process includes not only a behind-the-scenes evaluation of records, but also the interview of potential witnesses. There is one barrier that is unique to medical malpractice cases and affects the witness interview process. In many states, despite the fact that a patient has sued the physician for claimed mal-

practice, that patient is still entitled to claim the physician-patient privilege with respect to any other health care provider. Some states prohibit private meetings between the defense attorney and a patient's prior, subsequent, and current treating physicians without express written permission of the plaintiff. Needless to say, no plaintiff will voluntarily allow that communication without the plaintiff's attorney being present. In this setting, defense attorneys have their hands tied in trying to discover "off the record" what another physician might testify to if asked questions about cause and effect or damages. Keep in mind, however, that the defense can ask for a medical or psychiatric evaluation of the plaintiff if the plaintiff's medical condition is at issue.

Because of case law like this, in many states, a large part of the investigation can only be conducted through formal and expensive depositions, or during the trial itself. Defense counsel then, are "stuck" with reviewing the medical records. Rarely are these detailed enough to prepare counsel for questioning a particular witness or for determining whether other witnesses should be called. Some states have created an exception to the physician-patient privilege in medical malpractice or other personal injury cases in which the plaintiff's medical condition is a central issue. In these states, when a lawsuit is filed, the plaintiff is deemed to have waived his physician-patient privilege, and defense attorneys can meet privately with other treating physicians.

The Lawsuit and the Defendant Physician

The physician named in a lawsuit is referred to as "physician" or "Dr. so & so" until a process server delivers papers known as Summons and Complaint. These are the initial papers filed by the patient's (plaintiff's) attorney to start the lawsuit. The physician who is served with the complaint then takes on a new title — "Defendant."

In most states, once served with a complaint, the defendant has a certain number of days to respond in writing to the allegations, usually 21 or less. If insured, the defendant should immediately contact the insurance company so that it can retain a defense attorney to answer the complaint and proceed with developing the case. The physician often can request a particular attorney. The request is not a guarantee but often influences the decision of attorney assignments.

The physician who is not insured should select an attorney immediately, one who is experienced in handling the defense of medical malpractice claims. This experience and the attorney's contacts may make the difference in the outcome of the case. Like physicians, lawyers specialize. Likewise, even if the defense counsel is retained by the insurance carrier, the physician must feel confident in the attorney's abilities. There should be an easy flow of communication between attorney and client. As the case proceeds, the defendant needs to ask what is being done to defend the case to ensure that the attorney is taking an active interest in the matter and is not simply collecting fees for little or no work.

Once the attorney has been retained, the physician defendant should expect an early meeting to go over everything about the case. The physician should not hold back any information from the attorney. It is far better to discuss in private the potential weaknesses and the physician's concerns than be confronted with them for the first time in a deposition or on the witness stand in front of a jury.

The pretrial discovery process may include taking many depositions from the patient, family, friends, codefendant physicians, nurses, other prior or subsequent treating physicians, and expert witnesses. There is no formal requirement that the defendant physician attend any of these meetings. Transcripts of the entire proceedings are almost always prepared; thus, the questions and answers can be reviewed at a later date.

However, in most instances, the physician should attend as many of these deposition meetings as possible. This is particularly true when the physician has had any direct contact with a witness, including the plaintiff (patient), family members, or any other physician with whom the defendant spoke or consulted about the patient. Obviously, in the emergency department setting, the emergency nurses' depositions may also be taken.

The presence of the physician defendant at depositions is crucial for several reasons. First of all, although the physician cannot participate by asking questions directly of the witness, he can write out questions or indicate which questions the attorney should ask. Not only is the emergency physician an expert in his own right, he was the one who took care of that particular patient. The physician, better than the attorney

or perhaps anyone else, knows what occurred and is in an excellent position to help counsel follow up the witnesses' initial responses with other questions.

Second, for many witnesses, the defendant physician's presence tends to encourage honesty and minimize exaggeration. Third, attending the depositions allows the physician to see not only his own attorney in action, but also the plaintiff's. It helps clarify the case against the physician so that he can prepare for what will be asked of him in court.

Finally, even though the transcript of a deposition is available for later reading, a picture is still worth a thousand words. An emergency physician may see 25 to 30 patients per shift on perhaps 15 or more shifts per month. Recalling who a particular patient is two to five years later may be difficult. If the physician comes to the plaintiff's deposition, he can see the patient directly and hear the person's testimony. This is perhaps one of the best ways to refresh one's memory about past events.

Despite these important points, many defense attorneys do not encourage the physician's attendance because they do not want to disrupt the physician's schedule. Defendant physicians should make it clear to their attorneys that they want to attend as many deposition meetings as possible. In some instances, the plaintiff's expert may live out of town, and the question of travel expenses comes up. Generally speaking, insurance companies can be persuaded to pay these costs for the physician in order to have him present when a deposition is given.

Just as the plaintiff must have expert testimony to support a claim, the defense must have the same. Although the defendant physician can be qualified to testify on his own behalf, such a strategy is not preferred. The defendant's own testimony would be considered by most juries as self-serving, unless additional expert testimony is obtained from third-party physicians uninvolved with the case.

Picking experts for the defense is generally handled by the defense counsel. However, it is quite appropriate for the defendant to discuss possible candidates with the attorney. With rare exceptions, there should be no direct contact between the defendant physician and the prospective expert. Contact between the two could give their testimony an air of collusion. Also, there should be no preexisting friendship or close working relationship between the defendant and the expert to avoid the impression that the testimony was "developed" as a team effort. An expert should be an independent authority. If the expert appears to the jury to be unbiased, the testimony will carry greater weight.

Although there are plaintiff's experts who will say what they are paid to say, there are also defense experts, who in reviewing the case of a fellow physician will never find problems. From the defense side, retaining an expert who is too defense-oriented is dangerous. Such a person may not hold up well under cross-examination. It is important to have a reviewer who looks at the case with a very critical eye. Because both defendant physician and defense counsel should be aware beforehand of all potential weaknesses in their case, they should select a defense expert who can point out and raise the uncomfortable questions initially. Depending on the nature of these questions, such an expert may push the defense toward a settlement versus a trial, or vice versa.

The defendant should go over the opinions and comments rendered by the expert. After all, these are comments made by an outside observer who is relying on the medical records and perhaps some deposition testimony. Such comments may be quite revealing to the defendant and attorney. Even though different attorneys have different strategies in preparing for a claim, generally it is best to obtain an initial review or reviews as early as key records can be obtained. The expert's comments can be valuable to preparing the defense.

The Defendant's Deposition

This can be the most crucial part of the case. Preparing an hour before is rarely sufficient. By the time the physician's deposition is scheduled, he should have had at least one lengthy face-to-face meeting with the defense attorney at the beginning of the case. In preparation for the deposition, the physician and attorney should go over all the records and facts of the case in detail. The defense counsel may even role-play some questions that the plaintiff's attorney is likely to ask. To the extent events can be predicted, the attorney and defendant should cover every issue they can consider, regardless of how unlikely it may be, so that the area is at least touched on before the deposition.

Adequate preparation for the deposition is, in large part, the physician's responsibility. The physician need not study the area of medicine involved in the claim as if preparing for a board certification examination. On the other hand, as an emergency physician, he must understand the medical issues within the bounds of that specialty. Juries are likely to find it odd if the emergency physician appears to be a walking encyclopedia of subspecialty knowledge outside of emergency medicine.

At the very least, the physician must have thoroughly reviewed the medical records. In the average emergency department case, the records are relatively brief. There is no excuse for not knowing everything about a patient's chart before giving a deposition. This includes having a working knowledge of not only the emergency physician's notes, but also the triage notes, the nursing notes, the clerk's record of the chief complaint, the follow-up instructions, all laboratory test results, x-rays, and vital signs. The physician should know who made every entry and scratch mark on the chart.

The physician also should be aware that, in emergency cases, timing of events is almost always an issue. To the extent possible, the emergency physician should be so familiar with the chart that he can recreate it in the proper sequence and timing of events. Obviously, this cannot always be done. But to the extent it can be, it is immensely helpful to the defense to have a command of the case at the time of deposition.

Generally, the emergency physician should not speak directly with nurses, other physicians, or the hospital risk manager once the lawsuit has been instigated. Testimony based on such conversations does not look good to a jury because it gives the appearance of collusion or perhaps coercion.

Evidence Versus Fact Versus Truth

Although "evidence," "fact," and "truth" are often confused, in a court of law, it is assumed that these terms all mean the same thing. However, in actual practice, this is not necessarily the case. Scientific truth is rarely addressed in trial, and truth is not the actual end product of the legal system.

Evidence consists of the sworn testimony of witnesses and the introduction of exhibits, which are documents or other items presented to help prove or disprove a case. It may also include some testimony or items that the court simply tells the jury to consider as evidence. Although questions the attorneys ask the witnesses are not themselves evidence, the witnesses' answers are.

Most malpractice cases are tried before a jury, although some are conducted before the judge only. In either instance, the jury or judge becomes the fact-finder. The fact-finder determines the facts from the evidence received in open court. In instances where there is conflicting testimony, the fact-finder must decide which information provided as evidence constitutes fact.[6] The fact-finder, in other words, makes the determination of what is the truth. Obviously, what the jury or judge chooses to believe as fact or truth may not be at all.

In every state and federal court, there is a predetermined set of rules, known as the rules of evidence, that dictates what constitutes evidence. Most states have adopted the federal evidence rules for use in their state courts, with some modification. Typically, the rules of evidence have a purpose clause. For example, in Michigan, the rule reads as follows[7]: "These rules are intended to secure fairness in administration, elimination of unjustifiable expense and delay, and promotion of growth and development of the law of evidence and that truth may be ascertained and proceedings justly determined." The purpose of the rules of evidence is to determine what evidence will be admissible or presented to the fact-finder for consideration. Relevant evidence refers to evidence that tends to make any fact pertinent to a case more probable or less probable than it would be without the evidence.[8]

The entire scope of the rules of evidence is far too vast and complex to discuss in detail here, but all testimony and exhibits must pass the rules of evidence before they become admissible. By the nature of malpractice proceedings and the rules themselves, judges also have produced a large body of discretionary rulings regarding what constitutes admissible evidence. Thus, the determination of what is admissible could differ widely from judge to judge.

In general, admissible evidence includes all medical records generated by the defendants, as well as all other relevant medical records generated by other physicians. (Often, an exception is made in other medical records. Any diagnosis recorded in those records is not admissible and must be expunged from the record before submitting it to the jury.) Testimony from an eyewitness is admissible and relevant, as is expert testimony regarding the standard of care, breaches of standard of care, injury or damages, and the relationship between breaches of the standard of care and the injuries. For particular issues, attorneys, judges, and others must refer to the local pertinent rules of evidence, as well as case law defining what constitutes evidence.

Evidence may be introduced in the form of exhibits. There are three basic types of exhibits: originals, exact copies, and demonstrative evidence. Generally speaking, courts would rather have the original medical records than copies. By stipulation, often the copy is marked as an exhibit instead. Reasons for wanting the original might include the fact that originals generally are more legible and that it is easier to see when different pens are used to make the various entries.

A separate category of evidence is demonstrative or illustrative evidence. This category could include drawings of anatomy or a showing of a similar (but not the exact same) piece of equipment, such as an ECG machine, syringe, nasogastric tube, or other equipment used in the emergency department to help illustrate what the witness is talking about in describing a particular technique or event. Rarely are these demonstrative items admissible as evidence. Therefore, they cannot later be taken back into the jury room. But, they can be paraded before the jury during the course of trial to assist in the communication of the testimony.

Some of the most effective testimony is delivered with the assistance of colored markers and a large pad of paper on an easel. Jurors hear better and comprehend more if they can watch as well as listen. As the defendant physician or expert testifies, writing words or drawing (if only crudely) to emphasize or illustrate points is very helpful. Juries tend to remember such testimony more clearly when they deliberate at the end of the case.

The process of a trial can be viewed as an individual morality play. What the jury comes to believe may not be rationally based or reflective of true scientific thought. It may reflect more how well the plaintiff or defendant was able to capture the trust and sympathy of the jury. Although it is often difficult to know precisely what factors are most important for a jury in deciding a case, clearly, among the most essential are the testimony of the defendant physician and the image that physician presents to the jury.

Key Points and Conclusion

The following is a list of tips for successful presentation:

- There is no substitute for being prepared. Knowing the chart and medical issues well conveys confidence to a jury. The goal is to have jurors think that if they were sick, they would want you to be on duty in the emergency department when they sought treatment.
- First impressions can be lasting impressions. Dress conservatively and appear neat and clean. Expensive jewelry or expensive clothes tend to alienate jurors.
- Your conduct during the course of the trial is as important off the stand as it is on the stand. Maintain a professional appearance throughout. Making faces, joking, or appearing disgusted or disinterested will do little to help your case.
- Be present, if possible, for the entire trial. This demonstrates that you are taking the case seriously. If you are married, it is a nice touch to have your spouse present in the courtroom as much as possible. Conservative dress and professional appearance are important for your spouse as well.
- Always tell the truth. This admonition cannot be underestimated or overemphasized. Jurors have an uncanny way of knowing when a witness is not being truthful.
- During cross-examination, do not let the plaintiff's attorney put words in your mouth by paraphrasing earlier testimony. Force the attorney to restate the question, then respond to it.
- When your attorney makes an objection, listen to it. Such an objection may be a signal or message to you.
- When questions are asked "generally," make sure the answer distinguishes between the general question and the facts in the case at hand. Attorneys are masters at focusing on a portion of the facts that supports their case and leaving out pertinent facts that support the defense. As long as the answer given identifies the differences, the tactic will become clear.
- To the extent possible, do not succumb to plaintiff's intimidation tactics by responding in anger or with sharp words. With few exceptions, this response rarely works in the defendant's favor.
- You may be angry and hurt by being caught up in this legal process, but your frustration and anger should be expressed only in the privacy of your home or your lawyer's office. It should never be seen in the medical records, expressed in a deposition (on or off the record), or displayed in the courtroom in front of a jury.
- If the plaintiff's attorney asks you to comment on or refers to a document unfamiliar to you, take time to examine it thoroughly and to become familiar with its contents. If the plaintiff's attorney tries to prevent this examination, ask permission from the judge to review the material before answering questions about it.
- During the course of a trial, and particularly during depositions, avoid making any off-the-record comments regarding the case. Refrain from participating in any friendly conversation instigated by plaintiff's counsel. Comments made during these off-the-record sessions could come back to haunt you. Be polite, but remain on guard.
- If plaintiff's counsel attempts to impeach you by bringing up prior deposition testimony, take whatever time is necessary to read the prior statement in the context in which it was given. Chances are, there is a logical explanation for why you made one comment in the context of the deposition, and a seemingly different comment during the trial.
- Your choice of words in answering a question can be crucial to a case. In one emergency medicine trial, an otherwise defensible claim had to be settled because of a comment made during the course of deposition by the emergency physician defendant. Several hours into the deposition, after being asked several times in slightly different ways why a CT scan was not done, the emergency physician blurted out: "Not every drunk with a head injury deserves a CT scan." Although this statement was clearly made in frustration, it resulted in a settlement of several hundred thousand dollars that otherwise would not have occurred. Had that case been tried, the plaintiff's entire theme would be the prejudice of the emergency physician against alcoholics. It would have been an attack on the physician's credibility for the care he actually rendered in the case.
- If you feel tired, angry, or on the verge of losing your concentration or self-control, it is far better to request a break than to proceed.

- Do not think out loud when being questioned by the plaintiff's attorney. Before giving an answer, keep your thoughts private and formulate the answers mentally before giving them orally. Mumbling or informal comments may well wind up in the transcript during a deposition or may be heard by the jury during trial.
- If a question or a series of questions does not make sense, do not answer them. Ask for a rephrasing or clarification until the question is clear.
- As part of preparation, read all depositions taken in your case. Read certain depositions, particularly your own, repeatedly so the content becomes familiar and is easily recalled in the correct order and timing.
- When testifying before the jury, be careful to use words that every person can understand. After all, if jurors cannot understand you, they may well believe that the plaintiff did not understand you either.
- In many ways, a trial is a popularity contest. It is important for the jury to like you and identify with you. If they do, they will be less inclined to punish you for the care rendered to the patient.
- Never show disgust or disdain for the patient. Always refer to the patient with respect and caring. The winning edge in a case often is showing the standard of caring — not just the standard of care.

References

1. Michigan Standard Jury Instruction 2nd 30.01; *Sirila v Barrios*, 398 Mich 576 (1976); *Lince v Monson*, 363 Mich 135 (1961); *Robert v Young*, 369 Mich 133; 119 NW2d 627 (1963).
2. Prosser WL. *Handbook of the Law of Torts.* §67 at 472 (5th ed. 1984).
3. *Sullivan v Russell*, 417 Mich 398, 407 (1983); *Rick v Jaskolski*, 412 Mich 206, 211 (1981); *Francisco v Parchment Clinic*, 407 Mich 325, 327 (1979).
4. *Van Keulen and Winchester Lumber v Manistee and NR Co.*, 222 Mich 682; 193 NW2d 289 (1923); *Sutter v Biggs*, 377 Mich 80; 139 NW2d 684 (1966).
5. Fla Stat Ann §766.101(5) (West 1996). Medical review committee, immunity from liability.
6. McCormick CT. *McCormick's Handbook of the Law of Evidence.* §339 at 794-795 (2nd ed. 1972).
7. Mich R Evid 101.
8. Fed R Evid 401.

Chapter 24

Contracts in Emergency Medicine

Melvin E. Harris, MD
Daniel J. Sullivan, MD, JD, FACEP

The legal definition of a contract is a promise, or set of promises, the performance of which the law recognizes as a duty. A contract is entered into by "parties" — the legal terminology for the persons or entities who make the promises forming the contract. In common usage, the term "contract" has also come to mean a written document that specifies the details of an agreement that describes the working relationship between two or more parties.

Emergency medicine contracts have an important role in risk management in two principal ways:

- Contracts document the understanding of the parties at the beginning of the relationship. They can serve to limit risk that might otherwise result from a poorly functioning association or from a premature end to the association.
- Contracts describe the parties' relationships — their rights and duties with respect to each other and to third parties (e.g., patients, the public). The exact content of these provisions can expand or limit the liability of the various parties to the contract.

Risk management begins with the process of contract negotiation and continues through the careful drafting of the agreement. The negotiations should provide an adequate opportunity for all parties to identify, discuss, and resolve all important issues. Each party should carefully prepare a list of its most important (and contentious) issues for discussion with the other party or parties. In most cases, each party knows which items are most important to it; adequate time can then be allowed during negotiations to ensure that all parties have a common understanding about the most important items. Other issues will have lower priority and may allow the parties to be more flexible in their negotiations. The final written contract should reflect the negotiated agreement of the parties and clearly explain all significant items.

Case Studies

1

A physician just out of her emergency medicine residency signs her first contract with an emergency medicine contract group to work in a large community hospital. The contract contains a lot of boilerplate language and all the usual information about malpractice insurance, termination with and without cause, etc. She signs the contract after speaking over the telephone with an attorney friend who specializes in environmental law.

After her first few shifts, the physician decides that she has made a serious mistake. The emergency department is high acuity, at 40,000 patients per year in single physician coverage, with a physician's assistant in the main emergency department and a nurse practitioner in the fast track. According to the group's contract with the hospital, the emergency physician covers all inpatient cardiac arrests, newborn deliveries, and problems on the floors and reads floor ECGs and x-rays. The physician becomes fearful of working any more shifts, feeling that she is spread too thin and that her patients may be at risk. She reviews her contract for any information regarding the group's or the hospital's responsibilities.

2

A second emergency physician signs a contract with a group to provide emergency services at a local hospital. According to the contract, the group is responsible for providing the physician with malpractice insurance coverage in the amount of $1 million per incident.

That summer, a malpractice claim for misdiagnosis is filed against the physician. He then learns that his insurer had been placed into receivership several months earlier and that his emergency group had failed to obtain other coverage. The group tells the physician that he is not covered for this lawsuit. He contacts an attorney to find out if he has any right to demand enforcement of the group's promise to provide insurance coverage.[1]

3

Yet another emergency physician signs an employment agreement with a contract group to perform emergency medical services in one of the group's emergency departments. Under the agreement, on termination with the contract group, the physician is prohibited from performing emergency medical services for any hospital at which he has worked as an employee of the group. The contract contains a liquidated damages provision, whereby the emergency physician is required to pay $10,000 if he continues employment at the hospital after the termination of the group's contract.

The hospital to which this physician is assigned switches to a new provider group. The physician ends his employment with the old provider and continues to work at the hospital. The first provider sues for breach of contract, seeking payment of the $10,000 in liquidated damages provided for in the noncompete clause of the employment agreement.[2] He contacts an attorney to determine whether the noncompete provision in his contract is valid and whether he can do anything to avoid its enforcement.

Parties

Generally, there are three types of parties in emergency medicine contracts, as follows:
- Hospitals (or similar health care entities)
- Provider groups (e.g., national multihospital groups, smaller regional groups, single-hospital groups)
- Physicians

A contract is usually made by and between two of these types of parties (e.g., contracts between hospitals and provider groups, between provider groups and physicians, and between hospitals and physicians).

A party in a contract is sometimes represented by some other legal entity. For example, a hospital's role as a party may be fulfilled either by a large corporation that owns a number of hospitals or by a government-designated hospital district. Similarly, a physician may enter a contractual relationship through a professional corporation. These distinctions can be important because the rights, duties, and obligations under the contract generally will apply to the legal entities named as parties to the contract.

Contract Terms

Terms are the provisions or conditions determining the nature and scope of an agreement or contract. For example, a contract for the provision of professional medical services in a hospital emergency department typically contains and defines the following terms:
- Names and status of the parties
- Recitals of the general purpose of the agreement
- Duties and obligations of each of the parties
- Time frame encompassed by the agreement
- Mechanisms for renewal and/or termination of the agreement
- Notice provisions
- Hold harmless and/or indemnification provisions
- Restrictive covenants regarding the hiring of each other's employees
- Billing and payment procedures
- Reporting requirements
- Performance standards or criteria
- Statements regarding the confidentiality of all or part of the contract

Duties and Obligations of the Parties

In contracts involving emergency medicine, duties and obligations of the various parties typically include the following items.

Duties of the Hospital
- To provide an adequately equipped and staffed emergency department.

- To provide adequate backup for the emergency department by taking measures to ensure the availability of on-call attending staff and specialists.
- To provide adequate forms and clerical support to allow for proper and timely documentation of emergency medical treatment.
- To provide, through the hospital's medical staff and governing board, appropriate credentialing and privileging functions for physicians working in the department.
- To maintain an adequate system of medical records.
- To provide administrative support services, such as preparing and filing patient consent forms.
- To provide adequate ancillary medical services, such as laboratory, radiology, electrocardiography, respiratory therapy, etc.
- To provide adequate medical support services, such as backup or overread for ECGs, x-rays, etc., that are first read by the emergency physicians.
- To pay the other party for services provided on a timely basis (i.e., as stated in the contract).

Duties of the Provider Group

- To recruit physicians to work in the emergency department.
- To schedule physicians' work time in the emergency department so that no gaps in coverage occur.
- To facilitate the process in which physicians apply for and obtain hospital privileges to work in the emergency department (e.g., obtain completed application forms, verify licensure and DEA registration, verify education and certifications, obtain letters of reference).
- To provide a medical director for the emergency department.
- To pay the physicians who provide professional services in the emergency department.
- To keep records explaining costs incurred for those services for which payments are made under the Medicare or Medicaid programs (required by the U.S. Department of Health and Human Services).

Duties of the Physician

- To keep licenses, DEA registrations, and required certifications current.

- To be available for work in the emergency department and to work when scheduled.
- To perform professional services in accordance with standards of the profession and the rules, regulations, and procedures of the hospital and its medical staff.
- To apply for and maintain a medical staff appointment at the hospital.
- To prepare all documentation of medical services to ensure a timely and complete medical record and to facilitate billing for professional services.

Other Duties

The following duties may be assigned to any one party or all parties depending on the negotiated conditions:

- To keep the terms of the contract confidential except when disclosure is required by law or when specifically authorized by the other party.
- To provide professional liability (malpractice) insurance with specified limits.
- To bill for the professional services provided to patients.

Contracts in emergency medicine may assign to specific parties the responsibility for providing supervision and training of personnel, investigation of patient complaints, and peer review.

The responsibility for supervision of physicians in the emergency department depends on the nature of the relationship between the group and the hospital. If the physicians are employees, the hospital typically assigns supervisory responsibility to an administrative person or to the medical director. If the group is an independent contractor to the hospital, this responsibility is typically delegated to the medical director or, more generally, to the provider group. Some states prohibit hospital administrative supervision of medical providers to prevent what they view as the "corporate practice of medicine." Medical practice regulations in all states emphasize the importance of the physician's personal responsibility for decisions and actions involving medical practice.

Contracts should clearly delineate the responsibility for supervision of nonphysician personnel. The physician on duty should have final patient care authority, as this physician will certainly have ultimate responsibility. Supervision of department administrative personnel is usually the responsibility of the charge nurse, who reports to the head of nursing services and is indirectly accountable to the hospital administration. In a few emergency departments, the medical director has some direct responsibility for nonphysician personnel. Medical directors should make sure that all lines of administrative authority and responsibility are carefully documented.

Training of personnel can be designated as the individual responsibility of various professionals working in the emergency department, with specific requirements for their continuing education. Many hospitals will also wish to specify that the emergency physicians provide certain types of training for nurses, paramedics, and other personnel involved in the delivery of emergency care.

Patient complaint investigation is vital to risk management and public relations. The responsibility for managing complaints should be given to an individual who can and will administer the process fairly and consistently. If the medical director has good interpersonal skills, it often works best to assign this responsibility to the director. From a position of respect and authority, the medical director can involve staff physicians and other department personnel in responding rapidly and professionally to all patient complaints. Contract clauses outlining this responsibility should require written documentation of the outcome or resolution of every patient complaint.

Peer review of physicians is, by definition, the responsibility of other physicians. The hospital usually will want to stipulate that emergency physicians participate in peer review for the department. These activities (daily chart review, retrospective audits, etc.) are customarily coordinated by the medical director, who should ideally involve the other physicians. Information generated by such activities should be shared with all who can use the information to improve patient care and manage risk better. Written reports and documentation of such activity should be handled through regular hospital committee structures for peer review to protect the information from discovery in legal proceedings.

Breach of Contract and Remedies

The legal term for a party's failure to keep contract promises is breach of contract. Such a breach results when a party fails in some way to meet its duties or obligations, including failure to meet performance standards specified within the contract.

The consequences of a breach of contract can be serious. In such an instance, the non-breaching party may seek a legal remedy. When a court awards a remedy for a breach, it attempts to place the injured party in the same position it would have been in if the contract had not been breached.

The principal remedies courts may grant for breach of contract are as follows:

- Specific performance
- Injunction
- Money damages

When specific performance is the remedy, the court orders the breaching party to cure the breach, and the contract remains intact. Obviously, in contracts involving emergency medicine, this remedy is usually used only if the breach is not of such a serious and ongoing nature that the working relationship between the parties has been irreparably damaged.

Injunction is a remedy if the breach threatens to produce irreparable injury. The most frequent use of this remedy in contracts involving emergency medicine results from a breach caused by one party's breaking its promise not to hire the employees or independent contractors of the other party (i.e., violating its restrictive covenant). If the court deems the restrictive covenant reasonable, it may grant an injunction and order the employee or independent contractor not to work for the new employer.

Monetary damages awarded by courts as a remedy for breach of contract vary in kind and amount, depending on the circumstances of each case. The type of monetary damages most often involved in contract disputes are compensatory damages and liquidated damages.

Compensatory damages represent actual losses suffered by the injured party, including lost profits on the contract, the cost of securing substitute performance, and other losses caused by imperfect or delayed performance. Liquidated damages are a specific sum, to which the parties agree in advance, that can be recovered if the contract is breached. If the liquidated damages specified are unreasonably large or if the actual damages are easily determined, some jurisdictions will treat the liquidated damages as a penalty and refuse to enforce it.

The payment of monetary damages awarded by a court for breach of contract is enforced by the court. All parties entering into a contract must understand this potentially serious result of breaking promises made within the contract. In that regard, it is imperative that parties do not incur contractual obligations they cannot reasonably expect to meet.

In addition to the liability a party has toward other parties to a contract, there are some instances in which there may be unsuspected liability to other parties (i.e., entities or persons who are not actually parties to the contract). In contracts involving emergency medicine, this "unsuspected" liability most often involves patients or their heirs in questions of medical malpractice.

For example, suppose a party responsible for arranging and purchasing professional liability insurance with specified limits fails to do so. A plaintiff might still have rights through the original contract because, without the insurance in place, the plaintiff could be deprived of benefits to which he or she would otherwise have been entitled.

Another example of unsuspected liability might be created if a party failed to meet some performance criterion specified in the contract. Parties should be careful about terms of a contract that describe high goals and ideals of performance. The legal standard of care describes what an average, prudent physician would do in a particular case. A higher standard of performance derived from the language of the contract may create an opportunity for a third party to measure negligence based on the contractual standard rather than on the legal standard.

Termination

Contracts in emergency medicine usually contain specific provisions for either party to terminate the contractual relationship. The termination clause usually specifies termination procedures for alleged breach of contract by the other party and different termination procedures for reasons other than breach (i.e., termination without cause).

In each situation, the termination clause generally states how long services are to be provided after the notice of termination. For example, each party may be required to give the other party at least a 90-day notice of termination. This provides for a more orderly transition, giving time for the hospital to arrange for replacement services and for the physicians to find other employment.

Two important exceptions to the longer termination notice include the following:
- A breach by the physicians or provider group caused by a failure to cover shifts in the emergency department.
- A monetary default on the part of the hospital.

In the first instance, the hospital would not want to risk further damage by leaving its emergency department inadequately staffed for any significant period of time. In the second instance, the physicians or provider group would not want to continue to provide professional services for the hospital if they might never be paid.

Termination clauses dealing with breach of contract may provide a time frame during which the breaching party can "cure" or remove the breach and effectively stop the termination process. For example, such a termination clause might read: "In the event of a material breach by one party, the nonbreaching party may terminate this agreement upon 30 days' notice to the breaching party; provided, however, that if the breaching party substantially cures the breach within 10 days of having received the notice, the notice of termination shall be nullified and the agreement shall continue in full force and effect."

Noncompete Provisions

Many emergency physician groups routinely include noncompete clauses or restrictive covenant clauses that prohibit continued association of any of its emergency physicians in the hospital emergency department after termination of the emergency physician's contract with the group or the group's contract with the hospital. The rationale for such clauses is that it is unfair when an emergency physician group incurs the expenses to recruit and place physicians who are subsequently retained by the hospital or another physician group that assumes the emergency department contract. Such clauses are generally enforceable if they meet certain guidelines, as follows:
- Limited specifically to physicians.
- Reasonable duration (e.g., six months to one year).
- Restricted scope (e.g., to a particular hospital, community, or group).

The American Medical Association recently took a position to oppose noncompete or restrictive covenants. Several states have enacted legislation disallowing such covenants in physician contracts.

Courts first look to state law to determine whether there are any statutory restrictions against restrictive covenants. For example, in *Spectrum Emergency Care, Inc. v St. Joseph's*

Hospital and Health Center,[3] the court held that a posttermination restrictive covenant was invalid based on a review of North Dakota law.

In this case, Spectrum Emergency Care contracted with St. Joseph's Hospital to supply emergency physicians. The contract language restricted the hospital from directly hiring the physicians working for Spectrum. The agreements between Spectrum and the emergency physicians restricted them from working for the hospital for one year after the end of their contract.

Spectrum had the contract for several years. In 1989, two physicians working at the hospital approached the CEO, indicating they were unhappy with Spectrum and intended to find other employment. The hospital agreed to contract directly with these physicians and gave Spectrum notice of termination.

Spectrum sued the hospital and the physicians, alleging breach of contract. Looking first at the restrictive covenants in the physician contracts, the court noted that North Dakota law prohibits the use of language that attempts to restrain people from exercising a lawful profession. Looking to the hospital-Spectrum agreement, the court stated that to uphold the hospital's covenant would be to allow Spectrum to do indirectly what it could not do directly. Therefore, the court held the covenant not valid. As demonstrated by this case, a state law on point will invalidate a contractual restrictive covenant.

Prohibitions during the posttermination period generally evoke the greatest antipathy. Although they create a disincentive for a hospital to terminate a group, individual physicians often view them as "spoiler" provisions that unreasonably disrupt the physicians' professional and personal lives.

Legally, these posttermination noncompete provisions are problematic. Their enforceability varies according to state, geographic scope, limitations on practice, and duration, and perhaps other factors. Nonetheless, many groups have a strong financial incentive to attempt enforcement, and few individual physicians are willing to challenge it. The emergency physician should seek legal advice regarding the enforceability of these provisions in a particular state.

Posttermination noncompete provisions may take various forms. Some straightforwardly prohibit physicians from working in the emergency department for a fixed time. Others are structured as trade secrets provisions. The contract prohibits an individual physician from disclosing the group's confidential information, and both parties agree any attempt to negotiate with or stay at the hospital after termination would necessarily require a prohibited disclosure. Other noncompete provisions may be structured as a "recruitment fee" the physician must pay the group or as a "liquidated" or predetermined amount that the individual must pay the group for acknowledged damages, although they may be difficult to value.

In general, courts will err on the side of the practicing physician when evaluating a legal challenge to a restrictive covenant. If the covenant is too broad geographically or is defective in any manner, the court will modify or strike it. For example, in *PHP Healthcare Corporation v EMSA Limited Partnership*,[4] EMSA supplied emergency physicians to Millington Naval Hospital in Millington, Tennessee. The EMSA-physician contracts contained a termination clause on expiration of the EMSA-hospital contract and a restrictive covenant preventing the employees from continuing to work at the hospital as employees after the EMSA contract expired.

PHP, an EMSA competitor, was awarded the new contract with the hospital. PHP hired one of the former EMSA physicians after notifying EMSA that it considered the covenant unenforceable.

EMSA brought suit in federal court. The federal court looked to Florida law and held the covenant unenforceable under applicable law. The covenant was "over-broad," as it placed no geographic limit on the area of competition. EMSA appealed. The appellate court said that such covenants could be enforced if first, the enforcement was sought within a reasonable limited geographic area and second, the one seeking enforcement was still operating a "like business" in that area. The court found that because the contractual geographic area was Millington Naval Hospital, the covenant was not over-broad in geographic scope. However, EMSA was no longer operating a "like business" in the relevant area and, thus, could not enforce the noncompete covenant under Florida law.

Notice Provisions

Contracts should contain notice provisions that describe the method and place of delivery of notices or communications given by one party to another party. These clauses generally contain the official or legal mailing addresses of the parties. They also stipulate that the notices be written and sent by a method providing some proof that the recipient has received the notice (e.g., certified U.S. Mail or Federal Express).

Arbitration

Parties to a contract may wish to use arbitration to settle certain disputes that arise from performance or nonperformance of the contract. Arbitration is the legal process of submitting controversies or disputes to persons chosen by the parties themselves for determination. An arbitration clause in a contract should include the types of disputes to be submitted for arbitration (e.g., all disputes involving indemnification and restrictive covenants). The arbitration clause usually outlines the procedure for a party to request arbitration and defines the methods to select the arbitrators (e.g., an arbitrator selected by each party and one selected by those arbitrators). The clause generally indicates the degree to which the arbitrators' decision will be binding and stipulates the responsibilities of the parties regarding payment of expenses for the arbitration proceedings.

Arbitration can provide for a more rapid, cost-effective resolution of disputes than can a court-mediated settlement, with its attorneys, frequent delays, and complex rules of discovery. However, some parties may not want to sacrifice certain rights and protections provided by a court hearing, particularly when the disputes involve major financial risks.

'Law Effect'

If the formation or performance of a contract is illegal or contrary to the public interest, all or part of the contract may be void or not enforceable. Contract law holds that the public welfare is more important than the right of individuals to bargain freely. The legal system would undermine its own basic objectives if it enforced agreements that were illegal or contrary to the public interest.

Nevertheless, jurisdictions may vary in their application of this principle. When courts are considering the enforceability of contracts, the factors they take into account include the following:

- Ignorance of the facts and law (especially by one party).
- The degree to which the applicable portions of the contract are illegal, morally offensive, or damaging to the public good.
- The magnitude of the effect of illegal or offensive activities or contract provisions on the performance of those deeds central to the agreement.

In some cases, courts will apply the doctrine of severance when the illegal provision is not central to the agreement and does not involve serious moral turpitude. The court may choose instead to disregard the illegal portion and to enforce the rest of the agreement.

Provisions that might be deemed illegal or against public policy in contracts between hospitals and providers of emergency medical services include the following:

- Agreement by the providers to pay a portion of the professional fees received from federal resources to the hospital.
- Agreement by the provider to have its physicians screen patients and reject them for treatment or portions of treatment based on the patients' economic resources or other illegal criteria.
- Agreement by the provider to have its physicians admit to the hospital a minimum percentage of the patients treated in the emergency department.

Provisions in contracts between physicians and provider groups or hospitals that might be deemed illegal or against public policy include the following:

- Covenants not to compete that are too restrictive (e.g., agreement by the physicians not to practice medicine in a significantly large geographic area or for an unreasonable length of time after the contract has terminated).
- Agreement by the physician to delegate to subordinates practices beyond their qualifications or beyond those allowed under the state's medical practice act.
- In some jurisdictions, penalty clauses that require one party to pay the other a large sum of money for a certain act, without regard to a determination of actual damages.
- Illegal exculpatory clauses (escape clauses) that provide for a party to be excused from liability for harm caused either intentionally or recklessly.
- Illegal indemnification clauses.

Indemnification Clauses

Indemnification, or "hold harmless," provisions frequently are contained in emergency physician group or individual emergency physician contracts. These provisions define a commitment by one party to make good or repay another party to an agreement in the event of a specified loss.

Contracts between provider groups and hospitals often contain an "indemnify and hold harmless" commitment by the provider group to the hospital. This commitment means that if the hospital is brought into a malpractice lawsuit and has a judgment against it that is due solely to its vicarious liability for the acts of the physician (i.e., there is no contributory negligence on the part of the hospital or its employees), then the provider group is obligated to repay the hospital the amount of the judgment. The indemnification agreement might also provide for the payment of any legal expenses incurred by the hospital in defending itself in such a malpractice lawsuit.

A contract between a physician and provider group or hospital sometimes contains indemnification provisions similar to those described previously. For example, the physician agrees to repay the provider group or hospital for losses incurred by them that are due to the physician's negligent acts or omissions. On the other hand, contracts between hospitals and physicians or between hospitals and provider groups sometimes contain a commitment for the hospital to indemnify the physician(s) for any losses incurred as the result of the physician's participation in the peer review, credentialing process, or other administrative process.

When parties agree to indemnification provisions in contracts, they frequently attempt to achieve a reciprocal agreement whereby the indemnified party also agrees to indemnify the other party under certain conditions (e.g., a reciprocal commitment by the hospital to repay the provider group for losses it incurs due solely to negligent acts or omissions of the hospital or its employees).

Indemnification clauses sometimes limit the amount of the indemnification or repayment to the limits of insurance policies provided for the damages involved. For example, in the types of agreements described previously, the party providing the indemnification might limit its liability to the coverage limits of its professional liability (malpractice) insurance. Of course, to be certain that such a limitation provides any real protection, the indemnifying party should check its insurance policy to make sure that such indemnification is actually covered.

Illegal or unenforceable indemnification clauses include agreement by one party to repay another party for losses incurred as the result of its own intentional acts or illegal acts. Similarly, a party cannot indemnify a second party for the second party's losses or damages resulting from fines or civil penalties levied against it.

Indemnification clauses can be the source of a great deal of confusion and anxiety. Attorneys for various parties may have preconceived, fairly rigid opinions regarding their preferences for indemnification clauses. Disagreements in this area may even prevent a contract from being negotiated. Some comfort may be taken from the fact that, in addition to the unenforceable indemnification clauses described earlier, many jurisdictions will not allow a party to accept responsibility for another party's negligence — intentional or not. The same jurisdictions may prohibit parties from setting aside allocations of damages that have been determined by court proceedings. Therefore, when indemnification clauses are a major barrier to negotiations, the parties should obtain expert legal opinion regarding the rulings of local jurisdictions.

Interaction With Other Areas of the Health Care System

Contracts may contain provisions for interaction of emergency physicians with other areas of the health care delivery system, such as EMS transports, managed care plans, and provision of certain types of care for hospitalized patients. The nature of these relationships and their descriptions within the contract can affect the liability of each party.

Interaction with EMS transports and personnel usually involves radio communication with emergency physicians, who provide instructions for emergency care. Emergency physicians or provider groups also may be asked to supervise and train EMS personnel or to participate in the development of treatment protocols for use in prehospital situations. Such supervisory or educational activity can extend liability for alleged misdeeds of EMS personnel to the participating physicians, provider groups, and hospitals. These duties should be discharged with the same care as those delivered in the emergency department itself. Physicians involved in such activities should be certain that their professional liability (malpractice) insurance provides coverage for these circumstances.

In many ways, supervisory and educational interaction with EMS personnel has become a routine part of the practice of emergency medicine. As such, it may be covered automatically unless specifically excluded in an insurance policy. However, insurance obtained through many emergency medicine provider groups specifically excludes activities not covered in the provider group's contract for emergency medical services. In those circumstances, an agreement by the emergency physicians to provide EMS support for another party (e.g., a district EMS) might be deemed as outside the contract for emergency medical services for the hospital. This is particularly the case if payment for the EMS support is separate and is not mentioned in the contract for emergency department staffing. An insurance carrier might assert that it did not calculate or collect premiums for the EMS support services; therefore, the insurance coverage does not include those activities. When any question arises concerning insurance coverage in these areas, the safest course is to obtain written clarification from the carrier.

Many hospitals have important relationships with managed care plans (e.g., HMOs, PPOs, IPOs) and may require the emergency physicians to participate in the plans. However, contract language or actual practice should not permit procedures that may limit patients' access to adequate or timely treatment in the emergency department. For example, a policy may require that emergency physicians delay treatment or limit certain diagnostic procedures pending approval of a "gatekeeper," or screening physician, who has not seen the patient. Such a provision creates serious potential liability if a patient experiences an adverse outcome after an alleged unnecessary delay or incomplete evaluation.

Potential extension of liability also exists when physicians disagree regarding the nature of follow-up treatment a patient requires (e.g., specialist versus general practitioner). In these circumstances, the judgment of the emergency physicians should prevail. To do otherwise could give the impression that a patient suffered needless injury because medical services were withheld purely for economic reasons. This increases liability not only for the emergency physician, but also for the hospital and managed care plan that develop or permit such a practice.

Expansion of Duties

Hospitals (especially those with smaller emergency departments) sometimes wish to have the emergency physicians participate in medical emergencies involving inpatients. If such duties are to be included in the contract for services, it should be clearly stated that the emergency physician's primary duties are in the emergency department and that the emergency physician should not leave critically or seriously ill patients to treat hospitalized inpatients.

If this duty is described as a contractual duty of the emergency physician, it will be more difficult to use a Good Samaritan defense in the event of litigation. This will be especially true if the physician or provider group receives any compensation or fees related to this activity. Even if the Good Samaritan defense is not technically viable, it is more likely that a jury can be made to feel more sympathetic with a physician who acted of his own accord (i.e., beyond his duty) and did not charge for services. A reasonable approach from a risk management perspective might be to leave such an obligation out of the written contract but to have an understanding that such a service will be provided where no conflicts exist.

Many communities and hospitals have had a significant reduction in the availability of obstetrics services, causing a dramatic increase in the emergency physician's involvement in providing these services. As a result, the emergency physician's historical responsibility has expanded from simply checking obstetrics patients who are in labor or have acute medical problems and assisting with occasional precipitous deliveries, to monitoring and managing prolonged and often complicated labor and delivery. This has occurred because medical staff backup in obstetrics is unavailable or untimely. Medical malpractice exposure for the emergency physicians in such cases may potentially exceed policy limits. The emergency physician or the group should consider requesting contractual indemnification for any losses beyond the limits of the primary insurance policy.

Hospital administrators may be tempted to solve this problem by encouraging the emergency physicians or provider group to include obstetric duties in their contractual responsibilities. Such an arrangement, however, creates potential liability for the hospital, provider group, and emergency physicians, because it may fail to provide the optimum medical care for many obstetrics patients.

Case Discussions

1

On review of her contract, the emergency physician in the first case found a lot of boilerplate language but nothing specific as to the conditions of the emergency department, level of staffing, supervision of physician extenders, responsibility for out-of-department resuscitations, or responsibility for problems on the floors and reading floor ECGs and x-rays. There were no provisions for emergency physician call or backup, and no financial reimbursement or incentives for all of this extra work. She complained to the medical director, who told her "that's just the way things are." When the physician told the group she was going to complain to the hospital, they threatened to fire her for interfering with the group's hospital contract. The physician gave her 90-day notice of termination.

This physician learned a difficult lesson, one that all emergency physicians should be aware of before signing that first contract. Find out about the conditions of the emergency department and what your responsibilities are before signing the contract. Make sure there are contractual provisions for backup, additional coverage, and financial reimbursement, as necessary. And finally, when reviewing a contract for emergency services, find an attorney who is experienced in physician group contracts. Today, many attorneys have specific emergency medicine contract experience.

2

The physician in this case was advised to sue the group to demand specific performance of the contract provision providing insurance coverage. At trial, he won a judgment requiring the group to provide a defense for him in his malpractice case, insure him for any judgment in that case, and remit costs incurred in pursuing this declaratory judgment. The appeals court affirmed that judgment, stating that the group was obligated under contract to provide him with malpractice insurance, and had, in fact, done so until the policy was canceled. The company breached its duty by not obtaining other coverage.

The signed contract between the emergency physician and the group saved the day. It was not at all clear whether the physician could have prevailed if he had not had a signed contract in hand. Without the documents, the group might have been able to convince the court that no such promise had ever been made.

3

In the third case, the physician's attorney told him that it was not clear how a court would rule

on this posttermination contract restriction. In the absence of a state statute specifically on point, the courts will generally look to the specific agreement to determine whether it is overly broad geographically or represents an unreasonable restriction on the physician's ability to practice medicine in the community.

The trial court granted summary judgment in favor of the contract group. The appellate court affirmed, holding that the restriction placed on the physician's future employment was limited reasonably in duration and territorial effect while protecting the provider's interest. The physician was ordered to pay the $10,000 if he intended on continuing practice.

Key Points and Conclusion

This chapter discusses many of the standard or customary issues in contracts involving emergency medicine. The information presented here should help potential parties to a contract (e.g., hospitals, physicians, provider groups) gain a better understanding of these issues and help them prepare to negotiate and document their agreements.

All parties to a contract should seek legal assistance in drafting the final contracts. Although familiarity with the content of this chapter should greatly help each party in preparation and negotiation, the final review and approval of the contract by an attorney can be a valuable part of risk management.

References

1. *Ata Ulhaq v Trauma Services Group*, C-950955 and C-960141, Ohio 1st App Dist, Hamilton Co.
2. *Dominy v National Emergency Services Inc,*. 451 SE2d 472 (Ga Ct of App 1994).
3. *Spectrum Emergency Care, Inc. v St Joseph's Hospital and Health Center*, 479 NW2d 848 (ND 1992).
4. *PHP Healthcare Corporation v EMSA Limited Partnership*, No. 92-2342, US Ct App (4th Cir 1993).

Chapter 25

Peer Review

Hugh M. Barton, JD

Peer review can be generally defined by practicing physicians as the evaluation of the effectiveness and efficiency of services ordered or performed by other practicing physicians.[1] The term also encompasses decisions to grant or terminate medical staff membership or clinical privileges based on competence or professional conduct. Peer review is a fact of life in contemporary hospitals. A hospital owes a legal duty to its patients to exercise reasonable care in the selection and retention of physicians they permit to treat patients.

In most hospitals, this legal duty is fulfilled in the activities of a broad range of internal committee structures, each with specific responsibilities. Credentialing, which encompasses granting or refusing medical staff membership and delineating clinical privileges, is the most obvious. The next most obvious context is the disciplinary process, spanning the range from hearing minor complaints, to reducing clinical privileges, to terminating medical staff membership. Less obvious is the work of many hospital committees that address the wide range of issues regarding quality assurance and utilization review.

Proponents maintain that effective peer review, although it does to some extent impinge on the professional freedom of physicians, balances the physician's right to exercise medical judgment freely with the obligation to do so wisely. Proponents also advocate peer review as the only possible form of quality control for medical services because only physicians' peers are qualified to judge their work. On the other hand, peer review can be criticized as an inherent conflict of interest because physicians allegedly will not judge those who will judge them in return. Peer review also is faulted for not adequately reflecting the patient's point of view and for hiding evidence of malpractice behind a facade of privilege, thus shielding wrongdoers from well-deserved liability.

Peer review began as a learning process. Physicians presented cases to other physicians in teaching sessions in order to obtain other opinions as to proper case management. Everyone benefited: young physicians could hear the wisdom of their elders, and older physicians could learn new therapeutic techniques. These sessions gave way to more structured morbidity and mortality conferences, wherein responsibility for outcomes was fixed for purposes of accountability as well as teaching. The need for clinical data collection arose through the formal credentialing requirements of the Joint Commission on Accreditation of Healthcare Organizations (JCAHO), then known as the Joint Commission on Accreditation of Hospitals.[2]

This much is generally understood by physicians. What physicians often do not understand is the legal framework in which peer review now operates and the consequences of the decisions made. This chapter examines the legal background of peer review, those statutes that govern contemporary peer review, voluntary standards for peer review that have legal significance, and certain other legal doctrines that affect peer review. Also discussed are the laws that protect the confidentiality of peer review committee deliberations and records. Finally, some suggestions are presented for how to conduct peer review and preserve immunity and confidentiality.

The Legal Basis for Peer Review

Because there is no developed body of peer review law pertaining strictly to emergency physicians, the analysis in this chapter is based on statutory and case law common to all medical specialties.

General Common Law Rules

Although there is no legal duty to conduct peer review, there is a definite body of law regarding one person's liability for the negligence of another. This body of law, as developed by U.S. courts in the latter part of the 20th century, makes effective peer review somewhat of a necessity. The following is a brief review of the law of hospital liability that may give rise to a common law duty to conduct peer review.

Respondeat Superior. The first general rule is that a hospital may incur tort liability for the negligent acts of its employees and agents. This holds true regardless of the title and function of those employees and is based on the ancient English legal doctrine of *respondeat superior*, meaning "let the master answer." This rule of law has been carried over from feudal times and adapted to modern society.

Independent Contractor Status. The second general rule is that a hospital is not liable for the acts of independent contractors when no principal-agent relationship exists. Thus, the negligent acts of a physician who has medical staff membership at a hospital but is not an employee would not create a liability for the hospital. There are, of course, exceptions to both of these rules.

Exceptions to Common Law Rules

Corporate Liability. Under the corporate liability doctrine, a hospital owes its own set of independent legal duties to the patients in its confines. These include a duty to ensure that the hospital's medical staff is competent through a process of selection, review, and ongoing evaluation of those granted clinical privileges. The hospital also has a duty to provide an acceptable level of medical care to the patient.

The importance of this doctrine is demonstrated in *Darling v Charleston Community*

Memorial Hospital,[3] a case commonly cited as precedent for all hospital peer review responsibilities. The plaintiff, who had a broken leg, was taken to a hospital emergency department where a Dr. Alexander, who was on call, treated him. The leg was placed in a cast, and the patient was put in traction and admitted to the hospital. The next day, the plaintiff complained of soreness and discolored toes. Dr. Alexander modified the cast, but two days later he had to split the cast on each side. The plaintiff's leg was apparently cut in the process. He was transferred to another hospital two weeks later; an orthopedic surgeon ultimately amputated the leg below the knee. The surgeon later testified that the fractured leg had necrotic tissue resulting from swelling of the leg against the cast.

A lawsuit was filed against both hospital and physician, alleging negligence on four counts: allowing Dr. Alexander to do orthopedic work he was not qualified to do; not requiring a review of Dr. Alexander's operative procedures; failure of the medical staff to supervise the plaintiff's medical condition; and failure to require consultation after complications developed. It was also alleged that the hospital failed to meet licensing standards and its own bylaws and that such failure should result in liability for the hospital.

The court agreed, saying that modern hospitals do not merely furnish facilities in which physicians work, but that patients expect the hospital itself to cure them. The court also held that the manner of hospital operation demonstrates that this duty was undertaken by the hospital. The fact that there are licensing standards and bylaws provisions covering the issues raised demonstrates that it is desirable that a hospital assume a responsibility for patient care.

A hospital may be held liable for the negligent acts of independent contractor physicians if the hospital violates an independent duty of care. This point was demonstrated in *Park North General Hospital v Hickman,*[4] a Texas case in which the court determined that the hospital had an independent duty to exercise reasonable care in selecting its medical staff.

Apparent Agency. The second exception to the general common law rules is the doctrine of "ostensible" or "apparent" agency. For a hospital to be liable for the acts of independent contractor physicians under this rule, the hospital must either represent to the patient that the physician is the hospital's agent or fail to correct that impression. The patient, in turn, must rely on the physician's authority as an apparent agent of the hospital.

This doctrine is very important for physicians who work in emergency departments and for other hospital-based physicians. A patient who presents to an emergency department, in most cases, does not request a particular physician. The hospital, by having emergency physicians staff the emergency department, in effect, provides the patient with a physician. Thus, to the patient, the physician in the emergency department is apparently the agent of the hospital, even though the physician legally may be an independent contractor.

In *Smith v St. Francis Hospital*,[5] a malpractice case alleging the negligent misdiagnosis of appendicitis, the hospital attempted to deny liability on the grounds that its emergency physicians were independent contractors. In fact, the defendant physicians had a contract to staff the hospital's emergency department. The appellate court found that the contract between the hospital and the emergency group was simply an attempt by the hospital to avoid liability for its emergency department, even though the hospital maintained the same de facto control over the emergency physicians as it did over regular medical staff. The court noted the following factors to support its finding on the control issue:

- All of the emergency physicians were required to have hospital staff membership.
- All of the emergency physicians were required to be reviewed by the hospital.
- The hospital's quality of care guidelines were applicable to all of the emergency physicians.
- All of the emergency physicians were required to follow the hospital medical staff bylaws.
- The hospital had control over emergency department patient billings.
- The emergency physicians' fees were based on rates established by the hospital.
- The hospital's facility, supplies, instruments, and support services were provided to the emergency physicians at no cost.

These factors are likely to be present in many emergency department situations. The lesson is clear: even though physicians may be independent contractors, at least by virtue of their formal relationship with the hospital, if they are treated substantially the same as other medical staff members, or with more control as in the case of fees, then the hospital may be liable for their negligence under the doctrine of apparent agency. If that is the case, the hospital will natu-rally expect that effective peer review be performed to help prevent any acts that could be alleged as negligent.

State Law Basis for Peer Review

Most health care regulation begins at the level of state government. Thus, emergency physicians must examine the laws in their own states to understand medical peer review law and common law concerns. Typically, these laws are found in statutes dealing with hospital licensure and vary widely from state to state. The most basic type of approach — such as the old Oklahoma requirement that hospitals appoint "none other than good, competent, trained, and skilled physicians"[6] — is rarely seen these days. Rather, most states require hospitals at least to adopt bylaws and rules covering physicians' activities and to have such guidelines approved by the hospital's governing body, such as a board of directors or trustees. Following is a summary of the approaches of several large states.

California. California hospitals are required to have a formal, organized medical staff, with officers and bylaws. They must use JCAHO procedures for appointment and reappointment of medical staff.[7] The hospital may limit, restrict, or revoke the exercise of privileges for violation of the facility's rules when applied in good faith and nondiscriminatory manner.[8] It is even "unprofessional conduct" for physicians to practice in a licensed hospital unless two conditions are met: there is a formal medical staff with officers and bylaws, and the medical staff meets periodically to review and analyze their clinical experience, using medical records as the basis for such review.[9]

New York. In New York, physician credentialing and competence evaluations are part of a hospital's mandatory medical malpractice prevention program.[10] Physicians seeking hospital privileges must disclose any discontinuation of privileges at another hospital and any pending professional misconduct proceedings or any medical malpractice actions in New York or elsewhere.[11] It is an "improper practice" for a hospital governing body to refuse to act on an application for staff membership or privileges, exclude or expel physicians from staff membership, or curtail their professional privileges without stating the reasons. If the reasons are unrelated to patient care, the hospital must state the objectives of the institution or in what ways the character or competency of the applicant fails to meet hospital requirements.[12]

Florida. In Florida, each hospital must conduct peer review of its physicians as a condition of licensure.[13] Hospitals must have procedures that address such areas as the method for choosing membership of peer review bodies, adoption of rules of order, fair review of cases, and a mechanism to identify and avoid conflict of interest on the part of the peer review panel members. The statute also provides specific grounds to discipline medical staff members for unprofessional conduct, such as incompetence, habitual use of intoxicants or drugs, being found liable for medical malpractice, and failing to comply with the policies of a risk management or quality assurance program. Eligibility for staff membership is also determined by the applicant's "ability to work with others."

The procedures for such actions must be adopted pursuant to hospital bylaws and must also comply with the standards outlined by the JCAHO, Medicare and Medicaid Conditions of Participation, other appropriate private accreditation bodies, and the rules of the Florida Department of Health and Rehabilitative Services. A hospital's standards and procedures in considering applications for staff membership or clinical privileges are available for public inspection.[14]

Texas. The governing body of a Texas hospital is authorized to establish whatever rules, standards, or qualifications for medical staff membership as are deemed "necessary or advisable."[15] Such rules are to be "determined upon a reasonable basis, such as professional and ethical qualifications of the physician, upon standards that are reasonable, applied untainted by irrelevant considerations, supported by sufficient evidence, free of arbitrariness, capriciousness, or unreasonableness and do not differentiate solely upon the academic medical degree held by such physician."[16] The granting or refusal of medical staff membership is discretionary, although applications must be given "procedural due process." The rules provide a specific timetable for acting on completed applications.[15]

State laws affecting peer review vary in their coverage. Many states have different levels of overlapping regulation that reflect the legislature's concerns at the time of passage. For example, the requirement that a hospital governing body establish rules and standards for medical staff membership is nearly universal and can be viewed as part of a basic hospital regulatory scheme. However, laws that mandate periodic review of staff privileges and specific grounds to revoke such privileges are a second level of regulation and may have been enacted in response to liability concerns. Specific criteria for staff membership and privileges and some type of due process for applications are a third level of sophistication. These laws typically exist side by side in state statute books and must be construed together to obtain an adequate understanding of peer review under state law. Finally, different types of hospitals, such as facilities owned by a hospital district, may be subject to specific peer review statutes.

Federal Regulatory Basis of Peer Review

To receive Medicare reimbursement, a hospital must comply with Medicare's Conditions of Participation. The specific requirements do not use the term peer review; however, they govern activities usually considered within the scope of peer review. In many ways, the Medicare requirements mirror the basic level of state regulation described previously. Given that many state health departments perform Medicare inspections as federal contractors, it is not surprising that federal and state requirements are similar.

Medicare requirements are split between those imposed on a hospital's governing body and those imposed on the medical staff. The hospital's governing body must ensure that, in general terms, the medical staff is accountable to the governing body for the quality of care provided to patients.[17] The governing body must ensure that the criteria for medical staff selection are based on a physician's individual character, competence, training, experience, and judgment.[18]

The governing body also must implement an effective, hospital-wide quality assurance program. All medical and surgical services performed in the hospital must be evaluated as they relate to appropriateness of diagnosis and treatment.[19] The hospital must take "appropriate remedial action" to address any deficiencies found through its quality assurance program.[20]

Responsibility for the quality of medical care provided to patients is placed on the hospital medical staff. Thus, the medical staff is obligated to examine the credentials of medical staff candidates and to make recommendations to the governing body on the appointment of these candidates.[21] To guide the medical staff in this task, medical staff bylaws must contain criteria for determining the privileges to be granted and describe a procedure for applying the criteria to individuals requesting privileges.[22] Finally, the medical staff must conduct periodic appraisals of its members, such as recredentialing.[23] Thus, the Medicare law addresses the usual medical staff functions of credentialing and recredentialing, which have significant peer review components. Medicare law does not address the most extreme application of peer review, namely, disciplinary actions, although that idea is at least implicit. Medicare law also does not confer any sort of immunity for peer review activity; for that one must look to congressional enactments.

Voluntary Peer Review Standards

The JCAHO, through its annual *Comprehensive Accreditation Manual for Hospitals*,[24] promulgates various standards for all phases of hospital operations. Peer review is primarily imbedded in the medical staff subject matter area. Separate classes of medical staff membership, such as "active" or "courtesy" staff, are mandated. The medical staff is supposed to be organized and self-governing within a framework of bylaws.

In the JCAHO scheme, the primary function of the medical staff (besides patient care) is credentialing. Decisions on initial appointment and reappointment are based primarily on "criteria that are directly related to the quality of care" and competence but must also consider such specific matters as the following[24]:

- Previous or current challenges to licenses (medical and DEA)
- Termination of staff privileges at other institutions, whether voluntary or involuntary
- Involvement in professional liability actions
- Peer recommendations

The medical staff is required to follow a structured procedure for processing appointment and reappointment applications. Completed applications are to be acted on within a reasonable period of time. Decisions on reappointments or on revocation, recision, or renewal of clinical privileges are subject to a fair hearing and appeal process. Credentialing decisions ultimately are the task of the medical staff executive committee. The executive committee is responsible for making recommendations to the hospital governing body for approval. The governing body is ultimately responsible for medical staff credentialing, but no specific fair hearing or appeal process is mandated at that level.[24]

Note that the JCAHO accreditation standards do not treat emergency physicians as having special or separate classes of medical staff membership. Thus, emergency physicians are credentialed through the same process as other applicants for medical staff membership.

Hospitals perform peer review for a variety of reasons: to satisfy state licensure authorities, to ensure Medicare participation through accreditation programs, and to avoid tort liability to patients. But there is another side to peer review law: the nature and degree of potential legal liability that a hospital can incur to a medical staff member when it undertakes peer review either incorrectly or with flawed motives. Peer review thus presents hospitals and physicians with a double-edged sword. If they fail to perform peer review, they risk the loss of licensure and accreditation status. If they do perform peer review, they risk a lawsuit from a disgruntled physician if the process followed is not fair.

Federal Statutory Peer Review Standards

Patrick v Burget

Federal peer review law is shaped by the history of the case *Patrick v Burget*.[25] Briefly, the facts of the case are as follows.

In 1972, Dr. Timothy Patrick became an employee of the Astoria Clinic in Astoria, Oregon, and a member of Columbia Memorial Hospital's (CMH) staff. Later, he chose to go into private practice rather than become a clinic partner. The clinic refused to have any further professional dealings with him. He received no referrals, consultations, or back-up coverage.

In 1981, the CMH executive committee, following a complaint by a clinic physician, voted to revoke Dr. Patrick's medical staff privileges for substandard patient care. Dr. Patrick requested a hearing. A five-member hearing committee was appointed, chaired by the physician who initiated the earlier complaint. At the beginning of the hearing, Dr. Patrick requested that each member of the committee disclose any bias they might have against him, but the committee members refused. Dr. Patrick resigned his staff privileges rather than risk termination.

He then filed a lawsuit, alleging that the clinic partners violated antitrust laws by voting to revoke his staff privileges for the purpose of eliminating him as a competitor rather than to improve patient care. The issue went to a jury, who rendered a verdict against the clinic and awarded damages of $650,000 on two antitrust claims. Damages were trebled, as required by antitrust law.

The 9th Circuit Court of Appeals acknowledged that the Astoria Clinic had acted in bad faith during the peer review process. However, the court held that the clinic's process — regardless of motive — was immune from antitrust liability under the "State Action Exemption." The court made the ruling because Oregon had articulated a policy in favor of peer review and the state was, in fact, involved in supervision of peer review.[26]

In 1988, the U.S. Supreme Court reversed the appellate court decision. The Supreme Court held that, despite the policy in favor of peer review, no state agency reviewed, or even could review, the decision of a private hospital regarding medical staff privileges to determine if it complied with state regulatory policy.[25]

Reactions to the Supreme Court decision in *Patrick v Burget* were swift. The American Medical Association stated that it was inappropriate to apply the treble damages antitrust law remedy to peer review. The AMA warned of a "chilling effect" on the willingness of physicians to participate in peer review, utilization review, quality assurance, or any other evaluation of physicians.[27] A great deal of similar publicity occurred in the medical press.[28] Other reactions were less alarming. The American Hospital Association issued no formal response to the decision. Health care attorneys published explanatory articles but generally did not predict the end of peer review.[29]

The Health Care Quality Improvement Act of 1986

The Health Care Quality Improvement Act (HCQIA) of 1986 was a congressional response to the trial court's decision in *Patrick v Burget*. Congress specifically found that the threat of damage liability under federal laws, including treble damage liability under federal antitrust law, unreasonably discouraged physicians from participating in effective professional peer review. Consequently, Congress found that there was an "overriding national need" to provide incentives and protection for physicians engaging in effective professional peer review.[30]

HCQIA offers a two-part solution to these problems. First, it provides conditional immunity from liability as an incentive for physicians to participate in the peer review process.

Second, the National Practitioner Data Bank was established to track incompetent physicians as they move from place to place (this was pursuant to another specific congressional finding). A discussion of the reporting provisions is included in Chapter 12, "National Practitioner Data Bank."

Immunity for Peer Review Participants. If a peer review action (called a "professional review action") of a peer review body (called a "professional review body") meets the minimum standards set out below, then the peer review body, individual members (or staff) of the body, any person under a contract with the body, and any person who participates with or assists the body in peer review will not be liable in damages under any state or federal law for participating in that peer review action.

Thus, HCQIA protects peer review activity from claims of slander, libel, and tortious interference with a physician's ability to make a living, as well as from antitrust issues. The only exceptions are for lawsuits for damages under state or federal civil rights law and one type of antitrust law brought only by the government.

HCQIA protects peer review participants from damage awards but does not shield them from being sued or from having to stand trial in a lawsuit.[31] In addition, although providing immunity from damages, HCQIA does not provide immunity from lawsuits for injunctive or declaratory relief. This would allow a physician to bring legal action for reinstatement of his medical staff membership or clinical privileges if a professional review action is taken against him, so long as monetary damages are not sought. Physicians must look to their own state laws to determine if their legislature has discovered this loophole and remedied it with language that restricts any cause of action that arises out of peer review. Even in such cases where state law provides relief, it will be of benefit only in state courts. In the event that a lawsuit challenging a peer review decision is filed in or removed to federal court, the immunity provisions of the HCQIA generally govern that action.

Immunity for Witnesses. Protection is offered for those persons who provide information to peer review bodies unless the information is false and the person providing it knew the information was false. This protection covers informants and witnesses called to testify at peer review hearings. It appears that the protection for these individuals is broader than the protection extended to other participants in the peer review process. Unlike other participants, the informant or witness is not subject to civil rights liability.

The term "information" is somewhat ambiguous. Conceivably, a witness could provide information in the form of gossip and innuendo, which may be false, and still be protected, as long as the informant believed the information to be true. The absence of potential liability for defamation may cause peer reviewers to have little incentive to verify negative reports of a physician's conduct. The peer review committee's immunity is not conditioned on confirming the accuracy of the information they receive, other than to the extent that such committees must make a "reasonable effort to obtain the facts."[32]

Standards for Peer Review Actions. To be immune from damage claims, the following four criteria must be met:

- The action must be taken in the "reasonable belief" that the action was in the furtherance of quality health care. Thus, in order to prevail, a plaintiff must show that the peer review body lacked a reasonable belief in its actions.[33]
- The action must be taken after a "reasonable effort" to obtain the facts of the matter. HCQIA does not specify how much investigation the professional review body must conduct before its efforts are considered "reasonable."
- The action must be taken after "adequate notice and hearing procedures" are afforded to the physician involved, or "after such other circumstances as are fair to the physician under the circumstances."
- The action must be taken in the "reasonable belief" that it was warranted based on the facts known after a "reasonable effort" was made to obtain the facts, and after the adequate notice and hearing requirements were met. In any lawsuit relating to a professional review action, there is a presumption that these standards have been met unless the presumption is rebutted by a preponderance of the evidence.[34]

The Importance of Definitions

Physicians and hospitals should pay close attention to the way Congress defined terms in HCQIA. Otherwise, they may assume they have immunity when actually a defect in organizational structure or practice may place them outside the defined categories and leave them unprotected. Physicians and health care organizations should ask themselves six questions regarding their immunity under HCQIA.

First, does the peer review activity take place in a "health care entity"? That term includes not only a state-licensed hospital, but also any entity that provides health care services and that follows a formal peer review process. This includes a health maintenance organization or group medical practice, or a professional society (or committee thereof) of physicians or other licensed health care practitioners that follows a formal peer review process.[35]

Second, does the peer review activity concern a "physician"? HCQIA defines "physician" as a doctor of medicine, osteopathy, dental surgery, or medical dentistry, so long as they are legally authorized to practice by a state. The definition of physician also includes any person who claims to be authorized to practice as a physician even if that person has no authority to do so.[36] Thus, a decision to expel an imposter physician would be within the scope of HCQIA.

HCQIA does not pertain to other classes of licensed health care providers. Thus, immunity is not provided for actions relating to podiatrists, psychologists, chiropractors, optometrists, or allied health care professionals such as nurse midwives or anesthetists. Any immunity from legal action that such "allied health care practitioners" have would necessarily be governed by the licensure and registration statutes of their own states.

Third, is the peer review activity what HCQIA calls a "professional review activity"? In other words, does the health care entity do one or more of the following[37]:

- Determine whether an individual physician may have clinical privileges or membership in the entity.
- Determine the scope or conditions of such privileges or membership.
- Change or modify such privileges or membership.

The first two activities fit the traditional concept of credentialing. The third is more closely related to discipline.

Fourth, is the peer review activity conducted by what HCQIA calls a "professional review body"? A "professional review body" is the health care entity and its governing body, or any committee of the entity, that conducts professional review activity. A "professional review body" also includes any committee of the medical staff of the entity that assists the governing body in the professional review activity.[38]

Fifth, is the peer review action what HCQIA calls a "professional review action"? That is the action of a professional review body, when taken in the conduct of a professional review activity, that is also based on the physician's competence or professional conduct. There is, thus, a two-part test for immunity: the presence of a formal process that is coupled with a relationship to competence or conduct. A professional review action also includes the formal decision of a professional review body not to take an action or make a recommendation.[39]

However, HCQIA explicitly provides that certain types of activities are not professional review actions because Congress did not consider them to be based on competence or professional conduct. Thus, there is no HCQIA immunity for actions based primarily on the physician's fees, advertising practices, or other competitive acts to solicit or retain business. Nor is an action considered based on competence if it is based on any other matter not related to the competence or professional conduct of the physician.[40]

Sixth, does the result of the action "adversely affect" the physician's clinical privileges or overall medical staff membership? Under HCQIA, the action meets this requirement if it results in reducing, restricting, suspending, revoking, denying, or failing to renew a physician's clinical privileges or membership in a health care entity.[41] For example, the requirement that a physician seek consultations for all admissions or have monitors for surgical procedures where no such requirement existed before would be considered actions adversely affecting a physician's clinical privileges.

Adequate Notice and Hearing

One of the four standards for HCQIA immunity requires that the peer review action be taken after "adequate notice and hearing procedures are afforded to the physician involved." The health care entity is deemed to have satisfied the notice and hearing requirements if certain conditions are met (or voluntarily waived by the physician).

The physician who is identified for peer review action must be given written notice of the proposed action, the reason for the action, the right to request a hearing within 30 days of receipt of the notice, and a summary of the physician's rights at the hearing.[42] The physician who requests a hearing must be given written notice stating the time, place, and date of the hearing and a list of witnesses expected to testify on behalf of the professional review body. The hearing should not be less than 30 days from the date of the notice.[43]

The duty to act within a 30-day period applies only to the physician who receives notice of the proposed action. The health care entity is under no statutory deadline to set the date of the actual hearing after receiving the physician's request for a hearing. However, a long delay in setting the hearing, without an explanation, could be used to point out a lack of reasonableness and fairness in the hearing procedure. Any procedure, in other words, can be abused. The notice provisions do not contain an explicit requirement that the physician be given the right to "discover," or have a preview of the hospital's case, before the hearing.[44]

When the physician requests a hearing, the health care facility must hold the hearing before one of the following[45]:

- An arbitrator who is mutually acceptable to the physician and the health care entity.
- A hearing officer, appointed by the health care entity, who is not in direct economic competition with the physician involved.
- A panel appointed by the health care entity whose members are not in direct economic competition with the physician involved.

The hearing must be held by the facility itself and not by one of the peer review committees. For example, the quality assurance committee of a hospital emergency department would not be the proper body to hear a case against an emergency physician if the decision of that committee could result in a reduction of clinical privileges. It would, on the other hand, be an appropriate body to investigate an initial complaint, incident report, or other event that would trigger the formal peer review process. In any event, the quality assurance committee would not likely have the authority to suspend clinical privileges on its own account. Note also that the hearing officer and hearing panel options do not require approval by the physician under review.

HCQIA does not define what facts and circumstances constitute "direct economic competition." In determining whether the hearing officer or panel members are in "direct economic competition," the factors to be considered include whether the same specialty or same patient population is shared by the physicians. If it is difficult or impossible to find physicians who are not in direct competition with the affected physician, then it may be necessary for the health care entity to look outside its medical staff to comply with this requirement. This is a particular problem in rural hospitals with small medical staffs or in specialty hospitals that focus on psychiatric care and substance abuse. Under such circumstances, a health care entity might be well advised to establish a relationship with an outside firm or group that provides peer review on a contract basis.[46]

As stated previously, the physician must be given a list of his rights at a hearing. Under HCQIA, the physician has the right to be represented by an attorney or other qualified person, such as "physician counsel." The physician also has a right to have a record made of the proceedings and to obtain a copy for a reasonable charge. The physician (and presumably the attorney) has the right to call, examine, and cross-examine witnesses and to present evidence determined to be relevant by the hearing officer. Finally, at the close of the hearing, the physician has a right to submit a written statement to the panel or hearing officer.[47]

On completion of the hearing, the physician has the right to receive a written recommendation from the arbitrator, officer, or panel, including a statement as to the basis of its recommendations. The physician also has a right to receive a written decision of the health care entity, along with a statement of the basis for that decision.[48] Because HCQIA provides the physician with the right to receive these two written documents, there would seem to be some implicit recognition that the governing body will sit in a review capacity and render its own decision. In this regard, the law accords with common practice. However, the professional review body's failure to meet these requirements does not constitute, in itself, a failure to meet the adequate notice and hearing requirements of the standards for professional review actions.

The adequate notice and hearing requirements may be dispensed with in three situations:

- No adverse action is taken.
- An action is taken that restricts privileges for no more than 14 days, provided an investigation is conducted during that time to determine the need for formal peer review.
- Privileges are immediately restricted because of an imminent danger to the health of anyone, provided that subsequent

notice or "other adequate procedures" will follow.[49]

The first exception seems redundant. If there is no adverse action, no notice would be required. The second and third exceptions are, in a sense, different ways of saying the same thing. For example, an immediate restriction due to imminent danger would naturally be followed by an investigation.

Immunity for Peer Review Activity Under State Law

Immunity for peer review activity is usually conditional under state law. This is because the law, as a matter of public policy, does not often favor granting absolute immunities. And, any type of immunity can be abused. However, the trend is toward providing greater levels of immunity for peer review activities. This immunity, like that conferred by federal law, is usually made conditional on acting in "good faith," or "without malice," or some other subjective test of the peer reviewer's state of mind.

State law may mandate that specific peer review procedures be followed in order to obtain immunity. These may or may not be more detailed than those contained in HCQIA. Statutes enacted before HCQIA may have lesser due process guarantees but nevertheless provide immunity under state law.

State legislation may provide specific judicial procedures for combating frivolous peer review litigation. Would-be plaintiffs may be required to post a bond when filing a legal action. Common provisions include awarding attorneys' fees to prevailing defendants when the court finds that the lawsuit was frivolous, unreasonable, or in bad faith, and the provision that peer review defendants may file counterclaims either in the pending action or in a subsequent lawsuit.

Little litigation has occurred under these kinds of procedures, however. Although clearly intended to defer retaliatory lawsuits, it is unclear what evidence would justify a judicial finding that the original claim was frivolous. Simply because a lawsuit was ultimately unsuccessful does not mean it was frivolous. Emergency physicians should research the laws of their own states for specific provisions and limitations.

Liability for Peer Review Activities

Despite HCQIA, lawsuits challenging credentialing decisions are inevitable, because physicians whose hospital practices are restricted face reductions in income and professional stature. Serious quality-of-care problems may trigger adverse licensure actions as well. There is by now a large body of reported peer review cases in the United States. Most reported cases today turn on interpretations of HCQIA; however, a review of these cases indicates that successful judicial challenges to credentialing decisions are rare.

Effect of Improper Motive Allegations on HCQIA. In *Austin v McNamara*,[50] the plaintiff, Dr. Austin, was subject to an internal evaluation of his cases because of concerns about quality. His privileges were revoked by the hospital, and he requested a hearing before a "judicial review committee." The committee reinstated his privileges but did find that some of his care was substandard and recommended monitoring. Dr. Austin filed an antitrust lawsuit after he was reinstated, alleging a conspiracy to exclude him from practicing in the city.

The trial court found that the defendants were immune from liability under HCQIA, and the appellate court affirmed that holding. In doing so, the appellate court rejected the plaintiff's argument that the defendant's "hostile and contemptuous" treatment of him established an improper motive, holding that courts must determine HCQIA compliance objectively. Thus, bad faith is immaterial in a HCQIA analysis.

Effect of Additional State Law Requirements on HCQIA. In *Mann v Johnson Memorial Hospital*,[51] the laws of Indiana required that peer review hearings be composed solely of panels of medical staff members. The hospital bylaws, however, allowed the hearing to take place before a panel that included nonmedical staff members. The plaintiff brought a lawsuit, alleging that the hospital bylaws violated state law. The hospital defended its actions on the grounds that, because HCQIA does not specify the kinds of persons to be appointed to hearing committees, its bylaws complied with federal law.

The court held that, under HCQIA, a state may choose to provide greater procedural protections; that is, a state is not preempted from erecting higher due process guarantees than does federal law. Thus, the hospital bylaws were too broad under state law to support the procedure used.

Sufficiency of Antitrust Injury. In *Balaklaw v Lovell*,[52] the plaintiff physician's anesthesia group was replaced by a competitor after a bid-

ding process. The new group was granted an exclusive three-year contract with a six-month termination clause. After an unsuccessful internal appeal, the first anesthesia group filed a lawsuit, alleging that the exclusive contract was a conspiracy to drive them out of the market. The district court dismissed the action on grounds that the plaintiff had not alleged injury to competition, but only to itself and therefore lacked "standing" to bring an antitrust lawsuit.

On appeal, the plaintiff argued that the exclusive contract restrained trade in the relevant market and had no positive effect on competition. The court found that the market for anesthesiology services was national, not local; that the market had not been harmed by the new exclusive contract because plaintiff's group had previously provided them under a de facto exclusive contract; and that the exclusive contract did not foreclose competition due to its short duration.

Decisions Subject to Fair Hearing Requirement. In *Dutta v St. Francis Regional Medical Center*,[53] the plaintiff, a radiologist, challenged the hospital's termination of her privilege to practice in the radiology department after the hospital hired a new medical director and granted him exclusive privileges in the radiology department. The plaintiff requested that a review committee conduct a hearing on the loss of her privileges, but that request was denied. Plaintiff brought legal action for breach of her employment contract.

The trial court held that the plaintiff was not entitled to a hearing on the loss of privileges. The appeals court agreed, holding that the hospital bylaws granted a physician the right to a hearing only when a decision adversely affected staff member status or clinical privileges based on professional competency or conduct. In this case, the hospital was deemed to have made a business decision unrelated to competency or conduct. The fact that the plaintiff had not had her medical staff membership terminated, and that having staff membership did not guarantee clinical privileges, was also noted by the court.

The Extent of Due Process. In *Smith v Ricks*,[54] the plaintiff cardiologist's use of streptokinase was criticized, and the cardiology department's quality review committee recommended monitoring his performance on an ongoing basis. That decision was upheld by the medical executive committee. Later, the hospital learned that the plaintiff had been disciplined at another hospital for use of cardiac catheterization testing. Ultimately, the medical executive committee recommended that the plaintiff's privileges be terminated.

The matter wound up before the hospital's judicial review committee, which conducted a nine-day hearing and produced a 1,300-page transcript. Both sides were represented by legal counsel and a physician spokesperson. The hearing explored the question of bias by committee members. The judicial review committee recommended a two-year preceptorship, but the medical staff appealed to the board of directors. The board ultimately voted to deny the physician reappointment to the medical staff. The physician filed a lawsuit on antitrust grounds, alleging that a conspiracy of physicians was "out to get" him, but not challenging the substance of the peer review proceeding itself.

The physician complained that, because his attorney was not allowed to conduct cross-examination, he was denied the right to counsel. The trial court found that his attorney was present and that the physician's spokesperson conducted a cross-examination. In addition, the court found that the plaintiff was afforded a proper peer review procedure, contrary to his claim that he was not allowed to examine the hearing panel concerning their alleged bias against him. HCQIA requires only that panel members not be in direct economic competition with the physician under review. The panel's recommendation was due not to a conspiracy but to the physician's own substandard medical care. The court also found that the alleged competence (or lack thereof) of other physicians was not relevant to whether the hospital conducted a reasonable investigation.

The Ninth Circuit Court of Appeals affirmed the court's granting of the hospital's summary judgment under HCQIA, finding that the plaintiff's lawsuit was "at best without foundation and at worst frivolous." The Court of Appeals awarded $300,000 in attorneys' fees to the hospital.

Private Right of Action. A series of cases has held that HCQIA does not provide physicians with a private cause of legal action against a hospital for such matters as seeking hospital staff membership, being allegedly denied full representation and participation of counsel in peer review proceedings, or suspension of participation in a residency program. Rather, HCQIA was enacted to provide solely for immunity on the part of professional review bodies.[55]

Thus, as a practical matter, a physician seeking to challenge a hospital peer review action cannot simply file a lawsuit alleging that he was damaged because the technical provisions of HCQIA were not met and expect to prevail.

Racial Discrimination. The federal courts seem to be split on the issue of racial discrimination. One trend in case law is represented by *U.S. v Harris Methodist Ft Worth*.[56] In this case, the 5th Circuit Court of Appeals held that federal law prohibits racial discrimination with respect to decisions regarding physicians' staff privileges. Although this was not a case challenging a particular hospital decision, the court ruled that Title VII of the Civil Rights Act of 1964 applies to staff privilege decisions of all hospitals that receive Medicare or Medicaid reimbursement.

On the other hand, a ruling in the recent case of *Alexander v Rush North Shore Medical Center* offered a different view.[57] The plaintiff, Dr. Mark Alexander, an Egyptian-born Muslim, sued Rush North Shore Medical Center under Title VII of the Civil Rights Act, alleging discrimination in the revocation of his anesthesiology staff privileges at the hospital. The hospital argued that, as an independent contractor, Dr. Alexander was precluded from bringing a Title VII lawsuit. The appeals court agreed, holding that the relationship between an independent contractor physician and a hospital where he has staff privileges is too tenuous under an employee contractor analysis to allow a Title VII lawsuit.

Disability Discrimination. In *Ross v Beaumont Hospital*,[58] the plaintiff physician, a surgeon, filed a lawsuit challenging the termination of her medical privileges. In the action, she claimed she was terminated solely because of her medical condition of narcolepsy. Her lawsuit was based on alleged discrimination under federal and state laws that protect the handicapped, and on alleged discrimination based on her weight. The court, however, found that her medical condition was related to her ability to perform surgery and was not protected under the handicap statutes.

The court also found that there was evidence indicating that the physician's weight was a determining factor in the termination of staff privileges and that weight was not a bona fide occupational requirement for performing surgery. Despite this fact, there was evidence that the physician had engaged in abusive behavior toward hospital personnel over a long period of time. The court said that the evidence supported the conclusion that her staff privileges would have been terminated for her abusive behavior even if the hospital had not considered her weight.

The extent to which credentialing decisions are affected by the Americans with Disabilities Act (ADA) is still debatable, as there are no cases on point. Title I of the ADA protects employees who have disabilities from discrimination, but physicians who maintain staff membership and clinical privileges are usually independent contractors, not employees. Congress intended that case law interpreting the ADA be based on the Civil Rights Act of 1964, but federal courts are split as to whether the Civil Rights Act itself protects physician-hospital relationships.[59] In any event, hospitals are well advised to remove from their credentialing applications questions that have clear ADA implications in other contexts, such as: "Have you ever suffered or been treated for any mental illness or psychiatric problems?" Emergency physicians who are employed by hospitals in states that do not have "corporate practice of medicine" prohibitions and those employed by emergency medicine groups that contract with hospitals would be protected by the ADA.

Slander and Tortious Interference. In *Nanavati v Burdette Tomlin Memorial Hospital*,[60] the plaintiff was board certified in cardiology. He received staff privileges at Burdette Tomlin Memorial Hospital, where the defendant physician was the chief and sole cardiologist. The defendant was board certified in internal medicine but not in cardiology. As chief cardiologist, the defendant had effective control over the allocation of ECG readings, which represented a substantial source of income.

The plaintiff unsuccessfully demanded a share in ECG readings. At a medical staff meeting, he verbally attacked the chief cardiologist, demanding to know why a lesser-qualified physician could control the ECG readings. The plaintiff was allocated ECG readings several days per week but was still unsatisfied. He complained about the defendant's patient care and eventually made public statements about the quality of patient care at the hospital. One such statement was that the defendant physician's incorrect reading of ECGs had led to at least one death. The plaintiff also engaged in disruptive behavior with nursing personnel and other members of the medical staff. In turn, the plaintiff was accused of overbilling patients and prescribing unnecessary treatment.

The executive committee of the medical staff ordered the chief cardiologist to provide the plaintiff with more ECG readings each week; however, the chief cardiologist refused. The hospital attempted to terminate the plaintiff's staff privileges for his disruptive behavior three times, but each time, the decision was overturned by a trial court. Finally, the hospital was permanently enjoined from terminating the plaintiff on the particular misconduct charges at issue, holding that termination would be permitted only if the plaintiff's disruptive behavior had an actual, negative impact on patient care.

At the conclusion of the *Nanavati* case, the jury awarded the hospital $150,000 in compensatory and punitive damages against the plaintiff for defamation. The chief cardiologist was awarded $600,000 in compensatory and punitive damages against the plaintiff for defamation and a further $400,000 in compensatory and punitive damages for a claim of wrongful business interference. The jury awarded the plaintiff $1,050,000 in favor of his antitrust claims against the hospital.

The Third Circuit Court of Appeals vacated the awards and, in effect, returned the parties to the same positions they were in before the litigation began. The allegedly slanderous statements made by the plaintiff were held to be opinions that could not be the subject of a slander action. The antitrust award was overturned by the trial court because it was found that the hospital could not conspire with either its executive staff or individual physicians and therefore could not be liable for antitrust violation. The executive committee's action in recommending termination of plaintiff's privileges did not render it liable for antitrust violations. Furthermore, the plaintiff was found to have suffered no damages as a result of the hospital's brief revocation of his medical staff privileges.

Conducting Safe Peer Review

Because of the success of a few antitrust cases, hospitals and medical staffs must pay careful attention to their motivations when conducting peer review. HCQIA requires that, before immunity applies, peer review actions must be taken in the reasonable belief that the action will further quality health care. State law may define peer review in more specific terms, such as the evaluation of medical and health care services, including physician qualifications. Actions taken for purposes other than these may or may not result in a loss of immunity, even though they may be peer review in a broader sense.

In this regard, *Siegal v St. Vincent Charity Hospital*[61] is worth exploring. The plaintiff, an ophthalmologist, had a dispute with the hospital over a tract of land that both parties wanted to develop. The plaintiff went to a zoning hearing and publicly described the hospital's development plan as the "laughing stock" of other area hospitals. A short time later, the plaintiff was not reappointed as director of the ophthalmology department.

He allegedly retaliated by sending a letter to the local newspaper containing disparaging references to the hospital's expansion plans, and he privately threatened to sue the hospital. The medical executive committee then took a "corrective action" against the plaintiff for his allegedly disruptive conduct. The committee also sent him a "letter of admonition" urging him not to make further public allegations against the hospital, with which he complied.

The plaintiff later submitted his application for reappointment to the medical staff, as required in the bylaws. Both the credentialing committee and the medical executive committee recommended that he be reappointed, but the medical affairs committee, which was a committee of the board of directors, recommended that the plaintiff's reappointment be denied. The board of directors followed its committee's recommendation and denied the plaintiff's request for reappointment. Hearings followed in accordance with the bylaws, but no reappointment occurred. The plaintiff ultimately filed a lawsuit, alleging that the action was contrary to the bylaws.

At the trial court, a member of the medical affairs committee testified that there was no objection to the plaintiff's medical competence. The focus of testimony was on nonmedical matters, such as lack of cooperation, disparaging the image and reputation of the hospital, and disrupting the business activities of the board of directors. The trial court ordered that the plaintiff be reappointed on grounds that the hospital bylaws did not permit the kind of action taken.

The plaintiff further challenged the bylaws on grounds that Ohio case law does not recognize hospital bylaws provisions that allow disciplinary actions that are not reasonably related to a physician's skill, education, and competence. Furthermore, the bylaws were not based on objective criteria and were therefore invalid.

The Ohio Court of Appeals reversed the decision. The court held that the hospital's bylaws did permit the board of directors to review a physician's application for reappointment on grounds other than professional competency or skill. The issue was whether the standards used in reviewing bylaws were reasonably related to the operation of the hospital, including its business activities.

Another example is the case of *Cobb County Hospital Authority v Prince*.[62] A group of neurologists and neurosurgeons wanted to purchase a CT scanner and lease space within a hospital to operate it. The hospital declined this arrangement, and the plaintiffs located their scanner elsewhere. Meanwhile, the hospital purchased its own CT scanner. The hospital authority allowed the plaintiffs to move patients to their own scanner until the hospital's scanner became operational. At that point, the plaintiffs were informed that they could not move hospitalized patients to their outside scanner and revoked their staff privileges when they continued to do so. The plaintiffs sued, alleging that the hospital authority's decision was arbitrary and unreasonable.

The court found that the plaintiffs' medical judgment was not curtailed by the hospital policy. In addition, the resolution regarding use of outside diagnostic facilities was "reasonable and reflects a well intentioned effort . . . to deal with the intricate and complex task of providing comprehensive medical services to the people of our state." Although the hospital's decision was based on sound policy, in light of *Patrick v Burget*, peer review should obviously not be used for anticompetitive purposes. If the physicians had been subjected to adverse peer review action as a result of their business activities, another *Patrick* decision could have resulted.

Attention to Bylaws

Hospitals and medical staffs should review the HCQIA guidelines for the conduct of peer review, applicable state law, and their own existing bylaws. At a minimum, these bylaws should be amended to comply with the notice and hearing provisions of HCQIA if the particular state has not elected to ignore HCQIA and establish an equivalent one of their own.

The hospital's medical staff bylaws should establish a detailed hearing process to be followed in peer review cases. This process, especially that portion dealing with notice and timing, must be followed carefully. If the medical staff bylaws comply with HCQIA and are scrupulously followed, a claim of improperly motivated peer review will be more difficult to sustain. The fair hearing procedures should contain specific procedures that describe how the hearing should be conducted.

For example, the burden of proof can be allocated between the parties. California's statute has some interesting features in this regard. The peer review committee must initially present evidence that supports the recommended action. Initial applicants have the burden of proving their qualifications. The medical staff should consider allowing some degree of pre-hearing discovery consistent with state court decisions that grant discovery rights whether or not state statutes or medical staff bylaws contemplate them. Reviewing courts may reverse hospital decisions if they perceive that they were not fundamentally fair, despite following the letter of the bylaw.

At the conclusion of a contested hearing, the recommendations of the hearing panel should be set out in writing and given to all parties. At a minimum, this ensures compliance with HCQIA. The fair hearing section of the hospital's bylaws may require that certain "findings of fact" that will support the decision of the hearing panel be set forth in the report. This may help rebut later claims that the hearing panel's decision was reached rashly or without an adequate factual foundation.

When state law defines a "peer review committee" as a committee operating pursuant to written bylaws that must be approved by the governing board of a health care entity, a hospital administration should consider designating certain, or all, medical staff committees as peer review committees. In this way, if state law is otherwise vague about immunity, it is easier to argue that a certain committee's activities did constitute protected peer review activity. Medical staff bylaws often include the immunity and confidentiality provisions of state peer review statutes. Although the bylaws do not themselves confer immunity or confidentiality (that is a legislative function), the perceived advantage of including such language is to make the bylaws the beginning point for the defense of a lawsuit.

Involvement of Attorneys

When a hospital or other health care entity instigates a disciplinary proceeding against a physician that could result in the loss or termination of clinical privileges, legal counsel should be sought by those involved in the hearing process. Attorneys may be asked to participate in preparation for the hearing, including drafting the written notice of charges, preparing the evidence, and advising in the selection of witnesses. The role of the hospital's attorney (or other counsel brought in solely for purposes of the hearing) is not that of a prosecutor, but rather a procedural advisor to ensure that the proceedings are conducted fairly. The attorney should bear in mind the objectives of protecting both the consumers of health care and the physician involved against false or exaggerated charges.[27]

Attorneys advising the hearing panel and representing the affected physician should be allowed reasonable latitude in presenting evidence and cross-examining witnesses. However, intimidating tactics should not be permitted by the hearing panel.[63] As seen in the case of *Smith v Ricks*,[54] some hospitals allow the presence of counsel but restrict their involvement without any apparent HCQIA consequences. The decision to restrict counsel should be made by each hospital and its medical staff. When present, any such restrictions should be explained prior to the hearing to minimize both potential disruption and the argument that the affected physician was surprised by not having the restriction disclosed in advance.

The Hearing Panel

The section of the medical staff bylaws dealing with fair hearings should specify that the complainant (i.e., peer review committee, credentialing committee, etc.) will present its case first and then allow the affected physician an opportunity to respond to the charges.[63] To preserve the conditional immunity conferred by HCQIA and any applicable state statutes, the hearing panel should consist of physicians who are not in direct economic competition with the affected physician or who otherwise stand to gain something as a result of an adverse recommendation or decision regarding the affected physician. Although members of the hearing panel should be physicians who are respected in the medical community, they do not need to be practicing the same medical specialty as the affected physician.[27] On the other hand, they should not be so removed from the type of problem or problems involved that they cannot render an accurate decision. Physicians who are direct economic competitors of the affected physician may testify as witnesses, whether called by the affected physician, the hearing panel, or the hospital. However, the affected physician should not be deprived of privileges solely on the basis of adverse testimony by his economic competitors.

In any proceedings that may result in the termination of privileges, one or more physicians should testify who are not economic competitors or who do not stand to gain economically by an adverse action. They also should be knowledgeable in the treatment, patient care management, and areas of medical practice or judgment on which the adverse action is based.[27]

In an ideal world, physicians who have previous contact with the case or situation should not be allowed to serve on a peer review committee. This might include having acted professionally on the case, initiated a complaint, or served on any committee dealing with the case or situation, such as the executive committee of the medical staff.[27] This may be difficult to achieve in smaller hospitals. In any event, physicians with a history of conflict with the physician being reviewed may benefit economically or otherwise by that physician being disciplined. These persons should definitely be excluded from the review committee.[64]

In some cases, a peer review committee or panel may find that it cannot conduct a hearing because too many of its members are economic competitors with the physician involved. If so, the hospital should attempt to arrange for non-staff physicians, ideally having familiarity with peer review proceedings, to make up a special ad hoc committee for review purposes. The hospital might consider hiring a hearing officer who has some familiarity with the conduct of hearings, the rules regarding introduction of evidence, and the case law pertaining to medical staff disciplinary hearings.[64] Ideally, the affected physician and the medical staff should agree on which individuals from outside the hospital will hear the case. This approach can provide some assurance that the review process is fair and objective, as well as stop claims about economic competition.[64]

Conduct of Hearings

To ensure that a hearing not only appears fair but also is fair to the affected physician, the hearing panel should permit substantial latitude in the presentation of evidence, medical reference works, and testimony. The panel also should have discretion to set reasonable time limits on the proceedings.[27] A hearing on med-ical staff privileges should not take an inordinate amount of time, nor should the affected physician be permitted to protract the proceedings in the name of due process. A verbatim transcript of the hearing should be made available to the parties, with the costs shared by the hospital and the affected physician. This can be done by tape-recording the hearing; however, a court reporter is preferable.[27]

At the discretion of the hearing panel, witnesses may be requested to testify under oath.[27] Although there are no reported cases in which the issue of claimed perjury at a medical staff hearing has been raised on appeal, the administration of an oath or other intonement of responsibility to tell the truth may underscore the serious nature of the proceedings.

At times, an investigation indicates that a disciplinary proceeding is warranted to consider terminating (or restricting) a physician's clinical privileges. In such cases, the physician should not be permitted to resign until the hearing panel, based on testimony and evidence, decides for or against termination, regardless of whether the affected physician chooses to be present.[27] The affected physician should be informed that resignation under such circumstances will result in a report being filed with the National Practitioner Data Bank.

When the issue is the quality of medical care rendered, all witnesses should be admonished to testify as to the medical standards of the community. In other words, did the care given comply with the local standard of care? Physicians testifying about what they would have done under the circumstance are only giving their individual opinions and may not be representative of the medical community.

Although physicians who are in direct economic competition with the affected physician should not serve as hearing panel members, they may serve as witnesses.

Peer review committees should not simply "go through the motions" before recommending the termination of a physician's privileges. Likewise, the hearing panel should not rush through the process before imposing the actual termination. This careless use of the process may happen when the medical staff is dissatisfied with a particular physician and has decided the time has come to terminate the person. Evidence that the decision to terminate took place before the hearing may suggest to a reviewing court that the peer review process was not fair or objective.

In such a case, the reviewing court may depart from its usual role of examining the record to see if due process was followed, regardless of the actual decision. The court may rule that peer review was conducted in a manner that did not comply with the bylaws and thus violated due process. At worst, the court might find a conspiracy to violate a physician's civil rights or the antitrust laws. Similarly, standards of behavior should be imposed evenhandedly. If a physician with an abrasive personality is terminated for conduct that would be tolerated or merely reprimanded in a more well-liked colleague, then those peer review outcomes are likely to receive an unfavorable ruling at trial.

Where state law is unclear or weak about peer review immunity, peer reviewers may wish to consider obtaining insurance covering at least the defense costs of lawsuits. Most professional liability policies do not cover peer review proceedings and decisions. However, the hospital's own liability policies may provide some protection. Although insurance policies are unlikely to cover antitrust damages, some policies provide a defense to a lawsuit containing antitrust claims.[65] Hospital administrations should give some thought to having the hospital indemnify its peer review committees for damages incurred as a result of their service.

Preserving Confidentiality

To avoid having a court split hairs over which records are protected and which are unprotected, there should be evidence that letters requesting information, references, and the like on applicants for medical staff membership were prepared by or at the direction of the credentialing committee for peer review purposes. A reference to JCAHO credentialing standards might also be helpful in proving that the information requested is necessary to comply with such standards. Medical staffs might also give some thought to adding a section to their bylaws that declares that the records of the peer review committees are privileged and confidential in accordance with the laws of their state.

During the conduct of a peer review case, whether a simple committee meeting to discuss an incident or a formal hearing with counsel, confidentiality must be maintained. Committee chairs should remind participants that the matters discussed are confidential and should not be disclosed to anyone outside the meeting. When committees have long agendas at meetings and only part of the agenda relates to peer

review matters, members should be careful not to discuss the peer review issues except when they are raised. Any persons not connected with the peer review matter (e.g., invited guests, speakers) should be excused during these discussions. Committee minutes must be secured and, if necessary, redacted to remove confidential information if those minutes are to be reviewed by other committees (e.g., where a subcommittee reports to a larger committee). The same precautions should be taken at formal peer review hearings.

In a civil lawsuit related to peer review, if discovery of peer review records is sought, counsel may avoid disclosure by raising the appropriate privilege provision. Counsel should not assume that a reviewing court is familiar with the peer review privilege, nor assume that the court will recognize it without counsel having proved that the privilege attaches to the documents sought under the facts of the case. In other words, the peer review privilege must be actively urged before the court or it may be deemed to have been waived.

The Future of Peer Review

Economic Credentialing

Hospital credentialing processes are becoming increasingly responsive to reimbursement concerns. In 1982, Medicare changed hospital reimbursement to a prospective payment system, and physician's charges remained cost based. This change created a somewhat adversarial relationship between hospitals and physicians. In 1992, physicians also began being paid on a prospective basis. Discounted fees to managed care organizations affected this process as well where cost-saving strategies were used, such as denial of payment for "medically unnecessary services" and "substandard quality of care," even though the patient's treatment was within the traditional standard of care by which medical malpractice cases are judged. Health care entities realized that physicians' medical care decisions could make or break the hospital. This realization led to the concept that physicians' practice patterns could be scrutinized for economic as well as medical indicators.

This concept became what is now referred to as economic credentialing. Economic credentialing can be defined in two different ways:
- A system that measures physicians based on explicit cost or charge parameters. Under such a system, a physician might be

required to generate a certain amount of profit or to admit an economically favorable patient mix as a condition of retaining privileges.

- The evaluation of physicians based on individual utilization data, which illustrates not just financial issues but quality issues as well. Under such a system, physicians who use a large number of expensive procedures or tests might have such data factored into their review of credentials. This particular type of economic credentialing is becoming part of normal procedure in hospitals.

The ability to perform this kind of analysis is now commonplace. Most health care periodicals routinely carry advertisements from software vendors for products that will capture and collate any desired clinical data.

Legal Aspects of Economic Credentialing

Arguments for the legal authority to perform economic credentialing may stem from the general fiduciary duties of corporate entities or from the specific powers granted to various types of public entities that operate hospitals. For example, in most for-profit corporations, the officers and directors have a duty to exercise their powers solely for the benefit of the corporation and its stockholders. The governing bodies of hospitals often have authority to manage and control all matters relating to its government, discipline, contracts, and fiscal concerns and may adopt rules necessary to carry out the purposes of the hospital.

It can be argued that economic credentialing does not fit within the immunities of HCQIA. Review of a physician's use of hospital services, which does not reflect on the physician's medical judgment but does incur costs to the hospital, is probably not "based on the competence or professional conduct of the physician," as that term is traditionally understood. On the other hand, an argument can be made that any behavior subject to a hospital's bylaws, rules, and regulations and to a review at the hands of one of its various JCAHO-mandated committees is at least "professional conduct." The same kinds of arguments have to be considered in evaluating the liability for pure economic credentialing under state law. For example, if the cost of care is taken into account, is this "evaluating a physician's quality of care"?

Decisions to close departments or medical staffs, when motivated by financial as well as quality considerations, are a precursor to economic credentialing. For example, in *Desai v St Barnabas Medical Center*,[66] the plaintiff physician challenged a closed medical staff policy on grounds that it was arbitrary and capricious. The state supreme court held that a closed staff policy was rational if it was a legitimate exercise of the institution's duty as a public fiduciary, particularly where state law articulated a policy that hospital care be "efficiently provided and properly utilized at a reasonable cost." In *Redding v St. Francis Medical Center*,[67] two cardiologists filed a lawsuit when the hospital adopted bylaws that closed the cardiac surgical staff. The court held that legitimate hospital management decisions must outweigh vested interests of physicians even if individual staff members suffer adverse economic consequences.

Pure economic credentialing cases are more rare but often reach the same result. In *Knapp v Palos Community Hospital*,[68] a medical group brought a legal action to challenge the curtailment of the group's privileges. The basis of the action was the hospital's quality assurance reviews, which showed that the group had seriously overused hospital services, such as diagnostic tests, pacemakers, and pulmonary angiograms, and had made unsubstantiated diagnoses. In addition, the hospital found that the group's costs were 31% higher than those of other staff members.

Credentialing and Managed Care

Credentialing is rapidly becoming an issue for managed care organizations. The reason for this situation is the organizations' potential liability for failure to use reasonable care in selecting physicians or other providers as outside contractors and for referrals. In *Sloan v Metropolitan Health Council of Indianapolis*,[69] a staff model HMO was found liable for the negligent acts of a participating physician who provided services under an employment contract and a medical director who controlled staff physicians. In *Harrell v Total Health Care, Inc.*,[70] a primary care physician referred a patient to a urologist who was on the HMO's panel and who allegedly performed negligent surgery on the patient. The Missouri appeals court found that, although the HMO had established procedures for evaluating physicians who applied to be on the panel, the procedure was inadequate. Thus, the HMO breached what the court found to be a common law duty to conduct a reasonable investigation of physicians to ascertain their competence.

Economic Credentialing and Managed Care

State law varies widely in this area. In Texas, for example, although HMOs may not discriminate against providers on the sole basis of their type of license, neither are they required to use a particular type of provider, accept each provider of a category or type, or contract directly with providers. HMOs may set the terms and conditions under which health care services will be rendered by providers, and all providers must comply with the terms and conditions established by the HMOs.[71] Group model HMOs may selectively contract with providers, decline to contract, selectively contract for any or all covered services, and require enrollees to use specified providers.[72] With powers like these, HMOs are likely to engage in economic credentialing.

The trend today is clearly toward health networks, or integrated delivery systems. These are formally integrated groups of providers working together with a common vision and goal. They jointly provide services through an integrated continuum of preventive and primary care, inpatient hospital care, alternative inpatient care, ambulatory care, transitional care, and long-term or chronic care. Case management provides efficient, cost-effective, and seamless services to a defined or predetermined geographic area. There should be joint responsibility among providers and members (patients) for their health needs.[73] Under these situations, economic credentialing is likely to be an issue, because the network seeks to cut costs and use the savings in contract negotiations. But who controls the medical practice in these systems? Nonphysicians who control the day-to-day provision of health care can unduly influence the independent medical judgment of physicians.

One approach to this problem is to acknowledge the nonphysician's (i.e., hospital, insurance company) role in maintaining economic control in areas where they have expertise and authority. For example, they would retain the right to approve any financial decision of the organization, including but not limited to, approval of capital and operating budgets, expenditures, and any managed care contracts that involve some risk to the organization.

However, the governing boards of such networks should also have participating physician members who have a clear role in developing and approving bylaws. Those bylaws should provide that nonphysicians have no authority to interfere with the independent and professional practice of medicine by any physician employee or physician associated with the network, nor can they intervene in or interfere with any physician-patient relationship. As for peer review and credentialing, such bylaws should provide that all credentialing, quality assurance, utilization review, and peer review policies will be made exclusively by physician committees or groups.

This approach is not the same as an "any willing provider" approach to staffing HMOs. Despite the popularity of such tactics, organized medicine has mixed views about allowing any willing provider to contract with an organization because of the increasing number of physicians in managed care organizations. In 1993, the AMA adopted a resolution to use "all necessary resources" to secure a "willing provider" provision in a managed care reform bill. By 1994, the AMA had adopted another resolution in support of the proposed federal Patient Protection Act legislation. In recent years, the AMA has supported patient protection legislation that would provide, in part, the following:

- When economic considerations are used in credentialing, they must be based on objective criteria, which must be made available to applicants, participating physicians, and enrollees.
- There will be a due process appeal for all adverse decisions, using HCQIA criteria.

Twenty-four states have some form of "any willing provider" law, although state laws vary widely. Of these, 11 statutes cover pharmacy only, while nine govern all provider contracts. Some other states, like Texas, have taken the more restrictive Patient Protection Act approach through the insurance regulatory process.

Nonetheless, medical staffs will have to face the question of economic credentialing in the future. The use of computerized profiles that reflect a physician's resource consumption may be considered a valuable tool in determining whether the physicians reappointed to medical staff positions are managing their patients efficiently. Hospital administrations may well take the position that, if a physician is causing the hospital a financial problem, the hospital then has the right, or even the duty, to take that fact into consideration in reappointment decisions.

There remain many unanswered questions about a hospital's potential liability for economic credentialing. Whether such practices can withstand legal scrutiny will depend on many factors. One important factor will be the standards against which a physician's performance will be measured and how those standards relate to the quality of care rendered.

Key Points and Conclusion

Peer review is a shorthand term that describes a number of common yet important activities of physicians and hospitals. The term also describes an evolving set of legal rules that the courts do not as yet fully understand. Even though there is a rather large body of reported peer review litigation, the success of a few cases means that physicians must conduct peer review in a somewhat uncertain legal atmosphere. The anxiety that this causes is compounded by the larger threat of frivolous medical malpractice litigation that all physicians face in their everyday activities. On top of this, emergency physicians are particularly prone to lawsuits because of the wide variety of cases they handle and the often highly charged nature of an emergency department setting.

Despite the success of some notable antitrust cases, successful challenges to peer review decisions have historically been rare. Today, for better or for worse, there is a renewed and broader interest in the legal aspect of peer review. Fortunately for physicians in general and peer reviewers in particular, this interest, in many states, has been translated into new protections for peer reviewers. Such protections are of no use, however, unless participants in the process implement the procedural steps that inevitably accompany the enhanced level of protection. The impact of cost-conscious medical care on the peer review process and its potential liabilities remain to be determined.

References

1. Definition in "A Discursive Dictionary of Health Care," February 1976, prepared by the Staff of the Subcommittee of Health and the Environment, of the Committee on Interstate and Foreign Commerce, U.S. House of Representatives.
2. Watts C. From collegial to codified — the evolution of modern peer review. *Tex Med* 1995;(9):22.
3. *Darling v Charleston Community Memorial Hospital*, 211 NE2d 253 (1965) Cert denied, 383 US 946 (1966).
4. *Park North General Hospital v Hickman*, 703 SW2d 262 (1986).
5. *Smith v St. Francis Hospital*, 676 P2d 279 (Okla Ct App 1983).
6. Okla Stat Ann tit 19, §792 (West 1988).
7. Cal Health & Safety Code §32128 (West 1996).
8. Cal Health & Safety Code §1316.6.
9. Cal Business and Professions Code §2282 (West 1996).
10. NY Public Health Law, §2805-j (McKinney 1989).
11. NY Public Health Law, §2805-k.
12. NY Public Health Law, §2801-b.
13. Fla Stat ch 395.0193(1995).
14. Fla Stat ch 395.0191(4).
15. Tex Health & Safety Code §241.101 (Vernon 1996).
16. Tex Rev Civ Stat Ann, art 4495b, §1.02(9)(Vernon supp 1996).
17. 42 CFR §482.12(a)(5) (1994).
18. 42 CFR §482.12(a)(6).
19. 42 CFR §482.21(a)(3).
20. 42 CFR §482.21(c).
21. 42 CFR §482.22(b).
22. 42 CFR §482.22(c).
23. 42.CFR §482.22(a).
24. Joint Commission on Accreditation of Healthcare Organizations. *Comprehensive Accreditation Manual for Hospitals: The Official Handbook*. Oakbrook Terrace, Ill: JCAHO; 1995.
25. 108 S Ct 1658 (1988).
26. *Patrick v Burget*, 800 F2d 1498 (9th Cir 1986).
27. AMA Board of Trustees Report, MMM, A-88. AMA Annual Meeting, June 1988.
28. See, for example, O'Brien. Town left with little care. *American Medical News*, February 26, 1988.
29. See, for example, Bierig J. Peer review after *Patrick*. *J Health Hosp Law* 1988;21(6):135-139, and Hanson C. Does *Patrick v Burget* mean the end of peer review? *California Physician*, August 1988.
30. These findings are a direct rebuke to the Supreme Court, which dismissed arguments in favor of effective peer review in the closing words of the opinion: "[respondents and amicus curiae] contend that effective peer review is essential to the provision of quality medical care and that any threat of antitrust liability will prevent physicians from participating openly and actively in peer review proceedings. This argument, however, essentially challenges the wisdom of applying the antitrust laws to the sphere of medical care, and as such is properly directed to the legislative branch." Congress apparently took the Supreme Court at its word. California voted not to "opt out" of HCQIA in 1989. The California legislature found that the state's laws provide a more careful articulation of the protections for both those doing peer review and those subject to review, and better integrates public and private systems of peer review. California did not attempt to opt out of HCQIA's mandatory reporting provisions, which are discussed in Chapter 10, "Impaired Physician."
31. *Decker v IHC Hospitals*, 982 F2d 433 (10th Cir 1992); *Manion v Evans*, 986 F2d 1036 (6th Cir 1992); *Imperial v Suburban Hospital Ass'n Inc.*, 37 F3d 1026 (4th Cir 1994).
32. Jaffe CG. The health care quality improvement act: antitrust liability in peer review. *Tort Insurance Law J* 1989;24:571-592.
33. A "good faith" standard was originally proposed, but experts feared that it would be seen as a subjective test of the reviewer's state of mind. Therefore, "reasonable belief" was thought to impose a more objective standard. See House of Representatives Report No. 99-903, 99th Cong, 2nd Sess (A86), US Code Cong & Admin News 6384.
34. 42 USC §11112(a) (1996).
35. 42 USC §11151.
36. 42 USC §11151(8).
37. 42 USC §11151(10).
38. 42 USC §11151(11).
39. 42 USC §11151(9).
40. As previously noted, not all actions are considered to be peer review and would not fall into HCQIA's definition of a professional review action. Thus, if a hospital declines to grant staff privileges to a professional on the grounds that it does not have the required facilities to support

such specialty practice, that decision would not be one based on competence or professional conduct. As noted, there is a limitation that actions are not considered to be based on competence if they are primarily based on "any other matter that does not relate to the competence or professional conduct of a physician." It is questionable whether the act of a physician assaulting a patient or staff member in the hospital parking lot relates to the usual understanding of competence or professional conduct. To stretch the point somewhat further, a physician's indictment or conviction of Medicare fraud may or may not be related to competence or professional conduct.

41. 42 USC §11151(1) (1996).

42. 42 USC §11112(b).

43. 42 USC §11112(b)(2).

44. But see *Huntsville Memorial Hospital v Ernst*, 763 SW2d 856 (Tex App 1988). Although not discussing HCQIA, the Houston Court of Appeals held that, prior to a peer review hearing, a physician should be allowed to review all pertinent documents on which the hospital will rely, as well as other elements that are recognized by HCQIA. The California opt out legislation apparently recognizes the lack of specific discovery rights as a defect on HCQIA. Its remedy is to provide that the affected physician has the right to inspect and copy, at his own expense, any documentary evidence relevant to the charges that the peer review body has in its possession or control, as soon as is practical after the request for hearing is received. By the same token, though, the peer review body has the right to inspect and copy relevant material in the hands of the affected physician. These rights, and the procedural provisions to enforce them, may turn a peer review hearing into the medical staff equivalent of a full-blown courtroom procedure. The hearing could then be criticized as going far beyond the elements of administrative due process for these types of cases. See Section 809.2, California Business and Professions Code.

45. 42 USC §11112(b)(3)(A) (1996).

46. It is doubtful whether the facts in *Patrick* would have produced a different result under HCQIA. For example, the hearing panel in that case was composed of physicians in direct economic competition with Dr. Patrick.

47. 42 USC §11112(b)(3)(c) (1996).

48. 42 USC §11112(b)(3)(D).

49. 42 USC §11112(c).

50. *Austin v McNamara*, 979 F2d 728 (9th Cir 1992).

51. *Mann v Johnson Memorial Hospital*, 611 NE2d 676 (Ill Ct App 1993).

52. *Balaklaw v Lovell*, 14 F3d 793 (2d Cir 1994).

53. *Dutta v St. Francis Regional Medical Center*, 867 P2d 1057 (Kan Sup Ct, 1994).

54. *Smith v Ricks*, 31 F3d 1478 (9th Cir 1994).

55. *Evers v Edward Hospital Association*, 617 NE2d 1211 (Ill App 1993); *Hancock v Blue Cross-Blue Shield of Kansas*, 21 F3d 373 (10th Cir 1994); *Goldsmith v Harding Hospital, Inc.*, 762 F Supp 187 (SD Ohio 1991); *Doe v HHS*, 871 F Supp 808 (ED Pa 1994).

56. *U.S. v Harris Methodist Ft Worth*, 970 F2d 94 (5th Cir 1992).

57. *Alexander v Rush North Shore Medical Center*, Case No. 95-2782 (7th Cir, Nov. 25, 1996). In doing so, the court overruled its previous decision in *Doe v St. Joseph's Hosp. of Fort Wayne*, 788 F2d 411 (7th Cir 1986).

58. *Ross v Beaumont Hospital*, 687 F Supp 1115 (Mich 1988).

59. See Cultice P. Privileging: physicians are protected by the Americans with Disabilities Act. *J Health Hosp* 1995;28:163.

60. *Nanavati v Burdette Tomlin Memorial Hospital*, 857 F2d 96 (3rd Cir 1988).

61. *Siegal v St. Vincent Charity Hospital*, 520 NE2d 249 (Ohio App 1987).

62. *Cobb County Hospital Authority v Prince*, 249 SE2d 581 (1978).

63. Kelsay E. Protecting peer review activities. *PLICO News*, June 1989.

64. Hirschfield EB. Peer review pitfalls and how to avoid them. *The Citation* 1989;59(8):85.

65. Hanson C. Does *Patrick v Burget* mean the end of peer review? *California Physician*, August 1988.

66. *Desai v St. Barnabas Medical Center*, 510 A2d 662 (1986).

67. *Redding v St. Francis Medical Center*, 208 Cal App 3d 98, 255 Cal Rptr 806 (1989).

68. *Knapp v Palos Community Hospital*, 465 NE2d 554 (1984).

69. *Sloan v Metropolitan Health Council of Indianapolis*, 516 NE2d 1104 (Ind App 1987).

70. *Harrell v Total Health Care, Inc.*, 781 SW2d 58 (Mo 1989).

71. Tex Ins Code Ann, art, 20A.14(g) (West 1996).

72. Tex Ins Code Ann, art, 20A.06A.

73. From the ground up. *Hospitals*, June 5, 1993.

Chapter 26

Confidentiality

Mark M. Moy, MD, MJ, FAAFP, FACEP

Emergency physicians know that they owe their patients a responsibility to uphold the confidentiality of physician-patient communications. However, not every physician may be aware of the extent of this duty or the various exceptions to it. Patients assume that information given to physicians will not be transmitted without their knowledge and consent. Only with this trust can honest and open communication exist between the patient and the physician so that proper diagnosis and treatment can occur.

Reckless disregard of a patient's confidential medical information may subject a physician to legal penalties. Yet, in today's complex medical-legal climate, there are situations in which the physician may, and at times must, legally abrogate this responsibility. Maintaining a patient's confidentiality in these exceptional cases may even subject the physician to legal penalties. Emergency physicians need to understand when they must defend their patients' confidentiality, and when social considerations dictate exceptions to the general rule of confidentiality.

The sanctity of confidentiality in the physician-patient relationship has existed from the beginnings of medical practice. We physicians take the Hippocratic Oath, which reads as follows: "What I may see or hear in the course of the treatment or even outside of the treatment in regard to the life of men, which on no account one must spread abroad, I will keep to myself holding such things shameful to be spoken about."[1] According to the 1997 *Code of Medical Ethics* of the American Medical Association: "A physician shall respect the rights of patients, of colleagues, and of other health professionals, and shall safeguard patient confidences within the constraints of the law."[2] This duty of confidentiality has evolved from an ethical and professional obligation to a legal duty. The legal system has translated the right of confidentiality into medical licensure laws and state privilege statutes. Even the U.S. Supreme Court recognizes the right to privacy: ". . . one aspect of the 'liberty' protected by the Due Process Clause of the Fourteenth Amendment is 'a right of personal privacy, or a guarantee of certain areas or zones of privacy.' "[3]

The dilemma for physicians is that a patient's right of confidentiality is not absolute. In modern society, exceptions have evolved where public policy for the safety of all citizens overrides the treatment needs and rights of an individual patient. The courts have stated that "the protective privilege ends where the public peril begins."[4] Emergency physicians must recognize those situations in which such "public peril" allows them to breach their duty of confidentiality. The wrong decision can subject a physician to significant professional and legal liabilities.

Case Studies

1

While treating a patient in the emergency department, an emergency physician discovers that the patient has AIDS. The patient admits that he has not informed his wife of this fact. The physician feels a need to warn the wife of her risks of being infected with AIDS; however, he is unsure of possible legal repercussions from the patient for breach of confidentiality.

2

A maintenance worker falls asleep on the job. In response, the worker's supervisor sends him to the emergency department for a fitness evaluation and demands that he get a urine drug test. The emergency physician finds that the worker is positive for cocaine. He is unsure whether this information can be given to the employer.

3

The mayor presents to the emergency department with severe chest pains. He is evaluated in the department and admitted to the coronary care unit for further treatment. The emergency physician is immediately deluged with calls from the local media to comment on what happened to the mayor and on his condition and prognosis. The physician is unsure about what, if any, information should be released.

What Information Is Confidential?

All clinical information gathered by a physician during the course of treatment is protected by the duty of confidentiality. Confidential patient information includes not only oral communications, but also all examination findings, laboratory test results, x-rays, and any other medical tests. The information may be shared freely with other members of the immediate health care team, which includes nurses, house officers, technicians, orderlies, ward clerks, therapists, social service workers, patient advocates, and other health care personnel involved in the patient's care.

When responding to telephone inquiries from family, friends, or employers for information on a patient's condition, the physician should first obtain consent from the patient. The patient or designated family member may be asked to handle such telephone calls personally. If obtaining consent is not possible, the physician should divulge only general information, such as presence in the department and whether the patient's condition is stable.

Minors

In certain situations, minors have rights to confidentiality. In states where the legislature has enacted emancipated or mature minor legislation, physicians should permit a competent minor to consent to medical care and should not notify parents without the minor's consent. When a minor presents for medical care under a state's special treatment statute (e.g., contraceptive services, pregnancy-related care, treatment for sexually transmitted disease, drug and alcohol abuse), physicians must respect the minor's right to confidentiality. For minors who are emancipated, confidentiality of information disclosed during an examination, interview, or in counseling should be maintained just as it is for adults.[2] In Illinois, the Emancipated Minors Act defines a "mature minor" as "a person 16 years of age or over and under the age of 18 years who has demonstrated the ability and capacity to manage his own affairs and to live wholly or partially independent of his parents or guardian."[5]

Patient Transfers

Interhospital transfer of patient information raises confidentiality concerns. Emergency physicians often have urgent needs for medical information from other institutions. Frequently, transmission of medical information by fax or telephone is imperative to assist in the treatment of a patient in the emergency department. When possible, a release-of-information form signed by the patient or legal representative should be faxed first. When a signed waiver form is impossible to obtain, the releasing hospital must weigh the sensitivity of the requested information. Medical records concerning psychiatric or drug abuse treatment are highly sensitive. If the hospital releases such records, it probably risks violation of confidentiality; transmitting ECGs, x-ray readings, and laboratory results, however, seems reasonable.

Federal law may supersede a state's common law or statutory right to confidentiality. For example, the Emergency Medical Treatment and Active Labor Act (EMTALA)[6] dictates that medical records must accompany all patients who are transferred from one institution to another. These records include available history, physical examination, preliminary diagnosis, results of diagnostic tests, and treatment provided. Transferring a patient without this information would be a violation of the technical requirements of EMTALA. Health care providers can be confident that this transfer of medical records is not a violation of patient confidentiality.

Third-Party Requests

The complexities of modern medical practice necessitate the exposure of the patient's confidential medical records to numerous non-medical personnel, such as insurance company claim reviewers. A patient's consent to release medical records is required before release of information to insurance companies. Patients generally give permission for their medical records to be released to private agencies by signing routine waivers of confidentiality when applying for health insurance or when processing health care claims. This waiver allows the exposure of the records to secretaries, transcribers, and other employees of insurance companies. Insurance employees also have the responsibility to guard against misuse of this information, as their employers would be liable for violating the confidentiality of a patient's health records.

Occupational Medicine

Emergency physicians are becoming more involved in occupational medicine. When the emergency physician renders treatment for Worker's Compensation injuries, a physician-patient relationship is established even though the physician is paid by the employer. If the employee's illness or injury is work related, the release of medical information to the employer is subject to the provisions of Worker's Compensation laws. The physician must comply with the requirements of such laws, if applicable.[2] Implicit in the application for Worker's Compensation benefits is the surrender of confidentiality for that specific occupational injury or illness. For example, if a worker with an ankle injury also has a history of peptic ulcer disease, this latter information should be kept confidential. Information gained by the physician during preemployment physical examinations should not be divulged without prior patient consent. Even with authorization, the physician should release only that information which is reasonably relevant to the employer's decision regarding that individual's ability to perform the work required by the job.[2]

Federal and State Laws

Patient confidentiality is generally governed by state statutes and codes; however, there are federal statutes that cover medical confidentiality. The Drug Abuse and Treatment Acts and Comprehensive Alcohol Abuse and Alcoholism Prevention, Treatment and Rehabilitation Act impose rigorous requirements on the disclosure of information from alcohol and drug abuse treatment programs.[7] The federal rules apply to any disclosure, even acknowledgment of the patient's presence in a substance abuse program. With few exceptions, federal regulations prohibit disclosure of information concerning patients being treated for substance abuse or related conditions unless very specific patient consent elements are fulfilled.

Many states also have statutes that protect the confidentiality of committee reports involved in quality assurance and peer review activities. These laws are devised to allow free and candid discussions at quality assurance and peer review meetings without fear of discovery by others. The courts usually have been consistent in honoring the confidentiality of these meeting reports. However, in rare situations, courts have ruled that the reports or parts of the reports may be discovered. For this reason, care should be taken in the wording of a report to avoid any increase in liability exposure. Incident reports, although generally protected from discovery, may not always be protected. In *North Broward Hospital v Button*,[8] the court held that a hospital incident report was discoverable only on a showing of need and undue hardship in obtaining the substantial equivalent of the same information. In *Milynarsky v Rush-Presbyterian St. Luke's Medical Center*,[9] the court ruled that an incident report was discoverable because the report in question was not directly used for patient care. For more information in this important area, see Chapter 31, "Securing Risk Management Information From Discovery," and Chapter 38, "Incident Reports."

Breach of Confidentiality

Physicians may face disciplinary actions or have their licenses revoked for breach of patient confidentiality. For example, in Illinois, the state may "revoke, suspend, place on probationary status, or take other disciplinary actions when . . . [a physician] willfully or negligently violates the confidentiality between physician and patient except as required by law."[10] On the other hand, there are times when breaching confidentiality is required by law, such as reporting a patient for suspected child abuse. The Illinois Child Abuse Act states that "any physician who willfully fails to report suspected child abuse or neglect as required by this Act shall be referred to the Illinois State Medical Discipline Board for action. . . . "[11] These conflicting duties require that physicians become familiar with their own state statues.

In the past, state statutes regarding physician-patient confidentiality dealt solely with potential testimony at trial. This is called a "testimonial privilege," in which a physician may not divulge any physician-patient information (such as to opposing lawyers) without the consent of the patient. Most state evidence codes contain a testimonial privilege by which patients have legal rights to prevent the release of confidential communications with their physicians. A physician who receives a subpoena for release of information must first check to see if there is a release-of-information form signed by the patient. Without such a release, the physician should seek legal counsel before complying with the subpoena. A subpoena is not equivalent to a court order to release information, even though it is issued under the authority of the court.

Today, physicians are threatened with civil liability when there is a breach of confidentiality. In the early part of this century, there were only a few cases that dealt with physician-patient confidentiality issues. In a 1920s case, *Simonsen v Swenson*,[12] the court recognized a patient's right to sue but found that disclosure of a patient's syphilis was justified by public health concerns. The *Simonsen* court held that Nebraska's licensing statue, which stated that "a license may be revoked when a physician is found guilty of 'unprofessional or dishonest conduct,'" imposed a definite duty on the physician to refrain from divulging professional secrets.[12] The trend to hold physicians liable for breach of confidentiality gained momentum during the 1960s.[13]

A patient who is harmed by a physician's improper release of information (e.g., by losing a job, a spouse, or reputation) has a number of legal avenues to pursue when litigating against the physician. For example, based on the facts of the particular case, the allegedly injured party may sue the physician for invasion of privacy, breach of an implied contract of confidentiality, malpractice, defamation, and intentional infliction of emotional distress.[14] The legal basis for suing a physician for breach of confidentiality varies greatly from state to state. Physicians should consult with legal counsel for legal precedence in their states.

Statutory Duty to Disclose Confidential Information

Certain data on patient care and incidence of disease need to be maintained to safeguard public health. Collecting such data is deemed to be of greater societal importance than individual confidentiality rights. Such exceptions for government data collection are codified in state statutes where health care providers are required by law to report patient information to public health or law enforcement authorities. The following are examples of events or medical conditions that must be reported:

- Vital statistics, such as births and deaths, and causes of death on death certificates
- Communicable diseases, such as venereal disease, tuberculosis, and AIDS
- Child or elder abuse
- Occupational diseases, such as asbestosis
- Disabling illnesses, such as seizures (e.g., to driver's license agencies)

When reporting these types of patient information as required by law, physicians are legally immunized against liability. For example, the Illinois Communicable Disease Report Act states that "any medical practitioner or other person making such a report in good faith shall be immune from suit for slander or libel based upon any statements contained in such report."[15]

Emergency physicians frequently face confidentiality issues when dealing with law enforcement officials. Many states require the reporting of stab wounds or gunshot wounds, which imply criminal behavior. The Illinois statute is typical, imposing a duty on the physician or nurse to notify the local law enforcement agency "when it reasonably appears that the person requesting treatment has received any injury from the discharge of a firearm, or any injury sustained in the commission of or as a victim of a criminal offense. Any hospital, physician, or nurse shall be forever held harmless from any civil liability for their reasonable compliance with the provisions of this section."[16] In certain cases, physicians may safely report other findings to law enforcement officials when there is strong suspicion that a patient has committed a crime. For example, in *Bryson v Tillinghast*,[17] the Oklahoma Supreme Court ruled that a physician could not be sued by a patient for breach of confidentiality. In this case, a physician informed police about a patient who had a penile bite. This information led police to arrest the man for rape, which was a case they were investigating at the time. The patient was convicted of rape and sued the physician for breach of confidentiality. The court ruled that the disclosure was covered by public policy to protect the welfare of the community. However, this is a single ruling in one state. Physicians should still seek advice from hospital legal counsel before venturing into such sensitive areas.

In an effort to facilitate the prosecution of drunk drivers, some states have passed legislation that permits emergency physicians to release information to a police officer voluntarily without risk of "breach of confidentiality" liability.[18] For example, during the normal course of treatment, when finding positive alcohol or drug test results from patients injured in motor vehicle accidents, Illinois physicians, as of January 1997, are allowed to provide alcohol or drug test results to local law enforcement officers. In states where such liberties with confidentiality are legislated, the hospital should formulate policies on the proper protocol for releasing such information. For example, release of the blood alcohol level results should be documented in the chart, along with the name of the officer to whom the information is released. The information should be provided in writing rather than orally.

Duty to Protect Third Parties

In some states, physicians have a duty to break patient confidentiality when a "reasonably foreseeable danger" to a third party is present. When a physician fails to warn a third party of potential dangers and the third party suffers injury as a result, the physician can be charged with liability for negligence and breach of a duty to warn. The landmark case illustrating this situation is *Tarasoff v Board of Regents, University of California*.[4] Tatiana Tarasoff, a student at the University of California, was killed when a university psychiatrist failed to warn her that a patient of his had revealed a wish to kill her. The California Supreme Court found the employer of the psychiatrist liable for this failure to warn.

Different states view the scope of this duty in various ways. The California Supreme Court, in Tarasoff, ruled that only threats to specifically identified individuals created a duty to warn, so that there was no duty to warn a threatened group.[4] The Arizona Supreme Court, in *Tamsen v Wever*, ruled that foreseeable victims had to be warned even without specific threats.[19] The Washington Supreme Court, in *Peterson v State*, ruled that the duty to warn extended to unidentifiable victims.[20] The Vermont Supreme Court, in *Peck v Counseling Ser.*, extended this duty to include property damage.[21] An Illinois court, in *Kirk v Michael Reese Mem. Hosp.*, ruled that the physician only needed to warn identifiable

potential victims and not the general public.[22] Similarly, in *Purdy v Public Administration*, a New York court ruled that the physician had no duty to protect the public after an elderly woman patient injured a third party while driving from the health facility.[23] Because state interpretations of this developing area of law vary so widely, physicians should always seek legal counsel when these issues arise.

The duty to warn not only covers threats of violence, but also extends to a patient's medical condition, if it poses a danger to third parties. The general rule in many states is that a health care provider is liable for negligence if that provider permits persons to be exposed to and harmed by a communicable disease.[24] The duty to warn in this case includes individuals who may come into contact with the patient, health care workers, and even other patients.[25] In *Phillips v Oconee Mem. Hosp.*, the South Carolina Supreme Court ruled that a hospital could be sued by the parents of a girl who had died of meningitis after the hospital had failed to notify fellow students that meningitis had been diagnosed in a classmate.[26]

The duty to warn conflicts acutely with the duty of confidentiality when dealing with AIDS. Initially, AIDS was a fatal disease that killed rapidly and was mainly associated with homosexual men and intravenous drug abusers. A "leprosy mentality" developed, and AIDS patients encountered widespread discrimination in housing, employment, education, medical treatment, insurance, and other areas. AIDS patients, in turn, sought redress in the courts and legislature. Many state legislatures responded to this discriminatory treatment of HIV-infected patients by passing AIDS-specific legislation. Today, some statutes impose substantial fines or even imprisonment for unauthorized disclosure. In *Anderson v Strong Memorial Hospital*,[27] an AIDS patient sued the hospital, physician, and local newspaper for publishing a picture of him and revealing his condition. The trial court found that the patient's right to confidentiality included the protection of his identity, and the patient obtained damages of $35,000 from the physician and hospital. There is a fine line between maintaining confidential AIDS information and a duty to warn individuals who truly are in danger of contracting the disease.

Although state HIV statutes are generally written to provide confidentiality for HIV-positive patients, many include exceptions when the safety of others is involved. Most statutes allow the disclosure to professional personnel who become exposed to the patient in the normal course of their employment, such as police, EMS personnel, and health care workers. In *Johnson v W. Va. Univ. Hosps. Inc.*,[28] a security guard was bitten by an HIV-positive patient while trying to subdue him in the emergency department. The staff at the bedside knew the patient was HIV positive but did not warn the security guard. He sued the hospital and was awarded $1.9 million, despite the fact that he tested negative for HIV.

Personnel should be cautioned that this kind of information is given only for their own protection and should not be disseminated to anyone else. In *Doe v Shady Grove Adventist Hospital*,[29] a respiratory therapist disclosed a patient's HIV-positive test to a colleague, who then shared the information with the patient's family and friends. The court stated that the allegations, if true, violated the patient's right to privacy. Rape victims, caregivers, and adoptive or foster parents are also generally accepted as exceptions to AIDS confidentiality rules. The physician must recognize that the obligation to disclose may go beyond statutory authority to warn professional personnel.

The fatal consequences of contracting AIDS may create a Tarasoff-type duty for physicians to warn sexual partners of HIV-positive patients, who are most susceptible to exposure. In fact, some states have passed legislation that creates a duty to warn individuals who are likely to come in contact with a known HIV-infected patient.[30] The American Medical Association's Council on Judicial and Ethical Affairs allows notification of third parties at risk as a last resort. The Council advises a physician to do the following:

- Attempt to persuade the infected patient to stop endangering the third party.
- If persuasion fails, notify authorities.
- If the authorities take no action, notify the endangered third party.[31]

Some states place the duty to warn on the state health department and mandate that a physician who reports positive HIV test results to the state health department has fulfilled any duty owed to a third party. Emergency physicians should be aware that standards of confidentiality and disclosure vary from state to state. The prospect of successful treatment of AIDS in its earliest stages makes it more critical for physicians to warn third parties in a timely manner in order to protect their lives, safety, and well-being.

Reasonable Disclosures

Because of the emergency department's interaction with the community, emergency physicians are occasionally questioned by the media for medical information on public figures or in disaster situations. Emergency physicians should disclose only the most basic information, especially when public figures are involved. If the patient gives consent, the name, sex, address, occupation, marital status, and a general statement about medical condition may be released to the press.[32] In criminal cases, overdoses, and suicide attempts, no details should be given about the alleged motive, social status, or rumored evidence. In cases involving assault or rape, the identity of the victim should never be released.[33] The courts have accorded the media a "newsworthiness" privilege if the material reported is deemed to be of legitimate public interest. However, it is not at all clear whether a physician can claim this defense.

Case Discussions

1

Because some states have specific legislation related to AIDS confidentiality, physicians should consult with their hospitals' legal counsel. For example, in Illinois, notification of the spouse is allowed without creating a legal duty for the physician to do so. The Illinois HIV Disclosure Act states: "A physician may notify the spouse of the test subject, if the test result is positive and has been confirmed by a Western Blot Assay or more reliable test, provided that the physician has first sought unsuccessfully to persuade the patient to notify the spouse or that, a reasonable time after the patient has agreed to make the notification, the physician has reason to believe that the patient has not provided the notification. This paragraph shall not create a duty or obligation under which a physician must notify the spouse of the test results, nor shall such duty or obligation be implied."[34] For physicians in states that do not have specific legislation, the AMA ethical guidelines advise physicians to try to persuade the infected patient to notify the endangered party. If persuasion fails, the physician should contact public health authorities. As a last resort, the physician should notify the third party.[28] This scenario places a heavy burden on the emergency physician.

2

Fitness evaluations are common in safety-sensitive work settings, especially within the nuclear, chemical, and transportation industries. In this case, the company must have a well-developed drug testing policy approved by labor and management. If such a policy is in place, according to Department of Transportation regulations, the emergency physician may inform the employer of the name of the specific drug but not the quantity of the drug found.[35]

3

The emergency physician in this case must realize that, even though his patient is a local celebrity, the patient still has the right of confidentiality regarding his medical treatment and condition. The patient himself, or his appointed representative, must give consent as to what information may be released to the public. The hospital should designate one staff member, someone who is knowledgeable in the legalities of public relations, to be the designated spokesperson. Any press inquiry then may be channeled to this person without any variation or input from other hospital personnel. If the emergency physician were to "leak" information without the consent of the mayor, he would be breaching his duty of confidentiality.

Key Points and Conclusion

Medical practice traditionally has had an ethical duty to uphold a patient's right to confidentiality. This ethical responsibility has evolved into a legal duty. However, exceptions to this duty also have evolved, and physicians are obligated to breach confidentiality when public safety needs override patient rights. In the busy practice of emergency medicine, emergency physicians will find frequent situations where they are confronted with confidentiality issues. Although their first duty is to preserve patient confidentiality, they must also be aware of these exceptions. Emergency physicians need to consider the following key points about patient confidentiality:

- Laws vary greatly from state to state, so physicians should become familiar with the specific statutes in their own states.
- The environment of the emergency department makes it difficult for physicians to safeguard a patient's confidentiality in every case. However, this burden does not lessen the duty of the physician to preserve

all clinical information gleaned from a patient encounter.
- A patient who is harmed by a physician's breach of confidentiality has a legal right to sue the physician in civil court.
- Emergency physicians need to be aware of state laws governing the release of patient information in cases of suspected criminal activity.
- When the safety of a third party is involved, the emergency physician may have a duty to breach confidentiality to warn the third party of danger.
- Issues regarding AIDS confidentiality raise many conflicting duties for the physician. Emergency physicians need to be aware of applicable laws in their states.
- When dealing with the news media, the emergency physician needs to be cautious and avoid infringing on a patient's confidentiality rights, especially when treating celebrities and other public figures.

References

1. Edelstein L. *The Hippocratic Oath: Text, Translation and Interpretation.* 3(1943). (Supplements to the Bulletin of the History of Medicine No. 1).
2. Council on Ethical and Judicial Affairs, American Medical Association. *Code of Medical Ethics.* 1996-97 edition. Chicago: American Medical Association.
3. *Carey v Population Servs. Int'l,* 432 US 678, 684 (quoting *Roe v Wade,* 410 W 113, 152, reh'g denied, 410 UW 959 [1953]).
4. *Tarasoff v Regents of Univ. of California,* 7 Cal3d 425 (1976).
5. 750 ILCS 30/32.
6. The Emergency Medical Treatment and Active Labor Act (EMTALA, also known as COBRA), 42 USC §1395dd.
7. USCA §§290dd-3, 390ee-3 (West 1982 & Supp 1986).
8. *North Broward Hosp. v Button,* 592 So2d 367 (Fla 1992).
9. *Milynarsky v Rush-Presbyterian St. Luke's Med. Ctr.,* 572 NE2d 1025 (Ill 1991).
10. 225 ILCS 60/22.
11. 325 ILCS 5/4/02.
12. *Simonsen v Swenson,* 177 NW 831 (Neb 1920).
13. See *Hammonds v Aetna Casualty & Sur. Co.,* 243 F Supp 793 (ND Ohio 1965) ("The [public]policy is reflected in . . .The privileged communication statute."); *Clark v Geraci,* 208 NYS2d 564 (NY 1960) ("The duty of secrecy is implied by our statutory law."); *Humphers v First Interstate Bank,* 696 P2d 527 (Or 1985) (held that a mother who gave up her daughter for adoption may sue her doctor for breach of confidential relationship for revealing her identity to the daughter).
14. See generally *Breach of Confidence: An Emerging Tort,* 82 Colum L Rev 1426 (1982).
15. 745 ILCS 45/1.
16. 20 ILCS 2630/3.2.
17. *Bryson v Tillinghast,* 749 P2d 110 (Okla 1988).
18. 625 ILCS 5/11 – 501.4-1.
19. *Tamsen v Wever,* 802 P2d 1063 (Ariz Ct App 1990).
20. *Peterson v State,* 671 P2d 230 (1983).

21. *Peck v Counseling Serv.*, 499 A2d 422 (1980).

22. *Kirk v Michael Reese Hosp. and Medical Emergency*, 513 NE2d 387 (1987).

23. *Purdy v Public Administration v County of Westchester*, 514 NYS2d 407, 1987.

24. See *Hoffman v Blackman*, 241 So2d 752 (Fla. 1970), and *Skillings v Allen*, 173 NW 63, 143 Minn 323, 5 ALR 922 (1919).

25. See *Jones v Stanko*, 160 NE 456 (1928), and *Fostage v Corona*, 330 A2d 355 (NJ Super Ct Dec. 18, 1974).

26. *Phillips v Oconee Mem. Hosp.*, 348 SE2d 836 (1986).

27. *Anderson v Strong Memorial Hosp.*, 573 NYS2d 828 (NY Sup Ct 1991).

28. *Johnson v W. Va. Univ. Hosps., Inc.*, 413 SE2d 889, 897 (WVa 1991).

29. *Doe v Shady Grove Adventist Hosp.*, 598 A2d 507 (Md Ct Spec App 1991).

30. See Illinois Compiled Statutes Annotated, *Public Health Communicable Diseases AIDS Confidentiality Act*, 410 ILCS 305/9 (1995).

31. Council on Ethical and Judicial Affairs, American Medical Association. Ethical issues involved in the growing AIDS crisis. *JAMA* 1988;259:1360-1361.

32. Lucash PD, Koval K. The media and the emergency department. *Emergency Medical Services* 1981;10:30-32.

33. Larkin GL, Moskop J, Sanders A, et al. The emergency physician and patient confidentiality: a review. *Ann Emerg Med* 1994;24:1161-1167.

34. §410 ILCS 305/9 (a).

35. 59 *Federal Register* 7302

Chapter 27

Patient Consent

David L. Freedman, MD, JD, FACEP

In the medical treatment of all patients, patient consent is a key legal and ethical principle. Absent specific exceptions, consent must be obtained from all patients prior to treatment. Most medical and legal experts agree that this consent must be "informed." The doctrine of informed consent developed out of the understanding that patients have control over their bodies and are entitled to make their own decisions concerning medical treatment. The physician must remain mindful of the duty to obtain informed consent and be careful that it is not breached. Physicians must also be aware of the limitations of and exceptions to the doctrine, particularly in the emergency department where treatment without actual express consent may be required. As important as informed consent is, it is more important to remember that delayed treatment in an emergency, because of an inability to obtain express consent, is a much more serious medical-legal problem.

This chapter illustrates how different patient presentations dictate different levels and types of consent. Just as emergency physicians are broadly skilled and able to react under a variety of different clinical situations, they must also determine the type of consent required in any given case and be able to respond appropriately. Although legal doctrines regarding informed consent are obviously important, physicians should keep in mind that informed consent is really no more than a basic requirement of good ethical medical practice. The physician in this situation should be guided by the principle of *Cobbs v Grant*,[1] that "good medicine makes good law."

Case Studies

1

A 3-year-old boy is rushed to the emergency department by his babysitter. She says that the child has had a recent cough, cold, and ear infection. He had been doing well until the night before, when he spiked a fever to 103.5°F. That morning, she had found the child unresponsive in his bed and noticed intermittent seizure-type activity. Both parents are on vacation and unaware of the change in the child's condition. The emergency physician evaluates the patient and finds a barely arousable, septic-appearing child with a temperature of 105°F. He uncovers no obvious source of infection but is concerned about sepsis and meningitis. His attempts to reach the parents are unsuccessful.

The physician obtains all routine cultures and performs a lumbar puncture, which reveals grossly cloudy fluid. The child is immediately placed on IV antibiotics and admitted to the pediatric ICU. The spinal fluid culture for bacteria is subsequently reported as positive.

The boy has a stormy course in the ICU and only partially recovers, suffering severe neurologic sequelae. The parents later decide to sue the attending pediatrician and the emergency physician for their care of the child. They allege that the emergency physician provided substandard care and performed invasive procedures on their child without their consent.

2

An emergency physician is on duty in the emergency department when an ambulance arrives with a belligerent, obviously intoxicated man. Physical examination reveals a middle-aged man who has a large occipital skull laceration. The emergency physician determines that the wound requires repair, but no other obvious injury or focal neurologic deficit is found. The patient's blood alcohol level is twice the legal intoxication standard. The emergency physician explains to the patient that she needs to repair his head laceration. The patient refuses to consent to the procedure. The physician is not convinced that the patient is able to give or refuse informed consent. No family or friends are with the patient, nor can any be located.

3

A 15-year-old girl comes to the emergency department demanding treatment, stating that she believes she has contracted herpes and might also be pregnant. She refuses to allow staff to call her parents.

4

A 50-year-old woman is experiencing an acute myocardial infarction but adamantly refuses admission to the hospital. The emergency physician believes that the patient not only needs a coronary care unit admission, but also requires emergency thrombolytic therapy.

The emergency physician is afraid that if he tries to explain the risks and possible complications of thrombolytic therapy, the patient will refuse treatment. Reluctantly, the patient agrees to be admitted to the hospital. The physician then starts IV streptokinase without the patient's knowledge because he believes that the benefits of treatment outweigh the risks. The patient subsequently experiences a large intracerebral hemorrhage.

The Medical-Legal Perspective

What constitutes "informed consent" can best be understood by briefly reviewing the legal development of consent doctrine. Under U.S. civil and criminal law, individuals have a right to be free from nonconsensual touching by others unless an exception to the general rule applies (the doctrine of privilege, e.g., normal inadvertent touching in a crowded space). In most cases, however, a person who touches another without consent may be liable for the tort of battery.

The principle of consent also applies in the context of medical treatment. As the court held in *Schloendorff v Society of New York Hospital*[2]: "Every human being of adult years and sound mind has a right to determine what shall be done with his own body. . . ." Although informed consent doctrine has progressed significantly since Justice Cardozo wrote this opinion in 1914, his words continue to serve as a working definition of the rule.

Early consent cases were based on the theory of battery. If a surgeon performed an operation that had not been specifically consented to, such as operating on the left ear when the plan had been to operate on the right ear, the surgeon would be liable for battery.[3] This would have been true even if the left ear had been found to be more diseased than the right and the surgery was performed successfully. In *Mohr v Williams*,[3] the court held that "every person has a right to complete immunity of his person from physical interference of others, except in so far as contact may be necessary under the general doctrine of privilege . . . ."

Currently, the claim of battery, which is very difficult for the physician to defend, is seldom used in consent cases. Battery actions now tend to be limited to "situations where [the physician] fails to obtain any consent to the particular treatment, or performs a different procedure from the one for which consent has been given."[4] Under a battery theory, a plaintiff does not need to prove more than that a nonconsensual touching occurred. The plaintiff is not required to prove a bad result, substandard care, or even that the patient would not have consented to the procedure had the physician asked permission. The battery action can be attractive to plaintiffs for a number of reasons, including the fact that expert testimony may not be required, and plaintiffs may recover punitive damages even if actual damages are quite small or nonexistent.

Consent cases nearly always now proceed under a negligence theory, which requires that the plaintiff prove all of the elements of a negligence claim: breach of duty, substandard care, causation, and damages (see Chapter 23, "Malpractice and Civil Case Law"). These "lack of consent" actions are generally coupled with a claim of negligent treatment but, as this chapter addresses, can be pursued successfully without any proof, or even allegation, that the treatment itself was negligent.

Consent doctrine has progressed over the years from simple consent, that is, agreeing to a procedure despite no discussion of risks or alternative treatments by the physician, to the modern concept of informed consent, which requires physicians to give patients adequate information about the proposed treatment. The term informed consent was first used by the California Court of Appeals in 1957.[5] The court defined the duty of informed consent by saying that "[a] physician violates his duty to his patient and subjects himself to liability if he withholds any facts which are necessary to form the basis of an intelligent consent by the patient to the proposed treatment."[5] This case marked a transition from determining whether the patient had given simple consent to a more sophisticated two-step approach of determining whether the patient had given consent and also whether the patient had received adequate information in order to make an informed decision.

Types of Consent

Consent may be express, implied, or implied by law. In most cases, consent should be given expressly, that is, the patient specifically agrees either orally or in writing to the proposed treatment plan. It is not required to obtain express consent in writing, but a written document serves as useful evidence. Even express written consent is invalid in the case of inadequate disclosure, that is, if "material" information is withheld, or the consent is fraudulently induced. Implied consent occurs when the patient's action, or in some cases inaction, implies agreement to a procedure. For example, a man standing in an immunization line who, on reaching the front of the line, rolls up his sleeve and holds out his arm to the nurse to receive the shot, has implied his consent.[6] That person is not likely to complain successfully later that he received the shot against his will. Implied consent, although common in the emergency department (e.g., a patient holding out his arm to have his blood pressure taken), should never be used as an open invitation to perform risky or invasive procedures.

The standard consent form a patient signs when registering in the emergency department does not constitute informed consent. The courts do not read these blanket authorizations broadly as informed consent to specific procedures.[7] Furthermore, a signed consent form, preferably listing specific alternatives and risks, is evidence of informed consent but does not comprise the informed consent. Informed consent is the result of an ongoing discussion between the physician and the patient, not a signature on a form.

Consent is implied by law in emergency situations where express consent is impossible to obtain. For example, treatment of an unconscious trauma victim should never be delayed because of a lack of express consent. If the situation is an emergency and a "reasonable" patient would consent to the treatment if able, the physician should proceed. This type of consent covers all reasonable emergency treatment but does not extend to elective procedures. In addition, whenever feasible, emergency personnel should attempt to notify and ask permission from the patient's family members when the patient is incapacitated. This substituted consent may be obtained after the fact if immediate emergency treatment is required.

Standard of Disclosure

Physicians must meet a certain standard of disclosure to satisfy the doctrine of informed consent. This standard varies among jurisdictions. Two quite different standards are currently applied by U.S. courts. One is a physician-based standard, in which the plaintiff must prove that the physician failed to provide a level of disclosure that a reasonable practitioner in the same or similar community would have routinely made.[7] This standard bases the appropriate level of disclosure on professional custom.

Although professional custom is the standard generally applied in medical malpractice cases, many states have rejected this approach in informed consent cases. Those jurisdictions that reject the physician-based standard follow instead a patient-based standard, as first articulated in *Canterbury v Spence*.[8] In *Canterbury*, the court held that the proper measure of disclosure should not be measured by what physicians had always done, but by what a reasonable patient would require in order to make an informed decision. All "material" information that would affect a reasonable patient's decision must be disclosed. In this approach, a plaintiff must first prove that the physician failed to disclose material information about the procedure and second, that the patient would have refused the treatment if it had been disclosed. In addition, the plaintiff must also prove that a "reasonable patient" would have refused to undergo the procedure knowing about the material information. This more modern approach is commonly applied in informed consent cases, although further development may be constrained by legislative action.[9]

Congress and nearly half of the state legislatures have passed laws that affect informed consent. In some states, as part of tort reform, legislatures have mandated a physician-based standard of disclosure, sometimes overruling their courts' adoption of a patient-based standard.[9] In addition, some states legally require physicians to disclose specific risks, such as death.[10] Congress has mandated certain disclosures in the Emergency Medical Treatment and Active Labor Act (EMTALA), such as revealing the obligations of the law itself and the risks of a proposed transfer.[11] The Patient Self-Determination Act requires hospitals to provide patients with written information pertaining to their rights under state law to make decisions concerning their medical care and to use advance directives.[12]

What Must Be Disclosed?

The type of information a physician must disclose to a patient depends on the particular clinical situation, but certain generalities can be made.[7] The patient must be told what the diagnosis is. If there are other possible diagnoses, the physician should tell the patient what they are. The nature and purpose of treatment must be discussed, including the probabilities of success and failure. From a risk management perspective, physicians should always reveal the likelihood of a poor outcome so that the patient and family can be better prepared for it.

The risks and expected outcomes of the proposed treatment are key items the physician must address in appropriate detail. When unexpected risks and/or adverse outcomes materialize, patients and families are surprised and upset, and tempted to take legal action. A careful, unhurried discussion of the risks and the potential outcomes of treatment may help a physician avoid later claims alleging failure of informed consent, and also negligent diagnosis and/or treatment. Risks that require disclosure are those that would be material to a reasonable patient's decision.[13] A remote risk does not necessarily need to be disclosed[14]; however, that risk may not seem so "remote" to a jury after it has materialized. Any serious risk (e.g., death) should be discussed, regardless of how remote it is.

Alternative methods or approaches should be discussed if they are generally accepted in the medical community. The risks and potential benefits of these alternatives should be explained and compared to the proposed method of treatment. Even alternatives that the physician considers more risky should be addressed if a reasonable patient might select that alternative.[15] The consequences of refusing a proposed treatment should be discussed as well ("informed refusal").[16]

Discussions with patients and their families should always be in nontechnical language. A patient has not been informed, even if given all material information, if that information was not understood.[8] This is a legal requirement, as well as one dictated by good ethical medical practice. The standard of disclosure will be increased if a patient asks questions that go beyond what other patients might consider material.[7] For example, if a patient asks about remote or seemingly extremely minor risks, the physician should address those risks.

Obtaining patients' consent to participate in research projects or to undergo investigational treatment modalities requires a more formal method of informed consent. In these situations, the physician must explain to the patient that the proposed treatment is investigational, reveal anticipated risks, and acknowledge that other undisclosed risks are possible.[17] All research projects, other than simple surveys, should be approved by an institutional review board.

Who Has the Duty to Obtain the Informed Consent?

Laws governing informed consent are very specific about which medical personnel are required to obtain a patient's informed consent. This duty falls to the physician who actually provides the service. Courts have held this duty to be "nondelegable," meaning that it is not sufficient for a nurse or another person acting on behalf of the physician to obtain the patient's consent. Hospitals may have the duty to ensure that physicians obtain proper informed consent from their patients. If the physician is an employee or agent of the hospital, the hospital is vicariously liable and can be held fully liable for any negligence of its employee or agent. If the hospital is not vicariously liable, it will not be responsible for the negligent acts of the physician, but it may be held directly liable for not requiring its physicians to obtain informed consent from their patients.[18]

Who May Consent?

With adults, consent should be obtained directly from the patient being treated, with rare exceptions. In order to give consent, a patient must be competent, which is technically a legal determination. In the emergency department, however, emergency physicians often do not have the luxury of waiting for a court to litigate the competence of a patient. Emergency physicians must make judgments about a patient's ability to make decisions. The legal presumption is that an adult is competent unless proved otherwise. When a patient is not competent, any express consent must come from the patient's family or guardian.

Consent offered on behalf of an incompetent person depends on a number of factors. If an individual has been found legally incompetent and, as a result, a guardian has been appointed and is authorized to give consent on behalf of the patient, consent should be obtained from that judicially appointed guardian. If there is no appointed guardian, the situation is more complicated. In some cases, the patient will have appointed, by advance directive, a surrogate to make medical treatment decisions. Durable power of attorney and living will statutes vary among states. Some state legislatures have responded to the difficult situation where there is neither a guardian nor an advance directive by enacting family consent statutes. These statutes provide a hierarchy of family members who can give (or withhold) consent when a family member becomes incompetent.[7]

In states where there is no family consent statute, physicians have traditionally sought consent from the incompetent patient's closest family members. In the case of an emergency, this consent is not required legally, but implied by law. However, even if surrogate consent is not absolutely required and is not technically legally binding, it should be obtained, if possible. The patient's family members will appreciate being involved in the decision-making process. Communication is always a key component of risk management, and this conversation will help to avoid surprise and misunderstanding if a poor outcome is the result. If the patient's ability to make a decision is at all suspect, the physician should obtain the patient's and the family's consent to the proposed treatment plan. If the situation is not an emergency, or if the physician has any concern that the family is not acting in the best interest of the patient, court involvement may be necessary. In these situations, the emergency physician should consult with hospital counsel.

Minors do not have legal competence and are generally not able to give consent. In these cases, consent should be obtained from a parent or guardian. However, if an emergency exists, consent will be implied by law. Under the doctrine of *in loco parentis*, if a minor's parent or guardian is unavailable, those charged with the child's care may give consent in an emergency situation. Exceptions may be made for legally emancipated minors. State law generally dictates that "minors who are or have been married, who live apart from their parents and are financially independent, or who have children of their own, are considered as emancipated minors and are legally able to consent to their own health care, and where they have children, to the health care of their children."[19] In addition, there are specific exceptions in various state laws that allow minors to give consent for treatment of such conditions as pregnancy, sexually transmitted diseases, or chemical dependency.[20]

Consent law varies significantly from state to state, so emergency physicians must be aware of their own states' consent laws, both statutory and common. Although some informed consent concepts are universal, variations can be quite significant.

Liability for Failure to Obtain Informed Consent

Most informed consent claims are coupled with a claim of negligent treatment. That is, the patient claims not only that consent was not informed, but also that treatment was negligently provided and resulted in an injury. In some cases, however, a plaintiff may claim a failure of informed consent alone and will concede that the treatment provided fully met the relevant standard of care. In such a situation, the defendant physician may be held liable despite the absence of proof, or even claim, of actual negligent treatment.

A complete failure of consent may still lead to liability for battery. If the outcome is good and there is no proof of negligent treatment, the damages are likely to be nominal. However, if a complication develops, even if it is a commonly expected complication, the failure to disclose the possibility can lead to liability. An advantage to the plaintiff in a battery claim is that punitive damages may be awarded, even if actual damages are small.[7] In contrast, punitive damages are extremely unusual in negligence-based medical malpractice actions.

As previously mentioned, most informed consent cases are now brought under a negligence theory. In such cases, the plaintiff must prove not only that there was a failure to obtain informed consent, but also that damages ensued (i.e., the risk of the treatment materialized) and that these two elements were linked (causation). It is not necessary for the plaintiff, in a claim of failure to obtain informed consent, to prove any negligence in the actual performance of the treatment. For example, a physician may perform a lumbar puncture on a patient without telling the patient that headache is a possible adverse effect. If the patient subsequently develops a headache, the fact that the physician performed the lumbar puncture flawlessly is irrelevant. The materialization of the "uncommunicated hazard" is what creates potential liability.[8] The plaintiff could be awarded money for the damage (headache and associated losses) if it can also be proved that, had a reasonable patient been properly informed of the risk of headache, the reasonable patient would have refused the lumbar puncture. On the other hand, if the physician had properly disclosed the risk of the subsequent headache and then had performed the lumbar puncture according to the relevant standard of care, the physician would not be held liable if the disclosed risk occurred.

Case Discussions

1

The parents in this case have made two claims against the emergency physician: negligent treatment and failure to obtain consent for treatment. According to the facts of the case, the treatment was entirely appropriate: any delay in lumbar puncture or treatment would have been negligent. The physician should be able to defend against the informed consent claim, as the parents were not available and an exception to the requirement of express consent was present. Consent will be implied by law because of the child's critical illness, bacterial meningitis. Although there was a poor outcome in this case, it was not the result of any negligent treatment on the part of the emergency physician. In addition, the doctrine of *in loco parentis* could allow the physician to obtain consent from the babysitter. Never delay emergency treatment because of a lack of express parental consent.

2

This patient was not competent to give consent or to refuse treatment. He lacked capacity to make any significant decisions regarding his health care. Because there was no family available, the physician could have held the patient until he was sober and gave consent, or could have gone ahead and treated him. Even if the injury was not life-threatening, if a delay could have adversely affected the patient and a reasonable person would have given consent, the prudent approach would have been to treat the injury, as consent was implied by law. To allow the patient to leave without treatment not only would have been medically inappropriate, but also would have exposed the physician to liability for negligent failure to treat.

3

Most states allow minors to give consent for the treatment of sexually transmitted diseases and pregnancy. Physicians should make themselves aware of their state statutes that apply and the specific requirements of the law, for example, encouraging the girl to contact her parents. Although this situation did not present a life-threatening emergency, it was advisable to treat the patient after receiving her informed consent. In this case, the minor was mature enough to understand the informed consent discussion and the situation. According to federal law, all individuals presenting to the emergency department must receive a medical screening examination for the detection of emergency medical conditions.[11] The law does not distinguish among individuals based on age.

4

The physician, although well intentioned, clearly violated the doctrine of informed consent and will have difficulty defending his actions if sued. Competent adult patients must be allowed to make their own decisions after being presented with all the relevant information. Physicians have a duty to give patients their best recommendations, but they do not have the right to overrule the competent patient's decision, however irrational it might be. Had the risk of intracerebral bleeding been disclosed to the patient and she had consented to administration of the thrombolytic agent, the physician could not have been held liable for the occurrence of the CVA, absent negligent treatment. This failure to disclose now exposed him to liability for the damages of the CVA if the plaintiff could prove that, had the risk been disclosed, both the patient and the "reasonable patient" would have declined the treatment. This question will be posed to a jury, who will decide the issue in retrospect after knowing of the materialized risk.

Key Points and Conclusion

Effective and open communication with patients and their families is always beneficial. Legal issues aside, it is simply good medical practice. Poor communication by physicians commonly leads patients or their families to sue for malpractice. Most patients who are the victims of iatrogenic harm do not bring malpractice claims against their physicians.[21] It is the combination of a poor outcome and a lack of communication that makes patients and their families angry and litigious. Remember that we, as physicians, are advisors, not decision-makers, for patients. It is our role to inform patients and help them reach decisions regarding their health care.

References

1. *Cobbs v Grant*, 8 Cal2d 229, 104 Cal Rptr 505, 502 P2d l (1972).
2. *Schloendorff v Society of New York Hospital*, 105 NE93 (NY 1914).
3. *Mohr v Williams*, 95 Minn 261, 104 NW12 (1905).
4. *Logan v Greenwich Hosp. Association*, 191 Conn 282, 465 A2d 294.
5. *Salgo v Leland Stanford Jr. University Board of Trustees*, 154 Cal App2d 560, 317 P2d 170 (1957).
6. *O'Brien v Cunard Steamship Co.*, 154 Mass 272, 28 NE266 (1891).
7. Barry R. Furrow et al, *Health Law* (1995). *Wells v Van Nort*, 125 NE910 (Ohio 1919).
8. *Canterbury v Spence*, 464 F2d 772 (DC Cir 1972).
9. See, e.g., Ala Code §6-5-484 (1990).
10. See, e.g., Iowa Code Ann §147.137 (West 1989).
11. 42 USC §1395dd.
12. 42 USCA §1395cc(a)(l).
13. *Harbeson v Parke Davis*, 746 F2d 517 (9th Cir 1984).
14. See, e.g., *Shinn v St. James Mercy Hospital*, 675 FSupp 94 (WDNY 1987).
15. *Gemme v Goldberg*, 626 A2d 318, 326 (Conn App 1993).
16. *Truman v Thomas*, 165 Cal Rptr 308, 611 P3d 902 (Cal 1980).
17. See, e.g., *Estrada v Jacques*, 70 NC App 627, 321 SE2d 240.
18. See *Darling v Charleston Community Memorial Hospital*, 33 Ill2d 326, 211 NE2d 253 (1965) re: nondelegable hospital duties generally.
19. Douglas A. Hastings et al, *Fundamentals of Health Law*, at 118 (1995).
20. See, e.g., MCLA §333.5127(1).
21. Executive Summary. *Report of the Harvard Medical Practice Study to the State of New York* (1990).

Chapter 28

Duty to Warn Third Parties

Daniel J. Sullivan, MD, JD, FACEP

Emergency physicians regularly diagnose contagious disease, administer sedative or hypnotic medications, and manage violent patients and patients with medical conditions that may be unstable. Patients with these conditions may injure, disable, or even kill a third party after they leave the emergency department. Although the "duty to third party" law has rarely involved emergency physicians, in examining the court's reasoning in cases involving other physicians, there is no reason to think that the same considerations and rationale would not be applied in the emergency department environment.

Case Studies

1

A patient presents to the emergency department with an eye injury. The treatment for his injury, a corneal abrasion, includes placing a patch over the injured eye. Following discharge, the patient drives home in his car. On the way, he is involved in a collision with a man who is driving a motorcycle. The motorcycle driver is injured and subsequently sues the hospital and the treating emergency physician. He alleges that the emergency physician was negligent because he failed to warn the patient with the eye injury that he should not drive while wearing the eye patch.

2

A woman is suffering from a debilitating migraine headache. She takes a Percodan, but the pain does not stop. She goes to her private physician's office, and he administers Demerol IM. When she complains of nausea, the physician orders Tigan. Within the next hour, the woman leaves the physician's office, driving her own car. On her way home, she has a collision. The driver of the other car is badly injured. According to the woman's physician, roughly 70 minutes may have passed between the first injection and the accident.

3

A 25-year-old man is taken to the emergency department by ambulance because he is exhibiting violent and aggressive behavior in his home. On arrival in the emergency department, the man expresses homicidal ideation. He does not indicate intent to kill any one particular individual. The physician and nursing staff agree that the patient is dangerous to others, but for some reason, the patient is left unattended and unrestrained. He runs out of the emergency department, goes to his girlfriend's home, and beats her to death with a baseball bat. The woman's family sues the emergency physician for negligent failure to restrain the patient, which resulted in their daughter's death.

4

A 45-year-old woman presents for evaluation of an altered level of consciousness. The emergency physician examines her and diagnoses a drug overdose, but she actually is suffering from carbon monoxide exposure caused by a defective gas heater in her home. Within several days, the woman's husband dies from carbon monoxide exposure. As the plaintiff in this case, the woman claims she was not alerted to take appropriate steps to have the defective gas heater repaired and that failure to warn was the cause of her husband's death.

The Medical-Legal Perspective

Physicians are familiar with the concept of duty as it relates to medical malpractice actions, in which the physician-patient relationship creates a duty to provide reasonable care under the circumstances. The duty to provide reasonable care within the confines of the physician-patient relationship has been recognized in civil law in all states for many years. In contrast, the duty physicians may have to third parties is a relatively recent development. Emergency physicians should be familiar with the basic law of duty to third parties and the types of cases in which the courts have imposed a duty on the physician to keep third parties safe from harm.

The duty physicians owe to individuals outside the physician-patient relationship falls into the realm of tort law known as negligence, not medical malpractice. Plaintiffs frequently, and inappropriately, initiate these actions as medical malpractice claims. No claim for negligence can succeed in the absence of any one of the following elements:

- A duty of care owed by the defendant to the plaintiff.
- Conduct falling below the applicable standard of care amounting to a breach of that duty.
- An injury or loss.
- Causation.

As the injury to third party tort has grown and developed, the threshold issue in every jurisdiction has been the first element — whether the physician owes a duty of care to a third-party plaintiff.

As a general rule under the common or civil law, a person owes no affirmative duty, or obligation, to warn those who are endangered by the conduct of another.[1,2] That is, at common law, there was no duty to third parties. However, based on changing societal norms and creative lawyering, in certain situations, the law now imposes a duty on physicians to keep third parties safe from harm. As one judge put it, "the imposition of a legal duty reflects society's contemporary policies and social requirements concerning the right of individuals and the gen-

eral public to be protected from another's act or conduct."[3]

In the recent case of *Wilschinsky v Medina*,[4] the Supreme Court of New Mexico, for the first time, faced the question of whether a practicing physician in that state owes a duty to third persons who foreseeably may be harmed by a physician's negligence in treatment of a patient. In grappling with the concept of whether New Mexico should overturn the long-standing common law rule regarding obligations to third parties, the court researched the subject and had some interesting insight into modern health care, as follows[4]:

> The recent growth in use of outpatient clinics, day surgery units, and extensive office procedures is a new development in health care, unforeseen at the time when most state legislatures adopted malpractice legislation. It is encouraged by insurance policies that offer only partial coverage for patients admitted into hospitals overnight. As more extensive medical procedures are shifted to an outpatient setting, the risk of injuries to the general public from patients driving under the influence of drugs increases . . . .
>
> Changing societal conditions lead constantly to the recognition of new duties. No better general statement can be made, than that the courts will find a duty where, in general, reasonable men would recognize it and agree that it exists.

This is a new body of law, and it presents more questions than answers. A review of the legal literature reveals a very small number of cases, with just a few that specifically address the emergency department or the outpatient setting. The cases have fallen into four general categories:

- Duty to the driving public
- Contagious disease transmission
- Intended victims of violent crimes
- Miscellaneous

It is important to recognize that each state creates its own case law. In writing opinions, the state judges review cases from all over the country, especially now, as the tort is still in its infancy. However, one state's supreme court decisions have no direct bearing on the practice of emergency medicine in another state.

Duty to the Driving Public

In general, the duty to the driving public cases involve an emergency department patient, discharged in some compromised condition, who becomes involved in a collision with a third party. The injured third party then brings a lawsuit against the physician for negligent discharge, or failure to warn about the danger of driving in the compromised condition. Cases typically involve impaired vision, hypoglycemia, a seizure disorder, or altered level of consciousness from street drugs, alcohol, or emergency department parenteral narcotics.

In the first case study,[5] the defendant medical center filed a motion to dismiss the case, claiming that it had no duty to warn of such an obvious and apparent danger as driving while wearing an eye patch. The trial court dismissed the case and held that any duty to warn did not extend to the third party motorcycle driver. The court ruled that the physician had a duty to warn the patient for his own safety, but that such a duty did not extend to a third party who could be injured by the patient.

The appeals court disagreed and adopted the rationale of the growing body of third-party cases, which extend a physician's duty outside the physician-patient relationship. Thus, the court held that dismissal of the case was inappropriate. Although it was clear that an eye patch eliminates the use of one eye, the opinion of the court was as follows: "We cannot assume that the patient must have known that his driving would be materially affected. It is possible that the accident resulted from some effect of the eye patch known to the physician, but unknown to the patient." Having decided that, as a matter of law the physician had a duty to the third party motorcycle driver, the case was referred back to the trial court for a jury to determine if the defendant exercised reasonable care in connection with the alleged duty to warn.

This single case of failure to warn should not be assumed to create a national duty of care for emergency physicians. Over the years, millions of eye patches have been placed. Perhaps there have been related motor vehicle collisions, but there is only one case from one of 50 states available for review in the entire legal literature database. However, the case merits consideration. Perhaps the emergency department discharge sheet for eye injuries should contain a warning regarding driving and operation of machinery. Also, the court correctly pointed out that the potential for harm must be viewed from the patient's perspective, not that of the emergency physician or staff.

In determining whether a physician had a duty to a third party injured in a collision, the court in the second case study[4] made note of three things: the physician had administered drugs that could cloud a person's judgment and physical abilities and could create a risk to that person in driving a car; the patient was involved in a serious car collision within a short time after receiving medication; and the third party had received injuries from that collision.

The court held that the physician owed a duty to the driving public when he administered these drugs to the patient under these particular circumstances. Once the court determined, as a matter of law, that the physician had a duty to the third party and the driving public, the case was referred back to the lower court to determine if the other elements of the negligence action were present. The important issue is that the New Mexico Supreme Court opened the door for a duty to warn relationship between outpatient management involving parenteral pain or sedative medication and the third party driving public.

The impact of this ruling on the practice of emergency medicine is obvious. During a busy shift in the department, a dozen or more patients may receive pain medication or sedative or hypnotic agents. Great care must be taken to ensure that patients are monitored after injection and that warnings regarding driving and other potentially dangerous activity are given to the patient and documented in the record.

The Texas Court of Appeals reached the opposite conclusion in the case of *Flynn v Houston Emergicare, Inc.*[6] On January 6, 1988, at approximately 7:30 AM, Dr. Ron Kremer examined William Broadus in the emergency department of Houston Northwest Medical Center. Mr. Broadus complained of chest pain. Mr. Broadus testified that the night before, he had snorted cocaine. When he awoke at 5:30 AM, he felt a "heavy pressure in his chest" as if he were having a heart attack. He drove himself to the emergency department.

The physician took an ECG and a chest x-ray and placed Mr. Broadus on a cardiac monitor. Dr. Kremer concluded that Mr. Broadus was experiencing a "hyperadrenergic excess sympathetic state of stimulation secondary to cocaine use." Dr. Kremer prescribed Inderol and discharged the patient. Mr. Broadus then caused a rear-end collision with the plaintiff, Diane Flynn. Ms. Flynn alleged that Dr. Kremer was negligent in failing to admit Mr. Broadus to the hospital for observation and in failing to warn him not to drive for a specified period of time.

The Texas court reviewed several recent duty to third party cases from other jurisdictions. The court found that, in other jurisdictions, a duty to the driving public arose because the physician had created the impairment that resulted in injury to the plaintiff, as in the migraine headache and eye patch cases. The court held that there was no affirmative act by Dr. Kremer that had caused Mr. Broadus' impairment. Mr. Broadus' ingestion of cocaine caused the impairment that led to his automobile collision, and Dr. Kremer's care and treatment bore no relationship to that incapacity. Therefore, the defendants owed no duty to the public to warn Mr. Broadus not to drive following his ingestion of cocaine.

The reasoning of the three court decisions is interesting. The physician who placed an eye patch created the visual impairment and, thus, had a duty to the driving public. The physician who gave the drug created the impairment in level of consciousness, judgment, or reaction time and, thus, had a duty to the driving public. But if the patient creates the impairment, as in the cocaine case, the physician has no such duty. From the medical viewpoint, there probably is no difference how the individual became impaired. If the patient is impaired and needs a warning, why does it make a difference if it is an eye patch or a drug or alcohol ingestion? From the legal standpoint, however, extending the common law into new realms is a big issue. Typically, the process is slow and sometimes not completely logical.

In several of these cases, the courts discuss a duty to warn. There may be a duty to warn a patient not to drive with an eye patch, or after receiving certain medications, or after having a seizure or hypoglycemic episode. What happens if the patient ignores the warning and a third party is injured anyway? The courts are quite consistent on this issue: the duty is to warn the patient; thereafter, the physician is not liable if the patient does not heed the warnings. The physician incurs no duty to prevent a patient from driving. The mentally competent patient, once presented with the risks, is responsible for making choices.[7] If the patient has an abnormal mental status (e.g., alcohol intoxication), the physician may have a duty to restrain or use some alternative means to keep the patient from harming himself or others.

Contagious Disease Transmission

In everyday practice, the emergency physician has the difficult task of diagnosing and managing contagious diseases. When a patient presents with a communicable disease, the physician's immediate obligation is to attend to that person's needs. However, the physician must also consider the extent to which the communicable disease may spread and who may be subsequently affected.

Legal actions have alleged that a physician was liable to a third party for failure to diagnose the disease in a patient, for failure to inform a third party of the contagious nature of the disease, for negligently advising a third party that there was no danger of infection, and for failure to prevent the spread of the disease to the third party. For example, in the case of *DiMarco v Lynch Homes*,[8] the Supreme Court of Pennsylvania held that a physician had a duty and could be liable to a patient's sexual partner for failing to properly warn the patient about transmission of hepatitis B. The patient's boyfriend claimed that the defendant physicians were negligent for not warning the patient that having sexual relations within six months of the exposure could cause her sexual partner to contract hepatitis.

Although infectious disease experts may disagree over the time frame during which the disease can be transmitted, the point is that Pennsylvania has now created a duty to warn third parties when hepatitis is diagnosed. It is anybody's guess whether the Pennsylvania courts will limit this to the attending physician, based on the facts of the *DiMarco* case, or will be willing to extend the duty into the emergency department.

There may be a duty to warn following an exposure to a patient with meningococcal meningitis. Although there is no case law on point, the emergency physician diagnosing meningococcal meningitis may have a duty to warn the emergency department staff, family, classmates, and so on regarding the potential danger of exposure and recommendations for prophylaxis.

Emergency physicians taking care of known HIV-positive patients may have an obligation to warn emergency department and other staff of the potential danger of exposure.[9] Some state laws create a duty to warn third parties who may be in immediate danger from exposure to a patient with HIV who refuses to disclose the diagnosis.[10] In other states, there is a strict duty not to communicate HIV-related information. Statutes and regulations on this issue vary from state to state. The emergency physician should contact hospital or local counsel regarding the nature of the duty to report and the physician's obligation to third parties associated with HIV-positive patients.

There are cases from several jurisdictions related to transmission of hepatitis, herpes, and other sexually transmitted diseases. Most states have formal reporting systems for these conditions. However, emergency physicians would be wise to warn patients about the dangers of transmission or to refrain from contact until the patients' private physicians have had an opportunity to obtain culture results and review these issues.

Intended Victims of Violent Crimes

An area of duty to third party law with more limited application to emergency physicians is the duty to warn intended victims of violent crimes. These cases generally involve psychiatric patients who manifest violent intentions toward an individual or a potential group of individuals. It may be hard to imagine a court imposing liability on a physician who deals with mentally unstable patients only on an urgent or emergent basis. It is possible, however, when looking at relevant case law and the specific circumstances, that a court could find that an emergency physician had a duty to warn third parties or to report the patient to the appropriate authorities. At present, no cases involving emergency medicine duty to warn intended victims of violent crime have been reported in the legal literature.

The seminal case regarding duty to warn third parties is *Tarasoff v Regents of University of California*.[2] In *Tarasoff*, Prosenjit Poddar, a psychiatric outpatient at a University of California hospital, killed a woman named Tatiana Tarasoff. The woman's parents, the plaintiffs, alleged that two months before their daughter's death, Poddar told his therapist that he intended to kill a young woman fitting Tatiana's description. Although Poddar did not specifically name Tarasoff as his intended victim, the plaintiffs alleged that the therapist could have readily identified her. They alleged that the defendant negligently failed to protect their daughter from Poddar. The defendant contended on appeal that he was under no duty to ensure the safety of Ms. Tarasoff.

In analyzing the defendant's claim, the California Supreme Court stated: "As a general principle, a defendant owes a duty of care to all persons who are foreseeably endangered by his conduct, with respect to all risks which make the conduct unreasonably dangerous." The court noted that, under the common law, no one owes any duty to protect an individual who is endangered by a third person unless he has some special relationship with either the dangerous person or the potential victim. The California court found that a psychiatrist has such a "special relationship" to his patient.

The court also noted that the discharge of this duty may require the therapist to take one or more various steps, depending on the nature of the case. Thus, such a duty may call for him to warn the intended victim or others likely to apprise the victim of the danger, to notify the police, or to take whatever other steps are reasonably necessary under the circumstances.

In *Thompson v City of Alameda*,[11] the plaintiff sued the county for failing to warn the local police or "parents of young children within the immediate vicinity" about a juvenile offender who had extremely dangerous and violent propensities regarding young children. The person had indicated he would, if released, take the life of a young child residing in the neighborhood. He did, in fact, kill a young child soon after his release. The court pointed to *Tarasoff* in noting that, although the intended victim need not be specifically named, he or she must be readily identifiable. In *Thompson*, no particular victim was readily identifiable. The court also noted the lack of a direct and continuing relationship between the therapist and patient. Thus, the court declined to impose liability on the defendant to warn the community.

The court further noted that, because some psychiatric patients commonly make generalized threats, notifying the public of each threat would "produce a cacophony of warnings that by reason of their sheer volume would add little to the effective protection of the public." The only person likely to heed a warning is one who is personally threatened.

The third case study is fictitious, but it is fashioned after *Naidu v Laird*,[12] in which the plaintiff, Mrs. Laird, sued the defendants, who were psychiatrists employed at the Delaware State Hospital. Mrs. Laird's husband was killed when his vehicle collided with one driven by Mr. Putney, who had a long history of mental illness and apparently drove his car deliberately into Mr. Laird's vehicle. Mrs. Laird alleged that the defendants were grossly negligent and owed a duty to prevent the patient from causing injury to members of the public at large.

The Supreme Court of Delaware held that the psychiatrists did indeed have a duty because they knew or should have known that the patient's dangerous propensities presented an unreasonable risk of harm to others. This duty requires the mental health professional to initiate whatever precautions are reasonably necessary to protect potential victims of the patient. To that end, the court noted that a psychiatrist may have a duty to warn potential victims or a class of potential victims and/or control, to some appropriate degree, the actions of the patient. This represents a significant extension from *Tarasoff*. The court held there was a duty to a group of potential victims, and that the victim need not be readily identifiable.

The courts have not created a similar duty for emergency physicians. There is no case law establishing the emergency physician's duty to warn intended victims or a potential class of victims of a violent crime. No case has extended the duty beyond psychotherapists with an established physician-patient relationship. However, the emergency department certainly represents a high-risk area, with staff frequently caring for mentally ill patients who have dangerous propensities. It is not outside the realm of possibility that a court could impose a duty on an emergency physician who negligently releases a patient with clear homicidal intentions toward an identifiable victim and subsequently injures or kills that person. This ruling would represent a significant departure from existing case law.

However, remember that the court makes the law, and "changing societal conditions lead constantly to the recognition of new duties." If a patient is homicidal and wants to abscond, the emergency physician may have an obligation to restrain. Regardless of whether there is an identifiable victim, someone is at risk. If the facts are right, it would not be surprising for a plaintiff's attorney to bring a duty to third party negligence action against an emergency physician for such failure to restrain.

Miscellaneous

There are certain other third-party scenarios relevant to the practice of emergency medicine. These include exposure to carbon monoxide, seizure disorders, hypoglycemia, and discharge following use of drugs or alcohol.

In *Soto v Frankford Hospital*,[13] the fourth case

study, the plaintiff, Mrs. Soto, presented for emergency care after exposure to carbon monoxide. Because the cause of her problem was not identified, her furnace was not repaired, and her husband later died as a result of carbon monoxide poisoning. Mrs. Soto claimed that, because the treating physician did not make the correct diagnosis, she was not alerted to take appropriate steps to have a defective gas heater repaired. She contended that such failure to warn was the cause of her husband's death.

The court reviewed the body of case law and found several communicable disease cases and cases involving injuries to third parties by violent patients. The court held that this case was distinguishable because there was no communicable disease, and Mrs. Soto was not a dangerous or violent patient. The court felt that the physician did not have a duty to a third party because the situation did not involve a contagious disease or a violent patient.

It is hard to predict what the court would have found if the physicians had diagnosed Mrs. Soto correctly but simply failed to warn the family or the authorities. If an emergency physician diagnoses and treats a patient with carbon monoxide poisoning and it is clear that family and other tenants are being exposed, a court may find an obligation to warn or to report the matter to the local authorities.

Key Points and Conclusion

Duty to warn third parties is a fascinating, yet unpredictable area of medicine and law. The legal cases most directly applicable to emergency medicine are those involving a duty to the driving public. However, the correct approach in the practice of emergency medicine is to consider on a case-by-case basis if a particular therapy or treatment or the patient's underlying condition puts a third party or a potential class of third parties, at risk of harm. Where "reasonable people would agree that such a duty exists," the emergency physician should act. Here the appropriate perspective belongs to the reasonable person — the patient — not the emergency physician or a panel of judges.

References

1. Prosser WL. *Handbook of the Law of Torts*. §56 at 374 (5th edition, 1984).
2. *Tarasoff v Regents of University of California*, 17 Cal3d 425, 551 P2d 343.
3. *Kirk v Reese Hospital & Medical Center*, 117 Ill2d 507, 513 NE2d 387, 396-397.
4. *Wilschinsky v Medina*, 108 NM 511, 775 P2d 713.

5. 529 A2d 1364.

6. *Flynn v Houston Emergicare, Inc.*, 869 SW2d 403.

7. *Gooden v Tips*, 651 SW2d 364 (Tex App 1983); *Hasenie v United States*, 541 F Supp 999, 1011 (DMd 1982).

8. *DiMarco v Lynch Homes*, 525 Pa 558, 583 A2d 422.

9. *Johnson v West Virginia University Hospital, Inc*, 413 SE2d 889 (WVa 1991).

10. 410 ILCS 325/1 et seq.

11. *Thompson v City of Alameda*, 614 P2d 735.

12. *Naidu v Laird*, 539 A2d 1064, 1988 Del LEXIS 93.

13. *Soto v Franklin Hospital*, 478 F Supp 1134.

Chapter 29

Civil Commitment

Stephen A. Colucciello, MD, FACEP

The most difficult decisions regarding civil commitment fall squarely on the shoulders of the emergency physician. A desperate family faced with a psychotic relative, police struggling with a febrile, raving prisoner, paramedics coping with a dazed and babbling patient — all turn to the emergency department for help.

Commitment decisions are difficult for a variety of reasons, including complex or ambiguous statutes, the presence of occult medical illness, and lack of clear guidelines that identify a person who is a danger to self or others. Although psychiatric commitment may be lifesaving to the suicidal patient, it is a death sentence for a patient with meningitis who presents with acute confusion. Legal pitfalls abound. The emergency physician may be accused of improper restraint, violation of civil rights, or negligent failure to protect a third party. For these reasons, an understanding of the perils and pitfalls of civil commitment is essential to our practice.

The Medical-Legal Perspective

Physicians in all 50 states have the power to commit patients who are mentally ill and dangerous to themselves or others. Although laws regarding civil commitment vary from state to state, several themes apply.[1] The concept of "dangerousness," either to self or others, is central to commitment law. In addition, most states require that the person also have a mental disorder or mental retardation to be committed. However, mental illness alone is not grounds for civil commitment. Police frequently transport patients with chronic psychosis to the emergency department because of unusual or nuisance behavior. Such patients do not meet the criteria for involuntary commitment unless the physician documents dangerousness or makes a compelling argument for potential dangerousness. Some states use a "gravely disabled" criterion that allows physicians to commit psychiatric patients who are unable to care for themselves in the most rudimentary ways. Such profound helplessness represents a particular subset of danger to self.

Common law provides the legal premise for civil commitment under the aegis of "police power," which allows the state to ensure the safety of its citizenry. Under this doctrine, the state may protect those who are endangered by a violent, mentally ill person. In addition, the doctrine of *parens patriae* holds that under certain circumstances, an incompetent person may be cared for by the state, even if the treatment is against the person's will. In cases where life or limb is at risk, the mentally ill patient is considered like a child whose decisions are made by the state or its agent.[2]

There are several types of civil commitment. Judicial commitment is performed by a magistrate, who commits a person based on a petition, usually originated by a family member or police. Judicial commitment is reserved for those with psychiatric problems or incorrigible drug or alcohol abuse.[3] On occasion, the court may order a patient to undergo mandatory outpatient psychotherapy, particularly in the case of a chronically ill "revolving door" patient.[4]

Emergency physicians are rarely involved in the commitment of substance abusers, and they cannot order mandatory outpatient therapy. The emergency physician is generally involved with voluntary or involuntary civil commitment of mentally ill patients who pose a danger to themselves or others.

The emergency physician must be aware of the legal rights of committed patients. They have rights to counsel, to remain silent, to receive treatment in the least restrictive environment, to refuse certain treatments, and to have access to medical records under select conditions. Patients also have the right to refuse antipsychotic medication in the nonemergency setting. It is interesting to note that after the legal commitment process runs its course, most patients who refuse medication initially eventually do take it.[5]

Once patients are committed, they are transported or admitted to a psychiatric facility, where they may be held for a fixed period of time, usually 48 to 72 hours. After this time, the patient may appeal the commitment and has the right to a judicial hearing. In general, most patients do not appeal their detention.[6] When a hearing does occur, judges rarely overturn decisions made by physicians.[7,8] A judge is particularly unlikely to release a patient with schizophrenia and schizo-affective disorder or persons who are dangerous to others.[9] These appeals are rarely adversarial, and clinical concerns usually take precedence over legal issues.[10] In many states, the emergency physician is exempt from attending the hearings despite having originally committed the patient. Physicians may ask to be excused by signing a statement on the commitment papers. Interestingly, many civilly committed patients later admit that they needed to be hospitalized.[11]

Philosophical Issues

For decades, physicians, philosophers, jurists, and mental health activists have debated the philosophical issues associated with civil commitment. The medical perspective is utilitarian or paternalistic, arguing for what the physician sees as the best interests of the patient, while civil libertarians champion patient autonomy.[12] During the 1960s and 1970s, legal concerns generally emphasized patients' rights. Since 1980, there has been a shift toward ensuring community security, perhaps because of the significant rise in crime and homelessness.[13] These conflicting ideals have created ten-

sion, as the civil liberties of the mentally ill are balanced against the safety of the general public and the patient's need for appropriate therapy.[14]

The "dangerousness" criterion is the central theme of commitment law in most states. The patient's ability to respond to treatment, or even the patient's need for treatment, is not always the motivating force in the commitment process.[15] For better or worse, the dangerousness standard has created an increase in the number of patients with personality disorders and criminal histories who are committed to psychiatric facilities.[16] Whether the dangerousness standard mandates immediate risk, as opposed to potential for violence, is debatable. Some psychotic patients, especially those with paranoia, may not be acutely combative but have the potential for assaultive behavior as they deteriorate mentally. The "predictive deterioration" standard may be constitutional, and such patients may be committed even if they are not currently dangerous but are predicted to become dangerous in the near future.[17]

The dangerousness standard has been criticized by numerous authors. These opponents claim that violent patients with personality disorders or substance abuse problems do not belong in psychiatric treatment facilities because they may not be treatable.[18] Others maintain that modern commitment law is "legally and psychiatrically sanctioned coercive-paternalistic control of mental patients."[19] Others warn of "the peril of extending state control over persons who merely behave in socially obnoxious or unacceptable ways."[20]

The criminalization thesis supposes that mental illness has become a crime and leads to the frequent arrest of psychiatric patients.[21] Mental health activists argue that some individuals thought to be psychiatrically disturbed may be detained by the police on trivial charges to get them off the streets.[22] There also may be ethnic differences in civil commitment associated with police transport to the hospital.[23]

A final area of debate concerns consistency of commitment decisions. Because no gold standard exists, the decision to commit an individual patient is subjective. Some researchers believe that there is good interobserver reliability in assessment of dangerousness.[24,25] Others point out that the process of civil commitment is applied inconsistently and the rates of commitments vary greatly from year to year.[26] One study[27] showed only moderate agreement between emergency physicians and psychiatrists regarding the need for psychiatric admission. Unfortunately, there is no literature to demonstrate which group of physicians can better predict suicide or interpersonal violence. At least one author has said that "[t]he proposition that violence can be validly predicted clinically is seen as having little empirical support."[28] Physicians are more likely to disagree on the need for commitment when it involves patients with personality disorders who are acting out, or mentally ill patients who are disruptive and refuse treatment.[29]

Characteristics of Committed Patients

Although patients who are committed share certain common characteristics, these qualities vary among countries. For example, the criteria in England and Wales target older women; in the United States, younger men; and in Italy, a group balanced in age and sex.[30] In the United States, the patient who is manic, has grave psychiatric disability, or is psychotic is most likely to be committable from a variety of medical and legal perspectives.[31,32] Violent, young male schizophrenics who do not own homes are particularly likely to be committed.[33] Substance abuse also correlates with civil commitment, possibly due to unstable living conditions and organic mental illness.[34]

Malpractice Issues

Although the most immediate risk when dealing with psychiatric patients involves physical assault, there are medical-legal risks as well. Nearly 2% of closed claims against emergency physicians involve psychiatric issues, especially the failure to prevent suicide.[35] This malpractice trend began in the 1970s, when, for the first time, physicians were successfully sued for failing to recognize suicidal risk and for neglecting to take appropriate action to prevent suicide. Such "appropriate action" may include civil commitment and/or physical restraint.[36] The failure to prevent suicide results in the highest average indemnity in emergency medicine malpractice cases — an average of almost $400,000 per closed claim.[37] This figure surpasses even the average indemnity for failure to diagnose meningitis in children.

There are also legal risks when physicians fail to commit patients who pose a danger to others. If a physician does not commit a dangerous patient who later harms someone, the physician may be liable for injury to a third party. This is especially true if the physician is aware of a

Figure 1
Risk factors for suicide

Demographics
   White males > 65 years old
   Females > 60 years old
   Males 15 to 24 years old

Psychiatric disorder
   Major depression
   Bipolar disorder
   Schizophrenia
   Borderline personality disorder
   Panic disorder

Alcohol and substance abuse
   Alcoholism
   Drug abuse (particularly cocaine)

Past history
   Prior suicide attempts
   Terminal/chronic illness
   Chronic pain
   Physical or sexual abuse
   Recent discharge from psychiatric hospital

Family history
   Family violence
   Suicide in family

Social
   Firearm in home
   Living alone
   Separated, widowed, divorced
   Unemployed
   Recent personal loss
   Incarceration

Emotional state
   Hopelessness
   Chronic loneliness
   Fixation on death

From Colucciello SA, Hockberger RS. In: Rosen P, Barkin RM, eds. *Emergency Medicine: Concepts and Clinical Practice.* Fourth edition. St Louis: Mosby–Year Book; 1997. Used with permission.

Figure 2

Modified SAD PERSONS Score

			Points assigned
S	=	Sex (male)	1
A	=	Age (< 19 or > 45)	1
D	=	Depression or hopelessness	2
P	=	Previous attempts or psychiatric care	1
E	=	Excessive alcohol or drug use	1
R	=	Rational thinking loss	2
S	=	Separated, divorced, widowed	1
O	=	Organized or serious attempt	2
N	=	No social supports	1
S	=	Stated future intent	2

5 or less, questionable outpatient treatment
6 or greater, emergent psychiatric treatment/evaluation
> 9, psychiatric hospitalization

From Hockberger RS, Rothstein RJ. Assessment of suicide potential by nonpsychiatrists using the SAD PERSONS score. *J Emerg Med* 1988;6:99-107. Used with permission.

direct oral or written threat. In 1976, the court in *Tarasoff v Regents of University of California* determined that, when a patient tells a physician of intent to harm someone, the physician is responsible for warning the intended victim.[38] This duty to warn supersedes physician-patient confidentiality.

Although a physician may be liable for failure to commit, there are also medical-legal perils in the act of civil commitment. Physicians may be sued by patients or mental health activists for their commitment decisions.[39] Failure to follow statutory guidelines in the commitment process poses the greatest legal risk. Physicians are culpable when patients are deprived of their liberty by means of civil commitment without due process.[40] The courts mandate that physicians exercise "proper and ordinary care and prudence" when making commitment decisions.[41] The emergency department record is the best means of documenting "proper and ordinary care and prudence."

Emergency Department Management

Emergency physicians must determine a patient's "dangerousness" early during the emergency department encounter to prevent harm to other patients, staff, and visitors. Physicians should evaluate patients brought in by police for altered mental status or bizarre behavior as soon as possible. Patients who make suicidal statements and those who are actively hallucinating or severely agitated should be brought immediately to the treatment area by security officers. Emergency department protocols for managing suicidal and violent patients may standardize care and help avoid legal pitfalls.

Patient Searches

If the physician determines that a patient is suicidal or violent, security officers should search the patient and remove all dangerous objects. Five to 40 patients per 100,000 hospitalizations commit suicide while in the hospital,[42] and a far larger number assault emergency department staff. A search protocol may include confiscation of shoelaces and belts the patient could use to hang himself. Any experienced emergency physician can attest that patients who have attempted suicide by overdose invariably have the medication inadvertently placed within their reach by well-intentioned nurses, paramedics, or family members. Keep pill bottles, syringes, and laceration trays away from the suicidal or violent patient. The use of a handheld metal detector may reveal lethal devices disguised as harmless objects, such as a stiletto/pen or belt buckle/knife. The best solution to the problem of hidden weapons may be having the patient wear a hospital gown.

Patient Restraint

The Supreme Court decision of *Youngberg v Romeo* states that physicians may legally order patients to be placed in restraints if they exercise "professional judgment."[8,43] The dangerous patient can be restrained by security, or a designated security officer can act as a "sitter." A locked room or leather restraints are most effective. Having determined the potential for danger, the emergency physician who does not act to prevent escape may be liable if the patient gets away and either hurts someone or commits suicide.[44] For this reason, involuntarily committed patients should be treated in a locked unit.[45]

Chemical Restraints

The court in *Riese v St. Mary's Hospital* ruled that, absent a judicial determination of incompetence, antipsychotic drugs cannot be administered to involuntarily committed mental patients in nonemergency situations without their informed consent.[46] This right to informed consent does not extend to the emergency situation where life or limb may be threatened by failure to sedate. Emergency department patients who are acutely psychotic and uncontrollable cannot refuse tranquilizing medication. If the emergency physician clearly documents the need for chemical restraint, the medicine can be given safely from a legal perspective. Patients who wildly tug against physical restraints may suffer muscle breakdown and dangerous rhabdomyolysis unless sedated.

Voluntary Versus Involuntary Commitment

The decision to commit an individual patient is not always clear-cut. The physician must weigh many factors and consider the patient's dangerousness to self and others, the history of psychiatric illness, and the degree of disability and impulsiveness.[47,48] Physicians must also consider the resources (or lack of resources) available to the patient following discharge.

Some patients agree to voluntary psychiatric admission, an opportunity gratefully seized by the busy emergency physician because less paperwork is involved. As voluntary admission avoids involving the police, notaries, and courts, it has a seductive appeal. Unfortunately, numerous legal pitfalls are associated with voluntary admissions. Of greatest concern is the suicidal patient who initially agrees to a voluntary admission but changes his mind after leaving the emergency department. If a patient is truly suicidal or homicidal, this window for escape may prove fatal. The emergency physician should consider involuntary commitment of patients with a high "danger potential" (whether suicidal or homicidal) despite the patient's willingness to be admitted.

Another pitfall of voluntary admission is associated with issues of consent and competence. Only a competent patient may give consent for voluntary admission. In the U.S. Supreme Court case *Zinermon v Burch*, the court ruled that a mentally ill man was unable to give informed consent and could sue state officials who committed him to a state hospital using voluntary commitment procedures.[49] This case established that the legal process requires some type of procedure for determining whether voluntary patients are competent to consent to their admission.[50]

Suicidal Ideation

The emergency physician is usually the person who must decide whether to commit or release a potentially suicidal patient. Because suicide is a leading cause of death in the United States, the risk factors for completed suicide must be considered carefully (Figure 1). Ask the patient directly: "Do you intend to kill yourself?" Determine the lethal nature of the attempt, concomitant psychosis, degree of social supports, and whether a gun is kept in the home.

Scoring systems have been devised to predict the risk of suicide, but prospective studies demonstrate that they have limited utility.[51-53] It is frustrating but probably true that clinically predicting suicide in a given individual may be impossible.[54] One useful scoring system for the emergency physician, however, is the Modified SAD PERSONS Score (Figure 2). This scoring system may predict the need for hospitalization or consultation in the nonintoxicated patient at risk for suicide. In one prospective study,[55] no patient evaluated with this tool and sent home had committed suicide 6 to 12 months afterward. Nevertheless, a low SAD PERSONS score should not rule out civil commitment if the clinician still believes the patient to be at high risk.

Figure 3

Clinical pathway for civil commitment

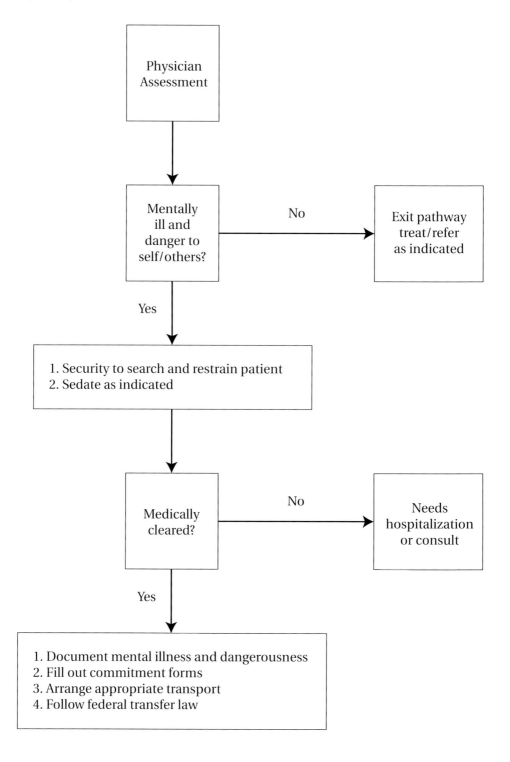

From Colucciello SA. Civil commitment, medical, legal and ethical. *Emergency Medicine Reports* 1997;18(6):55-64. Used with permission.

Not all patients who make suicidal gestures need to be committed. Although some physicians commit a patient based on a realistic appraisal of suicide risk, other physicians may commit based on the perceived legal risk to themselves if they do not do so.[2] Certain low-risk patients who make suicidal gestures may be sent home after careful evaluation and arrangement for follow-up. The law does not demand that the physician always be correct in either committing or discharging a patient; it insists that the physician demonstrate "professional judgment" and "reasonable care" in patient evaluation. Thus, physicians should carefully document their decision-making processes to avoid legal repercussions. The primary deterrent to a judgment against a physician in such cases is the well-documented emergency department record.[56] Despite the record's importance, emergency physicians frequently fail to document suicide risk.[57]

Studies demonstrate that patients who are involuntarily committed have a very high suicide rate,[58] but whether hospitalization has any impact on long-term survival is unknown. Civil commitment has never been proved to prevent suicide. In fact, some authorities believe that commitment may further injure the patient's psyche by promoting hopelessness, dependency, or rebellion.[2] Nonetheless, civil commitment is the current standard of care for the truly suicidal patient.

Dangerousness to Others

Scant literature exists regarding the emergency physician's ability to predict a patient's dangerousness to others. This threat is more likely to be associated with major mental illness, particularly psychosis, than is danger to self.[15,47,48] Patients with paranoid schizophrenia or manic-depressive disorder are particularly likely to be assaultive or homicidal.[59] Hallucinations featuring commands are especially dangerous if they instruct patients to injure themselves or others.

The emergency physician should obtain a history of prior violent behavior, particularly any recent violence. Patients who are violent in the two weeks prior to commitment are likely to be violent in the first 72 hours of hospitalization.[60,61] Ask the patient directly if he has ever been arrested for a violent crime (e.g., assault, rape, murder, armed robbery). A history of weapons possession by paranoid schizophrenics is also predictive of violent behavior.[62]

Figure 4

Pitfalls in civil commitment

Failure to recognize a patient's dangerousness to self or others.

Failure to search and restrain dangerous patients.

Failure to document dangerousness adequately.

Failure to perform adequate medical clearance, particularly if the patient is elderly or has abnormal vital signs.

Failure to use involuntary commitment when it is necessary (incompetent/psychotic patient, high danger potential), using voluntary commitment instead.

Failure to comply with federal patient transfer regulations.

From Colucciello SA. Civil commitment, medical, legal and ethical. *Emergency Medicine Reports* 1997;18(6):55-64. Used with permission.

Table 1.

Historical aspects of organic versus functional psychosis

	Onset	Age of onset	Hallucinations	Orientation
Organic	May be acute	Any age	Often visual	Often disoriented
Functional	Subacute to chronic	14 to 40	Usually auditory	Normal

From Colucciello SA. Civil commitment, medical, legal and ethical. *Emergency Medicine Reports* 1997;18(6):55-64. Used with permission.

Patients brought to the hospital by police tend to be violent, particularly if they are intoxicated.[63] Physicians must remember that persons restrained by police prior to arriving at the hospital usually require restraints in the emergency department. Increased motor activity, such as pacing, twitching, and clenching fists, often precedes violent acts.

Medical Clearance

A major pitfall in civil commitment is the act of sending a medically ill patient to a psychiatric facility. Unsuspected medical illness may account for 4% to 46% of apparent psychiatric disease.[64] A patient who is committed may undergo little or no further medical evaluation after leaving the emergency department. Most psychiatrists do not perform physical examinations, which means that the emergency physician is responsible for the medically ill patient who appears to have a psychiatric disorder.

Life-threatening medical illness may masquerade as new-onset psychosis. There is a frightening 10% mortality rate in committed patients within 19 months after hospitalization. Most deaths occur by suicide and in elderly, demented patients with underlying medical disease.[65] Look for evidence of organic disease in the history and physical examination (Table 1). New-onset psychosis is almost always preceded by prior psychiatric history and rarely manifests as an acute event. It first presents between puberty and age 40. Its sudden appearance (especially in people over 40) may herald infection, toxic or metabolic derangement, or mass lesion or hypoxia. Address abnormal vital signs, especially fever, in all candidates for civil commitment. The management of the geriatric patient who presents to the emergency department with an acute change in behavior is fraught with peril. The elderly are more likely to have a serious underlying medical illness as a basis for their psychiatric presentation than are younger patients.[65] Perform a mental status examination to assess orientation, affect, cognition, appearance, hallucinations, delusions, and suicidal or homicidal ideation.

Not all patients who are civilly committed require laboratory evaluation. The necessity and scope of any laboratory evaluation is dependent on the clinical presentation. A patient with a long psychiatric history who recently stopped taking his psychotropic medication and has stable vital signs and a normal physical examination probably requires no laboratory work. A patient with new-onset altered mental status and no prior psychiatric history, or one who is febrile, may require extensive diagnostic testing, including CT scan and lumbar puncture. A bedside measurement of glucose is the most important immediate test in a patient with new-onset abnormal behavior.

Consultation and Patient Transfer Issues

Some emergency physicians are fortunate enough to have a psychiatrist available to assist in commitment decisions. These on-call psychiatrists may come to the emergency department and assume management of the patient. In this situation, most potential liability arising from commitment decisions will be transferred to the psychiatrist. However, more often than not, psychiatric backup comes in the form of a psychiatric social worker or some other paraprofessional. Although these mental health paraprofessionals frequently provide valuable assistance, the emergency physician is the one responsible for the patient's disposition. If a patient commits suicide after being released by a psychiatric social worker, the emergency physician is at high risk for exposure to liability.[66]

If the accepting psychiatric facility is in the same institution as the emergency department, federal transfer laws do not apply. However, if the psychiatric facility is located elsewhere, the emergency physician must comply with all state and federal laws regarding transfer. According to the Health Care Financing Administration (HCFA) regulations, a patient who presents to an emergency department with a psychiatric complaint may have an emergency medical condition and is, thus, subject to federal law regulating transfers.[67] Under the Emergency Medical Treatment and Active Labor Act (EMTALA), a patient with an emergency medical condition must be medically and psychiatrically stable prior to transfer from an emergency department. If the transferring hospital has the ability to stabilize a psychiatric emergency, it must do so prior to transfer. The central issue is the definition of "psychiatrically stable." The use of chemical and/or physical restraints to prevent harm to self or others may qualify as a stabilizing intervention. In addition to stabilization, EMTALA mandates contact between the transferring and accepting facilities, along with the transfer of pertinent medical records (see Chapter 45, "EMTALA").

The actual physical movement or transport of a patient who has been committed may be problematic. The patient must be safely moved from the emergency department to a psychiatric facility that may be located some distance away. Some patients actively resist transport, and both physical and chemical restraints may be necessary. The safest method, both legally and physically, involves using a police or sheriff transport team. If the patient resists transport, the police are clearly empowered to prevent escape. However, the legal justification of hospital security to restrain a person during transport off hospital grounds may be questionable in some states.

Special Circumstances

Unusual circumstances are the norm when dealing with civil commitment. Certain problems that tend to recur in the emergency department are worth addressing here. Although no single "right answer" applies to the following dilemmas, certain broad principles are useful.

Family Issues

In general, family members who bring patients in for psychiatric evaluation are supportive of commitment.[32] More often than not, the family of a schizophrenic patient who is exhibiting bizarre behavior will insist on civil commitment. However, at times, the patient and the family will tell very different stories. The family may state that the patient is suicidal or homicidal, and the patient will deny it. Consider that some relatives of committed patients may have punitive attitudes toward the patient.[68] Accusations and counter-accusations may turn into a confusing "he said/she said" encounter for the emergency physician, which clouds the issue of who should be committed.

In general, the physician should err on the side of protecting life. In such situations, a history of psychiatric hospitalizations, the use of psychotropic medications, and prior suicide attempts may weigh heavily in commitment decisions.

On rare occasions, family members may adamantly oppose civil commitment. Although such devotion signals strong family support and a potential for outpatient management, a family cannot overrule a physician's commitment. Mentally ill patients who are truly and acutely dangerous to themselves or others should be hospitalized despite family objections.

Incarcerated Patients

Police may bring prisoners who have attempted suicide in jail to the emergency department for evaluation. Once such patients are medically cleared, they may return to jail under a suicide watch, with follow-up by the prison mental health services. Prisoners who attempt suicide do not necessarily require immediate psychiatric hospitalization.

System Abusers

Some patients feign suicidal ideation to obtain hospital services. The "hidden agenda" may include desire to escape cold weather or need for food. Such a patient may present to the emergency department stating: "I want to kill myself. Admit me to the psych floor." The emergency physician is not required to commit such patients but must perform an examination to determine true suicide potential. If such a patient wishes voluntary admission, this can be the responsibility of the admitting psychiatrist.

Commitment of Minors

Formal civil commitment is rarely used in the case of unemancipated minors. Parents or legal guardians may place a child into a psychiatric facility without the necessity of formal commitment. In some states, a minor may be voluntarily admitted without consent of the parent. Difficulties may arise if a minor presents to the emergency department after a suicide attempt and the parents refuse to have the minor hospitalized. If the emergency physician determines that the minor is truly suicidal, commitment may proceed despite the objections of the parent or guardian.

Intoxicated Patients

Many controversies surround the management of a suicidal or violent patient who is intoxicated. Although the violent alcoholic may show self-restraint while sober, the depressed alcoholic may remain a serious suicidal risk even when not drinking.

Many physicians and mental health professionals discredit suicidal statements a patient makes while intoxicated and will hold the patient in the emergency department until sober. If this patient does not exhibit suicidal ideation when sober, he will likely be released. This approach may be acceptable in the case of vague suicidal statements but is problematic in the face of a potentially lethal suicide attempt or a prior psychiatric history of severe depression. Alcoholics are impulsive and have a higher risk of suicide.

Managed Care Patients

Hospitals may have separate commitment processes for insured versus indigent patients. They may admit patients with certain insurance plans to their psychiatric units but transfer other patients depending on whether they are uninsured or belong to a particular managed care organization. Such economic transfers are regulated by federal patient transfer law.

At times, the needs of the patient run counter to the desires of managed care organizations.[69] These organizations may refuse payment for psychiatric hospitalization and ask that the patient be sent home to follow up with the primary care provider or a designated therapist. As always, the emergency physician's duty is to the patient, not to a third-party payer.

Key Points and Conclusion

Civil commitment poses many legal risks. The emergency physician must determine dangerousness and mental illness in patients presenting to the emergency department with altered mental status or psychiatric complaints. If a person is dangerous to self or others, the physician has a duty to act. Such actions may include a search for weapons, the use of physical and/or chemical restraints, medical clearance, and civil commitment. Careful documentation of the need for restraint and commitment provides the strongest defense in the case of subsequent litigation.

References

1. Faulkner LR, McFarland BH, Bloom JD. An empirical study of emergency commitment. *Am J Psychiatry* 1989;146:182-186.

2. Siegel K, Tuckel P. Suicide and civil commitment. *J Health Polit Policy Law* 1987;12(2):343-360.

3. Beane EA, Beck JC. Court based civil commitment of alcoholics and substance abusers. *Bull Am Acad Psychiatry Law* 1991;19:359-366.

4. Hiday VA, Scheid-Cook TL. Outpatient commitment for "revolving door" patients: compliance and treatment. *J Nerv Ment Dis* 1991;179:83-88.

5. Appelbaum PS. The right to refuse treatment with antipsychotic medications: retrospect and prospect [review]. *Am J Psychiatry* 1988;145:413-419.

6. Bradley C, Marshall M, Gath D. Why do so few patients appeal against detention under Section 2 of the Mental Health Act? *BMJ* 1995;310:364-367.

7. Hiday VA. Are lawyers enemies of psychiatrists? A survey of civil commitment counsel and judges? *Am J Psychiatry* 1983;140:323-326.

8. Mills MJ. Legal issues in psychiatric treatment. *Psychiatr Med* 1984;2:245-261.

9. Leong GB, Silva JA, Leong CA. Judicial discharge of involuntary patients. *Psychiatr Q* 1990;61:135-141.

10. Turkheimer E, Parry CD. Why the gap? Practice and policy in civil commitment hearings. *Am Psychol* 1992;47:646-655.

11. Edelsohn GA, Hiday VA. Civil commitment: a range of patient attitudes. *Bull Am Acad Psychiatry Law* 1990;18:65-77.

12. Chodoff P. Involuntary hospitalization of the mentally ill as a moral issue. *Am J Psychiatry* 1984;141:384-389.

13. La Fond JQ. Law and the delivery of involuntary mental health services. *Am J Orthopsychiatry* 1994;64:209-222.

14. Bloom JD, Williams MH. Oregon's civil commitment law: 140 years of change. *Hosp Community Psychiatry* 1994;45:466-470.

15. Bagby RM, Thompson JS, Dickens SE, et al. Decision making in psychiatric civil commitment: an experimental analysis. *Am J Psychiatry* 1991;148:28-33.

16. Miller RD. The criminalisation of the mentally ill: does dangerousness take precedence over need for treatment? *Criminal Behaviour Mental Health* 1993;3:241-250.

17. Slobogin C. Involuntary community treatment of people who are violent and mentally ill: a legal analysis. *Hosp Community Psychiatry* 1994;45:685-689.

18. Brouillette MJ, Paris J. The dangerousness criterion for civil commitment: the problem and a possible solution. *Can J Psychiatry* 1991;36:285-289.

19. Szasz T. Noncoercive psychiatry: an oxymoron: reflections on law, liberty, and psychiatry. *J Humanistic Psychol* 1991;31:117-125.

20. Meloy JR, Haroun A, Schiller E, et al. *Clinical Guidelines for Involuntary Outpatient Treatment.* Sarasota, Fla: Professional Resource Exchange, Inc; 1990.

21. Hiday VA. Dangerousness of civil commitment candidates: a six-month follow-up. *Law Human Behavior* 1990;14:551-567.

22. Bittman BJ, Convit A. Competency, civil commitment, and the dangerousness of the mentally ill. *J Forensic Sci* 1993;38:1460-1466.

23. Owens D, Harrison G, Boot D. Ethnic factors in voluntary and compulsory admissions. *Psychol Med* 1991;21:185-196.

24. Lidz CW, Mulvey EP, Appelbaum PS, et al. Commitment: the consistency of clinicians and the use of legal standards. *Am J Psychiatry* 1989;146:176-181.

25. Bursztajn H, Gutheil TG, Hamm RM, et al. *Parens patriae* considerations in the commitment process. *Psychiatr Q* 1988;59:165-181.

26. McNiel DE, Binder RL. Violence, civil commitment, and hospitalization. *J Nerv Ment Dis* 1986;174:107-111.

27. Garbrick L, Levitt MA, Barrett M, et al. Agreement between emergency physicians and psychiatrists regarding admission decisions. *Acad Emerg Med* 1996;3:1027-1030.

28. Kirk A. The prediction of violent behavior during short-term civil commitment. *Bull Am Acad Psychiatry Law* 1989;17:345-353.

29. Rissmiller DJ, Hogate PM, August D, et al. Commitment decisions: identification of indeterminate cases. *Crisis* 1994;15:110-115.

30. Segal SP. Civil commitment standards and patient mix in England/Wales, Italy, and the United States. *Am J Psychiatry* 1989;146:187-193.

31. Hoge SK, Sachs G, Appelbaum PS, et al. Limitations on psychiatrists' discretionary civil commitment authority by the Stone and dangerousness criteria. *Arch Gen Psychiatry* 1988;45:764-769.

32. McFarland BH, Faulkner LR, Bloom JD, et al. Family members' opinions about civil commitment. *Hosp Community Psychiatry* 1990;41:537-540.

33. Riecher A, Rössler W, Löffler W, et al. Factors influencing compulsory admission of psychiatric patients. *Psychol Med* 1991;21:197-208.

34. Sanguineti VR, Brooks MO. Factors related to emergency commitment of chronic mentally ill patients who are substance abusers. *Hosp Community Psychiatry* 1992;43:237-241.

35. Bongar B, Maris RW, Berman AL, et al. Inpatient standards of care and the suicidal patient. Part I: general clinical formulations and legal considerations. *Suicide Life Threat Behav* 1993;23(3):245-256.

36. Silverman MM, Berman AL, Bongar B, et al. Inpatient standards of care and the suicidal patient. Part II: an integration with clinical risk management. *Suicide Life Threat Behav* 1994;24(2):152-169.

37. Karcz A, Holbrook J, Auerbach BS, et al. Preventability of malpractice claims in emergency medicine: a closed claims study. *Ann Emerg Med* 1990;19:865-873.

38. Perlin ML. Tarasoff and the dilemma of the dangerous patient: new directions for the 1990's. *Law Psych Rev* 1992;16:29-63.

39. Miller RD. Grievances and law suits against public mental health professionals: cost of doing business? *Bull Am Acad Psychiatry Law* 1992;20:395-408.

40. *Samons v Meymandi*, 177 SE2d 209, 9 NC App 490. Anonymous. 1970.

41. *Kleber v Stevens*, 241 NYS2d 497, 39 Misc2d 712. Anonymous. 1963.

42. Hogarty SS, Rodaitis CM. A suicide precautions policy for the general hospital. *J Nurs Adm* 1987;17(10):36-42.

43. Rice MM, Moore GP. Management of the violent patient: therapeutic and legal considerations. *Emerg Med Clin North Am* 1991;9:13-31.

44. Korgaonkar G, Tribe D. Suicide and attempted suicide—a doctor's legal liability. *Br J Hosp Med* 1993;50:680-681.

45. el-Mallakh RS, Liebowitz NR, Patel K, et al. Impact of treating involuntarily admitted schizophrenics on an open unit. *South Med J* 1993;86:667-670.

46. Binder RL, McNiel DE. Involuntary patients' right to refuse medication: impact of the Riese decision on a California inpatient unit. *Bull Am Acad Psychiatry Law* 1991;19:351-357.

47. Segal SP, Watson MA, Goldfinger SM, et al. Civil commitment in the psychiatric emergency room. III. Disposition as a function of mental disorder and dangerousness indicators. *Arch Gen Psychiatry* 1988;45:759-763.

48. Segal SP, Watson MA, Goldfinger SM, et al. Civil commitment in the psychiatric emergency room. I. The assessment of dangerousness by emergency room clinicians. *Arch Gen Psychiatry* 1988;45:748-752.

49. Parry JW. The Supreme Court fashions new boundaries for involuntary care and treatment. *Ment Phys Disabil Law Reporter* 1990;14:198-202.

50. Winick BJ. Voluntary hospitalization after Zinermon v Burch. *Psychiatric Ann* 1991;21:584-589.

51. Clark DC, Young MA, Scheftner WA, et al. A field test of Motto's risk estimator for suicide. *Am J Psychiatry* 1987;144:923-926.

52. Motto JA, Heilbron DC, Juster RP. Development of a clinical instrument to estimate suicide risk. *Am J Psychiatry* 1985;142(6):680-686.

53. Goldstein RB, Black DW, Nasrallah A, et al. The prediction of suicide. Sensitivity, specificity, and predictive value of a multivariate model applied to suicide among 1906 patients with affective disorders. *Arch Gen Psychiatry* 1991;48(5):418-422.

54. Maris RW. Suicide and life-threatening behavior. Introduction. *Suicide Life Threat Behav* 1991;21:1-17.

55. Hockberger RS, Rothstein RJ. Assessment of suicide potential by nonpsychiatrists using the SAD PERSONS score. *J Emerg Med* 1988;6:99-107.

56. Perr IN. Psychiatric malpractice issues. *New Dir Ment Health Serv* 1985;25:47-59.

57. O'Dwyer FG, D'Alton A, Pearce JB. Adolescent self harm patients: audit of assessment in an accident and emergency department. *BMJ* 1991;303:629-630.

58. Engberg M. Mortality and suicide rates of involuntarily committed patients. *Acta Psychiatr Scand* 1994;89:35-40.

59. Beck JC, Bonnar J. Emergency civil commitment: predicting hospital violence from behavior in the community. *J Psych Law* 1988;16:379-388.

60. McNiel DE, Binder RL, Greenfield TK. Predictors of violence in civilly committed acute psychiatric patients. *Am J Psychiatry* 1988;145:965-970.

61. Litwack TR. Assessments of dangerousness: legal, research, and clinical developments. *Admin Policy Ment Health* 1994;21:361-377.

62. Shore D, Filson CR, Johnson WE, et al. Murder and assault arrests of White House cases: clinical and demographic correlates of violence subsequent to civil commitment. *Am J Psychiatry* 1989;146:645-651.

63. Perlman BP, Kentera A, Thornton JC, et al. Involuntary and voluntary psychiatric patients: a pilot study of resource consumption. *Am J Public Health* 1988;78:1347-1348.

64. Henneman PL, Mendoza R, Lewis RJ. Prospective evaluation of emergency department medical clearance. *Ann Emerg Med* 1994;24:672-677.

65. Shore JH, Breakey W, Arvidson B. Morbidity and mortality in the commitment process. *Arch Gen Psychiatry* 1981;38:930-934.

66. Armitage DT, Townsend GM. Emergency medicine, psychiatry, and the law. *Emerg Med Clin North Am* 1993;11:869-887.

67. 42 CFR §49.24(B).

68. Adams NH, Hafner RJ. Attitudes of psychiatric patients and their relatives to involuntary treatment. *Aust N Z J Psychiatry* 1991;25:231-237.

69. Petrila J. Who will pay for involuntary civil commitment under capitated managed care? An emerging dilemma "double jeopardy." *Psychiatr Serv* 1995;46:1045-1048.

Chapter 30

Good Samaritan Statutes

Vicky A. Trompler, MD, JD
David M. Siegel, MD, JD, FACEP, FACP, FCLM

Physicians and other medical personnel often find themselves in situations where they need to provide medical treatment at the scene of an accident or some other medical emergency. This can happen outside of the hospital or within a hospital setting. The Good Samaritan statute was developed to protect individuals from civil liability when they voluntarily provide emergency care. However, some caveats apply. The provider of care is not totally immune from liability. The statutes generally do not cover routine emergency medical practice, and the laws vary greatly from state to state. All physicians should understand how the Good Samaritan concept is covered in their state statutes and how it applies to their individual practices.

Case Studies

1

A physician is driving home after her shift in an emergency department. While stopped at a red light, she sees a sports car speed through the intersection and hit an elderly man crossing against the traffic. The man is thrown several feet by the impact of the car and lies unconscious on the street. The emergency physician runs from her car to the man and performs a quick assessment. She discovers that he has no spontaneous respirations or palpable pulses and has obvious head and chest injuries, as well as multiple fractures. She begins CPR and tells a bystander to call 911.

When the paramedics arrive, she identifies herself as a physician and assists in the airway control and immobilization, then helps establish an IV line. She diagnoses a tension hemo/pneumothorax and inserts a chest tube at the scene, retrieving a massive amount of air and blood. The man is transported to the local trauma center and is in the operating room within 45 minutes.

Despite heroic surgical intervention, the patient dies on the operating table. His family seeks legal action against the driver of the sports car, and against the emergency physician for alleged substandard care and treatment that contributed to the man's death.

2

A physician on duty at a small rural emergency department hears the paging operator signal a code blue in the hospital. He runs to the third floor and finds a middle-aged man in full cardiac arrest. He directs a long, involved resuscitation effort that results in the transfer of the patient to the coronary care unit on a respirator.

The patient dies after a protracted, complicated stay in the CCU. The patient's family decides to file a malpractice action against the private attending physician, as well as the emergency physician for his resuscitation efforts, which they allege contributed to the patient's death.

3

An off-duty emergency physician is attending the premier of a play. In the middle of the performance, a spectator collapses in the front row. The ushers ask any physician present to assist. The physician, despite encouragement from his friends, refuses to "get involved" because of the legal horror stories he heard about as a resident.

The patient dies at the hospital after a delay in the arrival of paramedics and prolonged treatment. The patient's family learns that the emergency physician was in the audience and was obviously competent and available to render emergency assistance. They file a lawsuit against him for failure to provide care, pointing out that the state's Good Samaritan statute would have protected him.

The Medical-Legal Perspective

Good Samaritan statutes encourage health care providers, and laypersons as well, to render emergency medical treatment, usually at the scene of an accident or medical emergency. To fully understand the importance of Good Samaritan laws, they must be viewed from their common law background.

Common Law Background

At common law, a passerby who finds another person in an emergency situation has no duty to render that person aid, absent a special relationship between the parties and unless the passerby caused the emergency situation. The passerby who chooses to offer aid, however, must exercise reasonable care to avoid further injury to the victim or increasing the victim's risk of harm. At common law, failure to exercise such care exposes the passerby to liability for damages caused by negligent acts or omissions. Thus, this "Good Samaritan" who tries to help may be liable for damages, while the "priest and Levite" who pass by have no liability.[1]

Development of Good Samaritan Statutes

Good Samaritan statutes vary from state to state in defining what kind of rescuer is protected (health care professional and/or layperson) and the degree of liability or standard of negligence applied to the person rendering care.[2] However, all have the same basic underlying theme and purpose. The development of these laws is succinctly described in a leading 1978 California case, *Colby v Schwartz*.[3] As articulated in this case, common law did provide some protection for the person who tried to help in an emergency. However, this protection was not

deemed sufficient to encourage would-be rescuers, as they could still be sued and found liable. Jury decisions could still be unpredictable and could fail to apply the lower standard of care criteria developed in common case law.

Therefore, legislators decided to codify the concept of a lower standard of care (reasonable but not grossly harmful or negligent) to settle the matter. As the judge in *Colby* summarized," . . . while the common law emergency standard of care operated to reduce the chances for a plaintiff's success at trial, it failed to discourage the commencement of malpractice actions. . . . The common law worked as a serious deterrent to the rendition of needed medical aid in emergency situations."[4] This situation prompted California to enact, in 1959, the nation's first Good Samaritan statute. Since then, every state has enacted some form of Good Samaritan legislation.[5]

An example of a typical Good Samaritan statute demonstrates what these laws generally accomplish, and perhaps more important, what they do not cover. Pennsylvania's Good Samaritan statute states: "Any physician or any other practitioner of the healing arts or any registered nurse, licensed by any state, who happens by chance upon the scene of an emergency or who arrives on the scene of an emergency by reason of serving on an emergency call panel or similar committee of a county medical society or who is called to the scene of an emergency by the police or other duly constituted officers of a government unit or who is present when an emergency occurs and who, in good faith, renders emergency care at the scene of the emergency, shall not be liable for any civil damages as a result of any acts or omissions by such physician or practitioner or registered nurse in rendering the emergency care, except any acts or omissions intentionally designed to harm or any grossly negligent acts or omissions which result in harm to the person receiving emergency care."[6]

There are numerous points to be made regarding this statute. First, it clearly refers to medical personnel and not to laypersons. (Pennsylvania has a separate section of the statute, sec. 8332, that applies to nonmedical personnel.) Also, it provides protection for the person who arrives at the scene of an emergency, or is present when one occurs, or who is called to the scene or whose duty it is to respond to such an emergency. It does not apply to the routine practice of emergency medicine in an emergency department or to the handling of emergencies as part of a regular job or duty.

The logic for this distinction is explored in the *Colby* case. The judge stated that physicians who treat patients requiring immediate care as part of their "normal course of practice" do not need the protection of immunity from civil liability to induce them to care for these patients; it is their job to do so. Also, the court pointed out that excusing these physicians from liability could lower their quality of care and would deny some malpractice victims legal remedies.[3] It must be noted, however, that there may be some extension of Good Samaritan liability protection in a few jurisdictions.[7]

In addition, the Pennsylvania law does restrict protection only to acts that are not intentionally harmful or grossly negligent. This statute reflects the reality that some standard of care exists in the emergency situation, although it is obviously a lower standard of care than in normal practice. However, other state statutes, such as the New Jersey Good Samaritan statute, contain broader protection and do not exclude grossly negligent or intentionally harmful acts.[8]

The Pennsylvania statute outlines a standard of care at the scene of an emergency that is not grossly negligent or intentionally harmful. This protects the physician who responds to an emergency in good faith and acts reasonably. According to Hattis, "there is hardly any case law in which a physician has been successfully sued for negligently treating a person in need of emergency care."[1]

Legal Issues

A summary of some of the legal issues involved in Good Samaritan statutes is presented by Veilleux.[9] Several of the salient points he discusses are presented here. In cases of liability lawsuits, a court must first decide if the physician involved had a preexisting duty to give emergency care. If such a duty is found to exist, the physician may not be protected by the Good Samaritan statute.[10] An example of a preexisting duty might be seen in a paramedic prehospital situation or in a case when a physician-patient relationship was already established.

The question also has been raised whether the Good Samaritan statute protection applies to on-call physicians in emergency situations. A Michigan case, *Gordin v William Beaumont Hospital*,[11] dealt with this issue. The court held that a surgeon who responded to an emergency department case but was not officially on call

was entitled to protection under the state Good Samaritan statute. The logical extension of this reasoning is that if the surgeon had been on call, he would not have received such protection. On-call duty might be deemed to create a preexisting duty to the patient.

The standard of care required by the physician is usually described as "ordinary and reasonably prudent"[12] or an even lower standard.[13] However, most statutes and case law do not protect the rescuer who is grossly negligent or who intentionally performs harmful acts.[14] Most statutes require that the case be a true emergency,[15] that the emergency has not been created by the person rendering the care,[16] and that, generally, the physician does not receive compensation for the care provided.[17]

No general duty to rescue exists in common law, although an argument can be made that there is an ethical duty to do so. Some authors have even argued for a legal duty to perform "easy rescue."[18] However, this would extend the liability of the physician rescuer and cut into the protection of the Good Samaritan statute. To date, this duty has not been extended, except in a few jurisdictions. A Vermont statute requires a person "who knows that another is exposed to grave physical harm" to give "reasonable assistance to the exposed person unless that assistance or care is being provided by others."[19] The person need not respond if the situation would place him in danger or peril or interfere with "important duties owed to others." The statute goes on to state that the rescuer will not be liable in civil damages unless "his acts constitute gross negligence or unless he will receive or expects to receive remuneration." Interestingly, the section specifically states that it does not in any way alter existing law with respect to the practitioner in reference to "acts committed in the ordinary course of his practice."[19]

Soon after the beginning of the nationwide Good Samaritan legislative movement in the early 1960s, some authors argued that the legislation would not be successful in encouraging physicians to render emergency aid because of ambiguities in the statutes and an exaggerated fear of legal actions. One author even contended that the statutes would be found unconstitutional. Instead, he recommended laws that would require physicians to render emergency care.[20]

Other authors have written on what the "ideal" Good Samaritan statute should include, for example, that the statute should apply to any physician, cover acts performed in good faith, involve gratuitous service, not protect gross negligence, and cover events at the scene of an emergency.[21] Some have argued for a uniform national Good Samaritan statute.[22]

An important aspect of liability involving the Good Samaritan statute is its applicability to in-hospital emergencies. *Colby v Schwartz* did not extend the California Good Samaritan statute protection to a hospital emergency surgical team. However, several jurisdictions have applied the Good Samaritan statute to in-hospital emergency situations.

In the recent case of *Hernandez v Lukefahr*,[23] a 2-month-old boy was brought into the emergency department with CPR in progress. Dr. Lukefahr, a pediatrician, was on another floor of the hospital when a nurse informed him of the hospital's emergency call over the loudspeaker for a pediatrician to go immediately to the emergency department. When Dr. Lukefahr arrived in the emergency department, he saw the emergency physician performing CPR on the infant. He proceeded to assist the emergency physician in attempting resuscitation. Dr. Lukefahr pronounced the infant dead when he noted that the pupils were fixed and dilated and the cardiac monitor showed no activity. The family stayed in the room with the infant and waited for the medical examiner. While they were waiting, they noticed some movement from the child. Approximately 1½ hours later, a pulse was found and the infant was transported to another hospital. A few days later, the infant died. The family filed a lawsuit, naming Dr. Lukefahr in the action. In the subsequent trial and appeal, the 14th District Court of Appeals of Texas found the state's Good Samaritan statute applicable as an affirmative defense for Dr. Lukefahr. This statute diminishes the standard of care by requiring wanton or willful negligence before it will permit liability.[24]

Another example of an in-hospital application of the Good Samaritan statute is demonstrated in *Pemberton v Dharmani*.[25] The plaintiff, Denise Pemberton underwent voluntary tubal ligation performed by Dr. Dharmani. During the surgery, Dr. Dharmani developed some difficulty viewing the left fallopian tube. He called another physician, Dr. Zarewych, and asked for his immediate assistance. Dr. Zarewych left the patients in his office and went to the hospital to assist Dr. Dharmani in the operating room. The next day, the pathologist determined that excised tissue was a section of colon rather than fallopian tube. Ms. Pemberton was taken back to surgery for a colostomy. Both physicians were sued for malpractice. Dr. Zarewych brought a motion for summary judgment, arguing under the Good Samaritan statute that he was immune from civil liability for ordinary negligence. The trial court granted Dr. Zarewych's motion for summary judgment, reasoning that the Michigan Good Samaritan statute was intended to apply when a physician responds in good faith to a request for emergency assistance, even though a life-threatening situation may not actually exist. Thus, this case demonstrates that not only can a Good Samaritan statute be applicable to in-hospital situations, but also to a situation that is not truly a life-threatening emergency.

Another California case noted that a separate California statute, other than Good Samaritan, was passed to provide immunity to a hospital rescue team.[26] The court refused to extend protection of the Good Samaritan statute to the Code Blue team department head. In this same case, however, the court did find that the head of the rescue team had acted in good faith, and the mere fact that there was some deviation from the American Heart Association guidelines in the resuscitation did not establish gross negligence. Therefore, the court held that this particular statute provided Good Samaritan protection to a Code Blue team. (For a general review in this area, see 64 *American Law Review*, 4th 1200.)

Good Samaritan statutes may apply to nonmedical or laypersons as well. The statutes characteristically refer to "any person" rendering aid. Likewise, the courts, in particular circumstances, may extend the liability protection to nonmedical rescuers.[15]

Good Samaritan Laws and Emergency Medicine

Good Samaritan statutes do not apply to the normal practice of emergency medicine by an emergency physician. In a normal emergency practice scenario, physicians are expected to handle emergencies because they are trained and equipped to do so. The physician owes a duty to patients presenting to the department. This duty can even be extended to emergency patients in the field, through preset or protocol EMS activities. It may even be extended occasionally to in-hospital emergencies.

Generally, the Good Samaritan protection for the practice of emergency medicine should not come into play when considering liability protection. Any physician must be cognizant of the local insurance requirements and of state Good Samaritan laws for any individual variations. As one author has stated, "it is foolhardy for physicians to conclude that Good Samaritan laws will provide them with blanket protection for liability in all emergencies."[27]

Case Discussions

1

This case represents the kind of aid that the Good Samaritan statute seeks to encourage. An emergency physician happened to be at the scene of an emergency and gratuitously provided care. She was obviously qualified to do so, and she was quick to summon aid and assisted the prehospital personnel. She performed rather invasive procedures at the scene of the accident. This might be the only argument the family would have against her.

However, following the facts of the case, it can be demonstrated with a degree of certainty that the physician acted reasonably and performed clearly indicated lifesaving measures. Assuming the state has a typical Good Samaritan statute, this physician, even though sued, would have been protected under the statute.

2

The extent of the emergency physician's liability in this case may well be decided by the individual state statute and court decisions, if any, regarding in-hospital emergency scenarios. One could argue that he had a duty to the emergency department but not to hospital patients. He responded as a "volunteer" to help in an in-house medical emergency. Assuming it was not his assigned duty to respond to a code blue, he may well be covered under a typical Good Samaritan statute and may escape any potential liability. On the other hand, if it is established that he had a duty to respond to in-house cases and was grossly negligent (failed to respond in a timely manner, for example), he may not receive Good Samaritan protection. The state may also have a particular statute that applies to in-hospital situations. In this situation, the statute would be the controlling authority to determine liability.

3

The Good Samaritan statute would have probably protected this physician if he had assisted in this case and acted reasonably. However, the statute does not create an affirmative duty to act in most jurisdictions. The physician may have a moral or ethical duty to respond, but in most states, under statute and common law principles, he has no obligation to do so.

Key Points and Conclusion

The Good Samaritan statutes passed by all state legislatures are intended to promote humanitarian assistance at the scene of an emergency. As a rule, they protect physicians (or in some cases, other health professionals or even laypersons) from liability if the rescuers act reasonably, in good faith, gratuitously, and without gross negligence or harmful intent. Society views these laws as a positive step toward helping emergency medical victims. Most groups, including medical associations, promoted their passage and continue to encourage their enforcement. The American College of Emergency Physicians has gone on record in support of this concept.[28]

Physicians must be familiar with the Good Samaritan statutes in their jurisdictions and how they apply to their practices. These statutes usually do not affect liability in routine emergency practice or change insurance liability needs of the average emergency physician. As always, individual state statutes and requirements must be consulted so the medical practitioner can practice and act in an informed manner.

- Good Samaritan statutes generally apply to emergency accident or illness cases, either inside or outside the hospital.
- These statutes, as a rule, do not apply to the routine practice of emergency medicine.
- Intentionally harmful or grossly negligent acts typically are not protected.
- Emergency physicians must be fully aware of their states' applicable statutes in order to understand the extent of duty assigned or protection afforded them in emergency cases.

References

1. Prosser WL. *Handbook of the Law of Torts*. §56 at 341-344 (4th ed, 1971).
2. Mapel FB, Weizel CL. Good Samaritan laws – who needs them?: The current state of Good Samaritan protection in the United States. *South Tex Law* 1982;21:327-354.
3. *Colby v Schwartz*, 78 Cal App 3d 885, 144 Cal Rptr 624 (1978).
4. *Colby v Schwartz*, 78 Cal App 3d 890, 144 Cal Rptr 624 (1978).

5. Morgan D, Trail W, Trompler V. Liability immunity as a legal defense for recent emergency medical service system litigation. *Prehosp Dis Med* 1995;10(2):82-91,89.

6. 42 Pa Cons Stat §8331 (a), 42 Pa Cons Stat §8332.

7. Florida Stat §768.13.

8. NJ Stat §2A: 62 A-1 (Supp 1983).

9. 68 *American Law Review*, 4th 294.

10. *Colby v Schwartz*, 78 Cal App 3d 885; *Emerg Phys Leg Bull* 1987;13(2).

11. *Gordin v William Beaumont Hospital*, 447 NW2d 793 (Mich App 1989).

12. *Botte v Pomeroy*, 438 So2d 544 (Fla App D4, 1983).

13. *Wallace v Hall*, 145 Ga App 610, 244 SE2d 129 (1978).

14. *Guerrero v Copper Queen Hospital*, 112 Ariz 104, 537 P2d 1329 (1975).

15. *Burciaga v St. John's Hospital*, 187 Cal App 3d 710, 232 Cal Rptr 75 (2d Dist, 1986).

16. *Flynn v United States*, 681 F Supp 1500 (DC Utah, 1988).

17. *Clayton v Kelly*, 183 Ga App 45, 357 SE2d 865 (1987).

18. *UCLA Law Review* 1983;31:252-293.

19. Duty to Aid the Endangered Act, Vt Stat Ann, tit 12, §519 (1973); Good Samaritan Law, ch 319, 1983, Minn Sess Law, Serv 2329 (West).

20. Good Samaritans and liability for medical malpractice. *Columb Law Rev* 1964;64:1301-1322.

21. Good Samaritan legislation. An analysis and a proposal. *Temple Law Q* 1985;38:418-432.

22. The Good Samaritan and the law. *Tenn Law Rev* 1965;32:287-293.

23. *Hernandez v Lukefahr*, 879 SW2d 137 (Tex App — Houston [14th Dist] 1994, no writ).

24. Texas Civil Practice & Remedies Code Ann 74.001(a), (Vernon Supp 1994).

25. *Pemberton v Dharmani*, 207 Mich App 522, 525 NW2d 497 (1994).

26. *Lowry v Henry Mayo Newhall Memorial Hospital*, 185 Cal App 3d 188, 229 Cal Rptr 620 (2d Dist, 1986).

27. *Emerg Phys Leg Bull* 1987;13(2):8.

28. Council Resolution 29, American College of Emergency Physicians, Board of Directors' Meeting, September 22-23, 1978.

Chapter 31

Securing Risk Management Information From Discovery

M. Elizabeth Sassano, MSN, JD

Emergency physicians and other department staff members are no strangers to the myriad risk management, peer review, quality assurance, and other administrative tasks designed to assess, monitor, or enhance the quality of the patient care they deliver. Although these activities support effective risk management and quality assurance activities, they also create an extensive paper trail of incident reports, committee minutes, surveys, and written recommendations. This flood of paperwork can be a problem to manage when staff must deal with requests from outsiders for access to or copies of this information.

Like other hospital employees, emergency department personnel may believe that all documents and information produced as a result of these activities are "privileged." They may also assume that this material may not be discovered — that is, reviewed by opposing counsel and potentially used as evidence against them — in a legal proceeding. This assumption may be accurate in some cases, but the rules governing discoverability of documents vary from state to state. What is protected in one jurisdiction may not be in another. As a result, each organization must first identify whether the privileged status of a document potentially exists and then take whatever steps are necessary to establish and protect that status.

Determining Privileged Status

The privileged status of hospital information has long been the subject of court proceedings.

Today, every state and the District of Columbia have enacted legislation addressing the issue of when and to what extent hospital activities (and the reports and other documents generated therefrom) may be exempt from public scrutiny. The legal parameters governing the privilege issue will continue to evolve as existing statutes are amended or challenged through litigation. Hospital personnel, therefore, must not only ascertain the scope of any privilege that may exist today, but also be alert for statutory changes and future court opinions that may refine, limit, or expand the nature and scope of the privilege granted.

The question of privilege is a difficult one for the courts to reconcile because it involves balancing two conflicting and important policy concerns: an individual's right of access to information and the need to keep certain information shielded from public disclosure. The importance of an individual's right of access is obvious. Internal hospital documents may contain information that could be valuable in assisting a plaintiff in preparing or proving a case. Ironically, for this very reason, hospitals and other health care institutions need to keep much of this information private. Certain hospital functions, notably peer review and quality assurance, are so sensitive that they must be protected from discovery in order to be carried out effectively. If such reports and data generated by these proceedings were made available for public scrutiny, the practice would undeniably chill the effectiveness of the quality assurance process. The free and candid exchange of information and opinion is essential. Health care professionals must be able to speak openly during internal review meetings without fear that their opinions and observations will later be used against them or their colleagues.

Committee Reports

Nowhere is the tension between an individual's right of access and the need for confidentiality more apparent than in the activities of hospital internal review committees (e.g., peer review, credentials, quality assurance). These committees perform a vital function by monitoring the quality of medical services and by ensuring that such services are rendered by competent practitioners in accordance with current medical standards. Consider, however, the impact on the jury in a malpractice action if a lawyer introduces a peer review report that is critical of the way a physician handled a previous emergency in a similar case. The report could be used to create a presumption of negligence — where actually none may have occurred.

Common Law Privilege

Recognizing the importance of the free exchange of information during these proceedings, some courts, such as those in *Bredice v Doctor's Hospital, Inc.* and *Dade County Medical Society v Hlis*,[1] acted early to adopt a common law privilege protecting medical review and quality assurance documents. Discovery of certain hospital and professional review documents was not allowed on the grounds that the public policy concern of preserving the freedom and candor of these activities outweighed any individual's right of access to such information.

Today, every state has codified the common law privilege articulated in *Bredice* and *Dade County* and prevents (or at least limits) the discoverability of documents arising from various review committee activities. Unfortunately, there is little consistency among the state statutes enacted, and their scope varies greatly from state to state.

Some are quite broad, such as the Illinois Medical Studies Act,[2] and protect a range of activities and data arising out of patient care audits, medical care evaluation, and utilization review, in addition to the work of hospital and medical staff committees performing similar functions. On the other hand, New Jersey's statute is more circumscribed and grants privileged status only to the data and information of utilization review committees.[3]

Adding to the confusion is the fact that, because it is not possible to categorize every type of information or document that might fall within the statutory privilege, most statutes refer to the protected activities and information in broad, often ambiguous terms. In those cases, the statutes themselves have become the subject of litigation as courts attempt to define their parameters. The ever-evolving body of case law that has developed in this area has made these statutes a moving target whose scope has been dramatically expanded or restricted depending on judicial interpretation.

Take, for example, the New Jersey statute that protects utilization review committee activities. A 1975 case held that a hospital's medical records and audit, tissue, and infection control committees did not perform a utilization review function and were thus denied privileged status.[4] However, a more recent case in that jurisdiction, noting the limitation of the statute, applied a common law public policy approach and granted privileged status to the evaluations and opinions of peer review committees.[5] A 1986 federal court decision in Kansas held that the JCAHO activities served a peer review function and, therefore, fell within the statutory protections afforded to peer review committee proceedings in that state.[6] Some courts have even gone so far as to deny access by state medical boards to physician peer review records afforded statutory privileged status.[7] Conversely, the Kentucky Supreme Court, in 1989, held that, despite the state's seemingly broad statutory protection of hospital committee proceedings, the records of peer review committees were discoverable by plaintiffs in medical malpractice actions.[8]

Applicability to Individuals

Most nondiscovery statutes afford protection only to the activities and proceedings of bona fide hospital or medical staff committees. As a result, it is questionable whether the activities of a risk manager, physician, or other individual or group acting independently (rather than as a member of a hospital's quality assurance or other standing committee) would qualify for statutory protection. A Pennsylvania court recently held that the report of an ad hoc committee formed to investigate an incident of patient violence was not privileged because the group did not serve an ongoing quality assessment/assurance function.[9] In states where the protection is afforded to committee activities only, individuals performing a risk management or quality assurance function should be made members of "protected" committees or should, at least, carry out their duties at the direction of such committees. In this way, the investigative findings will more likely be deemed as part of the bona fide quality control system and, therefore, be protected[10] from discovery.

Scope of Privilege

Equally important as the nature of the documents to be protected by a nondiscovery statute is the extent of the statute's protection. Some statutes offer an absolute privilege against discovery.[11] In other words, protected documents cannot be discovered under any circumstances.

In other jurisdictions, however, legislatures have determined that the need for confidentiality may not always supersede an individual's right of access. They have enacted statutes affording a limited or qualified privileged status to hospital committee documents. Typical among these statues is the Illinois Medical Studies Act,[2] which allows access to peer review documents in cases involving the granting or denial of clinical privileges to a practitioner:

> All information, interviews, reports, statements, memoranda or other data . . . shall be privileged, strictly confidential . . . except that in any hospital proceeding to decide upon a physician's staff privileges, or in any judicial review thereof, the claim of confidentiality shall not be invoked to deny such physician access to or use of data upon which a decision was based.[12]

Many states allow discovery of otherwise privileged documents in cases involving physician credentialing, particularly if such cases allege antitrust or discrimination on the part of the hospital or its committee members.

Federal Laws

In certain circumstances, federal law may override the privilege afforded by a state statute. In one notable example, *Robinson v Magovern*, a Pennsylvania Federal Court overruled that state's statute, which afforded an absolute privileged status for hospital peer review documents.[13] In this case, a federal antitrust action was brought by a physician who had been denied medical staff privileges. The court ruled (relying on federal laws governing evidence) that the need to obtain relevant information

superseded the protections afforded by state law. A Kansas Federal Court, also relying on the federal rules, similarly refused to allow the peer review process to shield behaviors allegedly conducted in violation of federal antitrust laws.[14]

Federal investigations of alleged violations of Medicare Medicaid law (e.g., conditions of participation, billing irregularities) most likely will not be subject to local statutes regarding privilege and confidentiality. It is quite possible that hospitals will be required to furnish confidential data, such as peer review and quality assurance records, as part of any such investigation. Given the federal government's recent emphasis on ferreting out health care fraud, such investigations and requests for information will likely proliferate.

There is yet another federal statute that is of particular importance to emergency medicine. The Emergency Medical Treatment and Active Labor Act (EMTALA) is a law that imposes stringent examination and treatment obligations on hospital emergency departments.[15] Organizations violating EMTALA may find themselves not only party to personal injury lawsuits brought by injured patients, but also party to administrative proceedings that could lead to substantial fines or even exclusion from the Medicare and Medicaid programs.

As part of its evaluation of a suspected EMTALA violation, investigators conduct an on-site investigation, usually unannounced, and ask to see a variety of emergency department and hospital records including, without limitation, the following:

- Emergency department log
- Representative sample of patient records
- Policy and procedure manuals
- Medical staff, emergency department, and quality assurance meeting minutes
- Quality assurance plan
- Selected credentials files

It is doubtful that a hospital will be able to rely on its local privilege laws to block federal investigators' access to these documents.

Even though there is a common law presumption that the records of hospital internal review committees are protected from discovery, hospital personnel must recognize that this presumption is rebutted by statutory and judicially established limits. Health care staff and hospitals must understand the full extent of their states' protections rather than assume, perhaps erroneously, that a privileged status exists. Organizations are well advised to consult with counsel to determine not only the extent of privilege granted in their respective jurisdiction, but also how best to respond to requests for records and data in situations where privilege may not apply.

Incident Reports

Incident reports are generally more discoverable than are review committee reports. One of the principal reasons for this is that incident reports usually are not specified as protected documents in nondiscovery statutes. In addition, because they are not typically generated by a standing committee, they will generally not qualify as protected committee documents.

If, however, the applicable state law expressly includes incident reports or does not require a document to be generated by a committee in order to qualify for privileged status, then a statutory privilege may apply. This is also true if the statute in question is so broadly drafted as to protect any document prepared in conjunction with the assessment of patient care services at a hospital.

Also, in some jurisdictions it may be possible to characterize an incident report as an attorney's work product or as subject to the attorney-client privilege, thereby protecting it from discovery. If available at all, however, the attorney-client or attorney work-product privilege will most likely apply only if the incident report is given to the hospital's attorney in conjunction with a claim pending against the hospital. (Note, however, that the attorney-client privilege may not be available in situations where an attorney is functioning as a claims investigator.)

On the other hand, incident reports prepared as a matter of course, rather than in response to an asserted or threatened claim, are not likely to be protected.[16] This is especially true if the reports are distributed among various hospital personnel. Furthermore, certain courts, notably those in Colorado and Texas, have permitted the discovery of investigative reports prepared by risk managers and investigators when the investigations took place before a claim was actually asserted or, at least, seriously threatened.[17]

The discoverability of incident and investigative reports, like those created by hospital internal review committees, varies depending on local law and judicial interpretation. Those responsible for such reports should consult with local counsel to determine what, if any, privilege may be available for these documents. If it is determined that such reports could be privileged if prepared a certain way or if sent to a certain individual (e.g., hospital attorney), then the necessary steps should be taken to ensure that the report falls within the available protections.

Given the likelihood of discovery, incident reports should be used judiciously. Take, for example, a situation in which an elderly patient falls out of bed and fractures her hip. The nurse caring for the patient insists that all bed rails were up when she last checked the patient. Imagine the impact on a jury, however, of an incident report prepared a few days earlier citing the nurse for leaving the patient unattended with the bed rails down. Although the patient suffered no harm, the report was prepared to call the nurse's attention to unsafe practice. If such a report is then presented to a jury, it will likely ensure a damage award in a negligence action. What was intended as a learning tool became a smoking gun.

Safeguarding Privileged Status

Once it has been determined that a particular document qualifies for privileged status, health care administrators and staff must follow certain safeguards to avoid its inadvertent disclosure. Even though a document may be privileged, inappropriate handling or dissemination may be interpreted as a waiver of the privilege and could result in its discoverability.

Also, staff must keep in mind that the privileged status of a particular document may not be immediately apparent or ascertainable. Therefore, hospital personnel should identify not only those documents that are clearly privileged but also those that are potentially privileged (i.e., items that may or may not be privileged depending on further research, statutory interpretation, or court ruling). The same safeguards that staff apply to clearly privileged documents should also be used in the handling and preparation of those that may become privileged.

In some instances, even privileged documents will often be the target of an attorney's request for production or subpoena. Strict compliance with the request may lead to the inappropriate disclosure of privileged information. Every organization should, therefore, have in place a system that carefully evaluates the validity and appropriateness of subpoenas and all third-party requests for information.

Preparation and Handling of Documents

The first step in protecting the privileged status of a document is to make sure it is properly prepared and identified so that it qualifies for the privilege. Assume, for example, that the state extends privileged status to quality assurance committee records. All of the committee's documents should be clearly identified with the committee name in order to qualify them for the privilege. They also should be marked confidential and should be kept in a locked cabinet or drawer, separated from other nonconfidential reports and documents. Access to the cabinet should be limited to the committee chair or other appropriate individual. Staff must be aware, however, that simply delivering or presenting an otherwise nonprivileged report to a committee whose activities are protected will generally not be enough to confer privileged status on the document presented. The document must have a more tangible link to the work or purpose of the committee.

Dissemination of Confidential Information

To the extent possible, copies of privileged and potentially privileged information should be given only to individuals with a legitimate "need to know." For example, any examination of privileged documents by committee members must be done in a way that preserves the privilege afforded to the documents. If meeting minutes are to be circulated to committee members for review prior to a meeting, the minutes should be hand-delivered or sent in sealed envelopes clearly marked confidential. It is preferable, however, not to distribute such documents until the meeting actually takes place. Following the meeting, all copies should be collected and destroyed so that only the original remains for the records.

When other persons or entities (e.g., hospital administrator or the board of directors) must be apprised of committee activities, it is preferable to present a summary report rather than to furnish duplicate copies of minutes or other committee documents. Insofar as possible, the report should not identify specific physicians, nurses, or patients.

A report about the activities of the quality assurance committee could note, for example, that the committee identified a problem with medication errors. It could further note that the committee had isolated the unit or the individual involved with the errors and had identified steps for remedial action. The report should not cite (unless otherwise necessary) the particular unit, hospital staff member, or patient involved in the incident.

The minutes of the board meeting (or meeting of any other group to which a committee report is presented) should note that a report was presented and should contain general information concerning the report contents. In no circumstances, however, should the minutes contain a copy or verbatim transcript of protected committee minutes or reports.

The Impact of Managed Care

As hospitals seek to associate with managed care organizations and third-party payers, they are frequently asked to prepare proposals outlining detailed information about hospital operations, particularly the quality of its patient care services. Requests for information about quality initiatives, clinical outcomes and other performance data, loss history, pending claims, litigation, and even case reserves are not uncommon. Individuals asked to provide information in response to these requests must consider carefully the extent to which such information may be privileged and the impact of its release on such privileged status.

Additionally, it is not uncommon for representatives from third-party payers to perform on-site review of patient records to verify services or to establish a care plan for a seriously ill or injured individual. Care must be taken to ensure both the identity of these reviewers and the patient's authorization for the review. Equally important, however, is the scope of the review. These individuals should not be given access to incident or internal committee reports, even if the reports contain insignificant information about the patient, the patient's condition, or prognosis.

A Final Caveat

Documents considered privileged today may become discoverable at some future date. Therefore, staff must exercise great care so that no privileged or potentially privileged document contains any information that, if discovered, would unnecessarily compromise the hospital or its committee members.

Committee discussions, particularly those involving peer review and credentialing matters, must be conducted and recorded in a professional manner. Reports should contain only objective data and a thoughtful analysis of the situation at hand. Committee meeting minutes should reflect what was done and what was decided at the meeting, not necessarily what was said. Peer review and credentialing committees must focus exclusively on a practitioner's performance, qualifications, and experience. Extraneous discussions regarding ethnic background, religion, race, sex, or the effect of an individual's practice on the economic interests of other practitioners on the hospital's medical staff are highly prejudicial and must be avoided.

Key Points and Conclusion

The issue of privilege as it relates to hospital committee and risk management documents is complex and ever changing. Those responsible for handling or collecting such information must consult with local counsel to determine what protections, if any, are available in a particular jurisdiction. Once it has been determined that a privilege does exist, hospital staff must take appropriate measures to safeguard the privilege.

However, because there will always be an element of uncertainty concerning the discoverability of risk management and related information, hospital personnel are well advised to treat all such information as privileged, while assuming for purposes of content that it will be discoverable. In this way, any privilege that may exist will be preserved. At the same time, if discovery is ever allowed, the staff will have created a good record. The hospital and its committee members will not be compromised by inappropriate or inflammatory statements in the record.

Finally, the emergency department staff must remember that the goal of hospital investigative and risk management activities is the promotion and maintenance of proper patient care. The reports and information prepared by individuals and committees carrying out such activities should reflect this goal.

The following list of do's and don'ts may be used as guidelines for dealing with confidential information and protecting it from discovery.

Do

- Work with local counsel to determine the scope and extent of state protections against discovery.

- Be aware of new laws or court cases that may affect such protections.
- Identify those documents that are privileged, potentially privileged, and clearly not privileged.
- Prepare and identify committee reports and other documents so that they fall within the protection of applicable nondiscovery statutes.
- Clearly label privileged or potentially privileged documents as confidential.
- Secure confidential materials in a locked cabinet.
- Limit access to confidential documents.
- Circulate committee reports and minutes to committee members only.
- Destroy extra copies of confidential documents after use.
- Provide directors with an executive summary rather than copies of committee minutes or reports.
- Establish protocols for handling requests for information, including subpoenas, from outside sources.

Don't

- Assume that all hospital committee reports will be automatically protected from discovery.
- Assume that incident reports are nondiscoverable.
- Forget to check the current status of laws governing discovery in one's state.
- Waive privileged status by inappropriate handling or inadvertent disclosure of confidential documents.
- Store confidential documents with those that are discoverable.
- Give copies of confidential documents to anyone who does not have a legitimate need for them.
- Circulate confidential documents through interoffice mail. If documents must be circulated, use a sealed envelope marked confidential.
- Leave copies of confidential documents lying around in offices or meeting rooms.
- Attach copies of privileged documents to reports that are discoverable.
- Include inflammatory or prejudicial remarks in committee discussions, reports, or minutes.
- Automatically comply with a subpoena before determining its validity and whether the documents requested are discoverable.

References

1. *Bredice v Doctor's Hospital, Inc.*, 50 FRD 249 (DDL 1970) and *Dade County Medical Society v Hlis*, 372 S2d (Fla App 1979).

2. 735 Ill Comp Stat Ann §5/8-2102 and 2102.

3. NJ Stat §2A:84A-22.8

4. *Young v King*, 344 A2d 792 (NJ Super Ct Law Div 1975).

5. *Bundy v Sinopoli*, 580 A2d 1101 (NJ Super Ct 1990).

6. *Fretz v Keltner*, 109 FRD 303 (D Kan 1986).

7. *Commonwealth v Choate – Symmes Health Service*, KNC 545 NE2d 116 (Mass 1989) and In Re: Petition of Attorney General, 369 NW 2d 826.

8. *Sweasy v King's Daughters Memorial Hospital*, 771 SW2d 812 (Ky Sup Ct 1989).

9. *Hankinson v Threshold, Inc.*, No. 1482 of 1992 (Pa Ct of Common Pleas, Westmoreland County, August 19, 1992).

10. *Flannery v Lin*, 531 NE2d 403 (Ill App Ct 1988).

11. Pa Stat Ann, tit 63, §§425.2 and 425.4 (Purdon).

12. 735 Ill Comp Stat Ann §5/2-2102

13. *Robinson v Magovern*, 83 FRD 79 (WD Pa 1979).

14. *Jiricko v Coffeyville Memorial Hospital Medical Center*, 700 F Supp 155a (D Kan 1988).

15. 42 USCS §1395DD (1995).

16. *John C. Lincoln Hospital and Health Center v Superior Court in and for County of Maricopa*, 768 P2d 188 (App 1929).

17. *National Farmers Union Property and Casualty Co. v District Court*, 718 P2d 1044 (Colo 1986); *Stringer v Eleventh Circuit Court of Appeals*, 720 SW2d 801 (Tex SC 1986); and *Morris v Texas Employers Insurance Association*, 759 SW2d 14 (Tex App 1988).

Additional Reading

Pozgar GD. *Legal Aspects of Health Care Administration*. 5th ed. Rockville, Md: Aspen Publishers; 1993:284-287.

Southwick AF. Peer review of professional practice. In: *The Law of Hospital and Health Care Administration*. 2nd ed. Health Administration Press; 1988:626-65.

Toyer GT, Salman SL, eds. Hospital law: theory and application. In: *Handbook of Health Care Risk Management*. Rockville, Md: Aspen Publishers; 1986:133-137.

Younger PA, ed. Medical records. In: *Hospital Law Manual: Attorney's Volume IIA*. Rockville, Md: Aspen Publishers; 1986:67-107.

Chapter 32

Handling and Securing Evidence

Michael T. Rapp, MD, JD, FACEP

The work of emergency physicians routinely includes making and documenting observations, collecting specimens, and ordering tests. All of these activities constitute collection of evidence, even though it may not be collected in contemplation of use in a court proceeding. In addition, both the victims of crime and its perpetrators come to the emergency department specifically for the collection and documentation of evidence.

Emergency physicians may be asked or even subpoenaed to appear in court to testify about evidence they have collected. Because of this, they need to know their legal rights and obligations and understand the proper methods of handling and securing evidence. For example, the physician's duty of confidentiality to the patient often is in conflict with efforts of police officers to obtain evidence to support potential criminal charges. The physician's duty of confidentiality does have limits and can be overridden by other societal obligations, including statutory requirements to report conduct, medical conditions, or injuries that may prompt a criminal investigation or possibly lead to state intervention to protect the victim.

Case Studies

1

A man involved in an automobile collision is brought to the emergency department for evaluation. During the examination, he admits to the emergency physician that he had had sever-al drinks shortly before getting in his car. The physical findings are consistent with alcohol intoxication, and the physician concludes that the patient is still intoxicated. A police officer says to the physician: "Is this guy drunk? Did he tell you he'd been drinking?" What is the physician's appropriate response?

2

A young woman comes to the emergency department and alleges that she has been raped within the past few hours. She refuses to contact the police, however, and says that she does not intend to make a report or seek to have the assailant prosecuted. The emergency physician knows that the patient has information that might help identify the assailant. How should the emergency physician proceed?

3

A 2-year-old boy is brought to the emergency department by his mother because of redness on the back of his hand. The mother offers no explanation for how the injury occurred, but simply that the child was playing and started crying. The emergency physician notices that the red lines on the back of the child's hand are similar to the size of an adult's fingers. The mother is well dressed, and the child appears healthy and happy. When confronted with the physician's suspicions that the redness represents a handprint, she remains pleasant and cooperative but denies that this occurred. The physician sees on the chart that she and her husband are both attorneys. Should the case be reported to the state authorities?

4

As part of a quality assurance program in a hospital that has been designated as a trauma center, the emergency department videotapes each trauma code. Later, the tape is reviewed in an effort to evaluate and improve the trauma care. One particular trauma patient admits to the staff that he killed another person during the fight that prompted his visit to the emergency department. This admission occurs before the police arrive. The police learn that a "confession" was made and recorded on videotape and ask that the tape be turned over to them. The hospital administration agrees, but the emergency personnel object on the grounds that the entire tape constitutes quality assurance material and should not be available to the police. The local prosecutor issues a subpoena for the videotape. Is it necessary to comply with the subpoena? Is the statement of the patient admissible in a criminal proceeding for murder?

Criminal Law

There are several fundamental differences between criminal law and civil law. Civil law is designed to offer restitution to a complaining party through a monetary award or injunctive relief that orders some specific action to be carried out. Criminal law is intended to punish the guilty defendant through fine or imprisonment. Because criminal law involves imposing punishment that deprives a person of liberty or property or both, a variety of protections and safeguards are built into the process to prevent an unjust outcome.

One example of the differences between criminal law and civil law is the standard of proof required. To support a verdict under civil law, a jury need find only that the "preponderance of the evidence" favors the claims made by the plaintiff. Under criminal law, however, the state is required to prove its case "beyond a reasonable doubt."[1]

Evidentiary rules are essentially the same for both criminal and civil conduct. However, the more demanding standard of proof in criminal law can make the exclusion of evidence that does not meet the evidentiary rule more critical to the outcome than in a civil case.[1] In addition, criminal cases tend to require a more strict adherence to evidentiary rules. This fact makes it even more important that emergency physi-

cians understand and comply with the rules of proper handling of evidence.

Real Evidence and Chain of Custody

Evidence, to paraphrase *Black's Law Dictionary*, is "proof" or "probative matter" presented at trial through testimony, records, documents, or concrete objects to support inferences pertinent to the issues in a trial.[2] A system of rules has developed that governs what materials may constitute evidence. Fundamentally, all rules of evidence are designed to keep out those items that are not sufficiently reliable to be considered by the jury or that may confuse or mislead the jury and thus outweigh their probative value.

Real evidence consists of physical or tangible items that in themselves can be used to infer guilt or innocence (e.g., a gun in a murder case). Special rules exist for the handling of real evidence because of the need to establish authenticity. It must be shown that the object offered in evidence is actually involved in the case and has not been altered.[3]

Some types of real evidence, such as a weapon, can be readily authenticated. It might be identified by serial number or by placing an initial on the weapon. Its basic characteristics prevent it from being altered. However, much of the evidence with which emergency physicians deal cannot be readily established as unique, and the evidence can be easily altered. Specimens obtained in the course of a rape examination are an obvious example. In view of this, emergency staff and their attorneys must assure the court that the results of the analysis of such evidence come from the specimens actually taken during the course of the examination and that the specimens were not altered. Otherwise, the court will not accept such material in evidence. The primary method of making this assurance is through a chain of custody.

A chain of custody consists of tracing who has handled or taken charge of the evidence from the time it was first obtained. This process demonstrates continuous possession of the object and that the object remained in substantially the same condition during each custodian's possession. As described by the Supreme Court of Virginia, "[t]he practicalities of proof do not require the Commonwealth to negate or exclude every possibility of substitution, alteration, or tampering. All that is necessary to establish a chain of custody is that the evidence afford reasonable assurance that it is the same and in the same condition as [it was] when first obtained."[4]

If the chain of custody cannot be shown, the evidence is subject to exclusion. For example, in *Robinson v Commonwealth*,[5] a sexual assault case in Virginia, the admission of the woman's panties and blouse was excluded because the prosecution could not document a chain of custody of the clothing from the time they were taken from the victim at the hospital until delivery to the laboratory for analysis. The court concluded that there was a fair probability that the items could have been contaminated. Therefore, they were not reliable as a source of scientific analysis, and the court excluded the evidence.

Safeguarding Physical Evidence

There are some practical suggestions that emergency department personnel should bear in mind when dealing with physical evidence. First of all, procedures should be developed to address such basic issues as sealing and marking evidence, keeping the chain of custody short, and keeping track of the transfer of items between custodians.[6]

One method to preserve common types of physical evidence in a legally acceptable manner is to place them in bags and label each bag with the patient's name and the date, then seal them and place the signature of the collector on each bag. Emergency department staff can then turn over the collected items, such as clothing, bullets, blood stains, and other small objects, to police personnel. The staff should obtain a receipt to document the name of the person who collected the evidence, the name of the person who received the evidence, and the signature of both, with date and time.[7] Another idea is to ask a local prosecutor to help the emergency department develop and establish procedures for handling criminal evidence. The prosecutor has a vested interest in making sure that evidence is handled properly.

Because of the need for consistency in handling evidence, states often set up specific procedures for collecting evidence, such as obtaining blood alcohol levels. Emergency physicians must become familiar with the specific procedures in their states. The procedures in Virginia, for example, include such details as specifying the qualifications of the person drawing the blood, describing the way the skin should be cleansed (which excludes anything containing alcohol), dividing the blood sample into two vials, and describing how each is to be handled. This procedure includes offering the person charged with a crime the opportunity to have the blood analyzed by a laboratory of his choice.[8]

The following chain of custody principles should be kept in mind by all emergency staff:

- Real evidence not unique or identifiable on its face requires chain of custody to establish its authenticity.
- Chain of custody must trace physical custody and show that the item remained essentially unchanged.
- Specimens that are alterable should be sealed and the container initialed.
- Receipts to identify each change of custodianship, including the giving and receiving parties, the date and the time, and the nature of the item, should be documented.

Patient Consent

The patient observations, testing, and treatment performed in an emergency department are normally done with either explicit or implied patient consent. At times, however, emergency physicians may be asked by the police to collect evidence without a patient's consent. Examples of recurring situations are removing drugs from a patient's stomach through a nasogastric tube, drawing blood alcohol tests, and removing a bullet from under the skin.

The extent to which evidence may be used in court depends not specifically on patient consent for what the physician has done but rather on the rules of evidence. For admission into evidence, these rules principally require relevance of the evidence to the proceeding, reliability, and the absence of any privilege, such as the physician-patient privilege. When evidence is obtained over the objection of the patient, the issue arises whether the protection of the Fourth Amendment to the U.S. Constitution has been violated. The Fourth Amendment prohibits unreasonable search and seizure by the state. Any evidence obtained in violation of the Fourth Amendment will be suppressed and will not be admissible in any criminal proceeding against the patient.

With regard to the Fourth Amendment, the U.S. Supreme Court has considered several cases that are relevant to emergency medicine. In a 1950s case, *Rochin v California*,[9] Los Angeles County sheriffs forced their way into the defendant's room because they suspected him of selling narcotics. Rochin grabbed certain capsules and swallowed them. The capsules were later forcibly extracted from his stomach through the use of a tube and an emetic, and the capsules were determined to be morphine. Finding these methods to obtain evidence as those that "shock the conscience," the Supreme Court found the Fourth Amendment violated and suppressed the evidence. In *Breithaupt v Abraham*,[10] a police officer ordered an emergency physician to draw a blood sample on an unconscious patient who had been involved in a motor vehicle collision that caused the death of other parties. The court sustained the police conduct. Finding no coercion or brutality and that venipuncture was a routine procedure, the court ruled that no violation of the Fourth Amendment had occurred. In *Schmerber v California*,[11] the court upheld the legality of a physician obtaining a blood specimen from a conscious patient over that patient's objection (with his attorney present) in a situation where the defendant was the only injured party. Again, noting that the blood was taken in a professional manner and constituted a relatively minor intrusion in bodily integrity, the Court refused to suppress the blood alcohol test and upheld the charge of driving under the influence of alcohol.

These Supreme Court cases indicate that blood alcohol levels obtained at the direction of the police without a search warrant and despite the objection of the patient can still be admitted into evidence. This is true provided the venipuncture is done in a professional manner without the active resistance of the patient. These cases, however, do not deal specifically with the issue of potential liability of the physician for performing the venipuncture itself. The Fourth Amendment regulates conduct of the state and therefore the police, not the physician. Moreover, even though today states typically have implied consent laws, whereby the operator of a motor vehicle impliedly gives consent to a blood alcohol test, this consent relates to the use of the evidence in potential criminal proceedings. It does not imply in law the consent that physicians need to perform a medical procedure.

For the physician, the risk of performing a venipuncture over the objection of the patient is liability for committing a battery. Under the civil law, "battery" refers simply to any touching without consent. Performing a venipuncture over the objection of the patient would clearly fall within the definition of a battery. The fact that the physician performed the test at the request of the police and that obtaining the test was not found to be an unreasonable search under the Fourth Amendment would not provide specific immunity to the physician in the event of a lawsuit for battery.

When an emergency physician is asked by the police to perform a venipuncture or other procedure to obtain evidence, the extent of a patient's active resistance is an important factor. If the patient strongly resists, the physician should not perform the procedure. If the patient objects but does not resist, the physician's best approach would still be to refuse to perform the procedure without the patient's actual and written consent. Exceptions to this recommendation are an actual court order mandating that the physician perform the procedure and specific immunity provided by statute.[12]

Reporting Requirements and Confidentiality

The relationship between a physician and a patient is private and confidential. Physicians are not at liberty to divulge information without the permission of the patient. This confidentiality is protected by both a common law (non-statutory) right to privacy[13] and by the physician-patient privilege.[1] Divulging confidential information without authorization constitutes a violation of the right to privacy, a tort (civil wrong), which is enforced by giving the patient grounds for a lawsuit against the physician. The physician-patient privilege, on the other hand, is an evidentiary privilege. That is, information obtained in the physician-patient relationship is "privileged," and the physician cannot be compelled nor permitted to disclose it, typically in a court proceeding. Thus, the concept of privilege can prevent information obtained within the physician-patient relationship from being used against the patient.

However, the confidentiality of the physician-patient relationship does have its limits. These include the common law duty to warn certain third parties of threats or risks to them even though learned within the physician-patient relationship (see Chapter 28, "Duty to Warn Third Parties"). In addition, other duties refer to specific statutory reporting obligations of physicians.

The physician-patient privilege is a creature of statute or court rule and not a privilege recognized at common law. Its limitations, therefore, are those of the statute or court rule in each state that creates the privilege. Therefore, emergency physicians should be aware of the scope of the physician-patient privilege within their states. Some states find the effect of the privilege to be rather narrow. In Virginia, for example, the physician-patient privilege does not apply to criminal cases, but only to civil cases. This allows confidential medical information to be subpoenaed for a criminal proceeding and requires it to be disclosed over the objection of the patient.

Other states apply the physician-patient privilege more broadly. In Illinois, for example, the relevant statute provides that: "[n]o physician or surgeon shall be permitted to disclose any information he or she may have acquired in attending any patient in a professional character, necessary to enable him or her professionally to serve the patient [with certain specific exceptions]."[14] For example, in one case,[15] a patient was charged with several criminal drug offenses on the basis of illegal drugs discovered by hospital personnel during medical treatment. Hospital personnel, in removing the patient's clothes to catheterize him, with police not present, discovered a small bag inside the defendant's underwear that apparently contained marijuana. They later turned the bag over to the police. During the trial, however, the physician-patient privilege was held to require that the evidence be suppressed.

In an analogous New Mexico case,[16] the appellate court suppressed a blood alcohol test. A patient involved in a motorcycle collision was taken to a hospital, where he refused the police officer's request for a blood alcohol test. However, a blood alcohol level was taken for medical reasons. A police officer asked about the results from an emergency department nurse, who showed him the results to be 0.104. Subsequently, the test result was subpoenaed and sought to be introduced to support a conviction for driving while intoxicated. Holding that the physician-patient privilege did apply, the court found the blood alcohol test results to be a confidential communication (information or knowledge gained by observation and personal examination of the patient), made for the purpose of diagnosis or treatment of the patient's physical, mental, or emotional condition. Therefore, by virtue of the rule of physician-patient privilege, it was inadmissible as evidence.

Finally, the obligations of physician confidentiality are limited by reporting statutes that require physicians to report certain types of information to public officials and law enforcement agencies despite their being learned in the physician-patient relationship. These include child abuse, elder abuse, communicable diseases, and in some states, spousal abuse (see Chapter 55, "Family Violence").

Following are examples of common emergency department encounters and suggestions for handling them appropriately.

Sexual Assault Investigation Report

The emergency physician must first obtain consent to perform a sexual assault examination and other medical-legal examinations involving adults. The information should be kept confidential. The physician should document consent, including permission to obtain a history and physical and pelvic examinations, to take specimens for laboratory examination, to take photographs (if necessary), to render treatment deemed necessary, to retain articles of clothing for evidence, and to release the information to the proper police authorities.[17]

When evaluating a patient who has allegedly been sexually assaulted, the first portion of the evaluation involves taking the history. (Details of what historical information should be obtained are available elsewhere.[17]) This history must be documented carefully. Although statements made by the victim can be introduced by the prosecution, they can also be used by the defense to defeat the prosecution. Make sure that all statements by the victim are recorded accurately.

In terms of the physical examination, the emergency physician should record the patient's general demeanor and carefully describe and document any evidence of bruising or other physical injury. Photographs may be taken, but this is probably best left to the police.

All states have procedures for handling sexual assault investigations.[1] The types of specimens required are similar but may differ slightly from state to state. Maintain the chain of custody with these materials. One method to keep the chain of custody as short as possible is to have one nurse involved in the process from start to finish. The nurse can collect specimens, such as hair samples and swabs, herself and assist the physician in the collection of samples that require a physician's participation.

If one nurse handles all the specimens, labels them, places them in a container, seals it, and hands it to the police officer, the chain of custody, at least in the hospital, can be established by one person. If the nurse also documents these steps on the medical report, the nurse may not need to appear in court at all, as the chain of custody and authenticity of the evidence will have been clearly established. The parties may stipulate in court that the requirements were met.

Child Abuse Report

The role of the physician in preserving evidence in child abuse cases can be very important. Not only should physical findings that indicate abuse be documented (and in the case of sexual abuse appropriate specimens obtained for analysis), but also verbal statements (evidence) should be documented.

In Virginia, for example, the process of collecting evidence is facilitated by a statute that gives the reporting individual the authority to talk with the child or sibling without the consent of the parent and to take photographs or x-rays without consent. Because the child may have difficulty being an effective witness in court, the Virginia statute provides for the introduction into evidence of the child's out-of-court statements in certain limited situations that are shown to possess particular guarantees of trustworthiness and reliability. The statements made to the physician describing abuse or identifying the abuser may assume extraordinary importance. For this reason, the physician should be careful to record the statements precisely and to note any factors that may help make the child's statements admissible either under state statutes or evidentiary rules.

An example of a traditional exception to the hearsay rule is statements made as "excited utterances" in response to traumatic events. The physician or nurse must carefully document such factors as the emotional state of the child, spontaneity of the statements, and the proximity in time to any abusive events. This information can be critical to getting out-of-court statements admitted as evidence.

The evaluation of a child for abuse presents different problems than for adults. The emergency physician may be less experienced in dealing with children and feel less comfortable in evaluating them for abuse, particularly if a court appearance is anticipated. Nevertheless, the medical evaluation can be essential in determining whether abuse has occurred.[18]

The hospital should have a protocol that addresses not only the patient's need for medical evaluation, but also the capabilities and roles of the emergency department and its staff. It may be preferable, for example, to limit the role of the emergency department to those aspects of the evaluation where timeliness is essential, rather than necessarily providing the definitive medical-legal report. This is particularly true when sexual abuse is suspected. Development of a protocol should include input from the social service agency responsible for investigating child abuse cases and from other pertinent medical staff departments, such as pediatrics and gynecology.

The emergency physician must be sure that the legally required notification of suspected child abuse is done. Occasionally, this step may be overlooked. For example, laboratory test results may be delayed that show the presence of a sexually transmitted disease in a child. Or, the police may bring a child in for evaluation of suspected abuse and the emergency staff may falsely assume that a report has already been made. Procedures should be developed to avoid such lapses.

As for history-taking, an important indicator of the possibility of abuse is a parent's or guardian's explanation that is inconsistent with the nature of the injury, or multiple explanations from different family members for the same injury. Accurate and detailed documentation of the explanations for suspicious injuries is very important. When the child provides information, exceptions to evidentiary rules may allow the child's statements to the physician to be considered at the hearing. To the extent possible, record the child's statements verbatim. Indicate in whose presence the child's statements are made. Reactions of the parent, or any effort of the parent to limit the child's history, are also noteworthy.

When conducting the physical examination, completeness is the watchword. Search for injuries beyond those suspected or obvious. The value of taking photographs cannot be overemphasized for documenting bruises or other visible injuries.

Child Sexual Abuse Report

Cases involving the sexual abuse of children can be among the most difficult to document, report, and prove.[19-23] The child may be reluctant to reveal such abuse or to offer any details. The occurrences may even be so strange that they are difficult for the examiner to believe.

Because of the nature of the evaluation, the

examiner must establish rapport with the child. This involves obtaining the history in a non-threatening environment. The examination must involve the cooperation of the child and should never be forced.[24]

The emergency department should determine which part of the evaluation will be performed by the emergency physician and which parts by other physicians. Usually, the emergency physician must perform a preliminary examination to look for signs of recent sexual abuse or other temporary findings, such as abrasions, bruises, redness, infection, or dried semen. This is particularly important because a child will hesitate to reveal all of the events that have occurred. On the other hand, when the examination is directed to more subtle signs of chronic sexual abuse, it may be better to defer to a gynecologist who has particular expertise in such evaluations.

A complete examination is important because the history often does not reveal the extent of the sexual abuse. Even when the history indicates that, for example, only vaginal contact has occurred, swabs should not be limited to the vaginal area but should also include rectal and oral cavities. Although completeness is essential, it should not be forceful. At times, general anesthesia or sedation needs to be considered to allow for the complete examination required.

Case Discussions

1

Because the physician-patient relationship is confidential, the physician in this case was not free to divulge such information as the patient's admission that he had been drinking or the physician's own conclusion that the patient was intoxicated. However, refusal to give such information to a police officer can create conflict with the police. Police officers can be quite insistent on obtaining information and may even suggest that the physician is under some obligation to provide it.

Occasionally, there will be a statutory obligation that overrides the general obligation of confidentiality, most commonly a reporting statute. But when there is no exception to the general principle of confidentiality known to the physician, the police officer should be asked to identify what the obligation is and even to provide a copy of the statute overriding confidentiality.

In some instances, the physician may be required to provide information in court, if subpoenaed. This would occur when the physician-patient privilege does not apply, as in a criminal case. However, the confidentiality obligation physicians owe to their patients is not necessarily identical to the physician-patient privilege. Even though the physician can be required to divulge the confidential information once subpoenaed during the prosecution of an actual case, that case cannot arise unless there are grounds to bring charges, and the preliminary procedures are satisfied. This situation is quite different from revealing confidential information before there are grounds for charging the patient with any crime and before the case actually gets to court.

As a general rule, therefore, the physician should courteously but firmly decline to give police officers any more than the most general information on patients. This could include telling officers whether the patient is to be admitted or released from the hospital and what the patient's general condition is.

2

A preliminary medical evaluation to identify and treat any injuries must be performed regardless of the victim's intention to report the crime. The decision whether to report a criminal act must be left to the victim in most cases. The exception is when there is a specific reporting statute covering, for example, child abuse or elder abuse or cases involving legal disabilities. When a minor is involved, the decision generally is left to the parents. If the patient is insane or mentally infirm, the decision is left to the next of kin or legal guardian.

The refusal of a competent adult to report a sexual assault at the time of examination can result in a complex situation for the emergency physician. On one hand, evidence must be collected at the time of the examination if prosecution is ever to be attempted. Not only will this prevent problems with chain of custody, but also specimens can be analyzed in a timely manner. Therefore, it is reasonable for the physician to insist that a report be made to the police if evidence is to be collected.

On the other hand, the victim may decide later to report the crime or may simply want evidence collected without reporting the sexual assault as a crime. Emergency physicians should have some procedure for at least documenting the presence of semen. To achieve this and to avoid problems with chain of custody, the physician may collect the specimen, carry it to the laboratory, look for evidence of motile sperm, and document the findings on the chart. Alternatively, laboratory personnel may come to the emergency department, collect the specimen, transport it, check for sperm, and make a report. Having one person handle the specimen prevents problems with chain of custody; nevertheless, it is important to document that the specimen was in the possession of one person at all times.

3

All states require physicians to report injuries when child abuse is suspected. These statutes protect the reporting persons, at least when the report is made in good faith. There is no doubt, then, that in these circumstances the physician is required to report suspected abuse in this case based on the nature of the injury and the lack of adequate explanations from the mother.

On the other hand, the physician cannot overlook the fact that parents find it highly stressful to be the subject of such a report and may be very resentful. The protection given to the reporting individual is not absolute. Document the basis for the report clearly. Because physical evidence of the injury will soon fade, take photographs of bruises, fractures, or other injuries. The relationship between the physician and the parent needs to be kept as cordial as possible to prevent the parent from alleging that the report was motivated not by a reasonable belief of child abuse but for some punitive reason.

4

Any information relevant to a court proceeding ordinarily will be admissible and subject to subpoena unless there is some exception to this general rule. The only exception will be some "privilege" that overrides the normal rule. Well-known privileges include the privilege against self-incrimination, the attorney-client privilege, and the physician-patient privilege.

This patient was not in police custody and made the admission voluntarily to medical personnel. Therefore, the privilege against self-incrimination will not apply. The statement was made in the course of medical treatment; thus, potentially, the physician-patient privilege will apply. This privilege derives from statute but not from common law, which recognizes no such privilege (in contrast to the attorney-client privilege.) As such privilege will be strictly (nar-rowly) construed and given effect only to the extent of the statute.

Some state statutes recognize no physician-patient privilege regarding criminal proceedings. In these states, the physician-patient privilege does not prevent the videotape from being subpoenaed for use as evidence in a murder trial. In states where the privilege does apply in criminal cases, it is likely that the physician-patient privilege will prevent the videotape from being introduced into evidence, as the confession occurred in the context of giving a medical history. Also, the videotape confession may be protected as part of a formal quality assurance process.

In this particular case, quality assurance was the purpose for creating the videotape. However, the purpose for which the material was sought to be subpoenaed was not to bring a proceeding against any medical personnel or the hospital. Moreover, it would seem possible to edit out the portion related to treatment and thereby limit what is presented in court to the "confession." As a result, the privilege to protect the quality assurance process was unlikely to defeat the subpoena.

On the other hand, the court may well limit what portion of the tape can be presented in evidence. The hospital can request a protective order, to prevent use or distribution of the tape and to delete material not directly part of the patient's confession. This case demonstrated that much of what happens in an emergency department involves collecting evidence that often will be relevant later when the patient is involved in a court proceeding based on the events that prompted the emergency department visit.

Key Points and Conclusion

Criminal law has a significant influence on the way evidence is collected and secured in the emergency department. When collecting evidence, the physician should conduct appropriate medical-legal examinations and ensure a proper chain of custody for all pertinent materials. The physician must be aware of and comply with state reporting requirements and must understand the evidentiary needs for the prosecution of cases based on such reports. Often, observations made and other evidence collected during the course of an emergency department visit will be relevant to court proceedings.

References

1. See generally, American College of Legal Medicine. *Legal Medicine*. 3rd ed. St Louis: CV Mosby and Co; 1995.

2. *Black's Law Dictionary*. 6th ed. 1990:555-557. See also, McLaughlin. *Federal Evidence Practice Guide*, Section 2.10. Matthew Bender; 1989.

3. *Black's Law Dictionary*. 6th ed. 1990:1264. Friend CE. *The Law of Evidence in Virginia*. 4th ed. 1993.

4. *Smith v Commonwealth*, 248 SE2d 805 at 808(Va 1978).

5. *Robinson v Commonwealth*, 183 SE2d 179 (Va 1971).

6. *Federal Evidence Practice Guide, supra*, Note 3 at 2-64.

7. Wiecking DK. The chain of custody. *Medico-Legal Bull* 1990;39(2):1-8.

8. Ann Code of Va §18.268.5-18.286.6 (Mitchie 1996).

9. 342 USC 165 (1952).

10. 352 USC 432 (1957).

11. 385 USC 757 (1966).

12. Police blood alcohol tests and the emergency physician. *Emerg Phys Legal Bull,* April 1989.

13. Prosser WL. *Handbook of the Law of Torts* 856 (5th ed, 1984, rev 1988).

14. 735 ILCS 5/8-802 (West 1992).

15. *People v Maltbia*, 210 Ill Dec 497, 659 NE2d 402, app denied 214 Ill Dec 327, 660 NE2d 1276 (3rd Dist 1995).

16. *State v Roper*, 122 NM126, 921 P2d 322 (NM App 1996).

17. George JE. Rape and the emergency department physician. *Emerg Phys Legal Bull* 1989;October:2.

18. Dorfman DH, Paradise JE. Emergency diagnosis and management of physical abuse and neglect of children. *Curr Opin Pediatr* 1995;7:297-301.

19. Schetky DH, Benedek EP. The sexual abuse victim in the courts. *Psychiatr Clin North Am* 1989;12:471-481.

20. Enos WF, Conrath TB, Byer JC. Forensic evaluation of the sexually abused child. *Pediatrics* 1986;78:385-398.

21 Ricci LR. Child sexual abuse: the emergency department response. *Ann Emerg Med* 1986;15:711-716.

22. Myers JE. Role of physician in preserving verbal evidence of child abuse. *J Pediatr* 1986;109:409-411.

23. Spencer MJ, Dunklee P. Sexual abuse of boys. *Pediatrics* 1986;78:133-138.

24. Levitt CJ. Medical evaluation of the sexually abused child. *Prim Care* 1993;20:343-354.

Chapter 33

Antitrust Law

Michael T. Rapp, MD, JD, FACEP

The federal antitrust laws are designed to eliminate practices that interfere with the free operation of competitive markets. They apply as fully to the business of health care and to the profession of medicine as they do to traditional business enterprises. Physicians need to be aware of the general provisions of the antitrust laws and the situations in which antitrust issues can arise.

Case Studies

1

The physicians in a midwestern state find that health maintenance organizations (HMOs) are becoming increasingly more unreasonable with respect to covering emergency department visits. Many deny payment unless the case is truly an emergency, and when they do pay, the amount often is very low. At a state chapter meeting, one of the members of the board of directors suggests that some emergency physicians "have priced themselves out of the market" and the HMOs are reacting as if all physicians charge unreasonably high prices. The board decides to develop a per-case charge for emergency care, at a reasonable level, and negotiate that price on behalf of the members of the chapter with as many HMOs as would be willing. Is this action permitted under the antitrust laws? What if the same action is taken with respect to the state Medicaid program?

2

At a meeting of another state emergency medicine chapter, during an open forum on managed care, one of the members complains that the prices paid by one of the HMOs are so low that she has decided not to conduct business at all with that HMO. She says: "I know I'm only one physician, and my group is only five physicians, but I really believe the only way to deal with this is to refuse to negotiate with them at all unless their terms are reasonable." What risk does such a position create for the chapter, the physician, and the group?

3

Five of eight independent groups of emergency physicians practice in an area with an equal number of hospitals with emergency departments. There is no other hospital within 100 miles, and there is virtually no overlap between the distant hospital and the local market. The five emergency groups decide to establish an independent practice association (IPA) to contract with managed care plans. Each group contributes $2,000 to fund legal fees to incorporate the IPA and the salary of the executive director to negotiate fee-for-service contracts.

Several of the groups have met with HMO representatives. The physicians are convinced that they can save the HMOs a substantial amount on emergency services if they work cooperatively on ancillary services. They have noted that often the laboratory tests and x-rays that the group physicians order are far more costly than the physicians' services. Some of these costs could be avoided without a reduction in quality patient care if there were better coordination of that care. A quality assurance and utilization review committee is established to develop protocols to reduce the required documentation in order to lessen the costs of providing services, to bill jointly for services, and to adhere to the protocols of the utilization committee.

Although not stated in writing, the groups are not expected to contract with the HMOs except through the IPA; in fact, no group has a contract with an HMO except through the IPA.

Is the IPA legal under federal antitrust laws? What if the number of groups is reduced to three, and the IPA provides in writing that it is not exclusive and the individual groups actively seek to participate in other IPAs? Further, what if the groups limit their payment arrangements with HMOs to capitation, or major fee withholds, that would be distributed to the IPA only if targets for utilization of x-ray and laboratory services are met?

4

A state chapter representing 85% of emergency physicians in the state decides to create a nonexclusive IPA that will negotiate non–fee-related aspects of contracts for members. The individual physicians will sign and negotiate their own individual contracts regarding fees. Does this arrangement violate the federal antitrust laws?

An Introduction to Antitrust Law

The federal antitrust laws of the United States are unique in their scope and vigor of enforcement. Their passage, more than 100 years ago, came in response to the massive aggregation of economic power that characterized the post-Civil War expansion of the U.S. economy and the ability to control pricing through "gentlemen's agreements" and trusts. The public, reflecting a deep-rooted political tradition hostile to the concentration of private power, demanded that something be done about trusts. Although the common law of England had condemned certain practices in restraint of trade, enforcement came only when a party to an agreement asked a court to void a restrictive provision of a business agreement. As such, the common law did nothing to prevent the formation of restrictive agreements. The Sherman Act empowered the federal government to take preventive action and placed the responsibility with the executive branch of government. Courts retained the important role of interpreting the broadly written statutes and of providing a forum for private enforcement.

In general, the intent of federal antitrust laws is to protect open markets, thus promoting competition. However, these laws are neither designed to protect any individual competitor nor even individual consumers. As for prices, antitrust laws prohibit price agreements but do not seek to promote any particular price levels. Rather, agreements by competitors to limit maximum prices violate antitrust laws just as much as efforts made to establish minimum prices. In addition, although monopolies represent the antithesis of competition, a monopoly itself is not forbidden, at least not when the monopoly is the result of superior competition. Enforcement of the antitrust laws often results in low prices with multiple effective competitors; however, these results are incidental to competition and are not the focus of the laws themselves.

Federal Statutes

Several statutes make up the federal antitrust laws. Of these, Section 1 of the Sherman Act[1] is of primary importance. It prohibits any combination or conspiracy in restraint of trade. Thus, its focus is to prevent concerted activity to restrain trade, not to regulate the conduct of a single business entity.

Section 2 of the Sherman Act[2] focuses on unilateral activity by prohibiting willful acquisition or maintenance of monopoly power. This is to be distinguished from growth or development of a monopoly as the consequence of a superior product, business acumen, or historical accident.

Section 7 of the Clayton Act[3] seeks to prevent acquisition of monopoly power through merger. It prohibits any merger acquisition that tends to lessen competition substantially or to create a monopoly. In furtherance of this goal, the Hart-Scott-Rodino Antitrust Improvement Act of 1976[4] requires premerger or preacquisition notification where parties meet certain size requirements.

Section 5 of the Federal Trade Commission Act prohibits "unfair methods of competition," which has been interpreted to encompass not only all Sherman Act and Clayton Act violations, but also restraints of trade contrary to the policy or spirit of those laws. The Act prohibits as well "unfair or deceptive acts or practice," which includes false or misleading advertisements or representations along with practices considered "unfair" to consumers.

Enforcement

There are three overlapping sources of enforcement of the federal antitrust laws: the Department of Justice, the Federal Trade Commission (FTC), and private civil actions. The penalties of enforcement can be severe.

Enforcement through the Department of Justice includes potential criminal penalties. Violation can result in imprisonment of individuals for up to three years, with monetary fines of up to $350,000 for each violation. Corporations face fines of up to $10 million per violation. FTC enforcement involves cease and desist actions and lawsuits for injunction or monetary fines. Its authority comes from the Federal Trade Commission Act.

Private enforcement occurs through lawsuits for damages filed in federal court. Originally, experts thought that civil action might be the principal means of enforcement for the federal antitrust laws. Even today, many believe that private legal action, except in the merger field, is more effective than government enforcement, at least in business areas to which the government does not give much attention.

Medical Practice and Antitrust Laws

Medical practice and health care were not the original focus of antitrust laws and their development. In fact, for many years, it was unclear whether the antitrust laws even applied to the practice of medicine. The legal issue was whether the practice of medicine, a learned profession, was a "trade" for the purpose of federal antitrust laws. In a 1943 case,[5] the Supreme Court avoided the question. Not until the 1980s was the question answered unequivocally, leaving no doubt as to the applicability of antitrust law to medicine. Today, health care has become the most active area of antitrust law development.

In addition to federal antitrust laws, there are also state antitrust statutes, which are enforced through lawsuits that state attorneys general may bring. Physicians need to be aware of the antitrust laws in their states, as merely adhering to federal law may not be enough to avoid antitrust liability.

Violations of the Sherman Act

Requirement of Combination or Conspiracy

A basic element of violation of Section 1 is the existence of a combination or conspiracy. Conspiracy is defined as an agreement of two or more persons to accomplish an unlawful purpose or a lawful purpose by unlawful means. The prevailing standard of proof is evidence that tends to exclude the possibility of independent action. As stated by the Supreme Court, there must be direct or circumstantial evidence that reasonably tends to prove a conscious commitment to a common scheme designed to achieve an unlawful objective. Independent, even consciously parallel behavior would normally be insufficient to meet the criteria for an antitrust violation, although it may raise suspicion of an unlawful agreement.

Still, few agreements in restraint of trade will be obvious. Enforcement agencies realize that their existence will often need to be inferred from the circumstances. Because of this fact, health care professionals seeking to avoid antitrust danger must not engage in or create circumstances that might reasonably lead to the conclusion that an agreement in restraint of trade exists. These circumstances might include an opportunity to conspire, for example, by attending a common meeting, followed by parallel or other conduct in the marketplace suggesting a conspiracy, coupled with an economic motive to engage in the alleged conspiracy.

Corporations

A corporation is an individual legal entity. As such, it cannot conspire with itself and, therefore, cannot violate Section 1 of the Sherman Act by itself. But corporations are fictitious entities and can act only through people. This raises the question as to when the actions of persons associated with the corporation can legally constitute a conspiracy.

Generally, officers, directors, or employees of the same corporation, when acting in their corporate capacity, are carrying out the work of the corporation and cannot be held to be conspiring with one another. Neither can a corporation conspire with its wholly owned subsidiaries. With respect to a hospital (a corporation), some jurisdictions have similarly held that a medical staff is deemed the agent of the hospital, with which the staff cannot conspire.

The fact that individuals form an incorporated entity does not preclude them from conspiring with one another through that vehicle, when it is merely an association of competing physicians who have separate economic interests. For example, courts have held that IPA members are capable of conspiring with one another, despite their organizational structure as a professional corporation.

Rule of Reason

The plain language of the Sherman Act makes "every" combination or conspiracy in restraint of trade illegal. But, as the Supreme Court noted, its plain reading is clearly too broad. Early after the statute's adoption, the Supreme Court fundamentally narrowed the Sherman Act by adopting the "rule of reason." This rule makes not "every" but only "unreasonable" restraints of trade illegal. The rationale for this limitation, as explained by Justice Brandeis, is as follows: "Every agreement concerning trade, every regulation of trade, restrains. To bind, to restrain, is of their very essence. The true test of legality is whether the restraint imposed is such as merely regulates and perhaps thereby promotes competition or whether it is such as may suppress or even destroy competition."

In outlining the various factors to be considered in determining whether a trade restraint was reasonable, the Supreme Court included facts peculiar to the business, the nature of the restraint, its effect or likely effect on the market, and the goals of the restraint. Today, these same factors are used to evaluate a restraint of trade for legality under the rule of reason.

Per Se *Violations*

Although the rule of reason was determined to be the general rule of construction of the Sherman Act, it was essential to develop a category of cases that did not require full rule of reason analysis to preserve judicial economy while enforcing the antitrust laws. The Supreme Court accomplished this by developing the *per se* rule, which describes a type of restraint that is conclusively presumed to be unreasonable and therefore *per se* illegal.

This *per se* concept was first applied to price-fixing. The Supreme Court pointed out that the aim of every price-fixing agreement — and result, if effective — is the elimination of one form of competition. Therefore, it is the power to fix prices, whether reasonably exercised or not, and the inherent ability to fix arbitrary and unreasonable prices that make such a restraint unlawful. Whether the prices actually agreed on are reasonable or unreasonable is immaterial. Over the years, the *per se* rule of prohibition has been extended from price-fixing arrangements to include group boycotts, tying arrangements, and horizontal division of markets.

Whether a restraint is classified in the *per se* category or in the rule of reason category is of critical importance. A *per se* violation cannot be justified on the basis of reasonableness; it is conclusively determined to be unreasonable. By contrast, for practical purposes, restraints that need to be evaluated using full rule of reason analysis are unlikely to be found illegal.

Price-Fixing. The sensitivity of price is of paramount importance under antitrust laws. As characterized by the Supreme Court, price is the central nervous system of the economy. To be guilty of price-fixing, an entity does not need to have either the actual ability to fix or control prices or any specific market power. Rather, the term "price-fixing" has come to be used in the broadest sense. It includes combinations or conspiracies to "raise," "depress," "fix," "peg," or "stabilize" price and encompasses agreements that may affect price, such as credit terms and discounts. Controlling maximum prices is just as unlawful as controlling minimum prices.

Price agreements for physician services have been held to constitute a *per se* violation of Section 1 of the Sherman Act. The seminal case on price-fixing of physician services is *Arizona v Maricopa County Medical Society*,[6] which involved setting maximum prices.

Group Boycotts. Restraints labeled as "group boycotts," or concerted refusals to deal on particular terms, are the second major type of trade restraint that has been classified by the Supreme Court as a *per se* violation. For this restraint, market power is important. This *per se* violation is particularly relevant to associations that provide a ready vehicle to refuse to deal with individuals or groups. Antitrust liability can result.

Horizontal Division of Markets. In horizontal market division, actual or potential competitors agree not to compete in specified territories or for specified customers. The consequence is to reduce the number of sellers in each affected market. The market division, when proved, is considered unreasonable *per se* on the theory that there is no other purpose to such an agreement except to have an effect on competition. The agreeing parties can gain no benefit unless the result is to give each a substantial degree of power in its own market.

Tying Arrangements. A tying arrangement is the sale or lease of one product (the "tying product") on condition that the buyer or lessee also buys or leases a second product (the "tied product"). The tying and tied products must, in fact, be separate, not merely parts of an overall product. Although the Supreme Court has held tying arrangements constitute a *per se* violation, the Court has made it clear that market power in the tying market is critical. The major Supreme Court case, and one pertinent to emergency physicians, is *Jefferson Parish Hospital District v Hyde*.[7] In this case, an exclusive contract between the hospital and an anesthesiologist was challenged as "tying" anesthesiology services to surgical services in a particular hospital. The contract, which precluded other qualified anesthesiologists from being part of the staff, resulted in patients being required to use anesthesiologists subject to the exclusive contract. The Supreme Court, finding no shortage in the area of other hospitals with competing services, upheld the contract. As a result of this case, there is little likelihood that a challenge to an exclusive contract will succeed on the basis of the federal antitrust laws, at least in any market area served by several hospitals.

Monopolization

Section 2 of the Sherman Act prohibits monopolization, attempted monopolization, and conspiracies to monopolize any line of trade or commerce. To be guilty of monopolization, one must first have monopoly power. Monopoly power is functionally defined as the ability of a competitor to restrict product output or increase price without incurring a significant loss of sales. Market share is the most important indicator of a defendant's degree of market power. Although it is difficult to establish any rule of thumb for market shares, a share of 68% or more has been held to be sufficient to constitute monopoly power; a market share below 50% generally has been considered insufficient.

In addition to market power, the competitor must have committed acts designed to achieve, maintain, or extend the monopoly unlawfully, or committed acts evidencing an intent to monopolize. Many exclusionary practices have been condemned by courts under Section 2 when the defendant satisfied the monopoly power requirements. These include such activities as predatory pricing (below-cost pricing meant to drive a competitor out of business), mergers to achieve a monopoly, purchase and shutdown of rivals' plants, and refusal to deal with a competitor.

Section 2 is an important antitrust provision in the health care area, but it applies only to large entities. It is generally not relevant to the average emergency physician.

Federal Antitrust Exemptions

There are several exemptions from the antitrust laws. The most important for the purposes of this discussion are the state action doctrine and the Noerr-Pennington doctrine. The state action doctrine exempts conduct that is directed by a state. The Noerr-Pennington doctrine exempts activity intended to prompt government bodies to take official action.

State Action Doctrine

This court-developed doctrine provides immunity for conduct that is authorized and regulated by a state acting in its sovereign capacity.[8] The doctrine provides immunity only where the private action follows a clearly articulated state policy and is subject to adequate supervision by the state or municipality of the state.

One example of how the doctrine has been applied is a California case[9] in which certain ambulance companies were found to be immune from antitrust liability when it was shown that their division of an operating area into exclusive territories was in compliance with the EMS Act. This action would otherwise be a horizontal division of markets and a *per se* violation.

In contrast, the immunity doctrine does not apply to a trade restraint prompted by action of the state but not directed by the state acting in its sovereign capacity. In *Goldfarb v Virginia State Bar*,[10] the Bar was held liable for enforcing a minimum fee schedule even though the Bar was established by the Virginia Supreme Court to allow that court to regulate the practice of law in Virginia. The U.S. Supreme Court pointed out that, although the Bar enforced the fee schedule, the Virginia Supreme Court had adopted ethical codes explicitly directing lawyers not "to be controlled" by fee schedules. The U.S. Supreme Court thereby concluded that enforcement of the fee schedule was inconsistent with the directives of the Virginia Supreme Court.

Noerr-Pennington Doctrine

The Noerr-Pennington doctrine is another court-established doctrine that provides antitrust immunity. It is based on the First

Amendment to the U.S. Constitution that guarantees the right of free speech, including the right to petition the government. The doctrine grants immunity for conduct that would seek to restrict competition through government action. In *Eastern Railroad Presidents Conference v Noerr Motor Freight*,[11] the Supreme Court held that antitrust laws did not apply to an alleged conspiracy among railroad companies that were campaigning the legislature to place anticompetitive restrictions on trucking companies. These restrictions would have put the railroads in a more favorable market position. As reiterated in *United Mine Workers of America v Pennington*,[12] the doctrine became known as the Noerr-Pennington doctrine.

By way of limitation, the Supreme Court has recognized a "sham" exception to the Noerr-Pennington doctrine. In *California Motor Transport Co v Trucking Unlimited*,[13] the Court held that a group of firms engaging in baseless and repetitive judicial or administrative actions in an attempt to harass or exclude a competitor was not granted immunity by the Noerr-Pennington doctrine. Moreover, the Court held that the Noerr-Pennington doctrine did not apply in *Allied Tube & Conduit Corp v Indian Head, Inc*[14] even though the electrical code in question, by practice, was adopted almost automatically by local governments. There, the association was found to have violated Section 1 of the Sherman Act because it allowed one group of competitors to dominate the process of adoption of the electrical code by the private standard-setting body to the detriment of another group.

The Medical-Legal Perspective

The great activity in health care antitrust law development may seem curious to many, because not until the 1980s were the antitrust laws clearly established to apply to the medical profession. However, this activity is more understandable when considering that health care now represents a large portion of the U.S. economy. Also, tremendous changes occurring in the health care marketplace are creating antitrust issues. Small, independent businesses face greater challenges because purchasing decisions are being made by larger and larger economic entities. When these companies seek alliances to become more effective in the marketplace, they inevitably encounter antitrust issues.

Rapid development of health care antitrust

law also means active enforcement. With this in mind, emergency physicians must have a basic understanding of the antitrust laws and be aware of the situations or risk factors likely to violate antitrust laws. By understanding the dangers, physicians can avoid antitrust law violation and know when to seek professional legal advice.

The three major areas of risk discussed here are professional associations, the hospital medical staff, and physician practice networks.

Professional Associations

Professional associations are popular with physicians. Scarcely a physician interest exists where there is not an association tailored to that interest. Associations provide a natural and needed forum for physicians to interact with each other, to keep up with the latest developments in the profession, and to have access to valuable educational opportunities.

The activities of associations also provide the following benefits to the public:

- They help set standards for products and services that can help improve quality and safety, making it easier for consumers to compare or combine products and services.
- They collect and disseminate information, such as industry product statistics, and offer advice on operating member businesses.
- They facilitate joint research on problems faced by the firms in the industry.
- They perform public relations activities involving joint generic marketing promotions activities.
- They lobby on public policy issues.
- They help mediate consumer complaints and provide public information.

Associations also provide a forum for members to discuss proposed or current laws that affect their industry. Because of their benefits to society, the activities of professional associations are given significant latitude. Still, these groups run a considerable risk of antitrust law violation, particularly if they stray into the area of *per se* violations. Principally, these involve group boycotts or limitations on price competition. Part of the risk to associations, at times, is a feeling by association members that they are equivalent to a labor union. But, associations cannot do what unions can. In fact, not even a union can collectively bargain with customers and suppliers in the marketplace, but only with its members' employers.

The major areas of antitrust risk for professional organizations include membership and credentialing, professional codes and self-regulation, statistical collection and distribution, standard-setting, and conduct of members.

Membership and Credentialing. The degree to which membership in an association is essential to being an effective competitor varies considerably. The more essential membership is in a given association, the more scrutiny will be given to the practices of the association to ensure that it does not unreasonably exclude competitors. A 1943 Supreme Court case involving a criminal indictment against the American Medical Association (AMA) and the Medical Society of the District of Columbia[5] provides an example. The AMA and the local medical society were able to exclude physicians from admitting patients in Washington, DC hospitals by threatening disciplinary actions, including expulsion of any AMA member who joined the staff of Group Health Association, Inc., a prepaid medical plan.

Certainly where membership is a significant business benefit to a competitor, association rules on membership should not seek to exclude competitors from access to the significant benefits of membership nor be overly broad in eliminating competitors. Membership standards should be organized so as not to be unduly restrictive and should reflect legitimate concerns regarding quality of care, cost containment, and efficiency. A purpose of the credentialing process cannot be to unreasonably restrict or boycott competitors. Due process should be available to ensure that no member is expelled arbitrarily or for anticompetitive reasons.

Professional Codes and Self-Regulation. The development of professional codes, criteria, and rules is a common activity for professional associations. They must be careful, however, to avoid any rule that would directly reduce competition, especially as it affects price. In *National Society of Professional Engineers v United States*,[15] for example, the association had an absolute ban on competitive bidding. Even though the ban was not enforced, the record of the case supported a finding that the association and its members pursued a course adhering to the competitive bidding ban through direct and indirect communication with members and prospective clients. The Supreme Court ruled that, although ethical norms that regulate and promote competition in professional services would fall within the rule of reason, doing

away with competition itself could not be justified.

In association cases involving physicians and dentists, rules that effectively restrict truthful, nondeceptive advertising have been the object of vigorous enforcement efforts. In the 1970s, federal enforcement efforts eliminated the restrictions in the AMA Code of Ethics on advertising, which had prohibited physicians from disseminating accurate information to the public about the price, quality, and other important competitive aspects of physician services. Even in 1996, an order was entered to prohibit the California Dental Association's interference with its members' truthful nondeceptive promotional activities, including categorical bans that would prevent dentists from advertising "low" or "reasonable" fees. The court found the ban illegal *per se*, even as imposed by a professional association.

In another noteworthy case,[16] a dental association adopted a rule forbidding members from submitting x-rays to dental insurers in conjunction with claim forms. Dental insurers requested x-rays in order to assist in determining whether dental care was appropriate. The rule was successful in particular communities where members were highly concentrated. It had the effect of eliminating competition among dentists in terms of offering cooperation with the requests of patient insurers. The rule was found to be an unreasonable restraint of trade, in the nature of a group boycott. The association's argument that evaluation of x-rays alone was not sufficient to evaluate the appropriateness of dental care was not sufficient to overcome the anticompetitive aspects of the restraint.

Rules of academic organizations also have faced antitrust enforcement. In a settlement with the Justice Department, the Association of Family Practice Residency Directors[17] agreed to stop using ethics rules that barred the use of individual economic incentives to attract prospective family practice residents and prohibited the use of certain other competitive recruiting practices. In commenting on the cases, Assistant Attorney General Anne K. Bingaman advised that professional associations must resist the impulse to use their collective power to restrict competition among their members.

Even the practices of law school faculty prompted action by the Justice Department against the American Bar Association (ABA), which was settled under terms that prevented the ABA from manipulating accreditation of law schools for the purpose of improving faculty salaries. The ABA had allowed accrediting committees to be turned over to professors, who used their control to force law schools to pay high wages and to provide expensive fringe benefits by refusing to accredit law schools that paid low salaries or failed to provide paid leaves for faculty. The Justice Department determined that the accrediting policy had nothing to do with guaranteeing students professional training and, in fact, forced students to pay higher tuition. The decree required the ABA to review accreditation standards on class size, institutional facilities, and other resources to eliminate any anticompetitive standards and to remove control over accreditation from law professors.

Statistical Collection and Distribution. Data collection and sharing are a frequent function of professional organizations. Given the risk that sharing or withholding certain information can lead to a trade restraint, associations must exercise care. They should follow a few general parameters with respect to statistical collection within the constraints of the antitrust laws. These parameters include the following:

- Voluntary not mandatory participation for those providing the information
- A legitimate business interest for the information
- Surveying for historical rather than projected data
- Using a procedure that preserves the confidentiality of the raw data from which aggregate results are compiled
- Sharing of the aggregate results not only with members, but also nonmembers
- Ultimately discarding the raw data
- Avoiding the collection of current price information

Any exchange of information regarding future prices, or exchange of information that would result in an agreement to fix prices, would be unlawful *per se*.

The recent statements of antitrust enforcement policy in health care issued by the Department of Justice and the FTC related to physician networks gives useful guidance to associations. These agencies provide "safety zones" — that is, they identify conduct that will not be challenged under the antitrust laws, absent extreme circumstances. One of these safety zones allows for the collective provision of non–fee-related medical data that may improve the purchasers' resolution of issues regarding the mode, quality, or efficiency of treatment. Provision of outcome data as to services proposed for coverage or suggested clinical protocols for adoption was included in the safety zone, so long as there was no attempt to coerce the purchaser, in the nature of a group boycott, into adopting the proposed coverage or clinical protocol.

As far as collective provision of price information or exchanges of price and cost information among providers, the safety zone was specifically limited to collected information managed by a third party. The information could not be shared with the competing providers, unless the information was at least three months old, where a minimum of five providers are involved, with none representing more than 25% of the aggregate. The aggregate information must not permit identification of the prices charged by any individual provider. This enforcement statement emphasized the importance of protecting against competitors discussing or coordinating provider prices or costs. Collective negotiations on price with a purchaser or purchasers by nonintegrated providers or any attempt at explicit or implicit coercion to accept collectively determined fees would likely constitute a *per se* violation.

Standard-Setting. The procompetitive advantages of associations establishing private standards include standardization of products to permit interchangeability, easier comparability, and improved safety. However, standardization might also deprive some consumers of a desired product, eliminate quality competition, exclude rival producers, or facilitate oligopolistic pricing by easing rivals' ability to monitor each other's prices. As with membership cases, efforts to enforce and not just agree on private product standards face more rigorous antitrust scrutiny.

The *Allied Tube* case[14] demonstrates the importance of having a fair procedure to adopt standards to avoid biasing the standard-setting process toward members with an economic interest in stifling product competition. In this case, members at a meeting were to consider a proposal to change the fire code to allow for plastic conduit. The association allowed the meeting to be "packed" by the steel conduit competitors. Predictably, the proposal was defeated. Ultimately, the U.S. Supreme Court held this action to be a *per se* violation, in view of the absence of a fair process, even though standard-setting cases are normally evaluated under the rule of reason.

However, a trade association can provide product or service information, even giving a seal of approval, especially when the group does not constrain others to follow its recommendation. For example, in a case involving the American Academy of Ophthalmology,[18] the court held that an organization's significant reputation does not reduce its freedom to speak out. The board of directors of the Academy endorsed the position that, at that time, refractive keratoplasty was "experimental" and urged the profession to use restraint until more research could be done. The court found no antitrust violation, pointing out that there was no associated disciplinary action and no efforts to get anyone, for example, hospitals, insurers, or medical societies, to take any adverse action with regard to its statement, nor to coordinate any activities with groups or parties independent of the Academy. The plaintiff contended only that the Academy's prestige influenced others' conduct. The case was contrasted with enforcement devices, for example, boycotting members who "fall out of step,"[15] or agreeing not to purchase or distribute certain products.[14]

Conduct of Members. An association can be also found guilty of an antitrust violation through conduct of its members, even when there is no actual involvement of the association through the authority of its governing structure. The doctrine of apparent authority provides that if a principal allows the appearance of an agency relationship, the principal can be held responsible for the conduct of the apparent agent, even though the agent has not been given any actual authority to act for the principal. A familiar example for emergency physicians is a hospital being held liable for the conduct of independently contracting emergency physicians when the hospital does not specifically inform the patient that the physician is not an employee of the hospital.

In the area of association antitrust law, the principal case applying this principle is *American Society of Mechanical Engineers, Inc v Hydrolevel Corp.*[19] This association promulgates numerous safety standards of great influence, many of which are incorporated by reference into federal regulations and state laws. One of its regulations involved fuel cutoff valves to prevent boiler explosions, and an association subcommittee had authority to respond to public inquires about this standard. Hydrolevel entered the market with an innovative device, which

was its only product. The volunteer chairman of the subcommittee contrived with the vice chairman, who worked for the major manufacturer of a conventional valve, to seek and issue an interpretation as to whether the Hydrolevel device met the association's standard. The interpretation criticizing the product went out on association letterhead over the signature of the employed staff secretary. The competitor used the interpretation against Hydrolevel in the market, and Hydrolevel went out of business. The association was held liable under the apparent authority doctrine, even though what the members had done was beyond their authority.

The *Hydrolevel* case teaches that associations must be alert to prevent individual members from engaging in anticompetitive conduct under the apparent auspices of the association. Further, based on the rulings in the *Allied Tube,*[14] the ABA, and the Association of Family Practice Residency Directors[17] cases, an association should not permit a group with homogenous economic interests to be delegated authority or dominate decisions that would allow the group to achieve anticompetitive ends. Rather, the association, to ensure even-handedness, must maintain authority as a whole over the actions of committees, at least in the area of private regulation.

Antitrust Compliance Program for Associations. The risk of antitrust law violation is significant enough that associations should develop antitrust compliance programs. Such a program should include a policy statement on antitrust law compliance, a compliance manual, and a formal orientation process. Each new group of association officers and directors should be thoroughly briefed on the antitrust danger areas and be made aware of the severe consequences of antitrust enforcement action.

A sound antitrust compliance policy should have the following characteristics:
- A strong commitment by the association's volunteer and executive leadership to ensure an attitude of respect for the antitrust laws throughout the organization
- A published statement of an association's position in favor of a continuing, consistent policy to comply with all applicable antitrust laws and to require that all volunteers and staff comply with these laws as well
- A simple, clear limitation of the prerogatives of volunteers and staff to communicate explicitly or implicitly in the association's name, such as in speeches and articles, as

well as in private communications, such as letter and telephone conferences

A compliance manual should include a summary of antitrust law, relate the potential applicability of antitrust laws to the activities of the organization or association, and state the antitrust compliance policy of the organization.

In view of the prohibition of the antitrust laws, associations need to be alert to discussions that members should avoid. The First Amendment protects a person's right to free speech, but not to engage in an unlawful conspiracy. Therefore, an association properly protects itself by prohibiting discussions from which a *per se* antitrust violation could be inferred. Such prohibited discussions would include the following topics:

- Raising, lowering, or stabilizing prices or fees
- Regulating production levels
- Affecting the availability of professional services
- Affecting allocation of customers or patients
- Encouraging boycotts of products or services
- Fostering unfair practices involving advertising, merchandising standardization, certification, or accreditation
- Encouraging anyone to refrain from competing
- Refusing to deal with a corporation because of its pricing or distribution practices

In contrast, many appropriate areas of discussion do not need to be controlled, such as the following:

- Reporting on general economic trends in the profession
- Describing medical advances or problems in relevant technology or research
- Demonstrating cost methods by which physicians can be more successful economically by acquiring better knowledge of costs
- Summarizing effective methods of marketing
- Providing education on various aspects of effective management
- Reviewing professional relations with state and federal governments

The American College of Emergency Physicians (ACEP) has adopted a policy on antitrust[20] that provides an example of a compliance policy. It is provided to new leaders and to persons who will be making presentations at ACEP educational programs. It is also included in each Board of Directors notebook in connection with meetings of the Board of Directors, as well as the Council.

Hospital Medical Staff

There are primarily two areas in which members of a hospital's medical staff can encounter difficulties with the antitrust laws. The first is in its official functions of credentialing, medical staff membership decisions, and peer review. The second area comprises other activities, often related to economic concerns, that are directly related to the medical staff's function of providing a self-governing structure to protect the quality of medical care rendered in the hospital.

Decisions made by the medical staff can be of critical significance to other physicians. Without hospital access, most physicians cannot effectively practice medicine. Even those physicians who have customarily practiced without the need for hospital privileges are now finding them necessary. More managed care organizations (MCOs) are requiring physicians to have hospital privileges before they can participate in the managed care plan.

The focus of the medical staff must be a legitimate interest in the quality of medical care in the institution and in the efficiency of the hospital's operations. To ensure that decisions are based on proper considerations, the hospital should develop formal processes that clarify the rationale for any adverse decision. The desire to limit competition cannot be a factor in the decision-making. Decisions made that have nothing to do with quality care or efficiency, for example, excluding osteopathic physicians as a group from medical staff membership, will expose the hospital and the medical staff to antitrust liability.

Peer review and corrective action procedures must reflect the findings of the seminal peer review case *Patrick v Burget*[21] (see Chapter 25, "Peer Review"). Briefly, *Patrick* was a successful lawsuit based on federal antitrust laws and the contention that the peer review process was used to stifle competition rather than to review the quality of medical care given. This case, which was eventually affirmed by the U.S. Supreme Court, nearly endangered the peer review process. In response, Congress ultimately enacted the Health Care Quality Improvement Act (HCQIA). Besides establishing the National Practitioner Data Bank, HCQIA provided for conditional federal antitrust immunity for peer review activities under the condition that procedures are developed to prevent unfairness or any anticompetitive motive in the peer review process.

To achieve antitrust immunity under HCQIA, adverse peer review action must be based on the reasonable belief that the action is taken to improve the quality of health care and is warranted by the facts. In addition, the peer review committee must give the practitioner an opportunity for a fair hearing, during which the facts on which the adverse action is based are made available. HCQIA specifies due process procedures, including a requirement that no member of the hearing panel can be in direct economic competition with the practitioner who is the subject of the hearing. Hospital bylaws and hearing procedures must comply with HCQIA to avoid federal antitrust lawsuits as a result of adverse peer review action.

Even then, because HCQIA provides only conditional immunity, the risk of federal antitrust liability still exists. For example, in *Boczar v Manatee Hospitals & Health Systems, Inc,*[22] an obstetrician successfully proved that a peer review action against her constituted an antitrust conspiracy, despite the committee's compliance with HCQIA. She produced evidence of conduct that no reasonable medical practitioner or hospital would consider as part of a legitimate peer review. This conduct, coupled with evidence of the members' economic motivation and their action's anticompetitive effect, proved her case.

A final note: HCQIA provides antitrust immunity only with reference to federal antitrust laws. State statutes may involve different legal presumptions and tests for liability.

In addition to the antitrust risk associated with peer review and credentialing or membership decisions, medical staffs face many of the same antitrust dangers as do professional associations. Members of hospital medical staffs meet often, both formally and informally, and have the opportunity to discuss the local health care market and economic conditions with other competing physicians who are active in the same market. This sharing of concerns can lead to joint decisions to take action that may have an anticompetitive effect.

A good example is the response of the medical staff of Broward General Medical Center to new competition from the Cleveland Clinic. In that case, the FTC in September 1991 charged the medical staff and its chief with having entered into a conspiracy to prevent or delay the expected competition through threats of boycott, refusal to deal except on collective terms, refusal to process applications for medical staff privileges sent by Cleveland Clinic physicians, and other anticompetitive activities. The medical staff signed a consent agreement to cease and desist from the alleged anticompetitive conduct.

Another case involved the Good Samaritan Regional Medical Center. The medical staff allegedly organized a boycott by its more than 500 members against the hospital. This induced the hospital to end its involvement in a multispecialty physicians' clinic that would have competed with the medical staff. The physicians, as alleged by the complaint, threatened to withhold patient admissions from the hospital and urged other physicians on the staff to do the same.

Both cases make clear the liability risks of using the medical staff to prevent or eliminate competition. Rather, the medical staff should limit its efforts to enhancing the quality and efficiency of the hospital.

Medical Practice Networks and Mergers

Traditionally, physicians have practiced as sole practitioners or in small groups. However, as third-party payers have become more aggressive in their efforts to control costs and MCOs have become a dominant market force, physicians have found that the traditional practice model puts them in a weakened position and makes it difficult to compete effectively in the marketplace.

One method of responding to the market change is to form a larger group by merging the practices of one or more physicians or smaller groups into a single larger entity, such as a single corporation or partnership. As long as the group's size does not raise Sherman Act Section 2 concerns or require advance reporting to the FTC, this approach is not a significant antitrust risk, because a single entity cannot conspire with itself.

A full merger provides the greatest safety from an antitrust perspective, but integrating previously independent practices can be very difficult. Many issues arise as physicians begin to put aside their autonomy and deal with the complexities of a much larger organizational infrastructure. As a result, maintaining economic independence often has more appeal to physicians and has led many to form networks rather than mergers. By maintaining their autonomy, physicians may develop economic alliances, but they retain their exposure to Section 1 of the Sherman Act.

Antitrust issues associated with physician networks were the focus of *Arizona v Maricopa County Medical Society*.[6] In this case, the local medical society established a maximum fee schedule, a practice the U.S. Supreme Court found to be a *per se* violation of the antitrust laws. The fact that maximum, and not minimum, prices were fixed was not significant.

Although the Supreme Court found the price agreement to be a *per se* violation, it pointed out that economic integration was an acceptable way for independent physicians to avoid illegal alliances. The Court explained that, if the providers can sufficiently integrate their practices and form a legitimate joint venture, their ancillary restrictions on competition may then be tested under the rule of reason. In *Maricopa*, the Court drew a distinction between the defendant foundation for medical care and "partnerships or other joint arrangements in which persons who would otherwise be competitors pool their capital and share the risks of loss as well as the opportunities for profit." The Court stated that "[i]n such joint ventures, the partnership is regarded as a single firm competing with other sellers in the market."

Although the Court suggested partial economic integration as a way to avoid a *per se* violation for price-fixing, the Court provided little guidance for determining when the provider members of a delivery system have sufficiently integrated their practices to avoid the *per se* rule. Generally, however, when courts analyze a joint venture, they apply rule of reason analysis. Joint ventures are considered lawful if any elimination of competition among the participants is limited to that which results directly from the partial integration of their functions. Thus, in this context, any agreement on prices must be a necessary part of the joint venture and can be no broader than necessary for that purpose. In addition, the market share of the participants as a group should be small, and the parties must not demonstrate a primary purpose or intent to restrict or eliminate competition.

Another significant case is the BMI case. Two associations of copyright owners (music composers) joined together in a royalty and blanket licensing agreement that allowed musicians to obtain a license to play compositions by paying a common license fee to the clearinghouse. Otherwise, the musicians would have to obtain a license from a musician on an individual basis. Although there was clearly agreement on price, the Court recognized the associations of composers as a new seller with a new product. The Court held there was no violation, in substance, because the procompetitive efficiencies of the arrangement permitted so much more music to be sold than would have been possible without the arrangement. The procompetitive efficiencies were clear, and the agreement on price was necessary to achieve them. Price agreement in this case was permissible even without a joint venture risk-sharing arrangement.

An analysis of the legality of physician networks stems from these two cases. Any network arrangement needs to be based on economic integration that results in procompetitive efficiencies. Apparent efficiencies resulting from the economic integration can take the case out of the *per se* category, even in the context of an associated agreement on price, and lead to analysis of the arrangement under the rule of reason. Although enforcement agencies do not generally apply full rule of reason analysis in these traditional *per se* categories, they do look for plausible efficiency justifications, with more extensive balancing as to reasonableness if the efficiency justifications are at least plausible. In evaluating networks, agreement on price must be incidental to the arrangement, not its basis.

If economic integration occurs without apparent procompetitive efficiencies, price agreements or efforts to stifle competition will be quickly condemned. Several cases demonstrate this.

In a 1994 case,[23] 10 Broward County, Florida, surgeons accepted a consent decree after they allegedly used their association as a vehicle to engage in collective negotiations on the fees and other contract terms without having integrated their services in any way nor created any efficiencies to justify their agreement to act collectively. When their terms were not met, they walked out, resulting in the closure of the trauma center at one of the hospitals for a period of months.

In another case,[24] the FTC brought an action that resulted in a consent decree and the dissolution of the Southbank IPA of Jacksonville, Florida. The IPA and its 23 obstetrician/gynecologist members were alleged to have engaged in a conspiracy to fix prices and boycott third-party payers; again, the group did not share financial risk or provide any new or more efficient services.

Finally, in a Virginia case settled by consent agreement, it was found that a group of physicians allegedly had agreed on reimbursement rates and other terms of dealing with third-party payers, then boycotted payers who did not meet those terms, thereby preventing any managed care plan from entering the area.

In short, IPAs and other ventures that serve essentially as vehicles to control or fix prices or to resist managed care through group boycotts will be challenged by enforcement agencies as *per se* violations of Section 1 of the Sherman Act. Groups of competitors can band together to form a joint venture, however, provided that the primary purpose is not to eliminate competition but to enhance it. This goal is accomplished most effectively by becoming a new competitor in the marketplace and offering a new product or service.

Antitrust Enforcement Policy Statements

What is the potential for the legality of various physician network arrangements to be challenged under the antitrust laws? This concern arises because, ultimately, most networks have some agreement on price. For this reason, the possibility for *per se* antitrust violation is real. What no one knows is when the enforcement agencies might consider a network as falling within the principles of the BMI case and be analyzed under the rule of reason.

This uncertainty has led the AMA to press for modification of antitrust laws to provide for general rule of reason analysis of physician networks. To demonstrate that legislative change is unnecessary, the Department of Justice and the FTC have tried to provide better guidance regarding how federal enforcement policies would apply to ventures that would result in lower health care costs.

To this end, the agencies have issued enforcement policy statements, one that addresses physician networks and one that addresses multiprovider networks. Both statements were revised in 1996. A physician network joint venture is defined as a physician-controlled venture in which the network's physician participants collectively agree on prices or price-related terms and jointly market their services. This includes such entities as IPAs and preferred provider organizations (PPOs). Multiprovider networks include all types and combinations of health care providers, including networks with a single type of provider. Networks that comprise only physicians are considered a particular category of multiprovider networks.

Physician Networks

The enforcement policy statement on physician network joint ventures can be summarized as follows. First, whenever a physician network is likely to produce significant efficiencies as a health care provider, any agreement on price reasonably necessary to accomplish the venture's procompetitive benefits will be analyzed under the rule of reason. Second, the statement establishes safety zones, which are, again, parameters for the network that are highly unlikely to raise substantial competitive concerns and will not be challenged under the antitrust laws, unless extraordinary circumstances exist. Third, the statement discusses the analysis of ventures that do not fall within the safety zone and emphasizes the point that being outside a safety zone does not make a venture illegal. Finally, the statement provides several examples of networks that are not likely to be challenged, and one example of a network that would be a *per se* violation.

A network must meet two basic requirements to qualify for safety zone protection. First, market share must be limited. For exclusive networks, the limit is 20% of the physicians in a given specialty with active hospital privileges in the relevant geographic market. For nonexclusive networks, the limit is 30%. An exclusive network is one that significantly restricts the ability of its members to affiliate with other physician network joint ventures and to contract individually with health insurance plans. A nonexclusive network does not impose any significant explicit or implicit restriction on the ability of its members to affiliate or contract with such other organizations. Second, the economic integration must be structured so that member physicians "share substantial financial risk."

Before the 1996 revisions, the safety zones explicitly recognized only two types of acceptable financial risk-sharing: capitation (in which physicians contracting with a health plan are paid a fixed amount per member per month regardless of the volume of services rendered) and withholds (in which a significant percentage of physicians' reimbursement is withheld unless the network as a whole meets predetermined cost-containment goals). In revising the statements, the enforcement agencies retained the requirement of sharing substantial financial risk. They view risk-sharing not as a desired end in itself, but rather as a clear and reliable indicator that a physician network involves sufficient integration by its physician participants to achieve significant efficiencies. In response to the request to broaden the safety zones, the agencies added other examples of arrangements of such risk-sharing beyond capitation and fee withhold financial incentives. They give an example of an additional payment method, which is an agreement among physicians to provide designated services for a predetermined percentage of premium revenue from a plan.

Another example is an alternative form of financial incentive, other than withholds, that establishes overall cost or utilization targets for networks with physician participants subject to subsequent financial rewards or penalties based on group performance.

Finally, the statements recognize the possibility that new types of risk-sharing arrangements will be developed. The statements suggest use of the expedited business review and advisory opinion procedures for organizers of physician networks who are uncertain whether their proposed arrangements constitute substantial financial risk-sharing.

The basic concern about the safety zones limitation was that any network in which physicians agreed on fees but did not fall within a safety zone was at risk of *per se* condemnation for blatant price-fixing. This was a real concern, because conduct subject to *per se* treatment cannot be defended on the ground that it had no anticompetitive consequences. In extreme cases, it could result in criminal prosecution and loss of professional license. Now, with the 1996 revisions, enforcement agencies have stated more explicitly that an arrangement that does not have safety zone protection does not necessarily raise antitrust concerns. Even though a network may fall outside antitrust safety zones, it still may have the potential to create significant efficiencies in health care delivery. If the physician integration through the network is likely to produce significant benefits for consumers and any price agreements (or other agreements what would otherwise be *per se* violation) by the network physicians are reasonably necessary to realize those efficiencies, then the network will be analyzed under the rule of reason.

Of particular importance is the fact that the revised statement goes beyond pure financial integration as a test for when rule of reason analysis may be appropriate. Instead, the statement now recognizes clinical integration as well. As set forth in the statement: "Physician network joint ventures that do not involve the sharing of substantial financial risk may also involve sufficient integration to demonstrate that the venture is likely to produce significant efficiencies. Such integration can be evidenced by the network implementing an active and ongoing program to evaluate and modify practice patterns by the network's physician participants and create a high degree of interdependence and cooperation among the physicians to control costs and ensure quality. This program may include: 1) establishing mechanisms to monitor and control utilization of health care services that are designed to control costs and assure quality of care; 2) selectively choosing network physicians who are likely to further these efficiency objectives; and 3) the significant investment of capital, both monetary and human, in the necessary infrastructure and capability to realize the claimed efficiencies."

With clinical integration as a basis for rule of reason treatment, the possibilities to develop fee-for-service networks are more flexible. Because a fee-for-service arrangement constitutes the primary basis for emergency physician reimbursement, it can benefit small independent groups of emergency physicians who might compete in the marketplace together on the basis of clinical integration when financial risk-sharing arrangements would be impractical or undesirable. For example, an independent emergency physician group that has a moderate market share in a community agrees on common utilization criteria, clinical guidelines, and protocols for handling managed care patients. Such an arrangement will provide both sufficient clinical integration of their independent practices and procompetitive efficiencies to prevent antitrust concern. Therefore, a reasonably necessary and related agreement on price for their services will be considered incidental.

For networks that approach sufficient integration to warrant analysis under the rule of reason, the actual analysis involves defining the relevant market, evaluating the competitive effects of the physician joint venture, evaluating the impact of procompetitive efficiencies, and analyzing any collateral agreements. Physicians must realize, however, that joint ventures that take the form of networks but which in purpose or effect are designed to impede competition will continue to be treated as unlawful conspiracies whose price agreements are *per se* illegal.

Factors that tend to corroborate a network's anticompetitive nature include statements evidencing anticompetitive purpose, a recent history of anticompetitive behavior, or collusion in the market, including efforts to obstruct or undermine the development of managed care. Other anticompetitive characteristics are networks that comprise a high percentage of local physicians where the marketplace does not justify such arrangements, the absence of any potential for generating significant efficiencies or otherwise increasing competition through the network, and the presence of anticompetitive collateral agreements without mechanisms to prevent the network's operation from having anticompetitive spillover effects outside the network.

Multiprovider Networks

The principles of analysis for multiprovider networks are much the same as those for physician networks. These include economic integration, either in the form of financial integration or clinical integration, that is likely to produce significant benefits for consumers. Also, any price agreements (or other agreements that would otherwise be *per se* violations) limited to what is reasonably necessary to realize those efficiencies will be evaluated under the rule of reason and will not be viewed as *per se* illegal. However, there are no safety zones for multiprovider networks. Multiprovider networks vary widely in their structures and relationships and new arrangements are continually being developed. As a result, the enforcement agencies are unable to establish a meaningful safety zone.

One point in the multiprovider network enforcement policy statement that is relevant to emergency physicians addresses networks of noncompetitors. As stated: "In a network limited to providers who are not actual or potential competitors, the providers generally can agree on the prices to be charged for their services without the kinds of economic integration discussed below." This raises the possibility, for example, of a network consisting of the emergency physicians group, the anesthesiology group, the radiology group, and the pathology group at a hospital developing a joint negotiating strategy and single negotiating representative to deal with an HMO interested in obtaining a contract with the hospital-based physicians at a given hospital. Assuming there is no competition or potential competition among the groups, agreement on prices would not be an agreement among competitors and should not be a restraint of trade.

Business review letters, or advisory opinions, provide a useful way to get specific approval of a proposed network plan. The agencies encourage groups and individuals to request such review when guidance is needed. Obtaining specific guidance can allow networks to proceed without significant fear of antitrust challenge. Also, the public has access to business review letters and advisory opinions, which provide even more opportunities to receive guidance on network arrangements that would be acceptable to the enforcement agencies.

Most of these opinions have been favorable. Of 13 business review letters issued on physician networks by the Department of Justice over a two-year period, only two letters were negative. In both cases, the primary reason for the unfavorable reviews was high market share. In one of the negative business review letters, the Department of Justice advised five groups of anesthesiologists based in Orange County, California, that it would not approve their proposal to deal jointly through a single price-setting unit with a managed care plan. The reason was that the arrangement would have resulted in there being only one reasonable alternative for consumers, which would have resulted in higher health care costs without any corresponding competitive benefits. Also, the proposed network would have made it difficult for MCOs to seek competitive prices by redirecting hospitals among the six major Orange County hospitals served by the groups. Each group had an exclusive contract.

The other negative letter addressed the proposal of a group of pediatricians who wanted to form a network representing 50% to 75% of primary care pediatricians in the relevant geographic markets. Interestingly enough, the high market share resulted when the Department of Justice failed to show that family practitioners were effective substitutes for primary care pediatricians, at least not based on the perception of MCOs in the market.

Business review letters and advisory opinions issued by the enforcement agencies are available on the Internet, as follows:
- Department of Justice, www.doj.gov
- Federal Trade Commission, www.ftc.gov

Case Discussions

1

Many physicians are naturally frustrated by the practices of HMOs and insurance companies, which at times may unilaterally decrease their payment schedules and present fee schedules to physicians as nonnegotiable. A natural response is to band together with other physicians with the goal of negotiating new fee schedules with one or more HMOs or insurance companies "from a position of strength."

Individual physicians or business entities can negotiate with an HMO and can decide individually to accept or reject a relationship on price or any other contractual term. In other words, the chapter in this case study, which represented competing individual physicians or physician group entities, decided on a "reasonable" price and negotiates on behalf of the competing physicians. This action would without question have been regarded as an agreement on price and would have been a *per se* violation of Section 1 of the Sherman Act. The fact that the price to be negotiated would have been reasonable or even low by market standards was irrelevant.

As for taking the same action with the state Medicaid program, the answer is different, provided it involves good faith petitioning of the government to adopt a payment proposal. Groups, even though they are competitors, can petition the government to obtain desired government action. For example, if the chapter had chosen to work with the state government, in good faith, to raise the fee schedule for Medicaid patients, or even to ask the state to require HMOs to raise their rates for emergency visits, this activity would not have been prevented by the antitrust laws. On the other hand, a group boycott of Medicare patients to force the state to adopt the rate proposal would have been a different matter.

2

One person can urge others to take individual action. The problem is that such activity, when it involves competitors, can appear to be a violation of antitrust law. It may be perfectly lawful for one competitor to urge another competitor to take a particular action. However, if the action, for example, involved raising prices, it would be strongly suggestive of an "agreement." If this activity results in a change in prices, an evaluating agency may determine that an agreement exists, which could prompt the agency to allege a violation of antitrust laws. An association should prevent such pricing discussions from taking place, given the fact that they do not serve a legitimate purpose of the association. Rather, they can lead only to either an actual agreement or an inferred agreement, even if one does not occur, and potential antitrust liability for the chapter, the physician who advocates the action, and the group.

3

An individual practice association, as the name implies, is a vehicle by which either independent physicians or independent physician groups engage in group business activity. The most clear-cut way to avoid any antitrust risk is to fall within a safety zone. To do so, a network that requires physicians to participate exclusively cannot include more than 20% of the active practitioners in a market. If the network is nonexclusive, it can include up to 30% of competing practitioners. Even if exclusive participation is not required by the terms of the network agreement, if members do not participate in other networks, the agencies will consider the network to be exclusive.

For emergency physicians, the extent to which other physicians are regarded as effective substitutes is an issue. Emergency physicians are not the sole providers of physician services in the emergency departments they staff. Urgent care centers and family physicians with walk-in practices compete for many of the same patients. Therefore, it might be possible to include others in the network, which would reduce the market share percentage that the network would be considered to represent.

In this case as presented, if there were no effective substitutes for emergency physicians, the percentage of participants was higher than required for the safety zones for either exclusive or nonexclusive networks. Even if the percentage met the 20% limit, the payment mechanism was fee-for-service without any financial incentive, such as a fee withhold. Therefore, the network would not have fallen within a safety zone.

With regard to the specific situation presented in this case, each physician's capital contribution was a potentially significant factor. The fact that major capital contribution was required to establish an entity suggested that the arrangement would have generated efficiencies; otherwise, the capital contribution would not have been needed. However, the amount seemed relatively small. If the capital contribution was required only to cover organizational costs, then this would have been consistent with an organization established to engage in price-fixing without procompetitive efficiencies. If the capital contributions were required to achieve major investment in developing utilization protocols, that is, activities specifically related to the efficiencies desired, then the capital contribution would have been more significant.

Even without capital contribution as an indication that the venture would have generated efficiencies, the network, as structured, had many features that were clearly procompetitive. The potential for cost savings was real. Moreover, a new competitive entity would have been created in the marketplace that would have been attractive to HMOs and achieved "clinical integration" to a large extent. As such, this network arrangement would probably have been evaluated under the rule of reason. One reservation was the size of the IPA, which encompassed 60% of the competitors in the market. However, if the percentage of competitors was reduced to a 30% nonexclusive network, it was likely that the network would have been acceptable to the agencies.

For network participants to avoid antitrust liability, they should fall within the safety zones. The alternative plan — a nonexclusive network that includes financial risk-sharing and limits compensation capitation or major fee withhold — would fall within the safety zone. This type of network could be implemented without significant fear of antitrust liability.

In a borderline situation such as this case, with limited insight as to what constituted sufficient clinical integration, the participants should have obtained a business review letter from the Department of Justice or an advisory opinion from the FTC. Nearly all such opinions have been favorable, except for those networks comprising a large percentage of the competition. The business review letter can create peace of mind before participants embark on a venture for which there are no models of approved networks.

4

The proposal here was in jeopardy because the network encompassed a large percentage of the competitors. On the other hand, there was no price agreement. Where only nonfee aspects of contracts were involved, the leeway allowed in terms of percentage of competitors was con-

siderably higher. Certain terms, such as gag provisions, definitions of emergency, utilization controls, or other contractual terms, may well be negotiated by such an IPA, as long as fees are not involved and competitive benefits are shown.

The antitrust enforcement policy statements provide an example of a nonexclusive IPA that involves 100% of the practitioners in a rural area without effective competition from the nearest big city. The proposed IPA, however, would limit its collective negotiation in behalf of all physicians to non–fee-related aspects of the contracts. Individual physicians and the local group practice would each determine whether to contract with third-party payers and negotiate their own individual contracts regarding fees. The competitive analysis provided in the statement emphasizes the nonexclusive nature of the IPA, which would allow individuals to contract separately from the IPA and with managed care plans not under contract with the IPA. In addition, the proposed IPA would serve a clinic that the managed care plan desires to open in a part of the county currently without medical services. To avoid antitrust liability, an IPA would need to show procompetitive efficiencies rather than just a desire to negotiate jointly, even for non-fee contractual items.

Key Points and Conclusion

- The federal antitrust laws apply fully to the practice of medicine.
- Penalties for violation of the antitrust laws are severe. They include criminal and civil penalties and expose physicians to damage awards in private lawsuits for three times actual damages and for plaintiffs' attorney fees.
- Physicians should be aware of the basic prohibitions of the antitrust laws and the laws' applicability so they will be alert to situations that create antitrust risk, particularly those activities that are considered illegal *per se*.
- Only unreasonable restraints of trade are illegal under the Sherman Act; however, *per se* violations are conclusively presumed to be unreasonable.
- The principal *per se* violations of the antitrust laws that apply particularly to physicians are agreements between competitors on price and joint refusals to negotiate.

- Association activities create significant risk of antitrust law violation, particularly the *per se* violation of joint refusal to negotiate. Associations should have a policy of antitrust law compliance and a program designed to ensure compliance with the antitrust laws.
- Medical staff should focus their activities on concerns of hospital medical quality and efficiency and avoid actions seeking to limit or control competition, particularly in credentialing. Staff engaging in joint activity designed to protect its members from the impact of the marketplace, other than through more effective competition, creates significant antitrust risk.
- Physician networks give independent physicians the opportunity to compete more effectively in the marketplace. Networks that involve either sharing of risk or other substantial procompetitive efficiencies and that constitute no more than a moderate share of the market can be legally formed, even though there is agreement on price. Networks viewed solely as vehicles to agree on price are illegal.

References

1. 15 USC 1.
2. 15 USC 2.
3. 15 USC 18.
4. 15 USC 18(a).
5. *American Medical Association v United States*, 317 US 519 (1943).
6. *Arizona v Maricopa County Medical Society*, 457 US 332 (1982).
7. *Jefferson Parish Hospital District No. 2 v Hyde*, 466 US2 (1983).
8. *Parker v Brown*, 317 US 341 (1943).
9. *A-1 Ambulance Service v County of Monterey*, 94-16704 (9th Cir 1996).
10. *Goldfarb v Virginia State Bar*, 421 US 773 (1975).
11. *Eastern Railroad Presidents Conference v Noerr Motor Freight, Inc*, 365 US 127 (1961).
12. *United Mine Workers of America v Pennington*, 381 US 657 (1965).
13. *California Motor Transport Co. v Trucking Unlimited*, 404 US 508 (1972).
14. *Allied Tube & Conduit Corp. v Indian Head, Inc*, 486 US 492 (1988).
15. *National Society of Professional Engineers v United States*, 435 US 679 (1978).
16. *FTC v Indiana Federation of Dentists*, 476 US 447 (1985).
17. *United States v Association of Family Practice Residency Directors District of Missouri*, May 28, 1996.
18. *Schachar v American Academy of Ophthalmology, Inc*, 870 F2d 397 (7th Cir 1989).
19. *American Society of Mechanical Engineers, Inc v Hydrolevel Corp*, 456 US 556 (1982).
20. Antitrust. ACEP Policy Statement, approved June 1996. To obtain a copy, call (800) 798-1822, touch 6, or go to www.acep.org.
21. *Patrick v Burget*, 800 F2d 1498 (9th Cir 1986).
22. *Boczar v Manatee Hospitals & Health Systems, Inc*, 993 F2d 1514 (11th Cir 1993).
23. Trauma Associates of North Broward, Inc, FTC C-3541 (1994).
24. Southbank IPA, Inc., 114 FTC 783 (1991).

Chapter 34

Fraud and Abuse

Gary W. Eiland, JD
Nancy C. LeGros, JD

Physicians and other health care professionals who provide medical care to beneficiaries of government-sponsored health care programs, such as Medicare, Medicaid, and CHAMPUS, have come under increased scrutiny over the past decade. Federal and state governments are seeking to control the costs associated with these programs. In addition to limitations placed on the levels of reimbursement, numerous fraud and abuse laws and regulations have been passed in an effort to expose and correct what is perceived as fraudulent behavior by providers.

Now more than ever, physicians must have a general knowledge of actions that may be violations of fraud and abuse laws or result in submission of what is considered a false or fraudulent claim for payment. Although some of the fraud and abuse laws have only limited application to emergency medicine, claims submitted on behalf of emergency physicians recently have been challenged based on the choice of CPT codes. Funding for federal antifraud enforcement programs has increased significantly, which means that physicians can anticipate increased review of the claims they submit.

This chapter focuses on the review and investigative activities conducted under the Medicare program to detect fraudulent or improper claims. The discussion also includes the federal sanctions for providers who are found to have committed fraud or abuse or to have submitted a false claim for payment under a government-sponsored health care program.

Role of the Medicare Carrier

The Health Care Financing Administration (HCFA) is the federal agency that contracts with private insurance companies to administer Medicare. Insurance companies responsible for the administration of the Medicare Part B program, which provides coverage for physicians' services, are referred to as Medicare carriers.

In addition to processing claims, each Medicare carrier has an important role in gathering and reviewing information used to maintain the integrity of the Medicare Part B program. Medicare carriers conduct a number of reviews to ensure the quality and medical necessity of services furnished to Medicare beneficiaries and to identify suspected cases of fraud or abuse.

Recent legislation contains provisions that enable the Secretary of the U.S. Department of Health and Human Services (DHHS) to contract with entities other than the Medicare carriers to perform these functions.[1] Through these reviews, the Medicare carriers also identify areas of policy weakness for action by HCFA or the Office of the Inspector General (OIG). The OIG is responsible for investigating suspected fraud and abuse cases, as well as initiating punitive actions against health care providers by referring criminal cases to the U.S. Department of Justice or by initiating civil monetary penalties or civil exclusion sanctions.

The Carrier's Medical Review Unit

Review activities at a Medicare carrier generally are carried out by the Medical Review (MR) Unit. The MR Unit is responsible for ensuring that Medicare beneficiaries receive only medically necessary and appropriate treatment. HCFA develops national coverage policies that establish the circumstances under which certain items or services are considered medically necessary. The MR Unit develops local medical review policies based on local patterns of utilization that may indicate possible overuse or misuse of a Medicare-covered item or service. National coverage policies and local medical review policies must be made public. Often, they are disseminated to providers through newsletter announcements.

Practices considered abusive rather than fraudulent are the primary responsibility of the MR Unit. In the *Medicare Carriers Manual*,[1] abuse is defined as "incidents or practices of providers, physicians, or suppliers of services that are inconsistent with accepted sound medical practices . . . resulting in unnecessary costs to the program, improper payment, or program payment for services that fail to meet professionally recognized standards of care or are medically unnecessary... Abuse involves payment for items or services when there is no legal entitlement to that payment and the provider has not knowingly and intentionally misrepresented facts to obtain payment."

Examples of abuse include the following[2]:
- Excessive charges for services or supplies.
- Medically unnecessary services (e.g., ordering a battery of diagnostic tests when only a few are needed) or services that do not meet professionally recognized standards.
- Exceeding the maximum allowable actual charge (MAAC).
- Billing Medicare patients at a higher fee schedule rate than for non-Medicare patients.
- Improper billing practices, including submission of bills to Medicare that are the responsibility of other insurers under the Medicare secondary payer regulation.

The goals of medical review include preventing inappropriate payments; identifying overutilization, abusive billing, and inappropriate care; educating providers to bill only for covered and medically necessary services to reduce inappropriate billing; and identifying overpayments.

Prepayment Review

Prepayment screens are designed to suspend the processing of Part B claims for services when these claims meet specific criteria developed by HCFA or the MR Unit to identify potential problems. Some screens are mandated by national coverage policy, and others may be developed locally by each carrier.

For example, HCFA mandates that carriers develop screens to identify claims in which more than one physician of the same or similar specialty or subspecialty bills Medicare for in-hospital services to the patient on the same date. Computer screens will automatically flag claims for manual review when the submitted charge exceeds a predetermined percentage of the Medicare prevailing charge or when the claim is for a given item or service and the frequency of such claims exceeds predetermined parameters. These parameters establish a threshold utilization level that triggers MR Unit review.

Screening parameters may be adjusted periodically by the carrier to ensure each parameter's effectiveness. Utilization guidelines describing the typical use of an item or service may be included in a national coverage policy or local MR Unit policy. These policies are available to the public; screening parameters are not.

Postpayment Review

A postpayment review identifies by locality and specialty those physicians whose utilization patterns differ from medically recognized standards, criteria, and norms. The process compares individual physicians statistically with other physicians in their specialty. The following standard postpayment data reports usually are generated every six months:
- The rate at which each provider and specialty bill a given item or service (expressed as the frequency billed per 100 Medicare patients for the six-month period).
- The rate at which an item or service was furnished to each patient who received the service.
- The percentage change in the total Medicare payment made to a provider for a given item or service from one six-month period to the next.

If a physician differs significantly from statistical norms, that physician will be placed under prepayment review for some or all services. This physician may also undergo a comprehensive medical review to determine whether corrective action, referral to the Fraud Unit, or other action is warranted.

A comprehensive medical review involves a thorough analysis of a sampling of a physician's processed claims. A comprehensive review begins with the selection of at least 15 Medicare beneficiaries who received the service under review. The MR Unit then requests the patients' medical records from the physician and obtains the payment history and other pertinent data relating to the service provided. The MR Unit reviews these documents to determine whether the service was medically necessary and whether the documentation supports the level of service billed. If the MR Unit finds that overutilization exists, it will instigate corrective action. This may include a warning letter, educational contact, overpayment assessment and recovery, prepayment screening of the physician's claims, and referral to the professional review organization or the carrier's Fraud Unit. The latter action may be taken if there is a pattern of abuse or if a provider has received warnings in the past. The case may be referred to the OIG if the practice pattern is not corrected.

Focused Medical Review

A focused medical review is used to examine areas where there is the greatest risk of inappropriate payments under the Medicare program. The impetus for a focused medical review often comes not from individual provider utilization data, but from trends in aggregate local utilization compared to other areas.

For example, the use of certain CPT codes may be more frequent in some regions than in others. The large volume of claims involved, however, makes individual reviews expensive and time-consuming. If the aberration cannot be explained by differences in the local Medicare patient population, the MR Unit analyzes aggregate local data to determine whether the item or service is being overused. If overuse is found, the MR Unit develops a local MR policy for the item or service and informs the medical community of the policy. Ideally, focused medical review enables the carrier to correct aberrations in utilization with minimal inconvenience to individual physicians.

Teaching Physician Documentation Audits

Intermediary Letter 372,[3] which formerly governed Medicare coverage and payment for services of teaching physicians, required that carriers make periodic checks of patient records.

The checks included an examination of admission, progress, and discharge notes to verify that physician services to patients furnished by teaching physicians in a teaching hospital met the appropriate attending physician coverage criteria and to recoup overpayments if a significant portion of the carrier's sample did not meet the criteria. Intermediary Letter 372 has been replaced by regulations adopted by HCFA in December 1995, effective July 1, 1996.[4] With limited exceptions, the regulations require the teaching physician to be present during the "key portion" of the service or procedure for which payment is sought. The *Medicare Carriers Manual* has not yet been updated to address enforcement procedures for the new regulations, but such procedures are likely to involve documentation audits of the teaching physician's involvement in the service or procedure. Special attention should be given to the new regulations if residents are assigned to the emergency department. The regulations also clarify coverage of services performed by "moonlighting" residents.

The Carrier's Fraud Unit

A Medicare carrier's Fraud Unit is responsible for preventing, identifying, and deterring fraud and abuse, although fraudulent activities are the unit's primary focus. Fraud is defined in the *Medicare Carriers Manual* as "the intentional deception or misrepresentation that an individual knows to be false or does not believe to be true and makes, knowing that the deception could result in some unauthorized benefit to himself/herself or some other person. The most frequent kind of fraud arises from a false statement or misrepresentation made, or caused to be made, that is material to entitlement or payment under the Medicare program."

Examples of fraud are as follows[1]:

- Billing for services or supplies not provided, including billing for "no shows."
- Misrepresenting a patient's diagnosis to justify services or equipment furnished.
- Altering claim forms to receive a higher payment amount.
- Deliberately applying for duplicate payment, that is, billing Medicare and the patient for the same service or billing both Medicare and another insurer to receive double payment.
- Soliciting, offering, or receiving a kickback, bribe, or rebate.
- Unbundling charges.
- Executing Certificates of Medical Necessity

for patients not personally and professionally known by the physician.

- Claiming a higher level of services than were actually furnished ("upcoding") or misrepresenting amounts charged for services, the patient's identity, or dates of service, etc.
- Submitting claims for noncovered services billed as covered services.
- Collusion between a provider and a patient or between a supplier and a provider that results in higher costs or charges.
- Using split billing, that is, billing procedures over several days when they were actually performed during a single visit.
- Using the adjustment payment process to generate fraudulent payments, for example, provider deliberately overbills for services and carrier employee generates adjustments without the patient's knowledge.
- Billing for "gang" visits, for example, a physician bills for 20 nursing home visits without providing specific services to individual patients.

At one time, some of these practices were included in the *Medicare Carriers Manual* as examples of abuse rather than fraud. Reflecting the current climate, the manual now notes that, although some of these practices may initially be considered abuse, they may evolve into fraud.

The Fraud Unit's activities include investigation and development of fraud cases; initiation of administrative actions to suspend or deny payments; referral of information or cases to other federal agencies, such as the OIG, Department of Justice, or the FBI; and identification and elimination of program weaknesses. The *Medicare Carriers Manual* provides that a carrier's Fraud Unit should not merely "react to complaints" but should "proactively seek out fraud" using a variety of internal and external sources for leads. These sources include aberrant utilization patterns detected through internal controls or postpayment reviews, referrals from Medicare beneficiaries, the MR Unit, the peer review organization, OIG, or HCFA, and activities highlighted in fraud alerts.

Random Reviews

Fraud Units routinely conduct reviews to determine the appropriateness of Medicare payments. Such reviews include the following:
- Random review of claims to determine propriety of payments.
- Telephone contacts with beneficiaries to confirm delivery of items and services.
- Random verification of physician licensure.
- Random verification of Certificates of Medical Necessity.
- Analysis of the following types of items or services: high frequency and high cost, high frequency and low cost, low frequency and low cost, and low frequency and high cost.
- Data analysis of local practices and claims compared to national and regional trends, beginning with the top 30 national services or procedures targeted for focused medical review, to identify fraudulent claims.
- Visiting providers on-site.

Investigations

Once the Fraud Unit determines that a given complaint, referral, or situation may involve fraud, it conducts a review of the provider's background, specialty, and practice profile. The provider may be contacted for discussion of the issue. (The *Medicare Carriers Manual* provides that Fraud Unit staff must identify themselves as such if contacting a provider suspected of fraud.) If further investigation is warranted, the Fraud Unit may review medical records or contact at least 10 Medicare beneficiaries to verify services or items furnished by the provider. If 40% of the beneficiaries contacted deny receipt of services billed by the provider, a strong potential for fraud is considered to exist.

Cases of suspected fraud are referred to the Office of Investigations within the OIG. The Office of Investigations is responsible for all criminal investigations conducted with the DHHS and is staffed with professional criminal investigators. The OIG may also involve the FBI, the IRS, and other law enforcement agencies in an investigation. Once the investigation is complete, and if the allegations of fraud are substantiated, the case is referred to the U.S. Attorney's office within the Department of Justice for civil or criminal prosecution.

According to the *Medicare Carriers Manual*, the following types of allegations should be referred immediately to the Office of Investigations:
- Carrier employee fraud.
- Cases in which an informant is a current or former employee of the suspected physician or supplier.
- Cases involving providers with prior fraud convictions or currently under fraud investigations or program investigations.
- Cases involving multiple carriers.

- Cases likely to receive widespread publicity or involving sensitive issues.
- Allegations of fraud involving federal employees, organized crime, or a third-party insurer with primary responsibility for health insurance coverage for a Medicare beneficiary.

If the Office of Investigations declines to accept a referral, the *Medicare Carriers Manual* provides that the Fraud Unit should continue to monitor the provider's activities, take appropriate administrative actions such as payment denial, and send a warning notice to the provider under review. Civil or administrative sanctions, such as exclusion from participation in the Medicare program, also may be pursued through the OIG. Finally, the *Medicare Carriers Manual* provides that the Fraud Unit can "shop the case around with other federal law enforcement agencies, such as the FBI, CHAMPUS, Railroad Retirement Board, or the Medicaid fraud control unit," if the Office of Investigations declines to accept a referral.

Payment Actions

The Fraud Unit is responsible for safeguarding the Medicare Trust Fund so that no payments are made to fraudulent providers. Payment may be denied for a specific claim if there is a substantive reason for the carrier to believe that an item or service was not provided or was not medically necessary, subject to the provider's right to appeal the denial. The carrier also may suspend claims already approved for payment if it has "reliable evidence" that the provider has submitted fraudulent claims or if the carrier needs time to determine whether allegations of fraud are credible. Generally, the carrier will inform a physician in advance of a proposed suspension and give the physician 15 days (or longer for good cause shown) in which to submit a statement as to why the suspension should not be put into effect. However, the carrier has the right to shorten the notice period prior to a suspension or, if there is "reliable evidence" of fraud or "willful misrepresentation," to provide no advance notice at all.

Overpayment Recovery

When it is determined that fraud or abuse has occurred, the Fraud Unit or the MR Unit can pursue recovery of claims paid. There is a four-year limitation on reopening a carrier's decision to pay a claim, but the limitation does not apply if fraud is involved.

A physician is liable for repayment of claims determined to be improper unless the physician is deemed to be "without fault." According to the *Medicare Carriers Manual*, a physician is without fault if he exercised reasonable care in billing for the item or service and in accepting the payment (i.e., the physician fully disclosed all material facts and had a reasonable basis to believe the payment was correct), or if the physician had reason to question the payment, he promptly brought the matter to the carrier's attention. If an overpayment is discovered subsequent to the third calendar year after the year of payment, the physician is deemed to be without fault unless there is evidence to the contrary.

Examples of circumstances that trigger physician liability for overpayments include the following:

- Use of an incorrect reasonable charge limitation.
- Receipt of duplicate payments.
- Received payment but did not accept assignment.
- Submission of erroneous information or failure to disclose facts material to the claim.
- Claims submitted for items or services that the physician should have known were not covered (generally, a physician is assumed to know policies or rules that are published in the *Federal Register*, disseminated to the medical community by the carrier, or sent by the carrier).
- An item or service furnished by an unqualified practitioner or supplier.
- Mathematical or clerical error other than proper assessment of the deductible.
- Lack of adequate documentation.

During a fraud investigation, a physician may offer to repay any amounts that are determined to be overpayments. However, the physician will be required to execute an agreement acknowledging that the repayment does not affect the right of the federal government to pursue appropriate criminal, civil, or administrative sanctions relating to the claims.

When determining the amount of an overpayment, the carrier is authorized to use statistical sampling. A sample of Medicare beneficiaries, bills, or services is readjudicated by the carrier and used as the basis for extrapolation of an estimated overpayment. This statistical sampling is used to project overpayments when claims are numerous and reflect a pattern of erroneous billing or overutilization, and when case-by-case review is not administratively feasible. Sampling and extrapolation procedures have been upheld as not arbitrary, capricious, or invidiously discriminatory.[5]

Statutory Provisions and Penalties for Violation

Federal government health programs contain numerous statutory provisions under which a provider may be sanctioned for program violation. The scope of many of these provisions was expanded by the Health Insurance Portability and Accountability Act of 1996.

In addition to the revisions noted below, this law provides for programs to enhance existing fraud and abuse enforcement activities. Under the Fraud and Abuse Control Program, the U.S. Attorney General and the DHHS Secretary, acting through the OIG, coordinate federal, state, and local health care antifraud enforcement programs. It also provides for the establishment of two other programs. Beneficiary Incentive Programs are designed to encourage Medicare beneficiaries to report providers engaging in fraud and abuse. The Medicare Integrity Program authorizes HCFA to enter into contracts with private entities to carry out fraud and abuse detection, cost report audits, utilization review, provider payment determinations, provider education, and a durable medical equipment list. Thus, in the future, entities other than Medicare carriers may carry out many of the claims reviews and investigations described previously.

Civil Statutes

The DHHS Secretary has the authority to exclude providers from Medicare and state health programs for program-related abuses.[6] This exclusion authority, which may be delegated to the OIG, is divided into two parts: mandatory and discretionary exclusions. The mandatory exclusion applies to individuals who are convicted of a Medicare- or Medicaid-related crime, a crime related to patient abuse, a felony conviction relating to health care fraud, or a felony conviction relating to controlled substances. A mandatory exclusion is for a minimum of five years but may be waived by the Secretary under limited circumstances. The Secretary also may waive a provider's exclusion under a state health care program on request from the state agency administering the program.

Discretionary exclusions may be issued to providers for other acts. A minimum period of exclusion is proscribed for certain offenses, subject to the Secretary's determination that a shorter or longer period is appropriate based on the circumstances.

Some of the offenses and circumstances that could result in discretionary exclusion include the following:

- Misdemeanor conviction relating to health care fraud or obstruction of an investigation (three years)
- Conviction for non–health care-related fraud, theft, embezzlement, or financial misconduct in connection with a government-funded program (three years)
- Misdemeanor conviction for controlled substances (three years)
- License revocation or suspension, or exclusion or suspension under a federal or state health care program (not less than the underlying exclusion or suspension)
- Claims for excessive charges or unnecessary services (one year)
- Fraud, kickback, and other prohibited activities
- Entities controlled or owned by an individual who has been sanctioned for health care-related offenses
- Failure to disclose required information
- Failure to supply requested information on subcontractors and suppliers
- Failure to supply payment information
- Failure to grant immediate access
- Individuals with an ownership or controlling interest in a sanctioned entity who know or should know of the action constituting the basis for the sanction, or a person who is an officer or managing employee of a sanctioned entity

The Civil Monetary Penalties Law[6] vests the Secretary with the power to levy civil fines for fraudulently submitted claims for Medicare or Medicaid reimbursement without initiating proceedings in the courts. Violators may be fined up to $10,000 as a penalty for each item or service fraudulently claimed and may be assessed up to three times the amount claimed for each item or service. An individual on whom the Secretary imposes a civil monetary penalty also may be suspended from participation in federal health care programs.

Civil monetary penalties may be imposed in the following situations:

- A claim is presented for an item or service that a person knows or should know was not provided as claimed, including habitual presentation of claims based on a code that the person knows or should know will result in greater payment than the code applicable to the item or service actually provided ("upcoding").

- A claim is presented for items or services and the person knows or should know the claim is false or fraudulent.
- A claim submitted is for a pattern of items or services that the person knows or should know are not medically necessary.
- An excluded individual retains an ownership or controlling interest in an entity participating in Medicare or Medicaid or serves as an officer or managing employee of a participating entity.
- A claim is presented for an item or service for which payment may not be made.
- A request for payment is presented that violates assignment, agreement with state agency or participating physician, or supplier agreement.
- A claim is presented for items or services incident to physician's services that were furnished or supervised by nonlicensed physician, when physician's license was falsely obtained, or when physician falsely represented board certification in a medical specialty.
- A claim is presented for an item or service furnished when claimant was excluded from program under which the claim was made.
- The physician knowingly and willfully bills a service in excess of the MAAC limits.
- A hospital, HMO, or competitive medical plan makes payments to physician as inducement to reduce or limit services provided to Medicare or Medicaid beneficiary under care of physician.
- A hospital and physician violate requirements concerning necessary stabilizing treatment and appropriate transfers of patients who have emergency medical conditions or are in active labor.
- A physician submits a bill for diagnostic tests performed by a supplier in excess of applicable deductible or coinsurance or not properly reimbursable to a Medicare Part B beneficiary.
- A physician or other provider knowingly, willfully, and repeatedly bills a Medicare Part B beneficiary for clinical diagnostic laboratory tests for which payment may be made only on an assignment-related basis.
- A physician or other provider offers or gives remuneration (including free items or services and waiver of coinsurance and deductible amounts, unless the waiver

meets certain standards) to induce individuals to order or receive items or services for which payment may be made, in whole or in part, under Medicare or Medicaid.

- A physician falsely certifies the need for home health services (this offense carries a maximum penalty of the greater of $5,000 or three times the amount of payment for home health services).

The Health Insurance Portability and Accountability Act of 1996 clarified the level of knowledge that must be found in order to impose a civil monetary penalty. A person generally must be shown to have "knowingly" presented a claim that the person "knows or should know" is fraudulent. "Should know" is now defined in the statute as "acts in deliberate ignorance" or in "reckless disregard" of "the truth or falsity of the information" at issue; "no proof of specific intent to defraud" need be shown.[6] The Act also expands the application of the Civil Monetary Penalties Law to federal health care programs not contained in the Social Security Act, such as CHAMPUS.

The Social Security Act also contains sanctions against providers who fail to comply with certain obligations. Enforcement of these obligations is the responsibility of peer review organizations. Providers are required to ensure that items or services they furnish or order will be provided in an economical manner and only when medically necessary, meet professionally recognized standards, and are supported by reasonable documentation. The Secretary has the authority to exclude a provider who fails to comply with these obligations from participation in the Medicare or Medicaid programs for at least one year, or to levy a fine of up to $10,000 for each instance of medically improper or unnecessary services.

In civil sanction cases, the OIG can proceed independently without involving a U.S. Attorney. The OIG has the authority to make factual determinations regarding the filing of false or improper claims and to impose civil exclusions, civil monetary penalties, or assessments. If the OIG proposes to impose a penalty and assessment or to suspend an individual from participation in a federal health care program, the OIG must notify the individual of the determination. At this point, the individual may request a hearing. The burden of proof is "preponderance of the evidence," the typical burden of proof for administrative matters as opposed to "beyond a reasonable doubt" required in criminal prosecutions. Except for illegal remuneration claims, no criminal intent needs to be proved — "reckless disregard" is sufficient to sustain a penalty. An administrative law judge is assigned to try the case, and no jury is involved. After the judge makes a decision, either party may file an appeal with the Departmental Appeals Board. Although judicial review of the board's decision is available, it will be reversed only if it is "arbitrary, capricious, an abuse of discretion, or not in accordance with the law." Administrative law judge decisions are not precedent, yet the agency may not be inconsistent nor depart from prior decisions without fully explaining its reason for doing so.

The False Claims Act

The False Claims Act[7] is a general federal civil statute that is being used increasingly as an enforcement vehicle for health care fraud and abuse laws. Originally enacted during the Civil War in response to fraudulent activities of government defense contractors, certain provisions of the law may be applied to the acts of submitting a false claim for payment under a federal health care program. These provisions provide sanctions for a person who does one or more of the following:

- Knowingly presents, or causes to be presented, to an officer or employee of the U.S. government, a false or fraudulent claim for payment or approval.
- Knowingly makes, uses, or causes to be made or used a false record or statement to get a false or fraudulent claim paid or approved by the government.
- Conspires to defraud the government by getting a false or fraudulent claim allowed or paid.
- Knowingly makes, uses, or causes to be made or used a false record or statement to conceal, avoid, or decrease an obligation to pay or transmit money or property to the government.

As used in this law, the term "knowingly" means actual knowledge of the falsity of a claim; deliberate ignorance of the truth or falsity of a claim; or reckless disregard of the truth or falsity of a claim.[7] Because actual knowledge of the falsity of a claim need not be shown to establish a False Claims Act violation, a physician may be found liable even if he has only minimal involvement in preparing and submitting claims for payment, if he acted in "reckless disregard" with

respect to the claim. A violation of the False Claims Act can result in civil penalties of $5,000 to $10,000 plus three times the amount of damages sustained by the federal government because of the person's act.

Enforcement of the False Claims Act is the responsibility of the Department of Justice. However, the law also provides for enforcement by private litigants — *qui tam* relators — who bring lawsuits on behalf of the government. The *qui tam* relator, or informer, brings an action under a statute that establishes a penalty for the commission or omission of a certain act. The *qui tam* relator must file the complaint under seal and submit a copy of the complaint to the Department of Justice, which has the option of intervening in the lawsuit. The complaint is not served on the defendant until the court orders it served, usually after the Department of Justice has made its determination of whether to intervene. A relator is entitled to receive a percentage of the proceeds from successful litigation of the case. The amount of the relator's share ranges from 15% to 30%, which can provide considerable incentive for a plaintiff to bring a complaint.

Criminal Statutes

The Social Security Act describes the following violations that may result in criminal penalties consisting of a $25,000 fine, five years' imprisonment, or both[6]:

- False statement, concealments, and conversions in connection with benefits or payments
- Illegal remuneration
- Misrepresentation of Conditions of Participation
- Illegal patient admission and retention requirements
- Knowing, willful, and repeated assignment or participation violations

Some sections of the Social Security Act were broadened by the Health Insurance Portability and Accountability Act of 1996 to apply to all health programs funded in whole or in part by the federal government, with the exception of the Federal Employees Health Benefit Program. The Act also contains provisions that require the Secretary to give guidance to providers regarding the application of health care fraud and abuse sanctions. Such guidance includes annual solicitation of proposals for modifications or additions to existing "safe harbors" that specify payment practices that will not be treated as violations, and issuance of advisory opinions as to the application of the law to specific activities and arrangements.

With respect to criminal laws other than those found in the Social Security Act, the Health Insurance Portability and Accountability Act of 1996 revised Title 18 of the U.S. Code to create a number of new criminal acts that carry monetary penalties and/or terms of imprisonment, generally from 5 to 10 years. These criminal acts are as follows:

- Theft or embezzlement in connection with any public or private health care benefit program.
- False statements in matters relating to public or private health care benefit programs.
- Health care fraud.
- Obstruction of criminal investigations of health care offenses.
- Laundering of monetary instruments.
- Authorizing injunctive relief and freezing of assets in cases involving federal health care offenses.
- Authorizing investigative demand procedures.
- Forfeitures for federal health care offenses.

How to Handle an Audit or Investigation

Routine inquiries on specific claims should be handled by the physician or the physician's business manager and billing staff. However, if the Medicare carrier or OIG initiates an audit or investigation, the physician should seek the advice of legal counsel knowledgeable in health law and in Medicare and Medicaid law and sanctions and how the Medicare carrier and OIG operate. This is especially true for complicated investigations involving multiple programs, agencies, and federal and state sanctions.

The physician and his staff always should maintain written notes of any conversations with the carrier that concern a particular claim, coverage, or payment issue. Any contacts with the carrier, OIG, or law enforcement personnel regarding an audit or investigation also should be documented. Generally, carrier personnel do not visit a provider on site without obtaining advance permission from the provider. OIG or law enforcement contacts can occur without prior notice. A physician may wish to inform the staff of their rights with respect to inquiries made by law enforcement personnel.

When first contacted by investigators, the physician should ask the following questions:

- Who are the investigators? Names, agencies, addresses, telephone numbers. Ask for official identification and make notes.
- What is the nature of the investigation? Target, subject matter, and authority.
- What information is being sought? For example, if normally confidential information, such as patient and medical staff records, are requested, what is the authority for examination?
- How long might the investigation continue?
- Will an exit conference be held? Will a report be issued?

The physician should call the hospital attorney and direct that the investigators schedule future contact through the attorney. The physician should implement an investigation response plan with the attorney and proceed with sensitized cooperation consistent with counsel's advice.

Compliance Programs

The term "compliance program" derives its name from Chapter 8 of the U.S. Sentencing Guidelines, which deals with the sentencing of corporate entities that are convicted of a felony or a Class A misdemeanor. Corporate entities can be found guilty of criminal conduct due to acts by employees. Under the Guidelines, a judge may consider certain aggravating or mitigating factors when determining the sentence of a corporate entity found to have violated a criminal law. One such mitigating factor is the existence of an "effective plan to prevent and detect violations of law." What such a "plan" is is a program that has been reasonably designed, implemented, and enforced so that it will generally be effective in preventing and detecting criminal conduct. The hallmark of an effective program is that the entity exercised due diligence in seeking to prevent and detect criminal conduct by its employees and other agents.

The Guidelines set forth the following seven requirements that must be met in order for a compliance program to qualify as an effective program:

- Reasonable compliance standards and procedures
- Appointment of a corporate compliance officer
- Exercise of due care in the delegation of discretionary authority
- Employee education and compliance training

- Ongoing monitoring and reporting systems
- Consistent and continuous enforcement of compliance standards
- Appropriate response to offenses; prevention of reoccurrences

Although an effective compliance program can reduce a criminal penalty, its greatest value lies in fostering compliance with the law and in preventing violations. Noncompliance with medical care laws, regulations, and instructions can have a potentially disastrous effect on a health care provider, especially if such noncompliance results in exclusion from participation in government health programs. Although development, implementation, and maintenance of an effective compliance program require significant time and effort, the program is worthwhile if it can prevent allegations of improper claims submission or violations of the fraud and abuse laws.

Key Points and Conclusion

Because of the increased audit and investigative activities of government regulators and law enforcement agencies, physicians and other providers should know about the scope of these activities. Routine review screens developed by Medicare carriers compare the services of one provider with the services of others in the same or similar specialty. Variations from the norm may cause a provider to undergo increased scrutiny, reviews, or investigations by various regulatory or review bodies. Ignorance of the law, regulations, or billing procedures is rarely considered a valid defense in case of a violation, particularly if information regarding the correct procedure or a particular coverage issue is publicly available. Physicians and staff must stay abreast of all Medicare and Medicaid regulations applicable to the physician's specialty and service area. Physicians should develop a response plan to guide the response to an audit or investigation. All staff members should be briefed regarding this response plan and clearly instructed concerning the referral of all inquires to the physician or person in charge.

References

1. *Medicare Carriers Manual*, HCFA-Pub. 14.
2. *Medicare Intermediary Manual* (HCFA-Pub. 13-3) Section 3956.1; *Medicare Hospital Manual* (HCFA-Pub. 10) Section 1096.2; *Medicare Skilled Nursing Facility Manual* (HCFA-Pub. 12) Section 106.2.
3. HCFA issued general payment guidelines for supervising physicians in a teaching setting in Intermediary Letter ("I.L.") No. 372 in April 1969, and issued subsequent clarifications of those guidelines in 1970 pursuant to a series of additional Intermediary Letters (i.e., Part A I.L. 70-7/Part B I.L. No. 70-2; Part A I.L. No. 70-25/Part B I.L. No. 70-2; and Part A I.L. No. 70-31/Part B I. L. Bo. 70-27, which, together with I.L. 372, are collectively referred to as "Intermediary Letter 372."
4. 60 *Federal Register* 6317.

Chapter 35

Alterations of the Medical Record

David L. Freedman, MD, JD, FACEP
Paul W. Kolodzik, MD, MBA, FACEP

The primary purpose of the emergency department medical record, like all medical records, is to communicate information about the care and treatment of a patient. The medical record also serves as a permanent business document, and as such, will be the subject of detailed scrutiny if a claim of malpractice arises against an emergency physician.

The medical record generally can and will be admitted into evidence at a malpractice proceeding.[1] It is the most important piece of evidence of the quality of emergency department medical care provided to a patient. A well-documented record is crucial to a physician's defense, and as such, its value depends on its completeness, accuracy, and timely preparation. Indeed, the well-prepared medical record is the simplest and most economical defense against a malpractice claim.[2]

Conversely, a medical record that is unavailable or "lost" poses an almost insurmountable obstacle to the physician's defense. Likewise, the improper alteration of a record, no matter how innocent the intent, is likely to be construed by the jury as a blatant attempt to conceal negligence and thereby avoid liability.

The issue of tampering with the medical record is compounded by the fact that, in some jurisdictions, the alteration or destruction of a medical record is considered a criminal offense and is punishable by fine, imprisonment, or both.

Case Studies

1

A 22-year-old woman comes to the emergency department on a busy Saturday evening with a chief complaint of pelvic pain of eight hours duration. After the patient is triaged, the emergency physician on duty sees her, takes a detailed history, performs a complete physical examination, including a pelvic examination, and orders appropriate laboratory tests. After reviewing the results of the laboratory tests and reexamining the patient's abdomen, the emergency physician diagnoses pelvic inflammatory disease. The patient is treated and discharged with instructions to follow up with her family physician within the next several days.

Shortly after discharging the patient, the emergency physician realizes that his documentation of the patient's pelvic examination has been entered on the chart of one of the many other pelvic pain patients he had seen that evening. He then realizes that the documentation of one of these other cases has been mistakenly entered on this patient's chart.

2

A 22-month-old girl is brought to the emergency department at approximately 3:00 AM by her mother, who says that the girl has a fever and left ear pain. The emergency physician on duty sees the patient and specifically evaluates her for meningitis. He notes that the patient is alert and playful, has no rash, and has a supple neck. The only positive physical examination finding is an inflamed and bulging left tympanic membrane. The emergency physician prescribes a course of amoxicillin after making the diagnosis of otitis media. He instructs the mother to monitor the girl for any changes in her condition and to follow up with her pediatrician within the next two days.

In the 24 hours following discharge, the girl's condition improves. However, subsequent to that time, she becomes gradually less alert. When seen by her pediatrician 2½ days after discharge, she is lethargic and has a petechial rash and obvious meningeal signs. She is hospitalized immediately and does recover but unfortunately has the sequelae of mild cognitive impairment and residual hearing deficit.

Two months after the patient's emergency department visit, the emergency physician is notified by the medical records department that a legal firm known to specialize in medical negligence cases has requested the girl's medical records. The emergency physician, who is able to recall the patient's visit and his evaluation of her condition in detail, is disturbed to find, on reviewing the medical record, that he had failed to document the patient's alert mental status, lack of rash, and supple neck.

3

A 28-year-old man presents to the emergency department with a laceration of the volar aspect of his right thumb, just proximal to the interphalangeal joint. During his evaluation of the patient's thumb, the emergency physician notes the loss of two point discrimination on the radial aspect of the thumb distally, as well as a decreased ability to flex the interphalangeal joint. On exploration of the laceration, a complete flexor tendon laceration is noted. The laceration is irrigated and closed with several loose sutures and a volar splint is applied.

The patient is referred to a hand surgeon and is instructed to follow up in two days. The patient's history, examination, exploration of the laceration, treatment provided, and discharge instructions given to the patient are well documented on the medical record in a complete, timely, and accurate manner.

The patient fails to follow up with the hand surgeon. Eighteen months later, the emergency physician learns that the patient has filed a claim of malpractice against him for failure to diagnose tendon and digital nerve laceration. He is able to recall the patient's visit, the injury, and his appropriate documentation of the care provided. Unfortunately, the medical records department informs him that the record has been lost.

The Medical-Legal Perspective

After a patient has a poor outcome, and particularly when a malpractice action has been filed, a physician's natural response is to review the involved patient's medical record. When that review reveals negligent treatment or inadequate documentation of appropriate treatment, the physician may be tempted to alter or even destroy the record. Despite this temptation, a medical record should never be covertly altered or destroyed. In rare instances, and only after legal consultation, a properly dated and initialed addendum to the record might be appropriate. Destruction of the record is never appropriate. No matter how much the record seems to support the plaintiff's claim of negligent treatment, the defendant physician's attorney will be able to present some type of defense. On the other hand, the physician's attorney will have extreme difficulty raising any credible defense if the record has been covertly altered or is unavailable for any reason. At the very least, covert alterations create an appearance of impropriety; at the worst, they create an impression of frank dishonesty, an impression that may be difficult or impossible to overcome. A missing medical record may lead to a legal presumption that it was destroyed by the defendant physician in an effort to avoid liability.

Many plaintiffs' attorneys have become quite sophisticated regarding medical malpractice litigation. They realize that medical records in general, and emergency department records in particular, are copied and sent to other physicians and departments, billing services, and insurance companies. Knowing the devastating consequences to a defendant physician of an apparently covert, self-serving alteration of a medical record, they will obtain the medical record from multiple sources in an effort to discover any such alterations. In addition, document examiners are used routinely by attorneys and have sophisticated methods of detecting alterations of records. The consequences of changing the medical record after the plaintiff's attorney has acquired an unaltered copy will be devastating.[3]

Altering the Medical Record

Numerous cases are reported that demonstrate the serious consequences of tampering with a medical record. A dramatic example of these consequences is seen in *Pisel v Stamford Hospital, et al,*[4] decided by the Connecticut Supreme Court. In this case, a 23-year-old woman with schizophrenia was admitted to a hospital psychiatric unit. Because she was in an agitated state, she was sedated and locked in a seclusion room. Four hours passed, during which time no staff member "entered [her] room or had any personal contact with her to assess her mental condition or alleviate her agitation." Following this four-hour interval, she was found wedged between a side rail of the bed and the mattress. Unfortunately, she was in cardiopulmonary arrest at the time she was discovered and died later that day. Several issues were raised in this case regarding the apparent negligence of the hospital staff. However, the issue pertinent to this discussion is the covert alterations of the medical record.

After the incident, it was obvious to the hospital staff that a significant risk management problem existed. In view of the facts of the case, defense of the staff's actions would have been difficult. The director of nursing at the hospital reviewed the medical record and, determining that it supported a claim of substandard care, "ordered the entire staff who charted the plaintiff's care to rewrite and change the hospital records pertaining to the care [Ms. Pisel] received on the morning of [her cardiac arrest]."[4] It was proved at trial that the original record had been covertly removed and a "revised" (exculpatory) record had been substituted. This alteration came to light when one of the nurses who had been forced to rewrite her note brought the situation to the attention of the hospital administration. According to the court, the revised record was demonstrably false and was in direct conflict with other records and with the testimony of the staff regarding the events on the day in question. The alteration was, in the court's words, "bungled."[4]

The consequences of this obvious, self-serving fabrication were disastrous to the hospital's defense. The Supreme Court of Connecticut upheld the trial court's instruction to the jury that they were allowed to infer from the medical record alteration that "the revision indicated a consciousness of negligence."[4] In other words, the jury could consider the alteration of the medical record essentially as an admission of liability. The court also upheld the $3.6 million judgment, which was four times larger than any verdict ever returned in the state of Connecticut up to that time.

An altered medical record can lead not only to the plaintiff winning the case, but also to an award of punitive damages. Punitive damages are seldom awarded in medical malpractice cases but are available in certain unusual circumstances. For example, punitive damages may be awarded when the malpractice is committed with "malicious intent."[5] To prove malice, the plaintiff must prove that the defendant intentionally altered or destroyed a medical record to avoid liability.[3] Punitive damages may be substantial and are not covered by liability insurance. Because the purpose of punitive damages is to punish the defendant rather than to compensate the injured party, public policy forbids insurance for punitive damages. Any payment of punitive damages will come from the defendant's personal assets. Even declaring bankruptcy may not relieve a person of this obligation.

The Ohio Supreme Court has dealt with the award of punitive damages in a medical malpractice case involving the alteration of a patient's record. In *Moskovitz v Mt Sinai Medical Center, et al,*[3] the court held that an award of $1 million in punitive damages was reasonable (compensatory damages in the case were $1.25 million). This was a case of alleged delay in diagnosis of an epithelioid sarcoma in a woman who subsequently died of metastatic sarcoma. The defendant orthopedic surgeon failed to perform a biopsy on a mass on the woman's leg, despite knowing that she had had tumors excised from the leg twice in the past. After observing the mass for more than one year, the orthopedic surgeon finally biopsied the lesion. It was malignant, and further workup showed that the cancer had already metastasized. A jury found that the surgeon was negligent and awarded $1.25 million in compensatory damages.

The facts of the case also showed that the surgeon had covertly altered his office records. He had deleted a sentence stating: "We will therefore elect to continue to observe" and had substituted a note that read: "As she [the patient] does not want excisional Bx, we will observe."[3] This alteration, had it been effective, would have relieved the physician of liability and placed the responsibility on the deceased patient. This fraud was prevented because the original, unaltered chart had been sent to a consultant before it was retrieved by the defendant physician and altered. It then had been sent to a second consultant. The unaltered copy of the original was obtained by plaintiff's counsel and doomed the defendant physician's case. This botched attempt to alter the chart rendered the physician's case essentially indefensible and resulted in an award of $3 million in punitive damages. This amount was later reduced to $1 million by the Ohio Supreme Court.

Any self-serving, covert, subsequent alteration of a medical record can change a potentially defensible case into a losing one. Dr. Figgie, the defendant in *Moskovitz*, may well have been negligent (in fact, he conceded this prior to trial), but his attorney could well have argued the element of causation. (To prevail in a malpractice action, the plaintiff must prove not just a breach of the standard of care, but the three other elements of a negligence action: duty, proximate causation, and damages.) If the tumor had already metastasized by the time Dr. Figgie first noticed it, his negligence in failing to perform a biopsy probably would not have been the proximate cause of the patient's death. However, the malicious alteration of the chart undoubtedly made the jury deaf to any arguments defense counsel tried to make.

Correcting Medical Records

To avoid the possible appearance of impropriety, any alteration in a medical record should be annotated appropriately. Errors in a medical record are not uncommon. When they occur, a timely correction should be made in accordance with standard protocols adopted by most medical records departments. When staff members adhere to such protocols, they decrease the likelihood that a correction will be used by a plaintiff to cast doubt or suspicion on the credibility of the record or of the physician who corrected the record.

Accepted methods of correcting erroneous medical record entries include the following recommendations[6,7]:

- Draw a single line through the incorrectly recorded information, making sure that the original entry remains legible. Entries should never be erased, made illegible, or covered up with liquid correction fluid. In fact, some departments do not allow the use of correction fluid for any purpose.
- Make sure the correction is dated, timed, and signed (initialed) by the person making the correction.
- Place an annotation near the correction indicating why the entry is being changed. For example, if a physician made an entry on the wrong chart, the explanation "error, wrong chart" or "error, wrong patient" would be appropriate.
- If possible and if concern for potential litigation warrants, make sure the correction is witnessed and initialed by another member of the staff.

Addenda to the Medical Record

Addenda to the medical record, made after the patient's visit, may be viewed skeptically by a jury. This is particularly true if the emergency physician adds the material after learning of potential litigation. Medical records are generally considered as having been prepared in "due course," that is, at the time of treatment. Therefore, records prepared days, weeks, or months after a patient encounter may be viewed as unreliable by a jury, especially if they appear to be self-serving.

The medical-legal literature is somewhat divided regarding the creation and attachment of such addenda to the medical record. Some experts argue that additional documentation may be appropriate, even after the emergency physician has become aware of a poor patient outcome and possible litigation, given the long delays that currently exist in the court system. Some would suggest that the physician should record all recollections about a case once a plaintiff's attorney subpoenas a medical record and then attach a separate addendum to the medical record that has been properly prepared and dated.[8] Others believe that such addenda to original records create the impression that the medical care provided was substandard; therefore, such entries are incriminating and should be avoided.[9]

A physician may want to record present recollections of a case while the memories are relatively fresh. This document need not, and in most cases should not, be attached to the patient's medical record. The purpose of the document is to refresh the physician's memory when, as is often the case, a lawsuit reaches the discovery and trial phase years after the actual event. The physician should discuss preparation of this document with counsel, who can help protect it from discovery. Depending on the advice of legal counsel, the physician can decide whether to add the document as an addendum to the patient's medical record.

Guidelines for the addition of such "late entries" have been adopted by most hospital medical records departments and should include the time and date of the addendum and the signature of the preparer. Any addendum to the medical record should accurately reflect the facts of the patient's visit and not simply be a self-serving addition that justifies the physician's action in retrospect. An addendum would be particularly appropriate in the difficult situation of a "lost" medical record, as the consequences to a defendant physician in such a situation can be catastrophic.

'Lost' Medical Records

Because the medical record is the most critical document in the defense of a medical malpractice claim, the loss of this document can be a devastating blow. If the record is not available to provide evidence that the medical evaluation and treatment were performed appropriately, the plaintiff's attorney will allege that these duties were not performed at all or were conducted in a negligent manner. Understandably, juries frequently agree with this assertion. In fact, the court may instruct a jury that they may infer, on the basis of the missing record, a consciousness of negligence on the part of the defendant.[10] If the court does not instruct the jury as to this inference,[11] the plaintiff's attorney may still suggest that the record was deliberately destroyed in an effort to conceal negligent action on the physician's part.

An often-cited case involving a lost medical record is *Carr v St. Paul Fire and Marine Insurance Company.*[12] In this case, a middle-aged man was discharged from an emergency department after presenting for evaluation of nausea, vomiting, and abdominal pain. He had been "evaluated" by a licensed practical nurse and two orderlies. The patient died one hour after discharge from the department, and a malpractice lawsuit was filed. The emergency department medical record could not be located and apparently had been destroyed on the evening of the patient's evaluation in the department. The court held that "the jury had a right to consider the impact that such destruction had in determining the actual facts." The court further stated that "no one knows the effect that such action [loss of the record] had on the jury, but the jury had the right to infer that had it been retained, it would have shown that a medical emergency existed."[12] Therefore, the jury was allowed to infer, with no direct supporting evidence, that the lost medical record indicated that the patient's treatment had been negligent.

Emergency physicians should never be a party to inappropriate alteration of a medical record by destroying it. Medical records are often misplaced as they circulate from the emergency department to the medical records department or the many other departments of the hospital. Emergency physicians should work closely with their hospitals' medical records personnel to ensure that all medical records arrive safely in the medical records department and are properly stored and safeguarded. Once a chart has been called for, in any type of legal action, the medical records personnel need to protect the chart from alteration. The usual and customary way is to have the chart duplicated and the original locked away.

Criminal Liability and Administrative Sanctions

Physicians are subject to administrative sanctions, criminal penalties, or both, for failing to properly maintain medical records or for fraudulently altering those records. Medical professionals may lose their professional licenses as a consequence,[13] as well as be denied the right to participate in federal programs, such as Medicare.[14] In addition to these administrative sanctions, a physician may be subject to criminal penalties under state law for the fraudulent alteration of a medical record.[15] All emergency physicians must know their hospitals' protocols regarding the preparation and storage of medical records in accordance with applicable state and federal statutes and regulations.

Case Discussions

1

Any correction of an error in documentation — in this case, recording part of the physical examination on the wrong chart — should be done in a way that will not suggest any impropriety. The procedure used to record the correction should be done so that, if a malpractice claim arises, the recording error cannot be used by a plaintiff to undermine the physician's credibility.

Proper correction methods are dictated by hospital policy. If information relating to one patient has been entered onto another patient's chart and is subsequently corrected, make sure that both charts have been properly corrected.

2

A case in which a patient is diagnosed with meningitis after a recent discharge from the emergency department always poses a serious risk management situation for the emergency physician. The challenge is even more difficult when the medical record reflects poor documentation of the patient's signs, symptoms, and physical findings at the time of treatment. In this case, given an apparent two-day interval until the development of any overt signs of meningitis, the physician may be able to defend himself successfully on the basis of a lack of proximate causation, if not compliance with the standard of care. However, any attempted covert alteration of the medical record after the patient's visit may allow the jury to infer consciousness of guilt and destroy any defense of the case.

In this case, the emergency physician must avoid the temptation to tamper with the chart. He should prepare dated notes of this patient's visit and discuss these details with his attorney. He should also discuss creating an addendum to the chart, appropriately dated and timed. Even if he does not enter an addendum to the medical record, the physician's prepared notes could be helpful to substantiate his detailed memory if the case comes to trial years later. Remember: by the time a chart is altered, copies of an emergency department medical record will likely have been distributed to other physicians and departments. Plaintiffs' attorneys are well aware of the effect that proof of a covert, self-serving alteration of a medical record will have on their case. They will seek to obtain all copies of the record in an effort to uncover such a prize.

3

This case demonstrates how emergency physicians, through no fault of their own, can be placed in jeopardy because the medical record is missing. In such cases, plaintiffs' attorneys will argue that the record was intentionally destroyed to conceal negligence. Emergency physicians must work closely with registration, billing, medical records, and other involved hospital personnel to be certain that emergency department records are properly processed, stored, and safeguarded.

In this particular case, the emergency physician and his counsel should pursue all avenues available to locate a copy of the original medical record. These might include contacting a third-party payer or the physician to whom the patient was referred in an effort to find a copy of the chart. Unfortunately, after such a long period of time, this might be difficult — the referral physician might have discarded the chart since the patient never showed up for follow-up. If these attempts are unsuccessful, the preparation of an addendum, as discussed in the previous case, may be appropriate and should be discussed with counsel. Unfortunately, the physician could be in a virtual no-win situation. On the one hand, any addendum will be dated after the institution of the lawsuit and will be seen as self-serving. On the other hand, if no addendum is entered and there is no medical record, the court may allow the jury to infer consciousness of negligence.

Key Points and Conclusion

Alterations of the medical record occur when the contents of a record are deleted or changed and when additions to the record are made. The record may also be altered by its intentional or unintentional destruction or misplacement. Any alteration of the medical record, or even the appearance of an alteration, poses a grave threat to the successful defense of a claim of malpractice. Emergency physicians may also be at risk for criminal prosecution if they fraudulently alter their medical records.

The emergency physician can guard against the potential increased liability pitfalls of medical record alteration by adhering to the following guidelines:

- Always prepare medical records in an accurate, timely, and thorough manner and store them properly. This should prevent claims of alteration from ever arising.
- Never covertly alter the medical record with deletions or additions or destroy the record.
- Prepare changes in the medical record in accordance with hospital policy; never conceal the original entries.
- Work closely with hospital personnel to ensure that emergency department records are appropriately processed and retained.

References

1. Medical records, offered into evidence for the truth of the material contained, are hearsay, and hearsay is generally excluded from evidence. They can be admitted, however, into evidence under an exception to the general rule excluding hearsay, usually under the regularly kept business record exception (See Federal Rule of Evidence 803(6)).

2. Glass LS. The medical record: shield or sword of Damocles? *Alaska Med* 1984;April-June:41-45.

3. See, e.g., *Moskovitz v Mt Sinai Medical Center*, 69 Ohio St3d 638, 635 NE2d 331.

4. *Pisel v Stamford Hospital, et al*, 430 A2d 1 (Conn 1980).

5. *Preston v Murty*, 32 Ohio St3d 334, 512 NE2d 1174 (1987).

6. Fox LA, Imbiorski W, Brewer E. *The Record That Defends Its Friends.* Chicago: Chicago Care Communications Inc; 1982.

7. Rines JT. The medical record and risk management. In: Kraus GP, ed. *Health Care Risk Management.* Owings Mills, Md: National Health Publishing; 1986.

8. Grayson MA. Risk management: new focus for traditional functions. *Hosp Med Staff* 1978;7:12-17.

9. Jorgensen T. Reducing malpractice claims through proper maintenance of medical records. *Med Malprac Cost Contain* 1980;1:303-313.

10. *Thor v Boska*, 38 Cal App 3d 558, 113 Cal Rptr 296, 301 (1974).

11. In *Brown v Hamid*, 856 SW2d 51 (Mo banc 1993), the Missouri Supreme Court did not allow evidence that the medical record was missing, ruling that this was a "collateral issue" and would cause jury confusion.

12. 384 F Supp 821 (WD Ark 1974).

13. See, e.g., *Weber v Colorado State Board of Nursing*, 830 P2d 1128 (Colo App 1992).

14. See, *Koh v Perales*, 570 NYS2d 98 (NY App Div 1991).

15. See, e.g., West's Ann Cal Penal Code §471.5, which makes intentional alteration a misdemeanor in California, and MCLA 750.492a, which makes it a felony in Michigan.

Chapter 36

The Medical Director's Role in Risk Management

Brooks F. Bock, MD, FACEP

Physician involvement in hospital risk management became mandatory effective January 1, 1989.[1] At that time, the Joint Commission on Accreditation of Healthcare Organizations (JCAHO) modified standards language pertaining to the development, support, coordination, and monitoring of risk management activities by hospital administration and medical staff. These standards pertain only to the risk management functions related to clinical and administrative activities designed to identify, evaluate, and reduce the risk of patient injury associated with medical treatment.

Clearly, these standards do not involve the full scope of risk management activities, which include visitors and staff and are also intended to:

- Reduce the risk of a malpractice lawsuit.
- Reduce the probability of a claim being filed after a potentially compensable event has occurred.
- Preserve the hospital's and the physician's assets once a claim has been filed.

It is within this larger context of risk management that the emergency department medical director and other staff members develop the policies and procedures that guide the risk management process. As is the case with all quality assurance activities, the JCAHO identifies risk management policy and procedure needs specific to a hospital. Policies and procedures are then delegated to specialty experts at the department level, with ultimate accountability assigned to the medical director.

Areas of Responsibility

The *Comprehensive Accreditation Manual for Hospitals*,[2] published by the JCAHO, provides guidance about a department leader's responsibility in quality assurance and risk management. The following standards are of note:

- LD.2 — Each hospital department has effective leadership.
- LD.2.6 — Directors continuously assess and improve their department's performance.
- LD.2.7 — Directors maintain appropriate quality control programs.
- LD.2.8 — Directors provide for orientation, in-service training, and continuing education of all persons in the department.

The director is charged with creating an environment or culture that enables a hospital to fulfill its mission and meet or exceed its goals. Directors support staff, encourage in them a sense of ownership of their work process, and hold them accountable for their performance. Department directors motivate staff to improve their performance continuously, thereby improving the hospital's performance and reducing the potential for adverse events.

Ultimately, department directors are responsible for the operation of their entire department, including the measurement, assessment, and continuous improvement of the department's performance. High-quality leadership can be seen in a department that operates effectively and efficiently.

Appropriate orientation of new staff is an important part of the risk management process.

Table 1

Comparison of risk management and quality assurance

Risk Management	Quality Assurance
Protects the financial assets of the hospital	Reflects a hospital's philosophy of providing quality care
Protects human beings and intangible resources	Improves the performance of all professionals and protects patients
Prevents injury to patients, visitors, employees, and property	Focuses on the quality of patient care delivered in the hospital
Reduces loss by focusing on individual loss or on single incidents	Sets the quality of care delivered against standards and measurable criteria
Prevents incidents by improving the quality of care through continuing and ongoing monitoring of hospital activities	Prevents future losses or patient injuries by continuous monitoring of problem resolution areas
Reviews each incident and the patterns of incidents through the application of the risk management process: risk identification, risk analysis, risk evaluation, and risk treatment	Searches for patterns of nonconformance with goals and standards using the following quality assurance processes: problem identification, problem assessment, corrective action, follow-up, and report of findings
Concerned with acceptable levels of care from a legal standpoint	Concerned with optimal level of care
Directed toward all persons, events, and environs in the health care setting	Directed toward patient care
Focused on legal, insurance, and risk financing activities	Focused on improving care

Mentors should be assigned to provide training and address any questions that arise. This orientation process should cover any issues that have the potential for adverse outcome.

To adhere to the JCAHO standards listed earlier, a hospital must have a system in place to identify risks regarding broad trends and specific cases. Broad trends might include falls, medication errors, and equipment problems. Specific cases might include adverse drug reactions, procedural complications, and unexpected deaths.

Once risks are identified, they must be analyzed, which will involve both peer review and recommendations. Risk analysis activities will naturally flow into risk reduction, which includes corrective action and programs aimed at prevention.

Finally, hospital staff should perform a follow-up assessment program to evaluate the effectiveness of risk management activities and to modify the overall process. A number of states, including Alaska, Colorado, Florida, Kansas, Maryland, Massachusetts, New York, North Carolina, Rhode Island, and Washington, have passed legislation or developed regulations requiring hospitals to implement risk management programs. In most of these states, the requirements are specifically designed to complement other quality assurance initiatives and are a condition for the state's hospital licensure. Seven of these 10 states provide immunity from liability only for those who supply information in risk management activities. This lack of immunity for those who work in risk management may be mitigated by ensuring that the conclusions of these activities be made a formal part of the quality assurance program.

Many hospital insurance companies require that insured staff implement risk modification or management programs. One company, MMI Companies, Inc., for example, focuses on identifying and eliminating preventable patient injuries in three high-risk areas: obstetrics, anesthesia, and emergency department services. The intention is to assist hospitals in evaluating their risk management policies and procedures.

Medical Directors and Risk Management

The medical director must know and understand the requirements of the JCAHO, state licensing authorities, and insurance companies to oversee the process of policy and procedure development and revision effectively. The medical director is responsible for establishing policies and procedures for quality assurance and risk management, activities that have overlapping functions and, at times, goals that are almost indistinguishable (Table 1).

A medical director is likely to have more experience with quality assurance than with risk management. Many medical directors have worked with their staffs to develop monitoring tools that establish standards of care for a particular clinical entity. The American College of Emergency Physicians has developed several clinical policies that are distributed nationally. The initial fear that physician-developed standards of clinical care may be used against them is warranted. These standards, which become policy, will be used in professional liability cases. However, the standards will both protect and implicate. Mistakes will occur; poor decisions will be made. It is hoped that the establishment of agreed-on clinical standards will lessen the potential for a plaintiff's expert to provide questionable or controversial testimony.

Debate exists as to whether issues committed to writing in the form of policy or procedure should be titled "guidelines" or "standards." Although each word is viewed as having a similar context, each carries a different emphasis. The word "standard" implies a minimal expectation or criteria to be met, while "guideline" indicates a general direction toward which one might aim. Currently, this debate has not been resolved, and different facilities use these words interchangeably.

Key Points and Conclusion

In today's health care environment, the role of medical directors in risk management is multifaceted. They are responsible for developing a process that identifies, analyzes, and reduces risk among staff and within the hospital. This process should be an ongoing activity, complement the quality assurance program, and involve other staff members with a goal of improving patient care. It should be regarded not as a burden but as the kind of activity that patients expect, pay for, and benefit from.

References

1. Joint Commission on Accreditation of Healthcare Organizations. *Accreditation Manual for Hospitals.* Oakbrook Terrace, Ill: JCAHO; 1990.
2. Joint Commission on Accreditation of Healthcare Organizations. *Comprehensive Accreditation Manual for Hospitals: The Official Handbook.* Oakbrook Terrace, Ill: JCAHO; 1996.

Chapter 37

Emergency Department Medical Record

W. Richard Bukata, MD

Purpose of the Medical Record: A Contrarian View

The emergency department medical record is a legal document that chronicles the course of a patient's medical evaluation, laboratory test and x-ray results, treatment, response to treatment, disposition, and follow-up instructions. Once generated, the record serves as the basis for communication to other health care providers concerning the care given to a patient. It is also a source of information for quality assurance monitoring and hospital and professional service fees. The medical record also has a major role in protecting the legal interests of the patient, the hospital, and the medical professionals who rendered the care.

The importance of producing a complete, thorough medical record that adequately meets these goals cannot be overemphasized. Although the record has several purposes, some are more important than others. For most patients, the quality of the medical record does not necessarily reflect the quality of care given. A physician may obtain a patient's history, perform an examination, and make a diagnosis of appendicitis without writing one word to record these steps. In many busy emergency departments, physicians often do their charting at the end of the shift because they are too busy to do it while there are patients to be seen. Although this practice is not the best way to generate records, it does not mean that patients fail to receive good care. In fact, the quality of care given to patients and the records describing that care are not dependent on one another.

Another reason the medical record is created is to communicate to other caregivers what has happened during the assessment, treatment, and disposition of a patient. However, there are only a few key items that other providers need to know. Follow-up physicians need to know the working diagnosis, what objective evidence supports the diagnosis, what treatment was given or prescribed, and, if the patient was discharged, what follow-up care was advised. All of these items can be indicated on a good set of follow-up instructions and, if provided to the physician rendering subsequent treatment, will allow for continuity of care.

Providing a copy of the patient's entire emergency department record to the follow-up physician may be desirable theoretically; however, surveying the emergency physician's actual history, physical examination, interval progress notes, nurses' notes, and so on, adds little to follow-up care. Nevertheless other substantial benefits can be attained when follow-up physicians receive legible (preferably printed) copies of emergency patients' records. These documents not only reflect positively on the quality of care provided to patients but also give members of the medical staff increased confidence in the service being provided by the emergency department in general, and by the emergency physician group in particular.

Another often-stated purpose of the medical record is to justify patient charges. When charges are challenged by payers, this is true. A detailed record that accurately describes the intensity and severity of a patient's condition and the degree of medical care and treatment rendered helps support the fees. In most cases, however, there is really no need for the medical record to contain anything but the appropriate ICD-9 and CPT codes. In fact, when electronic billing is used, the majority of the medical record is superfluous — only numbers are being transmitted back and forth between payers and payees. In medical facilities that exist primarily to treat indigent patients, the value of the medical record to support billing activities is virtually nil.

If emergency physicians could predict with 100% certainty that patients would suffer no adverse outcomes after being discharged or transferred from the emergency department and that the medical record would not be needed to justify patient charges, most emergency department records could be destroyed after several months. Unfortunately, this cannot be done; one of the most important functions of the medical record is to help protect the legal rights of the patient, hospital, and health care professionals who provided patient care. That function remains in force until the statute of limitations expires.

When the medical record is viewed in this light as a legal document, all its other functions automatically become well served. This "contrarian" view of the emergency department medical record is one that, when intellectually embraced, results in carefully crafted records that are detailed, yet succinct, and address all its intended purposes.

Required Elements

The Joint Commission on Accreditation of Healthcare Organizations (JCAHO) requires that a medical record be established and maintained on every patient seeking emergency department care. In addition, it requires that the record contain, as a minimum, the following elements:

- Patient identification (if not obtainable, the reason)
- Time and means of arrival
- Appropriate vital signs
- Documentation of pertinent history and physical findings
- Emergency care given prior to patient arrival
- Diagnostic and therapeutic orders
- Clinical observations, including the results of treatment
- Reports of procedures, tests, and results
- Conclusions reached on completion of examination and treatment
- Diagnostic impression
- Final disposition
- Patient condition on discharge or transfer
- Documentation of follow-up instructions

In addition to the JCAHO-mandated requirements, state health authorities may place their own requirements on the contents of the medical record. If emergency department records do not contain all the mandated components, they may be challenged as technically substandard. Other items commonly acknowledged to be important include the following:

- Presence of allergies to medications and chemicals
- Routine and current medications
- Likelihood of pregnancy, if germane
- Tetanus immunization history, if germane
- Name of the patient's private physician
- Documentation of prescriptions given to the patient
- Patient's signature acknowledging receipt and understanding of follow-up instructions

Regarding ownership, JCAHO clearly states that medical records are the property of the hospital and that hospitals are required to safeguard them. Release of the information in these confidential, legal records to unauthorized persons requires the written consent of the patient (or the patient's legal representative). Medical records can be removed from the hospital's jurisdiction and safekeeping only in accordance with a court order, subpoena, or statute. To ensure the easiest access to the most information about a patient, the "unit record system" of filing is advised. This system of record-keeping has all of a patient's records (both inpatient and outpatient) filed in one master record located at one place.

However, one patient document that should never be placed in the patient's medical record or have any reference made to it in the record is what is commonly referred to as an incident report. These privileged communications, detailing the investigation of circumstances surrounding adverse events involving patients (e.g., fell off table in x-ray, given wrong blood), should be entered only into the formal quality assurance program of the hospital to keep them undiscoverable.

Consent Issues

Early in an emergency department visit, the patient or a guardian is asked to sign a rather formal document often called "Conditions of

Admission." This document contains all the general consents and acknowledgments believed to be required or appropriate by the hospital's attorneys. The following items are commonly found in this document:

- Consent to medical and surgical procedures
- Advisory that the hospital provides only certain types of nursing care
- Explanation of the relationships among the hospital, private physicians, employed physicians, and contract physicians
- Statement regarding the release of information about the patient
- Policy concerning patient's valuables
- Financial agreement between the patient or guardian and the hospital
- Authorization regarding the assignment of insurance benefits to the hospital
- Advisory statement concerning the relationship between the hospital and selected health care service plans
- Advisory statement concerning the hospital's obligation to provide a certain amount of free care as mandated under the Hill-Burton agreement, if applicable

Typically, the hospital will use the same Conditions of Admission form for patients being admitted electively and for emergency department patients. Patients being admitted electively generally have the time and opportunity to read the "legalese" in these documents. However, it is generally unrealistic to expect patients presenting for emergency care to take the time to read the form. Fortunately, very few emergency medicine malpractice lawsuits have been brought concerning the consents and acknowledgments on a Conditions of Admission document. Because the signed document represents an agreement between the patient or guardian and the hospital, a copy of the agreement should be given to the person who signs it.

One area of significant concern regarding consent is the routine practice of sending copies of patients' emergency department medical records to their private physicians without the patients' explicit approval. This appears to be a clear breach regarding the unauthorized release of a patient record, an issue typically not addressed in the Conditions of Admission form. Specific situations in which patients may not want their private physicians to be aware of emergency department visits may include treatment for venereal disease or a request for a second opinion for a disorder already diagnosed by the private physician. If actual damages occur

as a result of this breach of propriety, litigation may follow.

The safest way to address this issue is to ask patients if they would like copies of their records sent to their private physicians. If they agree, they should mark and initial a "Yes" box beside this question on the Conditions of Admission form. If they do not, a "No" box should be checked and initialed by the patient. The purpose of the "Yes" and "No" boxes is to verify at a later date that the question was specifically asked and answered. If a private physician determines later that a patient was treated at the emergency department and asks why a copy of the record was not sent, the form will show that the patient specifically directed that the record be kept confidential.

Generating the Emergency Department Medical Record

Handwritten Records

Most emergency department records probably are still being handwritten by physicians, despite the fact that every other hospital-based specialty relies on transcribed reports. Even though emergency medicine is at high risk for malpractice exposure and everyone acknowledges that a detailed, legible record is among the most potent defenses against alleged malpractice, most emergency physicians are not provided with this basic tool to enhance their documentation. Even if malpractice concerns were not an issue, the disadvantages of the handwritten record are obvious. Copies of these records sent to patients' private physicians frequently are illegible. Such records do not allow emergency physicians to demonstrate the quality of their work.

The handwritten record is also a problem when it comes to billing. Physician charges typically are justified solely on the basis of the medical record. If these records are unduly brief and illegible and lack appropriate interval progress notes, they frequently will not support the fees being charged. Those approving payment of individual claims are likely to become increasingly frustrated trying to read illegible charts, and this may lead them to challenge or downcode a disproportionate number of claims.

The faults associated with a handwritten record are not solely related to the handwriting, but focus more on who is writing the record and how it is written. With rare exceptions, written records are produced by physicians — typically those with the least amount of time to generate the record, with the worst handwriting, and with the greatest distractions in the form of other patients waiting to be seen.

An emergency department scribe system is an innovative approach to the creation of high-quality written records. This system can offer major advantages over simple chart dictation systems. Typically, a "scribe" (often an LVN or EMT) is assigned to follow a physician around the emergency department. Usually, the physician and scribe go into the examining room together. As the physician elicits the patient history, the scribe records it. During the physical examination, the physician verbalizes all findings to the patient, and the scribe records them.

In a new twist on the scribe system, a specially trained EMT or paramedic uses voice-generated transcription technology to generate the physician's emergency department medical record. This system relieves physicians of the burden of having to learn how to use these computer programs, generates computer-quality records, and provides a personal assistant to help facilitate the physician's work. These systems clearly reflect the fact that excessive time spent by physicians on the charting process limits their ability to see additional patients and can seriously hamper their productivity. Systems that facilitate the work of physician and nurse charting, allowing these key individuals to treat more patients per unit time, are generally cost-effective.

Transcribed Records

Growing numbers of emergency departments are now reaping the benefits of the transcribed medical record system. In the early 1980s, one article[1] carefully documented the costs associated with transcribed medical records, including a transcriptionist's salary. In their review of almost 20,000 transcribed records, the authors found the average record contained 156 words (compared to the average 54-word length of a handwritten record). The dictation time for the average record was less than two minutes.

The article also noted that when the salary and benefits of a transcriptionist totaled $7.32 per hour, the cost of transcribing the average record was $1.03. It took approximately seven minutes to type, an average transcription time that has been documented by others. Generally, an average of four to five minutes of transcription time is required for every minute of dicta-

tion. Total transcribing equipment start-up costs were $2,605.[1] When salaries are updated to more contemporary levels and the record lengths increased for the mandated reimbursement-related documentation, the average cost per record increases to $2 to $2.50 per chart.

An ideal transcription system for the current practice environment would include the following elements:

Transcriptionists in the Emergency Department. Clearly, having a transcriptionist employed in the emergency department can be defended as the best of all worlds. Records generally can be transcribed as they are completed. When patients are admitted or transferred, they can be sent with copies of their legible, comprehensive, typed emergency department records.

Because it takes an average of only seven minutes to transcribe the typical emergency department record (perhaps 10 minutes given newer mandated charting requirements), the transcriptionist may be able to perform other functions, such as answering and placing telephone calls, coding charts, quality monitoring activities, placing orders for requested laboratory and x-ray tests, and so on.

Combining several duties into one position creates multifaceted and diversified jobs, increasing employees' job satisfaction (assuming that their overall workload is manageable). Using this model, even emergency departments with relatively light volumes can integrate transcribed records into their routines. Because the content of emergency department records is rather repetitive, individuals with basic typing and computer skills and a modest command of English can, with a little practice and training, quickly become excellent transcriptionists.

Twenty-Four-Hour Transcription Capabilities. Depending on department volume, it may not be economically feasible to have a transcriptionist in the department around the clock. One way to approach the goal of transcribing virtually all records is to have physicians dictate records when a transcriptionist is not present (typically from midnight until 7:00 AM). When the transcriptionist arrives in the morning, the records from the preceding period can be transcribed and held for physician signatures. Using this model, the records of patients who are to be admitted or transferred during the hours when the transcriptionist is not present are handwritten succinctly by the physician. This practice means that patients will carry a record with them that contains the essential data needed for immediate care. A more detailed record can be dictated for transcription at a later time.

Use of a Microcassette System. Microcassettes are small (2" x 1.25") cassettes that can be used in compact, handheld, inexpensive recorders (typically about $30 each). These cassettes can be attached easily to clipboards containing individual patient charts (use of Velcro fasteners on the clipboards and the microcassettes is an inexpensive yet effective technique). Because the cassette accompanies a patient's chart, the transcriptionist can easily see when a cassette is ready for transcription. When the cassette is not being transcribed, it is readily available to the physician, who may want to dictate interval progress notes once the initial history and physical examination are complete. This technique of using one microcassette per patient has been shown to be very effective and limits the potential for confusion and errors.

Use of Computerized Word Processing Programs. In the past several years, payers, particularly Medicare and Medicaid, have mandated that several specific items be documented in the record to qualify for various levels of payment. Because these mandates are highly detailed, payers' clerical personnel can easily audit compliance. Unfortunately, complying with these charting requirements has significantly increased the time and costs related to charting. Health care organizations have responded by finding ways to facilitate the charting process, largely through computerized charting programs.

Advantages and opportunities that computers offer include the ability to do the following:

- Transcribe the record onto the computer screen without having the physical chart on hand
- Verify spelling through use of a medical spell-check program
- Use preestablished "macros" for standardized paragraphs to avoid retyping repetitive information
- Perform a wide variety of automated tasks (e.g., quality assurance activities, ICD-9 and CPT coding, patient log, and generation of a wide variety of departmental statistics)

More recently developed programs allow patient histories and physical examinations to be documented through the use of mouse-selected choices on menus.

Computer-Generated Voice Recognition Emergency Department Records

As computer technology advances, the capability of systems that recognize human speech and directly translate it into typed records has evolved to a point where this approach is now increasingly practical. Systems currently available can recognize reasonably large vocabularies and can be programmed to recognize and decipher the unique characteristics of individual voices in about an hour. The integration of voice-recognition technology and preformatted templates of basic histories and physical examinations allow these systems to operate quickly. Instead of a record being all "free text," only those parts unique to the specific case at hand need be dictated into the computer.

Advantages of such systems over traditional dictation and transcription include substantial potential cost savings. A typical multiuser voice recognition system may have a one-time expense of $15,000 for computer hardware and software. In contrast, an in-department transcription system using a transcriptionist will likely cost $2 per record at 1997 rates, while commercial transcription charges are in the range of $5 to $7 per chart. After about 7,500 records, the voice-activated system would pay for itself compared to the cost of having a transcriptionist type approximately 3,000 records. Theoretically, all subsequent records using the voice recognition system would be "free." However, this calculation is only the case if generating such a chart takes the same amount of time for the physician as does free text dictation (which is not likely to be the case). Nor does this calculation factor in the time and costs of correcting errors. One recent study[2] found an error rate of 17% for English language terminology and 9% for emergency medicine terminology using the IBM Voicetype dictation system for emergency medicine.

Other potential advantages of computerized systems include 24-hour availability and greater reliability than human employees, who occasionally call in sick or take vacations. Because templates of standardized histories and physical examinations can be incorporated into these systems that are "chief complaint specific," physicians can be prompted to take and document thorough, accurate histories and to do appropriate physical examinations. These systems can be used to generate exemplary records, and their value as risk management tools makes them highly attractive. If malpractice insurance companies can be guaranteed that a significant percentage of records will meet these high standards and if such systems prompt physicians to consider and specifically look for known high-risk disorders, companies are likely to provide incentives and discounts for their use.

Attaining such goals, however, is not unique to the use of voice recognition technology. The essence of the system is the periodic prompting, and thus repetitive education, of physicians to watch out for high-risk situations and to generate careful, comprehensive medical records. These goals can also be achieved quickly by other systems designed to make physicians aware of minimum charting criteria per chief complaint and through rapid feedback when the charts do not contain the key items agreed on.

However, the use of voice recognition systems has several potential drawbacks. They are noticeably slower than standard dictation when physicians dictate free text. In addition, only one physician can use the system at a time. The system also takes time to adjust to different physicians' voices. Finally, physicians must be willing to invest the time to learn how to use these systems.

A final concern stems from the use of template histories and physical examinations. Although the advantage of these tools is their ability to encourage the physician to perform careful workups, they also may result in a record that significantly exceeds the actual extent of the history and physical examination performed. Although not unique to computer-generated records, the use of templates that require physicians to delete the elements of the history and physical that were not performed presents a temptation to create an exaggerated, if not actually fabricated, record. How a jury will view a machine-generated, generic record is another matter of concern.

Medical Record Do's and Don'ts

Make sure the record contains all the JCAHO and state-mandated elements. Even if you believe that some of the required elements are irrelevant to a specific case, it is best to have a record that meets the standards rather that one that can be loosely or technically defined as substandard.

Construct the chart so that key questions require answers. For example, in the area of the chart pertaining to allergies, have a "None" box that must be checked if, in fact, the patient has no allergies. A box labeled "Allergies" that is left blank and does not have a "None" box is potentially ambiguous. If left empty, does it mean there were no allergies or does it mean the question was never asked? The same would apply to "Medications," "Possible Pregnancy," "Family Physician," and so on.

List the patient's occupation in a prominent location. It would be helpful to know that the patient being treated for a hand injury is a professional musician or personal injury attorney. To suggest that a heightened level of concern is not appropriate in these cases is unrealistic.

Read and acknowledge the nurses' notes. They should be succinct, factual, and objective with a minimum of judgmental elements. Patients find it annoying when physicians appear not to know why they are in the emergency department after they have told their story to two or three other members of the emergency department staff. The nurses' notes often provide important information that may otherwise not be appreciated. If there is a conflict between the nurse's assessment and yours, the conflict must be addressed early.

For example, a nurse may record a judgment that a child is "lethargic"; however, in your assessment, this may not be the case. Make extra efforts to document all the elements of your assessment indicating that, at the time of your examination, the child did not appear to be lethargic. Serial reassessments that continue to document the lack of lethargy would be helpful.

The entire health care team must be aware of the "danger" words and use them judiciously. The goal is to generate a medical record that is totally internally consistent with the final diagnosis and disposition. Achieving this goal is more difficult when several individuals are recording their judgments on the record and yet only one — you, the physician — is making the final decisions. Emergency department staff should make it a priority to record carefully considered comments that will not preclude patient discharge independent of the outcome of the complete assessment. In short, the physician's review of the nurses' notes is an absolute necessity. If not done in the emergency department, it may be done in court.

Pay particular attention to vital signs. Vital signs are straightforward, easily quantifiable measurements of certain essential body functions concerning the respiratory, cardiovascular, and thermoregulatory systems. Timed, initialed vital signs are a standard part of the emergency department medical record. Most patients with minor complaints generally have one set of vital signs taken. Frequently, there is little relationship between the patient's complaint and the medical necessity to take vital signs. Such cases typically include those patients with minor soft tissue or orthopedic injuries.

In these situations, emergency department staff may be tempted to take vital signs for granted, a lapse that may land the staff and hospital in medical-legal hot water. Specifically, when routine vital signs are taken, the patient may be noted to have a blood pressure of, for example, 170/105. If the patient's minor presenting problem is treated without rechecking his blood pressure before the visit ends, the risk of problems arising later can be high. If the patient has a CVA two months after the emergency department visit and was not advised to seek follow-up care for high blood pressure, the basis for a malpractice claim may exist.

The routine failure of emergency department staff to act on the discovery of significantly elevated blood pressures was documented in a study of three hospital emergency departments.[3] In this study, 5% of patients did not have their blood pressures taken. Of those who had it taken, approximately 20% showed elevated blood pressure. Appropriate recognition and referral for further evaluation occurred in only 64% of these cases. A particularly alarming finding was that only 28% of those with a diastolic pressure of 110 mm Hg or more were referred.[3] In short, the importance of advising a patient of a significantly abnormal test or measurement and the need for follow-up care cannot be overstated. These facts must be stated on the chart and on the follow-up notes.

Common charting deficiencies include the lack of timely documentation of serial vital signs in appropriate cases and the failure to note therapeutic actions and responses to substantive changes in vital signs. Vital signs are important objective markers of a patient's status. If they are not measured at appropriate intervals consistent with the severity (or potential severity) of a patient's illness, the lack of serial vital signs can be a significant source of future embarrassment if there is an unexpected adverse outcome.

Discharging a patient who has substantially abnormal vital signs (particularly high pulse or respiratory rate) can be risky when the quality of care needs to be defended. A case could reasonably be made that an adult patient with respiratory complaints who is discharged with a respiratory rate in the 30s has been released prematurely or inadequately treated. Vital signs obtained prior to discharge that objectively measure any improvements in the pulse, respiratory rate, and/or blood pressure will go a long way in defending a discharge disposition.

Chart the times that events occur in the emergency department record. This information can be used either to defeat or support a liability claim. When a medical record is scrutinized in the process of evaluating whether a malpractice claim should be filed, the chronology of emergency department events surrounding the care of the patient sometimes becomes an important issue. Failure of nurses and physicians to act in a timely manner may serve as one of the key issues in the claim.

To the extent that appropriate timely action can be documented in the record, physicians and nurses should include the times at which key observations and actions take place. It is an accepted general practice to indicate the times of emergency department entry and discharge, initial and subsequent vital signs, interval progress notes by the nurses and physicians, when various treatments were given, and when important communications occurred.

Obtain and document an appropriately detailed history. The recording of symptom chronology, pertinent past medical history, risk factor assessment, previous treatment, and key positive and negative historical facts are important elements in documenting the level of concern and thoroughness in patient care. An unduly abbreviated, barely legible note will convey a sense of carelessness and haste to a jury evaluating the merits of a plaintiff's case. A similar view may be taken if you refer to the nurses' notes with the familiar phrase "as above" as a substitute for recording your own history. In addition, be careful to review the initial nurses' notes to make sure all significant items are addressed in your history.

Perform and document a thorough physical examination. Patients expect to be examined and will base a significant portion of their judgments concerning the care, concern, and thoroughness of the physician on the quality of that examination. If they perceive that your examination is cursory and incomplete, they may feel that you provided substandard care if an adverse outcome occurs. Tell the patient (or family member) what you are looking for and what you find during an examination so that the patient or family members will understand the many items being assessed.

When treating young children, be particularly careful to describe in their charts their behavioral status — response to stimulation, level of activity, curiosity, and playfulness. These behaviors represent key factors in determining whether a child is seriously ill. If these items are not documented, the record cannot be used to show that the child did not appear toxic on discharge.

Do not give anyone cause to view the record as anything but truthful. A common yet usually inappropriate notation in emergency department charts is the abbreviation "PERRLA." When asked by a patient's attorney what the "A" stands for and whether "accommodation" was specifically tested, the unwary emergency physician who uses this abbreviation may appear to the jury to have documented something not actually done. The attorney can then suggest that perhaps other parts of the record are equally untrue.

A more blatant example is the recording of "cranial nerves II-XII normal." Physicians who use this short-cut phrase when recording neurologic examination findings should be fully prepared to describe the name, function, and method of testing these cranial nerves and affirm that the described tests were all performed. They also should be prepared to answer whether this neuroanatomy was reviewed after being named in the lawsuit and be expected to hear the plaintiff testify as to whether all such tests were, in fact, performed.

Such cases are another example where the transcribed record will serve the physician well. Within seconds, a detailed neurologic examination can be recorded that does not require the use of potentially embarrassing abbreviations. The physician can quickly mention all the functions that were checked in a more specific manner (e.g., ". . . extraocular movements normal without nystagmus, pupils midrange, equal and reactive, facial motor function intact with no asymmetry and normal sensation present . . .").

Never use terminology that demeans the patient. Medical humor is often used to release tension or to vent frustrations. Under no circumstances, however, should the physicians or nursing staff include these remarks on a chart. When an attorney asked a nurse, in front of a jury, the meaning of the abbreviation "SPOS," which had been written in the chart concerning a plaintiff, she greatly prejudiced the jury against

her when she said it stood for "subhuman piece of shit." Stories of emergency departments that have made rubber stamps depicting turkeys to be used on selected patients' charts indicate the level to which such inappropriate and high-risk behavior can be taken.

Likewise, the use of words such as "obnoxious," "filthy," "drunk," or "belligerent" reflect a degree of hostility toward the patient that is easily discerned by laypersons. The use of more professional and less demeaning terms is clearly advantageous to the professional staff, while the use of inappropriate terminology may come back to haunt them.

Generate interval progress notes. A review of emergency department medical charts will quickly indicate that physicians commonly believe recording interval progress notes is the nurse's job. The physician, on the other hand, typically documents the history, physical examination, diagnostic and therapeutic orders, diagnosis, and follow-up instructions.

For example, a patient may have been in the emergency department for four hours for the treatment of a refractory asthma attack. During that time, the patient will have received multiple treatments, including, perhaps, IV fluid therapy, steroids, and inhalation treatments with a variety of drugs. For the physician not to comment in the record regarding the patient's course and response (or lack of response) to treatment is most inappropriate. If the nurses are the only ones charting interval progress notes of any sort, the physician will have relinquished the prerogative to detail the course of treatment.

As the physician, you would hope to agree with the content of the nurses' notes; however, remember that such notes are just that — nurses' notes. They do not take the place of your interval progress notes. Interval progress notes are not only important for the documentation of the patient's course, but also essential for the defense of "holding time" or "critical care time" charges.

Even minor cases are well served by the inclusion of "summary/medical decision-making" notes. In one or two brief sentences, you can dictate that: ". . . an ice bag was applied to the ankle, and upon ascertaining the lack of GI sensitivity, a prescription for ibuprofen was given for pain. X-ray was read by the radiologist as showing no fracture, and an elastic wrap was applied. The patient was instructed in the use of crutches and will follow up with his physician in two days."

Document recognition of significant laboratory, x-ray, and ECG abnormalities. Although emergency physicians commonly rewrite data from laboratory slips onto patient charts, the more cost-effective technique is to note only the significantly abnormal findings or, perhaps, to refer to them in the discharge summary note. When you interpret x-rays or ECGs, record these interpretations on the chart. Because there is so much inconsistency in interpreting ECGs, it may be best to describe any suspected abnormalities in equivocal cases rather than be committed to an interpretation of "normal" or "abnormal."

A detailed diagnosis and a disposition consistent with the diagnosis are very important. This is one of the basic rules of emergency department charting — the diagnosis and disposition must be medically in keeping with the charted history, physical examination, and interval progress notes of all the individuals who entered this information on the chart. If any substantive disagreement or conflict exists in the chart regarding potentially serious issues, the chart may be used against those who generated it. The diagnosis should reflect the intensity and severity of the patient's condition as well as possible.

Medicare and other insurance programs allow emergency physicians the prerogative of using a special group of ICD-9 "diagnoses" that are essentially a restatement of symptoms. Examples include "abdominal pain" (780.9), "painful urination" (788.1), "numbness" (782.0), "myalgia" (729.1), "dyspnea" (786.09), and "confusion" (298.9), among others. The use of such "symptom" diagnoses in conjunction with other diagnoses will allow insurance carriers and others to comprehend more fully the severity and intensity of a patient's problem and may be used when a more specific diagnosis is not known.

Some emergency physicians have a habit of putting "rule out" diagnoses down when discharging patients. The value of this practice is unclear, but the potential dangers associated with its use are very real. A "rule out — R/O" is a term typically used in the care of inpatients to capsulize the thoughts of the admitting physicians regarding possible diagnoses to be considered or rejected in a patient whose condition is unknown. It implies that the listed diagnoses will be systematically ruled out.

Emergency physicians do not rule out the diagnoses typically listed as "rule outs" when patients are discharged. If any of the diagnoses on the list of "rule outs" is potentially serious or typically requires immediate admission to the hospital, patients cannot be sent home until these diagnoses have been ruled out. Therefore, a patient whose condition is diagnosed as "nonspecific chest pain, R/O chest wall pain vs. new onset angina" cannot be discharged. Nor can the patient with "nonspecific abdominal pain, cannot exclude R/O appendicitis" unless early follow-up is guaranteed.

Emergency physicians and other staff will occasionally generate charts that have certain "danger" words and phrases that will preclude the discharge of a patient. For example, the chart of a discharged infant may contain the words "toxic," "lethargic," or "apathetic" as recorded by the physician or the nurses. Such terms in the record may be a liability for the attending staff if the child is subsequently found to have meningitis. Likewise, the chart of the 28-year-old man who has new-onset chest pain charted as "heavy pressure associated with nausea and sweating" could present a similar risk. Unless a rather heroic effort is made to dilute the influence of "danger" words or phrases, once written they tend to invalidate any final diagnosis that appears to warrant discharge.

Never let lack of space be used as an excuse for inadequate documentation. Most emergency department patient records require only the space available on one 8 $\frac{1}{2}$ x 11 sheet. However, a few of these records, for the sickest patients or those who have been in the emergency department the longest, may have charts that require two or three pages.

A jury generally has little sympathy for a physician who writes notes in the margin and on areas of the chart not intended for physician notes, or whose handwriting becomes progressively smaller and less legible, or whose notes become more cryptic as he runs out of room to write. Physicians should not hesitate to use a second or even third page. Forms designed specifically for this purpose should be readily available at all times. With a dictated record, this issue is seldom, if ever, a problem.

Correct charting errors and enter addenda properly. If a word or series of words placed on a chart is subsequently found to be incorrect, draw a single line through the incorrect words. Above that line, write the word "error," initial the correction, and enter the time and date. The error should never be completely blotted out or covered over so that it is no longer legible. The plaintiff's attorney could easily suggest that the obliterated part of the record is hiding self-incriminating information.

At times, a large section of the chart is in error (as typically occurs when a physician inadvertently writes an entire history and physical on the wrong chart). In such cases, you can generate an entirely new record that contains all the information that was previously entered correctly (e.g. nurses' notes, vital signs, clock-in times) along with the correct entry by the individual who made the original error. In these instances, the nurses are asked to copy over their original notes and create a record identical to the first up to the point of the error. This problem also arises occasionally when a medical history and physical examination are printed onto the wrong chart as the result of a transcription error.

If a patient's chart needs to be supplemented with information obtained after the fact, an addendum should be made. The addendum should not appear to have been written at the time the chart was originally generated. All addenda should be specifically identified as such, with the time and date noted. Occasionally, addenda will be self-serving notes added to the record to defend in more detail why a certain action was taken or to elucidate certain findings. When this occurs, word the addendum to avoid suggesting an inappropriate or unethical motive behind its addition.

Emergency physicians and staff should never alter the record after the fact in a way that would indicate or suggest an intent to deceive the reader. Once this type of change has been made known to a jury (and plaintiff attorneys have many ways to seek out and identify altered records), the defendant physician can expect no mercy. His credibility is totally destroyed, and it becomes easy for the jury to make the logical leap from "liar" to "bad doctor" to "guilty."

The treating emergency physician should try to be the last person to enter data on the chart. Being the last person to make chart entries allows you the opportunity to scan the notes of the other documenters and to be aware of everything that has been recorded. Make a special effort to identify charting inconsistencies or other potentially problematic areas that may indicate internal conflict in the record.

Discharge Instructions

Discharge instructions are a vital and integral element of the emergency department medical record. Many claims against emergency physicians succeed because the plaintiff's attor-

neys are able to demonstrate that the physician failed to give discharge instructions to patients, clearly telling them when and under what circumstances follow-up care was needed.

There are two general types of follow-up instructions — "mandated" and "as needed" follow-up.

Mandated Follow-Up

Mandated follow-up is the easier type to prescribe because the patient does not have to make any decisions. The patient is given a specific day or time when the mandated follow-up is to occur. If the emergency physician feels it necessary and appropriate, the follow-up physician can be contacted in advance to help ensure that the prescribed follow-up care will occur.

Besides situations in which the need for mandatory follow-up is obvious (fractures, pregnancy, sutured wounds), it should also be advised when simply relieving a patient's symptoms may not resolve the initial problem. One good example of this is the patient with abdominal pain that is not adequately explained. Pain often temporarily subsides when the pressure in a distended appendix is relieved by rupture. Certainly in this situation the patient will have taken a turn for the worse although the symptoms have become less painful. Another example is the 1-year-old child whose condition is diagnosed as otitis media. Even though symptoms of the ear infection may have resolved, the physician should mandate follow-up if a persistent effusion exists that may result in subsequent hearing and learning difficulties. The same rationale applies to the 4-year-old girl with a first urinary tract infection.

In short, certain conditions require mandated follow-up despite the apparent resolution of the immediate symptoms. Emergency physicians must be aware of these disorders so that inappropriate, as needed follow-up will not be advised.

One potential problem with mandated follow-up is that it can be overused. Some physicians routinely prescribe mandated follow-up in an effort to limit their perceived malpractice risk. This practice of defensive medicine does not take into consideration the fact that the patient and family members may have to miss work to see follow-up physicians, or that they will incur additional medical costs, or, to a certain extent, that ethical issues may be raised concerning unnecessary referral. Many self-limiting disorders treated by emergency physicians do not warrant mandated follow-up. The disorder will simply run its natural course. Emergency physicians are paid to use their skills and training to treat and advise their patients. They are not performing this job well if they are unwilling to advise "as needed" follow-up when it is perfectly appropriate and ethical to do so.

One final word about mandated follow-up. Physicians should always instruct the patient orally and state in writing on the discharge instructions to seek care sooner than the prescribed time if any problems arise, such as new symptoms or recurring or worsening symptoms.

As Needed Follow-Up

As needed follow-up is the more difficult of the two to prescribe because the patient is required to make certain judgments. In this regard, disease and injury processes can progress in four ways: the symptoms can persist, improve, or worsen, or new symptoms can develop. If each of these four options is addressed by as needed follow-up instructions, safe discharge can be anticipated.

A patient who develops new or worsening symptoms should be advised to return to the emergency department immediately that day if unable to see a follow-up physician. If physicians offer patients anything but a same-day option to be reassessed, an attorney can construe this as advising the patient to delay getting proper treatment. Persisting symptoms require follow-up if they last a specified amount of time.

For example, mild ankle sprains typically resolve in 7 to 10 days. Patients whose symptoms persist longer should be advised to seek follow-up care. The patient given antibiotics for exudative pharyngitis typically will feel much better within two to three days. If symptoms persist longer than three days, follow-up is indicated.

Who Provides Follow-Up Care?

After defining when and under what circumstances follow-up care should be sought, the next thing to do is establish who will provide this care. Customarily, emergency physicians will refer patients to their private physicians or, if a specialist is required, call the private physician for a specialist referral. Emergency department staff can include on the discharge instructions the name and telephone number and address of the physician who will provide follow-up care. If a patient does not have a private physician, give the patient the name, address,

and telephone number of the appropriate call panel physician. This practice varies throughout the country. In some areas, physicians are obligated by medical staff rules to accept referrals from the emergency department. In other locales, on-call physicians may pick and choose those patients whom they wish to follow up in their private practices.

In either situation, discharge instructions should ensure that needed follow-up always takes place. All such instructions should advise patients to return to the emergency department if they are unable to receive follow-up care in the appropriate time or to go to some other medical facility where care will definitely be provided (e.g., a county or municipal hospital) if they are unable to arrange local follow-up care. These options must be offered so patients will not be medically stranded and so that complications or a worsening disease process can be identified and treated in a timely manner for the benefit of the patients and, potentially, of the physician.

Discharge Instructions Do's and Don'ts

Provide instructions in plain, simple language. Most follow-up instruction sheets are written by physicians. They must understand that these instructions are intended primarily for the patients, and only secondarily for physicians. Thus, these instructions must be written at a level most patients can be expected to understand. One study[4] indicated that fully half of the 105 emergency department patients studied at the University of Virginia Medical Center may have had reading levels too low to understand patient-directed emergency department materials.[4]

Another practice to avoid is the use of medical abbreviations and lingo or Latin phrases. "FU in AM with PMD" is likely to be incomprehensible to the typical emergency department patient. Use of such phraseology may show a jury just how inadequate a physician's instructions were to the patient.

When an emergency department consistently treats a significant minority of patients who speak a language other than English (e.g., Spanish), failure to provide discharge instructions in this language may be viewed as discriminatory, as well as dangerous from a medical-legal perspective. When non–English-speaking patients are discharged from the emergency department, it is useful from both a medical and legal perspective to have a translator or family member present who can speak the language of the patient (see Chapter 8, "Communication Barriers in the Physician-Patient Relationship").

Always record the name of the translator on the discharge instructions or on the main body of the emergency department record in the event that a claim is later filed and the issue of language differences becomes part of the case. Clearly, it is wiser to use a hospital employee rather than a family member to serve as the "official" translator. If a claim is filed and the content and quality of the discharge instructions become a factor in the case, the translator will make a better witness for the hospital.

Include on the discharge instructions the working diagnosis so that both the patient and follow-up physician will know what is believed to be wrong with the patient. It is not uncommon to see a patient returning for follow-up care who seems to have no idea what the initial diagnosis was. This failure of communication is less likely to occur if the diagnostic impression is written in plain language on the discharge instructions. Use terms likely to be understood by the patient — "bladder infection" instead of "cystitis," "middle ear infection" instead of "otitis media."

Some physicians have chosen to use "softer" words than diagnosis on their emergency department charts and discharge instructions, perhaps to convey to the patient a certain tentativeness. Then, if the diagnosis ultimately proves to be different from the one listed by the emergency physician, the patient may be less likely to believe that an error was made. To this end, physicians have used phrases such as "impression," "preliminary diagnosis," and "provisional diagnosis." Whether this approach achieves its purpose is purely speculative; however, it may be appropriate to consider using it.

Indicate on the discharge instructions what care was specifically rendered in the emergency department. When the patient takes the discharge instructions to the follow-up physician, this information tells the physician what was done in the emergency department, what prescriptions the patient was given, and what test results, if any, are pending. The value of this practice is obvious. Many times, a patient will not go to the physician identified for follow-up care. Even if the patient goes to the physician to whom a copy of the chart was sent, the chart copy may arrive after the patient has presented for follow-up care.

In this regard, the practice of routinely giving patients copies of their laboratory reports, ECGs, and a list of x-rays taken can also help to facilitate their follow-up care. Listing the x-rays taken is especially helpful for patients who have sustained multiple trauma and who may complain of areas of soreness on subsequent visits to their physicians. Follow-up physicians can then quickly determine via the discharge instructions whether an x-ray was taken of a certain area.

If a case can be made for providing all this information, should the patient also be given a copy of the chart to take to the follow-up physician? Generally, the chart is unnecessary when patients are given discharge instructions that already contain the key information follow-up physicians need: diagnosis, results of laboratory tests and x-rays, a copy of the prescription, a list of pending tests (if any), and the treatment given in the emergency department. If patients look at the chart and read their own history and physical examination results, they are likely to be bewildered by such terminology as "SOB 40 y.o. obese female who appears older than stated age . . ." Their confusion and concern can cause needless anxiety and potentially result in problems for the emergency physician.

Provide specific instructions regarding home care for the patient's injury or illness. These instructions can range from brief written notes of questionable legibility to computer-generated multipage documents. There are two points of view regarding such instructions. The first is to keep the instructions brief with heavy emphasis on the basics (e.g., for minor orthopedic-type injuries, ice, elevation, rest, limiting use, and brief information regarding nerve and circulatory checks). The second point of view can be summarized as "the more the better" school. Typically, emergency departments that adopt this position send parents home with separate instruction sheets for fever, vomiting, diarrhea, and upper respiratory tract infection treatment when a child with all of these findings is discharged. A major area of concern with this practice centers on the parents' ability and inclination to read and understand multiple sets of instructions.

The safest discharge instructions are those that do not rely heavily on a layperson's judgments about potentially vital issues. "Are the pupils really unequal? What are the pupils anyway?" "Is it OK to vomit once at home after a head injury but not twice?" "How slurred does the speech have to be before we should see the doctor?"). As noted previously, whether instructions are detailed or brief, they should always be given with the caveat, both orally and in writing, that the patient or parent should call or return to the emergency department if they have any questions or concerns.

A word about the advantages and drawbacks of computerized discharge instructions. The computer is a wonderful tool to generate discharge instructions of consistent quality and completeness. Currently, there are multiple suppliers of computer programs for this specific purpose. Some can generate prescriptions and discharge instructions in foreign languages (usually Spanish). All can assist emergency physicians in their task of providing patients with first-rate discharge instructions. However, because computers make it so easy to give patients information concerning their diagnosis, home care, potential adverse effects of their prescriptions, and so on, it is easy to overload patients with information and to obscure essential instructions in a deluge of "nice-to-know" data. The critical criteria in judging effective discharge instructions remain the appropriateness of the information provided — it gives enough information but not too much, is written in plain language, and relies only minimally on a layperson's judgment to make important medical decisions. The true measure of an effective set of discharge instructions is the degree to which these goals are met, whether the instructions are computer-generated or otherwise.

Don't be confused about who is responsible for providing follow-up instructions — the treating physician is always responsible. This issue is frequently debated in emergency medicine circles, with the major concern being whose "job" it is to give out the discharge instructions. Although this task may be delegated to the nurses by physicians, physicians are responsible for ensuring that both specific and general follow-up instructions are conveyed to the patients and that any questions patients may have are answered appropriately.

Physicians must always appreciate how vital the "closing" of an emergency department visit is to the patient. This is the opportunity to summarize the entire visit regarding diagnosis, home treatment, follow-up care, questions, and concerns about related issues —"Can I go to work?" "Can I change the dressing?" "When?" "You do remember I'm allergic to penicillin, don't you?") — and the acquisition of last-minute information — "Actually, I have been having some aching in my chest lately, too." "Come to think of it, my brother had a bad headache like mine, and he was told he had something like a brain aneurysm." The "signing out" of a patient is the final opportunity to address unanswered concerns, to reinforce the attitude of caring hopefully instilled during the visit, and to let patients know that they are appreciated. To delegate this important opportunity to others does not seem judicious when practicing the high-risk specialty of emergency medicine.

Explain why the patient or parent is signing the discharge instructions. It is common emergency department practice to have the same individual who gives the instructions sign them as well. The name of any translator should be documented either in the chart or on the discharge instructions. When patients or parents sign discharge instruction sheets, they should know that their signatures mean they have received and understood the instructions. A statement to this effect can be printed next to the signature block.

Keep a copy of the completed discharge instructions in the patient's record and give the original to the patient or parent. Some emergency departments keep the original and give the copy to the patient. The potential problem associated with this practice relates to legibility issues: why should the copy in the medical records department be the most legible one? Remember: the discharge instruction sheet is a document for the patient's medical benefit. The patient should receive the best copy. Also, because a copy of the discharge instructions is in the patient's record, it is reasonable to assume that the original must have been given to the patient. When the original is in the patient's record, it is less clear who received a copy or if, in fact, a copy was ever given to the patient.

Sometimes patients leave without receiving their written, signed discharge instructions. When this occurs and the patients were orally advised of all they needed to know but simply forgot to take the instruction sheet with them, a note should be placed in the chart indicating that oral discharge instructions were given. Ideally, emergency department staff should call patients to tell them they forgot their discharge instructions and to offer to answer any further questions.

Occasionally, a patient may leave without receiving either written or complete oral instructions. Emergency department staff should try to contact these patients immediately so that the key items can be reviewed. Place a note in the chart mentioning that a call was made, who was spoken to, and what was discussed.

Sometimes, patients will not have a telephone, or the number listed will be incorrect. In the case of incorrect telephone numbers, emergency department staff can call directory assistant in an attempt to ascertain the number. Although certain patients will purposely give wrong numbers when registering, it is equally possible that the registration personnel may have made an error when recording the number given by the patient. Thus, staff should contact the telephone company to check the number and then document in the medical record that this action was taken. A jury would be suspicious of any emergency department staff if they failed to make the most basic efforts to locate a telephone number.

Key Points and Conclusion

A substantial portion of the practice of emergency medicine is the generation of medical records. Just as there is both an art and a science to patient care, so, too, is there an art and a science to the creation of the medical record.

Generating the medical record is an acquired skill born of the basic understanding that a legal record is being created that must serve the providers of care as well as the patient. When the medical record and discharge instructions are viewed as primarily legal documents created to detail the assessment and care of a patient, along with recommended follow-up, all the other functions of the medical record will be well served. All who are authorized to make entries into a patient's chart must understand the potential importance of the legal record they are creating, the need for carefully considered entries, their responsibility to chart appropriately, and the potential consequences of their actions.

References

1. Klimt CR, Becker S, Fox BS, et al. A transcribed emergency record at minimum cost. *Ann Emerg Med* 1983;12:556-558.

2. Zemmel NJ, Park SM, Schweitzer J, et al. Status of Voicetype Dictation for Windows for the emergency physician. *J Emerg Med* 1996;14:511-515.

3. Glass RI, Mirel R, Hollander G, et al. Screening for hypertension in the emergency department. *JAMA* 1978;240:1973-1974.

4. Powers RD. Emergency department patient literacy and the readability of patient-directed materials. *Ann Emerg Med* 1988;17:124-126.

Chapter 38

Incident Reports

Charles L. Zeller, Jr., MD, FACEP

An incident, or occurrence report is a form or process used to describe and document situations or actions — occurrences — that deviate from routine or are inconsistent with established emergency department patient care practices or functions. Most hospitals use incident reports to document a variety of occurrences, for example.

If an event occurs that warrants documentation in an incident report, the report should be completed as soon as possible by everyone involved to ensure accurate and thorough reporting. High-quality patient care and safety must be the guiding concerns.

Confidentiality

Incident reports often contain sensitive information about patient care, information that can be legally damaging to emergency department staff and the hospital. For this reason, the existence and contents of an incident report must be kept strictly confidential. Incident reports are an integral part of hospital quality assurance programs and are protected by statute in every state.[1]

Confidentiality, with respect to an incident report, means protecting it from discovery or from being admitted into evidence in a lawsuit. It also means keeping the contents of an incident report known only to personnel specifically approved to address them. Many states have laws that specifically outline the process by which occurrence reports are protected. For example, a hospital can declare that an incident

report was prepared to advise its legal counsel of potential liability and as such represents an attorney's "work product," or privileged information.

Unnecessary written or oral reference to an incident report or to its contents jeopardizes confidentiality, contributes to potential negative repercussions, and takes away from its potential to benefit patient care practices. All staff should be educated about incident reports — what they are, why they are important, and why unnecessary discussion about them should be avoided.

Why Incident Reports Are Useful

Why, then, if incident reports must be kept confidential and are so potentially dangerous, do so many hospitals across the country use them. Incident reports have many purposes and uses, the most important of which are risk management and loss prevention. First, they can help pinpoint shortcomings in emergency department procedures, employee skills and knowledge, and staff behavior. In some cases, incident reports also provide valuable information to improve risk management efforts, such as documentation in potential or active liability situations or other efforts to identify and prevent high-risk occurrences.[2,3]

Second, when data from incident reports are gathered and analyzed appropriately, trends can be identified and this new insight may result in system or procedural changes. For example, individual accounts or a series of accounts may lead to employee training or education in a specified problem area to reduce or eliminate errors in the future.

Third, small trends discovered through data analysis can be used to evaluate new emergency department systems. For example, if the nursing staff decides to change staffing patterns, incident report trends could reveal what impact these changes have on patient care.[4-6]

Finally, incident reports can be the catalyst for obtaining more information about an incident that later results in litigation.

How to Complete Incident Reports

Procedures for filing incident reports and collecting data have undergone major changes in recent years. The document that used to be several pages long and produced multiple copies has been replaced with a more abbreviated form that is circulated much more selectively. Some hospitals used different forms for different types of incidents and different people. Now, a single form that can be used for all incidents is more common. More recent advancements include computer-automated or-generated reporting. With these systems, reporting, data collection, and collation are easier, but confidentiality and security are controversial.[7,8]

As an early step, establish criteria to determine what types of occurrences should be documented in an incident report — injury or potential injury to a patient? Operational issues? Medication errors? Then, determine what information each report should include. The types of data collected can vary significantly from hospital to hospital, and particularly from one region or state to another. At a minimum, however, each report should include the following basic information:

- Description of the incident
- Specific names, dates, times, and witnesses
- Any clinical impact, if known
- Remedial actions taken
- Follow-up recommendations

There is no place in an incident report or the medical record for judgmental opinions or the assignment of fault, blame, or accountability. For example, do not include statements such as: "I made a mistake when I . . ." or "I felt badly because I was wrong when I . . . ." Keep the information objective and to the point.

The incident report form itself should be user-friendly and flexible enough to adapt to a changing environment or needs. Consider in-service training for personnel to ensure proper and concise report completion. All staff should be educated and trained and committed to completing reports correctly.

Using the Data

Data can be useful only if they are properly collected and collated, and then properly interpreted, distributed, evaluated, and applied. Merely compiling information without careful study and dissemination is not useful. The use of data should be delineated in emergency department policy. Designated emergency department personnel should have access to the data and be responsible for evaluation and feedback. The information gathered must complete the feedback loop to ensure that the data become an asset. Only through adequate data can staff behavior be altered and outcomes improved. Ideally, the department's "culture" will create an atmosphere for positive change and maximum benefit.[9]

Equally important in a discussion of how to use data is how not to use data. As a general rule, data should not be used for disciplinary purposes or punishment.

Physician Credentialing

One of the most controversial uses of incident report data is in physician credentialing. To some, this application contradicts the premise that the information should not be used for punitive purposes. The temptation by risk managers to use incident report data, however, is overwhelming. The argument is often made that "past incidents" translate to "past performance" and, therefore, predict future behavior.

For this reason, incident reports must contain only objective, accurate information. They must be stored securely and evaluated and interpreted only by appropriately designated, objective, nonprejudicial persons. Specifically, a physician's actual credentials folder should never contain quality assurance material — only credentialing facts. The physician's hospital recredentialing folder, which is outside the peer review loop, may be both discoverable and admissible.

Preventing Discovery

No issue associated with incident reports is more challenging than how to prevent them from being "discovered" or used in litigation. Some basic guidelines can provide a measure of "protection" from discovery.

First, minimize the number of copies generated and the number of people receiving them. As a general rule, do not encourage photocopying reports. Confidentiality can be ensured only if people treat data as such. Second, ensure that the reports pass only through appropriate, preestablished hospital channels. Review these channels periodically.

Some specific rules of civil law traditionally have been used to protect incident report discoverability in the process of medical malpractice litigation.[10]

The first rule is referred to as privilege. Privilege is defined as the protected interaction between client and legal counsel. This position is strengthened if reports follow only previously established routing pathways — and weakened if multiple administrative and other personnel have had access to the reports.

The second rule, work product, applies to any note, working papers, reports, memoranda, or similar materials that are specifically prepared for an attorney or by an attorney, in anticipation of litigation. These documents are protected from discovery.

Other actions can be taken to minimize discovery. As previously discussed, incident reports should not be used for disciplinary purposes. Absolutely no references should be made to the reports in patient medical records, and they must not be stored with patient medical records. A simple but potentially helpful practice is to state clearly on the incident report form that the filing is being investigated for possible use by legal counsel.

Despite the risk of discovery, do not lose sight of the fact that the primary purpose of emergency department incident reports is to improve patient care. Timely, strict adherence to hospital policy and proper labeling of reports will help prevent discovery. The emergency physician should contact legal counsel to determine applicable local rules regarding the discoverability of incident reports.

Recently, the Joint Commission on Accreditation of Healthcare Organizations (JCAHO) implemented a formal approach to address adverse patient occurrences within accredited organizations. (Depending on the organization's control over the precipitating events, the organization can get an "accreditation watch" as opposed to a "conditional" accreditation. Some legal advisers say this may jeopardize the protection of confidentiality for peer-reviewed material.) The JCAHO's position needs to be assessed by case and by state.[11]

Key Points and Conclusion

Incident reports are important documents that have useful and important roles in an emergency department's risk management efforts. The data collected must be specific and stated objectively. These reports should be kept strictly confidential and distributed only to authorized personnel with periodic review and training.

The ability to protect data from discovery requires specific common sense applications of basic rules of law and confidentiality, such as the following:

- Incident reports are part of the quality assurance peer review system.
- Ensure confidentiality by labeling materials properly and training staff.
- Do not make reference to the incident report on the patient's medical record.
- Incident reports should present only facts — never conclusions as to fault or harm.
- A physician's hospital folder or credentialing folder should never contain incident reports or any other peer review materials. These should be kept in a separate folder.
- To avoid discoverability, use wording in all materials that complies with state statutes for protection of peer review material.

References

1. Dwyer JS. Hospital incident reports: protected from discovery? *Hosp Prog* 1982;October:38-39.
2. Puetz K. Development of an incident reporting system. *QRB* 1988;14(8):24-50.
3. Connaway NI. The legalities of home care: incident reports in home health agencies. *Home Healthcare Nurse* 4(3):9-10.
4. Cohen M, Davis N. Pharmacists must receive all incident reports involving medications. *Am J Hosp Pharm* 1993;50:1575-1576.
5. Camac K, Fisher M, McIlwrath M, et al. Quality improvement through use of medication incident reports. *The Lamp* 1994;May:12-13
6. Hartwig S, Schneider P. Use of severity-indexed medication error reports to improve quality. *Hosp Pharm* 1994;29(3):250,280-211.
7. Crowner M, Peric G, Stepcic F, et al. A comparison of videocameras and official incident reports in detecting inpatient assaults. *Hosp Community Psychiatry* 1994;45:1144-1145.
8. Coleman J, Peixoto C, Tyler T. User-friendly, low-cost incident reporting software available. *Hosp Secur Safety Manage* 1995;16(8):13-14.
9. Parisi L. Implementing a CQI approach to incident reporting. *Advisor* 1994;9(4):4-5.
10. Dollar C. Promoting better health care: policy arguments for concurrent quality assurance and attorney-client hospital incident report privileges. *Health Matrix* 1993;3(259):259-308.
11. The Joint Commission. *J Qual Improve* 1995;21(10):542-548.

Chapter 39

In-House Emergencies

William D. O'Riordan, MD, FACEP

The emergency physician, through medical staff policy or contractual arrangements, is often required to be a member of a hospital's critical care team. This team provides medical care to hospitalized patients and, occasionally, to outpatients whose conditions require immediate assessment and treatment. These "emergent" or "urgent" situations range from managing a cardiopulmonary arrest, to assessing a patient who has fallen out of bed, to verifying and pronouncing patient death.

The emergency physician who provides this type of service assumes numerous risks — negligence in the assessment and treatment of nonemergency department patients, claims of abandonment by emergency patients whose conditions deteriorate while the emergency physician is gone, violations of state, county, or public health and safety codes, and so on. The emergency physician's liability exposure can extend beyond the actual time it takes to treat a nonemergency department patient if the attending physician does not respond within an appropriate time frame.

An emergency physician group or an emergency physician who assumes responsibility for assessing and treating nonemergency department patients also has a duty to make sure that the hospital has the proper equipment, medications, and supplies strategically located throughout the facility. These must be immediately available when the emergency physician responds to an emergent call, as in the case of a cardiopulmonary arrest.

In some cases, the independently contracting emergency physician group has an agreement with the hospital that the emergency physician is covered under the hospital's malpractice insurance policy. In other cases, the emergency physician group has a specific clause in its insurance policy that extends the coverage to nonemergency department patients. If the issue of insurance coverage is not specifically addressed, emergency physicians could find that they are uninsured for the care and treatment of nonemergency department patients. Even when emergency physicians have contractual agreements to provide services to hospitalized patients, they should never assume that such services are protected against liability. All the states and the District of Columbia have "Good Samaritan" laws; however, these statutes vary considerably from state to state and do not preclude a lawsuit being filed against the emergency physician — nor do they protect the physician against nonfeasance. As a result, emergency physicians must make sure that the services they provide for in-house emergencies are covered by malpractice insurance or are in some other way protected against liability.

Case Studies

1

A 15-year-old boy is hospitalized for atypical rubella, dehydration, and fever. On his third hospital day, the patient is found with his head wedged between the guard rail and the mattress in the midst of a grand mal seizure. Eighteen minutes later, a code blue is called. The code blue team, consisting of an emergency physician and emergency nurse, arrives three minutes after the code is called. The emergency physician performs a brief assessment of the patient. A few minutes later, the seizure activity stops, and the emergency physician goes back to the emergency department.

Four minutes later, the patient has a second seizure. Another code blue is called, and five minutes later, the team returns. The patient is nasotracheally intubated, and IV diazepam and a small dose of phenytoin are administered. Despite these interventions, the seizure activity continues for another 30 minutes. The patient suffers a severe hypoxic insult to his brain and recurrent seizure activity.[1]

2

Late one night, a nurse on a medical-surgical unit asks an emergency physician to come up and assess a patient, a 46-year-old man who apparently is experiencing repeated episodes of hematemesis. The patient had undergone an exploratory laparotomy 18 days before to control hemorrhage from a bleeding gastric ulcer and had bled again six days earlier. At that time, the patient was treated for the hemorrhage.

The emergency physician responds and performs an assessment of the patient. Vital signs are blood pressure 90/60 and pulse 156. The emergency physician orders laboratory tests and a type and crossmatch for 6 U of packed RBCs. He asks the nursing staff to place a nasogastric tube and begin iced-saline lavage, then orders the patient transferred to the ICU. The emergency physician then calls the patient's internist and the surgeon who performed the operation. He cannot reach the internist, so he calls the internist's partner. Fifteen minutes later, he reaches the surgeon and advises him of the patient's severe bleeding. Neither the internist nor the surgeon comes into the hospital to assess the patient.

The next morning, the internist sees the patient briefly at 9:00 AM. At 10:30 AM, the patient goes into profound shock. After a prolonged resuscitation, the patient is taken to surgery. He is subsequently shown to have a severe ischemic insult to his brain.[2]

3

A 10-month-old child is undergoing an elective air arthrogram for a congenitally dislocated hip in the pediatric section of the radiology department. During the procedure, several attempts are made to enter the hip joint, and small amounts of air are injected into the area of the joint. After 10 tries, the radiologist cancels the procedure.

A few minutes after the last injection of air, while the radiologist is taking some "spot films," the child suffers respiratory arrest followed by cardiopulmonary arrest. A code blue is called. Emergency physicians from the pediatric section of the emergency department, located one floor below the x-ray department, respond and attempt to initiate advanced cardiac life support measures. Unfortunately, there is no pediatric resuscitation equipment available. An emergency nurse runs downstairs to the emergency department to get the pediatric intubation equipment. After intubating the patient, the emergency team takes the child to the pediatric emergency department, where they establish IV access, administer medications, and perform a successful resuscitation. Subsequently, however, the child exhibits signs and symptoms of having suffered a severe ischemic injury to the brain.[3]

Establishing Responsibility for Patient Care

Because emergency physicians possess a well-recognized expertise in cardiopulmonary resuscitation, they frequently assess and treat patients who have emergent and urgent medical conditions. Medical staff members and administrators of acute health care facilities recognize this expertise and have come to rely on emergency physicians to assess and treat inpatients whose conditions are believed to be rapidly deteriorating. As a direct result, emergency physicians are placed in a position of double jeopardy when the care and treatment they render to inpatients and outpatients require them to leave the emergency department.

In hospitals that do not have full-time house officers or residency training programs, the emergency physicians should carefully define their responsibilities regarding the treatment of in-hospital and outpatient "emergencies" with the medical staff and the hospital's administration and board of directors. As a part of any agreement with the medical staff and hospital administration, the term "emergency" should be defined as narrowly as possible to prevent the abuse of the emergency physician by medical staff members and nursing personnel. The responsibilities of the attending physician must also be clearly defined so that the emergency physician will not assume the medical and, hence, legal responsibility for a patient's ongoing care after the emergency.

The most efficient way to define the emergency physician's role in responding to inpatient and outpatient emergencies is to adopt policies and procedures. These policies should originate in the emergency department or emergency services section and be approved by the medical executive committee and adopted by the board of directors or trustees. Such policies might include the following language: "The emergency physician's primary responsibility is the assessment, treatment, and monitoring of all patients who enter the emergency department. In the event that an inpatient or outpatient suffers a cardiopulmonary arrest and/or exhibits signs or symptoms that would be expected to lead to death and/or a loss of limb or serious morbidity, the emergency physician will respond to the emergent condition. After assessing the patient, the emergency physician will order emergently needed diagnostic tests and treatment and summon the attending physician. The attending physician or the physician on call for the attending physician will respond to an in-house life-threatening emergency as would any other staff member when called to do so."

One likely dilemma is that an emergency physician who is the only physician on duty will be caught between treating an unstable emergency department patient and responding to an inpatient or outpatient emergency. In this situation, the emergency physician's primary obligation is always to the emergency department patient. A policy that addresses this dilemma should be submitted to and approved by the medical staff's executive committee and adopted by the board of directors.

Such a policy might contain the following language: "The emergency physician's primary responsibility is always to the patients in the emergency department. In the event the emergency physician is called to assess and treat an inpatient or outpatient who is in emergent need of assessment, treatment, and care and, at the same time, there is an unstable, critically ill, or injured patient in the emergency department, the emergency physician's primary responsibility will be to the emergency department patient. If, in the emergency physician's judgment, the in-house patient is in greater need of the emergency physician's attention and there are no other physicians in the hospital to respond to inpatient or outpatient emergencies, the emergency physician will respond to the in-house emergency."

In situations where the in-house patient is not in immediate danger of death or when the emergency physician cannot leave the emergency department, the in-house patient can be taken to the emergency department.

The contract between an emergency physician or group and a hospital without house officers and/or residency training programs should reflect the language previously suggested for the medical staff policies concerning inpatient and outpatient emergencies as well as the attending physician's responsibility to respond to such emergencies. The emergency physicians who are employed by a hospital should also have a section in their employment contract specifically outlining these areas.

In those cases where emergency physicians accept responsibility for being a member or the leader of the hospital's cardiopulmonary resuscitation team, they should make sure that resuscitation equipment, medications, and supplies required for advanced cardiac life support measures are immediately available to them. Providing and maintaining equipment and medications are the hospital's responsibilities.[4,5] Therefore, the emergency physicians should define, through medical staff policy, the hospital's responsibility for the purchase, maintenance, and proper placement of these resources. The team must be able to implement advanced cardiac life support measures within minutes of an emergency call.

Such a policy may be worded as follows: "Because successful cardiopulmonary resuscitation has been correlated with the rapid implementation of advanced cardiac life support measures, the hospital will provide sufficient equipment, supplies, and medications to enable the resuscitation team to implement advanced resuscitation procedures on all inpatients and outpatients within a time frame that complies with nationally recognized standards. The emergency department committee will determine the strategic locations for this equipment and the manner and frequency with which these supplies will be checked."

This policy, once passed by the medical executive committee, must be submitted to the board of directors or trustees for adoption. The emergency physicians should request that the hospital's responsibility for purchasing and maintaining the resuscitation equipment be included in their contracts or service agreements.

In some cases, an emergency physician group will contract to provide emergency services for an acute care facility, or an emergency physician will be employed by a hospital with full-time in-house physicians and/or a residency training program in internal medicine, anesthesia, or general surgery. In such instances, the physician or group should carefully define its obligations to nonemergency inpatients and outpatients who develop emergent and urgent conditions. In the past, house officers and residents have assumed responsibility for responding to these emergency situations. However, as a result of emergency physicians' recognized expertise in cardiopulmonary resuscitation, the trend has been to require the emergency physician to act as the team leader in all cardiopulmonary arrests. If the contracting group agrees to have its emergency physicians act as team leaders in these cardiopulmonary arrest situations, then the group inherits the same risks as the contracting group does in hospitals that do not have in-house physicians or residency training programs.

This specific problem can be addressed by the emergency department committee. Committee members can recommend to the medical executive committee that all house physicians as well as residents be certified to a provider level in ACLS. The result of such a policy can be to shift the team leader responsibility to the house officers or residents, relieving the emergency physicians of any nonemergency department responsibility. Some emergency physician groups have agreed to train in-house physicians to expedite the transfer of this responsibility. If such a policy is adopted by the medical executive committee and by the board of directors, the emergency physician group should amend its contract to reflect this change in their responsibility. Similarly, the emergency physician employee's personal service agreement or contract should be changed.

Transferring Patient Care to Attending Physicians

The procedure for transferring the responsibility for ongoing patient care from the emergency physician to the attending physician should be delineated by hospital policy. A simple method to determine whether a patient's physician has arrived is for the emergency physician to write an order asking the nurses to notify him when the attending physician arrives. Likewise, a notification can be sent if the attending physician does not physically assess the patient within a specific period of time. If the attending physician does not respond, the emergency physician can call the physician again.

What should the emergency physician do when the attending physician or the physician on call does not respond to care for the patient? Because the failure of a physician to respond can be a critical liability issue, the emergency physician must be able to handle this problem in an appropriate and timely manner. For example, if the attending physician does not assume care of the patient within a reasonable time after being notified by the emergency physician or does not respond despite repeated calls, the emergency physician should call the chair of that physician's department or service and ask for help. If the chair cannot be contacted, then the chief of the medical staff should be asked to help. Some emergency physicians are reluctant to do this because they want to avoid the political problems that may result. However, failure to act needlessly increases the liability exposure of the emergency physician and the institution. Emergency physicians must consider the best interests of their patients in these situations.

Good Samaritan Protection

All of the states and the District of Columbia have passed Good Samaritan legislation. These laws, in one form or another, allegedly protect from liability the health care provider who responds to a cardiopulmonary arrest or other medical emergency situations. However, most Good Samaritan laws apply to out-of-hospital emergencies. In those states that provide in-hospital protection, if a contract specifically agrees to let a physician act in an emergency, the physician is no longer a Good Samaritan but simply a paid employee or independent contractor who has a contractual duty to provide medical care. Although the courts have affirmed these Good Samaritan laws, they do not prevent a physician or nurse from being sued. Because state laws differ in scope and meaning, physicians and staff should become familiar with the law in their states.

Insurance Coverage

The emergency physician has a very real liability exposure when assessing and treating inpatient and outpatient emergencies. For this reason, the emergency physician or group must be absolutely sure to have liability coverage for providing emergency services to nonemergency department patients. If the physician or group is required to provide its own liability coverage for these services, the policy should contain specific language not only defining such terms as "emergent" and "urgent" conditions, but also clearly stating which conditions will and will not be covered. Special attention should be given to the policy's coverage of obstetrics emergencies and other potentially high-risk conditions.

Many state supreme courts have ruled that the board of directors or trustees is ultimately responsible for emergency patient care in an acute care facility.[6-9] If the emergency physicians are handling inpatient and outpatient emergencies for the good of the hospital, then the hospital should be willing to provide liability coverage for the emergency physicians' services for nonemergency department patients.

The following specific language might be inserted into the emergency physician's or group's contract: "The emergency physician will be considered an agent of the hospital when requested to assess and treat an inpatient or outpatient by a member of the medical staff or an agent of the hospital. As an agent of the hospital, the emergency physician acting in such a capacity will be covered under the hospital's liability policy."

It is true that the emergency physician employed by the hospital is considered an agent of that hospital. Nonetheless, this physician should have a specific section in any contract with the hospital that addresses participating in the care and treatment of in-house emergencies as well as rendering care to outpatients in other departments. The reason for including this language is that a hospital could claim that the physician was acting outside the terms of the employment agreement and, therefore, would not be covered for responding to a nonemergency department event.

Documentation

The emergency physician who responds to in-house emergencies should carefully document what takes place and record a brief history, past medical history, medications and allergies, and a physical examination, including the vital signs. Also, the exact time the emergency physician arrived should be recorded in the progress note or dictation, along with the diagnosis and an emergency interim treatment plan. Other important steps to take and carefully document include what time the attending physician was called, a brief summary of the conversation, and a notation that the patient's physician was asked to come to the hospital to assume care for the patient.

Writing or dictating this information for inclusion in the patient's medical record will ensure that anyone who subsequently reviews the record will see that the emergency physician was responding to the emergency only and that the attending physician was to be responsible for all subsequent care.

The importance of handwritten or dictated progress notes concerning the emergency physician's response cannot be overemphasized. This information is the most important defense the emergency physician has if a claim is subsequently made by the patient or the patient's family, or if the attending physician fails to respond to the hospital's call. In particular, the emergency physician should record what was said to the attending physician in case there is a discrepancy in their accounts of the interaction.

If at all possible, emergency physicians should review the nurses' notes, and the cardiopulmonary resuscitation (code blue) sheet if a cardiac arrest has occurred, before writing or dictating their own notes. This step will help prevent conflicting statements in various records. If the emergency physician believes that a nurse has made a mistake in a nursing entry, a correction can be made on the same date the event took place.

Case Discussions

1

This case illustrates that emergency physicians must act in accordance with recognized standards of care when assessing and treating emergency conditions in hospitalized patients. The boy's parents alleged that the emergency physician acted below recognized standards of care for emergency physicians because he failed to assess and treat their son as he would have if he had come to the emergency department with a history of a first-time seizure lasting 18 minutes. They claimed that the seizure recurred as a direct result of the emergency physician's negligent care the first time he responded, and that the seizure activity continued because he administered suboptimal doses of anticonvulsants.

Despite the fact that the assessment and treatment rendered to this patient might be considered to fall under the state's Good Samaritan act, such an argument will not be made on the emergency physician's behalf. First, he failed to act the first time he saw the patient. Second, the nurses' notes pertaining to the emergency physician's first visit indicated that he said he did not consider the patient's seizure activity an emergency.

Third, his progress note did not mention the first time he saw the patient. Because nonfeasance, or the failure to act, in an emergency situation is not included in this state's Good Samaritan statute, and because the alleged failure to act was potentially a significant causative factor in the resulting damage, the physician's attorney believed that the Good Samaritan law does not apply.

2

In this case, the window of liability is dramatically increased because the internist and the surgeon failed to come to the hospital to see the patient after the emergency physician performed an assessment, instituted emergency treatment, and wrote orders. The plaintiff alleged that, because the emergency physician was the last physician to examine the patient until approximately 9:00 AM the following day, his responsibility continued until the internist got there. The plaintiff also claimed that, because the internist and surgeon did not respond appropriately, the emergency physician's conduct was causally related to the patient's severe hypoxic ischemic CNS injury caused by excessive bleeding.

Once again, the handwritten progress note was critical to the documentation of events that took place during assessment and treatment. This case is an outstanding example of why the emergency physician's notes must include the time the attending physician was notified, as well as the fact that the physician was asked to respond. Unfortunately, the emergency physician's progress note did not include any reference to the request that the attending physician or surgeon come to see the patient. The emergency physician testified that he "assumed" they came to the hospital to see their patient. Such assumptions frequently result in the emergency physician's inclusion in medical malpractice cases.

3

The obvious question in this case is why isn't the pediatric section of the radiology department equipped for ACLS measures? When an emergency physician or group agrees to be responsible for nonemergency department cardiopulmonary resuscitation and inpatient and outpatient emergencies, the emergency physician and the hospital are both responsible for making sure that the necessary equipment is immediately available.

In this case, the highly skilled emergency physicians who responded to the cardiopulmonary arrest could not implement advanced resuscitation measures. Instead, they had to transport a child who was in cardiopulmonary arrest down a flight of stairs while performing closed chest compressions and ventilation. The failure of both the physicians and the hospital to make sure that appropriate equipment was readily available was indefensible from a moral, medical, and legal perspective. Furthermore, the lack of equipment excluded use of this state's Good Samaritan law.

Key Points and Conclusion

Requiring emergency physicians to respond to patients outside the emergency department is a potential legal nightmare. To reduce the potential liability, emergency physicians should narrow the scope of these functions as much as possible in the following manner:

- Develop a policy that specifically outlines the scope of emergency physicians' obligation to nonemergency department patients. This policy should be approved by the medical executive committee and adopted by the hospital's board of directors or trustees.
- Develop a policy that outlines the obligation of the attending physician or designee when the emergency physician assesses and treats a nonemergency department patient and then asks the attending physician to come to the hospital to assume responsibility for that patient's care.
- Include in the physician's contract the hospital's responsibility to provide and maintain resuscitation equipment, medications, and supplies in readily accessible locations throughout the hospital.
- Define the roles and responsibilities of the emergency physician in relation to house officers and residents in responding to in-house emergent and urgent medical conditions. Attempt to transfer all inpatient and outpatient care and responsibility to these physicians after they have received appropriate training.

- Outline in the contract the roles and responsibilities for emergency physicians' care and treatment of nonemergency department patients. Because the emergency physician is providing these services for the benefit of the hospital, the hospital's liability policy should cover the emergency physician for this nonemergency department function.

The most important point for the emergency physician to realize concerning the care of non-emergency department patients is that every time emergency physicians respond, they place themselves in double jeopardy. Doing so could result in a potential claim of abandonment by an emergency department patient, in addition to the legal exposure created by treating the nonemergency department patient.

The emergency physician must never assume that a Good Samaritan law will afford protection from a lawsuit. This law potentially will protect the individual only from a judgment. Good Samaritan laws do not protect physicians from a failure to act.

References

1. *Rous v Greater Bakersfield Memorial Hospital*, (1984) KCSC:CA;195204.
2. *Gorton v Palmdale Hospital Medical Center*, (1985) LACSC:CA;NOC5436.
3. *Nguyen v Los Angeles County Harbor UCLA Medical Center*, (1986) LACSC:CA;C537628.
4. *Wade v John D. Archbold Memorial Hospital*, 166 Ga App 487, 304 SE2d 417 (1983), rev'd on other grounds.
5. *Medical & Surgical Memorial Hospital v Cauthorn*, 229 SW2d 932 (Tex Civ App 1949).
6. *Jackson v Power, Alaska Supreme Court*, 743 P2d 1376 (1987).
7. *Courtreau v Dodd, Arkansas Supreme Court*, 299 Ark 380, 773 SW2d 436 (1989).
8. *Thompson v Nason Hospital*, 527 Pa 330, 591 A2d 703 (Pa 1991).
9. *Pamperen v Trinity, Wisconsin*, 144 Wis2d 188, 423 NW2d 848 (1988).

Chapter 40

House Staff

William D. O'Riordan, MD, FACEP

Emergency medicine residents and residents in other medical specialties who rotate through the emergency department may not always have direct supervision when providing patient care. In these situations, patients can be at risk of receiving substandard emergency care. In some programs, faculty members rely on retrospective chart reviews instead of direct supervision to ensure that patients receive appropriate care. Unfortunately, this type of review does not identify a potentially adverse event until after it has occurred. This is fertile ground for litigation.

Residents often are not aware of the legal pitfalls in emergency medicine, probably because residency programs do not always provide risk management education as a part of their curriculum. To sensitize residents to potentially costly malpractice situations and frequent claims areas, hospital administrators should make sure that risk management becomes an integral part of residency training programs.

In general, resident physicians, like the faculty and attending clinical staff, learn about and obtain professional liability insurance through the emergency medicine training program. Residents should be made aware of exceptions to liability coverage. Unless the insurance coverage is fully explained to them, these physicians could unknowingly practice outside the scope of their coverage and not be covered for malpractice claims.

Also, emergency medicine residents are not always aware of department policies designed to ensure that patients receive proper care. By making residents aware of department policies

and guidelines, their exposure to potential liability situations can be minimized.

A serious new liability issue is billing for patient care services provided by residents. Medicare Part B services can be billed only if the supervising physician is directly involved in providing such care. Billing without providing such supervision is viewed by the Office of the Inspector General as fraud and may be a criminal act. Malpractice insurance does not cover such wrongdoing. Ignorance of hospital billing procedures is no defense for the physician.

Case Studies

1

A 25-year-old man is riding his motorcycle to work when he is struck by a car. He is unconscious for approximately one minute at the scene and is transported to a community hospital's emergency department for assessment and treatment. The patient is found to have a fractured ulna and is subsequently transferred to the county hospital's emergency department. Prior to being transferred, the patient becomes agitated and complains of a severe headache. An emergency physician administers 50 mg of meperidine and hydroxyzine immediately before the patient leaves.

The patient arrives at the county hospital three hours after the accident. He is initially assessed by a second-year family practice resident. During the initial assessment, the patient complains of severe headache, confusion, and vomiting. The resident calls another family practice resident who is rotating through the orthopedic service. This second resident assesses the patient and notes that he is slightly lethargic and is vomiting. He applies a cast to the patient's fractured arm and sends him to x-ray.

Approximately 1½ hours later, the patient returns from x-ray in a comatose state. He is intubated and a CT scan is performed, which is initially interpreted as being normal by a third-year family practice resident who is rotating through the neurosurgery service. The patient is admitted to the hospital's ICU. At 5:00 PM that same day, an attending neurosurgeon assesses and begins treating the patient, and he is later found to have sustained a severe CNS injury.[1]

2

A 64-year-old woman is referred to an acute care community emergency department by her internist after she complained of having a severe headache. The emergency department is hosting emergency medicine residents from a local medical school training program. A PGY-2 resident assesses the patient and obtains a history that notes an abrupt onset of a severe, right temporal headache accompanied by vomiting and neck pain. The patient tells the resident that she had a cerebral aneurysm clipped 6½ years prior to admission. The resident orders a head CT scan, which the radiologist interprets as normal. The resident attempts to call the patient's internist but is unsuccessful.

The resident consults with the attending emergency physician, who has not seen the patient. They decide that the patient does not need a lumbar puncture because she probably has a tension headache. The attending physician then cosigns the chart, and the patient is discharged and advised to see her internist as necessary. Six weeks later, the patient pays the bill for the emergency physician's services.

Ten weeks later, the patient experiences another severe headache, and shortly thereafter lapses into a deep coma and dies.[2]

3

A man presents to an emergency department complaining of fever, nausea, vomiting, and diarrhea. A family practice resident rotating through the emergency department assesses the patient and orders laboratory tests and chest and abdominal x-rays.

The emergency physician faculty member who is overseeing the resident assesses the patient and reviews the x-rays with this resident and two surgical residents. They agree that the films reveal a nonspecific ileus. The patient is admitted to the surgical service, observed, rehydrated, and discharged 24 hours after admission. Approximately 28 hours later, the radiologist reads the film and discovers a left lower lobe infiltrate consistent with acute pneumonia. He calls the emergency physician, who in turn notifies the surgical resident in charge of the surgical service.

The patient returns to the emergency department the next day with fever, fast heart rate, elevated respiratory rate, and slight hypotension. He is admitted but soon becomes severely hypotensive, suffers a seizure, and subsequently is found to have sustained a severe CNS injury.[3]

The Medical-Legal Perspective

Under the doctrine of *respondeat superior*, the employer is responsible for employees' malfeasance (wrongdoing, misconduct) and nonfeasance (failure to act). Because residents are employees of the health care facility where they are receiving their postgraduate education, they are almost always covered by the teaching facility's liability insurance policy. When a resident rotates through a community hospital's emergency department as part of the training program, the liability insurance for the resident can be provided through the teaching facility, the community hospital, or by the insurance policy that covers the emergency physician group. Residents must be made aware that if they work outside their training programs, they are usually not covered for alleged acts of negligence under the umbrella of the residency training program policy.

Faculty members and nonpaid clinical physicians who donate time to a training program are usually covered under the doctrine of *respondeat superior*. On occasion, an independently contracting physician group will provide emergency physicians for the emergency department training program. In this instance, the insurance coverage for the group can be provided through the hospital's or the group's policy.

When a medical negligence lawsuit is brought against an emergency medicine resident and a faculty member, the institution, and not the individual physician, is usually the named defendant. In cases where an individual is named, the coverage is still provided by the institution's policy.

Supervision

The expertise of residents varies from the first-year resident, who is a newly graduated, unlicensed, inexperienced physician, to third- and fourth-year emergency medicine residents, who usually possess a high degree of skill and knowledge. In order for the teaching facility's emergency department patients to receive appropriate care and to reduce the liability exposure of its residents, the physicians in training must be carefully supervised. This practice can help inexperienced physicians meet the same standards as those followed by fully trained and experienced emergency physicians. Concurrent supervision by the faculty is the most important factor in maintaining high-quality patient care and in preventing the emergency medicine resident from being sued for negligence.

Emergency medicine residents who have recently graduated from medical school and are entering their first year of residency training must be monitored at all times. They are not licensed to practice medicine anywhere throughout most of the United States. A fully licensed, experienced emergency physician faculty member must actively assess every emergency department patient along with the first-year resident. This approach will help hospital staff fulfill their responsibility to patients and comply with state and federal laws of licensure.

The second-year resident who becomes licensed and obtains a DEA number, theoretically, can practice emergency medicine without supervision. However, in reality, an emergency physician in the second year of training still lacks experience in the assessment and treatment of acutely ill or injured patients. As a result, the second-year resident is more prone than the experienced emergency physician to acts of commission and omission.[4]

In many jurisdictions, there is legal precedent that physicians in training should be held to the standards possessed by other physicians with similar training.[5,6] This concept, coupled with the resident's lack of clinical experience, makes direct supervision even more critical. Another factor that supports concurrent monitoring of all second-year residents is that the emergency department record must be cosigned by a faculty member or a member of the attending staff. The teaching faculty member who cosigns the record, in effect, approves both the content of the record and the assessment and treatment rendered to the patient.

One of the highest risks for an emergency medicine residency program is the practice of having residents from other medical specialties rotate through the emergency department. Frequently, these physicians have not been exposed to the initial assessment and treatment of acutely ill or injured patients. As a result, the potential for catastrophe is very high. This possibility is even greater when nonemergency medicine residents are asked to assess and treat emergency conditions that fall outside the scope of their specialties. Because these residents have limited emergency medicine exposure, they require careful and aggressive monitoring.

When a resident reaches the third year and beyond, monitoring usually decreases; however, the faculty member who cosigns a patient's records without seeing the patient may share legal responsibility for the resident's mistakes in diagnosis, treatment, and other actions. If there is a negligence claim, the cosigning physician may be named as a defendant and be subject to the rigors of discovery and trial.

Medicare Reimbursement

In accordance with regulations adopted by the Health Care Financing Administration (HCFA), Medicare will pay on a fee schedule basis only for services personally furnished by a physician who is not a resident or when a physician presence requirement is met. When a resident participates in a service furnished in a teaching setting, physician fee schedule payment will be made only if a teaching physician is present during the key portion of any service or procedure for which payment is sought. However, in some circumstances, the teaching physician's presence is not required for the entire duration of the patient encounter.[7]

What this means is that if the emergency physicians' group or health care facility bills the patient for the emergency physician's services and the faculty member or attending staff has not seen the patient, the faculty member may be exposed to criminal charges under the Medicare and Medicaid fraud and abuse laws[8] (see Chapter 34, "Fraud and Abuse").

The federal government, through HCFA, has demonstrated an intent to audit every academic facility nationwide, or have a facility conduct a self-audit, to enforce these regulations. In mid-1996, one university hospital and faculty foundation entered into a $12 million settlement agreement with the government for failing to document teaching physician participation in patient care and for not documenting services consistent with charges.[9] The lesson here is that the teaching physician's presence during the key portion of services or procedures should be properly documented.

On a related note, HCFA has modified its limitations on Graduate Medical Education (GME) funding of certain residency programs. HCFA will pay full GME funding for three years of an emergency residency program. It will pay only at 0.5 full-time equivalents for the fourth year of a four-year emergency residency.[10]

Chart Review

As previously mentioned, some programs use retrospective chart reviews instead of concurrent supervision to monitor residents. As a risk prevention mechanism, chart review does not compare favorably with direct supervision. Even with 100% retrospective chart review within 24 hours of the patient being assessed, a potentially adverse event can occur by the time the chart is reviewed. For example, the condition of a chest pain patient who is discharged and later develops a myocardial infarction, or the child with early meningitis who is mistakenly sent home, will usually have deteriorated by the time the retrospective review indicates a potential adverse event.

Retrospective chart review is an excellent way to determine the quality of the resident physician's documentation. But, when it comes to assessing compliance with established clinical standards of care, policy, and procedure, or identifying residents who lack knowledge in specific clinical areas, retrospective reviews cannot match direct supervision. Direct supervision, on the other hand, provides a way to immediately intervene on a case.

Another risk-reduction tool for the emergency department is to provide residents with lectures specifically addressing the high-risk and frequent claims areas. These presentations should stress the importance of high-risk or frequent claims areas and sensitize the resident physician to the subject.

Policy Development

The Joint Commission on Accreditation of Healthcare Organizations (JCAHO) mandates that emergency care facilities develop and implement standards of care for each clinical department or service section that is to be integrated into the department's quality improvement plan.[11] To increase residents' awareness of the specific clinical areas associated with expensive and frequent claims, emergency department residents, with faculty supervision and input, could develop their own standards of care for these specific clinical subjects. From a patient care and risk management perspective, the development of such standards or guidelines would further alert the resident to potential liability hazards.

In emergency medicine residency training programs, lines of authority should be established both among the residents and between the full-time and part-time faculty. Usually the senior resident acts as the spokesperson for the residents and meets regularly with the faculty's resident liaison. By establishing lines of communication, problem areas within and outside the department that may impair patient care or lead to litigation can be resolved before they become the basis for a medical negligence claim.

In training centers with multiple specialty training programs, there may be disagreements among various house staff members of different training programs concerning patient care issues. Therefore, policies should be developed and approved by both the faculty physicians and residents. These policies, in turn, should be read and approved by the faculty chairperson's committee or by the medical executive committee of the hospital and finally adopted by the board of directors.

One of the policies that should be developed is a policy to resolve disagreements between the emergency medicine resident and other residents about the disposition of emergency department patients after consultation with a physician in another specialty. Such a policy might be worded as follows: "In the event of a disagreement between the emergency medicine resident and a house officer of another specialty concerning the disposition of an emergency department patient, the senior emergency medicine resident will be contacted by the emergency medicine resident and will attempt to resolve this dispute. If there is no resolution of the problem, the senior resident will contact the on-call faculty member, who will assume responsibility for the patient's disposition."

Policies should also be in place regarding response times for on-call resident physicians in other specialties, for preliminary and final radiographic interpretations, for laboratory response times, and for any other area affecting emergency patient care. Such policies should be approved by the medical executive committee and the board of directors. Patient care policies must be part of the residents' and faculty's methods available to help prevent potential liability situations from occurring.

Case Discussions

1

This case is a good example of what can happen when residents are unsupervised. The second-year family practice residents, who were rotating through emergency medicine and orthopedics, failed to recognize the severity of the patient's neurologic signs and symptoms. When they finally called for neurosurgical assistance, the first responder was a third-year family practice resident who had little experience in diagnosing or treating the acute phase of closed-head injuries. Despite the fact that all three residents were in critical patient care positions, not one of them was being supervised.

The residency training program in this particular facility did not meet the basic obligations that an acute care facility has to its patients, that the physician in training must be directly supervised by a faculty member in that particular specialty. The substandard care rendered to this patient is an example of what can occur when concurrent supervision policies are not in place and the resident is left unsupervised. Besides the lack of monitoring, the attending neurosurgeon did not respond adequately, as evidenced by his late arrival.

2

This case illustrates the responsibilities of the attending or supervising emergency physician and what can occur when the attending physician fails to evaluate a patient personally who has a potentially catastrophic condition and who has been seen by an emergency medicine resident. Because this incident occurred in a community emergency department, it was obvious that the attending physician was not following an established policy or guideline concerning his responsibility to the patient. It may also have indicated that the training program had not developed and distributed a policy concerning the attending's responsibility to the patient and to the resident.

Another important point is that, even though the attending never saw this patient and only consulted on her condition, he cosigned the emergency record, thus approving the resident's assessment and treatment. By cosigning the chart, the attending physician assumed a significant amount of the medical and legal responsibility for the patient's outcome. This can result in significant legal exposure. Because the attending physician had not evaluated the patient, he had to rely totally on the accuracy of the resident's documentation in order to defend himself.

Another area of grave concern is the fact that the attending physician actually billed for his services even though he never evaluated the patient. Under the HCFA guidelines, billing for his professional service is fraudulent.

By not following simple protocols and recognized standards in the assessment and treatment of this patient, both physicians were unnecessarily exposed to the potential for a negligence claim for the wrongful death of the patient. This emergency physician and his own medical group have exposure for a potential criminal complaint for billing the patient for a service he did not provide.

This case demonstrates the need for emergency medicine training programs to develop policies and procedures concerning billing, emergency residents, and supervision. Also, before an emergency physician group in a community hospital agrees to become affiliated with a training program, the group must decide how it is going to monitor the residents to comply with federal and state laws.

3

This case illustrates why emergency medicine postgraduate training programs must develop policies addressing a variety of patient care issues and what consequences can occur if they are not in place. Most facilities with emergency medicine training programs also have other specialty training programs. To avoid losing valuable diagnostic information that these specialty programs can provide, a clear policy must be established about how such information can be communicated to the emergency physicians and then to the patient.

The radiology and emergency department policies for this facility addressed how soon a radiologist's final interpretation should be delivered to the emergency physician. However, the policy did not state who should be contacted when the physician's preliminary interpretations were incorrect and the patient had been admitted to the hospital. Although there was conflicting testimony about the timeliness of the radiologist's final interpretation, all parties agreed that the delay violated both departments' policies.

After the emergency physician was notified, she elected to call the surgical resident rather than to contact the patient, who had already been discharged from the hospital. As a result, it was alleged that the patient's pneumonia remained untreated and resulted in the patient going into septic shock. In a teaching facility, the policies concerning diagnostic tests should always be directed toward informing the patient. The responsibility for this task should never be transferred to another physician in another training section.

Key Points and Conclusion

Emergency medicine residents are particularly vulnerable to risk exposure because of their inexperience. The chance for a malpractice claim increases even more when residents are held to the same patient care standards as an experienced physician would be in that same specialty. To ensure that emergency department patients receive care consistent with the prevailing standards, the following measures are suggested:

- The resident should be concurrently monitored or actively supervised by a member of the faculty while that resident is assessing patients in the emergency department. The faculty physician must realize that signing the chart without being directly involved does not equal supervising care.
- The resident from a specialty other than emergency medicine, who is rotating through the emergency department, should be monitored in a manner similar to the first-year emergency medicine resident.
- Retrospective chart review, although useful, is not a substitute for direct supervision. A credentialed staff physician is always ultimately in charge of a patient's care and must bear that responsibility.
- The faculty must determine the risks and benefits for emergency patients receiving unsupervised emergency medicine resident care from third- and fourth-year residents as well as the potential legal consequences of the faculty members signing the charts without evaluating the patients.

- Billing for a resident's services in the absence of a faculty member's assessment must be considered a high risk for faculty members. The federal government and many states are actively pursuing physicians under the doctrine of fraud when they render bills for services in which they have not been directly involved.
- Medicare should not be billed for a teaching physician's services unless that physician was present during the key portions of the procedure or services. The physician's presence should be properly documented.
- The resident, faculty, and attending clinical faculty are customarily covered for liability purposes under the doctrine of *respondeat superior*; however, variations in the insurance coverage of the residents and of the nonpaid clinical faculty members do occur. Residents should be informed of all exceptions concerning liability coverage. Even if their financial obligations are met, they are not exempt from being reported to the National Practitioner Data Bank.
- The resident and faculty must have efficient lines of communication at all times. Representatives from each group should meet frequently to discuss and solve patient care problems before they result in an adverse event. Policies should be implemented that solve potential disputes before they result in an injury or death. Similarly, a policy must be developed for ancillary service responses to the emergency department needs.
- The resident physician from another specialty who is called to the emergency department to evaluate a patient is still a resident. No patient should be treated and discharged by such a resident unless the emergency physician agrees with that resident's recommendation. Disputes on how the patient should be managed should be resolved between the emergency physician and the resident's supervising physician or outside attending physician according to established policy.

References

1. *Kirk v Redlands Community Hospital*, (1985) SBSC:CA;222882.
2. *McCarthy v Bitter*, (1990) LASC:CA;NC003541.
3. *Carter v County of Riverside*, (1984) RCSC:CA;180879.
4. Rusnak RA, Stair TO, Hansen K, et al. Litigation against the emergency physician: common features in cases of missed myocardial infarction. *Ann Emerg Med* 1989;18:1029-1034.

5. *McBride v United States*, 462 F2d 72 (9th Cir 1972).

6. *Hilyer v Hole*, 114 Mich App 38, 818 NW2d 598 (1982).

7. 60 *Federal Register* 63124, 63186 (42 CFR §415).

8. Public Law No. 95-142, 91 Stat 1185 (codified as amended in scattered sections of 42 USC) 1981.

9. Kelly AB, Saunders BL. Fraud and abuse. *Health Law Digest* 1996;24-9:37-38.

10. 61 *Federal Register* 46166, 46225 (42 CFR §413.86).

11. Joint Commission on Accreditation of Healthcare Organizations. *Comprehensive Accreditation Manual for Hospitals: The Official Handbook*. Oakbrook Terrace, Ill: JCAHO; 1996.

\

Chapter 41

Consultations

William D. O'Riordan, MD, FACEP

Emergency physicians are recognized by their peers, the public, and the courts as having the skills necessary to stabilize emergency patients until specialized, definitive treatment, if needed, can be obtained.[1] To facilitate patient care, emergency physicians often request consultations from physicians in other specialties. Failure to request appropriate specialist care when such a consultation is necessary may be viewed as negligence on the emergency physician's part.[2-4]

Consultations are not limited to hands-on assistance. If a particular specialist who is needed for the treatment of an emergency patient is not on the hospital's medical staff, then telephone consultation may be necessary. If such consultations are available and the emergency physician does not attempt to use them, then the emergency physician has not fulfilled the medical-legal obligation to the patient.

Sometimes a patient's private physician will demand to be notified before a consultant is called in, or will order treatment when recognized standards call for a different or specialized approach. In these situations, the patient's health and safety may be jeopardized. The emergency physician who simply follows these orders may also be in jeopardy — and at risk for a claim of negligence. Similarly, sometimes an emergency physician and a consultant will disagree about the severity of a patient's illness or injury or about appropriate disposition. If a patient experiences a poor outcome because an emergency physician blindly accepted and followed the recommendation of a consultant, that emer-

gency physician can be held liable.

On occasion, differences of opinion between emergency physicians and consultants can take a more troublesome turn, especially if the consultant is not addressing the emergency patient's medical condition appropriately, or worse, is behaving abnormally. Such aberrant behavior can result in injury to a patient, so the emergency physician may need to intercede on the patient's behalf. The emergency physician who does not act in these situations can be liable for the acts of the consultant physician.

Case Studies

1

A 25-month-old girl is brought to an acute care emergency department at approximately 4:30 PM for treatment of a possible tricyclic antidepressant overdose. According to the parents, the child ingested the pills at about 3:30 PM. They called their pediatrician, who advised them to take the child to the hospital where he has privileges, even though this hospital is an hour away from the family's home. The pediatrician did not order ipecac.

The patient is initially assessed by the triage nurse, who notes that her condition is normal. There are no pediatric beds available in the emergency department, so the parents and the child are sent to the waiting room. Fifteen minutes later, the child's mental status suddenly deteriorates and she has a grand mal seizure. The patient is brought into the emergency department, where she is assessed by the emergency physician. The seizure activity continues; she is intubated and given IV phenobarbital.

At approximately 5:30 PM, the pediatrician comes to the emergency department to consult in the child's care and treatment. She experiences repeated seizure activity and a prolonged hypotensive episode. Capillary and arterial blood gas measurements obtained during the hypotensive event indicate a severe metabolic acidosis; however, bicarbonate is not ordered by the emergency physician or the pediatrician.

The pediatrician calls in a neonatology consultant, who then orders physostigmine. At approximately 6:45 PM, the patient is transferred by helicopter to a children's hospital. She has sustained a severe CNS injury.[5]

2

A 39-year-old insulin-dependent diabetic presents to an emergency department with rapid respirations, a fast pulse, and a low normal blood pressure. The patient's family practitioner is called, and he asks the emergency physician on duty to evaluate the patient and initiate treatment. The emergency physician performs an examination and orders diagnostic tests, which indicate that the patient is hyperglycemic. An arterial blood gas measurement reveals that he is hypoxemic and hypocapnic and has a severe metabolic acidosis. The patient receives 500 mL of a crystalloid solution over the course of one hour.

The emergency physician calls the family practitioner back to tell him the results of the diagnostic tests, and the family practitioner says that he will come to the emergency department to assume the patient's care. Forty-five minutes pass before the family practitioner arrives, and in the meantime, the patient's mental status deteriorates. By the time the family practitioner sees him, the patient is disoriented regarding name, time, and place and is severely tachypneic. One hour and 45 minutes later, two consultants are called to assess and treat the patient. Despite aggressive therapy, the patient dies.[6]

3

After having an argument with her boyfriend, a 17-year-old girl ingests 190 tablets of 200-mg Theo-Dur and a large quantity of an antihistamine. Two hours after the ingestion, the girl's mother finds her unconscious and calls 911. She is transported to the nearest Level II emergency facility.

In the emergency department, the patient is given ipecac, which produces 112 pills and some pill fragments. After the emesis, 30 g of charcoal is administered. A theophylline level is ordered; several hours later, the laboratory technician informs the physician that it is greater than 44 µg%. No quantitative determination is ordered.

While in the emergency department, the patient is alert but agitated and has a fast pulse and rapid respirations. She is admitted to the ICU of the service of her family's physician, and the emergency physician writes the admitting orders. While in the ICU, the patient's pulse gradually increases, and is at 150 by 8:00 AM the next morning. When the family practitioner evaluates her, he orders diazepam for her nervousness and agitation, requests a psychiatric consultation, and leaves the hospital for the weekend.

Two hours later, an ICU nurse asks the emergency physician to come up and evaluate the patient, whose pulse has risen to 196. The emergency physician orders a β-blocker and tries, unsuccessfully, to contact the family practitioner. One hour later, the patient goes into status epilepticus. The emergency physician returns to the ICU with a cardiologist. The patient subsequently suffers repeated episodes of grand mal seizure activity, and late in the afternoon goes into cardiopulmonary arrest. Early in the evening, a neurologist and a nephrologist evaluate the patient and note signs and symptoms of severe CNS injury.[7]

The Medical-Legal Perspective

The legal relationship between a consultant physician and an emergency physician is an interesting one. By definition, a consultation is the advice and counsel requested from another physician, usually one who has had training in a specific field. This advice given to an emergency physician by a consultant physician is supposed to be based on a higher level of expertise than the emergency physician possesses. However, the emergency physician's legal, moral, and ethical responsibility is to the patient — not to the hospital or other members of the medical staff. For this reason, the failure of an emergency physician to request the most appropriate medical specialist to consult in the treatment of a patient with an emergent or urgent medical condition could be considered substandard care.

The courts have recognized that the emergency physician's function is to evaluate and stabilize emergency department patients until appropriate consultants can provide definitive care.[1] If an emergency physician requests a consultation from a physician who does not have the background and training to care for the patient's emergent or urgent condition, the emergency physician can be held partially responsible for any of the consultant's acts of commission or omission. Similarly, an emergency department patient may need immediate care and treatment by a specific type of specialist. If the patient has a private physician and that private physician does not have the skills necessary to treat the condition, the emergency physician should call in an appropriate specialist, regardless of the private physician's wishes.

In some cases, an emergency physician may refer a nonurgent emergency patient to a consultant physician for evaluation in the physician's office. Whether this act renders the emergency physician potentially liable for the acts or omissions of that consultant physician has been addressed by the courts for physicians generally, but not specifically for emergency physicians. A Missouri court ruled on this issue and rendered the following opinion: "A referral of a patient by one physician to another competent physician, absent partnership, employment, or agency, does not impose the liability on the referring physician."[8]

Barriers to Effective Consultations

Why would an emergency physician not call in appropriate consultants? There are several reasons. Many medical staffs have policies that require the emergency physician to call the patient's private physician first before contacting any consultants, regardless of the patient's condition. Such a policy unnecessarily delays definitive care, which can result in severe complications or even death. At times, a patient's private physician may claim to have the requisite skills to treat the condition and will assume responsibility, even though a consultant's care would be at a higher level of expertise. In such a situation, the emergency physician can be held liable if the patient is denied the appropriate level of care.

Hospital policies to address this issue could be worded as follows: "The emergency physician is a medical specialist trained to recognize and initially treat emergent and urgent medical conditions that can lead to a patient's death, loss of limb, or morbidity if timely care is not administered. Because the hospital and its medical staff attempt to provide the best possible medical care to all their patients, the emergency physician will request an appropriate specialty consultation when, in the opinion of the emergency physician, the patient is in emergent or urgent need of specialized care. If a patient's private physician is on the medical staff of the hospital, this physician will be contacted as soon as the patient's condition allows."

Differences of Opinion

Emergency physicians frequently ask for telephone or hands-on consultations on such issues as diagnosis, treatment, and disposition. Telephone consultations carry a higher risk for the emergency physician because the consultant has not physically assessed the patient. In these situations, if the consultant's assessment and advice could, in the emergency physician's opinion, place the patient at risk, the emergency physician should ask the consultant to come to the emergency department to evaluate the patient.

Even after a consultant has done a hands-on evaluation of an emergency department patient, there may still be a disagreement about appropriate treatment and disposition. When this happens, the emergency physician must take additional steps to ensure the emergency patient's well-being. First, the emergency physician and the consultant should discuss their differing opinions in private. If this discussion does not resolve the problem in the patient's best interests, the emergency physician must present the two opinions to the patient or the patient's family. If the patient or family accepts the consultant's advice and treatment plan, then the patient's care should be transferred to the consultant physician and the chain of events documented in the patient's medical record. This documentation should reflect that, after a thorough discussion, the patient or family has elected to follow the consultant's care. It should also reflect that the consultant has assumed full responsibility for the patient's care. These notes should never be inflammatory, but should simply state the facts.

If the patient or family is undecided about the course of treatment, they should have the opportunity to get a second opinion. If a second consultant agrees with the first consultant, then the emergency physician's obligation to the patient has been fulfilled. Once again, the emergency physician should document these steps and decisions in the patient's record.

Sometimes obtaining a second consultant

opinion can be difficult or even impossible. The emergency physician may have no alternative but to notify the director of the emergency department and the chair of the particular medical specialty department or service involved. By notifying the chair of the consultant physician's department, the emergency physician transfers the responsibility of obtaining a second opinion directly to the appropriate medical staff leader. If the department chair cannot obtain a second consultation, he is then obligated to assess the patient personally and make a treatment recommendation.

Arguments between the emergency physician and consultant physicians in front of or near a patient can reduce the patient's confidence in the medical staff and care given. Making negative statements about the nurses or ancillary or support personnel is also high-risk behavior. When such behavior is noted, the emergency physician should talk with the consulting physician in private and explain how such behavior increases liability exposure. These incidents should be reported to the emergency department director and to the chair of the consultant physician's department or service.

Inappropriate Behavior by Consultants

The emergency physician assumes even more legal exposure when a consultant physician exhibits bizarre or inappropriate behavior while performing a consultation on an emergency patient. When abnormal behavior is identified or suspected, the emergency physician should speak in private with that physician and try to evaluate the consulting physician's mental status. If, in the opinion of the emergency physician, there is even a remote possibility that the emergency patient's care will be compromised, the emergency physician should immediately contact the chair of the consultant physician's department or service and ask that person to come to the emergency department to assess the physician. Keep in mind that these actions could be challenged in a defamation lawsuit based on alleged damage to the consultant physician's reputation. Therefore, any action by the emergency physician should be based on personal observation of abnormal conduct. Carefully document the event and identify other witnesses.

If the chair of the consultant physician's department is not available, the emergency physician should follow the chain of command of medical staff leadership. Specifically, the chief or president of the medical staff should be asked to come to the emergency department immediately to handle the situation. The emergency physician who does not act after recognizing such aberrant behavior has not fulfilled the obligation to the emergency patient and, as a result, could be contributing to an adverse patient outcome.

A physician's abnormal behavior patterns are a quality assurance issue. Most medical staff bylaws and hospital quality assurance policies require that behavior abnormalities on the part of any physician on a medical staff be reported in writing to the chair of the consulting physician's department or service and to the quality assurance chair and the chief of staff. All correspondence should be marked "Quality Assurance Matter, Private and Confidential: To Be Opened and Read by Addressee Only" to protect confidentiality.

Patient Referrals

Another potential medical-legal nightmare is the referral of a nonurgent emergency department patient, whose private physician is on the medical staff, to an appropriate but different medical specialist's office.

Perhaps the best approach to this situation is to ask patients or family members if they have ever been cared for by a specialist in the required field. If the patient has seen such a specialist in the past, the emergency physician can refer the patient to that physician, then inform the patient's private physician. If the patient has never seen such a specialist, the private physician should be informed of the emergency physician's opinion regarding definitive care. If the private physician insists on seeing the patient, the family should be told that the patient needs to be seen by a specialist. The patient's emergency department medical record and the aftercare instruction sheet should document this advice.

The emergency physician should use all available resources when assessing and treating emergency patients. When a specific medical specialty or subspecialty is not available, the emergency physician and nurses must have immediate access to regional and even national sources of information where the recommended treatment can be obtained. For example, consultants are always available at poison centers. If the emergency physician fails to use these resources and, as a result, contemporary standards of care are not met, the physician's care will be considered substandard.

Conflict Resolution

Because disagreements between emergency physicians and consultants can lead to political problems for the emergency physician or group, the emergency department committee should develop a conflict resolution policy. This policy must be submitted for approval to other clinical departments and finally to the medical executive committee. Such a policy should recognize the potential for disagreement between emergency physicians and consultants and provide an efficient mechanism for resolving such disagreements.

The conflict resolution policy could be worded as follows: "In the event that an emergency physician and a consultant disagree concerning the care, treatment, or disposition of an emergency department patient and the emergency physician believes that the patient's outcome could be adversely affected by the adoption of the consultant specialist's recommendations, the emergency physician should initially discuss these concerns with the consulting physician in private. If their difference of opinion cannot be resolved after such a discussion, the patient should be informed of the disagreement and given an option of following the consultant physician's advice or of having a second opinion from another physician in that same specialty. In the event that a second consultant's opinion cannot be obtained, the chair of the consulting physician's department or service will be asked to render a second opinion in order to resolve the disagreement."

Once this policy is approved and implemented, the emergency physician has an approach to dealing with these disagreements that has been accepted by the medical staff leadership and by the hospital's board of directors or trustees.

Case Discussions

1

There are two obvious questions in this matter. Who was the physician in charge of the ongoing care and treatment of this emergency patient? Why wasn't the regional poison center contacted by either the emergency physician or the pediatrician? The plaintiff alleges that neither physician was in charge of the patient's care and that neither the emergency physician nor the pediatrician was familiar with the contemporary care and treatment of this toxicologic emergency.

Because the emergency department record and the pediatrician's progress note implied but do not state who was in charge, it appeared that no one was. If neither physician was familiar with the standard of care of tricyclic antidepressant ingestions in a 25-month-old child, then they should have tried to get information by calling a specialist. Unfortunately, neither physician attempted to contact the local poison center or seek advice from the nearby children's hospital.

2

In this case, the emergency physician's transfer of the care and treatment of the patient were allegedly substandard. This patient was admitted in critical condition, yet an appropriate consultant was not called immediately by the emergency physician to intercede on the patient's behalf. Obviously, the patient needed acute medical care above the level that could be offered by the family practitioner.

The emergency physician's failure to call the appropriate consultants resulted in a significant delay in definitive treatment. Because the emergency physician's obligation was to the patient and not to another medical staff member, the emergency physician's liability exposure is significant. The emergency physician must always act in the best interests of the emergency patient — not in the best interests of a medical staff member or the hospital.

3

This case is an outstanding example of an emergency physician following a policy that was written for the benefit of the medical staff and not for the emergency patient's well-being. Specifically, the policy required the emergency physician to admit this patient — who was in critical condition — to the service of a family practitioner, who obviously had no knowledge in the assessment and treatment of such a toxicologic emergency. The emergency physician who initially assessed the patient also did not seek consultation from the regional poison center and allegedly did not understand the severity of the ingestion, as evidenced by the care rendered to the patient.

This case illustrates two points. First, the emergency physician's contract should state that, if by following the rules established by the hospital the physician is sued for an inappropriate referral, the hospital will bear all liability and pay all costs attending such an action. In this way, the hospital must live up to its responsibilities when establishing such protocols.

Second, an emergency physician who does not understand the potential consequences of an ingestion must attempt to determine the severity of a clinical situation by consulting with area resources if no specialists in that area are on the hospital's medical staff. The emergency physician who follows a policy that obviously is not in a patient's best interests is violating the moral and ethical obligations to the emergency patient. Policies that restrict the emergency physician's ability to act on the patient's behalf are not acceptable.

The emergency physician who evaluated the patient in the ICU did not summon consultants, who were urgently needed. This physician requested a cardiology consultation but certainly should have contacted other specialists, including poison control, for advice.

Key Points and Conclusion

Emergency physicians frequently call on other specialists to provide definitive care for emergency patients. When an emergency physician's ability to obtain an appropriate consultation is compromised, the emergency physician assumes unnecessary risk.

- Policies should be developed that address the patient's needs and not simply the convenience of physicians. Once approved by the medical executive committee, these policies should be adopted by the board of directors or trustees.
- The emergency physician who requests a consultation must realize that these consultations are only advisory. The emergency physician is still morally and legally responsible for the care and treatment of the patient and therefore must exercise his own best judgment in rendering care.
- In the event that the emergency physician disagrees with a consultant physician and thinks a particular recommendation could be harmful to the patient, the emergency physician must act on behalf of the patient's well-being.
- Physicians should follow a conflict resolution policy that has been passed by the medical executive committee and adopted by the board of directors or trustees.

- If the emergency physician witnesses any abnormal behavior on the part of consultant physicians, these incidents must be reported to medical staff leadership for immediate intervention. The emergency physician also should document such events in a manner that protects the confidentiality of the quality assurance process.
- The emergency physician should not be required to make certain referrals based on hospital custom. Policy must allow the emergency physician to choose the type of consultant required and to seek that care as expeditiously as possible.

References

1. *Dalgo v Landry,* 424 So2d 1159 (La App 1982).
2. *Kiniry v Danbury Hospital,* 439 A2d 408 (Cohn 1981).
3. *Johnson v St. Bernard Hospital,* 79 111 App 3d 709, 35 Ill Dec 364, 399 NE2d 198 (1979).
4. *Ritondo v Pekala,* 275 NJ Super 109, 645 A2d 802 (NJ Super 1994).
5. *Kaufman v Pomona Valley Community Hospital, et al,* (1982) LACSC:CA;EAC 50512.
6. *Hicks et al. v Santa Monica Hospital Medical Center, et al,* (1982) LACSC.CA;WEC 62328.
7. *Likes v Pacoima Memorial Hospital,* (1980) LACSC.CA;NWC 88214.
8. *Mincey v Blando,* 655 SW2d 609 (Mo App 1983).

Chapter 42

On-Call Lists

William D. O'Riordan, MD, FACEP
Gregory L. Henry, MD, FACEP

Since publishing new hospital standards in 1996, the Joint Commission on Accreditation of Healthcare Organizations (JCAHO) no longer classifies emergency departments into four levels of care. In fact, JCAHO has abandoned all classification systems for emergency departments.[1] Likewise, requirements for on-call physician specialists are not specified in the new JCAHO standards as they had been under the previous standards. Therefore, there are no specific JCAHO guidelines about on-call responsibilities of staff physicians.

The lack of specific guidelines, however, is made irrelevant by the Emergency Medical Treatment and Active Labor Act (EMTALA), also known as "COBRA." EMTALA is now the on-call policy standard for every hospital in the United States.[2] This federal law requires hospitals to provide on-call physicians to help treat patients who present to emergency departments. The law does not directly mandate physicians to take call, but it does require hospitals to provide on-call physicians. Physicians accept on-call responsibility according to medical staff bylaws and department rules and regulations.[3] The provision of on-call physicians is the responsibility of the hospital — not of the emergency physicians.

The Health Care Financing Administration (HCFA) promulgated regulations to enforce EMTALA. According to these regulations, physicians on the hospital staff must be available for the treatment of patients presenting to the emergency department regardless of whether they had been previously obligated by the hospital to provide these services.[4] The hospital and the medical staff must understand these responsibilities and the tremendous liability imposed on the hospital for failure to comply. Hospitals must put in place policies, procedures, and availability standards using reasonable and appropriate guidelines. Hospitals that fail to do so or that adopt standards that cannot be met may be in jeopardy for failure to follow their own rules.[5]

A physician who is on the emergency department's on-call panel has an important obligation to help maintain a high level of patient care. When an on-call physician does not respond to a call for assistance from the emergency department, or refuses to care for an emergency patient, or demands that the patient be transferred to another acute care facility, the patient and the physician and the hospital are placed at very high risk. If the patient needs immediate intervention by the on-call physician and such care is denied or delayed, the patient may die or suffer serious damage from an illness or injury.

When an on-call physician refuses to respond and other medical staff members will not get involved, then the emergency physician may have no other choice but to transfer the patient to another acute care facility. If this transfer is not completed in an appropriate manner, federal and state actions can be taken against the emergency physician and the hospital.

The number of uninsured and underinsured persons presenting to emergency departments has risen sharply in the past few years. Large numbers of patients receive primary care in emergency departments[6] because emergency departments are one of the few remaining entrances to the health care system. As a result, more physician specialists are withdrawing from the on-call lists at Level II emergency facilities. As the number of medical staff physicians participating in on-call lists declines, the legal exposure of emergency physicians and hospitals increases. This situation, in turn, requires the boards of directors of these facilities to make changes to address the needs of emergency department patients.

In many hospitals, however, medical staff bylaws or policies do not specifically address the on-call physician's responsibility to emergency department patients. Consequently, emergency physicians in these facilities do not have a way to solve the growing problems associated with on-call lists. Hospitals that do not have on-call physician policies are at risk of violating EMTALA. Hospitals solve their problems in many ways. Some have obtained cross-coverage in several specialties from other hospitals. No hospital is expected to maintain on-call capability for services it does not provide. For example, hospitals that do not have neurosurgery or hand surgery, for example, are not expected to have such specialties on the call list. Therefore, arrangements should be in place so that patients can be transferred quickly to the facility where proper care can be received.

Case Studies

1

A 16-year-old boy falls off a cliff and is evacuated by air ambulance to a nearby emergency department, arriving shortly after midnight. The patient is assessed by the emergency physician, who orders x-rays, CBC, and urinalysis. After reviewing the x-rays, the emergency physician determines that the patient has several fractured thoracic and lumbar vertebrae; other injuries include abrasions to the face and scalp and a large laceration on his back. The on-call orthopedist is summoned and admits the patient to his service about 2:00 AM. The emergency physician writes admitting orders for the orthopedist. Results of the urinalysis are not obtained before the patient is admitted.

Several hours later, the patient voids grossly bloody urine. The nurse calls the emergency physician, not the admitting orthopedist. The emergency physician does not notify the orthopedist or order any diagnostic tests. When the orthopedist makes rounds later in the morning,

he finds the nurse's note about the urine and the results of the urinalysis. He immediately calls for general surgery and urology consultations. Despite surgical intervention, the patient loses both kidneys and has multiple complications and a prolonged postoperative course.[7]

2

A 24-year-old man is running across a street shortly after midnight and is hit by a car. His forehead hits the windshield, and he is thrown an unknown distance. When the paramedics arrive, the man is unconscious and hypotensive. The paramedics immobilize his head and neck, fit him with a pneumatic antishock garment, start two IV lines, and transport him to the nearest larger acute care facility.

In the emergency department, the patient is documented as having alcohol on his breath, a depressed mental status, compound fractures of both lower extremities that are noted to have "no a/n/v loss," and a negative Babinski sign. A cross-table lateral cervical spine x-ray visualizing C-1 through the top of C-6 is interpreted by the emergency physician as normal. After completing the initial evaluation, the emergency physician summons a general surgeon.

Shortly after the surgeon arrives, the patient suffers a respiratory arrest and is intubated by the emergency physician. The surgeon assesses the patient and leaves the emergency department, allegedly to change clothes, but he does not immediately return to care for the patient. Approximately 1 1/2 hours later, while still in the emergency department awaiting surgery, the patient suffers a cardiac arrest. Following resuscitation, the patient is taken to the operating room; he is in pulmonary edema and is promptly given furosemide. The anesthesia record indicates that the patient received approximately 14,000 mL of fluid and 2 U of packed RBCs during the time he was in the emergency department. Following surgery, the patient is found to be a quadriplegic.

The emergency department log indicates that, during the surgeon's absence, the emergency physician assessed a patient with a possible myocardial infarction and a patient who had ingested a large dose of chlorpromazine.[8]

3

A 23-year-old man involved in a fight is struck in the head and loses consciousness for approximately two to three minutes. He is subsequently evaluated at a nearby emergency department.

Cervical spine, skull, and mandibular x-rays are obtained and preliminarily interpreted as normal by the emergency physician. The patient is discharged.

Two days later, the patient returns with complaints of increasing headache, lethargy, and disorientation. He is evaluated by the emergency physician and admitted to the service of the internist on call. The emergency physician writes admitting orders, which include an order for Percodan. The patient is unable to sign the "Terms and Conditions of Admission" and is placed in a general medical unit.

Approximately three hours later, the patient is found comatose. He is transferred to the ICU and subsequently transported by ambulance, with a nurse in attendance, to a hospital 30 minutes away for a CT scan. The CT scan reveals an intracerebral hemorrhage and cerebral edema. After the patient returns to the first hospital, a neurosurgeon is contacted; however, this physician does not respond. The patient is then transported by air ambulance to a Level I facility, where he is taken to the operating room for a craniotomy. The patient sustains extensive CNS injuries.[9]

How On-Call Systems Work

Theoretically, an emergency department on-call system is a way to ensure that emergency patients who need to be admitted or who require follow-up care receive definitive care from physicians who have the appropriate training and background. In a hospital that does not have specialty coverage 24 hours a day, an on-call system also serves as a referral service for emergency department patients. This approach ensures continuity of care for the patient's condition. In most acute care facilities, participation in the on-call panel is part of the physician's medical staff privileges. In some facilities, it is a separate privilege that must be approved by the emergency department committee and the medical executive committee.

In facilities that do have 24-hour coverage, emergency department backup often includes medicine, surgery, orthopedics, obstetrics/gynecology, pediatrics, and anesthesiology. In major trauma centers, these physicians are immediately available, and rapid response times usually are not a problem. But even in major medical centers, response from other medical specialties often varies.

The number of medical specialties represented in an on-call list differs according to facility location and the size of the medical staff. Usually, family practitioners, internists, pediatricians, obstetrician/gynecologists, general surgeons, orthopedists, urologists, and perhaps ophthalmologists, otorhinolaryngologists, and psychiatrists rotate on the on-call panel. In addition, major medical facilities with large medical staffs usually have thoracic surgeons, neurosurgeons, plastic surgeons, and hand surgeons on their on-call lists.

The amount of time that an on-call physician is on duty varies from specialty to specialty. Physicians in specialties such as family practice, internal medicine, general surgery, orthopedics, pediatrics, and obstetrics/gynecology usually serve on the on-call panel for 24 hours. Other specialties, summoned much less frequently, can be on call for up to one week or longer.

The Medical-Legal Perspective

Some medical staffs do not require their physicians to participate on the on-call panel. In hospitals that provide a disproportionate share of emergency care to underfunded and nonfunded patients and that make on-call participation voluntary, the number of physicians on the on-call list has decreased dramatically. As a result, coverage in vital specialty areas is inadequate. This situation sharply increases emergency physicians' and hospitals' potential for exposure to administrative sanctions and liability.

When an emergency department's on-call panel is understaffed, patients in need of emergent intervention may die or suffer great harm. When a patient is in need of a specialist's care but no specialist will respond, the emergency physician may be forced to transfer the patient to another facility as the only way to save the patient's life. If such a transfer is denied by the receiving facility and the patient is sent to that facility anyway, then the on-call physician can be charged with an EMTALA violation. EMTALA creates an affirmative obligation for hospitals to report known violations to HCFA within 72 hours.[11]

EMTALA is not the only source of on-call responsibility. Many states have laws that require a certain level of physician participation in on-call services. The emergency department must consult with hospital administration as well as legal counsel to understand the ramifications of both EMTALA and state laws with regard to on-call responsibilities.

The courts have ruled that the hospital's

board of directors or trustees is ultimately responsible for a patient's well-being.[11,12] In more than one recent case, the board of directors has been found to be responsible for negligent care of patients needing emergency care.[7,13-15] At times, a hospital cannot solve its on-call panel vacancy problems through the medical executive committee or the administration, nor can the emergency physician provide appropriate patient care because of these on-call panel vacancies. In such cases, the medical executive committee should formally notify the hospital's board of directors in writing of this deficiency and its potential adverse effects on the quality of care. By formally notifying the board of directors, the medical executive committee shifts a significant portion of the responsibility for solving this problem to the board, which has a nondelegable duty to do all it can to ensure quality patient care.[7]

Response Time

A common problem is the on-call physician who does not respond to a page or telephone call from the emergency department within an acceptable amount of time. Many emergency facilities require the on-call physician, who is not required to be in the hospital, to answer and respond within at least 30 minutes from the emergency physician's initial call. If the on-call physician does not respond, the emergency physician must have an alternative for obtaining definitive care for emergent or urgent patients.

When developing a policy to address this situation, include language that allows the emergency physician considerable latitude in obtaining a physician's services for an emergency patient. For political reasons, the policy should be developed by the emergency department committee, then submitted to and approved by medical staff departments that participate on the on-call panel before it is presented to the medical executive committee. This approach will allow each department to comment on or amend the proposed policy before it is approved then adopted by the board of directors.

A policy pertaining to the response of on-call physicians might read as follows: "If a physician on call to the emergency department does not respond to the emergency physician's telephone call within 30 minutes, the emergency physician can call other medical staff members of the same or similar specialty. If, after calling a second physician there still is no response, the chair

of the department or section will be asked to respond immediately. If, in the opinion of the physician, the patient's condition warrants immediate medical or surgical intervention, the emergency physician can call any physician in the needed medical or surgical specialty in order to meet the acute needs of the patient."

Refusal to Treat

An area of increasing concern for emergency physicians is the on-call physician who refuses to care for an emergency patient based solely on the patient's insurance status. Even though the emergency physician cannot definitively treat the patient, the responsibility for the patient's care and well-being remains with the emergency physician until an appropriate physician specialist assumes hands-on care for the patient.[16]

To minimize legal exposure, emergency physicians must have a way to solve this problem. One way is to include a provision in the medical staff bylaws, which is either added to the conditions of the medical staff membership section or placed in the emergency department manuals. Such a bylaws addition might read as follows: "A medical staff member who is serving as an on-call panel member for the emergency department must care for an emergency patient regardless of the patient's financial classification when requested to do so by the emergency physician." Such a policy must be approved by both the medical executive committee and the board of directors or trustees.

In general, an emergency physician contacting an on-call physician creates a duty of care to the patient just as if the on-call physician had treated the patient initially. For example, when a subscriber of a particular health care plan presents to a participating hospital emergency department and the plan's physician on call is consulted about treatment or admission, the courts will usually find that a physician-patient relationship exists between the physician and the insured.[17]

Disagreements About a Patient's Care

Sometimes an emergency physician and an on-call physician will disagree concerning the assessment, care, and disposition of an emergency patient. When such circumstances occur, emergency physicians must remember that they should always act in the patient's best interests. Initially, the emergency physician should discuss the matter in private with the on-call physician in an attempt to resolve it. If the disagreement cannot be resolved, the patient, or the patient's family if the patient is a minor, must be informed of this disagreement and given an opportunity to accept the on-call physician's recommendation or request a second opinion. The American College of Emergency Physicians has a policy regarding medical staff responsibilities in the emergency department that emphasizes this close interrelationship between emergency physicians and on-call physicians.[18]

If the patient accepts the on-call physician's recommendations, the emergency physician's obligation has been fulfilled. Document the patient's acceptance of the on-call physician's advice. If the patient is undecided and requests a second opinion, the emergency physician should attempt to obtain the opinion of a physician in the same specialty as the on-call physician. If the second opinion is the same as the on-call physician's, then the emergency physician's obligation to the emergency patient has been fulfilled. Once again, the emergency physician should document what has occurred. When a second opinion cannot be obtained, the chair of the on-call physician's department should be asked to resolve the situation.

When documenting these events, always be objective and avoid inflammatory statements. The on-call physician and any other physicians assessing the patient should be asked to document their findings and opinions by dictating a formal consultation so that a permanent medical record is created. If the emergency physician accepts the on-call physician's opinion even though his opinion is contrary to the on-call physician's, the emergency physician could be named a defendant in a lawsuit if an adverse event occurs. The patient could allege that the emergency physician did not offer any options concerning the patient's care.

The emergency department should have a policy outlining what steps should be taken when there is a disagreement between the emergency physician and the on-call physician concerning the care, treatment, and disposition of an emergency patient. This policy should be submitted to the other medical staff committees for their discussion and amendments before it is submitted to the medical executive committee, then forwarded to the board of directors or trustees for adoption.

Such a policy might read as follows: "When a difference of opinion exists between the emergency physician and an on-call panel member concerning the care, treatment, and disposition of an emergency department patient, the emergency physician is obligated to discuss in private these differences with the on-call physician. If these differences cannot be resolved, the patient should be advised and given an option of following the on-call physician's advice or obtaining a second opinion. If the patient accepts the on-call physician's recommendation, then the emergency physician has fulfilled his or her obligation to the patient. If, on the other hand, the patient requests a second opinion, then the emergency physician should attempt to obtain a second opinion. If the opinion of a physician in the same specialty cannot be obtained, the department or section chair will be asked to resolve the issue."

A similar problem can occur when the emergency physician has a telephone conversation with the on-call physician and the on-call physician advises that the patient can be safely discharged. The emergency physician who disagrees with this decision but discharges the patient anyway is legally responsible for the patient after the discharge because the on-call physician did not physically assess the patient. When faced with this situation, emergency physicians must remember that their responsibility is always to the emergency patient.

A policy that would address this problem might read as follows: "When the emergency physician believes that a patient is in need of admission and, via telephone communication, the on-call physician disagrees and advises the emergency physician to discharge the patient, the emergency physician will ask the on-call physician to come to the hospital to assess the patient. If the physician refuses to come to the hospital when asked to do so, then the emergency physician will contact the chair of that physician's department or section and ask the chair to intervene."

Admission Policies

In some hospitals, medical staff or emergency department policy mandates that all emergency patients who need to be admitted from the emergency department will initially be admitted to a specific medical specialty. The specialty, in turn, will obtain consultants as deemed appropriate by the admitting physicians. The net effect of such policies is increased cost to the emergency patient and increased risk of mistakes being made in assessment and treatment. Emergency physicians who are burdened with such an inappropriate policy should attempt to change it to one that addresses the patient's needs rather than those of the physician. Until such changes are made, the emergency physician should not hesitate to modify the policy according to the patient's needs.

Physician Impairment

The emergency physician's responsibility to the patient includes protecting the patient from an impaired on-call physician. When the emergency physician has reason to believe that the on-call physician is mentally or chemically impaired, the emergency physician must take action to protect the patient. This can be done by assessing the physician in private and by asking the physician's department chair to come to the emergency department immediately. The chief of the medical staff should also be notified. A confidential written report must be submitted to the impaired physician's department chair, the quality assurance chair, and the chief of staff. Otherwise, the emergency physician and the hospital can be liable for any injuries the patient sustains after the impaired physician assumes care.

Follow-Up Care

In most emergency departments, the on-call physician has a valuable role in follow-up care. If the on-call physician does not provide such care, the emergency physician can be accused of abandoning the patient if an adverse event occurs. If one or more of the on-call physicians refuse to perform follow-up care, then arrangements must be made with other health care providers in the community to ensure proper outpatient care. If no provider for follow-up care can be arranged, the medical staff should be advised that emergency physicians may have to see patients for follow-up care to prevent an allegation of abandonment.

Case Discussions

1

This case illustrates that the emergency physician must assess patients according to recognized standards and use the on-call list in a manner consistent with national standards of care. Specifically, the plaintiff alleges that the emergency physician did not obtain a urine specimen and failed to call the on-call general surgeon shortly after the patient was admitted

into the emergency department. As a result, the extent of the patient's injuries were not recognized in a timely manner. Yet another allegation is that the emergency physician should have insisted that the orthopedist come to the emergency department to assess the patient. If this had been done, the orthopedist would have discovered the extent of the patient's injuries and would have called a general surgeon.

In this case, the emergency physician extended his responsibility for the patient by writing admitting orders. The plaintiff's emergency medicine experts provided an opinion that the emergency physician was negligent in failing to respond when he was informed of the patient's grossly bloody urine.

2

In this case, the emergency physician assessed and treated the patient and summoned the on-call general surgeon to assume responsibility for the patient's care. After the on-call surgeon arrived in the emergency department, he suddenly disappeared and, according to his own testimony, did not return. After the general surgeon left the department, the emergency physician assessed and treated two potentially critically ill patients.

As a result of the general surgeon abandoning the patient, the transfer of responsibility became a critical issue. During this time in the emergency department, the patient received approximately 7,000 mL of the 14,000 mL of crystalloid and colloid solution. Obviously, the emergency physician and nurse should have realized that the surgeon was not taking care of the patient and retrieved the surgeon or summoned another surgeon to the emergency department.

Emergency physicians should not make assumptions about the transfer of responsibility for care to other treating physicians. The emergency physician should carefully discuss transfer of responsibility with the other treating physician and should document the discussion. Also, the time the responsibility is transferred should be documented in the physician's notes and the emergency nursing records.

3

This case illustrates the use and misuse of on-call panels and inappropriate policies for admitting patients from the emergency department. When this patient returned to the emergency department 48 hours after the original traumatic event, he exhibited obvious clinical signs and symptoms of an expanding intracranial lesion. Instead of calling a neurosurgeon to the emergency department to evaluate the patient or transferring the patient to an appropriate facility with neurosurgical and CT scanning capabilities, the emergency physician admitted the patient onto the medical floor under the supervision of an internist.

The emergency physician subsequently testified that he was required to admit all patients to one of a group of four internists regardless of the patient's diagnosis. Obviously, this emergency physician did not fulfill his duty to the patient when he followed this policy. He also allegedly did not act in the best interests of the patient by failing to determine if the hospital had neurosurgical capabilities or CT scanning equipment.

Key Points and Conclusion

Since the passage of EMTALA, the federal government has set an absolute standard for the role and responsibility of on-call physicians with regard to their relationship to emergency department patients.

Emergency facilities often require on-call physicians to respond within 30 minutes of the emergency physician's call. Because patients in life-threatening conditions frequently do not have the luxury of waiting 30 minutes, the emergency physician, through various medical staff committees, must develop policies that address patient needs. Medical staff policies that do not properly address these needs should be changed. Policies also should be developed to resolve disagreements between on-call physicians and emergency physicians and for dealing with on-call physicians who behave inappropriately.

Some hospitals with voluntary on-call panels have experienced the withdrawal of medical staff members from these panels. They should, through the medical executive committee, formally notify the board of directors of the catastrophic effects that such vacancies can have on emergency patient care and request that the board resolve this glaring deficiency.

The fact that on-call physicians are the ostensible agents of the hospital has clearly been established in multiple legal cases. The hospital, therefore, bears an agency responsibility for those physicians who represent them.

References

1. Joint Commission on Accreditation of Healthcare Organizations: *Comprehensive Accreditation Manual for Hospitals: The Official Handbook.* Chicago: JCAHO; 1996.
2. 42 USC 1395dd.
3. 42 USC 1395cc(a)(1)(I)(iii).
4. *Burditt v Department of HHS,* 934 F2d 1362 (5th Cir 1991).
5. 59 *Federal Register* 32100.
6. Macy J, Jr. The role of emergency medicine in the future of American medical care. *Ann Emerg Med* 1995;25:230-233.
7. *Jackson v Power,* Alaska Sup Ct, 743 P2d 1376 (October 16, 1987).
8. *Del Rio v Beverly Hospital,* (1982) LACSC:CA;C406044.
9. *Caplinger v La Miranda Community Hospital,* (1978) LACSC:CA;C242125.
10. 42 CFR 489.53(a)(10).
11. *Darling v Charleston Community Hospital,* 33 Ill2d 326, 211 NE2d 253 (1965).
12. *Pedroza v Bryant,* 101 Wash2d 226, 677 P2d 166 (1984).
13. *Courtreau v Dodd, Arkansas Supreme Court,* 299 Ark 380, 773 SW2d 436 (July 3, 1989).
14. *Thompson v Nason Hospital,* 527 Pa 330, 591 A2d 703 (Pa 1991).
15. *Pamperen v Trinity,* 144 Wis2d 188, 423 NW2d 848 (May 31, 1988).
16. *McNamara v Emmons,* 36 Cal App2d 199, 204, 97 P2d 503, 507 (1939).
17. *Hand v Tavera,* 864 SW2d 678 (Ct App Tex 1993).
18. Medical Staff Responsibility for Emergency Department Patients. ACEP Policy Statement, approved June 1993. To obtain a copy, call (800) 798-1822, touch 6, or go to www.acep.org

Chapter 43

Admitting Orders

Peggy L. Goldman, MD, FACEP

In general, medical orders establish which physician is responsible for the care of a patient. When a patient is admitted to a hospital, the attending physician occasionally will ask the emergency physician to write admission orders. This practice is potentially dangerous because the emergency physician generally does not provide continuing inpatient care.

Nevertheless, many emergency physicians are obligated by policy or practice to write "holding" orders for patients who are admitted to the hospital through the emergency department. In these situations, the emergency physician can better serve the patient by writing brief, time-limited orders to cover the period of transition of responsibility from the emergency physician to the attending physician.

Case Studies

1

A 6-year-old boy is brought to the emergency department because he has a high fever and a sore throat. He is able to swallow his saliva but resists speaking because of pain. Examination of the pharynx reveals mild erythema. A soft tissue lateral film of the neck is interpreted as being normal. The emergency physician calls the attending physician and arranges for the child's admission to the hospital. His diagnosis is "tonsillitis, possible epiglottitis."

The attending asks the emergency physician to write admission orders for IV fluids and antibiotics. The child is admitted to the hospital at midnight. Four hours later, the emergency physician is called to the child's hospital room and finds the child in cardiac arrest. Resuscitation attempts are unsuccessful, and the child is pronounced dead as the attending physician arrives.

2

An 87-year-old man with multiple medical problems is brought to the emergency department by his son because he has been weak and unable to care for himself. The patient is confused, but the son says that his father has "been forgetful for years." The patient is cachectic and dehydrated and exhibits signs of a urinary tract infection. The emergency physician calls the attending physician and speaks to his office nurse. Arrangements are made to admit the patient to the hospital. The nurse asks the emergency physician to write holding orders for the patient until she can get in touch with the attending to have him see the patient in the hospital. The emergency physician writes admission orders for a soft diet as tolerated and IV fluids and antibiotics. The next morning, another physician on staff calls the emergency physician to tell him that the patient has developed pulmonary edema. The attending physician still has not come in to see the patient, and IV fluids are still running.

3

A 43-year-old man presents to the emergency department late one evening with symptoms of an acute abdomen. The emergency physician believes that surgery is required and calls the on-call surgeon, who suggests that he will come in to see the patient promptly. However, the surgeon does not come in, and the patient dies the next morning as the result of a ruptured abdominal aneurysm. The emergency physician is cited for a violation of the Emergency Medical Treatment and Active Labor Act (EMTALA) because he did not stabilize the patient before sending him to the ICU and did not ensure that the surgeon performed an examination. The hospital and the on-call surgeon are also cited.

The Medical-Legal Perspective

The emergency physician's role in the delivery of medical care is to deal with a patient's urgent or emergent problems — not to provide ongoing primary care. Providing a medical screening examination, stabilizing the patient's condition, and referring that patient to another physician for definitive care is an approach that meets the standard of care.[1] The American College of Emergency Physicians (ACEP) defines the role of the emergency physician in a similar way.[2-4]

In most hospitals, staff physicians are allowed to admit patients without seeing those patients in their offices first. How soon after admission the attending physician must see the patient is usually specified in hospital bylaws and often depends on whether the patient is admitted to an ICU. Such a patient is clearly the responsibility of the admitting (attending) physician and the hospital. When a patient is admitted to the hospital from the emergency department, however, responsibility for the patient is not always clearly defined. The emergency physician usually examines the patient, discusses the case with the attending physician over the telephone, and occasionally writes admission orders.

The problem with this procedure is that the emergency physician's orders direct the care of the patient after this physician is no longer available for consultation. The emergency physician cannot be expected to leave the emergency department in order to give continuing care to admitted patients.

The attending physician often does not see the patient until the next day. If the patient does not do well, the attending physician may claim that the emergency physician was responsible for the poor result because he was the only one to see the patient and wrote the orders. The emergency physician, on the other hand, does not periodically check on the patient after admission and is not usually notified by the nurses about changes in the patient's condition.

In too many cases, however, the ultimate responsibility for the patient is ambiguous, and everyone is blamed when something goes wrong.[5] Some experts believe that emergency physicians should never write admission orders for attending physicians or specialists because doing so involves the emergency physician in the management of patients in medical units remote from the emergency department, where the liability risk is increased.[6]

ACEP believes that quality patient care occurs when there is no ambiguity as to which physician is responsible for a particular patient's care. Because medical orders, in general, establish which physician is in charge of a patient's care, and because emergency physicians generally do not provide continuing inpatient care, ACEP has endorsed the principle that emergency physicians should not be involved in writing orders that extend responsibility for a patient beyond treatment in the emergency department. Hospital policies should clearly delineate responsibility for writing admission orders and guarantee that the patient be seen in a timely manner by the attending physician.[7]

When asked to write holding admission orders as a courtesy, the emergency physician must consider the possibility that the request is driven by what is convenient for the attending physician rather than by the urgency of the patient's condition. Emergency physicians are becoming more sensitive about the need to cooperate with the attending medical staff in order to ensure collegiality and job security and deal with the reality that most physicians do not want to leave a busy practice or come to the hospital in the middle of the night. As a solution, some hospitals, managed care organizations, and emergency departments provide in-hospital physician services that allow primary care physicians to delegate the care of their patients to an in-house physician. This solution is designed to promote quality medial care, be more cost-effective in the managed care environment, and create a better outpatient practice environment. In hospitals that do not have these physician services, the emergency physician may have to agree to write brief admitting orders.

On the other hand, however, writing holding orders can expedite patient care in some situations. Emergency physicians can extend their liability in a controlled manner by writing brief holding orders that have time limits, that deal only with the acute situation, and that allow for appropriate transition of responsibility to the attending physician. These orders should clearly state who is the attending physician of record, and how to reach that person. If the emergency physician elects to cooperate with the medical staff by writing admission orders, they should be written carefully. Remember: this agreement to retain some responsibility for the patient's care outside the emergency department will require time and may prevent the emergency physician from providing prompt care for other emergency patients. In any case, writing for full doses of routine medications is not required.

Case Discussions

1

All too often there is a nebulous period of time in a patient's care when it is unclear who is responsible for that patient immediately following admission to the hospital. This gray area starts when the emergency physician calls the attending physician, continues through the technical transfer of responsibility for the patient, and should end when the attending physician examines the patient in the hospital. Refusing to write admitting orders sometimes seems trivial. Why should an attending physician get out of bed and spend an hour doing something the emergency physician can do easily in five minutes?

Some emergency physicians believe that complaints made by attending physicians who are frequently asked to evaluate or to admit patients at inconvenient times will jeopardize their job security. However, a courtesy to the attending physician may not truly serve patient care, particularly if it extends the time that elapses from examination in the emergency department to the time the patient is seen by the attending physician in the hospital.

2

Emergency physicians should never assume that messages to on-call physicians have been transmitted correctly. In this case, there was a contributory culpability of the nurses in failing both to recognize a worsening condition and to notify the appropriate physician. However, the emergency physician was still liable for not ensuring the proper transfer of medical responsibility and for being the last physician of record.

It was unclear whether the attending physician violated a hospital bylaws requirement of a time limit in which to see the admitted patient. If the emergency physician's admission orders had been written to expire in several hours, the nurses on the floor probably would have tried harder to contact the attending physician and have him come to the hospital.

3

Orders by the on-call physician to admit a patient to his or her service without the attending physician coming in to see the patient has resulted in EMTALA citations. When a patient with an emergency medical condition requires "stabilizing treatment" by an on-call specialist, the on-call physician must respond in person in a timely manner to attend to the patient. Because the Health Care Financing Administration (HCFA) has not specified the appropriate response time, the determination of whether the on-call physician responded quickly enough will be made according to the hospital policy.

The legal standard places a heavy responsibility on the emergency physician to enforce EMTALA compliance.[7] In many hospitals, medical staff bylaws must be amended to adequately address the changing obligators of the staff under EMTALA. Not only are the requirements much more stringent for the policies regarding on-call physicians, but how soon after admission the patient must be seen as well as physician responsibilities in the transfer process of emergency to attending physician must be addressed.

Key Points and Conclusion

Medical orders establish which physician is in charge of a patient's care. Emergency physicians must observe the following guidelines to ensure proper patient transfer and to avoid liability:

- Ideally, the emergency physician should not be involved in writing any orders that extend responsibility for the patient's care beyond treatment in the emergency department. When admission orders are written by the emergency physician, they should be time limited and provide for clear transfer of responsibility to the attending physician.
- According to EMTALA, on-call physicians are required to respond to emergency department requests for consultation or patient care in a timely manner.

References

1. *Dalgo v Landry*, 424 Sol12d 1159 (La Ct App), writ denied, 429 So2d 133 (La 1983).

2. Emergency Care Guidelines. ACEP Policy Statement, approved September 1996. To obtain a copy, call (800) 798-1822, touch 6, or go to www.acep.org.

3. Definition of Emergency Medicine. ACEP Policy Statement, approved April 1994. To obtain a copy, call (800) 798-1822, touch 6, or go to www.acep.org.

4. Core Content for Emergency Medicine. ACEP Policy Statement, approved December 1996. To obtain a copy, call (800) 798-1822, touch 6, or go to www.acep.org.

5. Fish RM, Ehrhardt ME. *Preventing Emergency Malpractice*. Oradell, NJ: Medical Economics Books; 1989.

6. Frew SA. *Patient Transfers: How to Comply With the Law*. Second edition. Dallas: American College of Emergency Physicians; 1995.

7. Writing Admission Orders. ACEP Policy Statement, approved October 1993. To obtain a copy, call (800) 798-1822, touch 6, or go to www.acep.org.

Chapter 44

Telephone Orders From Private Physicians

Peggy L. Goldman, MD, FACEP

During the course of a routine day in an office-based practice, some patients require treatment that is not available in the physician's office. In these situations, many physicians send patients to the emergency department and call in orders for the necessary treatment. This is a workable arrangement as long as these patients receive a medical screening examination in the emergency department before the telephone-ordered treatment is rendered. The problem is, the medical screening examination may not be provided.

Despite the fact that federal law requires that all patients presenting to the emergency department receive a medical screening examination to determine whether emergency medical conditions are present,[1] some hospitals still have policies — or time-honored practices — that allow these "private" patients to be treated without being evaluated in the emergency department. From a patient care perspective, this practice carries a degree of risk even when the patient comes directly to the emergency department from the private physician's office — and an even higher degree of risk when the private physician has not seen the patient at all, as is commonly the case at night and on weekends. From a medical-legal perspective, the degree of risk is equally high: both can result in missed diagnoses, and both represent potential violations of the Emergency Medical Treatment and Active Labor Act (EMTALA). These violations can lead to civil monetary penalties and termination from the Medicare program for both the physician and the hospital.

Private physicians who rely on the emergency department to provide this type of care to their patients often do not understand the extent of liability that the hospital and the emergency physician can incur when a patient receives treatment by telephone order without first undergoing an emergency department medical screening examination. Those who do not understand are the ones who ask emergency department staff to "skip the exam" so their patients "won't have to be put through it again" or have to "wait around the emergency department all night just to get a shot." Hospital policy should require that all patients who present to the emergency department for treatment undergo a medical screening examination first, regardless of requests to the contrary made by private physicians.

Case Studies

1

A 52-year-old woman is suffering from persistent back pain caused by a work-related injury. She has had surgery more than once, but without relief of her symptoms. In an effort to control the back pain, her newest physician has prescribed methocarbamol and oxycodone in addition to the glutethimide she is already taking. She has become increasingly dependent on these drugs but still has severe back pain.

On a Saturday night, her physician calls the emergency department to prescribe an injection of meperidine and hydroxyzine. He also asks the triage nurse to take care of getting the patient refills of her pain medications. The patient arrives in the emergency department and receives the injection. However, the pharmacy refuses to fill the narcotic prescriptions without a physician's signature. The triage nurse takes the prescriptions to the emergency physician and says: "Sign these so we can discharge her. We need the bed."

The emergency physician signs the prescriptions and the patient is discharged. Later that night, she takes a lethal overdose of acetaminophen, salicylate, oxycodone, and alcohol.

2

During the seventh month of her first pregnancy, a 21-year-old woman is seen in her obstetrician's office for abdominal pain. The pain is crampy and associated with some nausea but no vomiting. The obstetrician determines that the woman is in premature labor and sends her home.

When the woman continues to experience pain, the obstetrician sends her to the emergency department and calls in orders for her to be examined by the resident obstetrics house physician. The orders include performing a fetal monitoring strip, which if negative, indicates that she can be sent home. The woman is examined by the house physician, the monitoring strip is obtained, and she is sent home by the nursing staff. The emergency physician signs the chart.

Three days later, the patient returns to the emergency department in septic shock. After a stormy course in the ICU, she dies from adult respiratory distress syndrome; the fetus also dies. An autopsy reveals generalized peritonitis secondary to a perforated appendix. A multimillion-dollar lawsuit is filed against all parties concerned, including the emergency physician.

3

A 24-year-old patient who has chronic migraine headaches receives Schedule II controlled substances in the emergency department after her private physician calls in telephone orders. A medical screening examination is not performed, resulting in an EMTALA citation.

The Medical-Legal Perspective

Private physicians use telephone orders because they believe this approach will expedite patient care and reduce health care costs.

However, when the treatment of a patient's acute illness is dictated only by telephone order, the patient is at considerable risk. In the absence of a medical screening examination, critical aspects of the patient's condition can be missed.

Any time a person presents to an emergency department, the hospital is required by law to provide a medical screening examination, even if the person is not examined by the emergency physician. The most conservative risk management position is to require an emergency physician to examine every patient who presents to the emergency department. According to EMTALA, screening examinations must be offered to all patients regardless of their ability to pay and regardless of whether their insurance plans or managed care organizations will pay for the visits.[1] This requirement is very clear — and often in direct conflict with an attending physician's request that a patient be treated without an emergency physician evaluation.

Ideally, the private physician who needs to order medication or treatment should do so in writing. In practice, however, this is not always possible. If telephone transmission is the only option, the nurse who takes the orders should read them back to the physician to be sure there is no miscommunication.[2] The act of one physician signing a prescription on behalf of another physician with the notation "per telephone order" (of the other physician) probably does not create a physician-patient relationship.[3] However, some courts have determined that an implied physician-patient relationship is established when a physician signs an order in a hospital setting, even if the physician has not had any contact with the patient.[4]

The primary risk of following telephone orders without performing an examination is that the emergency physician may be treating a condition that has been misdiagnosed by the private physician. More than two thirds of emergency medicine medical malpractice actions involve the failure of an emergency physician to diagnose a patient's condition.[5] One article in the literature[6] describes the case of a 28-year-old woman with recurring headaches who had been diagnosed as having migraines based on her previous history and physical examination performed by her family physician. When she visited the emergency department, she usually received an injection of meperidine and hydroxyzine by telephone order. Because the private physicians at this hospital did not want the emergency physicians to bill their patients, hospital policy allowed that patients would be seen by an emergency physician only on request of the patient's private physician or if the patient's condition suddenly worsened while in the department. In this case, the patient had unequal pupils, but the emergency physician was not informed of this fact (or even of the patient's presence) until she became comatose some time after she arrived. The patient eventually died of a ruptured intracranial aneurysm, which may have been the cause of her headaches all along.

The attorneys in this case claimed that the emergency physician had a duty to provide reasonable care to patients in the emergency department. The conservative position is to assume that once a patient is physically in the emergency department, a duty to treat that patient is established. Every patient is entitled to a medical screening examination, which was not performed in this case. In some jurisdictions, the emergency physician has been held responsible for any patient presenting to the emergency department.[7-9]

In another case, a woman presented to an emergency department with nausea, vomiting, and abdominal pain. The nurse obtained the patient's history, took her blood pressure, and called the emergency physician, who was not present in the department. Relying on the nurse's assessment, the emergency physician prescribed medication over the telephone for what he believed was a urinary tract infection. The next day, the woman's appendix ruptured, requiring two hospitalizations and operations.[10] In this case, the telephone order was made by the emergency physician rather than the private physician. It can be argued that in this case the nurse provided the medical screening examination. However, whether the emergency physician is in or out of the department, a failure to diagnose a condition may result in a malpractice case. The malpractice case is less defensible for the emergency physician if a careful examination of the patient has not been performed.

Facilitating the treatment of private patients by using telephone orders can be cost-effective and appropriate. However, one lawsuit for a poor outcome can negate years of cost-effectiveness. The law allows for mistakes in judgment provided the judgment is based on competent evaluation. Still, many hospitals allow physicians to treat emergency patients over the telephone without examining them and without requiring emergency department evaluation,

which leads to potential liability for the emergency physician, the attending physician, and the hospital.

Where does the American College of Emergency Physicians (ACEP) stand on this issue? According to College policy,[11] telephone orders for emergency department patients dictated by physicians from outside the department can affect the quality of medical care patients receive and can create legal liability for emergency physicians. For this reason, the College endorses these three principles:

- Hospital policy should specify that all patients who come to the hospital for emergency care should be provided with an appropriate medical screening examination in the emergency department.
- When a patient comes to the emergency department for planned nonemergency services, hospital and emergency department policy should specify the criteria for dictating and accepting telephone orders.
- These criteria should clearly identify the types of patients, medical conditions, and services for which telephone orders can be accepted and the allowable interval between the patient's last examination by his physician and the request for emergency department treatment.

ACEP policy also acknowledges that the federal Drug Enforcement Administration prohibits dispensing controlled substances from emergency department stocks for treatment of patients by telephone order.

Case Discussions

1

In this first case, both the attending physician and the emergency physician responded inappropriately to the patient's complaints and request. Each physician felt compelled "to do something" — and that "something" was prescribe medication. In hindsight, however, they both did too much. Emergency physicians are often caught in the difficult position of doing too much or doing too little at the request of a patient or another physician.

In most instances, an emergency physician will prescribe narcotics simply as a conscientious response to a patient's complaints of severe pain. Remember: the complaint of pain is subjective and may be exaggerated, or even fabricated. Handling a patient who demands excessive medication is very difficult. The emergency physician in this case would have been better off examining the patient himself, refusing the prescription, or asking the private physician to come to the emergency department to do so.

2

This case represents a common scenario in emergency medicine — the "bounce-back" or "repeater" patient — someone who seeks care for the same complaints more than once in a short period of time. The risk associated with these patients is labeling them with their original diagnoses then not considering the possibility that some other conditions — more serious ones — are actually causing the symptoms. Unfortunately, the approach to these patients on subsequent visits is often to perform a superficial examination, or not to have them seen at all by the emergency physician. All return visits should be considered a "red flag" that the correct diagnosis was not made or that proper instructions were not given to the patient.

A compounding factor in this case was the evaluation performed by the obstetrics house physician. When another physician sees a patient and makes a diagnosis, it is easy to feel secure that the diagnosis is correct. This may be particularly true in a teaching institution, where the attending emergency physician is responsible for the supervision of house officers who are medical residents in an academic teaching program. Unfortunately, emergency department staff members sometimes develop biases about "repeaters," especially if they suspect drug-seeking behavior. Although this attitude is sometimes justified, the physician must remember that almost every serious medical condition is easier to recognize once it has worsened. Physicians must set aside their biases and give each patient a fresh look.

3

The enactment of EMTALA greatly increased the emergency physician's scope of responsibility to see all patients who present to the emergency department and provide them with medical screening examinations. The continuing growth of managed care creates even more pressure. Many hospitals rely on telephone triage systems to compete in a managed care environment, but these systems must be managed carefully in order to provide quality care and avoid excessive malpractice risks.[12]

When a patient arrives at the emergency department, telephone orders are not a replacement for a medical screening examination. The medical staff should understand this federally mandated requirement. One solution is to adopt a policy that all patients who register in the emergency department must be seen by a physician before they leave. This policy would eliminate the problem of a private physician sending in patients for telephone-ordered injections without any physician evaluation.[13] Do not assume that a private physician will leap to the defense of an emergency physician when a lawsuit is involved.[6] In fact, a desirable contract provision would require that all patients be evaluated by an emergency physician. This would prevent private physicians from using the emergency department as a private clinic.

Key Points and Conclusion

Telephone orders dictated by physicians from outside the emergency department for patients who are currently being seen in the department can result in significant harm to the patient and liability risk to the emergency department staff and health care facility.

Keep the following guidelines in mind to minimize risk:

- By federal law, every emergency department patient must be provided a medical screening examination to determine whether an emergency medical condition exists.
- In those circumstances where telephone orders are acceptable, hospital policies should specify the criteria for dictating and accepting telephone orders, having them countersigned, and allowing for the medical screening examination.
- Hospital policies should prohibit telephone orders for medications on the controlled substances list.

References

1. 42 USC 1395 dd.
2. Creighton H. *Law Every Nurse Should Know*. 111 4th ed, 1981.
3. *Bass v Barksdale*, 671 SW2d 476 (Tenn Ct App 1984).
4. *Giallanza v Sands*, 316 So2d 77 (Fal App 1975).
5. Rogers JT. *Risk Management in Emergency Medicine*. Dallas: American College of Emergency Physicians; 1985.
6. Henry GL. Problem: a private patient in the ED. *Emerg Med* 1986;129.
7. Nobel JJ. The duty to render emergency care. *Emerg Med Ambul Care* 1987;9(6):2.
8. Negligence suit settled for $500,000. *American Medical News*, April 3, 1987.

9. George JE. Duty to treat. *Emerg Nurs Legal Bull* 1981;7(3):2-6.

10. *Bartimus v Paxton Community Hospital,* 458 NE2d 1072 (Ill App 1983).

11. Telephone Orders in the Emergency Department. ACEP Policy Statement, approved January 1997. To obtain a copy, call (800) 798-1822, touch 6, or go to www.acep.org.

12. Providing Telephone Advice from the Emergency Department. ACEP Policy Statement, approved August 1995. To obtain a copy, call (800) 798-1822, touch 6, or go to www.acep.org.

13. Blaylock P. Medical malpractice trends in the ED. *Emergency Department News,* June 1985.

Chapter 45

EMTALA

Robert A. Bitterman, MD, JD, FACEP

"There's no better way of exercising the imagination than the study of law. No poet ever interpreted nature as freely as a lawyer interprets truth." — Jean Girandoux (1882-1944).

The Emergency Medical Treatment and Active Labor Act (EMTALA)[1] is a federal law that governs the delivery of hospital-based emergency medicine in the United States. It sets a standard of care for emergency services and grants federal rights to individual patients and other hospitals if that standard is not met.

Congress enacted EMTALA as part of the Consolidated Omnibus Budget Reconciliation Act of 1985, which is how it came to be known as the "COBRA" law. It is also referred to in the literature as the Patient Transfer Act, the "Anti-Dumping Law," Section 1867 of the Social Security Act, or COBRA Section 9121. The original intent of the law was to prevent private hospitals from transferring, or "dumping," medically unstable, indigent patients to public hospitals.[2] Today, economically motivated transfer issues are but a fraction of the vast scope and pervasive impact EMTALA has had on emergency medicine. It now functions as an antidiscrimination statute, designed to prevent discriminatory treatment of emergency patients, and raises contentious issue for emergency physicians in their dealings with hospital administrators, managed care entities, and other members of the medical staff, particularly on-call physicians. It has spawned vexatious litigation and civil penalties from state and federal regulators, as well as new theories of tort recovery for plaintiffs' attorneys.

EMTALA is actually a condition of participation in the Medicare program. By accepting Medicare payment, hospitals "voluntarily" agree to abide by EMTALA. Hospitals that do not accept Medicare funds do not have to comply. Emergency physicians should remember one key concept, which is the underlying theme of this chapter: if any emergency department practice treats one class of patients, such as Medicaid patients, managed care patients, or private patients, differently than any other class of patients, such disparate treatment is probably illegal under EMTALA.

From a risk management perspective, compliance with EMTALA actually helps physicians manage the only real risk they face — the risk to the life and well-being of patients. Knowledge of this law will help emergency physicians create policies and implement procedures that are in the best interest of patients from the time they present at triage through examination, treatment, and stabilization, and to discharge, admission, or transfer.

Case Studies

1

A 35-year-old woman presents to the emergency department with a chief compliant of migraine headache. An emergency nurse triages the patient and calls her private physician, who tells the nurse to send the patient to his office. The patient is not examined by the emergency physician on duty; the nurse does not inform the physician of the patient's presence prior to sending the patient to the private physician's office. An hour later, the patient returns, and the private physician calls the emergency department with orders to give the patient 75 mg of meperidine IM and 75 mg of hydroxyzine hydrochloride IM for her headache. A nurse administers the medication and allows the patient to leave the emergency department without an examination by the emergency physician. Six hours later, the patient returns by EMS after a seizure and later dies from a sub-arachnoid hemorrhage. The family brings a wrongful death action against the hospital for failure to provide the patient with an appropriate medical screening examination.

2

A 22-year-old woman presents to the emergency department with a complaint of lower abdominal pain. She is a member of a local HMO. Her vital signs are blood pressure 130/55, pulse 110, respirations 20, temperature 99°F. The triage nurse asks the patient to wait until authorization is obtained from her HMO primary care physician. The physician calls back 45 minutes later and denies authorization for the patient's emergency department visit. He tells the nurse to send the patient to his office. The triage nurse relays the physician's instructions to the patient, who is not pleased with the course of events but leaves the emergency department to go to the physician's office. Two hours later, the patient is sent back to the emergency department with a blood pressure of 80/50. She is taken to the operating room for removal of a ruptured ectopic pregnancy.

3

A 60-year-old man with a history of hypertension presents to the emergency department with sudden severe, searing chest and back pain. An ECG is normal, and a chest x-ray reveals a widened mediastinum. An immediate CT scan demonstrates an acute aortic dissection. The hospital does not have a surgeon on staff capable of repairing the dissection. The emergency physician calls the patient's primary care physician (PCP) to arrange a transfer. The PCP contacts the hospital contracted to provide services for his MCO enrollees. This hospital is unable to accept the transfer because it has no ICU or recovery beds available and is currently on bypass status to EMS. The PCP asks the emergency physician to keep the patient until a bed

opens up at the MCO hospital, which he expects to occur in two to three hours. The emergency physician initially agrees but recontacts the PCP two hours later because of difficulty controlling the patient's hypertension. The PCP reaffirms the MCO hospital's closed status, then denies authorization when the emergency physician asks to transfer the patient to a different facility.

The emergency physician calls another hospital anyway. This hospital is fully capable of managing the patient's aortic dissection but refuses to accept the patient until authorization is obtained from the MCO. After another 90 minutes of arguments and still no bed available at the MCO hospital, the PCP relents and authorizes the transfer. Twenty minutes after reaching the hospital, the patient arrests and dies.

The Medical-Legal Perspective

EMTALA imposes three legal duties on hospitals:
- If any individual comes to the emergency department, the hospital must provide an appropriate medical screening examination to determine whether an emergency medical condition exists.[3]
- If a hospital determines that an emergency medical condition does exist, then the hospital must either stabilize the medical condition or transfer the patient to another hospital that is capable of stabilizing the medical condition.[4] Hospitals must provide on-call physicians to help stabilize patients.[5]
- Hospitals with specialized capabilities or facilities must accept appropriate transfers of patients who require such specialized services if the hospital has the capacity to treat the individual.[6]

Several of the terms used to describe these legal duties — "medical screening examination," "emergency medical condition," "stabilize," transfer" — now have legal definitions that may mean something frightfully different than what is understood by physicians and other hospital personnel. Compliance with these legal definitions will usually be judged by an unsympathetic jury, aided by hindsight, in the context of a patient suffering an adverse medical result. In fact, as the judge stated in *Burditt v U.S. Department of Health and Human Services*[7]: "The statutory definition renders irrelevant any medical definition."

Transfer Defined

According to EMTALA, the term transfer

means "the movement (including the discharge) of an individual outside a hospital's facilities at the direction of any person employed by (or affiliated or associated, directly or indirectly, with) the hospital, but does not include such a movement of an individual who (A) has been declared dead, or (B) leaves the facility without the permission of any such person."[8]

Emergency Department Discharges. Under EMTALA, all patients discharged from an emergency department are considered, from a legal perspective, to have been transferred, and all the transfer requirements of the law apply. Sending a patient home who is determined retrospectively to be unstable is considered a transfer of an unstable patient, and as such, a violation of law. To avoid such retrospective analyses, emergency physicians must document that no emergency condition was found and that the patient was stable on discharge.

The section of the medical record designated for recording the patient's condition on discharge should include boxes for no "emergency medical condition" (EMC) and "stable" rather than the "good," "fair," "serious," "critical," "deceased" options normally found and recommended by the Joint Commission on Accreditation of Healthcare Organizations (JCAHO). Compliance with JCAHO standards is irrelevant and no defense for an EMTALA claim.

Inpatient Discharges. Also according to EMTALA, any patient admitted through the emergency department and later discharged from the hospital also has been transferred. In the seminal case *Thornton v Southwest Detroit Hospital*,[9] a woman presented to an emergency department with a stroke. She was admitted, treated as an inpatient for three weeks, then discharged. Her condition worsened after she left the hospital, so she sued the hospital under EMTALA, claiming that the hospital failed to stabilize her and transferred, or "dumped," her out of the hospital. The hospital argued that the law only applied to discharge from an emergency department and that, once admitted, the patient was no longer covered by EMTALA. The appellate court, however, held that emergency care must be provided until the patient's emergency condition is stabilized, regardless of where the patient is in the hospital. The court stated that "hospitals may not circumvent the requirements of [EMTALA] by admitting an emergency room patient to the hospital, then immediately discharging the patient."[9] Thus, patients admitted through the emergency department and later discharged from the hospital have been transferred according to EMTALA, a fact that often goes unrecognized by hospitals and our admitting colleagues.

This interpretation of the law probably applies only to patients who are admitted through the emergency department, and not to patients admitted in other ways, but the issue is still somewhat unsettled in the courts.[10]

Other "Transfers." The EMTALA definition of transfer also applies to any patient sent from triage to a physician's office, an urgent care clinic, or a managed care facility. Even if, for example, a security guard or housekeeper comments to an incoming patient: "It's so busy in there. The ED is three or four hours behind. You might as well come back later," that patient has been legally transferred. Note that the definition says: ". . . movement of an individual outside the hospital's facilities at the direction of any person affiliated with the hospital."[8]

Fortunately, the government has decided that if the patient is dead or leaves without permission, then the hospital has not legally transferred the patient.[8]

Emergency Medical Condition Defined

The law defines an emergency medical condition as existing if a patient has ". . . acute symptoms of sufficient severity (including severe pain) such that the absence of immediate medical attention could reasonably be expected to result in placing the individual's health in serious jeopardy, serious impairment to bodily functions, or serious dysfunction of any bodily organ or part."[11] A pregnant woman who is having contractions has an emergency medical condition if "there is inadequate time to effect a safe transfer to another hospital before delivery, or if the transfer may pose a threat to the health or safety of the woman or unborn child."[12]

This is vague, broad language. Does a child with a two-inch scalp laceration have an emergency medical condition? What if it is bleeding? Does an 18-year-old college student with a fever and sore throat have an emergency medical condition? What if it is a "high" fever and a "bad" sore throat? Competent physicians can reasonably disagree whether certain symptoms are acute, immediate, or serious enough to be emergency medical conditions.

The Health Care Financing Administration (HCFA), the agency charged with investigating and enforcing EMTALA, offers little help in determining exactly what conditions are emergency conditions. One exception is that HCFA specifically defines psychiatric disturbances and/or symptoms of substance abuse to be sufficiently severe medical symptoms to warrant the label emergency medical condition.[13]

HCFA routinely substitutes the judgment of its regulators for that of the examining emergency physician, retrospectively deciding that a patient was suffering from an emergency medical condition, then citing the hospital for failure to stabilize that condition it did not believe existed in the first place. For example, a major trauma center released a patient with a crush injury to the base of the nail bed on his nondominant pinky finger. There was no reported open fracture or loss of extension. HCFA determined that patient had an emergency medical condition when he left the emergency department because the finger injury was a "serious impairment to a bodily part." It then cited the hospital for failure to stabilize an emergency medical condition prior to transfer (remember, discharge is a transfer). In another case, a Virginia hospital released a patient with a fractured wrist and patella. The patient was evaluated, x-rayed, and appropriately splinted and arrangements were made for the patient to follow up with an orthopedic surgeon. While in the emergency department, the patient received injectable pain medications and a prescription for adequate narcotic analgesia. HCFA cited the hospital, stating that the patient had "severe pain" when discharged and, therefore, had an emergency medical condition that was not stabilized prior to transfer. There seems to be a trend with "severe pain" cases, in which HCFA substitutes its judgment for that of the emergency physician in determining whether the patient's pain was adequately controlled and could be treated on an outpatient basis.[14]

Fortunately, the federal appellate courts, which hear the civil damage lawsuits under EMTALA, expressly prohibit such retrospective analysis. The courts hold that a hospital must have actual knowledge that a patient is suffering from an emergency medical condition for it to be held liable under EMTALA for failure to stabilize that condition.[15] The courts, in essence, refuse to let EMTALA be a federal malpractice act, and instead hold that the "failure to diagnose an emergency medical condition" is a malpractice claim to be brought in state court under ordinary malpractice laws.[15]

The disparity between the HCFA standard for investigating hospitals and the standard the courts use for allowing civil lawsuits is unsettling. But, until HCFA mends its ways, or a hospital sues to obtain a court order restraining HCFA, hospitals and physicians will have to live with the dichotomy and contest HCFA's factual determinations on a case-by-case basis. Hospitals are very reluctant to confront HCFA because of the cost and adverse publicity involved, and because the enforcement process leaves them only 23 days to come into compliance or risk losing their Medicare provider agreement with the federal government.

The problems associated with definitions emphasize the critical importance of emergency physicians documenting the presence or absence of an emergency condition during all patients' initial emergency department evaluations. Although physicians may not be able to avoid HCFA's misapplication of the law, they can protect themselves and their hospitals from civil liability.

To What Hospitals, What Persons, and Which Physicians Does EMTALA Apply?

All hospitals that participate in the Medicare program must comply with EMTALA,[1] which includes about 98% of all hospitals in the United States and U.S. territories. Some Veterans Administration hospitals do not participate in Medicare and, thus, are exempt. Some private hospitals, generally private psychiatric hospitals, do not accept Medicare patients. Physicians' offices, public health centers, clinics, and independent freestanding urgent care centers are also exempt, even if they accept Medicare funds, because they do not meet the Medicare legal definition of a hospital. Thus, a facility must meet the definition of a hospital and must accept Medicare funds to be obligated under EMTALA.

If the hospital does participate in Medicare, the law covers "any individual" who presents to the hospital's emergency department, not just Medicare beneficiaries. The passage of EMTALA was the first congressional action to use the Medicare program to regulate the delivery of health care services to non-Medicare patients.[16]

All physicians who treat patients in a Medicare-participating hospital, not just emergency physicians, are subject to the legal duties of EMTALA. The fact that on-call physicians and admitting and consulting physicians are obligated under the law is not well known outside the emergency medicine community. The duties attach to physicians by virtue of their accepting medical staff privileges at a Medicare-participating hospital.

Who Is Not Covered?

After the medical screening examination, if a patient is found not to have an emergency medical condition, that patient is no longer covered by EMTALA. Similarly, patients who presented with an emergency medical condition that was subsequently stabilized, as defined by law, are not covered. A patient who does not have an emergency medical condition is defined as being stable, and further examination and treatment are no longer dictated by the law. Because emergency medical condition and stabilized are now defined legally, it is extremely important for physicians to use these legal terms to document a patient's condition in the medical record.

The Medical Screening Examination Requirement

The purpose of the medical screening examination (MSE) is to determine whether a patient has an emergency medical condition. There are many issues and many questions concerning the MSE requirement.

Who Is Entitled to the MSE?

The law states that "any individual" who "comes to the emergency department" and a "request for examination or treatment" is made on behalf of the individual must be provided an MSE.[3]

"Any Individual." The courts have interpreted this language literally: anyone who presents to the emergency department must be screened.[17] Whether the patient is indigent, a member of a managed care plan, covered by Medicare or Medicaid, or a private patient of a medical staff attending physician is irrelevant; the hospital must provide all the MSE. Illegal aliens are also entitled to the MSE, much to the chagrin of border hospitals. The courts have stuck to the plain language of the law, noting that it does not state "any U.S. citizen."[18]

EMTALA also invalidates state consent laws for minors. If a 13-year-old babysitter brings a 2-year-old child to the emergency department and requests an examination or treatment for the child, the hospital must provide the MSE. EMTALA is federal law, and under the U.S. Constitution's Supremacy Clause, federal law preempts conflicting state law. Certainly, the hospital should attempt to contact the child's parents, but it should not delay the MSE to obtain consent from the parents, regardless of how trivial the child's complaint initially appears. If the MSE reveals no emergency medical condition, then the hospital can wait on the parents before proceeding with further evaluation and treatment.

"Comes to the Emergency Department." HCFA regulations state that anyone on hospital property is deemed to have "come the emergency department" for purposes of EMTALA. HCFA further defines hospital property to include "ambulances owned and operated" by the hospital.[19]

If enforced, the HCFA interpretation would significantly disrupt regional trauma and EMS systems. If a hospital-owned ambulance (and certainly this includes a hospital-owned helicopter) participates in the EMS network, then the hospital's ambulance would have to return patients to its own hospital for the mandated MSE, regardless of whether it is clearly in the patient's best interest to be taken to a closer or more appropriate facility. An argument can be made that an ambulance directed by the EMS medical alert zone is not "operated" by the hospital, or that the patient did not request examination or treatment at that hospital, or that HCFA is overreaching in its reading of the statute. Until a court logically rules otherwise, the HCFA interpretation is the existing law.

However, sometimes physicians simply must do what they believe is in the patient's best interest and worry about the regulatory or legal consequences later. Which would you rather defend to a jury of your peers: diverting a patient to a needed trauma center or closer facility, or taking an action because some HCFA bureaucrat without any medical training, expertise, or experience told you to?

Non–hospital-owned ambulances and helicopters directed by a hospital's telemetry base station are not deemed to have "come to the emergency department" of that hospital.[20]

"Request for Examination or Treatment." The request for examination or treatment of a patient can be made by anyone on behalf of the patient. The request does not have to come from the patient. Police requests for blood alcohol testing do not require an MSE, as long as no "request for examination or treatment" is made. The nurse or physician involved should specifically document that the patient did not request examination or treatment for any medical condition.

Who Must Perform the MSE?

The law does not specify whether a physician, nurse, or other health care provider must perform the MSE. HCFA requires that the screening examination be performed by "qualified medical personnel" and requires the hospital's governing body designate who is a qualified person to perform medical screening.[21] HCFA wants to hold the governing body "properly accountable for this function."[22]

Nurse triage is not an MSE. The purpose of triage, as it is practiced in most hospitals, is to ascertain the nature and severity of a patient's complaint and to determine the order in which patients are seen by a physician. The purpose of the MSE is to determine whether the patient has an emergency medical condition. HCFA and the courts have uniformly held that triage of patients does not constitute an EMTALA-mandated medical screening examination. HCFA has cited many hospitals for violating EMTALA when its triage nurses evaluated patients and then referred them out of the emergency department to a managed care clinic or a physician's private office.[23]

Some hospitals, notably the University of California, Davis, allow specially trained nurses, under direct physician supervision, to perform screening examinations. These examinations are not triage examinations; they are much more extensive and are directed at determining whether the patient is suffering from an emergency medical condition.[24] HCFA reserves the right not to accept the hospital's designation of "qualified medical personnel" and may determine retrospectively, based on the circumstances and the patient's condition, that the designated person did not have sufficient medical training or expertise to conduct the MSE.[25] In fact, HCFA has cited some hospitals for not having a physician conduct the MSE, even though the hospitals had designated nurses capable of performing that examination.[26]

The position of the American College of Emergency Physicians (ACEP) is that screening examinations should be performed by a physician.[27]

To What Extent or Scope Should the MSE Be Performed?

If triage is not sufficient, how extensive must an examination be to constitute an MSE? Federal courts hold that the examination must be "reasonably calculated to identify critical medical conditions."[28] Because the stated purpose of the MSE is to determine whether an emergency medical condition exists, the hospital should conduct whatever examination is necessary, "reasonably calculated," to make that determination. It may take only a visual glance to rule out an emergency medical condition in a patient with a rash. But, if it takes a CT scan and a lumbar puncture to decide whether a patient with the "worst headache of my life" has a subarachnoid hemorrhage, then those tests and procedures are part of the federally mandated MSE. Similarly, if it takes an on-call surgeon to decide if a patient has an acute abdomen, then that surgical evaluation is an integral part of the MSE.

EMTALA was specifically amended in 1989 to add that hospitals must provide the screening examination within the capabilities of the hospital's emergency department, "including ancillary services routinely available to the emergency department."[29] Thus, if the emergency department usually has ultrasound, CT scanning, V/Q scans, and the like available, then it must use those resources if necessary to determine whether a patient has an emergency medical condition. This also means that the emergency physician who is undecided must use on-call physicians to help make that determination. The law specifically requires hospitals to provide on-call physicians to help determine if patients are suffering from emergency medical conditions and, if so, to help stabilize those conditions.[5]

Hospitals should clearly identify and define what ancillary hospital and physician services will be routinely available to its emergency department.

What Exactly Is an 'Appropriate' MSE?

Appropriateness, like nature, is "a mutable cloud which is always and never the same."[30] EMTALA does not define what constitutes an "appropriate" MSE. To quote one appellate court judge: "Appropriate is one of the most wonderful weasel words in the dictionary, and a great aide to the resolution of disputed issues in the drafting of legislation. Who, after all, can be found to stand up for 'inappropriate' treatment."[18]

Courts hold that not only must the screening examination be reasonably calculated to identify emergency medical conditions, but also that the exact same level of screening must be uniformly provided to all patients who present with substantially similar complaints. The courts base their analysis on the stated goal of the law: to prevent disparate treatment among patients. In the two seminal cases of *Cleland v Bronson Health Care Group, Inc,* and *Gatewood v Washington Health Care Corporation,* the courts held that appropriate means "care similar to care that would have been provided to any other patient, or at least not known by the providers to be in any way insufficient or below their own standards"[18]; and that what is appropriate is determined "not by reference to particular outcomes, but instead by reference to a hospital's standard screening procedures."[31] The other circuits have followed the analyses of Cleland and Gatewood, generally stating that "the hospital satisfies the requirements . . . if its standard screening procedures apply uniformly to all patients with similar circumstances."[32]

The only area in which the courts have disagreed is the issue of whether an improper motive is necessary for a hospital to be liable under EMTALA. The 6th Circuit Court of Appeals, as in *Cleland,* imposes liability for disparate treatment only if the hospital had an illicit motive.[18] Every other circuit has imposed liability for disparate treatment regardless of the hospital's motivation, citing the plain language of the law, which does not include motive as a necessary element to be liable under EMTALA.[32]

Managed care plans frequently expect hospitals to provide different levels of screening for their enrollees. They often ask the hospital merely to "eyeball the patient" or perform a clinical examination sufficient to determine whether the patient can be safely triaged to a managed care facility. Neither HCFA nor the courts condone this practice, emphasizing again the antidiscriminatory nature of the law.

One illustrative example may be helpful: A 4-month-old infant presents with fever, cough, and wheezing. The child does not appear to be in extremis and clinically seems sufficiently stable to be sent to a managed care facility two blocks away, where a physician is willing and able to see the patient. However, assume that, normally, to evaluate whether the child is suffering from an emergency medical condition, the emergency physician will obtain a pulse oximetry reading and order a chest x-ray. If the hospital fails to provide these tests for managed care patients before sending them to the managed care facility, then it deviates from its standard screening protocol and its actions violate EMTALA. It is precisely this type of differential treatment that the courts have determined is

not allowed, regardless of the hospital's rationale for treating one class of patients different from another.

Similarly, hospitals cannot set up separate and different screening procedures for Medicaid managed care patients. Some states, hospitals, and managed care entities believe that the "waivers" allow them to alter emergency care of Medicaid patients to accommodate managed care techniques and cut costs. However, these waivers do not allow the states to circumvent the requirements of EMTALA. Hospitals and emergency physicians who participate in such disparate Medicaid screening do so at their own peril. Just in the past year, HCFA has cited hospitals in West Virginia, Georgia, and Colorado for performing differential screening examinations of Medicaid patients.

There is one significant advantage of the courts' interpretation for emergency physicians. The courts hold that the critical element of an EMTALA claim is not the adequacy of the screening examination, but whether the screening examination performed deviated from the hospital's customary procedures to evaluate patients with similar conditions.[33] As long as the hospital and physician act in a manner consistent with standard customary screening procedures, they will not be held liable under EMTALA, even if that standard is inadequate under the state's malpractice law. The courts are not allowing EMTALA to become a federal malpractice law and are concerned more with the process of the examination rather than its outcome. Hospitals and physicians will not be held civilly liable for failure to stabilize an emergency medical condition that has not been discovered.[33]

Unfortunately, HCFA, unlike the courts, feels perfectly comfortable second guessing the judgment of physicians. It has cited numerous hospitals by not accepting the judgment of the examining physician, instead holding that the physician failed to detect an emergency medical condition and, therefore, failed to stabilize that emergency condition prior to "transferring" the patient from the emergency department — regardless of whether the emergency physician found an emergency medical condition or believed that the patient was stable at the time of discharge.

What If a Managed Care Plan Refuses to Authorize a Patient Visit?

Managed care organizations (MCOs) provide

(or deny) authorization for payment only. They cannot authorize or deny treatment. Whether an MCO has authorized payment for an emergency department visit is irrelevant under EMTALA.

According to HCFA regulations, managed health care plans "cannot deny a hospital permission to examine or treat their enrollees, they may only state what they will and will not pay for, and regardless of whether a hospital is to be reimbursed for the treatment, it is obligated to provide the services specified in COBRA."[34]

The hospital must provide the mandated screening examination regardless of whether it will be paid by the MCO and regardless of whether the MCO is able to see that patient immediately at its own clinic. Because the authorization is for payment only and not treatment, MCOs have no EMTALA liability for denying someone an MSE. Only hospitals have a legal obligation to provide the MSE, and they will be held to that standard regardless of the financial pressures placed on them by MCOs.

Can Emergency Department Personnel Wait for MCO Authorization Before Performing the MSE?

No. Waiting for an MCO gatekeeper to call and authorize payment for a patient's visit is an EMTALA violation. The law contains a "no delay" provision, which reads as follows: "A hospital may not delay provision of an appropriate medical screening examination or necessary stabilizing treatment . . . in order to inquire about the individual's method of payment or insurance status."[35]

When Congress passed this law, it recognized that care delayed is care denied. If hospitals were not prohibited from delaying screening examinations or stabilizing treatment to patients without guaranteed payment, the purpose of EMTALA would be defeated. Hospitals, for economic reasons, would treat paying patients first and force those without insurance to wait.

The HCFA implementing regulations mirror congressional intent regarding this no delay provision. Although the regulations do allow emergency departments to follow reasonable registration processes, including requesting information about insurance, HCFA specifically states that such procedures must not delay or impede provision of the MSE or necessary treatment, and the same registration procedures must be applied equally to everyone.[36]

Hospitals that delay a patient's access to the MSE while waiting for a return telephone call and authorization are violating the law and may be investigated, cited, fined, and potentially even terminated from participating in Medicare.

Does a No Delay Provision Mean Hospitals Cannot Tell Patients That Payment Was Denied?

The answer to this question is unknown. Many hospitals correctly triage patients without asking about their insurance status. The emergent patients are taken directly to the emergency department, examined, and treated. Nonurgent patients are sent to the waiting room and are provided the MSE in the order in which they arrived — a perfectly appropriate approach because it is nondiscriminatory. While the patients are waiting to be seen, the hospitals obtain insurance information and call the MCOs for authorization of the services requested. If the MCO calls back and denies payment authorization after the patient is examined, treated and released, so be it. If, however, the denial is obtained before the patient is examined, then these hospitals inform the patient of the payment denial and leave the decision of whether to stay up to the patient.

There are two legal pitfalls in this apparently reasonable scenario. First, if the patient chooses to leave the emergency department after being told of the payment authorization denial and, thus, refuses the MSE, the hospital must handle the interaction very carefully to avoid EMTALA liability. Patients do have the right to refuse the MSE. However, the federal courts presume that the patient requested emergency care and place the burden of proof on the hospital to demonstrate that the patient either explicitly revoked the request for treatment or that the hospital offered the screening examination and the patient refused and left the hospital voluntarily.

As HCFA requires in its rules and regulations, the hospital must "take all reasonable steps to secure the individual's written informed consent to refuse" the screening examination.[38] Hospitals should have the patient sign a "Refusal to Be Screened" form (Figure 1). The hospital must inform the person of its obligations under EMTALA and explain the benefits of the offered screening examination and the risks involved in refusing that screening examination before obtaining the patient's signature. If the patient refuses to sign the form, a hospital representative should document that the MSE was offered

Figure 1

Sample form for patient's refusal to be screened

●   ●   ●   ●   ●

Informed Consent to Refuse Examination, Treatment or Transfer

I understand that the hospital has offered: (Check all that apply.)

A. ☐ To examine me (the patient) to determine whether I have an emergency medical condition, or

B. ☐ To provide medical treatment or to provide stabilizing treatment for my emergency condition (AMA), or

C. ☐ To provide a medically appropriate transfer to another medical facility.

The hospital and physician have informed me that the **benefits** that might reasonably be expected from the offered services are:

_____

_____

and the **risks** of refusing the offered services are:

_____

_____

Physician Documentation

☐ The patient appears competent and capable of understanding risks.

☐ Alternative treatments discussed with the patient.

☐ Patient's family involved.   ☐ Family not available.   ☐ Patient does not want family involved

Signature of Physician _____

I understand that if I refuse the offered services, I am doing so against medical advice. I understand that my refusal may result in a worsening of my condition and could pose a threat to my life, health, and medical safety. I understand I am welcome to return at any time. I choose to refuse the offered services.

Signature/Patient or Legally Responsible Person _____

Print Name _____ Address _____

City _____ State/Zip _____ Date _____ Time _____

Witness/Signature _____ Print Name _____

Patient or person legally responsible for patient was offered but refused to sign form after explanation of their rights and the risks/benefits of the services offered:

Hospital representative who witnessed refusal to sign _____

Date _____ Time _____

Carolinas HealthCare System
Informed Consent to Refuse Examination, Treatment, or Transfer

ADDRESSOGRAPH

White/Medical Record   Yellow/Risk Management   Pink/Q/A

4243
E(0696)BG

and the person refused to accept the examination and refused to sign the refusal form.

The second caveat is that HCFA believes that telling patients they may have to pay for the offered services is economic coercion. HCFA is cognizant of the economic duress of this process and warns hospitals as follows: "Hospitals should not attempt to coerce individuals into making judgments against their best interest by informing them that they will have to pay for their care if they remain."[39] Several organizations insist there is no statutory authority for this HCFA interpretation; in fact, this is often referred to as "HCFA's gag rule." These organizations believe that patients should be given financial information so they can make informed decisions about how, where, and when to obtain health care services. HCFA has convened a panel of experts to examine this issue and other issues regarding interpretation and application of EMTALA but has not yet changed its position. There has been no litigation associated with this practice, so there is no precedent to guide a hospital in assessing the risks associated with informing patients of managed care denials.

State laws further complicate the issue of informing patients of financing consequences. Some states, including California, Florida, and Maryland, prohibit authorization calls from occurring until after the patient is provided the MSE and any necessary stabilizing treatment.[40] Emergency physicians must understand their own state laws before deciding whether to inform patients of authorization denials.

Can an MSE Be Performed Outside the Emergency Department?

After triage, many hospitals send pregnant women with isolated, pregnancy-related complaints to a labor and delivery (L&D) area outside the emergency department for evaluation and treatment. The L&D examination constitutes the hospital's MSE for these patients. These protocols comply with EMTALA as long as all patients with these complaints go to L&D for their MSE. If only private patients or only Medicaid patients or only managed care patients go to a designated L&D area and all others remain in the emergency department or are sent to a different L&D area, discriminatory treatment in violation of EMTALA has occurred.

The same considerations apply to an urgent care or fast track setting, whether hospital-based or within the emergency department. The parameters for distributing the patients must be

nondiscriminatory and based only on medically indicated triage criteria.

However, patients must not be sent outside the hospital to receive the MSE. Several hospitals have been cited for failure to perform an MSE because they triaged patients to a private physician's office or a managed care clinic at the request of the patient's physician.[26]

Rural hospitals that do not have an emergency physician on duty 24 hours a day often have nurses triage patients who present to the emergency department and then contact the hospital's on-call physician. In many of these situations, the patient is sent to the on-call physician's office for examination and treatment. HCFA condemns such a practice, holding that the on-call physician must come to the emergency department in all cases to perform the MSE in the hospital's emergency department.[23]

Stabilization

After performing the MSE, the emergency physician must determine and document the presence or absence of an emergency medical condition. Only when the hospital actually determines that the patient has an emergency medical condition do the EMTALA stabilization and transfer requirements kick in. If an emergency medical condition is found, the hospital must provide further medical examination and treatment, within the staff and facilities available to the hospital, required to stabilize the emergency medical condition. If the hospital cannot stabilize the patient's condition, then it must transfer the patient to a hospital that can.[41]

Stabilized Defined

Because Congress passed EMTALA to prevent inappropriate transfers, the legal language defines stabilization in reference to the ability to move patients safely between hospitals.

The term "stabilized," according to the law, means that no material deterioration of the emergency medical condition is likely, within reasonable medical probability, to result from or occur during the transfer, or that the pregnant woman with contractions has delivered (including the placenta).[42]

This is an objective standard that will be judged under a professional standard of care measure, just as ordinary malpractice claims are. However, only when a patient's condition actually deteriorates sometime during or after a transfer and the patient experiences an adverse outcome will the issue of stabilization arise. It will appear likely, particularly in hindsight, that the patient was not completely stabilized prior to transfer.

Staff and Facilities Available

Hospitals must use all ancillary personnel, diagnostic testing, and other resources at its disposal in an attempt to stabilize the patient's condition. This requirement includes the use of any on-call physician whose services may be necessary to help stabilize the patient. These stabilization efforts must be conducted before any transfer occurs, even though MCOs may pressure the hospital to do the least amount possible before it transfers the patient to the MCO facility for definitive treatment.

No Delay Provision

Similar to the requirement that the MSE must not be delayed because of the patient's insurance status, any necessary stabilizing treatment must not be delayed for insurance reasons. If the hospital determines that the patient has an emergency medical condition, it cannot wait to provide stabilizing treatment to obtain authorization from an MCO or to arrange a transfer to a managed care facility. Stabilizing treatment must be provided the same way it would be for any other patient.

Other Stabilization Issues

In the case of Baby K,[43] the 4th Circuit Court of Appeals ruled that a hospital must provide respiratory support to an anencephalic infant despite the fact that all examining physicians felt intubation and ventilation were "inappropriate medical treatment" and morally and ethically wrong. The court noted that the plain language of EMTALA requires mandatory stabilization regardless of moral or ethical considerations and held that Congress was the appropriate branch of government to remedy this concern. This case raises issues in the care of terminally ill patients when advance directives are not immediately available in the emergency department.

When and if a patient is stabilized has significant ramifications for hospitals and physicians. Once patients are stabilized, EMTALA no longer applies and hospitals are free to deny further treatment or transfer patients for purely economic reasons. On-call physicians can refuse to treat or admit stable patients and insist they be transferred because of lack of insurance or as requested by MCOs. Other hospitals do not have to accept stable patients in transfer. However, a physician cannot refuse to come in to determine whether a patient has an emergency medical condition until an MCO authorizes the consultation, because doing so would delay examination or stabilization of the patient for insurance reasons.

Whenever emergency physicians determine and document the presence of an emergency medical condition, they should always document whether the patient has been stabilized prior to discharge, admission, or transfer.

Physician On-Call Requirements

EMTALA is now the on-call policy of every hospital in the country. The law requires hospitals to provide on-call physicians to help care for patients presenting to their emergency departments.[5] The law does not directly mandate that physicians take call. Physicians only voluntarily accept EMTALA responsibilities by agreeing to participate in on-call coverage for the emergency department in the hospital's medical staff bylaws and department rules and regulations.[7]

Which Physicians Must Take Call?

HCFA regulations specify that physicians generally available to patients at the hospital are considered to be available for the treatment of patients presenting to the emergency department regardless of whether those physicians had previously been obligated by the hospital to provide emergency services.[44]

For example, if ophthalmologists or urologists regularly admit patients, provide consultations, and perform surgery at the hospital, then the service of an ophthalmologist or urologist must be provided when needed by patients in the emergency department.

When Must On-Call Physicians Respond?

On-call physicians must respond to the emergency department whenever they are needed to help determine if a patient has an emergency medical condition or whenever they are needed to help stabilize a patient already diagnosed with an emergency medical condition. On-call physicians are part of the emergency department's capabilities — "ancillary services routinely available to the emergency department" — to determine if the patient has an emergency medical condition.[44] The law directly states that they must be available to provide stabilizing treatment.[5]

On-call physicians must respond regardless of whether the patient belongs to an MCO with which they participate. For example, the emergency physician examines a patient and believes the patient has appendicitis or an acute abdomen. The emergency physician asks the on-call surgeon to come in and evaluate the patient to determine if an emergency medical condition exists. This surgeon must come to the emergency department and examine the patient. If the surgeon decides that the patient does have appendicitis or an acute abdomen, both of which are emergency medical conditions, then the surgeon must proceed with stabilizing treatment, which generally is immediate surgery. If the on-call surgeon refuses to come in or asks the emergency physician to transfer the patient to a hospital that participates in the patient's managed care plan, then he has violated EMTALA. Why? Because he has failed to provide an MSE and stabilizing treatment and has inappropriately transferred the patient from the hospital.

When an on-call physician's obligations are triggered is determined by the emergency physician. Thus, whether patients have emergency medical conditions and when and if they are stable can be contentious issues between emergency physicians and on-call physicians.

The law also requires the on-call physician to respond within a "reasonable period of time."[5] Again, the emergency physician decides what is reasonable. The emergency physician who is caring for an unstable patient must decide how long is a reasonable period of time to wait for the on-call surgeon before making other arrangements to stabilize the patient. If the emergency physician has to transfer a patient because of the unavailability or the refusal of the on-call physician, the hospital must send that physician's name and address with the patient to an accepting facility, with the obvious ramifications.[45]

Obviously, hospitals, their medical staffs, and the emergency department must cooperate to provide on-call services to emergency patients. The hospital and the medical staff must be educated in their on-call responsibilities and implement policies and procedures to meet those duties. Similarly, hospitals should carefully identify which physician services will be available to the emergency department and at what times they will be available. Hospitals should draft those policies, procedures, and availability standards carefully, using words such as "reasonable" or "appropriate" and avoiding specific time frames, such as "within 30 minutes." Otherwise, they will hold themselves to a standard they may not be able to meet and expose themselves to liability for failure to follow their own rules.[46]

Transfer of Unstable Patients

Before transferring any patient out of the emergency department, the emergency physician must first determine if the patient is stable, as defined by law. EMTALA regulates the transfer of unstable patients only; it does not apply to the transfer of stable patients. If no emergency medical condition is found, the patient is considered stable. The determination of whether a patient is stable must be made at the time of transfer to be valid under the law.[47]

An emergency physician can transfer unstable patients for only one of two reasons: either the transfer is medically indicated or the patient requests it.

Medically Indicated Transfers

A transfer is "medically indicated" if the reason for the transfer is to obtain a higher level of medical care necessary to treat the patient's condition, a level of care that is not available at the transferring facility. For example, to obtain needed neurosurgical services when the transferring facility does not have a neurosurgeon on staff.

To effect a medically indicated transfer in compliance with EMTALA, the emergency physician must do the following[47]:

- "Certify" that the benefits of the transfer to the patient outweigh the risks of the transfer.
- Obtain the patient's informed consent.
- Arrange an "appropriate transfer" as defined by law.

Transfer Certification. The transfer certificate is a legal document that must be completed carefully. It must be in writing and should include the statutory language as follows: "Based on the information available to me at the time of this transfer, the medical benefits reasonably expected from the provision of appropriate medical treatment at another medical facility outweigh the increased risk to the individual and, in the case of labor, to the unborn child from effecting the transfer."[47] Figure 2 includes a sample transfer certificate.

The physician must write a summary of the risks and benefits on which the certification is

Figure 2

Sample form for medically indicated transfer, with transfer certificate

Medically Indicated Transfer
(To be completed by Transferring Physician)

NOTICE OF HOSPITAL RESPONSIBILITIES

Pursuant to Title 42 U.S.C., Section 1395dd(c)(l)(A)(i), you are hereby notified that this hospital has the following responsibilites under the law:

* This hospital must provide a medical screening examination to any person presenting at the emergency department to determine whether the patient suffers from an emergency medical condition or from pregnancy with contractions present.

* In the event that an emergency medical condition or pregnancy with contractions is present this hospital must provide such additional medical examinations and treatment as may be required to stabilize the medical condition (to stabilize a pregnancy with contractions present the hospital must deliver the baby and the placenta), except in the case where the benefits of transfer outweigh the risks that may arise from or during transfer.

* In the event the hospital deems it in the best interests of the patient (or in the case of pregnancy, the unborn child) to transfer the patient to another medical facility, the hospital must require your physician to execute a transfer certificate complying with the standards of the law, and further must provide a medically appropriate transfer of the patient.

PHYSICIAN'S CERTIFICATE OF TRANSFER

A. MEDICAL CONDITION IDENTIFIED

Check Box No. 1 <u>or</u> No. 2

☐ 1. Patient screened - no emergency medical condition identified

☐ 2. Patient screened - an emergency medical condition was identified

Diagnosis_____

C. TRANSPORT (do both)

☐ Appropriate transfer initiated for patient

☐ Patient transfer order form completed

B. STABILIZATION

If checked Box No. 2 in A., then check <u>one</u> of the following:

☐ 2a. **Stabilization established:** the patient's emergency medical condition has been treated such that within reasonable medical probability no material deterioration of the condition is likely to arise from or during the transfer of the individual, or with respect to the pregnant woman who is having contractions, the woman has delivered (including the placenta).

☐ 2b. **Stabilization not established:** The patient is not stable, but the transfer is medically indicated and in the best interests of the patient.

D. ANALYSIS OF BENEFITS VS RISKS OF TRANSFER

BENEFITS:_____   RISKS:_____

_____   _____

☐ Obtain level of care not available at this facility   ☐ Worsening of your condition or death if you stay here

Also, all transfers have the risks of traffic delays, accidents during transport, rough weather, rough roads, and the limitations of equipment and personnel in the vehicle, all of which potentially endanger the health, medical safety, and survival of the patient.

E. ☐ Based on the above and my personal judgement, I hereby certify that based on the information available to me <u>at the time of transfer,</u> the medical benefits reasonably expected from the provision of approriate medical care at another medical facility outweigh the increased risk to the individual and in the case of a woman in labor, the unborn child, of the transfer.

Physician's Signature _____ Physicians Name_____ Date _____ Time _____

IF NO PHYSICIAN IS PRESENT: RN'S Signature_____ Date _____ Time _____

RN'S Name _____ on verbal order of Dr._____ **PHYSICIAN MUST COUNTERSIGN WITHIN 48 HOURS.**

PATIENT CONSENT TO TRANSFER

I hereby consent to transfer to another facility. I understand that it is the opinion of the physician responsible for my care that the benefits of transfer outweigh the risks of transfer. I have been informed of the risks and benefits upon which this transfer is being made these risks and benefits and consent to transfer.

Signature of Patient or Responsible Party_____ Date _____ Time _____

Signature of Witness _____ Date _____ Time _____

Carolinas HealthCare System
Medically Indicated Transfer

ADDRESSOGRAPH

White/Medical Record   Yellow/Transfer with Patient   Pink/Q/A

4240
E(0696)BG

based.[48] These risks and benefits should be expansively documented; failure to include all foreseeable risks can invalidate a patient's informed consent. The physician's certification must be based on information available at the time of transfer, not when the physician initially examined the patient. Thus, an unstable patient should be reevaluated just prior to transfer to ensure that the transfer is still medically appropriate.

The physician should certify that the transfer is medically indicated only if the patient is being transferred to a facility with physician or hospital resources that are not available at the transferring facility. Transfers of unstable patients to facilities with lesser capabilities or those reasonably the same as the transferring facility are violations of EMTALA.

Similarly, a hospital should not transfer a patient to a hospital mandated by an MCO unless the transferring hospital cannot handle the patient's condition and unless the MCO facility has the necessary resources and physicians available to manage the patient's condition and foreseeable complications.[49] Otherwise, the transferring hospital is liable under EMTALA for failure to arrange an appropriate transfer.

For hospitals that do not have an emergency physician on duty in the emergency department at the time of the transfer, a "qualified medical person" may sign the certification. This person must consult with the physician who will be responsible for determining that the benefits of the transfer outweigh its risks and be responsible for the transfer.[50] That physician must later countersign the certification.[50]

Informed Consent. The hospital should obtain informed consent and a signature on the transfer form from the patient and/or the patient's family prior to transfer. The informed consent should also include the nonmedical risks of transfer, such as risks associated with helicopter or ambulance transport. If the patient or a family member is physically unable to consent at the time of transfer, the physician should proceed with the transfer, assuming that implied consent is present under the emergency doctrine.

Appropriate Transfer. The third element of a legal, medically indicated transfer is the arrangement of an "appropriate transfer," as described later.

Patient-Requested Transfers

An unstable patient may ask to be transferred from the emergency department to a different hospital for further stabilizing treatment. Transfers at the request of the patient's private physician, the request of the patient's MCO, or simply to be closer to home all constitute patient-requested transfers: the patient chooses to leave for one of those reasons. The transfer is not to obtain necessary medical services unavailable at the transferring hospital.

The distinction between a patient-requested transfer and a medically indicated transfer is important because the legal elements and the liability exposure of the two types of unstable transfers are distinctly different.

To legally transfer an unstable patient who requests transfer, the hospital must do the following[51]:

- Inform the patient of the hospital's legal obligations under EMTALA.
- Inform the patient of the risks and benefits of transfer, including the travel risks such as motor vehicle collisions or delay secondary to weather or mechanical breakdown.
- Obtain the request for transfer and the reason for transfer in writing.[52]
- Obtain the patient's informed consent, with the patient's signature indicating that the patient is aware of the hospital's obligations and the risks and benefits of the transfer.
- Arrange an "appropriate" transfer.

Figure 3 is a sample form for documenting all of these requirements for a patient-requested transfer. According to HCFA, patient requests for transfer should be unsolicited. It is concerned that patients may be induced to request transfer if they are told they will be financially liable for the services rendered if they remain.[53]

Effecting an Appropriate Transfer

According to EMTALA, transfers of unstable patients, whether medically indicated or patient requested, must meet certain conditions to be considered appropriate and legal. The five elements specified in the law are as follows[54]:

- The transferring hospital must provide medical treatment, within its capacity, that minimizes the risks to the individual's health and, in the case of a woman in labor, the health of the unborn child. This means that the hospital does whatever it can to stabilize the patient while waiting for the transfer to occur. This includes the use of on-call physicians, who may not want to come to

Figure 3

Sample form for patient-requested transfer

Transfer Requested by Patient
(To be completed by Transferring Physician)

NOTICE OF HOSPITAL RESPONSIBILITIES

Pursuant to Title 42 U.S.C., Section 1395dd(c)(l)(A)(i), you are hereby notified that this hospital has the following responsibilities under the law:

* This hospital must provide a medical screening examination to any person presenting at the emergency department to determine whether the patient suffers from an emergency medical condition or from pregnancy with contractions present.

* In the event that an emergency medical condition or pregnancy with contractions is present this hospital must provide such additional medical examinations and treatment as may be required to stabilize the medical condition (to stabilize a pregnancy with contractions present the hospital must deliver the baby and the placenta), except in the case where the benefits of transfer outweigh the risks that may arise from or during transfer.

* In the event that the hospital deems it in the best interests of the patient (or in the case of pregnancy, the unborn child) to transfer the patient to another medical facility, the hospital must require your physician to execute a transfer certificate complying with the standards of the law, and further must provide a medically appropriate transfer of the patient.

PHYSICIAN'S FINDINGS, RECOMMENDATIONS, AND EXPLANATION OF RISKS AND BENEFITS

A. MEDICAL CONDITION IDENTIFIED

Check Box No. 1 <u>or</u> No. 2

☐ 1. Patients screened - no emergency medical condition identified

☐ 2. Patients screened - an emergency medical condition was identified

Diagnosis _____

B. STABILIZATION

If checked Box No. 2 above in **A**, then check <u>one</u> of the following:

☐ 2a. **Stabilization established:** The patient's emergency medical condition has been treated such within reasonable medical probability no material deterioration of the condition is likely to arise from or during the transfer of the individual, or with respect to the pregnant woman who is having contractions, the woman has delivered (including the placenta).

☐ 2b. **Stabilization not established:** The patient has not been stabilized, however, the <u>patient</u> has requested transfer to another hosptial in writing after being informed of the hospital's obligations and risks of transfer under COBRA.

C. RECOMMENDATION

Check BOX No. 1 <u>or</u> No. 2

In the treating physician's opinion, transfer of the patient at this time is:

☐ 1. Not a significant threat to health and safety of the patient

☐ 2. A significant threat to the health and safety of the patient

D. TRANSPORT (do both)

☐ Appropriate transfer initiated for patient

☐ Patient transfer order form completed

E. NOTICE OF RISKS AND BENEFITS OF TRANSFER

You are hereby informed that the possible risks and benefits of transfer to the patient at this time include:

RISKS: _____   **BENEFITS:** _____

☐ **Worsening of current medical condition**

☐ **Possible death**

Also, all transfers have the risks of traffic delays, accidents during transport, rough weather, rough roads, and the limitations of equipment and personnel in the vehicle, all of which potentially endanger the health, medical safety, and survival of the patient.

PATIENT-INITIATED REQUEST FOR TRANSFER

I understand and have considered the hospital's responsibilities, the risks and benefits of the transfer, and the physician's recommendation. I request upon my own suggestion and not that of the hospital, physician, or anyone associated with the hospital that I (the patient) be tranferred to:

_____

The reason I request transfer is _____

Signature of Patient or Responsible Party _____ Date _____ Time_____

Signature of Witness _____ Date _____ Time_____

Carolinas HealthCare System
Transfer Requested by Patient

White/Patient Record   Yellow/Transfer with Patient   Pink/Q/A

4242
E(0696)BG

ADDRESSOGRAPH

the emergency department and take care of patients who are about to be transferred.

- The receiving facility must have available space and qualified personnel for the treatment of the individual and must have agreed to accept transfer of the individual and provide appropriate medical treatment. Emergency physicians should speak with a physician who is authorized to accept transfer patients for the receiving facility and ascertain that the facility has the appropriate space, equipment, and personnel to handle the patient's condition. To transfer, for example, a neurosurgical patient to a hospital that does not have a functional CT scanner would be an EMTALA violation.

- The transferring hospital must send to the receiving facility copies of all medical records and diagnostic studies available at the time of the transfer, including records related to the individual's condition, observations of signs or symptoms, preliminary diagnosis, treatment provided, copies of any informed written consent or physician certification, and the name and address of any on-call physician who refused or failed to appear within a reasonable time to provide necessary stabilizing treatment. Never delay a transfer while gathering tests, studies, and medical records to send with the patient. When necessary, fax machines can solve paperwork issues and taxicabs can transport x-rays. The name and address of an on-call physician who refused or failed to appear must be included whenever such a situation led to the patient being transferred. If the emergency physician fails to send along the name and address of the on-call physician, the emergency physician violates EMTALA and is subject to fines and liability.

- The transfer must be effected through qualified personnel and transportation equipment, as required, including the use of necessary and medically appropriate life support measures during transfer. The mode of transport and the equipment and personnel selected to transfer the patient must be sufficient to manage effectively any foreseeable complication of the patient's condition that could arise en route. The transfer may require flying the patient by helicopter with a physician and nurse in attendance or using an ordinary car with a

family member. Each case will depend on the patient's individual circumstances, but this will be another physician action that will be judged retrospectively. Physicians should carefully document the transfer decision-making processes. For example, in the case of *Owens v Nacogdoches County Hospital*, the hospital paid $50,000 in emotional distress damages for transferring an obstetrics patient in early labor in a "1976 Pinto in bad condition" even though no complication occurred en route and no harm came to the patient or her baby. In fact, the woman was not even admitted at the receiving facility and did not deliver until four days later.[55] The court felt that the patient should have been transferred in an ambulance with a nurse or physician in attendance, just in case the patient delivered.

- The transfer must meet such other requirements as the Secretary of Health and Human Services may find necessary in the interest of the health and safety of individuals transferred. To date, the regulations contain no new mandates from the Secretary.

Transfer of Stable Patients

Stable patients can be transferred for any reason, including economic reasons. Patients who do not have an emergency medical condition are considered stable, so the transfer of these patients is not governed by EMTALA. Legally, when transferring stable patients, the hospital is not required to arrange an appropriate transfer or have the physician certify the transfer. However, hospitals should arrange all transfers as appropriate transfers. This provides uniformity in hospital policy and practice, ensures that the hospital routinely adheres to EMTALA transfer requirements, and conforms to the expected standard of care for transfers.

For example, reconsider the case of the emergency physician who was concerned a patient had acute appendicitis. The on-call surgeon appears and, in his judgment, determines that the patient does not have appendicitis at that time but needs to be admitted and further evaluated over time. The surgeon estimates that the patient should be reexamined in four to six hours. Because the patient is determined not to have an emergency medical condition at that time, the patient is considered stable. It would be allowable to transfer this patient to another

Figure 4
Sample patient transfer order

● ● ● ● ●

Patient Transfer Order
(To be completed by Transferring Physician)

Patient Name _____

Reason for Patient Transfer (complete either Section A _or_ B, but not both).

| ☐ A. Unstable Patient (check either Box 1 _or_ Box 2.) | ☐ B. Stable Patient |

A. Unstable Patient (check either Box 1 _or_ Box 2.)
1. ☐ Patient requested transfer in writing after risks & benefits explained
2. ☐ Transfer medically indicated in patient's best interest

If checked Box 2, then check either Box 2a _or_ 2b.

B. Stable Patient
☐ Transfer medically indicated
☐ Patient requested transfer
☐ HMO   ☐ Private doctor
☐ Other_____

2a. ☐ Our hospital has provided medical treatment within its capacity to minimize the risk to the individuals health and, in the case of a woman in labor, the health of the unborn child; and the treating physician has certified that the medical benefits reasonably expected from the transfer outweigh the risk to the patient from effecting the transfer.

2b. ☐ Our hospital has not provided medical treatment within its capacity because an on-call physician has refused or failed to appear within a reasonable period of time to provide further examination or necessary stabilizing treatment; and the treating physician has certified that at this time the medical benefits reasonably expected from transfer outweigh the increased risks to the patient from the transfer.

Name and address of On-Call Physician _____

For the reasons listed above, I direct that the patient be transferred with the following instructions:

1. ☐ The receiving hospital/physician have agreed to accept this patient in transfer and confirm the availibility of adequate equipment, and qualified personnel necessary for the treatment of this individual.

Destination Hospital _____ Accepting Physician _____

Date _____ Time _____

2. ☐ Copies of available medical record, tests, orders, consents, certification, and radiographic studies to accompany patient.

3. Mode of Transfer ☐ BLS/Ambulance ☐ ALS/Ambulance ☐ Neonatal Unit ☐ Helicopter ☐ Car ☐ Other_____

4. Additional personnel, equipment, or life support services required to accompany patient:_____
_____
_____

5. Medical Orders : _____
_____

6. If radio on-line medical direction is necessary during transfer, control to be exercised by:

☐ This hospital   ☐ Destination hospital   ☐ Other _____   ☐ None necessary

7. Physician's Signature _____   Physician's Name _____

Date _____ Time _____

TO BE COMPLETED BY HOSPITAL STAFF:
Name of Transfer Agency _____ Person Contacted _____
Contacted By _____ Date _____ Time _____
Time of Arrival _____ Time of Transfer _____
NOTES:

Carolinas HealthCare System
Patient Transfer Order

ADDRESSOGRAPH

White/Patient Record   Yellow/Transfer with Patient   Pink/Q/A

4241
E(0696)BG

facility for economic reasons, such as the patient's concerns about his MCO. Compare this situation to one in which the patient has obvious appendicitis. The necessary stabilizing treatment is an operation. The hospital cannot transfer the patient to the MCO facility to have the operation performed. Doing so would constitute a failure to stabilize the patient prior to transfer and a delay in stabilizing treatment based on the patient's insurance status, both of which are EMTALA violations.

The most effective way for the hospital to comply with federally mandated transfer requirements and definition of an appropriate transfer is to use carefully drafted transfer forms and a transfer checklist. Figures 2, 3, and 4 are samples of such forms, and Figure 5 is a sample checklist. Use of the forms documents whether an emergency medical condition was found and if so, whether stabilization was achieved. Such documentation protects the hospital from subsequent EMTALA liability. The courts have uniformly held that a hospital and examining physicians would not be held liable for failure to stabilize any emergency condition that it failed to diagnose.[15] In essence, the thought processes and methods of documenting clinical findings and patient conditions in emergency medicine have been recast by EMTALA. Emergency physicians should document using the terms "presence or absence of an emergency medical condition" and "presence or absence of stabilization" as those terms are defined by EMTALA.

As noted earlier, all patients discharged from the emergency department are considered to have been transferred. Assuming the emergency department discharges only stable patients, the law no longer applies, and emergency department personnel do not need to complete transfer forms. For all patients discharged from the emergency department, emergency physicians must document stability in words that mirror the language of the law. Then, the emergency department can continue to use the standard discharge forms and instructions rather than complete EMTALA transfer forms "transferring" the patient home.

One caveat: HCFA believes that patients discharged from the emergency department and sent directly to physicians' offices, such as patients with fractures or ophthalmologic conditions, are still unstable and must be appropriately transferred and the appropriate forms completed. This unsettling interpretation has not yet been addressed by the courts. Proper discharge documentation in the medical record and in the discharge instructions that contains the elements of an appropriate transfer should be adequate to protect the hospital and the physician. In reality, the elements of an appropriate transfer under EMTALA reflect common sense and sound medical practice of arranging follow-up for patients who need further diagnostic or therapeutic modalities after leaving the emergency department.

Transfer of Psychiatric Patients

The impact of the law on the transfer of psychiatric patients deserves special comment. The question arises when hospitals have on-call psychiatrists and inpatient psychiatric units but admit only insured patients, transferring uninsured patients to a designated state or county psychiatric facility. (For the purpose of this discussion, assume that these patients have undergone an appropriate MSE and any medical condition identified has been treated. In other words, the patients are "medically clear" and only their psychiatric conditions need further attention.)

HCFA specifically defines psychiatric manifestations as being sufficiently severe symptoms to constitute an emergency medical condition.[13] As such, psychiatric patients have a legally defined emergency medical condition that must be stabilized before any transfer can occur.

Apparently, HCFA believes that, for a patient to be psychiatrically stable, the psychiatric condition must be treated definitively. For example, a suicidal patient must be cured of suicidal intent. In an advisory opinion, HCFA stated that the hospital's on-call psychiatrist must come to the emergency department to evaluate such a patient and admit for further treatment the patient who is indeed suicidal.[26] If HCFA is correct, because EMTALA is federal law and preempts state laws, it would render irrelevant state programs set up for the inpatient treatment of psychiatric patients.

However, this HCFA position appears to be far overreaching. What is it about psychiatric patients that leads physicians to conclude that they are suffering from an emergency medical condition? It is the fact that their conditions represent a danger to self or others. If that emergency condition can be stabilized, then the patient can be transferred, even for purely economic reasons, to a state mental health facility. Reread the definition of stabilized: ". . . that no

Figure 5

Sample transfer checklist

The following items must be complete prior to the transfer of any patient from our facility to another acute care facility. Check off items done; send completed checklist to Q/A.

A. Examinations and Treatment

❏ Medical screening examination (MSE) performed, to the extent possible considering the Emergency Department's capabilities and ancillary services and/or on-call physicians available, to determine if the patient is suffering from an emergency medical condition (MSE is only for ED cases), and/or

❏ Treatment provided, including any necessary stabilizing treatment, to the extent possible within the resources and physician personnel available to our facility.

B. Interaction With Accepting Facility

❏ Transfer accepted by appropriate physician and documented on the Patient Transfer Order form.

❏ Transfer accepted by receiving facility.

❏ Receiving hospital has adequate space and qualified personnel to appropriately handle the patient's medical condition.

C. Forms to Complete Prior to Transfer (See transfer form instructions included in this packet):

❏ If this is a **patient-requested transfer:**

    ❏ Complete the **Transfer Requested By Patient** form, *and*

    ❏ Complete the **Patient Transfer Order** form

    or

❏ If this is a **medically indicated transfer:**

    ❏ Complete the **Medically Indicated Transfer** form, *and*

    ❏ Complete the **Patient Transfer Order** form

D. Transfer Procedure

❏ Arrange transfer of the patient through qualified personnel and transfer equipment as appropriate to the patient's condition.

❏ Send copies of pertinent patient records with patient to receiving facility.

    ❏ Tests: ❏ Labs   ❏ X-rays   ❏ ECGs   ❏ Monitor strips   ❏ ABGs

        ❏ Others: _____

    ❏ Medical records

    ❏ Transfer forms

❏ Obtain patient's vital signs and reassess patient's medical condition just prior to the time of transport and document in medical record.

❏ Give nursing report to receiving hospital.

❏ Send patient's belongings with the patient.

❏ Notify patient's family.

RN Name: _____

Signature: _____

Date: _____   Time: _____

Imprint patient's ID here.

Send complete checklist to Q/A.

material deterioration of the emergency medical condition is likely, within reasonable medical probability, to result from or occur during the transfer of the individual from a facility."[42] If the patient is rendered incapable of harming self or others, then that patient should be considered stable according to the language of the law. Restraining the patient appropriately, either through chemical or physical means, clearly prevents that patient from hurting self or others. Therefore, if the physician can ensure that the patient is properly restrained so that the patient cannot harm self or others, then a reasonable interpretation of the law would allow that such a patient is stabilized and that EMTALA requirements have been met.

In these cases, documentation must track the language of the law. Compliance with EMTALA, or ordinary malpractice, will be reviewed retrospectively with the knowledge that the decision was based on the patient's lack of financial resources. Hospitals must carefully select which patients are transferred for economic reasons, ensuring that such transfers occur smoothly and without any substantial risk of harm to the patient.

The advisory committee HCFA recently convened recommended HCFA change its interpretive guidelines to define stability regarding the transfer of psychiatric patients to read exactly as noted above: "The psychiatric patient is considered to be stabilized when he/she is protected and prevented from injuring him/herself or others; for example, the patient is adequately restrained, either chemically or physically." HCFA, though, has not yet adopted the advisory committee's recommendation.

Accepting Transferred Patients

EMTALA enables hospitals to obtain stabilizing treatment for patients who they are unable to stabilize because they lack the necessary resources. EMTALA requires hospitals that can stabilize patients' emergency medical conditions to accept these patients in transfer. Specifically, the law reads as follows: "Hospitals with specialized capabilities or facilities shall not refuse to accept appropriate transfers of individuals who require such specialized capabilities or facilities if the hospital has the capacity to treat the individual."[6]

ACEP was instrumental in this 1989 amendment to prevent the widespread practice of tertiary care hospitals refusing to accept patients in transfer who did not have insurance, a practice that came to be known as "reverse dumping."[16]

"Specialized Capabilities or Facilities." EMTALA does not define what are specialized capabilities or facilities, but the term almost certainly applies to any hospital that has the resources or physician services necessary to manage the patient's emergency medical condition and that are not available to the transferring hospital. The purpose of this nondiscrimination clause is to forbid hospitals to refuse patients on any rationale other than the physical inability to provide the necessary care for the patient.

"Capacity." A hospital may refuse an appropriate transfer only if it does not have the capacity to treat the patient's condition. HCFA defines capacity very generously to include the hospital's past practices of accommodating additional patients in excess of its occupancy limits.[56] If the hospital is not closed to its local EMS system, it probably is not at capacity according to EMTALA.

"Appropriate Transfers." Hospitals are only required to accept "appropriate" transfers. Even if a hospital does have the capacity to manage a patient's condition, if transfer to that hospital is not clearly in the patient's best medical interest, then the hospital does not have to accept the patient. For example, if the transferring hospital clearly has the staff and resources to handle the patient's problem, or if it needs to provide stabilizing treatment before transferring the patient, then the requested hospital may refuse the transfer. A trauma center can refuse a multiple trauma patient with a tension pneumothorax until the transferring hospital places a chest tube, assuming the transferring hospital is capable of inserting chest tubes. However, hospitals that refuse patients in these instances better be right. It is almost certainly safer to make recommendations on how to handle a patient prior to transfer while simultaneously accepting the patient, and thus not delay appropriate transfers or be viewed as refusing to accept the patient for a non medically indicated reason.

Unacceptable reasons for refusing patients in transfer include the following: the patient lacks insurance; the hospital does not participate in the patient's managed care plan; the patient's physician is not on staff at that hospital; the patient received services at a different hospital previously; physician convenience. Also, hospitals may not refuse patients because they are from out-of-county, out-of-state, or

Figure 6
Sample notification of patient rights under EMTALA

IT'S THE LAW!

IF YOU HAVE A MEDICAL EMERGENCY OR ARE IN LABOR

YOU HAVE THE RIGHT TO RECEIVE,

within the capabilities of this hospital's staff and facilities:

• An appropriate medical SCREENING EXAMINATION

• Necessary STABILIZING TREATMENT
(including treatment for an unborn child)

and if necessary

• An appropriate TRANSFER to another facility

even if

YOU CANNOT PAY or DO NOT HAVE MEDICAL INSURANCE

or

YOU ARE NOT ENTITLED TO MEDICARE OR MEDICAID

This hospital (does/does not) participate in the Medicaid program.

outside the hospital's defined referral service area. The law does not provide for such territorial safe harbors. However, hospitals are not obligated to accept transfers from hospitals located outside the boundaries of the United States.[56] (Compare that with a hospital's obligation to provide an MSE to an illegal alien who presents to its emergency department, regardless of whether that person came from outside the borders of the United States to present to the emergency department.)

Hospitals are under this duty to accept patients in transfer even if the patients' insurance or managed care plans will not authorize payment for care.[49] Refusals of transfers on the basis of patients' insurance status are totally illegal.

A hospital must carefully designate who may accept or refuse requested transfers on its behalf. Some hospitals allow their on-call physicians to accept or reject requests to accept patients in transfer. In these cases, the physicians are acting as agents of the hospital, and if they refuse to accept a patient for an inappropriate reason, that refusal will be attributed to the hospital and the hospital will be liable for violating EMTALA. Compare this liability with the practice of physicians who accept or reject patients in their private practices, which is perfectly legal. An appropriate policy would be to designate the emergency department staff to accept or reject all transfer requests from other emergency departments or outpatient facilities. Generally, emergency staff members are knowledgeable about what resources and personnel are available to the hospital at that time and have experience arranging such transfers. Also, patients are frequently "advertised" as needing one subspecialist and later determined to need a different subspecialist; after evaluating the patient, the emergency physician can marshall the appropriate hospital resources and personnel to handle the patient's condition.

The EMTALA nondiscrimination clause also applies to requests for transfer from hospital inpatient units, as well as transfer requests from emergency departments. In these situations, hospitals should designate either the on-call physicians or a small group of physicians who are knowledgeable about EMTALA and facile with the transfer process. The hospital's legal counsel and risk management personnel should be involved in drafting a procedure for the hospital to ensure compliance with the law.

Additional Obligations

Compliance Policies

Hospitals are expressly required to adopt and enforce policies to ensure compliance with EMTALA.[57] The hospital's quality assurance activities, both for the emergency department and hospital-wide, should include review of transfers in and out of the hospital as well as other EMTALA issues.

Central Log

Hospitals must maintain a central log of all patients presenting to the emergency department requesting examination or treatment. The log must contain the name of the patient and the disposition, including whether the patient refused treatment, whether the hospital refused to provide treatment, whether the patient was admitted, treated, and stabilized or transferred, or discharged.[58] Although not technically required, hospitals should also include the date and time of the patient's presentation as well as the other information required by JCAHO.

Medical Record

A medical record should also be kept for all patients presenting to the emergency department.[19] If a hospital uses other locations than its emergency department to perform screening examinations, such as the labor and delivery unit, then those areas must also keep a log and a medical record of patients presenting for examination and treatment.

The hospital must maintain medical records for patients transferred to or from the hospital for a period of five years from the date of transfer.[59] Hospitals must also have systems to retrieve these transfer records for HCFA to review on request.

Signage

The hospital must conspicuously post a sign in the emergency department specifying the rights of persons under EMTALA and whether the hospital participates in the Medicare or Medicaid program (Figure 6).[60] Even the exact content, size of the sign, and point size of the writing on the sign are specified by HCFA.[61]

Reporting EMTALA Violations

A hospital must report to HCFA "anytime it has reason to believe it may have received an individual who has been transferred in an unstable emergency medical condition from another hospital in violation of . . . [EMTALA]."[62] The American Hospital Association contends that HCFA's reporting mandate is not supported in the language of the statute. However, HCFA has already cited one New York hospital for failure to report an EMTALA violation by another hospital.[63] Emergency physicians should report suspected EMTALA violations to their hospital legal departments; the reporting requirement rests with the hospital. Hospital legal counsel and risk management should at least address the issue in some manner.

Enforcement

HCFA is charged with enforcing EMTALA requirements and investigating potential violations. HCFA uses state survey agencies to conduct the actual investigations, and HCFA's regional offices decide whether hospitals have violated the law.

Termination From Medicare

If a regional office finds that a hospital has violated EMTALA, it has the power to terminate the hospital's Medicare provider agreement with the federal government, a certain death penalty for any hospital.

The official position of HCFA is that any EMTALA violation constitutes an "immediate threat to patients' health and safety," and it instructs its regional offices to implement 23-day termination procedures in all cases any time they believe a hospital has violated EMTALA.[64] If the hospital "comes into compliance" within 23 days, that is, solves the identified problems and properly disciplines the offending physicians and hospital personnel to HCFA's satisfaction, HCFA will stop the termination process. Hospitals really have only 19 days: the official letter of final termination is sent on day 19 and effective on day 23, and between days 19 and 21, HCFA will place notification in local newspapers informing the public it is terminating the hospital from the Medicare program.[65] These termination proceedings contain absolutely no due process, and there is no right to a pretermination hearing. HCFA's decision to terminate the hospital based on medical negligence is made solely by nonmedically trained HCFA regional administrators.

However, many of HCFA's regional offices use 90-day, not 23-day, proceedings, and many use peer review organizations to obtain medical opinion prior to terminations. But, there is widespread inconsistency among HCFA's 10 regional offices.

To date, HCFA has investigated approximately 2,500 complaints of hospitals alleged to have violated EMTALA. HCFA now investigates more than 400 hospitals a year, and the numbers are increasing. In only about 25% of the investigations is the hospital actually found to be in violation of EMTALA.[66,67]

Approximately a dozen hospitals have been permanently terminated from the Medicare program, although a few of those were later recertified to participate.[66,67] HCFA's goal is not to destroy hospitals, but to force them into compliance with the law and, thus, deliver medical services that do not jeopardize the health and safety of patients.

Physicians, too, may be terminated from the Medicare program under the standard of a "gross and flagrant, or repeated" violation. HCFA defines a gross and flagrant violation as one that presents an imminent danger to the health, safety, or well-being of the individual who seeks emergency examination and treatment or places that individual unnecessarily in a high-risk situation.[68]

Civil Monetary Penalties

If HCFA finds that a hospital has violated EMTALA, it refers the case to the Office of the Inspector General (OIG) for potential civil monetary penalties. The case also is referred to the Office of Civil Rights (OCR), which will investigate whether the hospital still has "community service assurance" provisions under the Hill-Burton Act of 1946. Hill-Burton provided construction and modernization grants to hospitals that, in turn, promised to provide emergency services to persons who worked or lived in the hospital's service area regardless of their ability to pay for those services.[69] The OCR may also investigate whether a hospital has violated an individual's civil rights.

The OIG can impose a maximum civil monetary penalty of $50,000 per violation against physicians. The penalty for a hospital with more than 100 beds can be as high as $50,000, and $25,000 if less than 100 beds.[70] The standard for imposing monetary penalties is ordinary negligence. There does not have to be improper motive, and the patient does not have to have suffered harm. These fines are like criminal traffic violations: he who is caught speeding pays the fine, regardless of whether he intended to speed or if anyone was injured as a result of his speeding. Of note is the fact that the fine is for each violation: a single patient encounter can result in multiple violations and multiple fines.

Only a small percentage of hospitals and physicians have actually been fined by the OIG. Unlike HCFA's investigation process, the OIG must conduct professional peer review before making its determination. At least one third of the time that HCFA believes a violation is present, the OIG either finds that no violation existed or finds other evidentiary or public policy reasons not to impose fines. However, the OIG is years behind HCFA in concluding its determinations, which means that the number of fines to date does not reflect the growing number of investigations. The fines have ranged from $1,500 to $150,000 for hospitals and $2,500 to $20,000 for physicians.[66,67]

Also, a number of states, including Texas, California, New York, and Tennessee, impose criminal penalties against hospitals and physicians who violate their state equivalents of EMTALA.[71]

Civil Actions by Hospitals

Hospitals that are "dumped on" in violation of EMTALA may sue the transferring hospitals for financial losses that result from treating inappropriately transferred patients.[72]

Civil Enforcement by Individuals

Any person who is harmed as a direct result of a hospital violation of EMTALA may sue the hospital for damages available under that state's personal injury and malpractice laws.[73] This plaintiff can be not only the patient, but also others, such as family members, who suffered personal harm as a direct result of the violations, including emotional distress, loss of consortium, or wrongful death.[28]

Only hospitals, not physicians, can be sued for damages under EMTALA, and hospitals are directly liable, not vicariously liable, for its physicians' actions. The courts hold that the plain language of the law does not include the physician.[74] However, contractual indemnity provisions and common law indemnity give hospitals the right to seek recourse against physicians whose actions resulted in the hospital's liability.[75]

EMTALA substantially extends hospital and physician liability exposure in a number of ways. Plaintiffs have the right to sue the hospital in either federal or state court, whichever forum they believe is most beneficial to them. Because

EMTALA is federal law and preempts conflicting state laws, it allows plaintiffs to sue under EMTALA and bypass all state malpractice procedure hurdles, essentially rendering irrelevant state tort reform measures painstakingly enacted over the past two decades. For example, some states have one-year statutes of limitations[76]; EMTALA's statute of limitations is two years.[77] Thus, plaintiffs can use EMTALA to avoid a state's short filing time. Similarly, state notice provisions, discovery limitations, review panels, mandatory arbitration, and even sovereign immunity or Good Samaritan immunity are all preempted if the action is brought under EMTALA rather than state malpractice law.[78]

Probably most important is the preemption of expert witness qualifications. Some states, such as North Carolina, require expert witnesses to be in the same specialty as the defendant and have actively practiced that specialty for at least the year prior to the date of the alleged malpractice.[79] If the plaintiff brings the EMTALA claim in federal court, the federal expert witness rules apply, not the state's. The federal rules are generally more liberal than state rules.

Contrary to state procedural laws, state substantive laws on damages are not preempted by EMTALA. For example, state caps on damages available for pain and suffering remain intact. In the now-famous case *Power v Arlington Hospital*,[80] a woman was awarded $5 million for the hospital's alleged violation of EMTALA. The federal district court reduced the award to $1 million, the maximum allowed under Virginia's malpractice damage cap. The reduction was upheld by the 4th Circuit Court of Appeals and denied review by the U.S. Supreme Court.[81]

Case Discussions

1

HCFA cited the hospital in the first case study for failure to provide the patient an MSE at both the initial visit and the return visit. Under EMTALA, physicians cannot send a patient to the emergency department for medications or for other treatments without the hospital providing an MSE at the time the patient presents. It is irrelevant that a physician examined the patient immediately before sending her to the emergency department: the hospital must provide an MSE to "any individual" who "comes to the emergency department" requesting examination or treatment.

2

In the second case study, HCFA cited the hospital for delaying the patient's MSE while it waited for the gatekeeper to call back. It also cited the hospital for failing to provide the MSE once authorization was denied. The hospital let the patient go to the MCO office without properly obtaining the patient's informed consent to refuse the MSE at the hospital. Moving patients away from the emergency department for completion of the MSE is a risk management minefield. Consult hospital legal counsel before implementing any such process.

3

In the third case study, the emergency physician had the duty to stabilize any patient presenting to the emergency department with an emergency medical condition. Because the emergency physician was unable to stabilize the patient because of a lack of resources available to him, he had to arrange for an appropriate transfer to a facility that could stabilize the patient's condition. It was perfectly reasonable to call the patient's managed care physician to help arrange the transfer. However, EMTALA's no delay provision states that he cannot delay stabilizing treatment because of the patient's insurance status. Once it was determined that the MCO hospital was unable to accept the patient in transfer, it was not appropriate for the emergency physician to wait a few hours for a bed to open up there. He should have thanked the PCP for his efforts and then simply called another hospital that was capable of handling the patient's condition, which, under EMTALA's nondiscrimination provision, would be required to accept the patient in transfer.

The MCO hospital has no liability in this case. It had no available beds and was not accepting local EMS units, clearly demonstrating that it met the law's definition of "at capacity." The second hospital, however, clearly violated EMTALA. It refused to accept the patient in transfer on grounds other than its capacity or that the transfer was inappropriate. Refusing to accept the patient in transfer until authorization is obtained from the MCO also violates the no delay provision.

The PCP has no liability under EMTALA: his authorization is for payment only, not treatment. EMTALA liability rests solely with the hospital regardless of the MCO's pressures to control medical decision-making or movement of patients between facilities.

Even if the MCO had authorized the transfer and the second hospital had agreed to accept the patient, that hospital still violated the no delay provision by delaying the patient's access to stabilizing treatment while waiting for the authorization.

Key Points and Conclusion

The singular purpose of EMTALA is to prevent discriminatory treatment of any person seeking emergency care. Hospitals must screen all who present, stabilize all those with emergency medical conditions, and transfer patients it cannot stabilize to a hospital that must accept the patient if it has the capability and capacity to stabilize the patient's condition. Remember the mantra: no disparate treatment.

The law creates many difficulties for emergency physicians — potential conflicts with hospitals, on-call physicians, and managed care plans, new civil liabilities, potential civil penalties, disruptive investigations by misguided federal regulators. Education, collaboration, and guidance of expert legal counsel can resolve issues with medical colleagues, hospitals, and managed care. Understanding the legal definitions of medical terms and recognizing a new paradigm of medical decision-making and documentation can bridle plaintiffs' lawyers. Always acting under one paramount ethos, the "best interest of the patient," may hold HCFA at bay, at least until the vagaries and inconsistencies in the application of the law are worked out with HCFA and in the courts. Never violate tenets of proper patient care to comply with what HCFA or anyone else says is the law.

Fortunately, from a risk management perspective, knowledge of EMTALA gives emergency physicians the power to create systems of delivering emergency care that minimize the only real risk that matters — the risk to the health and safety of the patients they serve.

- Adopt and enforce a hospital EMTALA policy. Monitor compliance through emergency department and hospital-wide quality assurance efforts.
- Educate the appropriate staff, including on-call physicians and physicians involved in transfers out of or into the hospital, as well as the entire emergency department staff.
- Create a standard medical screening examination process. Formally designate who will perform screening examinations. Define the hospital's standard medical

screening examination process for patients presenting to the emergency department, then be sure it is uniformly applied to all individuals. The scope of the MSE should be reasonably calculated to determine if the patient has an emergency medical condition. Do not delay the screening examination or stabilizing treatment to ask questions about insurance or seek payment authorization from an MCO. Triage all patients, then examine and treat them in the order determined solely by their medical acuity. Obtain written informed consent from any patient who refuses the MSE.

- Provide on-call physicians to the emergency department. The hospital and medical staff, in its rules, regulations, and bylaws, must commit in writing to provide on-call services within reasonable response times to the emergency department.
- Create a system for transferring patients. Build formal transfer agreements with nearby higher-level facilities to accept patients in transfer. Implement formal procedures for all transfers, using transfer packets with instructions, checklists, and properly drafted transfer forms.
- Create a system for accepting patients in transfer. Formally designate who can accept transfers on behalf of the hospital. Define the resources and capacity of the hospital, the times when those resources are available, and parameters controlling rerouting or closure to EMS.
- Review administrative and medical records procedures. Maintain a central log and medical record on each person who presents to the emergency department seeking medical care, even if the patient is not actually seen in the emergency department. Maintain a record of all transfers into and out of the hospital for at least five years. Post signs in the emergency department that outline the hospital's EMTALA obligations. Inform hospital legal counsel whenever the emergency department receives a transfer of an unstable patient in a materially different condition than described by the transferring facility. The hospital may have to report the incident to HCFA.

References

1. 42 USC 1395dd.
2. HR Rep No. 241 I, 99th Cong, 1st Sess 27 (1986).
3. 42 USC 1395dd(a).
4. 42 USC 1395dd(b).
5. 42 USC 1395cc(a)(1)(I)(iii).
6. 42 USC 1395dd(g).
7. *Burditt v Department of HHS*, 934 F2d 1362 (5th Cir 1991).
8. 42 USC 1395dd(e)(4).
9. *Thornton v Southwest Detroit Hospital*, 895 F2d 1131 (6th Cir 1990).
10. *James v Sunrise Hospital*, 86 F3d 885 (9th Cir 1996); *Urban v King*, 43 F3d 523 (10th Cir 1994); *Smith v Richmond Memorial Hospital*, 416 SE2d 689 (Va), *cert denied*, 113 S Ct 442 (1992); But see, *Reynolds v Mercy Hospital*, 861 F Supp 214 (WDNY 1994).
11. 42 USC 1395dd(e)(1)(A).
12. 42 USC 1395dd(e)(1)(B).
13. 42 CFR 489.24(b).
14. HCFA citations against St. John's Hospital in Detroit and Augusta Medical Center in Fishersville, Virginia.
15. *Summers v Baptist Medical Center Arkadelphia*, 91 F3d 1132 (8th Cir 1996); *Vickers v Nash General Hospital, Inc*, 78 F3d 139 (4th Cir 1996).
16. Bitterman RA. A critical analysis of the federal COBRA hospital "antidumping law": ramifications for hospitals, physicians, and effects on access to healthcare. *University of Detroit Mercy Law Review* 1992;70:125-190.
17. *Brooker v Desert Hospital Corp*, 947 F2d 412 (9th Cir 1991); *Cleland v Bronson Health Care Group, Inc*, 917 F2d 266 (6th Cir 1990); *Gatewood v Washington Healthcare Corporation*, 933 F2d 1037 (DC Cir 1991).
18. *Cleland v Bronson Health Care Group, Inc*, 917 F2d 266 (6th Cir 1990); *Roberts v Galen of Virginia, Inc*, 1997 US App Lexis 6554 (6th Cir) April 9, 1997.
19. 42 CFR 489.24(b).
20. *Johnson v University of Chicago Hospitals*, 982 F2d 230 (7th Cir 1992); *Miller v Medical Center of Southwest Louisiana*, 22 F3d 626 (5th Cir 1994).
21. 42 CFR 489.24(a), 42 CFR 482.55.
22. 59 *Federal Register* 32099.
23. Bitterman RA. Recent EMTALA citations demonstrate recurring themes. *Patient Transfer News* 1995;3:3,7.
24. Derlet RW, Kinser D, Ray L, et al. Prospective identification and triage of nonemergency patients out of an emergency department: a 5-year study. *Ann Emerg Med* 1995;25:215-223.
25. 42 CFR 489.24(a).
26. Frew SA. *Patient Transfers: How to Comply With the Law.* Second edition. Dallas: American College of Emergency Physicians; 1995.
27. Medical Screening Examinations. ACEP Council Resolution, approved June 1987.
28. *Correa v Hospital of San Francisco*, 63 F3d 1184 (1st Cir 1995).
29. 103 Stat 2154, 2245 (1989).
30. *Correa v Hospital of San Francisco*, 63 F3d 1184 (1st Cir 1995) quoting, in part, Ralph Waldo Emerson in *Essays: First Series* (1841).
31. *Gatewood v Washington Healthcare Corporation*, 933 F2d 1037 (DC Cir 1991).
32. *Eberhardt v City of Los Angeles*, 62 F3d 1253 (9th Cir 1995); *Baber v Hospital Corp*, 977 F2d 872 (4th Cir 1992); *King v Ahrens* 16 F3d 265 (8th Cir 1994); *Rupp v Anadarko Memorial Hosp*, 43 F3d 519 (10th Cir 1994).
33. *Holcomb v Monahan*, 30 F3d 116 (11th Cir 1994).
34. 59 *Federal Register* 32116.
35. 42 USC 1395dd(h).
36. 59 *Federal Register* 32099.
37. *Stevinson v Enid Health System, Inc.*, 920 F2d 710 (10th Cir 1990).
38. 42 CFR 489.24(c)(2).

39. 59 *Federal Register* 32101.

40. Fla Stat 395.1041(3)(h) 1994; Calif SB 1839, September 1994; MD Health-Gen Code Ann 19-701 (1993).

41. 42 USC 1395dd(b)(1)(A)&(B).

42. 42 USC 1395dd(e)(3)(B).

43. In the Matter of Baby K, 16 F3d 590 (4th Cir 1994).

44. 59 *Federal Register* 32100.

45. 42 USC 1395dd(c)(2)(C).

46. *Marks v Mandell*, 477 So2d 1036 (Fla Dist Ct App 1985).

47. 42 USC 1395dd(c)(1)(A)(ii).

48. 42 CFR 482.24(d)(1)(ii)(B).

49. Wood JP. Emergency physicians' obligations to managed care patients under COBRA. *Acad Emerg Med* 1996;3:794-800.

50. 42 USC 1395dd(c)(1)(A)(iii).

51. 42 USC 1395dd(c).

52. 42 CFR 482.24(d)(1)(ii)(A).

53. 42 CFR 489.24(c)(4).

54. 42 USC 1395dd(c)(2).

55. *Owens v Nacogdoches County Hospital District*, 741 FSupp 1269 (ED Texas 1990).

56. 59 *Federal Register* 32105.

57. 42 USC 1395cc(a)(1)(I)(I).

58. 42 CFR 482.20(3).

59. 42 USC 1395cc(a)(1)(I)(ii).

60. 42 USC 1395cc(a)(1)(N)(iii).

61. Department of Health and Human Services, HCFA, Interim Manual Instructions Recommending Publication of Sign, Transmittal #IM-90-1, June 1990.

62. 42 CFR 489.20(m).

63. Frew SA. First hospital cited for failure to report EMTALA transfer violation. *Emergency Physicians Monthly*, October 1996.

64. Department of Health and Human Services, HCFA, Interim Instructions Clarifying Implementation of Section 1867 of the Social Security Act 90-52, Memorandum, December 1990.

65. 42 CFR 489.53.

66. Stieber JD, Wolfe SM. Update on "Patient Dumping" Violations. Public Citizen's Health Research Group, October 1994.

67. Levine RJ, Guisto JA, Meislin HW, et al. Analysis of federally imposed penalties for violations of the Consolidated Omnibus Budget Reconciliation Act. *Ann Emerg Med* 1996;28:45-50.

68. 42 CFR 1003.105(a)(1)(ii)(c).

69. 42 USC 216,300 m-4,300-1(6).

70. 42 USC 1395dd(d).

71. Tex Rev Civ Stat Ann art 4438a; Cal Health & Safety Code Section 1317.5; NY Pub Health Law Section 20805(b)(2)(B); Tenn Code Ann Section 68-39-303.

72. 42 USC 1395dd(d)(2)(B).

73. 42 USC 1395dd(d)(2)(A).

74. *Eberhardt v City of Los Angeles*, 62 F3d 1253 (9th Cir 1995); *Baber v Hospital Corp*, 977 F2d 872 (4th Cir 1992); *King v Ahrens*, 16 F3d 265 (8th Cir 1994); *Gatewood v Washington Healthcare Corporation*, 933 F2d 1037 (DC Cir 1991); *Delaney v Cade*, 986 F2d 387 (10th Cir 1993).

75. *McDougall v Lafourche Hospital Service District*, 1993 WL 185647 (EDLA).

76. Ohio Rev Code Ann Section 2305.11(B); Ky Rev Stat Ann Section 413-245; Tenn Code Ann Section 29-26-116; Wash Civ Code Ann Section 4.16.350.

77. 42 USC 1395dd(d)(2)(C).

78. *Power v Arlington Hospital*, 42 F3d 851(4th Cir 1994); *Brooks v Maryland General Hospital, Inc*, 996 F2d 708 (4th Cir 1993); *Griffith v Mt Carmel Medical Center*, 842 F Supp 1359 (D Kan 1994); *Helton v Phelps County Regional Medical Center*, 817 F Supp 789 (ED Mo 1993); *Reid v Indianapolis Osteopathic Medical Hospital*, 709 F Supp 853 (SD Ind 1989).

79. NC Gen Stat 8C-1, Rule 702 (1996).

80. *Power v Arlington Hospital*, 42 F3d 854 (4th Cir 1994); But see, *Cooper v Gulf Breeze Hospital Inc*, 839 F Supp 1538 (ND Fla 1993).

81. *Power v Alexandria Physicians Group Ltd*, No. 96-527, *cert denied*, 65 USLR 3398 (US Dec 2, 1996).

Additional Resources

Council Resolutions and Policy Statements of the American College of Emergency Physicians. Current versions available from ACEP, (800) 798-1822, touch 6, or go to www.acep.org.

- Appropriate Interhospital Patient Transfer. Policy Statement, September 1992.
- Managed Health Care Plans and Emergency Care. Policy Statement, March 1993.
- Medical Screening Examination. Council Resolution, June 1987.
- Medical Staff Responsibility for Emergency Department Patients. Policy Statement, June 1993.
- Payment for Services: Prior Authorization. Council Resolution, November 1987.

"Frequently Asked Questions on the EMTALA." Answers to 30 common questions on EMTALA can be found on the Internet at the Web site of the law firm of Andrews, Fosmire, Solka, & Stenton, P.C.: www.afss.com/medliab.htm. It was written by M. Sean Fosmire, Esq.

Furrow B. An overview and analysis of the impact of the Emergency Medical Treatment and Active Labor Act. *J Legal Med* 1995;16:325-355. Health lawyer's view of the effect of EMTALA on patient care and access to care.

Luce G. *Defending the Hospital Under EMTALA: New Requirements and New Liabilities*. Washington, DC: National Health Lawyers Association; 1995. Addresses primarily the hospital's response to a HCFA administrative review for potential EMTALA violations and defense of EMTALA claims in court.

Patient Transfer News. ACEP review and commentary on legislation, regulations, and court interpretations on EMTALA and other laws that affect patient transfers. ACEP regularly obtained HCFA's records and investigative materials pertaining to EMTALA violations through the Freedom of Information Act (5 USC 552). The attorneys and physician-attorneys on the editorial panel reviewed these reports and periodically published summaries of the violations of EMTALA by hospitals. Published quarterly March 1993 through June 1996. Back issues available. (800) 798-1822, touch 6.

Chapter 46

Disposition and Follow-Up

Hugh F. Hill III, MD, JD, FACEP, FCLM

Emergency medicine differs from traditional office-based practices beyond the obvious distinctions. Internists' doorways are not often cluttered with ambulances offloading patients in extremis. Surgeons do not usually manage several critical patients at the same time. Even intensivists, who do multiple-case management, have more control at the intake portal. Behind these obvious differences lie even more stark dissimilarities in approach to patient care and realistic time management and practice organization.

Less obvious to other specialists but well understood by every emergency physician are patient-centered differences. Emergency physicians usually have only one brief opportunity to identify and respond to a patient's problems. The patients themselves are usually more of an unknown: will she follow up? Is he reliable? Risk management in emergency medicine also differs significantly from traditional medical practice. Emergency staff have no control and often little influence over what happens after the patient is discharged. Whereas time is a diagnostic tool for most office-based physicians, time and its passage after a patient is discharged from an emergency department do not work to the benefit of the physician who will not see that patient again. A substantial portion of the emergency department's risk is determined by what happens, or does not happen, after a patient leaves. An understanding of the differences in that risk compared with office practice will help make the hazards recognizable and, thus, preventable.

This chapter focuses on the impact these differences have on disposition decisions and their extraordinarily important confederates: follow-up possibilities and realities. The formulation of an exit plan is appropriately linked to the physician's best guess about what will happen after the patient leaves the emergency department; follow-up alternatives must be part of the disposition decision.

Case Studies

1

A 39-year-old man presents to the emergency department with a three-day history of fever and abdominal pain. The emergency physician diagnoses a urinary tract infection (UTI), prescribes Bactrim, and advises the patient to follow up with his family physician in two to three days.

The man does not see his physician but stays home for six days. When he returns to work, he looks sick enough that his employer arranges for him to see the company physician. The patient complains of continued chills and fever and has developed hives. The company physician prescribes Benadryl and changes the antibiotic to tetracycline.

Twelve days after the initial emergency department visit, the man goes to another hospital emergency department. There, the physician diagnoses a continuing UTI and obtains blood for culture. Two days later, the patient is admitted to the second hospital; the diagnosis is

"UTI/septicemia." A urine culture test is negative, but the blood culture grows *Streptococcus* B. A heart murmur is detected, and mitral valve subacute bacterial endocarditis progresses to embolization and mycotic cerebral aneurysm.

Two months after the patient's initial complaints, one of the brain's arteries has tripled in diameter. The artery is successfully repaired, and two weeks later the mitral valve is replaced. After surgery, the patient experiences a collapsed lung, a myocardial infarction, and sepsis. His blood pressure falls sharply on the fifth postoperative day, causing the arterial graft to collapse. As a result, the patient suffers a stroke and right hemiparesis.

The patient files a lawsuit, naming all the physicians and both hospitals involved in his care. He later drops some of the physicians from the lawsuit, and the court dismisses some others. The company physician settles out of court for $600,000. The case goes to trial against the sole remaining defendant — the first emergency physician, whose only involvement was during the patient's initial visit to an emergency department.

2

Four days after falling and injuring his head and neck at work, a 38-year-old man seeks help at a walk-in clinic. The physician on duty, a board-certified internist, sees the patient after he is checked in and evaluated by a triage nurse. The patient gives a history of impact to his neck and complains of pain and tingling radiating down to his right hand. The physician palpates the patient's neck and checks his upper extremity reflexes. The left trapezius is in spasm and tender. The physician diagnoses "muscle spasm" and sends the patient home, advising him to refrain from heavy lifting and to take aspirin and Flexeril.

The patient stays at home until the symptoms worsen 22 days after injury. The pain is more severe and radiates into the right leg. He goes back to the same clinic but is evaluated by a different physician. As he is getting on the examination table, he collapses. Neurologic deficits are obvious, and he is transferred to the clinic's parent hospital. There, a myelogram reveals a C4 to C5 disk herniation. Surgery is unsuccessful, and the patient remains a quadriplegic. He sues the parent hospital and the physician who initially diagnosed muscle spasm.

3

A 47-year-old woman presents to the emergency department with a migraine headache. The emergency physician performs a neurologic examination, which reveals nothing unusual, and orders Demerol and Vistaril by injection. The patient has had migraines before, but this time, unlike her usual episodes, she does not obtain complete pain relief an hour after the injection. The emergency physician calls the patient's private physician, who decides to admit her. He asks the emergency physician to write the orders, but the emergency physician politely declines and hands the telephone to a nurse to take verbal orders. The patient is admitted to the floor with instructions for neurologic checks every hour.

In the early morning, the patient's condition worsens. A CT scan reveals a large left intracerebral bleed. She survives but suffers hemiparesis and cognitive impairments. Her husband sues the hospital and the attending physician. The hospital, citing requirements of its insurance carrier, files a claim against the emergency physician, alleging that if there were negligence, it was his failure to obtain a CT scan when the patient was admitted.

4

A 23-year-old man presents to the emergency department with an obvious case of hives. The history reveals no cause, and his symptoms resolve with Benadryl and epinephrine. Because he has no anaphylactoid manifestations, he is sent home with more Benadryl, advised not to drive, and told to see his family physician the next day.

The next morning, the patient calls his family physician and says that he is having difficulty breathing. The physician tells him to double the Benadryl. Late that afternoon, the patient's wife calls EMS, and an ambulance takes her husband to the emergency department in severe respiratory distress. Intubation is impossible, so a tracheostomy is performed.

When the family physician comes in, the wife asks why more had not been done after the initial telephone call. Specifically, she asks: "Why wasn't he on steroids?" The family physician hesitates and says: "I thought he was. At least, I mean, he should have been."

The patient's wife writes a scathing letter to the hospital and the state medical society and consults an attorney to consider filing a lawsuit.

The Medical-Legal Perspective

Emergency physicians often express dismay about the extent to which they may be legally responsible for what happens to patients after they leave the emergency department. The reasons for this extended liability are found in the basic theoretical underpinnings of the United States' tort law system of compensation, in public policy and political considerations, in a misapplication of a legal principle, and practical realities.

A claimed act of negligence in the emergency department can be associated with subsequent injury in several ways. A disease or condition might worsen, or it might take an unusual turn and develop into a rare complication. The problem or its complication can result in serious consequences in the life of the patient or the lives of family, friends, or others. Even if the condition does not worsen or the patient does not develop complications, a failure to prevent or shorten the effects of illness or injury can be claimed as injury. Finally, some intervening event can aggravate, fail to mitigate, or stimulate injury. All these can happen in the hospital or after discharge.

The Realities

The prosaic facts of litigation in the United States explain much of the emergency department's vulnerability for postvisit deterioration. Consider the sequence of events that precedes a malpractice lawsuit or some other complaint:

- Something goes wrong.
- Prior events are reviewed as the patient or family asks: "Why?"
- An attorney is engaged to review the case and asks himself or a consulting expert if the case has merit.
- If the attorney files lawsuit, he names everybody that might be to blame. "Everybody" often includes contact with an emergency department at some point. If the attorney misses a potential defendant and the named defendants point to that missed party, the attorney is vulnerable to a legal malpractice action. The attorney also hopes that multiple defendants will panic and blame each other.

The Theory

The tort law system is intended to compensate victims. A person behaving reasonably who is hurt by another person who is not behaving reasonably should not have to bear the costs of the harm. If someone is injured, the person who should pay for that injury is the person who was in the best position to prevent it. This is the economic efficiency argument for assignment of financial responsibility for injury. The deterrent effects of personal injury lawsuits, touted by the plaintiffs' bar, are secondary.

However, in the legal literature and in the minds of judges and attorneys, there is a strong bias in favor of the presumably innocent victim as against the presumably wrongdoing, negligent party. In any gray area, such as degree of contributory fault, that bias influences a decision about who should pay and how much. In other words, a patient can behave very stupidly and still not completely absolve health care professionals of accountability. Further, systems of tort compensation have evolved in many states to allow comparative negligence. In the older law, a plaintiff could not pursue any other causal agents if the plaintiff were at all at fault. Newer schema hold various tortfeasors liable by percentage. In extreme jurisdictions, the plaintiff can collect all from any one defendant, leaving that defendant to recoup from the others, including penniless, or judgment-proof, codefendants.

Evidence is weighed delicately in civil law personal injury cases. Juries are instructed to decide guilt by a mere preponderance of the evidence, that is, 51%. However, once it is decided that the defendant was negligent, all reasonably foreseeable damages are laid to that defendant's charge. Oliver Wendell Holmes said it plainly: "The measure of the defendant's duty in determining whether a wrong has been committed is one thing, the measure of liability when the wrong has been committed is another."

Causation

The question of cause and effect in personal injury cases is not always easy to answer. Every harm that follows a negligent act cannot be said to be caused by that act. Subsequent injuries can be too remote in time, or too many intervening (or potentially intervening) influences can blur the connection between the act and the injuries. Eventually, it becomes neither fair nor practical to hold the tortfeasor responsible.

Foreseeability

To what extent, chronologically and circumstantially, does responsibility extend from the original act? The law uses the concept of foreseeability, in other words, could the outcome or the eventual injury have been anticipated? Note both the tense and degree of possibility in this question. "Could" it have been foreseen at the time of the act?

A case that all law schools use to teach the concept of foreseeability is *Palsgraf v Long Island R.R. Co.*[1] The facts of this case are as follows: Ms. Palsgraf stood at one end of a railway platform. At the other end of the platform, a man tried to catch a departing train. As the railway's employees helped him on board, a package he was carrying fell on the rails. It contained fireworks, which exploded and knocked some scales onto Ms. Palsgraf and injured her. She sued the Long Island Railway and won.

The appeals court upheld the verdict, but the New York State Supreme Court reviewed and reversed it. Chief Justice Cardozo's opinion explained that there can be no negligence without duty and that the employees, unable to foresee that their actions might endanger Ms. Palsgraf, owed her no duty. Justice Cardozo said that causation, remote or proximate, had nothing to do with the case.

The dissenting opinion by Justice Andrews expressed a more general notion of duty, not individual-specific or owed to Ms. Palsgraf. Justice Andrews wrote that an act which unreasonably threatens the safety of others should make the doer liable for all its proximate consequences. Thus, the specific individual hurt or the particular kind of hurt does not matter, and only the relationship between cause and effect is important in determining liability. Justice Andrews then discussed the futility of using philosophical models of causal connection and suggested a common sense approach: "What we do mean by the word 'proximate' is that, because of convenience, of public policy, of a rough sense of justice, the law arbitrarily declines to trace a series of events beyond a certain point. This is not logic. It is practical politics." Over time, the dissenting views of Justice Andrews have prevailed and are today the law.

Against this background, judges and juries decide how distant from the emergency department visit the responsibility of the practitioner and the institution extends. It is this potential for extended liability that risk management efforts must address. Justice Andrews in *Palsgraf* did leave a few clues: "There are some hints that may help us. The proximate cause, involved as it may be with many other causes, must be, at the least, something without which the event would

not happen. The court must ask itself whether there was a natural and continuous sequence between cause and effect. Was the one a substantial factor in producing the other? Was there a direct connection between them, without too many intervening causes? Is the effect of cause on result not too attenuated? Is the cause likely, in the usual judgment of mankind, to produce the result? Or, by the exercise of prudent foresight, could the result be foreseen. Is the result too remote from the cause, and here we consider remoteness in time and space."

One might, not unreasonably, interpret this "standard" to include almost everything. This is the rational approach to risk management of disposition and follow-up decisions: recognize that liability can attach for a considerable length of time and a significant number of possible adverse outcomes.

Case Discussions

1

The patient's attorney did not specifically argue that the emergency physician should have diagnosed the endocarditis. With the support of expert testimony, he claimed that the emergency physician was negligent in diagnosing the patient's problem as a simple UTI and in failing to obtain blood and urine cultures. (The emergency physician expert testifying for the plaintiff said only that a urine culture was standard.) The plaintiff's experts said that this failure led to a delay in diagnosis and treatment of the endocarditis.

The jury agreed and awarded the plaintiff $720,000, finding the company physician 60% at fault, the emergency physician 20%, and the patient himself 10% for not adhering to the emergency physician's follow-up instructions. The court entered judgment against the emergency physician for $144,000 (20% of the total), plus prejudgment interest.

The emergency physician appealed, arguing that the company physician's negligence was an "intervening" cause of the patient's injury. Defendants are not responsible for the consequences of their negligence if an unforeseeable subsequent cause of the damage intervenes. But, the appeals court ruled that the company physician's acceptance of the UTI diagnosis was foreseeable.[2]

This emergency physician's liability highlighted a particular vulnerability for all emergency physicians. If follow-up care after an emergency department visit is flawed, problems are compounded and damages are aggravated. Courts routinely hold, as in this case, that the first physician could have foreseen the subsequent negligence.

Recognize the lack of control in patient follow-up. Managing the risk of liability for the care rendered by subsequent physicians or medical staff is more difficult for emergency physicians because options are limited. Emergency departments have on-call lists for unassigned patients and policies for patients who already have physicians. Emergency care providers are rarely permitted to recommend what they think is the best available follow-up. At times, referrals to on-call physicians may not represent optimal care. Patient care concerns dictate that no patient be referred for follow-up to a known-to-be dangerous source. In general, however, the emergency physician's level of anxiety does not rise to the level of refusing to follow policy (which creates a different set of risk management problems) or demanding that a practitioner be taken off the on-call list. The quality of follow-up treatment and the associated risk depend on the standard of care available in the community.

These concerns are not staff or community dependent. Patients may choose someone else with whom to follow up or may choose alternative healers, such as nonallopathic physicians or physicians whose practice approach is unusual. Such a choice loosens the foreseeability connection but does not necessarily break it. Standard discharge instruction routines and the documentation thereof must take these risks into account.

Sometimes, heightened risk can be anticipated. A particular patient, the nature of a particular clinical problem, and what the emergency physician knows about the planned source of follow-up care may all be sources of increased risk. When the emergency physician anticipates increased aftercare difficulties, the emergency department staff should make their instructions and documentation more detailed and specific. The patient should be told why follow-up is necessary, and the risks of noncompliance should be communicated and recorded. One technique to use when the quality of follow-up is suspect is to tell the patient (and write down) what steps the follow-up physician should take if the condition fails to improve or worsens. Some colleagues may feel insulted or "second guessed," but the better physicians will appreciate the

warning. For example, emergency physicians commonly say something like: "If your wrist still hurts next week, you may need another x-ray." This serves to warn the patient, buffer disappointment at a late-discovered fracture, and encourage proper follow-up care.

The emergency physician in this case could have advised the patient that simple UTIs in healthy middle-aged males are rare, that cultures could become necessary, and that a urology workup would be required regardless.[3] The time required for the emergency physician to inform the patient and to document this information, even multiplied by several patients in a shift who need detailed follow-up instructions, is a bargain compared with the time and aggravation involved in defending a lawsuit.

2

When this case went to trial, counsel for the plaintiff argued that if the patient had been adequately advised, he could have avoided quadriplegia. The plaintiff's expert testified that if the patient had returned to an emergency department in three days for evaluation of continued symptoms, the "proper medical procedure would have required" x-rays. The x-rays would have been negative, said the expert, and emergency physicians would then have obtained a CT scan, which would have shown bulging disks, leading to immobilization and earlier surgery.

The jury returned judgment for $6,660,720 and found the patient 13% responsible for his condition. On appeal, the award was upheld. The state supreme court ruling read as follows: "Most importantly, [the physician] should have told the plaintiff to return in two or three days if the pain continued." In the state where this happened, winning plaintiffs are entitled to prejudgment interest. This means that their award is compounded by the interest they would have earned had they received their money the same day they filed the lawsuit. The thinking behind this rule is that it encourages settlement of valid claims. By the time the appeal ended, the total award exceeded $13 million. The hospital involved was a charitable organization, and in this state, such organizations are limited in liability to $20,000. The rest was the physician's responsibility. The upper limits of his insurance policy were not reported.[4]

The hospital's emergency department and its satellite clinic now include standard warnings in their discharge sheets. Patients are advised of parameters by which to judge their progress.

Most are given definite follow-up dates. Discharge planning now presumes nothing about patient compliance or intelligence. Even the most obvious warnings are recorded.

3

The emergency physician and his emergency department colleagues were incensed at the position taken by the hospital. One of the emergency contract group's managers explained that the hospital had a right to defend itself this way. The plaintiffs proposed a settlement that appealed to the hospital, offering an opportunity to end the case. The hospital administrator told the contract group to settle. The group held meetings with its own attorney, who explained that the emergency physician and the group did have some exposure if the case went to trial. In this state, which subscribed to the concept of comparative negligence, a jury might ascribe a small percentage of liability to the physician, especially if an emergency expert said that the standard of care requires a head CT scan under these circumstances, even in off hours. The group agreed to pay half the settlement, and the hospital paid the other half.

Admitted patients are now thoroughly worked up in the emergency physician's emergency department. Unless the attending physician comes in to take over the care, very few diagnostic tests are put off that might possibly be helpful. If an attending physician objects and verbally cancels any workup, the emergency physician's order is left on the chart with the notation: "Canceled by order of Dr. [name]."

Is this an overreaction? Although this response is not practical in most facilities, it is understandable that these physicians felt caught between the contract group and hospital. Third-party actions arise when one defendant drags someone else into the case and says: "Their fault, not mine!" That finger-pointing defendant then becomes a plaintiff as to the third party. Where hospital boards and administrations are estranged from their medical staffs, and where staffs do not identify with or integrate emergency physicians, these third-party claims are more likely (see Chapter 24, "Contracts in Emergency Medicine," and its comments on indemnification clauses).

Although it is highly desirable to avoid writing admitting orders, one drawback to this policy is the lack of control that results (see Chapter 43, "Admitting Orders"). To avoid this dilemma, make a suggestion to the admitting physician and note this in the emergency department record. Initially, such suggestions are not likely to be well received by admitting physicians, who are already perturbed that the emergency physician is not writing orders. Once the attending staff is accustomed to this policy, however, such suggestions may be more easily offered. The way in which these suggestions are made is an art refined by a generation of emergency physicians who elevated the specialty from the status of servant to colleague, an art that young residency graduates may wish, at times, to acquire. For example, the admitting physician might be advised as follows: "I don't want to write orders on your patient, but I will call the radiologist and CT tech for you so you can go back to sleep."

Emergency physicians should cultivate collegial relations, know the group's and hospital's policies, and offer documented suggestions.

4

Investigations into this complaint confirmed that the patient had been treated properly. The wife's attorney called a physician friend to get an objective opinion about the case. The friend explained that most emergency physicians would not use steroids in this situation and that the emergency department care was within standard. The attorney advised the wife not to pursue legal remedy.

For a time, the emergency department group decided to call attending physicians on all patients to seek their approval for discharge and treatment plans and informally explain the specific reasons for this new policy. After enough late-night calls and complaints from patients about delays in emergency department care, the policy was reduced to encouraging occasional calls. This particular patient's family physician, however, is still called day and night, for every patient, and the conversations are carefully documented.

The importance of cordial and mutually trusting medical staff relationships is higher on emergency physicians' risk management "wish list" than on that of other specialties. The physician who has a long-standing relationship with a patient is less likely to be the target of anger and frustration than is the emergency physician, with whom the patient and family have but brief contact during stressful circumstances. Accordingly, it is easier for other medical staff to try to redirect ill will from themselves toward the emergency physician.

Although the clinical picture might suggest

one response, the "risk picture" might suggest a more cautious response. The frequency with which a simple case of hives progresses to or recurs in the form of a more dangerous reaction might be insufficient to dictate special warnings, but warning a patient about the signs of anaphylaxis is never contraindicated. Printed instructions, if used, might advise the patient to return or call his own physician immediately if certain symptoms or signs appear. If printed instructions for this common problem are not available, at least give the patient the written admonition: "Return if worse."

The "slippery slope" argument is sometimes offered in response to advice to warn. In simplified form, the question is this: "Because there's a risk of anaphylaxis, aren't you obligated to administer prophylaxis? You're giving the warning, so aren't you admitting there's a risk?" This is parallel to the argument offered decades ago regarding ECGs in the emergency department: if there's enough of a possibility of a heart attack to warrant an ECG, and because a negative ECG doesn't rule out a myocardial infarction, aren't you obligated to admit everyone on whom you perform an ECG? This is a false syllogism and a true failure to discriminate in degree, not in kind.

The likelihood of a complication or adverse event can be enough to suggest warning the patient, but not so likely as to create even minuscule added risk. To treat (or to refrain from treating) for risk management purposes is to confuse self-defense with the superior medical value of the patient's best interest if that decision adds even the slightest risk for the patient. But the extra time and effort put into educating and documenting are ethically unencumbered medical-legal defense practices. For this patient, the risk did not rise to the level of requiring even the minimal cost and complication rate of steroids, but it did rise to the level of suggesting warnings.

Emergency physicians should provide patients with guidelines for measuring their problems. This patient's condition, for example, was not expected to progress to involve his respiratory pathway, intestinal mucosa, circulatory integrity or become toxic necrolysis. This expectation means the patient can be discharged, but still, this patient could be the rare case. Tell the patient what to expect and what to do if things do not go as expected. This approach is superior when it is not practical to provide a laundry list of warnings. If anything unexpected happens, for better or for worse, the patient knows to contact someone.

Discharge and Follow-Up Recommendations

The law will allow a jury to hold emergency physicians responsible for postdischarge and postadmission problems. These problems may have only a tenuous connection with the alleged error in the emergency department. As a result, emergency department staff must make every effort to manage this extended and extensive risk. At a minimum, excellent documentation of the emergency team's efforts is required.

At the basic level of triage, where the emergency physician must differentiate those patients who require immediate admission from those who do not, the database is necessarily limited. In the emergency department environment, the emergency physician cannot be assured of patient or caregiver reliability, nor judge accurately if the complaints match the symptoms. The emergency physician should be more willing to admit a patient than the patient's own physician for any given complex of complaints and findings. If the patient is discharged, does the chart adequately reflect the logical basis for this decision?

Although they are less common, situations occasionally will arise where the attending physician who knows the patient will recognize a seemingly minor complaint or finding as significant. The clues to these occasions are in the history ("Dr. Jones always admits me for this.") or in the chart ("This is the 14th hospital stay for this problem for this patient."). These situations may also be identified if the emergency department policy is to call attending physicians for unclear cases. If attending physicians are called only for patients who require admission, then they are not being called enough to manage emergency department risk. The physician who will see the patient next should be part of the planning process. That physician is also the first and most likely critic of emergency department care if he has not "bought into" the plan.

For a patient referred to the emergency department "for admission," call the referring physician promptly. If admission is desirable or inevitable, the subsequent emergency department workup can be directed and ministerial. The propriety of such family physician referrals and that physician's medical management can be questioned later if necessary. Based on the communication with the family physician, the patient expects to be admitted. The risk of sending such a patient home, even when completely justified medically, is enormous.

When patients, families, or charts give a history of multiple admissions, unless the problem is obviously self-limited and unrelated to past history, the emergency physician should call the attending physician. This should also be done when it is not entirely clear that the patient's condition allows discharge or requires admission. The choice is rarely a cold alternative between admission or no care at all. In making disposition decisions, a variety of options is available. In recent years, more resources have become accessible, such as home health services referrals.

The emergency physician must consider the full range of choices when making a disposition. There are "in between" clinical situations for which "in between" solutions are best. The availability of these alternative responses offers more choices at discharge, but also burdens the emergency physician with greater responsibility to document the rationale behind any decisions. It is not enough to record why something was not done (unless all possible "somethings" are covered). Plaintiffs' attorneys find it easy to propose some seemingly simple, inexpensive alternatives to the emergency physician's choice.

Consultants can be asked to come in and see patients. The emergency physician can ask the patient to see a consultant in the office or back in the emergency department at some set time and have staff arrange the appointment. Patients can be asked to wait and be observed in the emergency department area or in the reception area. They can even be asked to come back to the emergency department to see the emergency physician at a scheduled time. Keep in mind the following question: does it appear on the face of the record that the disposition decision made was the best out of the full range of choices available?

Once the decision is made to discharge a patient directly from the emergency department, the physician's thinking should shift. At discharge, the question is: "What can we do to protect the patient after he leaves?" This is not to suggest that responsibility should or does extend to this degree of paternalism. Rather, this approach and this question focus clinical considerations in a way beneficial to the patient and consistent with good risk management. The instructions given to a patient and family at the time of discharge are a basic tool for managing the risk of extended liability (see Chapter 47, "Discharge and Follow-Up Instructions"). Good discharge planning transfers some of the responsibility for care to the patient. Conscious shifting of the responsibility for patient care must be a part of every medical professional's medical-legal tool kit, especially when that shift involves asking competent patients to assume their rightful share.

Several questions, always worthy of consideration, become critically important at discharge.

- What if I am wrong? The patient's problem could have been misdiagnosed or its severity unrecognized. Hubris kills.
- What if the patient behaves irrationally? The emergency physician cannot assume that the patient will act with common sense or recognize or respond appropriately to an unexpected change in condition.
- What if something goes wrong later? How will it look in retrospect? Some problem may arise that could be made to look as if it had been missed or ignored in the emergency department.
- Finally (and this is the hardest question), what if the physician who follows up on this problem is not competent to handle the specific problem? Not all private physicians practice alike, yet the emergency physician's risk in part depends on their abilities.

Most emergency department patients should receive instructions to follow up with a named resource. The follow-up should be for a specific date or dates and not "prn." Emergency department patients generally believe that they have an urgent or emergent problem when they come to the emergency department or call 911. In general, problems of that degree of severity should have follow-up. If the problem and the patient appear to be appropriate for discharge from all further care, at least admonitions, such as "seek help for any change in condition," are in order. As in the second case study, patients can ignore significant manifestations of serious illness or injury for prolonged periods. This delay can compound treatment errors, which may be attributed to the emergency care providers. Patients discharged with instructions to follow-up "if needed" should be given a time frame and specific limits for clinical signs and symptoms.

Unfortunately, too many emergency physicians regard telephone calls back into the emergency department from patients seen earlier as a distraction or intrusion. Similarly, return visits, sometimes derisively termed "bounce-backs," are a source of dismay. Unscheduled return visits within 72 hours are rightly viewed as quality improvement review triggers, provoking the question: "Should anything have been done differently in the earlier encounter?" Emergency physicians should look at patients who come back with complications, problems, or even questions related to an earlier emergency department visit as presenting the emergency department staff with a second chance.

In fact, calls from recently seen emergency department patients should be regarded as a blessing and treated as such. They are an opportunity to correct potentially high-risk misunderstandings, to monitor the patient's progress, and to recognize postdischarge problems and intervene before harm is done. The emergency physician, when on the telephone with a former patient, should have someone pull the chart and record the basic content of the conversation, especially if any advice is given to the patient. The on-duty physician should gladly accept the interruption represented by patient or family calls, including those about patients seen recently by colleagues, and should expect colleagues to do the same when they are on duty.

Return visits, scheduled or not, give emergency physicians a taste of the risk control and loss prevention tools their office-based colleagues enjoy. This gift becomes even more significant when a patient comes back for evaluation of a complication or problem related to an earlier visit. The situation is now much more in the department's control than is usually so, and relations with the disappointed patient can be repaired and any sequelae optimally limited. Welcome such return visits. Thank the patient for coming back to the department.

An important aspect of liability often overlooked by emergency physicians is injured third parties. The term comes from contract law and refers to persons outside the primary relationship between the first two parties, the physician and patient. In some states, emergency physicians and departments have been held liable for damage done to third parties by patients who have been discharged from the emergency department (see Chapter 28, "Duty to Warn Third Parties," Chapter 53, "Patients With Altered Mental Status," and Chapter 54, "Use of Restraints").

On rare occasions, a question arises regarding the emergency staff's duty to warn third parties of possible harm that a patient may cause them.[5] Generally, however, the emergency department staff can mitigate this liability. The staff should warn the patient against behaviors that might endanger third parties. Thus, for example, discharge forms should contain indications that patients should not drive or operate machinery under the influence of soporific drugs or while an eye is patched. This step may seem obvious, but both of these circumstances have led to successful lawsuits against treating physicians.

Patients should not be discharged from the emergency department when they face inescapable harm, if there are any other alternatives, including a social admission or agency referral. If a battered spouse insists on returning to her abuser, emergency personnel cannot force her to act intelligently but should ensure that she is aware of whatever alternatives are available. Child and elder abuse victims require special discharge planning. Battered children should not be released to the custody of the batterer.[6]

Emergency staff might easily carry this assumption of responsibility further than is legally required. If more is taken on, it must be done prudently. Emergency staff sometimes feel they are standing on the barricades, defending everyone against everything. However, they must not accept and create legal duties where unnecessary or become resentful or overwhelmed and fail to fulfill existing duties.

Obtain the patient's cooperation with discharge plans. This task involves careful negotiation. The patients' right to put their own health at risk should not put the emergency department at risk, but it does. "How to minimize this risk?" should be the question, as it cannot be eliminated. First, give the patient your best advice. If follow-up tomorrow is optimal, say so and, especially if the patient seems reticent, say why. Second, listen to the patient's response. If he seems unwilling to follow your advice, he could be frightened, unconvinced of the dangers involved, angry that he's not getting what he wants, or not responsive for any number of other reasons. Third, find out what follow-up the patient is willing to do. If this is unacceptably more hazardous than the ideal follow-up, initiate informed refusal measures (see Chapter 48, "Refusal of Care"). Fourth, document the potential risks and the particular patient's circumstances.

Send discharged patients who refuse to leave back to the waiting room. If the emergency department bed must be vacated to make space for other patients and the patient refuses to get off the gurney, consider moving it to another site, such as the hallway. Forcing a patient who does not want to be discharged off the premises entirely is problematic. Even though such a patient is technically a trespasser,[7] he has an opportunity to harass even a flawless emergency department. Involve the on-call administrator in such cases and expect help, not more burdens. Alternatively, if the patient is a danger to others (and lacks the mental disorder that could lead to civil commitment), a documentable basis for forced eviction, even from the waiting room, exists.[8]

Key Points and Conclusion

Recognizing and managing the medical-legal risks associated with a departing patient is possible. All that is really required is for the entire emergency department staff to recognize that liability extends beyond discharge or admission. An appropriate sense of responsibility for patient welfare beyond those doors will help to reduce risk and to support the department's primary goal — quality patient care.

- The law will allow a jury to hold emergency physicians responsible for postdischarge and postadmission problems even though these problems may have only a tenuous connection with the alleged error in the emergency department.
- The emergency physician should be more willing to admit a patient than the patient's own physician might be, for any given complex of complaints and findings.
- Use the family or attending physician often, particularly in cases referred "for admission," or if patients have required multiple admissions.
- There are "in between" clinical situations for which "in between" solutions are best.
- Consider using consultants in formulating discharge plans.
- The instructions given to a patient and family at the time of discharge are a basic tool for managing the risk of extended liability.
- Most emergency department patients should receive instructions to follow up with a named resource. The follow-up should be for a specific date or dates and not "prn."
- Emergency physicians should look at patients who come back with complications, problems, or even questions related to an earlier emergency department visit as presenting the emergency department staff with a second chance. Patients who come

back to the emergency department offer a risk management opportunity.

- Warn the patient against behaviors that might endanger third parties.
- Patients should not be released from the emergency department when they face inescapable harm, if there are any other alternatives, including a social admission or agency referral.

References

1. *Palsgraf v Long Island R.R. Co.,* 248 NY 339, 162 NE 99 (Ct App 1928).
2. *Bandel v Friedrich,* No. A-104-87T1 (NJ Supp App July 19, 1989).
3. The Bandel care report as published in *Emergency Department Law,* 1981;1(16):1. Adapted with permission of the publisher, Business Publishers, Inc, 951 Pershing Drive, Silver Springs, MD 20910-4464. (800) 274-6737. Fax: (301) 589-8493. E-mail bpinews@bpinews.com and Web site: www.bpinews.com.
4. *Harlow v Chin,* 40 Mass 697 (1989). A form of this case report and analysis appeared in *Emergency Department Law,* 1989;1(21):1,5-6. Adapted with permission of the publisher, Business Publishers, Inc, 951 Pershing Drive, Silver Springs, MD 20910-4464. (800) 274-6737. Fax: (301) 589-8493. E-mail bpinews@bpinews.com and Web site: www.bpinews.com.
5. Kiscina SF. *Medical Law for the Attending Physician: A Case-Oriented Analysis.* Carbondale, Ill: Southern Illinois University Press; 1982:276.
6. *Landeros v Flood,* 551 P2d 389 (Calif 1976).
7. *Lucy Webb Hayes National Training School v Geoghegan,* 281 F Supp 116 (DDC 1967).
8. The patient who refuses to leave. Practical guidelines. In: MacDonald, et al. *Health Care Law: A Practical Guide.* Matthew Bender; 1989.

Chapter 47

Discharge and Follow-Up Instructions

Hugh F. Hill III, MD, JD, FACEP, FCLM

Of all patients who are treated in the emergency department then discharged with follow-up instructions, most should, and some will, follow up by visiting their own physicians or clinics. However, they often do so at a time related more to convenience than medical necessity. Some patients will decide for themselves whether any follow-up care is necessary, but many are unwilling or are insufficiently informed by emergency department staff to make a conscious choice. A few will completely ignore discharge and follow-up instructions, and their symptoms may continue or worsen, possibly with serious results. Only a small fraction will remember everything they were told in the emergency department and precisely follow instructions.

What is interesting about patients' imperfect compliance is that those who sue often claim to have extraordinarily good memories of exactly what they were told or not told. Emergency department staff, on the other hand, must rely on charted notes not only for documentation of what happened, but also for clues to help refute these claims.

The emergency department team has little control over what patients do after they leave the emergency department. Discharge and follow-up instructions are tools for influencing patient behavior. Documentation of those instructions is an opportunity to shift some of the risk for subsequent medical problems to where it should lie — with the patient.

Case Studies

1

A 4-year-old boy has experienced several days of "sniffles" and one day of fever before his mother brings him to the emergency department. She cannot see the child's pediatrician because of an outstanding bill.

The emergency physician confirms the patient's symptoms and notes normal activity level, with good oral intake. Rectal temperature is 39°C, and the examination is fairly nonspecific. The emergency physician notes that one tympanic membrane is redder than the other. Based on this finding and the history of biphasic illness, he diagnoses otitis media. The mother says that the child has a history of ear problems, and she is not surprised by the diagnosis.

The emergency physician prescribes oral antibiotics and tells the mother to take the child to the pediatrician if he does not get better in two or three days. He also tells her to take him to the pediatrician in two weeks to make sure the infection has cleared. The child takes his first dose of the antibiotic in the emergency department and is discharged.

The emergency physician is shocked to learn later that the boy is admitted to another hospital 11 days later with a diagnosis of meningitis. Severe brain damage is already evident; the boy is suffering nearly uncontrollable seizures and has a poor prognosis. The physician notifies his insurance carrier that a lawsuit might be filed.

2

A 55-year-old man with a history of asthma is having difficulty breathing, and his wife takes him to the emergency department.

The emergency physician performs an initial evaluation and indicates on the chart that the patient does not seem to be in any trouble. Respiratory rate is 24 breaths/minute; both nursing and physician notes indicate that the patient is in no acute distress. He is treated and released. The patient's wife asks the physician whether it is wise to discharge her husband and is assured that there is no danger.

The patient makes the three-hour ride home in the cold air, at 6,000 feet above sea level. He dies soon after getting home. The wife sues the physician and the hospital. She testifies later that her husband's condition on release was serious and that he had looked ashen and blue.

3

A 35-year-old man sustains an injury at work when he is struck on the knee by a coworker with the flat part of a shovel. He goes to the emergency department for treatment. The emergency physician examines the patient's knee and orders x-rays, which are negative. Physical examination reveals no signs of ligament or cartilage tear, only considerable tenderness and swelling. The physician orders a knee immobilizer and crutches and tells the patient to see an orthopedic physician in two days. He prescribes an aspirin-codeine combination for pain and discharges the patient with his x-rays.

Two days later, on his way to the orthopedist's office, the man hits another car head on and is killed instantly. The prescription bottle for pain killers, with the emergency physician's name on the bottle, is found on the seat of the car. The woman who was driving the other car suffers a neck injury that requires almost daily follow-up care. Her insurance company decides to investigate the man's estate to see if damages can be recovered. However, the man was penniless. They investigate the possibility of suing the physician and request the related medical records. The medical records department notifies the hospital's risk manager, who alerts the emergency department. The physician and the hospital attorney review the chart for possible vulnerability.

4

An 11-year-old boy is struck on the head in a fistfight at the school playground. He rides his bicycle home, then his father takes him to the local emergency department. The boy is examined by the nursing staff, an intern, and a pediatrics resident. A contusion is apparent, but plain films reveal no fracture. He has a headache, is irritable and lethargic, and vomits twice.

There is a dispute about whether the boy should be admitted, at least in part because of a mistaken belief that his pediatrician does not attend at that hospital. The director of the pediatrics clinic, attending another patient in the emergency department, tells the boy's father to take him home. This physician instructs the father to watch for pupillary dilatation and to make sure that his son can be aroused from sleep. However, the preprinted instruction sheet for head injury, which includes all the usual instructions and precautions, is not given to the father.

The father takes the boy home and observes him closely. He reads in a first aid book to watch for slow pulse. When the boy's heart rate falls from 44 to 40 and one pupil "blows," he rushes him back to the hospital. Surgery is performed and the boy survives, but he is left a quadriplegic and mute.

The Medical-Legal Perspective

Consider what happens when a patient or family member goes to a lawyer's office. If the injuries are costly enough and if the fee is potentially high enough to interest the attorney, the medical records are reviewed. Although inadequate, incomplete, or even erroneous follow-up and discharge instructions are not the best focus for an attack by plaintiffs, they will be used if needed.

As always, the physician's foremost concern is patient care. However, it is not the only concern. Risk management considerations should loom large in communicating and recording discharge and follow-up instructions. In fact, risk management efforts can be justified by general patient care criteria, as part of the department's determination to stay open, healthy, and focused. Legal cases associated with poor outcomes following emergency department discharge demonstrate three things:

- Arranged follow-up care is safer than leaving the responsibility for aftercare to the patient's discretion.
- Specific instructions regarding follow-up care are safer than "prn" advice.
- Failure to provide follow-up instructions or parameters is rank error.

Physicians should understand how discharge and follow-up instructions play out in the legal process as it unfolds. First, considerable time usually passes between the emergency department visit and the trial. This delay and its effect on the reliability of memory make recorded instructions critically important.[1] Second, in contrast to the modern trend in health care, in which patients demand more information and control, it is difficult to shift the responsibility for health to patients. If a patient's decision to ignore follow-up instructions was not an informed decision, the responsibility — and the risk — may not transfer out of the emergency physician's hands. Finally, despite attacks and protestations by the plaintiff's attorney, a patient's signature on the discharge instruction sheet usually helps to prove that the patient should be held responsible for knowing what the instructions meant and for the risks of disregarding them.

The long delay between the emergency department visit and trial tends to favor plaintiffs in any contest of memories. Years later, the physician, nurse, and paramedic are unlikely to recall any specific patient unless there was some dramatic event associated with the encounter. The plaintiff is generally only one of thousands of patients seen that year. But to the patient and family, the visit and the care received were isolated, unusual events. Both plaintiff and defendant may be regarded by jurors as self-serving in their recollections. The credibility of their memories, however, can differ depending on whether the event was something jurors feel that a witness should remember. A written record of what was said to the patient and family at discharge can be vital. Most of the time, these conversations are recorded in ignorance of the subsequent problem that leads to legal action. On the scale of credibility, this documentation is an effective counterweight to the heavy burden of overcoming the patient's or family member's memory. Imagine facing a particularly lengthy, vigorous cross examination without the discharge instruction record, and its importance is revealed.

Shifting risk to the patient is difficult in health care risk management. Although the concept of shifting liability risk to a third party who may be injured is often applied, for example, to industry and public access exposure, the responsibilities of health care professionals limit their use of this technique. When a sign is posted such as "Enter at your own risk," the party placing the sign is attempting to hand off the jeopardy to the reader. Legal doctrines shift risk as well, in ways that both reflect and influence behavior. For example, "assumption of the risk" is the doctrine that applies when someone voluntarily enters a dangerous situation. Thinking about the risk-shifting potential of discharge instructions will help emergency physicians analyze and respond to case specifics, such as a patient's questionable ability to understand discharge instructions.

To transfer risk and responsibility effectively, the instructions must be clear, and the patient must understand them. Even perfectly complete and thorough discharge instruction sheets may not be enough. Emergency department staff must explain carefully to the patient the risks of disregarding the instructions to make sure the shift of responsibility is secure and to avoid a claim of uninformed refusal.

Informed refusal fits within those patterns of legal analysis that recur in many settings and are applicable to a variety of medical situations. Informed refusal relates to the concept of informed consent. In this paradigm, a patient's acceptance of treatment is not "informed" unless the patient knows the risks and benefits of the proposed treatment and the alternatives. Emergency department staff worry less about informed consent than do surgeons because the law implies consent in emergency situations (see Chapter 27, "Patient Consent"). Reasoning that a rejection of recommended treatment is a decision comparable to acceptance of treatment, courts have held that these refusals must also be informed, that is, that patients must understand the risks and benefits of the proposed treatment and the alternatives, including the alternative of refusal.

In practice, emergency department nurses and physicians routinely inform worrisome patients about the risks of refusal. The patient with chest pain who wants to go home, the person with an anaphylactic reaction who is afraid to use steroids, the woman with abdominal pain who refuses a pelvic examination — these are all examples of patient encounters in which physicians and nurses will warn patients without prompting, simply out of an honest concern for the patients' welfare. This pattern of response should be institutionalized, however, so that it is used regularly for all patients who refuse care even when that refusal does not appear to be dangerous. If the emergency department were a race track, these patients would have yellow flags out every time they came around. They are already, by definition, a problem, and the fact that their own choice creates or worsens their poor outcome will not necessarily relieve the emergency physician of all responsibility. Too often, the cry is raised: "If only I had been told that . . ."

The informed refusal analysis also guides the documentation of discharge instructions. The patient who is not told why an instruction is important may simply ignore it and defeat the intended protective effect. Discharge and follow-up instructions should be sufficiently detailed and clear so that if the patient or family refuses to follow the instructions, that refusal is, by legal standards, informed.

Signed discharge instruction sheets are better than a note on the chart stating what the emergency staff told the patient. In general, in legal terms, an individual may be more easily charged with knowledge of a signed document than an unsigned one. Signing something is a serious act, not to be taken lightly, and most people understand this. In medical situations, however, much more so than in commercial contexts, it is possible for people to claim that they did not understand what they were signing. Even so, the signature still has some effect. Lawyers speak of individuals being "put on notice." A signed document is more likely to put a patient on notice of its contents than is a simple note in the chart.

Complete and clearly written discharge and follow-up instructions can reduce the emergency department's liability risks that result from disappointing outcomes patients may experience after leaving the emergency department.[2]

Case Discussions

1

The hospital's and emergency physician's insurance carriers investigated the case, attempting to do so without alerting the patient's family. However, neither carrier was surprised when the family filed a lawsuit. The boy had survived but in a severely debilitated state. The family demanded several million dollars in compensation.

Initially, the hospital assigned nuisance value to the claim, and the emergency physician's insurer refused to discuss settlement with the plaintiff's lawyer. Depositions were taken, and the defense learned that the boy improved in the first week after treatment started. The mother testified that she ran out of the antibiotic after one week and did not have money to get more. She testified that the boy seemed to lose energy about 9 or 10 days after the emergency department visit and that his temperature went back up. Because the principal manifestation of illness was a decrease in the boy's usual level of activity, the mother was more relieved than concerned. She said that when her son collapsed and she called an ambulance, the physicians at the receiving hospital started treatment immediately but told her it might be too late.

The defense team asked the trial judge to dismiss the case because the plaintiffs had not yet produced the expert statement required in their state. The plaintiff's lawyer explained the delay to the court's satisfaction and was given 15 days to produce a letter. On the 15th day, the defense received a statement from an emergency physician who believed the standard of care had been violated. The expert witness said that the mother should have been told to seek help immediately if her son became worse. This error, the expert witness said, lulled the boy's mother into a false sense of security and, as a result, deprived the boy of a chance of early diagnosis and cure.

Over the emergency physician's objections, the two insurance companies settled with the family, agreeing to a total payout of $1.2 million. The defense did not negotiate for a commitment to refrain from publicizing, and the settlement was reported in the local press.

As a result of this lawsuit, the hospital's standard form discharge instructions were changed to include, in bold type and in Spanish and English, the phrase: "If you get worse or do not improve as expected, call for medical attention immediately." The emergency physician now gives discharge instructions without making any assumptions about the recipient's prior knowledge or experience.

This scenario is liberally adapted from an actual case, and the core of the story is true. Cases of this specific type have fallen off dramatically with the use of *Haemophilus influenzae* vaccines, but the lessons apply more broadly.

2

The defense in this case relied on the medical record to defeat the lawsuit. Apparently, the patient had been regarded as so stable that no repeat or discharge vital signs were documented. Neither were any objective tests of his pulmonary status performed.

Before trial, the plaintiff was willing to accept $650,000 to settle, but the defense refused. The defense attorneys were confident when they were called to the courthouse to hear the jury's verdict. They were shocked when the foreman announced a verdict for the plaintiff in the amount of $4 million.

The defense team announced its intention to appeal and to seek a new trial. The parties entered new settlement negotiations, only now with a $4 million verdict factored in. Initially, the hospital had said its insurance covered the emergency physician up to $8 million. After the verdict, his lawyer learned that there had been a mistake: his client was only covered up to $2 million. Amounts in excess of that sum were in dispute. The attorney believed the emergency physician's case was good and that there had been errors to justify a new trial, but the disputed coverage put the situation in a different light. He had to recommend settlement up to the $2 million limit to avoid possible personal exposure for the physician. The plaintiff accepted $2 million to avoid risking an appeal and possible new trial.[3]

This case demonstrates how much weight a jury can put on the testimony of families and friends about what happened during an emergency department visit. The defense attorney later said that the plaintiff's witnesses were solid and believable. Additionally, their recollection that they had asked the physician about the wisdom of discharging the patient was supported by the physician's testimony that he had reassured them.

Any objective evidence of the patient's condition on discharge would have helped — forced vital capacities, ABGs, even discharge vital signs and improved respiratory rate. If the patient's condition did not seem to warrant such testing, the family's concerns might have stimulated a reevaluation.

In general, whenever anything seems out of the ordinary, including a discrepancy between family and professional perceptions, extra caution is required. The expression of that extra caution might take the form of testing, or it might be enough to document the thinking involved. The defense position would have been enhanced significantly by a note in the chart saying: "Family states worse than usual, desires admit. Condition stable to me because . . ."

3

In this case, the emergency physician realized that his interests and those of the hospital might not be identical, so he consulted his own counsel. His lawyer advised cautious cooperation. In the meeting with the hospital's attorney, the emergency physician explained that the patient, who was partially immobilized, should not have been driving. The attorney asked if warnings not to drive were standard with narcotic prescriptions, and the physician admitted that they probably are, or at least an expert could be found to say they are. The attorney said he believed that there was potential exposure and advised notification of the insurance carriers. He explained that the physician and the hospital might be sued by the patient's estate or by the injured woman.

The emergency physician's insurance carrier interviewed him and opened a file, but they decided not to set aside reserves until more was known. The company asked him not to talk with the hospital's attorney again, except through their lawyers.

The hospital's attorney reported that the injured woman's policy only allowed the company to recover from any insurance the patient might have had, but not against anyone else. The patient had lived alone, and no family or friends were managing the estate. The injured woman was reported to be content with the insurance company's payment of her medical expenses and was not inclined to sue anybody for anything. The hospital, the physician, and the insurers are all waiting for the statute of limitations to expire on this case.

The physician's emergency department now uses an updated version of their old discharge instruction form. The new one contains much more standard language and covers situations such as the one in this case. At least one phrase is displayed prominently and is invariably circled by the physician whenever he prescribes any medication that may cause drowsiness: "Do not drive or operate machinery if you are taking medication."

4

The father's allegations in the malpractice lawsuit were for wrongful discharge. Hospital policy had required that the printed form be given to pediatric patients. Evidence adduced at trial showed that both the resident and the intern had wanted to admit the patient, but an unidentified person in the hospital's admitting office had told the examining intern that the child could not be admitted because his private physician did not have privileges there. The jury awarded the plaintiff more than $4 million.

This case, *Niles v City of San Rafel*,[4] was based on events that happened in the 1970s. Although it is difficult today to overlook the clinical misjudgment in this case, remember that, in the 1970s, one substantial body of opinion held strongly that patients with closed head injury who did not have a documented history of 10 or more minutes of unconsciousness did not need to be admitted for observation. Concepts of regional referral centers were only beginning to be widespread, and most hospitals could not gear up for nocturnal neurosurgery much faster than this. But just as it is difficult to base a malpractice defense effort on the inevitability of the outcome, it is also unwise to base a risk management strategy only on the cases where intervention is well proved to improve results. Even though handing the father the policy-required form would not have resulted in an earlier operative intervention, a tight causal connection is not always required by a jury empathetic toward a seriously hurt plaintiff.

Policies not followed are traps. They may never be sprung, but they can cause disaster. If compliance with a policy cannot be enforced, consider revising or dropping that policy. If a policy is not followed for a reason, document that reason.

Key Points and Conclusion

Follow-up and discharge instructions are designed to offer the patient guidance and advice for follow-up care. They are handed to the patient in written form to help the patient remember what the staff said. These instructions are also designed to reduce liability for the emergency department, the staff, and the hospital if the patient or family member later sues. For this purpose, discharge instructions are in written form as an evidentiary record of what the patient was told.

With an understanding of this dual purpose, fashioning solid discharge instructions should be easy, although somewhat time-consuming. However, it is time well spent. Emergency staff must be trained to use some of their precious emergency department time to avoid serious medical-legal risks later on.

When developing instructions, emergency physicians and staff should start by assuming that all emergency department patients will need some sort of follow-up (see Chapter 46, "Disposition and Follow-Up"). They should keep in mind that patients must be given some indication of the staff's reasoning behind the instructions and that their concern is for patients' well-being. The staff should assume little or nothing about patients' understanding of their conditions or their ability to use common sense or respond to the obvious. The discharge form may be all that stands between the staff and a lawsuit.

Finally, physicians and staff should reread the instruction sheet and ask themselves the following questions:

- Does the patient have specific instructions about what to do?
- Are there conditions or limits stated to guide the patient?
- Are there warnings of what not to do?
- Is there some indication of what the physician is thinking? What is the physician's concern that requires follow-up care?
- Should the risks of noncompliance be recorded?
- Are the adverse reactions of patients' conditions covered adequately in the instructions?
- Does the form clearly state that patients must seek help if there is a change for the worse, if they are concerned about a symptom, or if they are not progressing as expected?
- Do the form's other standard disclaimers and warnings apply? If so, they should be circled or otherwise highlighted. ("Your x-rays will be reviewed by a radiologist in the morning." "If results of lab tests or cultures are not available when you leave the emergency department, they will be reported to your doctor." "Don't drive or drink alcohol if you are taking medication.")
- Should the form be explained to someone else — a friend or family member?
- Emergency department staff must keep a copy of discharge and follow-up instructions and make sure they are as secure as the medical record itself. Work slips should be handled similarly. There is at least one reported case of a lawsuit against an emergency department resulting from a discrepancy between the work note and the discharge instructions.

Keep in mind the possible future use of these documents. As the centerpiece of a malpractice defense, they must be created and treated appropriately.

References

1. Greenberg. *Avoiding Malpractice in Emergency Medicine.* Wayne, Pa: Greenleaf; 1989.

2. See, generally, Focus: Discharge Instructions, *Emergency Department Law*, 1989;1(21):8.

3. *Hospital Underwriting Group v Summit Health*, USDCMD Tenn, No. 3:88-0297, July 5, 1989. This case report and analysis is adapted from *Emergency Department Law*, 1989;1(17):5-6. It is reprinted as adapted with permission of the publisher, Business Publishers, Inc, 951 Pershing Drive, Silver Springs, MD 20910-4464. (800) 274-6737. Fax: (301) 589-8493. E-mail bpinews@bpinews.com and Web site: www.bpinews.com.

4. *Niles v City of San Rafel*, 42 Cal App 3d 230, 116 Cal Rptr 733 (1974).

Chapter 48

Refusal of Care

Dan M. Mayer, MD
Daniel J. Sullivan, MD, JD, FACEP

Patients who refuse emergency care present the emergency physician with a wide array of challenging situations. In the past, the typical "refusal" was initiated by the patient either after being evaluated by the physician (against medical advice, "AMA"), or from the waiting room after having "waited too long" (left without treatment, LWOT, or LWBS, left without being seen). With the increased prevalence of managed care, patients presenting to emergency departments are now faced with preauthorization decisions, which often result in patients refusing emergency services.

Patients refuse care for a variety of reasons. Many of these situations are easily managed with a basic understanding of the law. Others are more difficult because the law does not address every situation. In some instances, case law has just begun to address the relevant issues.

Why Do Patients Refuse Medical Care?

Researchers have identified and published the typical reasons that patients refuse medical attention[1,2] and have developed a useful profile of "reluctant" patients. These patients usually are upset because of misunderstanding, anger, or fear. This misunderstanding is often exacerbated when patients cannot understand the language used by the health care provider to explain the problem. Patients are already upset about being ill and having to come to the emergency department. Their anger is then directed toward the physician or the treatment plan.

When interviewed, many patients say that they left the emergency department because they disagreed with the assessments and treatment plans of the physician or because they felt that their problems were not as severe as stated by the physician.[3,4] Narcotics abusers and drug-seekers often become angry because their need for drugs is not fulfilled.

Patients with chronic illness, such as asthma, epilepsy, and diabetes, displace anger related to their illness onto the physician. Patients with anxiety disorders and feelings of helplessness or panic may express anger, especially when no easily treatable organic illness is found. Patients who are under the influence of alcohol or drugs, or who exhibit suicidal or homicidal behavior, frequently refuse treatment. Others reject care out of fear of further pain, previous bad hospital experiences, discovery of a serious diagnosis, or because they feel that interns and residents are "practicing" on them. Finally, some patients are unable to prioritize their lives, equating potentially lifesaving medical treatment with personal responsibilities, such as feeding the cat or locking up the house.

Studies of hospital patients who sign out AMA reveal that emergency department patients have the highest rate of AMAs.[5-7] Denial of illness or suspicion of the legitimacy of the treatment or diagnostic procedure being recommended were the most common reasons for refusal in these patients. In many of these cases, the treating physicians appeared to take the easier path to discharge "difficult" patients who refused treatment and signed out AMA rather

Figure 1

Clinical situations in which patients may be treated against their will

- New change in mental status.

- Intoxication, hypoxia, acidosis, or any other metabolic derangement.

- Dementia (surrogates may make decisions, except in some emergency situations).

- Suicidal or homicidal ideation or intent.

- Acute organic brain syndrome.

than to determine the patients' reasons for refusal. They rarely consulted psychiatrists.[7] Patients were found to lack clear information and understanding about their diseases and the risks of refusal.

One study[3] of patients who refused emergency department treatment found that chest pain was the most common presenting complaint in the patients who left AMA. In this study, disagreement with the physician was the most common reason for refusing care. The documentation of the refusal was poor in one third of the cases, yet most patients were satisfied with the encounter. Another study[4] compared patients with chest pain who left AMA midway in their clinical presentations with those who were subsequently discharged or admitted by the emergency physician. The risk of complications and death was similar in the two groups.

Ethical Issues

The problem of refusal of care arises because health care providers must balance the autonomy of the patient against the interests of the state in maintaining its citizens' life and health. Patient autonomy requires that patients be allowed to refuse any care that they find objectionable, for whatever reason. This right, within limits, has been upheld repeatedly by the courts.[8]

The state has an interest in preserving life; of protecting the lives of innocent third parties, such as the fetus, children, "incompetents," and other dependents; and of preventing injuries to third parties. This beneficence principle may result in the physician restraining a patient and forcing care against the patient's will. The physician's interest is protection from liability related to negligence lawsuits involving patients who have refused care and subsequently suffered a poor outcome, or inappropriate use of restraint and legal action based on battery or false imprisonment. Balancing these interests is the challenge of managing patients who refuse care.

Consent and the Right to Refuse Care

A patient's right to be informed and give consent for any medical treatment is a standard part of medical care. Informed consent includes disclosure of the nature of the disorder; the proposed intervention; the likely benefits, risks, and discomforts; the possible alternatives; and the risk of receiving no treatment. These issues must be presented to patients in a manner that they can easily understand and attest to by signing a form.[9]

First stated by Justice Cardozo in *Schloendorf v Society of the New York Hospital,* the concept of informed consent has been upheld and expanded in many subsequent court citations.[10-18] The fundamental issue involved in the refusal of care dilemma can still be summed up in Justice Cardozo's famous statement: "Every human being of adult years and sound mind has the right to determine what shall be done to his body."[12] The same rules of informed consent that apply to allowing treatment also must be applied in the refusal of care. Patients must clearly understand the recommended treatment, the risks of not being treated, the possible outcomes, and all reasonable alternatives.

State courts use one of two basic standards that dictate the amount and type of information that must be communicated to provide an informed consent or informed refusal. The first standard is set by the "reasonable medical practitioner." It is that quantity and detail of the information given to patients that would be imparted by a "reasonable practitioner" using generally agreed-on medical standards. The standard defined by the court is "measured by those communications a reasonable medical practitioner in that branch of medicine would make under the same or similar circumstances," as established by expert medical evidence.[13] The second standard is a "reasonable patient standard." In other words, a consent or refusal is informed if that decision is one that "a reasonably prudent person in the patient's position" would make if "adequately informed of all the significant perils."[14]

The autonomy interests of patients who refuse care can be addressed easily by explaining the risks and alternatives and then allowing the patient to make an informed decision. Patients who cannot understand all the ramifications of refusal cannot, by definition, make an informed refusal of care. These include patients intoxicated by drugs or alcohol, those unable to communicate or in coma, those with an organic mental disorder that prevents them from acting in a manner that is totally protective of their life interests, actively psychotic patients, and others (Figure 1).[19]

The debate over a patient's right to refuse care was reviewed by a presidential commission in 1983.[20] Growing out of the ethical issues that resulted from the increased technology of medicine, the commission attempted to set a series of guidelines under which practitioners could determine which patients could be allowed to forego these new technologies and (possibly) die as a result. Weighing the competing positions of unconditional patient autonomy and absolute physician authority, the commission developed a compromise position in which the operational term was "shared decision-making." Also defined was a continuum on which patient decision-making could be judged. This went from unconditional patients' rights on one hand to total physician authority on the other. Parallel to that were other continua of disease severity (minor to life-threatening) and futility (easily treated with success, to failure no matter what treatment was employed), which could apply to each individual situation.

This continuum of "shifting severity" led to a "shifting standard of competency" to be applied in all cases of refusal. The location of patients on the continuum depends on the severity of the illness, the urgency of treatment, and the patients' ability to deliberate about the choices offered and come to an ultimate decision. This decision must then be supported by the patients' values and, ultimately, the implications that refusal of treatment would have on their lives. Simply put, minor medical problems, in which there is little ultimate effect on patients' lives, allow for greater patient autonomy to refuse care. Conversely, the physician has a duty to provide a more in-depth discussion of values for cases in which the outcomes are more dire. The most intoxicated alcoholic may easily be allowed to refuse to have a minor laceration sutured, but an articulate university professor who attempts to refuse care for a myocardial infarction must pass the most stringent series of tests before being allowed to refuse care.[21] This second patient must be fully aware of the nature of the illness, including the inevitable results of letting nature take its course. He must then be able to articulate his wishes and knowledge clearly to the health care provider and demonstrate how this refusal is consistent with a deeply held value system before being allowed to refuse treatment.

Determining a Patient's Capacity to Refuse Care

The patient who refuses potentially lifesaving care must first have the capacity to understand the ramifications of refusal. There are several bedside tests that can be applied to test capacity. These can be summarized into determinations of orientation and judgment. Appelbaum and Grisso[22] have developed a com-

Figure 2

Model quations for the assessment of psycholegal capacities

Ability to Render a Choice

1. Have you decided whether to go along with your doctor's suggestions for treatment? Can you tell me what your decision is? (Can be repeated to assess stability of choice.)

Ability to Understand Relevant Information

1. Please tell me in your own words what your doctor told you about:
   a. the nature of your condition.
   b. the recommended treatment (or diagnostic test).
   c. the possible benefits from the treatment.
   d. the possible risks (or discomforts) of the treatment.
   e. any other possible treatments that could be used, and their risks and benefits.
   f. the possible risks and benefits of no treatment at all.
2. You mentioned that your doctor told you of a [percentage] chance the [named risk] might occur with treatment. In your own words, how likely do you think the occurrence of [named risk] might be?
3. Why is your doctor giving you all this information? What role does he/she expect you to play in deciding whether you receive treatment? What will happen if you decide not to go along with your doctor's recommendation?

Ability to Appreciate the Situation and Its Consequences

1. Please explain to me what you really believe is wrong with your health now?
2. Do you believe you need some kind of treatment? What is treatment likely to do for you?
3. What do you believe will happen if you are not treated?
4. Why do you think your doctor has recommended [specific treatment] for you?

Ability for Rational Manipulation of Information

1. Tell me how you reached the decision to accept [reject] the recommended treatment?
2. What were the factors that were important to you in reaching the decision?
3. How did you balance those factors?

From Appelbaum PS, Gutheil TG. Interviewing the alleged incompetent. In: *Clinical Handbook of Psychiatry and the Law*. Second edition. Baltimore: Williams & Wilkins; 1991. Used with permission.

prehensive set of questions based on the findings of the presidential commission, which specifically test a patient's capacity to make an informed refusal (Figure 2). Although some form of determination of capacity should be applied to emergency department patients who want to leave AMA, there is no standard required test or series of formal mental status tests.

The clinician seeks an operational measure of capacity that can easily be applied in a busy emergency department. Patients must be oriented to person, place, and time and be able to engage in extended conversation about their illnesses and treatment goals. This automatically excludes patients who are uncooperative and noncommunicative, or who have a clearly altered mental status (see Chapter 53, "Patients With Altered Mental Status"). The physician must then explain the diagnostic possibilities and the proposed treatments to patients in language that will be understood by the "prudent layperson." Patients must demonstrate, by paraphrasing the information just given by the physician, that they understand the diagnosis, reasons for the treatment offered, risks and benefits of the treatment offered, and the likely result of refusing treatment. They should be asked how a poor outcome will fit into their lives, or how their values permit them to make the decision to refuse.

Patients' desires and rationale for refusal must remain constant over time. This means at least long enough for the interview to be completed. The rationale for refusal should remain unchanged with repeated questioning. Impaired judgment may occur because of denial, psychiatric illness, cognitive impairment, or delusional states, such as paranoia or an acute organic mental disorder. Impairment because of drugs, organic illness, dementia, or florid acute psychosis will substantially reduce patients' rights to refuse care in the emergency setting.[22]

Bedside tests, such as the Short Portable Mental Status Questionnaire,[23] Mini Mental Status Examination,[24] and the Cortical Function Assessment Test,[25] are useful tools to determine the presence of an organic mental syndrome.[23-26] They test patients' ability to recall several objects over a brief period of time, draw simple shapes, recognize objects or words, spell common words, and manipulate numbers. The physician can assess thought content and process, concentration, affect, and mood during the history and discussion of patients' reasons for refusing care. The emergency physician is not obligated to apply a formal test of mental status in all situations. However, some sort of bedside determination of thought processes should be applied and documented on the medical record before patients are allowed to refuse care.

Testing internal consistency requires that two further requirements be met. The first is that patients can explain their own beliefs about their conditions and the reasons why they think the physician is requesting further diagnosis and treatment, thus comparing their own reasons for refusal with the physician's reasons for compliance. Second, patients must be able to tell the physician how and why they came to these conclusions. They should be questioned about the factors that led them to make their decisions. This is a measure of patients' values regarding treatment. These skills are often absent in psychotic, phobic, and manic patients, as well as those with organic disorders, and would invalidate their right of refusal.

Patients' values may not be the same as or even palatable to the physician. The important part of the physician's judgment is that patients' views are strongly held, persistent through interviews, and internally consistent. The patient who refuses relatively benign care for a potentially fatal problem should be asked to give the name of someone who would be aware of these strongly held beliefs. Attempt to contact that person and verify those beliefs, with the patient's consent. These include the patient's family, close friends, religious leaders, physicians, and even personal attorneys, who when contacted may convince the patient to agree to care.

The process of determining capacity should be nonthreatening to patients. It is always good practice to allow family members and friends to witness the procedure. They may become allies in attempting to change the patients' minds to allow treatment. At the least, they will be witnesses to the physician's attempts to provide care and patients' refusal of those attempts.

Some patients may appear to be confused about their desire for or against treatment, as evidenced by inconsistency in their statements regarding treatment. This ambiguity may be a form of diminished capacity or simply loosely held beliefs resulting from never having carefully examined life values and goals. In this setting, diminished capacity must be assumed in refusal situations that are potentially life-threatening. If the need for treatment is less immediate, a psychiatrist may be called to help patients clarify their values.

Psychiatrists are not legal experts on declaring patient competency. A declaration of competency, or lack thereof, can be done only by a court of law.[27,28] The psychiatrist is usually consulted to help the emergency physician verify patients' capacity to understand proposed diagnoses and treatment procedures. Part of this determination is a requirement to test the consistency and internal validity of the reasons for refusal. In our reality as emergency physicians, this is a time-consuming task and one that cannot be done easily in a busy emergency department. Requesting psychiatrist assistance for capacity determination allows patients time to clarify goals and gives the emergency physician insight into the patients' thought processes.

If a patient refuses to cooperate with the evaluation by not giving the emergency physician an adequate history or allowing an examination and the physician feels there is an immediate threat to patient well-being, it may be inferred that there is sufficient indirect evidence of impairment of capacity. It may then be concluded that the patient would probably be found incompetent by a court.[28] This is simply a statement of the "emergency exception" to consent, which allows immediate treatment even against a patient's will.

Patients Who Leave Against Medical Advice

Traditional AMA forms contained only a blanket release from liability. A modified AMA form (Figure 3) should include statements describing the potential diagnosis, recommended treatment, and risks of nontreatment, including possible death and any reasonable alternatives. The actual words used on the AMA form should be clear and in simple terms that patients can understand.[29,30] Generally, patient comprehension of medical forms is limited due to intelligence level and the use of medical terminology in the form. Ask patients to read the statements on the AMA form aloud. The more serious the consequences, the more inclusive the documentation should be. Patient records should include descriptions of all attempts made by the physician to change patients' minds and the process by which patients' capacity to refuse care was assessed. This process may be shortened in cases in which the refusal has a less serious outcome.

Patient signatures should be obtained on a firm, flat surface and should be "characteristic" of the patient. The discharge is then completed in

Figure 3
Sample AMA form

Albany Medical Center Hospital
Release for Leaving Hospital Against Medical Advice

Patient name:_____

Date of service: _____

PATIENT IDENTIFICATION PLATE

I, _____ , hereby certify that I am leaving (PRINT NAME) Albany Medical Center Hospital against the advice of the attending physician, giving the physician in charge of my case, the Albany Medical Center Hospital, and its staff an absolute release from all responsibility for any damage resulting from my leaving the hospital against medical advice.

I have discussed my refusal with Dr. _____ and I have reached this decision by myself. No one has forced me to make this decision.

I understand the following:

1. The potential diagnoses include: _____

2. The recommended treatment/tests include: _____

3. Alternatives to treatment include: _____

4. The expected benefit(s) of the treatment/tests include: _____

5. The risk(s) of no treatment/test include: _____

Comments:

I understand that if I change my mind, I can receive treatment at any time even though I am signing this refusal of care against medical advice.

Patient signature:_____ Date signed:_____ Time signed: _____

Witness signature: _____ (Print name) _____

Physician signature: _____ (Print name) _____

Date signed: _____

Used with permission from the Albany Medical Center Hospital, Albany, New York.

the same way as for any other patient. An "uncharacteristic" signature can suggest that the patient was suffering from an organic mental disorder at the time of refusal. Emergency physicians should write discharge instructions as if patients had completed treatment and should give these instructions to patients with a copy of the AMA form. Patients should be informed that they may return for additional medical care at any time without prejudice. Follow-up care with the physician on call or of their choice should be recommended.[21] Patients must be given oral and written instructions not to engage in any activity that could be potentially dangerous. This includes driving an automobile if the patient is intoxicated or has any illness that could impair sight, coordination, or judgment. Patients who are impaired (e.g., significantly intoxicated) should be discharged only if accompanied by responsible third parties. Otherwise, patients should be held for observation.

A properly executed AMA form with appropriate documentation of the process of determining capacity and fully informing patients will protect the physician from successful negligence actions in cases of patient refusal. It also protects patients from reckless action. By asking patients to read the medical information and understand the issues of risk and benefit from treatment, they will be forced to clarify their goals and values at the point of refusal. However, the form is not a guarantee against successful liability action. As in any other situation, reasonable and prudent medical care is the best defense against a lawsuit and the standard against which any specific medical practice will be measured. The presidential commission recognized that an overly strict interpretation of informed consent would become an unreasonable burden for the physician.[21] Nowhere is this more applicable than in the emergency department. If a treating physician has any doubt that a patient's refusal is not fully informed and the outcome is potentially disastrous, reasonable therapeutic restraint is necessary and, with careful documentation, would be totally defensible.

Patients Who Leave Before Being Treated

Patients who leave before receiving emergency department treatment pose similar problems to those who actually complete the major part of their care and sign out AMA. Patients who leave from the waiting room are generally labeled as LWOT or LWBS. Patients who have entered the emergency department, are in the process of care, and then leave without notifying the emergency department staff are generally known as absconders, or patients who are absent without leave (AWOL).

There are several areas of potential exposure to liability for emergency department staff in these situations. The first is in the appropriateness of the triage to the waiting room. In lawsuits involving plaintiffs who LWOT, the retrospective evaluation will focus on the adequacy of the triage process. Patients are sent to the waiting room because there are no places for them in the emergency department. If the emergency department is not busy, they are seen immediately. If it is very busy, they are asked to wait. Triage staff must be carefully trained in prioritization based on severity of illness. The triage nurse or other nurse or physician should reevaluate waiting room patients at regular intervals. Patient advocates are quite helpful in explaining delays to patients and in alerting staff about patients preparing to LWOT.

Patients who abscond from the emergency department during treatment without notifying the care providers present another type of medical-legal risk for the emergency physician. In general, these patients have chosen to leave of their own free will and without notifying the emergency department staff. Although it would appear on the surface that there is minimal, if any, medical-legal risk involved in this situation, these patients present with the same medical-legal problems (and some unique ethical problems) as other patients who refuse care. In most of these situations, if the staff had known that a patient was going to leave without treatment, they would have initiated the AMA process and would have tried to anticipate the patient's leaving the emergency department AWOL. An indiction that a patient may leave suddenly is when the patient becomes increasingly agitated or impatient with the care given. Early recognition of these patients may help reduce the number of AWOL situations.

Documentation of these patient encounters should include the time patients were last seen and a notation that they left without warning. If attempts were made to stop the patient, that should also be documented.

If a patient leaves suddenly and without warning, attempt to determine if the patient is a danger to self or to others. Patients in this group include those with possible organic mental disorders, alcohol intoxication, unstable medical problems that could cloud decision-making, and suicidal or homicidal ideation. If there is any possibility that the patient may be a danger to self or others, the police should be notified and recruited to help find and return the patient to the emergency department. In some cases, restraints will be required, but most often, the patient will return, albeit reluctantly, for treatment. When the patient is returned to the emergency department, the AMA process can be formally carried out, if it is appropriate.

Special Categories of Patients Who Refuse Care

Psychiatric Patients

Most psychiatric patients are currently treated as outpatients. They often present to the emergency department for medical care without the presence of supervising staff. They are often brought in by police, EMS crews, or bystanders who notice that they are "acting funny." They should be presumed competent to refuse care, and their capacity to refuse should be determined by the previously described rules. Patients who refuse to allow even a medical screening examination must be held against their will until they allow either treatment or formal mental status testing. A mentally ill patient who is in a community residential facility may be discharged to a facility staff member who can vouch that the patient is at baseline and will assume responsibility for supervising the patient. The staff member can sign the AMA form with the patient and agree to return the patient if any deterioration occurs. Or, a psychiatrist can be consulted to determine capacity. Psychiatric patients' rights to refuse psychotropic medications generally have been upheld by the courts.

Homeless Patients

Homeless or "street" people may be brought to the emergency department against their will under orders from local politicians or civil authorities to remove them from the streets. Even though such a patient has not asked to be brought in for care, the emergency physician is still required to conduct a screening examination as with any other emergency department patient, according to EMTALA.[31] If no current problem is noted after the medical screening examination, no further care is needed. If an abnormality is found and the patient refuses additional care, the refusal should be handled in the same way as for any other patient. The physician is under no obligation to force additional care on a patient who clearly has a normal mental status and denies the presence of any physical complaints. The political problems that lead to this situation must be dealt with by emergency department management and community leaders.

Narcotics Abusers

Narcotics abusers who attempt to leave after reversal of narcotic overdose may present an example of coerced refusal. Reversing the narcotic makes them uncomfortable enough and gives them an uncontrollable desire to get more drugs. Their refusal becomes based solely on this fact and will (usually) prevent them from understanding that they may lapse into unconsciousness again when the naloxone wears off. They are angry that the high has been reversed and will try to leave in order to get high again. Naloxone has a shorter half-life than heroin or other narcotics, and the patient is at risk for a recurrent respiratory arrest.[32]

Narcotic reversal may cause patients to become violent and can produce acute withdrawal, vomiting, pulmonary edema, uncontrolled hypertension in patients who use heroin and cocaine, and other potentially life-threatening adverse effects. Emergency department staff should anticipate these problems by restraining these patients before administering naloxone, and then closely observing them immediately afterward. Administering a small dose of naloxone to prevent respiratory arrest but not to wake such a patient is another option.

The patient who asks to leave AMA after waking up must be assessed for capacity but should be held in the emergency department for at least one half-life of naloxone. The risk of recurrent respiratory arrest is certain, and discharge would constitute a risk of self-harm.

Alcoholic Patients

Many instances of missed diagnosis occur in alcohol intoxication cases. Emergency physicians treat a disproportionate number of alcohol-intoxicated patients. Most often seen during night shifts, they are difficult to evaluate because they present with a complex set of medical problems and have an altered mental status. Alcoholics and alcohol-intoxicated patients are prone to head and neck injuries and frequently present with atypical signs and symptoms of these injuries. They represent a significant risk of misdiagnosis.[33,34]

In general, when treating such a patient, if a blood alcohol level is drawn, the physician typically orders repeat levels, holding the patient until the level is at or below the state legal limit of intoxication. An important caveat is that once the patient demonstrates mental competence and there is no apparent life threat, the emergency physician has no legal right to detain the patient any longer. Thus, although many emergency physicians work with the legal limit of alcohol in planning discharge, the mentally competent individual has the right to refuse further care, regardless of the alcohol level.

If a blood alcohol level is not drawn, the patient can be assessed clinically for resolution of intoxication or a coexisting condition and may be discharged when the physician is able to document competence. This is generally accomplished through an evaluation of mental status and a physical examination.[34]

The emergency physician should assume that the intoxicated patient does not have the capacity to consent to or refuse treatment and has a life-threatening problem. Therefore, the emergency physician should perform a complete patient evaluation, or in EMTALA parlance, a medical screening examination. A relatively liberal restraint policy will allow proper evaluation of these patients and prevent them from leaving AMA or AWOL (see Chapter 54, "Use of Restraints").

Violent Patients

Violent patients, or those who are shouting obscenities, disrupt any emergency department. They often refuse care as well. There is a correlation between violence and acute organic brain syndrome. These patients should be treated with reasonable therapeutic restraint. The AMA form should not be used to get rid of unwanted violent patients.[35] Extremely violent patients may harm emergency department staff, and attempts to convince them to stay for treatment may be difficult.

If emergency department staff make reasonable attempts to prevent such a patient from leaving, they have no added duty to remain in harm's way to treat a violent patient. If the patient can be retained for a short time, police may help the emergency department staff restrain the patient. If not, staff should document the fact that the patient was not restrained because of fear of harm to emergency department personnel. The patient should be allowed to "escape," and the police should be notified and told that the patient may be a threat to self or others. Police should also be asked to return the patient to the emergency department in their custody.

Religious Objections to Treatment

Consent issues take on constitutional proportions when religious beliefs are concerned. The general rule is that competent adult patients have the right to refuse any treatment on any grounds, including religious ones.[16,36]

The Jehovah's Witness refusal of medical care is the stereotypical example of religious practices at odds with medical opinions. Although many religious groups refuse certain types of medical treatment, Jehovah's Witness followers firmly believe that transfusion of blood will result in a loss of eternal life, based on interpretation of biblical passages. They do not accept transfusion of whole blood, packed cells, white cells, or plasma or autotransfusion of predeposited blood. However, many will permit use of albumin, immunoglobulins, hemophiliac preparations, crystalloids, hetastarch, or IV iron dextran, as well as dialysis, use of heart-lung equipment, and intraoperative salvage if extracorporeal circulation is uninterrupted. If the use of fluorinated blood substitute becomes available, this practice would not be objectionable to members of this religious group. In addition, organ transplant is not specifically prohibited.

Transfusion or other treatment can be authorized over patients' objections if there is a question of patients' competency, or if the state demonstrates a compelling and overriding interest, or if the refusal is not contemporaneous and informed.[37] Therefore, transfusions *may* be authorized in Jehovah's Witness followers or members of other religious groups who are not competent adults, who have dependents, or are pregnant, or in those for whom there is reasonable doubt of the strength of their religious convictions. These patients or their families should be advised in advance of the pending transfusion.

Courts have held that any refusal of lifesaving medical treatment must be contemporaneous and informed to be enforced. For example, in *Werth v Taylor*,[36] the court held that a patient's prior refusals to permit blood transfusions, which were made before the necessity for transfusion arose and in contemplation of routine dilatation of the cervix and curettage of the uterine lining, were not contemporaneous and informed. Thus, the physicians who gave the patient a blood transfusion when she was under anesthesia determined that transfusion was necessary to save the patient's life. This did not constitute assault and battery, regardless of whether the physician failed to obtain her husband's permission.

Patients who refuse care on religious grounds present very difficult medical-legal issues. When confronted with such a situation, the emergency physician should immediately contact the hospital administrator or hospital attorney to help work through these issues. In many cases, the hospital must immediately appeal to the courts for assistance in determining whether the patient does, in fact, have a right to refuse care.

Refusal of Care and Managed Care Organizations

The advent of managed care has resulted in an entirely new set of problems associated with refusal of care. Some managed care patients present to the emergency department and are then told over the telephone by the managed care organization (MCO) representatives that the charges for their emergency care will not be covered by the plan. This usually occurs when such a patient is being registered in the emergency department, after triage but before being seen by any medical care provider.

The MCO has an interest in minimizing costs while delivering quality care. The balance between reducing costs and maintaining or improving quality is a difficult one, and the behavior of MCOs varies in this regard. The emergency department has become a site of care that most MCOs find expensive and not cost-effective. Some have set up 24-hour urgent care centers to manage patients who think they have an emergency and who in the past would have gone to the emergency department. Most MCO policies deny coverage for unauthorized emergency department services. Although they all manage this problem differently, the overall goal is to minimize emergency department care.

The typical scenario involves a patient who presents to the emergency department and at the time of registration notifies the clerk that he is a member of a certain MCO. He is then informed that the MCO in question does not automatically authorize care at that emergency department unless there has been prior approval by the MCO staff. Approval is usually provided by a clerk or a nurse at the MCO, a person who has not seen or examined the patient.

According to EMTALA, this patient must receive a medical screening examination and stabilizing treatment within the capabilities of the hospital.[31] This potential patient must be offered a medical screening examination, regardless of his MCO's coverage decision. However, like many patients, he may decide to leave the emergency department at this point and refuse any further care. EMTALA specifically states that hospitals do not have a duty to provide a screening examination to patients who make an informed refusal of care.[38] Denial of a screening examination or stabilizing treatment, however, is a violation of the law.

Emergency department staff should not delay provision of a medical screening examination while calling the MCO unless the patient refuses to proceed with the visit until the coverage decision is made. In general, financial information may be gathered while the medical screening examination is being performed as long as it does not delay examination and appropriate stabilization (see Chapter 45, "EMTALA").

The hospital should have a formal, written procedure for the refusal process. In general, this should follow the procedures for patients who leave AMA. Patients should be offered the examination and treatment regardless of his ability to pay or whether the MCO authorizes payment. If patients still refuse care, they should be asked to sign a formal informed refusal document. If they will not sign the document, that fact should be documented, and the chart should become part of the permanent medical record. These "managed care" refusals must be listed in the emergency department central log to comply with other aspects of the EMTALA regulations.[39]

Advance Directives

The U.S. Supreme Court has determined that a competent person has a constitutionally protected liberty interest to refuse medical treatment.[16] The Court concluded that the U.S. Constitution would grant a competent person a constitutionally protected right to refuse lifesaving medical treatment, including nutrition and hydration. This is accomplished through advance directives, or directions that individuals give about the kind of health care they wish to have or not to have if they ever lose the ability to make decisions for themselves. Advance directives provide statutory authority for refusal of certain types of medical care.

Advance directives allow for greater patient

autonomy regarding end-of-life decisions. They represent a legislatively authorized way to refuse care. There are problems, however, with the application of advance directives in the emergency department.

A survey of outpatients at the Massachusetts General Hospital[40] found that many patients did not have advance directives in place. More than 90% of these patients and slightly less than 60% of nonpatient members of the general public wanted advance directives. There were no differences in the percentages of those wanting advanced directives among age groups or by health status. The major perceived barrier to the issuance of an advance directive was lack of physician initiative. Emergency physicians must understand the different types of advance directives, the function of each, and their application to the refusal of care situation.[41]

The Patient Self Determination Act[42] was passed in response to the public debate over the right to accept or refuse medical treatment and the use of advance directives, as publicized in *Cruzan v Director, Missouri Department of Health*.[16] The law was intended to increase people's ability to make treatment decisions, especially for end-of-life decisions, when they may lack the mental capacity for decision-making. The law mandates that health care providers and health care organizations that participate in Medicare and Medicaid give all adults for whom they provide medical care written information about their rights to make health care decisions under states law. This includes the right to refuse treatment and formulate advance directives. This information must be documented in the patient's medical record, and the staff and community must be educated about advance directives. The law also prohibits discrimination by health care providers based on the execution of an advance directive. Compliance is monitored as part of the Medicare and Medicaid program. Violators may be suspended from participating in those programs. There is no funding to help health care providers meet these obligations.

There are two kinds of advance directives: living wills and health care powers of attorney. In general, advance directives will discriminate between providing comfort care in contrast to life-sustaining treatment. Comfort care is any medical or nursing intervention designed to treat pain and discomfort. Such treatment is not given simply to postpone death. Life-sustaining treatment, on the other hand, is any medical or surgical intervention that is principally designed to prolong life or to delay the process of dying.

Living wills are legal documents that give patients the power to give advance direction to physicians regarding their care. They often begin with a general admonition to discontinue life-sustaining treatment under certain conditions. They may state what treatment patients will allow and are usually only effective when these patients have terminally ill conditions.

A terminal condition is generally defined as being irreversible and incurable and is usually determined by a patient's private physician and confirmed by a consulting physician. It is caused by disease, illness, or injury; recovery is unlikely, and death will occur imminently if life-sustaining treatment is not administered immediately.

The durable power of attorney for health care is a document used in some states to specify an agent to help patients make health care decisions. Generally, patients state their preferences and make specified limitations on their agents' powers. These documents take effect when patients are no longer able to make their own health care decisions.

The courts are increasingly upholding the validity of a properly executed advance directive.[43,44] In these cases, courts have declared that medical care providers must honor any requests by a patient's power of attorney (POA) to withdraw treatment. They have often added that the health care providers will be absolved from criminal or civil liability for complying with a POA's request. Courts have also upheld living wills executed in other states.[45] At the same time, failure or refusal to implement an advance directive does not necessarily automatically allow legal action against the health care provider.[46] In fact, some statutes give health care providers the right not to comply with advance directives as a matter of conscience and to transfer the care of such a patient to a provider who will comply with the patient's wishes.[47]

The durable POA is believed to be the best choice for most patients who can identify friends or family members to make health care decisions consistent with their wishes. More flexible and comprehensive than the living will, it simply designates an agent to make decisions, while a living will specifies the decisions ahead of time. It also does not require that a patient have a terminal illness. Used with a living will that has been appropriately modified, the durable POA controls the situation until it becomes unenforceable for any reason, at which time, the modified living will takes over. This situation can occur if the agent is unable or unwilling to serve or if the patient lives in a state that does not recognize health care durable POA. Emergency physicians should become aware of the types of advance directives allowed in their states.

Several states have passed medical surrogate laws, which specify who can make decisions for incompetent patients when they leave no advance directives. Surrogate laws provide a "pecking order" of decisionmakers who have the right to consent to or refuse treatment for an incompetent, terminally ill family member.[48]

In the event that a patient does not have an advance directive and the state does not have medical surrogate legislation, the physician may have to rely on a "do not resuscitate" order to withhold treatment. In certain instances of irreversible or terminal illness, CPR, intubation, or other treatment may be medically futile or so contrary to the patient's wishes or expectations as to be unjustified. If the patient lacks decision-making capacity regarding treatment, a surrogate may make the decision based on the patient's previously expressed wishes or, if those wishes are unknown, in accordance with the best interests of the patient.[49]

Refusal of Care for Children

Unless a minor is emancipated, or is a "mature minor," or has one of the special conditions covered by a state's "special treatment statutes," a minor is not cognitively or legally capable of giving or refusing consent for medical treatment.[50] The young child who refuses a laceration repair typically is not a problem. The parents and the physician agree on treatment, and the child is overruled.

Problems typically arise when adolescents refuse care. This situation often presents a significant dilemma for emergency physicians. For example, a mother presents to the emergency department with her 16-year-old daughter. The mother believes that the child has had sexual intercourse and asks the physician to perform a pelvic examination. The 16-year-old adamantly refuses examination. The case clearly presents an ethical and legal dilemma. The refusal of care should be respected. The 16-year-old is probably old enough to understand her actions. She certainly understands the nature and purpose of the examination. State law also supports the minor when presenting for sexually transmitted diseases (STDs) and pregnancy. States are increasingly recognizing a minor's right to pri-

vacy. The emergency physician should evaluate and document the patient's developmental state and maturity. The refusal should be accepted under the mature minor exception, or it may be covered under one of the specific treatment statutes with regard to pregnancy or STDs.

In those jurisdictions that recognize the mature minor, the minor has the same right as a competent adult to refuse life-sustaining treatment. In the Illinois case of *In Re E.G.*,[51] a 17-year-old leukemic Jehovah's Witness was permitted to refuse a lifesaving transfusion. However, not all jurisdictions recognize the mature minor doctrine. For example, in the case of *In Re Long Island Jewish Medical Center*,[52] a New York court refused to adopt the mature minor doctrine and recommended that the legislature or appellate courts adopt a doctrine with an appropriate procedural safeguard.

Refusal of care cases involving minors can be complex, and there are many gray areas. For example, a 15-year-old boy with leukemia refuses a blood transfusion, or a 17-year-old girl with vaginal bleeding and lower abdominal pain decides to leave AMA before being evaluated for ectopic pregnancy. These are difficult issues, and emergency physicians should request assistance from hospital administration or counsel.

When a Parent Refuses Medical Care for a Child

Generally, state and federal courts support parental control over the basic matters affecting their children. However, when parental actions have resulted in inadequate medical care, the courts have stepped in to decide between parents' wishes and physicians' concerns. Under the doctrine of *parens patriae* (the state's paternalistic interest in children), the state will not allow a child's health to be seriously jeopardized because of the parent's limitations or convictions. Parents do not have the authority to forbid saving their children's lives. Courts invariably rule in favor of physicians who claim that parents are denying standard medical care to their children.

Under the doctrine of *parens patriae*, the state represents the best interests of the child. The state also looks to the child abuse and neglect statutes, which provide for protective custody when the child has not received medically indicated treatment.

Once again, the emergency physician is empowered by understanding the law. If parents withhold consent and there is a threat to a child's life, the emergency physician should take temporary protective custody based on child neglect. Explain to the parents that this is a medical obligation under the law that you will immediately report to the hospital administrator, hospital attorney, and the local child protection agency. The parents will typically stand down and allow care to proceed. Even in situations where the child's life may not be threatened but severely impaired, the courts usually will order medical treatment over the parents' objections. Remember: the emergency physician is protected from civil and criminal liability under the child abuse and neglect statutes. Emergency physicians may be hesitant to take custody, but it should not be for fear of liability.

If there is no life threat and no potential for serious impairment, the parents' refusal should be respected. The refusal should be informed and well documented. In this context, informed means that one or both parents have a normal mental status, understand the risks of refusal, have had an opportunity to ask questions, and have decided to leave AMA. They should then complete an AMA form.

At times, parents will refuse care based on claims of religious freedom. The First Amendment issue of religious freedom does not change the analysis. The typical example is the 14-year-old boy, a victim of a car collision, who has internal bleeding. He is in shock and needs blood. The emergency physician has typed and crossmatched the patient's blood and has contacted the surgeon to go to the operating room. The parents intervene and refuse to consent to the blood transfusion. The courts have held that denying medical care to a child is not within the parents' First Amendment right of freedom of religion. In *State v Perricone*,[53] the court said: "The right to practice religion freely does not include the liberty to expose . . . a child . . . to ill health or death. Parents may be free to become martyrs themselves. But it does not follow that they are free . . . to make martyrs of their children . . ." In *Re: The Petition of Allen Town Hospital-Lehigh Valley Hospital Center in the Matter of J.S.S.*,[54] a Pennsylvania court ordered a pregnant mother, who was a member of the Jehovah's Witness faith, to undergo a blood transfusion to save the life of her unborn child. The Pennsylvania Court of Common Pleas issued a court order in which it held the following: the mother had the legal right to refuse consent to administration of blood products, even if it was likely she would die without such treat-

ment; she did not have the right, however, to refuse consent to transfusions or administration of blood products if the unborn child were likely to die, to be stillborn, or suffer irreversible physical injury as a result.

In another case, *In Matter of McCauley*,[55] the court applied the best interest test and determined that the child should receive treatment when the parents refused to consent to medical treatment on religious grounds. When children are at risk, emergency physicians should take temporary protective custody, provide care, and report to the appropriate individuals and agencies.

In more difficult cases, such as the management of terminally ill patients, there are many ethical and legal uncertainties. In the previous car collision case, clearly, blood administration is in the best interest of the child. But in other cases, such as a minor who has leukemia and a life-threatening anemia, the best interest analysis is far more difficult. Here, the emergency physician must discuss the case with the patient's private physician and may need to temporize care until reasoned judgment from additional decisionmakers (e.g., lawyers, ethicists) can be brought to bear.

It is noteworthy that, in the past 30 years, no cases have been reported in which a parent has successfully sued a physician for providing non-negligent care to an adolescent without parental consent.

Refusal of Prehospital Care

Some patients who call EMS will refuse treatment or transport to the hospital. The reasons for such refusal are probably the same as for patients in the emergency department, with the addition of those patients for whom EMS was called without their knowledge. Handling these problems in the prehospital milieu is more difficult, as there are increased stressors and outside pressures in the "street" that are not present in the emergency department. Situations involving patients under the influence of alcohol or drugs or who have altered mental status based on the substance use are more common. Some patients want to delay treatment because the EMT is not a physician. Prehospital patients whose violent behavior poses a threat should be restrained as in the emergency department. EMS personnel should call the police to help them restrain these patients.

Prehospital providers should be instructed to inform patients of possible diagnoses and the

Figure 4

Required documentation for patients who leave AMA

- Orientation to time, place, and person.

- Evidence of organic mental disorder.

- Ability to understand complex information.

- Understanding of the illness and potential results of nontreatment.

- Ability to repeat the risks and benefits of treatment and refusal.

- Internal consistency of the decision, that is, how the refusal and possible adverse outcome fit into the patient's life (must be present in cases with high potential for loss of life or limb if care is refused).

- Presence of witnesses to the refusal.

- Patient's signature on the AMA form.

dangers of delaying care. This instruction should be given in plain language, and the providers should be sure that patients understand the information. Using allies at the scene, contacting family when able, and in general "selling" the need for treatment is the next step. If patients are not clear about the consequences of their refusal, this could be regarded as a shift in their attention over a brief period and is grounds for continuing efforts to obtain their consent to treatment or for bringing them in against their will.

Physicians who are providing online medical direction should be contacted and given the opportunity to talk to these patients or family members over the radio to convince them to come to the hospital. The information to determine such a patient's capacity can usually be obtained simply by asking if the patient appears to be acting in an unusual way at the time. If all attempts to obtain the patient's consent fail, a fully documented refusal of medical assistance form should be filled out. The threshold for bringing patients to the hospital against their will should be fairly low. The sample hospital form described earlier (Figure 3) can be modified for prehospital use.[56]

The online physicians are ultimately responsible for the care of these patients, even though they have not seen or possibly even heard about the patients. Physicians' responsibility for directing prehospital care begins with the appropriate training of prehospital providers in how to determine a patient's capacity to refuse care. The online function continues whenever prehospital providers sign out someone who refused medical attention, and these providers should be educated to contact the online physician in all these cases. Each EMS system must perform regular quality assurance reviews and track refusal of care cases. EMS administrators can then develop mechanisms for minimizing these cases and for ensuring that those carried out are done with the least risk to the providers and to the system.

Key Points and Conclusion

Patients who refuse medical care pose many medical-legal risks when they leave the emergency department. Although patients who possess capacity have the right to refuse medical care and physicians have no right to impose this care in most cases, those patients who do not possess capacity must have treatment performed against their will. The rules of determination of capacity, and then signing patients out AMA should be closely followed, and proper and fully informed refusals documented. EMTALA requires emergency departments to provide medical screening examinations of all patients who present for care, including those who are members of MCOs. Other situations involving alcohol-intoxicated patients, psychiatric patients, narcotics abusers, minors, patients with religious objections, and patients with end-of-life advance directives present their own unique problems. A complete working knowledge of the issues and risks associated with AMA care is part of the emergency physician's armamentarium.

- Patients who have capacity for decision-making have the right to refuse care under many situations.
- Emergency physicians must understand the principles of testing patients' capacity and apply these principles to the situation of a patient refusing medical care.
- Patients who lack capacity to refuse care may be held in the emergency department and restrained, if necessary, and given the appropriate and needed medical care.
- Patients who possess capacity and refuse care should have this capacity documented, be signed out AMA, and given proper discharge instructions.
- Every attempt should be made to detect patients in the waiting room who are getting ready to LWOT and to encourage them to remain to seek care.
- EMTALA requires that a medical screening examination be given to everyone who presents to the emergency department, even if payment authorization is refused by an MCO.
- Most situations of patient refusal on religious grounds are appropriate, except when the decision involves a minor or a pregnant woman.

References

1. Swartz M. The patient who refuses medical treatment: a dilemma for hospitals and physicians. *Am J Law Med* 1985;11:147-194.
2. Schlauch RW, Reich P, Kelly MJ. Leaving the hospital against medical advice. *N Engl J Med* 1979;300:22-24.
3. Dubow D, Propp D, Narasimhan K. Emergency department discharges against medical advice. *J Emerg Med* 1992;10:513-516.
4. Lee TH, Short LW, Brand DA, et al. Patients with acute chest pain who leave emergency departments against medical advice: prevalence, clinical characteristics, and natural history. *J Gen Intern Med* 1988;3:21-24.
5. Long JP, Marin A. Profile of patients signing against medical advice. *J Fam Pract* 1982;15:551-556.
6. Jankowski CB, Drum DE. Diagnostic correlates of discharge against medical advice. *Arch Gen Psychiatry* 1977;34:153-155.
7. Appelbaum PS, Roth LH. Patients who refuse treatment in medical hospitals. *JAMA* 1983;250:1296-1301.
8. Dunn JD. Risk management in emergency medicine. *Emerg Med Clin North Am* 1987;5:51-68.
9. Iserson KV, Sanders AB. Autonomy and informed consent. In: Iserson KV, Sanders AB, Mathieu DR, et al, eds. *Ethics in Emergency Medicine*. Baltimore: Williams & Wilkins; 1995.
10. Brock DW. Informed participation in decisions. In: Iserson KV, Sanders AB, Mathieu DR, et al, eds. *Ethics in Emergency Medicine*. Baltimore: Williams & Wilkins; 1995.
11. Elliott J. More support for refusing medical treatment. *JAMA* 1980;243:506-507.
12. Rozovsky FA. *Consent to Treatment: A Practical Guide*. Boston: Little, Brown & Co; 1984.
13. *Cobbs v Grant*, 8 Cal2d 229, 502 P2d 1, 104 Cal Rptr 505 (1972).
14. *Wooley v Henderson*, 418 A2d 1123, Maine Sup Ct (1980).
15. *Truman v Thomas*, 611 P2d 902, Cal Sup, 165 Cal Rptr 308, 27 Cal3d 285 (1980).
16. *Cruzan v Director, Missouri Department of Health*, 110 SCt 2841, 111 LEd2d 224 (1990).
17. *Canterbury v Spence*, 464 F2d 772 (DC Cir 1972).
18. *Crisher v Spak*, 471 NYS2d 741, Sup Ct, 122 Misc2d 355 (1983).
19. Appelbaum PS, Lidz CW, Meisel A. *Informed Consent: Legal Theory and Clinical Practice*. New York: Oxford University Press; 1987.
20. Drane JF. Competency to give an informed consent. *JAMA* 1984;252:925-927.
21. Mayer D. Refusal of care and discharge of "difficult" patients from the emergency department. *Ann Emerg Med* 1990;19:1436-1446.
22. Appelbaum PS, Guisso TG. Model questions for assessing patients' capacities to consent to treatment. In: Appelbaum PS, Gutheil TG, eds. *Clinical Handbook of Psychiatry and the Law, Second Edition*. Baltimore: Williams & Wilkins; 1991.
23. Pfeiffer E. A short portable mental status questionnaire for the assessment of organic brain deficit in elderly patients. *J Am Geriatr Soc* 1975;23:433-441.
24. Folstein MF, Folstein SE, McHugh PR. "Mini-mental state". A practical method for grading the cognitive state of patients for the clinician. *J Psychiatr Res* 1975;12:189-198.
25. Herst LD. Emergency psychiatry for the elderly. *Psychiatr Clin North Am* 1983;6:271-280.
26. Litovitz GL, Hedberg M, Wise TN, et al. Recognition of psychological and cognitive impairments in the emergency department. *Am J Emerg Med* 1985;3:400-402.
27. Buchanan AE. The question of competence. In: Iserson KV, Sanders AB, Mathieu DR, et al, eds. *Ethics in Emergency Medicine*. Baltimore: Williams & Wilkins; 1995.
28. Gutheil TG. The right to refuse treatment: paradox, pendulum and the quality of care. *Behav Sci Law* 1986;4:265-277.
29. Powers RD. Emergency department patient literacy and the readability of patient-directed materials. *Ann Emerg Med* 1988;17:124-126.
30. Logan PD, Schwab RA, Salomone JA III, et al. Patient understanding of emergency department discharge instructions. *South Med J* 1996;89:770-774.
31. Emergency Medical Treatment and Active Labor Act, 42 USC 1395dd(a).

32. Neal JM. Complications of naloxone (lett). *Ann Emerg Med* 1988;17:765-766.

33. Marx J. Alcohol and trauma. *Emerg Med Clin North Am* 1990;8:929-938.

34. Simel DL, Feussner JR. Does determining serum alcohol concentrations in emergency department patients influence physicians civil suit liability? *Arch Intern Med* 1989;149:1016-1018.

35. Johnson R, Trimble C. The [expletive deleted] shouter. *JACEP* 1975;4:333-335.

36. *Werth v Taylor*, 475 NW2d 426 (Mich App 1991).

37. *Norwood Hospital v Munoz*, 564 NE2d 1017 (Mass 1991).

38. 42 USC 1395dd (a)(2).

39. 42 CFR §489.20(b) (1995).

40. Danis M, Southerland LI, Garnett JM, et al. A prospective study of advance directives for life-sustaining care. *N Engl J Med* 1991;324:882-888.

41. Lydon DR. New rules govern a patient's "right to die" *Emerg Med Rep Leg Brief* 1991;2:93-100.

42. PL 101-508 §4206, 4751; 42 USC 1395 (cc) et seq.

43. *Rettinger v Little John* (No. 9CVD455, Forsythe, North Carolina General Court of Justice, September 2, 1991).

44. *Re: Ray* (No. 9-2202ca A, Circuit Court of Oskaloosa, Florida, July 29, 1991).

45. *Zodin v Manor* (No. 90082007, Cobb County (Ga) Superior Court, November 2, 1990).

46. *Anderson v St. Frances/St. George Hospital, Inc.*, No. A-89087, Common Court of Pleas, Hamilton County, Ohio, July 25, 1992.

47. Ohio Rev Ann: 337.6(B), 233.0(A) (Anderson 99 Supp).

48. Illinois Health Care Surrogate Act, 755 ILCS 40/1 et seq.

49. American Medical Association, Council on Ethical and Judicial Affairs, Code of Medical Ethics. *Current Opinions with Annotations No. 2.22*. Chicago: AMA; 1996.

50. Lawrence JD. Consent for minors. *ED Leg Lett* 1997;8:1-12.

51. *In Re E.G.*, 549 NE2d 322 (Ill 1989).

52. *In Re Long Island Jewish Medical Center*, 557 NYS2d 239 (1990).

53. *State v Perricone*, 37 NJRep 463, 181 A2d 751 (1962).

54. *Re: The Petition of Allen Town Hospital-Lehigh Valley Hospital Center in the matter of J.S.S.* (No. 1990-1492, Common Court of Pleas of Lehigh County, Pennsylvania, Orphans Court Division, December 13, 1990).

55. *In matter of McCauley*, 565 NE2d 411 (Mass 1991).

56. Holroyd B, Shalit M, Kallsen C, et al. Prehospital patients refusing care. *Ann Emerg Med* 1988;17:957-963.

Chapter 49

Nursing Care Standards, Practice Guidelines, and Protocols

Barbara C. Sexton, RN, MSN, CNS

Standards of care, practice guidelines, and protocols have a prominent role in risk management. The American Nurses Association (ANA) defines standards of care as authoritative statements by which the nursing profession describes the responsibilities for which its practitioners are accountable. Consequently, standards reflect the values and priorities of the profession.[1] They are the yardstick that measures the qualitative and quantitative value of nursing care. Standards also reflect the minimal requirements that define an acceptable level of care and provide criteria for assessing competent practice. Virtually all malpractice cases involve issues of whether a caregiver complied with standards of care in a given situation.

Practice guidelines and nursing protocols are mechanisms for ensuring that safe, appropriate, and consistent care is provided.

Case Studies

1

Late one night, a 26-year-old man is brought to the emergency department after being found sitting on a street corner. He is very intoxicated and combative. His speech is slurred and he is ataxic. He admits to drinking heavily but denies any other drug use. Because of his belligerence, EMS personnel are not able to take his vital signs.

On arrival in the emergency department, he is responsive to pain and able to speak and move his extremities. There are no signs of trauma. No vital signs are taken. He is placed on a gurney on his side to "sleep it off." Documentation between 10:45 and 11:30 PM, when the patient is found cyanotic and apneic, is sparse and contradictory. The emergency physician later reports that the nurse found the patient unresponsive and apneic at 11:05 PM. According to the patient's chart, he was pronounced dead at 12:07 AM after 30 minutes of resuscitation. At autopsy, his blood alcohol level was 0.39%.

2

A young mother and father take their two sons to the emergency department in a rural county in Maryland. Both boys have rashes and fever. The mother tells the emergency nurse that she picked two ticks off her younger son several days before. The nurse fails to document this information in the chart or to tell the physician. The husband, along with other witnesses, later confirms that this information was given to the nurse.

The boys are diagnosed with measles and discharged. Two days later, they return to the emergency department because of unremitting fevers. The rash has spread to cover their arms and legs as well as the torso and head. A different emergency physician is on duty. After examining the children and conferring with the family pediatrician, the emergency physician sends the boys home with the same diagnosis. Six days later, the younger child is found dead. Postmortem examination reveals Rocky Mountain spotted fever. The older boy is treated and recovers.

3

A young woman goes into labor at approximately 1:00 PM. One hour later, she and her husband leave home to drive to the hospital. During the drive, the frequency and severity of the contractions escalate alarmingly. She describes sudden, severe abdominal pain and a feeling of "tightness."

They arrive at the hospital at 4:00 PM. On arrival, she tells the nurse what occurred en route to the hospital. She is placed in a room until 5:00 PM, when she is taken to the operating room. The OB unit has a policy of putting fetal heart monitors on all women in labor; however, on this occasion, one is not used until 5:07 PM as the woman is prepped for an emergency cesarean delivery. The baby is born with severe brain damage following a placental abruption. The nurse later testifies that she believed at the time that both of the unit's monitors were in use. However, the nurse admits that she did not look for one.

Sources of Standards

Nursing standards of care come from a variety of sources. The three major sources are professional nursing associations, regulatory agencies, and health care institutions.

In 1973, the ANA published its standards of clinical nursing practice,[1] which were generic and applied to all nurses in all practice settings. The focus of the standards was the nursing process and addressed assessment, diagnosis, outcomes identification, planning, implementation, and evaluation. Over the years, nursing specialty organizations have proliferated and each specialty has developed its own standards. In 1983, the Emergency Nurses Association (ENA) published the *Standards of Emergency Nursing Practice*. By 1990, because of the lack of consistency in the development of standards, the ANA decided to reexamine and revise its standards. Task forces of representatives from specialty nursing organizations were formed, and a consensus was reached as to purpose, definitions, and a framework for developing standards of care.

Also, in 1990, legislation was passed establishing the Agency for Health Care Policy and Research (AHCPR), which was charged with the responsibility of developing practice guidelines, standards of quality, performance measures, and medical review criteria. Expert panels are selected to work on various topics. The panels are multidisciplinary and always include consumer representatives.[2] To date, there have been more than 20 guidelines developed on various clinical topics.

ENA's *Standards of Emergency Nursing Practice*,[3] now in its third edition, has adopted ANA's standards as the basis for further development of emergency nursing specialty standards. In addition, ENA says that its standards constitute recommended goals and general guidelines of care, education, and experience levels for emergency nurses but do not constitute a legal or regulatory document.[3] This position is in keeping with the national trend toward the development of practice guidelines. Regulatory agencies, both government and private, have had a profound effect on the development of standards. The Joint Commission of Accreditation of Healthcare Organizations (JCAHO) sets standards for patient care with measurable clinical outcomes.

Institutional standards are developed and described through polices and procedures, job descriptions, the activities of risk managers, and continuous quality improvement programs. Standards set by institutions are determined by legal, political, economic, and staff educational variables in the organization. The focus of institutional standards is on care delivery systems and their improvement.[4]

Finally, Medicaid and Medicare services and peer review organizations have all used reimbursement to exert their influence on the development of standards of care.[1]

Definitions

Nursing care standards, practice guidelines, and protocols are terms that are often used interchangeably, which creates much confusion. Over the years, different types of health care organizations have developed their own standards of care independently, with no consistency in frameworks and definitions. The following is a discussion of the similarities and differences among standards, protocols, and guidelines.

Standards of care are statements that describe the level or degree of quality considered adequate for practice. Standards address the process of nursing care and focus on the nurse.

Practice guidelines, as described by the ANA,[1] are systematically developed statements based on available scientific evidence and expert opinion. They focus on patient outcomes rather than on the process of care. Unlike standards, which are generic, guidelines center on the care of a patient with a specific clinical condition.

Protocols evolved out of policies and procedures. A policy is an overall plan to accomplish general goals. A procedure is a step-by-step plan to implement the policy. Nursing protocols originally were used to provide direction in the use of equipment. They were eventually expanded to include clinical processes, as well as technical aspects of care. For example, protocols for the setup and use of the hypothermia blanket evolved into protocols for management of the patient with altered body temperature.[5]

Guidelines and protocols differ from one another in a number of ways. Guidelines are more generalized than protocols and allow for more flexibility and interpretation.[4] Guidelines guide the practitioner through the decision-making process, whereas protocols are a series of "how to" instructions. Because of the language used, deviation from a guideline is more easily defended in malpractice litigation than is deviation from a protocol. Words such as "usual," "relative criteria," and "generally," which are used in guidelines, allow more latitude for exceptions. Protocols, which follow a "cookbook" set of instructions, allow for less variation in application and are more predictable in outcomes.

Development

When developing protocols and guidelines, the people who will be using them must be involved in the planning process. The planning committee should be multidisciplinary when the protocol or guideline will affect other health care professionals. For example, when planning a protocol for the care of a victim of domestic violence or child abuse, the committee should include representatives from social services and security. Protocols and guidelines should be based on scientific evidence, and development should begin with a review of the literature.

Standards of care, guidelines, and protocols must be reviewed and updated continuously to remain current with new technologies, treatment practices, and legislation. Guidelines and protocols must reflect what is actually done. In the case of *Parker v Southwest Louisiana Hospital Association*, the hospital's protocol for monitoring infants was visual observation every 10 to 15 minutes. Most of the staff failed to comply with this protocol. The American Academy of Pediatrics standard for visual observation was every 20 to 30 minutes. When an apparently healthy baby suffered a respiratory arrest, the nurses were found to be negligent. They were held to the higher standard.[6]

Crafting precise guidelines and protocols is a challenge. If they are written with language that is too inflexible, there will be no room to exercise judgment. For example, if an EMS protocol states that all trauma patients are to have an IV started in the field, any failure to do so, even if the injury is minor or the hospital is less than one minute away, is a deviation from the protocol, opening the way for litigation. Instead, the protocol might be worded as follows: "An IV may be started in the field," or "Starting an IV in the field will be considered."[7] On the other hand, guidelines should not be worded too generally. They should clearly describe in what circumstances they are to be used. If written too broadly, guidelines may be applied incorrectly.

Case Discussions

1

In the case of *Feeney v New England Medical Center*,[8] the hospital and nurses were found liable. The court noted that the standard of care was not met. The nurses failed to take vital signs, properly assess the patient, or monitor him throughout his emergency department stay.

2

In the case of *Ramsey v Physicians Memorial Hospital*,[9] the nurse was found negligent, as she was responsible for assessing the patient and communicating significant information to the physician throughout the patients' emergency care experience.

3

In the case of *Nelson v Trinity Medical Center*,[10] the hospital was found liable because the nurse failed to follow the hospital's established protocol for monitoring women in labor. Failure to do so resulted in fetal distress, which was not discovered in time to prevent injury.

Key Points and Conclusion

Practice guidelines and protocols may improve patient care. Because scientific evidence and the consensus of experts support them, practice guidelines and protocols promote safe, efficient, and legally defensible care. In litigation, the practitioner is judged against a standard of care. But which standard? Standards and guidelines come from many sources and can create a legal minefield. The fact that an institution takes the time and effort to develop and implement guidelines and protocols shows a concern with quality and safety issues. It is a proactive approach in providing quality patient care. An organization should not promulgate policy guidelines and standards it does not intend to follow.

References

1. Taylor JW. *Implementation of Nursing Practice Standards and Guidelines.* Washington, DC: American Nurses Publishing; 1995.

2. Smith T, Popovich J. Health care standards: the interstitial matter of quality programs. *J Nurs Care Qual* 1993;8(1):1-11.

3. Donatelli N. *Standards of Emergency Nursing Practice.* St Louis: CV Mosby Co; 1995.

4. Gawlinsk A. Practice protocols development and use. *Crit Care Nurs Clin North Am* 1995;7(1):17-23.

5. Lyer PW, Camp NH. *Nursing Documentation: A Nursing Process Approach,* St Louis: CV Mosby Co; 1991.

6. Aiken TD. *Legal Ethical and Political Issues in Nursing.* Philadelphia: FA Davis Co; 1994.

7. Azzara A. Assessing your protocols. *Emergency* 1995;27(4):32.

8. *Feeney v New England Medical Center Inc,* 615 NE2d 585 (1993).

9. *Ramsey v Physicians Memorial Hospital Inc,* 373 A2d (1979).

10. *Nelson v Trinity Medical Center,* 419 NW2d 886 (ND 1988).

Chapter 50

Triage

Paul A. Craig, RN, JD

Understanding the risks of triage requires moving beyond the battlefield metaphor. Triage today is more than simply sorting the wounded. It is a "hot spot" of liability risk where the expectations of various people intersect. Every patient, even the least acutely ill, expects prompt, courteous, quality care. Government regulators expect all patients to be screened for emergency medical conditions regardless of their ability to pay and without having their treatment delayed while someone checks their insurance status. Managed care plans expect to cut costs and maybe even bypass the emergency department entirely. The only way for hospitals to survive in this competitive health care marketplace is to find a way to balance these competing and often conflicting interests. Successful emergency departments begin balancing these interests and managing the associated risks at triage.

The Medical Model

The medical model of triage, prioritization by acuity, has historically been the beginning and end of triage. Accurate assessment of patient acuity and appropriate prioritization of patient flow will always be the central risk management issues associated with triage.

Triage personnel have a pivotal role as gatekeepers to a hospital's emergency services. Their ability to recognize quickly the presentations of patients with life-threatening conditions becomes the cornerstone of risk management in the medical model of triage. Many conditions requiring urgent or emergent treatment may have subtle presentations: the middle-aged smoker with indigestion may be having a myocardial infarction and need prompt thrombolytic therapy; the young woman with abdominal pain may have an ectopic pregnancy; the elderly man with back and abdominal pain may have an abdominal aortic aneurysm that is about to rupture.

Triage staff also can have an important role in the emergency department's approach to critical illness. They can minimize the "door-to-needle" time, shortening the gap between arrival at the emergency department and effective treatment of an emergency condition. Triage staff can administer an initial nebulizer treatment to a patient with asthma, order an ECG and cardiac enzymes on a smoker who complains of indigestion, and perform a pregnancy test on a woman with abdominal pain.

The biggest risk in this medical model is that triage staff will fail to identify patients for whom "seconds to minutes" can influence the outcome of intervention, and that these patients will wait their turn in the waiting room and the opportunity to intervene on a timely basis will be lost. To manage this risk, emergency departments can provide the following to triage staff:

- Advanced training in patient assessment
- Clear triage protocols
- Ongoing quality monitoring

This approach to managing the malpractice risks of triage also is reflected in a policy of the American College of Emergency Physicians,[1] which says: "The triage and screening of each patient who enters the facility seeking care must be performed by a physician or by a specially trained registered nurse, nurse practitioner, or physician assistant in accordance with the Emergency Medical Treatment and Active Labor Act policies delineated in the medical staff bylaws or by the hospital board of trustees. Policy guidelines should be developed collaboratively by the medical director of emergency services and the director of emergency nursing . . . Immediate evaluation and stabilization, to the degree reasonably possible, must be available for each patient who presents with an emergency medical condition."

Formal guidelines for triage personnel that clearly delineate the conditions and presentations that warrant bringing a patient "straight back" for treatment may reduce the risk that critically ill patients will go unrecognized and slip through the cracks. Guidelines that are overly general or limited in scope may result in inconsistent application if staff members' interpretations vary.[2] If there is no measurable basis for staff accountability, then chart audits and other quality assurance monitoring devices become less useful. In contrast, guidelines that are overly specific and set unrealistic standards may be used against the emergency department in a malpractice action or government administrative investigation. A balance must be struck that provides solid direction and parameters for triage decisions but permits a certain degree of discretion or "wiggle room."

No set of triage protocols can prevent individual errors in judgment.[3] However, they can reduce many of the attendant risks of triage. To be effective, triage protocols must be based on commonly accepted categories of acuity, must dictate the timing and allocation of patient flow according to these acuity categories, and must specify minimum intervention and documentation requirements within each category. Triage personnel should be regularly monitored for compliance with protocols, accuracy of assessment, and adequacy of documentation. A system of regular and ongoing triage chart audits should be established to monitor compliance with triage protocols and to provide continuing education.

The Triage-Registration Interface

The medical model of triage is only one piece of the risk management puzzle. Another key piece, which has a major impact on patient perception and satisfaction, is the efficiency of the interface between triage and patient registration. It is has become an axiom in health care that "perception is everything." An efficient interface between triage and patient registration may help reduce the risk of patients turning into plaintiffs. In emergency departments that have well-run triage and registration programs, these two pieces fit together hand in glove. Emergency departments that do not have a well-run triage-registration interface may experience frequent patient complaints and an increased risk of malpractice claims and adverse regulatory enforcement action.[3]

Without careful design and management, triage can become a narrow channel that constricts patient flow. At times of peak patient volume, the triage-registration interface can become a real bottleneck, which increases the turbulence of patient flow and escalates patient dissatisfaction.[4] To enhance patient flow, improve patient satisfaction, and reduce malpractice risk, the objectives of the triage-registration interface must be examined and possibly redefined.

The common objectives of the triage-registration interface for all emergency departments, regardless of size or sophistication, include timely collection of essential patient information, generation of accurate patient medical records, and medical evaluation and prioritization of patient care. Any attempt to analyze or redesign the triage-registration interface should focus on three fundamental risk management issues related to information-processing:

- The sequence of information-gathering
- The accuracy of medical and billing documentation
- The efficiency of information intake, with a focus on reducing duplicative information-gathering

There are many different approaches to the sequence of information-gathering, but there is little debate about the gold standard, or best practice, from a risk management point of view: it is always the best practice for each patient to undergo the medical triage evaluation before registration clerks collect the demographic and insurance information required to generate a medical record file.[3,5] First, this practice reduces the department's risk of violating the Emergency Medical Treatment and Active Labor Act (EMTALA). Second, it greatly reduces the risk that subtle but significant injuries or medical conditions will go unrecognized and destabilize or deteriorate while patients are waiting for registration personnel to perform their functions. Finally, depending on the "people" skills of the triage personnel, the practice of letting patients see a "medical person" before they see clerical staff may help reduce their anxiety and, in turn, the department's risk associated with patient dissatisfaction. Satisfaction at the triage level can help create a positive perception for the entire emergency department visit.

In a perfect world, the gold standard of triaging patients before registering them would be followed around the clock. However, circumstances may dictate following a reverse order. It is not uncommon for emergency departments to use dedicated triage personnel only during certain peak hours and not during periods of lower patient volume or staffing. Conversely, in periods of unusually high patient volume or acuity, the sequence may have to be reversed if triage personnel cannot process patients fast enough or have to assist with patient care.

Whatever the cause, whenever registration precedes triage, the emergency department's professional staff must organize their activities, realizing that this sequence increases their risk. Other safeguards must be employed to expedite the postregistration triage evaluation. For example, protocols for registration personnel should include simple categories of chief complaints that require a nurse to conduct an abbreviated triage evaluation. Registration personnel should receive regular inservice education on common clinical presentations of emergency conditions.

Registration and triage personnel must have open lines of communication and should be under common lines of supervision. In some emergency departments, registration personnel are hired by and report to the business office, central registration, or some other department. To facilitate the level of communication and coordination of activities required to manage the risks of triage, staff members who are in charge of the emergency department should have the organizational authority to directly and actively supervise registration personnel.[5]

Triage to Other Departments or Hospitals

Historically, the vast majority of patients who present to the emergency department have been registered, examined, and worked up in the emergency department before being transferred to any other department within the hospital. Recently, however, it has become increasingly common for hospitals, particularly those with an expanded array of ambulatory care services, to permit patients to be triaged directly to other areas of the hospital.[3] Patients may be triaged to a fast track or chest pain unit that is under the control of the emergency department, but in some hospitals, they may also be triaged directly to occupational medicine or Medicaid managed care clinics that are separate and physically distinct from the emergency department. This practice is fraught with risk for both malpractice liability and regulatory noncompliance.

Malpractice Risk

Triaging patients directly to other departments may advance the efficiency and cost-effectiveness of the delivery of hospital services, but it is not without malpractice liability risk. Before engaging in this advanced form of triage, certain risks must be carefully analyzed. The most significant risk is that the emergency department evaluation will be attenuated, increasing the likelihood that triage personnel will fail to recognize urgent or emergent conditions. Triage to other departments may compound the risk of treatment delays, which increases the need for diligence in performing the triage assessment. Therefore, department policies must be designed to promote the performance of an adequate triage evaluation, which should be documented according to approved standards before the patient is sent to another department.

Some patients who present to the emergency department and expect to be examined in the emergency department will feel that they are being "shunted" to a lesser level of care or that they are not being taken seriously. Triage personnel must be sensitive to this public relations aspect of triaging patients to other areas of the hospital and must adequately explain treatment options to these patients.

Finally, hospital policies must be developed to promote cooperation and communication among departments and with patients. These policies must establish an adequate system of communication regarding the census, staffing, and hours of operation of departments to which patients are triaged. Patients who are sent to clinics that are operating beyond capacity or short staffed are likely to complain about not being seen in the emergency department. Patients who are sent to a clinic shortly before it closes and are forced to return to the emergency department will complain as well.

Regulatory Risk

Most, if not all, emergency physicians have a working knowledge of EMTALA,[6] which is often referred to as the "antidumping act." However, there has long been confusion regarding how triage fits into EMTALA's statutory structure. EMTALA creates two legal duties that are relevant to triage. The first requires the hospital to provide an "appropriate medical screening examination" to any patient who comes to the emergency department requesting examination or treatment. The second duty exists when a screening examination reveals an emergency medical condition. Then, the hospital must, within its capabilities, either provide further examination and treatment required to stabilize the patient, or make an "appropriate" transfer (as defined by the statute and regulations) of the patient to another facility.

The Health Care Financing Administration (HCFA) published guidelines[7] in 1995 that clarify a number of issues related to triage. Unlike the statute itself or the regulations promulgated by HCFA, HCFA guidelines do not have the force of law. They are internal directives to HCFA investigators that contain agency interpretation of certain key regulatory provisions and may provide significant guidance for risk management programs. It must be noted that some HCFA regional offices have very narrowly interpreted EMTALA, departing from the terms of HCFA guidelines. Certain regional offices and state agencies have adopted enforcement strategies inconsistent with the HCFA guidelines. As a result, emergency physicians must exercise caution in drafting EMTALA compliance policies and should always consider the precedent of local agency enforcement actions before changing practice patterns.

The most significant of these issues is whether the triage evaluation fulfills EMTALA's medical screening examination requirement. The HCFA guidelines answer this question as follows[7]:

Individuals coming to the emergency department must be provided a medical screening examination beyond initial triaging . . . A screening examination is not an isolated event; it is an ongoing process. The record must reflect ongoing monitoring in accordance with the individual's needs and must continue until the individual is stabilized or appropriately transferred.

Triage begins the screening process but does not, in and of itself, complete it. The triage evaluation does not qualify as an EMTALA medical screening examination, in part, because the two serve different purposes. The scope of triage is limited by its narrow purpose of prioritizing patient care delivery.[8]

The HCFA guidelines address two other related questions: can a patient be sent to other departments or other facilities, directly from triage, for the screening examination? Is there a risk of an EMTALA violation if a patient leaves the emergency department after being triaged but before being examined by a physician or some other practitioner authorized under hospital policy to conduct the EMTALA screening examination?

According to the guidelines, patients may be sent to other departments within the hospital from triage without risking an EMTALA violation. However, patients may not be sent to any other facility until the screening examination has been completed. The HCFA guidelines read as follows[7]: "Emergency services need not be provided in [the emergency department] . . . For example, it may be the hospital's policy for nurses to meet an individual at a helicopter pad or ambulance dock, or to direct all pregnant women to the labor and delivery area of the hospital. Hospitals may use areas to deliver emergency service which are also used for other inpatient or outpatient services. Emergency examinations may require specialized equipment located in other areas of the hospital . . . [However] It is not acceptable to refer individuals who have not been medically screened to a location outside the hospital for their screening examinations. The hospital itself must be the site of an examination which is sufficient to determine whether or not an emergency medical condition . . . is present."

If patients are to be sent from triage to other departments for screening examinations, the risks of delay and communication breakdowns must be addressed. Hospital policies must be developed regarding interdepartment communication and the timely acceptance of patients sent from the emergency department. These policies must establish limitations on the types of patients or presenting complaints that may be triaged away from the emergency department. They should also define the circumstances that require approval or consultation of an emergency physician before triage to another department.

The Triage Evaluation

The scope of triage activities varies among emergency departments, and sometimes even within a department, depending on its census. At a minimum, triage personnel function as traffic directors, or they conduct spot checks of patients based on their chief complaints and general appearance.[9] The brevity of the triage evaluation may increase the risk that significant conditions will be missed or underappreciated. Conversely, many triage systems are comprehensive, with triage personnel conducting detailed examinations, sending patients to x-ray, sending specimens for laboratory analysis, and initiating treatment.

Although more comprehensive triage evaluations tend to decrease the risk of emergency conditions going unrecognized, the time required to conduct these evaluations may contribute to the bottleneck in patient flow, causing other patients to wait unnecessarily. For many years, the trend was to increase the complexity of triage evaluations. More recently, some emergency departments have started to scale back in an attempt to increase the efficiency of patient flow. Many emergency physicians have begun to ask, for example, whether a full set of vital signs is necessary for every sprained ankle or injured finger. Remember: the purpose of triage is to sort patients and prioritize care, not to make a final evaluation. The scope of the triage evaluation may be limited by its purpose. Because there is little consensus on this issue, emergency staff must be cautious when drafting protocols that call for less of anything, especially documentation.

Documentation

Whatever the scope of the triage evaluation, it is not complete until it is adequately documented. Those who design emergency department triage protocols must also evaluate the triage documentation form. This form must provide adequate space for documentation of a focused history, physical evaluation, and limited overall assessment.

The design of the triage form should be analyzed from a risk management perspective. Triage forms that use comprehensive checklists reduce the need for lengthy narrative and provide for rapid and efficient documentation of a head-to-toe evaluation of body systems.

An optimally designed form will "force" triage staff to ask important questions by requiring them to check off boxes. For example, these forms typically contain check-off boxes for last tetanus shot or last menstrual period. Properly designed, check-off box forms not only prompt the triage staff to ask the question, but also prompt other emergency department staff to follow up with appropriate treatment. Properly designed triage forms may also facilitate documentation of the prioritization category into which a patient has been placed for easy reference by the charge nurse and other emergency department staff. Emergency department staff must realize that failure to provide adequate documentation of the factual basis for triage prioritization can greatly increase both malpractice liability risk and regulatory risk.

Waiting Times

Even efficiently run emergency departments become backlogged from time to time. A wide range of internal and external factors can create prolonged waiting times between triage and examination and treatment, which can increase both the risk of malpractice liability and the risk of EMTALA violations. Both of these risks are implicated when patients get tired of waiting and leave before they have been screened and treated.

There are two general principles in managing the risks of prolonged waiting times in the triage area. First, the triage staff must continue to monitor and regularly reevaluate patients until they leave the waiting area and are taken to a treatment area. This is particularly true for certain groups of patients, including children with fevers, patients with abdominal complaints or head injuries, and intoxicated patients. However, timely reevaluation of patients in the waiting room (and documentation of the reevaluation) is often neglected. The reasons may be obvious: when the emergency department is backlogged, triage personnel are often busy with incoming patients. Notwithstanding the pressures that make this task difficult, the regular reevaluation of patients subjected to prolonged waiting times before physician examination is an essential risk management tool. Emergency departments should develop and comply with protocols for the scope and timing of recommended reevaluations based on presenting complaint and acuity category. Because of the difficulty in accomplishing this objective, administrators should review compliance with those protocols regularly.

The second risk management principle is flexible staffing. At times, triage may become so busy that the usual staffing pattern is insufficient. An emergency department can manage this by giving the charge nurse or emergency physician the discretion to increase triage staffing temporarily. This may be accomplished by reassigning staff nurses, paramedics, or emergency department technicians to triage during periods of unusual volume and delay. Often, triage will be backlogged because the emergency department itself is so swamped that all staff members are too busy to help. Under these circumstances, emergency departments will need to find ways to pull emergency staff to triage. At other times, when triage is backlogged because patients are not moving or inpatient beds are not available, emergency staff should be temporarily reassigned to triage.

Patients Who Leave Prematurely

Despite the best efforts of staff to improve patient flow and reduce waiting times, a certain percentage of patients will get tired of waiting and leave. Patients who leave before treatment is complete fall into two groups: those who "LWBS," that is, leave without being seen (or "LWOT," leave without treatment), and those who leave "AMA," or against medical advice. Both groups of patients present obvious malpractice liability risks. In addition, both groups may present the risk of an EMTALA violation.

In *Correa v Hospital San Francisco*,[10] the 1st Circuit Court of Appeals ruled that a hospital violated EMTALA when a patient LWBS after a prolonged wait following emergency department registration. Although other factors may have influenced its decision, the court stated: "In this case, [the hospital's] delay in attending to the patient was so egregious and lacking in justification as to amount to an effective denial of a screening exam." In a private lawsuit involving EMTALA, the allegation that the patient was effectively denied a screening examination because she waited so long to see a physician will have strong prejudicial jury appeal. Witness the *Correa* court's caustic comment that the patient "went to the hospital in critical condition and received only a high number and a cold shoulder."

The HCFA regulations appear to present a more narrow perspective of when prolonged emergency department waiting times constitute an EMTALA violation or patient "dumping." The guidelines read as follows[7]:

If a screening examination reveals an emergency medical condition and the individual is told to wait for treatment, but the individual leaves the hospital, the hospital did not dump the patient unless,

• The individual left the emergency department based on a 'suggestion' by the hospital, and/or

• The individual's condition required immediate attention but the hospital was operating beyond its capacity and did not attempt to transfer the individual to another facility.

Risk Management Recommendations

There are four aspects to managing the risks of patients who fall into the LWBS category. First, as discussed earlier, every effort must be made to improve patient flow and reduce the overall number of patients who leave prematurely. When patient flow is impaired for any reason, patients must be regularly reassessed according to their triage classifications. Regular reassessment not only reduces the risk that an emergency medical condition will go unrecognized and deteriorate, but also reassures patients that they are not being ignored.

Next, when patients inform emergency department personnel that they intend to leave, the staff must make reasonable efforts to convince them they should stay and be examined. An emergency physician should become directly involved and speak to the patient personally whenever possible. Explain the risks of leaving without a full examination in terms the patient can understand. A continuing offer of examination and treatment should be documented. A brief chart entry to document the patient's overall condition, mental status, and competence to refuse treatment should be made before the patient leaves.

When reasonable attempts to get the patient to stay have failed, reasonable effort must be made to document their informed refusal of care.[11] A patient's withdrawal of a request for examination or treatment or informed refusal of consent for further examination or treatment may terminate the hospital's obligations under EMTALA. In general, HCFA investigators are instructed as follows: "In cases where an individual . . . withdrew the initial request for a medical screening examination and/or treatment for an emergency medical condition and demanded his or her transfer or demanded to leave the hospital, look for a signed informed refusal of examination and treatment form . . . If the individual . . . refused to sign the consent form, look for documentation by hospital personnel that states that the individual refused to sign the form."[7]

EMTALA regulations spell out particular requirements for the documentation of informed refusal, as follows: "The medical record must contain a description of the examination, treatment, or both if applicable, that was refused . . . The hospital must take all reasonable steps to secure the individual's written informed refusal . . . The written document should indicate that the person has been informed of the risks and benefits of the examination or treatment, or both."[7]

The emergency department should maintain a log of all patients who leave prematurely and initiate a call-back system to contact these patients no later than the following day. Information about these patients can be recorded in an easily retrievable form for quality assurance purposes. Tracking and trending of these patients may supplement other information sources when department staffing and budgeting decisions are made.

Triage and Managed Care Patients

Despite its original legislative intent, EMTALA is not limited to Medicare or Medicaid patients or the uninsured and underinsured. EMTALA is in effect whenever any patient, including those who are insured through an HMO or other managed care organization (MCO) comes to an emergency department requesting examination or treatment. Application of EMTALA to managed care patients brings emergency department regulatory risk management practices into direct conflict with business risk management practices. These conflicting risks must be balanced carefully.

One of the most well-known cost-containment mechanisms used by many MCOs is the requirement that patients, with certain exceptions, obtain preauthorization for emergency department treatment.[12] Frequently, managed care patients do not call for preauthorization before they come to the emergency department. Not uncommonly, an MCO will deny authorization, prompting the patient to leave the emergency department before examination and treatment are completed. The risk of managed care patients subjecting an emergency department to EMTALA citations exists every day. EMTALA regulations do not prohibit an emergency department from obtaining insurance

information or making inquiry into method of payment as part of a reasonable registration process, as long as the hospital does not delay screening or treating the patient to verify the information.[13]

Likewise, nothing in the statute, regulations, or HCFA guidelines prohibits an emergency department from calling or instructing a patient to call an MCO for authorization, as long as examination or treatment is not delayed to obtain the authorization. However, some state agencies have adopted an extremely narrow interpretation of permissible registration processes and have cited certain hospitals for EMTALA violations because the emergency department called for preauthorization. It may be argued successfully that such agency interpretations are overly zealous and inconsistent with the law. Those arguments have to be made retrospectively, during administrative or court hearings, following allegations of a statutory violation, at significant expense to the hospital.

The HCFA guidelines do make several references to managed care patients. The essential point is that MCO denial of authorization does not release a hospital from its obligations under EMTALA.[14] The guidelines read as follows: "A hospital may not refuse to screen an enrollee of a managed care plan because the plan refuses to authorize treatment or to pay for such screening and treatment . . . A managed health care plan (e.g., HMO, PPO) cannot deny a hospital permission to treat its enrollees. It may only state what it will or will not pay for. Regardless of whether a hospital will be paid, it is obligated to provide the services specified in the statute and this regulation."[7]

The tension between business risk and regulatory risk may be managed prospectively by a variation on one of three basic approaches. Some hospitals have taken an ultraconservative approach to EMTALA risk management. These hospitals have decided to not permit their employees to call MCOs, or instruct patients to call for preauthorization at any time during the emergency department visit. Although this approach eliminates regulatory risk, there is the alternative risk that payment will be denied, which will create ill will between the hospital and local MCOs as well as patients. However, in areas of the country where HCFA or state agencies have adopted strict enforcement tactics, this approach may be the most prudent option.

Some experts advocate an intermediate approach, which involves calling the MCO after the medical screening examination has been completed.[8] This approach eliminates or greatly reduces any regulatory risk but does little to reduce the business risk of denial of payment. In fact, this approach may actually increase the likelihood of payment denial in instances where the screening examination has ruled out an emergency medical condition. Some states have provided some relief from the dilemma of the EMTALA/MCO interface in the form of "prudent layperson" statutes, which limit MCOs' ability to deny payment for emergency screening. These statutes bar MCOs from denying payment based on the final diagnosis.[15]

A third alternative is to call the MCO, or instruct the patient to call following triage but before the actual screening examination. This approach, which is used in numerous emergency departments, reduces business risk but does not eliminate the risk of EMTALA violations. If this approach is used, the emergency department must scrupulously adhere to a policy that examination and treatment will not be delayed pending MCO authorization. Policies must be developed to manage the risk created when managed care patients choose to leave the emergency department following MCO denial of payment. Ongoing department monitoring of managed care patient records must provide documentation that care was not delayed.

There is a common misconception that an emergency department has complied with EMTALA, if, after triaging a managed care patient, emergency department personnel document that the patient was sent to a physician's office outside of the hospital as directed by the MCO, following denial of authorization. Managed care patients should not be sent to offices outside the hospital following a denial of authorization, without receiving the same medical screening examination provided to all other emergency department patients who present with the same symptoms unless their informed refusal is documented.

Key Points and Conclusion

Triage is a critical step in the emergency department encounter. In order to create an effective department risk management program, the triage system must be given high priority. "Seconds-to-minutes" type emergencies must be recognized by triage personnel. Constant vigilance is necessary in the waiting room. Emergency department staff must work with hospital administration to develop and follow EMTALA-related policy. Regarding evaluation and documentation, triage staff must strike a delicate balance — not too much or too little.

Finally, triage must be viewed as a rapidly changing environment. The emergency department supervisor must address staffing requirements in triage to optimize patient flow.

References

1. Emergency Care Guidelines. ACEP Policy Statement, approved September 1996. To obtain a copy, call (800) 798-1822, touch 6, or go to www.acep.org.

2. VanBoxel A. Improving the triage process. *J Emerg Nurs* 1995;21:332-334.

3. Scott VL. Triage and patient flow. In: Hellstern RA, ed. *Managing the Emergency Department—A Team Approach*. Dallas: American College of Emergency Physicians; 1992.

4. Wears RL. Introduction. In: Harwood Nuss AL, ed. *The Clinical Practice of Emergency Medicine*. 2nd ed. Philadelphia: JB Lippincott; 1996.

5. Ramsey FE. Enhancing patient flow. In: Hellstern RA, ed. *Managing the Emergency Department — A Team Approach*. Dallas: American College of Emergency Physicians; 1992.

6. 42 USC 1395dd (1992); Regulations codified at 42 CFR 489.24.

7. Interpretive Guidelines and Investigative Procedures for Responsibilities of Medicare Participating Hospitals in Emergency Cases, HCFA, 1995.

8. Berry MC. The impact of COBRA on clinical decisions. Presented at the 18th Annual Conference of the American Society for Health Care Risk Management, September, 1996, San Francisco.

9. Rice M, Abel C. Triage. In: Sheehy SB, ed. *Emergency Nursing Principles and Practice*. St Louis: CV Mosby Co; 1992.

10. *Correa v Hospital San Francisco*, 69 F3d 1184, 1995 US App LEXIS 30978 (1st Cir 1995). (Case also involved allegations that hospital attempted to "shunt" patient after scrutinizing her insurance card.)

11. Karcz A. Managed care and emergency care: a risk management perspective. *J Healthcare Risk Manage* 1994;Fall:30.

12. Craig P. Health maintenance organization gatekeeping policies: potential liability for deterring access to emergency services. *J Health Hosp Law* 1990;23:135-146.

13. 42 CFR 489.24(c)(3).

14. Keeping COBRA MCOs from slowing triage. *ED Management*, June 1996.

15. See, e.g., federal Access to Emergency Medical Services Act of 1997, HR 815, also known as the Cardin Bill, which has served as a model for many of the state statutes.

Chapter 51

Nursing Documentation

Barbara C. Sexton, RN, MSN, CNS

An estimated 90 million patients are seen in emergency departments across the country each year. Emergency departments are, for a variety of reasons, a high-risk area for malpractice litigation. Malpractice claims may take years to come to trial. The likelihood of a physician or nurse remembering a brief encounter with a particular patient seen several years earlier is very small. For this reason, juries view the chart as the best evidence of what happened. Good charting may not help the physician or nurse who has been negligent, but poor or incomplete documentation can make a good practitioner look incompetent.[1]

Before the 1950s, nurses' notes were seen primarily as a means of communication between nurses or between nurses and physicians. Nurses' notes were not considered part of the permanent medical record and were not preserved by medical records personnel once the patient was discharged.[2] In the past 40 years, there have been dramatic changes in nursing practice in general and in documentation in particular. In the 1970s and 1980s, the American Nurses Association (ANA) and the Emergency Nurses Association (ENA) published recommended goals and general guidelines of care based on the nursing process.[3] Federal regulatory agencies, such as the Health Care Financing Administration (HCFA), and private accreditation bodies like the Joint Commission on Accreditation of Healthcare Organizations (JCAHO) have all turned to nursing documentation as a way to measure compliance with legal guidelines and regulatory requirements.[4]

The primary purpose of nurses' notes is the recording and communication of pertinent patient information. All patient care should be recorded in a concise, coherent, and chronological manner. Good documentation paints a picture of what happened and what the results were, tying together the contributions of all health care providers.

The second purpose of nurses' notes is to ensure appropriate reimbursement from government agencies, insurance companies, and other third-party payers. To obtain reimbursement, all physician orders must be documented in the nurses' notes as having been carried out. If an order is not charted, third-party payers regard it as not needed or not done.

A third purpose of nurses' notes is documentation used in various types of legal actions. Charts may be reviewed in civil lawsuits, such as personal injury cases. They may be used in guardianship proceedings or competency hearings. Nurses' notes may even be used as evidence in criminal cases, such as sexual assault.[5]

Case Studies

1

A mother takes her daughter to a neighborhood clinic because the child is listless and feverish. The child is examined and discharged with several prescriptions. Three days later, when the child shows no improvement, the mother takes her to a nearby emergency department. The emergency nurse records on the emergency record the word "fever" but does not document any vital signs. The mother tells the emergency physician that the child has a fever and a head cold and has been coughing. A chest x-ray is performed and a diagnosis of bronchopneumonia is made. The patient is discharged with prescriptions.

Twenty-four hours later, the mother returns to the emergency department with the child. The child now complains of a stiff neck and refuses to eat. A different emergency physician examines the child and performs tests and makes a diagnosis of spinal meningitis. The child is admitted to the hospital and dies four days later. The physician later testifies that he was unaware that the child had been examined and treated three days earlier for the same complaint.[6]

2

A 71-year-old nursing home patient is transported to the emergency department by paramedics. Earlier that day, she had been found unconscious on the bathroom floor by an attendant. The paramedics report to the triage nurse that they found her slightly disoriented and sitting in bed. Vital signs are blood pressure 92/58, pulse 50 and irregular, respirations 28 and shallow, rales bilaterally, and temperature 102.6°F orally. The triage nurse communicates this information to the primary nurse, but the primary nurse records it as: "Fever for one day, weak, and possible stroke." The vital signs are recorded as normal.

When the physician examines the patient, he finds that she is alert and oriented to name, place, and time. He records all systems as being within normal limits. The laboratory report reveals a blood glucose level of 42. After appropriate treatment is rendered to correct the hypoglycemia, the physician encourages the patient to be admitted for a workup. She refuses admission, and the physician sends her back to the nursing home for follow-up treatment by her private physician.

3

A young pregnant woman presents to the emergency department at 8:30 PM and is taken to obstetrics. The receiving nurse documents an assessment and examination. The patient is placed on a fetal heart monitor; normal fetal heart tones are recorded. At 9:30 PM, the nurse calls the attending physician at home and notifies him of the arrival and status of the patient. At 10:15 PM, the nurse is unable to obtain fetal heart tones and notifies the attending physician of this at 10:20 PM. At 10:30 PM, the attending physician is contacted again en route to the hospital and advised that the membranes have ruptured and meconium staining is noted. The patient is prepped for an emergency cesarean delivery. The child is delivered at 11:40 PM but is stillborn as a result of respiratory distress syndrome and acute visceral congestion.[7]

The Medical-Legal Perspective

In malpractice litigation, the verdict of a case often hinges on the quality and credibility of the nurses' notes. The appearance of the chart and its content can strongly influence a jury. Illegible handwriting, misspellings, and the use of nonstandard abbreviations can make a good practitioner appear incompetent. Even more important, improperly corrected errors (e.g., obliterated entries, whited-out portions of the chart, or recopied notes), can make a nurse or physician appear dishonest. For example, in *Ahrens v Katz*,[8] missing and contradictory documents and whited-out sections of the nurses' notes convinced the jury that the nurse and physician were guilty of fraud.

Nurses' notes must reflect a continuity of care from admission to discharge. Accurate documentation of times is especially important in the emergency department. The times of arrival, triage, all examinations performed, and all care rendered must be documented. This documentation protects against charges of undue delays in treatment that frequently are the basis of malpractice litigation.

All documentation must be complete and correct. Nurses must record all pertinent information received from patients and should communicate findings with the physician both orally and in writing in the nurses' notes. In *Kenyon v Hamner*,[9] a physician was found liable when a nurse failed to chart that a patient's blood type was O-negative. A second pregnancy five years later produced a stillborn infant because the mother had not been given $Rh_0(D)$ immune globulin after the first delivery.

Physicians must be sure to read the nurses' notes. They must reconcile any apparent discrepancies and variances between medical and nursing observations and address all abnormal findings.

Documentation Standards

Which information is recorded in the nurses' notes and when is determined by professional standards and emergency department policies and procedures. The following are suggestions for emergency department nursing documentation based on the ENA's Standards of Care.[3]

Triage Nurse

Beginning with triage, the nurse rapidly and systematically collects information related to the patient's chief complaint. This information is used to identify and record patient needs. The nurse initiates a nursing diagnosis and plan of care and assigns the patient a priority level. Nurses' notes document a focused assessment, vital signs, and any care rendered (e.g. splinting, ice). The triage nurse is responsible for ongoing reassessment of patients in the waiting room as needed and as defined by hospital and emergency department policies.

Primary Nurse

Once a patient is admitted to an emergency treatment area, the primary nurse performs and documents an initial assessment, identifies a nursing diagnosis, and implements the plan of care. Reassessments and vital signs are repeated and recorded at regular intervals, which are determined by emergency department policies and/or subsequent events.

The nurse documents in the nurses' notes all medical examinations and nursing interventions (e.g., medications, procedures, therapies, diagnostic tests) and any consultations (visits or telephone). Interventions by other caregivers (e.g., social services, respiratory therapy) are noted as well.

The nurse should record, in a timely manner, responses to all treatments and therapies. The nurse should also record any treatment instructions or teaching given to patients and family and the response. The nurses' notes should document discharge instructions regarding what was taught and to whom, as well as the patient's level of understanding and condition on discharge.

Types of Nursing Documentation

One common excuse for poor documentation is that it takes too much time away from patient care. To help alleviate this, the time spent charting can be reduced by using a standardized format. Formats are a way of organizing information to make it concise, accurate, and timely. There are several common formats in use today. Examples include narrative charting, problem-oriented records, focus charting, and PIE charting.

Narrative Charting. Narrative charting is the oldest format in use. It organizes information in chronological order and has the advantage of being quick and easy to use in emergency situations.

Problem-Oriented Records. Developed in the early 1970s, problem-oriented records with "SOAPIE" notes are based on a medical model and focus on specific patient problems. Information is organized as follows:
- Subjective data
- Objective data
- Assessment
- Plan of action
- Interventions
- Evaluation of the interventions

Focus Charting. Focus charting, developed in 1981, is a method of identifying patient concerns and organizing narrative documentation around key words that may be a nursing diagnosis, a sign or symptom, or a condition. Notes are organized in a "DAR" framework, that is:
- Data
- Action
- Response

PIE Charting. Developed in 1984, PIE charting organizes documentation into three components:
- Problems
- Interventions
- Evaluations

The problem is written as a nursing diagnosis. The interventions are all actions taken, and the evaluations evaluate the success of the interventions.

The format used in nurses' notes is a matter of institutional preference. All are equally effective when used correctly. Other types of documentation especially useful in the emergency department are flow sheets and checklists. They help nurses gather and organize needed information about a patient. They are also useful as reminders for monitoring ongoing assessments and nursing care needs, such as for the patient in restraints. They are most helpful in readily identifying trends or changes in a patient's condition. When flow sheets are used consistently and correctly, information documented on the flow sheet does not need to be repeated in the nurses' notes.[10-12]

Case Discussions

1

The hospital in the first case, *Reynolds v Swigert*,[6] was found liable under the doctrine of *respondeat superior*. The court observed that one of the allegations of negligence against the hospital was that the emergency nurse had a duty to obtain an adequate medical history of the child, check the patient's vital signs, record this information on the emergency record, and call this information to the attention of the emergency physician. Expert witnesses testified that it is the nurse's responsibility to do so without being told and that this is the standard of practice in emergency departments throughout the country.

2

According to the nursing home's report to the paramedics, the patient initially was found unconscious. The primary nurse receiving this information did not accurately communicate it to the physician. However, the physician should have read all nurses' notes and paramedic run sheets and questioned the personnel involved.

Emergency department personnel must communicate all patient information when multiple parties are involved. This practice helps clarify conflicting information. All abnormal vital signs must be addressed. This patient needed to be admitted for a complete workup. The nursing home and her private physician should have been informed of the patient's unwillingness to stay. On discharge, the emergency physician should have documented the patient's condition, medications prescribed, and follow-up for the nursing home staff.

3

In the third case, *Mariano v Tanner*,[7] accurate and timely nurses' notes reflected ongoing monitoring of the patient and prompt reporting to the physician. The time when problems developed was pinpointed and all actions taken from that point on were appropriate to the patient's needs. Because the staff kept meticulous nurses' notes, the hospital, physician, and nurse were held not liable.

Key Points and Conclusion

Emergency department managers must ensure clear, concise, and complete nursing documentation. To improve compliance with good documentation practices, follow these suggestions:

- Use continuous quality improvement monitors to assess the quality and completeness of nurses' notes.
- Develop policies and procedures that clearly define documentation needs and requirements.
- Conduct periodic inservice training and other risk management activities to ensure compliance with department policies and standards of care.

Charting guidelines for physicians:
- Read nurses' notes.
- Reconcile all discrepancies and variances in notes of other caregivers.
- Document legible entries.
- Ensure all orders are written before signing the chart.
- Address all abnormal vital signs and laboratory test results.
- Correct errors and add late entries in an approved manner. Never attempt to correct anyone else's documentation.

Charting guidelines for nurses:
- Use a consistent format.
- Document frequently.
- Individualize charting.
- Do not be redundant.
- Sign all entries.
- Write legibly, and time and date all entries.
- Record only on the proper forms.
- Chart in chronological order. Late entries can be added, but note that fact when charting.
- Do not erase or write between lines. For errors, draw a single line through the entry and write "error."
- Eliminate bias from charting. Be nonjudgmental.
- Be specific. Avoid vague terms like "large amount," "apparent," and "seems."
- Be honest.

References

1. Iyer PW. Thirteen charting rules. *Nursing* 1991;21(60):40-45.

2. Iyer PW. *Nursing Documentation. A Nursing Process Approach.* St Louis: CV Mosby Co; 1991.

3. Donatelli NS, Flaherty L, Greenberg L, et al. *Standards of Emergency Nursing Practice.* Third edition. St Louis: CV Mosby Co; 1995.

4. Taylor JW. *Implementation of Nursing Practice Standards and Guidelines.* Washington, DC: American Nurses Publishing; 1995.

5. Feulz-Harter SA. Documentation principles and pitfalls. *JONA* 1989;19(12):7-9.

6. *Reynolds v Swigert,* 697 P2d 504 (NM).

7. *Mariano v Tanner,* 497 So2d 1066 (La).

8. *Ahrens v Katz,* 575 F Supp 1108 (Ga).

9. *Kenyon v Hamner,* 688 P2d 961 (Ariz).

10. Milstead J, Rodriguez-Fisher L: Legally defensible effective charting. *Crit Care Nurse* 1992;12(6):103-105.

11. Fischbach FT. *Documenting Care Communication: The Nursing Process and Documentation Standards.* Philadelphia: FA Davis Co; 1991.

12. Sullivan G. Legally speaking. *RN* 1996;59(4):61.

Chapter 52

EMS Support and Communication

Ellen F. Wodika, MA, MM
Paul A. Craig, RN, JD

Sometimes emergency physicians are reluctant to become involved in EMS support and communication activities because of a concern that these activities might increase their professional liability exposure. An analysis of the professional liability involved in EMS activities should take into account three important considerations. First, the frequency and severity of the risk of a lawsuit are relatively low. Lawsuits against physicians arising out of EMS support and communications are infrequent, and the judgments and financial settlements typically are relatively small.[1] Second, in most states, there are significant sources of legislative immunity that may shield physicians from or provide valuable defenses against EMS-related lawsuits. Finally, a physician's risk exposure related to EMS can be both identified and controlled.

The key factors to consider when analyzing a physician's EMS risk exposure include the following:

- Physician liability for directing EMTs, including potential vicarious liability
- Risk issues in patient management: consent, refusal, the use of restraints, do not resuscitate (DNR) orders
- EMS project medical director's responsibilities
- Statutory immunity for paramedics: Good Samaritan, EMS Act

The Medical-Legal Perspective

A review of the literature indicates that physicians are seldom named as codefendants in EMS cases and that the dollar value of litigated claims is relatively small. In one 10-year study,[1] only one case was filed in 24,096 incidents. Another study,[2] conducted in Chicago, found one lawsuit for every 27,371 patient encounters and one lawsuit for every 17,995 transports. A third study,[3] involving a national review of EMS appellate cases from 1987 through 1992, observed that physicians were named as codefendants in only 9 of the 86 cases heard in appellate court (Table 1).

The two major areas of risk exposure for physicians are liability for directing EMTs "online" over the telemetry radio and fulfillment of EMS administration responsibilities by EMS Project Medical Directors (PMDs). The risk exposure for PMDs involves certain elements of "offline" direction, such as training, ongoing skill development, and performance assessment of EMTs and nursing staff. These offline activities may include development, implementation, and evaluation of standing orders and protocols.[4]

Plaintiffs may rely on two legal theories related to online medical direction when seeking to hold emergency physicians personally liable for injuries allegedly caused by EMTs. First, a plaintiff may seek to hold the physician directly liable for negligence, claiming that the telemetry medical orders violated a physician's standard of care. Second, a plaintiff may claim that a physician is indirectly liable for the EMTs' acts or omissions under the doctrine of vicarious liability. Under the theory of vicarious liability, one person (typically a corporation), who is known

Table 1

Litigation against emergency physicians involved in EMS[3]

Physician role	# Physicians named as codefendants (86 cases)
Emergency department treatment	3
In-house treatment before transfer	2
Emergency department treatment and direct medical control	2
Direct medical control	1
Medical director	1
Total cases with physician named as codefendant	9

as the "principal," becomes liable for the acts or omissions of another person, known as the principal's agent/employee. The theory assumes that the principal's control over the agent is sufficient to hold the principal liable for the conduct of the agent/employee without any further proof that the principal was actually negligent in hiring, training, or supervising the agent/employee. This is the theory under which a EMT's employer, either a municipal fire department or private ambulance company, may be held liable for the EMT's actions.

Because EMTs are not employed by emergency physicians, the theory must be creatively stretched under an old common law extension of vicarious liability theory, known as the "borrowed servant" doctrine.[5] This doctrine uses a legal fiction (i.e., a solution contrived by the courts) that an employee of one entity temporarily becomes the "borrowed" employee of another. Applying this doctrine to cases involving emergency physicians and EMT's, the theory would be that the EMT becomes the "borrowed" agent/employee of the physician because the physician temporarily controls the actions of the EMT over the radio. Actual appellate case law applying this doctrine to this relationship is scarce. However, in theory, the doctrine could impute any paramedic negligence to the physician.

Online Direction

The physician who directs an EMT radio call assumes responsibility for managing the following:

- Online medical direction
- Patient rights: refusal of treatment, use of restraints, DNR orders, advance directives
- Continuity of patient care and diversion to closest facilities

Online Medical Direction

Online medical direction is real-time management of patient care. Direction and supervision include specifying and monitoring the assessment and interventions provided by the paramedic. These responsibilities require clear, unambiguous, and direct communication from the physician to the EMS provider. In many cases, the EMS provider may have already implemented preapproved protocols and standing medical orders (SMOs) before contacting the physician in the base or resource hospital. The physician providing online direction must be familiar with the local system's SMOs and must review the appropriateness of EMTs use of SMOs in particular cases.

When a patient arrives at an emergency department, the run report and prehospital communication can be compared to the physician's findings to affirm the quality or note the deficits in prehospital services provided. On occasion, direct follow-up with EMTs may be necessary to obtain an accurate account of certain patient assessments, the reasons for certain treatment decisions, or the efficacy of treatment. A follow-up to online direction may include teaching and assessment of the EMS providers' services. The EMS system should delineate whether this role is voluntary or required. If the physician has reason to doubt the competency of EMS providers, such as their knowledge base, judgment, or skills, the physician may have some responsibility to report these concerns to the EMS provider's employer and EMS PMD.

Patient Rights

The simple and incontrovertible legal maxim, that a competent patient has the right to consent or to refuse medical care, can take many complicated twists in the context of prehospital EMS care. For example, a patient may be intoxicated and uncooperative but may also have life-threatening injuries. Decision-making in this context is extremely difficult. Most emergency physicians believe that, in the prehospital context in general, the risks of nontreatment almost always outweigh the risks of treating patients against their will. If doubt remains regarding the patient's mental status, the prudent approach is to transport and treat.

Field Determinations of Competence. In cases where a patient is awake and responsive, the question is whether that patient is competent to understand the nature of the medical condition and the risks of refusing treatment and transportation. Emergency physicians directing EMTs over the radio are seriously limited in their ability to make the medical assessment of competency. Instead, they must rely on the judgment of EMTs. However, documentation of ambulance runs must provide some objective basis for the physician's determination of competency or incompetency. Given the time constraints and limitations of radio communications, a simplified approach to the determination of competency must be developed.

Frequently, the requirements for the field determination of competence are specified in local EMS protocols. These protocols should be strictly followed. At a minimum, patients must demonstrate that they are alert and oriented to person, place, and time. In addition, they must show in some way that they understand the seriousness of their conditions and the risks of refusal of care. Sometimes compromises are needed. On occasion, a balance can be struck, allowing the patient to refuse invasive prehospital treatment in return for an agreement to be transported to the nearest facility for a more accurate determination of competence by emergency department staff and possible treatment.

Treatment Without Consent and the Use of Restraints. Generally, emergency physicians advocate respect for a competent patient's right to refuse treatment. However, under certain circumstances, prudent risk management may lead an emergency physician to order the involuntary transportation of an apparently alert and oriented patient who is refusing treatment. This should happen only if circumstances amounting to "good cause" support a physician's belief that the patient's lucidity may be transient or that the patient may not have a genuine understanding of the seriousness of the emergency medical condition. For example, a diabetic patient awakens from a severe hypoglycemic episode, during which he caused a serious automobile collision. Any evidence of head injury or a blood sugar level that may be partially corrected and relapse may justify treatment without consent.

Whenever patients with emergency medical conditions show that they do not understand their conditions or the risks of refusal of treatment, they should be transported to the closest appropriate facility in the least restrictive type of restraint necessary for safe transport. Restraints are also typically used with uncooperative patients who are either intoxicated or have a history of mental illness and are either incompetent and reasonably believed to have an emergency medical condition, or there is reason to believe they are either a danger to themselves or others or they are unable to care for themselves. Any time patients are transported against their will and in restraints, EMS personnel should anticipate scrutiny of their documentation and leave a written record that details the objective basis for their actions.

DNR Orders and Advance Directives. Historically, advanced cardiac life support and CPR have been initiated in the prehospital environment to all patients in cardiac arrest unless the patient was decapitated or had rigor and/or dependent lividity in an environment of normal ambient temperature. Over the past decade, in the wake of a number of "right to die" legal decisions and the enactment of the federal Patient Self Determination Act,[6] advance directives, such as living wills and durable powers of attorney for health care, and DNR orders have become increasingly prevalent. Although these types of documents are generally acted on in hospitals, long-term care facilities, or hospices, it is not uncommon for EMTs to encounter them in the field.

The requirements of a properly drafted and executed advance directive are determined by state law. Likewise, the determination of whether an EMT may rely on an advance directive or DNR order is dictated by both state law and local EMS policies and directives. For guidance on this issue, emergency physicians should contact their local EMS systems or hospital counsel.

According to the American College of Emergency Physicians (ACEP), there are three circumstances under which CPR should not be initiated[7]:

- Obvious signs of death are found.
- A valid DNAR [do not attempt resuscitation] order is documented, consistent with local policy, and is produced at the scene.
- The patient's physician takes direct responsibility for withholding resuscitative efforts.

Continuity of Care and Ambulance Diversion

EMTs, particularly those who are employed by private ambulance companies under contract with particular health care facilities, commonly radio base station hospitals to request permission to transport a patient to a specific destination. The choice may be determined by patient request, location of the treating physician, recent discharge from a hospital or its ambulatory services, or availability of specialty programs, such as a hospice.

Complying with the patient's choice of destination is within the physician's discretion. The physician's decision should be based on the patient's condition, availability of EMS resources to transport the patient, and availability of appropriate medical services at that destination. Emergency physicians should keep in mind that a base station's response to the EMTs' request to transport to a particular destination may have a significant impact on continuity of care and insurance reimbursement issues. For these reasons, and because honoring the request generally follows patient, family, and private physician expectations, such requests should generally be respected.

However, if the patient has an unstable emergency medical condition that requires advanced life support, local EMS regulations and traditional medical wisdom may dictate patient transport to the closest hospital. In this case, the patient's expectation of transport to a particular hospital often comes into direct conflict with prudent medical judgment and safe EMT practice. When it genuinely appears that transportation to the requested facility will seriously jeopardize a patient's safety, several steps should be taken. First, little time should be wasted deliberating. A reasonable attempt should be made to obtain consent from the patient or family for transport to the closest hospital. If the patient is competent or if there appears to be competent documentation of a guardianship or power of attorney, have the appropriate individual sign a release after informing that person of the risks of transport beyond the closest hospital. Finally, if a release cannot be obtained and an unstable emergency condition exists, transport the patient to the closest comprehensive emergency department for stabilization.

The Emergency Medical Treatment and Active Labor Act. Generally, the prehospital EMS system exists outside the scope of and is not directly regulated by the federal Emergency Medical Treatment and Active Labor Act (EMTALA). There are two notable exceptions. First, EMTALA applies to ambulances actually owned by hospitals.[8] Once a patient is inside a hospital-owned ambulance, the patient is considered to have arrived at the hospital for purposes of triggering EMTALA's screening and stabilization provisions (see Chapter 45, "EMTALA"). Second, EMTALA applies when an ambulance is being used to transfer a patient with an unstable emergency medical condition from one hospital to another.[8] Under these circumstances, a hospital has a statutory duty to transport patients with emergency medical conditions using qualified medical personnel, which may require the presence of a nurse or physician.

Malpractice plaintiffs have unsuccessfully attempted to get around the immunity provided by state statutes by arguing that prehospital radio direction of EMTs and hospital bypass or diversion decisions are regulated under EMTA-

LA. In *Johnson v University of Chicago Hospitals*,[9] a federal district court in Chicago originally ruled that a hospital's direction of EMTs in the field amounted to arrival at the hospital for purposes of establishing EMTALA liability and that diversion of a patient may have been a violation of EMTALA. The case prompted an uproar in EMS circles, and several hospital and medical organizations filed briefs in support of the hospital on appeal. The theory was that application of EMTALA to prehospital EMS could disrupt trauma center networks and have many unintended consequences. The district court's decision was overruled by the 7th Circuit Court of Appeals, which ruled that EMTALA did not apply to radio contact between a hospital and EMTs in the field.

Administrative Liability

According to ACEP, in its policy statement *Medical Direction of Prehospital EMS*,[10] one of the primary roles of a PMD is to ensure quality patient care. A PMD's risk exposure is based, in part, on the obligation to fulfill these administrative duties. To minimize risk exposure, PMDs should document how they discharge their administrative responsibilities, including quality improvement (QI) and risk management functions. QI and risk management are essential parts of good management. Some view them as flip sides of the same coin. The goal of a QI program is to improve services. This goal is achieved by setting, monitoring, and revising EMS policies and patient care protocols to keep pace with evolving standards of care.

The goals of a risk management program are to prevent untoward events or incidents that have the potential to result in lawsuits. Untoward events or incidents are occurrences that result in outcomes contrary to patients' expectations. Together, EMS QI and risk management programs can proactively reduce the frequency and severity of patient dissatisfaction and untoward events. Alignment of EMS QI and risk management programs with patients' and consumers' expectations may be the PMD's best opportunity to stay out of the legal foray.

Relevant EMS quality standards include time criteria, protocols, knowledge, and skills.[11] QI monitoring should include regular review of radio communications, response times, run sheets, and outcome of resuscitation efforts.[12] Additional quality indicators that should be considered include diverted patient transports, noncompliance with patient-requested transport destination, patient satisfaction, and receiving facility emergency physicians' and staff satisfaction.

These quality issues map certain EMS risk exposures. The following are specific examples of occurrences that should be tracked and trended:

- Death of patient prior to arrival of EMS team
- Death of patient prior to arrival at health care facility
- Failure of base or resource hospital emergency physician or staff to provide appropriate medical direction
- Failure of health care facility to report patient condition appropriately
- Threat of violence to EMS team during patient extrication
- Treatment or medication errors
- Patient complaints
- Problems related to equipment and supplies
- Motor vehicle collisions during patient transport

Statutory Immunity

There are three potential sources for immunity for EMS providers and emergency physicians involved in EMS support and communication:

- Sovereign immunity
- EMS Act immunity
- Good Samaritan statutes

The scope of immunity provided by these statutes and the applicability to certain classes of providers varies widely from state to state. Therefore, emergency personnel should contact local counsel to determine the applicable immunity and Good Samaritan protections.

Sovereign Immunity

Sovereign immunity originated in English common law and has been carried over into the statutory schemes of both federal and state governments. Sovereign immunity generally protects government and other public agencies and their employees against tort law claims. Under most sovereign immunity statutes, the government permits certain exceptions to the doctrine, permitting a plaintiff to sue a state agency without recovering from the individual state employee under government tort claims act provisions. These provisions typically provide a narrow window of time in which to file a lawsuit and a number of procedural and substantive limitations on tort recovery. Many sovereign immunity statutes provide "good faith" immunity, barring a plaintiff's right to recover for injuries unless the plaintiff can prove the state employees' actions demonstrated "bad faith." Many courts have ruled that sovereign immunity and many other restrictions on lawsuits against public entities protect many public and municipal EMS providers.[2]

EMS Act Immunity

Many states' statutes that authorize their EMS systems and set certain EMS standards also contain provisions that are similar to sovereign immunity provisions. Some states shield EMS providers from liability unless their actions constitute gross negligence (New York) or willful and wanton conduct (Illinois) or conduct inconsistent with EMT training (Michigan).[13]

These laws tend to protect individuals who are certified, licensed, or authorized to provide emergency and nonemergency medical services during approved training or in the normal course of conducting their duties. In addition, they may protect persons, organizations, and institutions who administer, sponsor, authorize, support, finance, educate, or supervise EMS personnel. Although most of these acts protect both public and private EMS personnel, some of these immunity provisions are available only to persons with certain classes of licenses, and others are available only to public or volunteer providers.

Good Samaritan Protection

Good Samaritan statutes usually provide broad immunity for individuals who render emergency care. Sometimes, there are limitations on the circumstances under which the care must be rendered, such as at the scene of an accident. The parameters of these laws tend to include the following:
- Good faith actions
- Services that are neither billed nor reimbursed

Key Points and Conclusion

To date, lawsuits against physicians arising out of EMS support and communication activities have been infrequent, and the awards typically have been small. Although the risk of large professional liability losses arising from this aspect of emergency medicine may not be great, several steps can be taken to reduce the likelihood of claims. Risk management of EMS oversight and communications should address these four key issues:
- The physician's risk exposure is based on the medical direction provided to the on-scene

EMS provider. Background issues involve monitoring the integrity of EMT training and supervision. Immediate issues involve managing the adequacy of radio communication and orders and monitoring of EMS personnel assessment skills and appropriate use of SMOs.
- Generally, emergency physicians advocate respect for a competent patient's right to refuse treatment. Local EMS protocols should be complied with strictly. Risk management also includes monitoring documentation of parameters of competence and informed refusal.
- The PMD's risk exposure is based on the obligation to fulfill administrative duties. Systematic maintenance of documentation files is a key component of risk management. QI and risk management programs should include monitoring that will alert the PMD to problems and opportunities for improvement.
- The three potential sources of immunity for EMS providers and emergency physicians involved in EMS support and communication are sovereign immunity, EMS Act immunity, and Good Samaritan statutes. Because these statutes vary from state to state, local counsel should be contacted for specific information.

References

1. Soler JM, Montes MF, Egol AB, et al. The ten-year malpractice experience of a large urban EMS system. *Ann Emerg Med* 1985;14:982-985.
2. Goldberg RJ, Zautcke JL, Koenigsberg MD, et al. A review of prehospital care litigation in a large metropolitan EMS system. *Ann Emerg Med* 1990;19:557-561.
3. Morgan DL, Wainscott MP, Knowles HC, et al. Emergency medical services liability litigation in the United States: 1987 to 1992. *Prehosp Dis Med* 1994;9(4):214-220.
4. Saunders C, Hearne T. Pre-hospital emergency services. In: Saunders CE, Ho MT, eds. *Current Emergency Diagnosis and Treatment*. 4th ed. Norwalk, Conn: Appleton and Lange; 1992.
5. Ayres RJ Jr. Legal considerations in prehospital care. *Emerg Med Clin North Am* 1993;11:853-867.
6. Public Law No. 101-508 Section 4206, 4751.
7. 'Do Not Attempt Resuscitation' Directives in the Out-of-Hospital Setting. ACEP Policy Statement, approved September 1994. To obtain a copy, call (800) 798-1822, touch 6, or go to www.acep.org.
8. Emergency Medical Treatment and Active Labor Act Final Regulations, *Federal Register*, pp. 32075-32308, June 22, 1994.
9. *Johnson v University of Chicago Hospitals*, 1992 WL 259404 (7th Cir Ill).
10. Medical Direction of Prehospital Emergency Medical Services. ACEP Policy Statement, approved October 1992. To obtain a copy, call (800) 798-1822, touch 6, or go to www.acep.org.

11. Polsky SS, Weigand JV. Quality assurance in emergency medical service systems. *Emerg Med Clin North Am* 1990;8:75-84.

12. Lilja GP, Swor R. Emergency medical services. In: Tintinalli JE, Krome RL, Ruiz E, eds. *Emergency Medicine: A Comprehensive Study Guide*. Third edition. New York: McGraw-Hill Inc; 1992.

13. Morgan DL, Trail WR, Trompler VA, et al. Liability immunity as a legal defense for recent emergency medical services system litigation. *Prehosp Dis Med* 1995;10(2):82-89.

Additional Reading

Ethics in management: emergency medical services need NOT resuscitate. *Nurs Manage* 1996;27(1):50-52.

Harrawood D, Shepler P, Gunderson M. Risk Business: EMS needs risk management. *JEMS* July 1995:30-34.

Maggiore WA. Withholding resuscitation: the medical, legal and ethical concerns. *JEMS* July 1991:94-98.

McDowell R, Krohmer J, Spaite DW, et al. Guidelines for implementation of early defibrillation/automated external defibrillator programs. *Ann Emerg Med* 1993;22:740 – 741.

Page JO. The portability of EMS liability. *JEMS* July 1991:6.

Polsky S, Krohmer J, Maningas P, et al. Guidelines for medical direction of prehospital EMS. *Ann Emerg Med* 1993;22:742-744.

Rice MM. Legal issues in emergency medicine. In: Rosen P, ed. *Emergency Medicine: Concepts and Clinical Practice*. 3rd ed. St Louis: CV Mosby Co; 1992.

Shanaberger CJ. Case law involving base-station contact. *Prehosp Dis Med* 1995;10(2):75-80.

Shanaberger CJ. The legal file: what price patient restraint? *JEMS* October 1993:69-71.

Wolfberg D. Law, policy, and politics: beyond negligence — is provider immunity good for EMS? *JEMS* October 1994:28-30.

Wolfberg D. Law, policy, and politics: refusing emergency medical care — how far do a patient's rights go? *JEMS* January 1995:133-136.

Wolfberg D. Law, policy, and politics: wrongful resuscitation: getting sued for saving lives. *JEMS* October 1995:76-77.

Chapter 53

Patients With Altered Mental Status

Hugh F. Hill III, MD, JD, FACEP, FCLM

There is a wide variety of causes for altered mental status, and as wide a variety of responses. However, the risk management analysis for the initial approach to the patient is the same regardless of etiology. Emergency departments receive patients with nearly every form of mental aberration, from acute psychosis to amnesia, with and without organic components. In some cases, the cause may simply be an unusual reaction to illness or injury; in others, cultural and emotional responses must be distinguished from thought disorders. The nature of emergency medicine is such that these patients represent a significant portion of every department's patient load. They also represent a special problem and a special risk to emergency department staff and the hospital.

The clinical problem of determining mental capacity parallels the legal problem of adjudicating competence. The law reflects conflicting values in society. Patients with altered mental status present the dilemma of paternalistic care versus freedom and self-determination. The primary legal issues of this dilemma as they relate to emergency care professionals are the torts of battery and negligence. Treating patients without their consent is a tort recognized by the law that will not be mitigated by proof of good intentions. Failure to treat a patient who lacks the mental capacity to refuse is also actionable at law; once sufficient mental impairment is proved, withholding needed care cannot be defended successfully based on the fear of being sued for treating without consent.

Patients with diminished mental function present risk management questions that are not fully answered by the old adage "just take care of the patient." There is no safe middle ground between the two opposing demands. The emergency physician must make a clear choice: is the patient competent to make decisions about care, or must treatment be rendered without the patient's consent?

In addition to the clinical issues raised by a patient's incompetence, risk management efforts must address the implication of partially diminished mental capacity. The patient's family members or attorney, or the patient's condition itself, may suggest that the patient cannot understand or appreciate what he is told. When people do something "crazy" to themselves or others, there is an obvious implication that they are "crazy." Similarly, if people fail to act reasonably regarding their own health, the issue of diminished capacity arises, even without family or friends there to prompt the physician. A suspicion of incompetence is often part of an emergency physician's reaction when medical advice is rejected.

Only a little imagination is required to foresee the risk management challenge created by patients who refuse necessary care. If the refusal of care results in patient injury, the patient or family may suggest, in retrospect, that the patient's choice must have been the result of misunderstood instructions or an inability to understand them. If the former is true, then the emergency physician faces accusations that of failing to adequately inform the patient. If the latter is true, the physician will be accused of failing to recognize or respond to mental impairment. As with other risk problems, once the damage occurs, the situation, in retrospect, will appear to have been obvious. A plaintiff's lawyer will work hard to create the "realization" in jurors that "no sane patient would have risked this if he had been told what would happen!"

Patients with real or possible altered mentation are a major clinical challenge and risk management problem for emergency departments. For both reasons, they require an amount of staff time disproportionate to their medical problems. This chapter addresses the risk management aspects of caring for and disposition of these patients in and from the emergency department. It also covers the subject of discharge instructions for patients with reduced or altered mental capacity.

Identifying patients who must be cared for immediately without their permission is as important as recognizing patients whose competence may be questioned outside the emergency department. Either the decision to treat or the decision to respect the patient's idiosyncratic choice can be questioned. Both require aggressive risk management efforts; potential accusations of error must be anticipated with both choices.

Case Studies

1

On two consecutive days, the wife of a 32-year-old man notices that her husband is acting oddly. His statements and behavior are sufficiently bizarre that she suggests he see a psychiatrist. The man tells the psychiatrist, "I know I am God" and "I also know how to go through doors without being seen and without being hurt. I just have to slow my molecules completely down." The psychiatrist's diagnosis is "schizophrenic reaction with ideas of reverence agitation." He prescribes Haldol and Artane. The patient takes the first dose of Haldol and leaves the psychiatrist's office, promising to return later. The psychiatrist calls the patient's father to discuss the man's problems.

The patient drives away alone, apparently intending to return to work. More than an hour later, the fire department's emergency squad finds him sitting on the sidewalk, with his car also partially on the sidewalk. The fire and rescue officers describe the patient's state as "sluggish" and take him to the nearest emergency department.

On arrival, the patient is properly registered, and the nurses' history notes that he had taken Artane and Haldol and felt dazed. The emergency physician examines him and determines that the problem is a reaction to medication. The patient is advised to stop taking the medication and to discuss his condition with his own physician.

The patient is discharged from the emergency department in the early afternoon. His whereabouts are unknown until about an hour later, when he jumps to his death off a bridge onto an interstate highway. Given the number of pills still in their bottles in his pockets, it is clear that he did not take any more of either medication.

The patient's wife sues the hospital, the emergency physician, and the psychiatrist. The psychiatrist settles, and the case goes to trial against the emergency physician and the hospital.

2

A 62-year-old man is committed to a state mental health facility after a long history of manic-depressive behavior. As a result of drug treatment in the facility, he develops permanent tardive lingual and oral facial dyskinesia. He sues, claiming that he never consented to the use of Prolixin and Mellaril.

The state hospital's physicians respond that the patient was already committed and his consent was not possible or required. The defense asks the judge to throw out the case, and he grants the motion, saying: "I don't see how in the world a treating psychiatrist could be held to such a rule requiring informed consent, and I don't believe they are." The plaintiff appeals to the state's supreme court.

3

A 52-year-old man has presented to a particular emergency department many times. The routine is always the same: EMTs respond to a report of a person exhibiting strange or bizarre behavior in a public place. The emergency department staff has seen the patient so often that they do not pay much attention to his antics. On each arrival, he is interviewed briefly by the physician and placed in restraints while the paperwork for commitment is completed.

One day when the patient is brought in, however, a new emergency physician is on duty. She has not seen the patient before and asks the nursing staff to disrobe him so that she can perform an adequate examination. One nurse explains that no examination is necessary: "The other physicians just fill out the forms. Besides, this guy is dangerous if you get too close." The physician decides against following the nurses' recommendations and calls for security to help disrobe the patient.

The examination is mostly unremarkable except for some proptosis and fullness about the neck. The patient's vital signs indicate tachycardia and hypertension, but he is struggling against the restraints. The physician orders a drug screen and thyroid panel but has to draw the blood herself because of the patient's reputation for violence. The nearby state mental hospital refuses to take the patient until the tests are reported, which delays the transfer and further aggravates the nursing staff.

The laboratory test results indicate hyperthyroidism. The physician cannot understand why no one seems pleased that she has uncovered a possible medical cause for the patient's aberrant behavior. In fact, the department's risk manager schedules a meeting with her.

4

A young man presents to the emergency department with a known mental disorder. The emergency department staff initiates a transfer to another hospital. The patient never arrives at the receiving hospital, and the emergency department staff hears that he later shot someone. Remembering the *Tarasoff* case, they are not surprised when the shooting victim sues the emergency department for releasing the patient.

The Medical-Legal Perspective

As with most jurisprudential issues, the historical and cultural anthropological approach to medical law governing the care of patients with impaired mental capability can be enlightening and can provide a framework for recall and analysis. The general law of medical malpractice grew out of the earliest consumer protection cases, which appeared in English judicial opinions more than 200 years ago. Against this expectation is balanced another great common law principle — the right to be left alone. What does the law expect of emergency care professionals when the patient may be impaired? Many of the answers are found in the definitions and applications of the terms used.

Malpractice law, as with other tort law, is developed by judges. Courts give opinions in disputes, attempting to follow or distinguish prior comparable decisions. Rarely, and only in recent cases, are laws passed to control the outcome of these disputes. Malpractice law grew out of a line of cases that addressed protection of people to whom judges said defendants owed a special duty. These people were lodgers in public houses and travelers on coaches operated by businesses; the defendants were the innkeepers and common carriers. The people lodged or carried were vulnerable to the individuals or businesses into whose hands they delivered themselves. This vulnerability, coupled with the power and responsibility of the coach, barge, or innkeeper, was cited by judges articulating a special duty beyond the normal sense of decent behavior in the business relations of equals. Thus, the law did not focus as much on the rights of hostellers, carriers, or healers, but rather on their responsibilities.[1]

Over time in other cases, this same notion of a special duty was applied in other areas, including the healing professions. The duty that courts held defendant physicians owed patients in early malpractice cases drew on these even earlier cases requiring the protection of those who had entrusted their safety to others. Reverberating down through the centuries, this notion of protection conflicts with modern expectations of autonomy and respect for the individual's own choices.

Against this paternalistic background, contrast the Anglo-Saxon legal principle of the right to be left alone. Once available only to those with the money and power to demand it, a more egalitarian application of this right has developed over time. Some years ago, the U.S. Supreme Court found a "right to privacy" in the "penumbra" of the Constitution. A powerful force behind the deinstitutionalization movement that emptied state mental hospitals (and exacerbated and confused the economic homeless issue) a quarter century ago was its appeal to a sense of rights, including a right to make, without interference, choices most would regard as crazy. In law, an unwanted touch, regardless of the intent of the toucher, creates a right to sue for the one touched.

Problems for emergency medicine providers in this area arise in a subset of clinical situations. If a patient is desperately sick and refuses care, it is easier to say that refusal indicates incompetence. At the other extreme, if there is no immediacy at all, a determination as to the patient's mental capacity can be safely deferred. But when the medical need is urgent and not the result of a condition that arguably impairs the person's mental faculties or is likely to deteriorate into an emergent situation if the patient is allowed to refuse care or to select a suboptimal option, then the emergency physician must exercise judgment and manage risk.

When addressing mental capacity, the law asks: "Capacity to do what?" General competence is not usually the issue. The legal question is more likely to be specific to an act or decision, such as the capacity to make a will.[2] An individual's ability to handle personal financial affairs is not necessarily the same as the ability to make basic decisions about terminal care, for example. These distinctions are important to family physicians and other professionals with a longer term relationship with patients and families. Emergency physicians are more concerned with only one kind of mental capacity, which often requires a rapid determination: can the patient make decisions for himself? If the patient lacks the mental capacity for decision-making, refusal can be subsequently made worthless on proof of a patient's lack of capacity. No amount of time devoted to documenting patient counseling regarding the risks of refusing care can offset the legal liability.

The legal model diverges from medical reality in that a legal determination of mental capacity requires more time than most emergency departments have available. In the law, an "emergency" decision about mental status requires hours, at least. A judge or magistrate holds a bedside hearing, soliciting arguments on both sides of the question and hearing medical testimony about the patient's mental status. The medical professional opinion does not always prevail. In the emergency department, faced with patients who want to leave or who refuse immediately needed treatment, the staff must make a quick decision. They often do not have time to gather other information or obtain consultation, and even then must balance benefit to the patient against risk of violent confrontation.

By training and inclination, emergency physicians want to push needed treatment on the unwilling and indecisive. But the law expects that individual rights will be respected. Patients who come in on their own or call 911 rarely present this problem. They may balk at some procedure or insist on a therapeutic protocol of their own choosing, but their capacity to understand and make an informed choice is usually not in question. More often, a patient with significant mental status change does not come to

the emergency department of his own volition. Despite the limited time available and the fine distinctions required regarding capacity for the specific function of consenting to or refusing emergency care, the emergency physician must arrive at a rational decision, taking into account clinical and societal demands. In addition to harming the patient by violating his basic rights, the physician who is contemplating ordering treatment against advice must also consider patient and staff safety. If the patient is forced, will he be hurt? Will the staff or other patients be injured?

If the patient is held or treated against his own wishes and the diagnosis of mental incapacity was unreasonable, liability is greater than for simple medical negligence. Such restraint or treatment is an intentional tort, not a simple professional error. Without any real harm done at all, the patient so mistreated can win a lawsuit. In that circumstance, the damages would be minimal, but unpermitted treatment triggers a kind of strict liability for the physician who orders treatment that results in any injury. In a medical negligence case, the plaintiff must prove that the defendant made a mistake, an act, or omission that violated the standard of care. Once battery (i.e., unpermitted treatment) is proved, the defendant can be held liable for all resulting harm, without any showing that the care was ill chosen or below the standard of care. Thus, an adverse reaction to well-chosen and indicated medications, for example, can be blamed on the physician.

A quick reminder of how the law deals with suicide and homicide risks will provide a clue to the law's notion of the limits of individual freedom. State statutes on this subject use language akin to "present danger to self or others." Patients, to be committed, must clearly suffer from a mental disorder and be a fairly immediate threat to themselves or others.[3] In this context, then, a patient's foolish decision cannot alone justify declaring the individual incompetent, but it may help indicate that the patient meets commitment criteria. The emergency physician must still reach the conclusion that the patient lacks the requisite capacity before holding or treating the patient against his wishes. Nevertheless, the refusal of obviously needed care is potential evidence of impairment and should be recorded.

The general approach to questions of capacity to refuse treatment must involve a determination of the patient's ability to anticipate or to understand and appreciate the consequences of his actions.[2] This inability does not have to be permanent; temporary incapacity secondary to correctable causes can be a satisfactory justification for forced treatment.

The primary question should be this: is the concept of informed consent or refusal meaningful for this patient at this time? If the patient has the capacity to give or withhold consent, then the patient must be dealt with as any other rational being, including allowing terminally stupid decisions. If the patient lacks the capacity, then the patient must be protected, even against himself. If a competent patient will consent (or at least not object) to medical intervention, then protectionist measures can be used, and more treatment options become available for the emergency physician.

Use of the terms "competence" and "capacity" suggests that one term is more general than the other. If a patient is declared incompetent and adjudicated as such by a court, a guardian will likely be appointed who exercises all powers to accept or decline recommended treatment. Court-declared general incompetence allows a presumption that the patient has no authority left and can refuse nothing. Without such broad definition, incapacity is a minute-to-minute, circumstance-specific decision. A patient may lack the capacity to refuse admission but can understand and appreciate risk sufficiently to refuse something else, such as a lumbar puncture.[4]

The caring medical professional's inclination is to slant any close cases toward whatever allows clearly needed care to be administered. But even the most paternalistic ethical structure respects autonomy principles and balances them against need and evidence of incapacity for at least a subset of cases. Although the moment of making difficult decisions will come at different times for different emergency physicians, it will come. If principles and definitions are clear and well considered ahead of that time, the emergency physician will be less likely to err from a risk management perspective, as well as from an ethical one.

Patient Management and Documentation

Patients with possibly altered mental status are a special legal hazard to the emergency department. As a result, the documentation associated with their care must be particularly thorough. The following specific points might have to be addressed in the medical record.

Mental status is a threshold consideration for many reasons, not just for discharge. This possibility can affect the reliability of the patient's history and even features of a physical examination. Charts that bear some indication that altered mental status may exist are extremely dangerous when they show no corresponding or countervailing assessment, nothing to indicate that altered mental status was considered and rejected. Most important, if the patient is able to understand what is being said but the situation still suggests mental impairment, the emergency physician must document mental status.

Careful questioning that reveals the patient's mental state and ability to understand and follow discharge instructions is part of taking a good history. Some patients' impaired status is apparent; others will have their impairment revealed or suggested only after investigation. The breadth and depth of this inquiry is implied by the law's formulation "knew or should have known." The emergency physician will be charged with acting on the basis of knowledge that could and should have been reasonably obtained.

The chart should reflect some assessment of the patient's mental status or at least some response to any recorded suggestion that the patient may have an altered mental state. The suggestion may appear somewhere other than in the physician's notes, such as in nurses' notes or attached EMS sheets. If anything on the chart raises the question of an abnormality in mental status, is the question answered?

When clinical circumstances suggest a patient has altered mental status, some effort to obtain information or confirmation from someone other than the patient is necessary. Risk management dictates that these efforts be documented. Even if they yield no useful information, they should be recorded. The absence of any history of problems may be helpful, and the documented effort makes the emergency department team's attitude and thoroughness clear. This contact can also be useful on the positive side — confirming consent that the possibly impaired patient is willing to give but may be invalid. If the nearest relative is available, that person's formal consent to emergency care for the patient should be sought and documented, if the patient allows the information to be released.[5]

Assessment of a patient's mental status is not something that takes place at any one point. It changes with observation and additional information from other sources. The assessment can change when certain negatives appear, such as a low blood alcohol level in an apparently intoxicated patient. Even without the added information to trigger a reassessment, a diagnosis of altered mental status itself should stimulate continued and periodic reevaluation. Flow sheets should be a part of every patient's record when the diagnosis is altered mental status. Physicians should ask themselves: does the chart reflect periodic reassessment of patients with altered mental status?

The patient who turns out to be in an altered mental state is at least arguably unreliable. When this is a consideration, or if the patient's condition in retrospect might be viewed as impaired, then accepting an uncorroborated history from the patient can be made to appear foolish. The emergency physician should get some confirmation of the important features of the medical history, for example, locating someone who will say whether the patient is deviating from usual behavior.

Sometimes, patients must be treated, often with sedatives or tranquilizers, before every step in the preformulated process can be completed. Establishing that treatment was needed on an emergency basis is probably less difficult for an emergency facility than for a chronic care facility.[6] To avoid a consent problem, the physician should document the emergency nature of the treatment and not assume a patient is incompetent to refuse medication simply because that patient has been, or is being, committed. An involuntarily committed person may be capable of understanding the risks and benefits of proposed treatment. Medication forcibly administered must be necessary and documented as such to preserve the patient's life or to avoid serious harm to the patient or others.[4]

Patients may need emergency intervention before the physician can complete the evaluation of mental status. Mental impairment does not preempt the emergency exception doctrine. If action must be taken immediately to prevent irreparable harm, take it.[7] If emergency intervention is necessary, the emergency physician should thoroughly document the reasons for immediate treatment.

If the situation is truly a medical emergency, and "if there is any doubt as to the patient's mental competence or whether the patient has had sufficient opportunity to give a knowing, informed consent, emergency treatment should be given until such time as the situation can be clarified."[8] If the possibly mentally impaired patient deteriorates to become a true emergency after arrival in the emergency department and before assessment of competency is completed, treat unless there are advance directives to the contrary.

The emergency department's risk manager, when reviewing charts of involuntary patients, should scan for therapeutic or safety interventions, including medication as well as restraints. If the patient was treated, does the documentation sufficiently establish that the treatment was urgently required?

Obtaining additional history from others raises confidentiality concerns. The physician should try to get what is needed without revealing information about the patient. The patient can be asked to permit conversation with others about the case. Privileged communications with other health care providers, such as EMS providers or the patient's own physician, is always permitted. Making contact with another responsible person involved with the patient can be critically important if discharge is being considered. The team may have to give discharge instructions and warnings to the patient's friends or family members.

A period of observation may be in order. Not only does this buy time to get more information, but the patient's condition may fluctuate and even clarify. Many lawsuits in this area include evidence of rapid evaluation and discharge; the implication of inadequate treatment in a short stay is often used by malpractice plaintiffs. The observation period implies the opposite, that the emergency physician is acting in a careful and concerned manner. The countervailing argument, that long stays mean severe conditions, seems to appear only when the patient has been in the emergency department for evaluation for more than 10 hours.

Discharging the patient with possibly altered mental status is a medical-legal minefield. Discharge instructions, even if well documented, can be nullified as a malpractice defense if the patient could not understand what was said. If the emergency team knows that the patient may be deemed impaired but does not believe that admission is required, then special efforts to communicate discharge instructions are advisable. One useful tactic is to inform a competent family member or friend, although this raises confidentiality issues.[9] Most patients will allow at least limited information to be communicated to someone of their own choosing, but their permission should be secured. The emergency physician should record advice and warnings given to that other person and have that person sign the discharge sheet along with the possibly impaired patient. If the patient refuses to consent to contact family or friends, the physician should warn of the risks this entails, document the refusal, and reconsider the wisdom of discharging the patient.

All the other features of sound risk management should also be considered with altered mental status, with special emphasis on techniques used to address unclear cases. The emergency physician should consider asking a consultant to see the patient or obtain laboratory confirmation of suspected drug reactions or abuse. All of the available options may be less than optimal when a possibly impaired patient is discharged. The best choice among them may be apparent at the time, but the chart must document the decision thoroughly so as to withstand the retrospective examination that will occur in the event of a poor outcome.

Retrospective and ongoing review of these patients' charting should not stop with quality assurance. Risk management analysis of at least a significant sample must confirm that documentation is sufficient and pointed enough to protect the department, the hospital, and the individual physicians and nurses. The risk manager might review all charts of committed patients for adequate documentation of examination, including patients sent to the emergency department for "medical clearance" before admission to psychiatric facilities. The nursing and physician staff review at least cumulative statistics of these cases at monthly meetings in many departments.

Above all, emergency physicians should remember that their documentation must justify their decisions. So many "foreseeable" events can happen to these patients during their stay or after discharge. Physicians may want to construct their records as if these foreseeable events may actually occur. In that way, the record will show that the physicians had ample reason to commit or discharge all patients who appear to have altered mental status. They will also be able to justify treatment decisions in a way that can minimize their liability risk.

Case Discussions

1

The jury's verdict came in for the defendants in this case, but the patient's wife appealed on the grounds that the trial judge had refused to allow certain statements into evidence. The plaintiff had attempted to introduce statements made by bystanders about the patient's condition at the sidewalk. The trial judge said these were hearsay — statements made outside of court offered to prove the truth of the content of the statement — and excluded them. The appeals court, however, agreed that these statements were offered for a legitimate purpose: to try to prove that the emergency physician knew or should have known that the patient was acting dangerously. A new trial was ordered.[10]

Given the history suggesting the patient's possible mental impairment, the emergency physician and the staff might have anticipated that standard operating procedure on discharge would be insufficient. If they believed that the patient could understand and appreciate the risks of failing to heed the instructions, then this should have been noted. If they did not believe he understood, then he should not have been discharged. Other health care professionals will assume that the physician believed the patient competent and therefore special notation was unnecessary; some will reason from the psychiatrist's office discharge that emergency department discharge without consultation was appropriate. However, jurors may not.

In this case, the diagnosis of medication reaction for a behavioral complaint raised liability issues. Although the court record did not indicate whether the emergency physician and the staff evaluated other choices before discharge, other choices were probably available:

- Eliciting information from EMTs or the police who were at the scene
- Calling the psychiatrist
- Holding the patient for observation until the suspected drug reaction cleared
- Calling the patient's family, if permitted by the patient, for information or to give discharge instructions

Even if these efforts yield no useful information, they should be recorded. The absence of any history of problems is helpful, and the documented effort makes the emergency department team's attitude and thoroughness clear.

If the emergency team had known this patient was impaired but not sufficiently so to require admission, then they should have made special efforts to communicate discharge instructions. When the history and medication suggest impairment, the safer practice is to treat the case as one where the question of impairment can be raised, even if it is clearly not a problem in the emergency department. Note that the psychiatrist had already called the patient's father. If the emergency physician had informed the father, more information would have been forthcoming and warnings delivered. Confidentiality obligations prevent unpermitted communications unless the patient is adjudicated or declared incapacitated or, perhaps, being evaluated for incapacity under what some states call "an emergency petition."

This case raised several caution flags, giving the emergency department staff and physician a number of opportunities to intervene to manage and reduce risk. Sometimes when the answer seems apparent, the clinical situation itself has to trigger extra precautions. A possibly impaired patient should prompt more thorough documentation.

2

The appeals court reversed the verdict and allowed the plaintiff to go to trial against the physicians. Unless a patient's incompetency has been decided by a judge, committed patients are entitled to care under the usual standards, including consent standards, the appeals court explained. Federal courts, for example, have consistently held that an involuntarily confined mental patient still maintains a constitutional right to reject potentially harmful antipsychotic medications.[11] Today, this is less of a problem for state and private institutions; reformed commitment laws require hearings and judicial review for long-term involuntary confinement and intervention.

Emergency and involuntary administration of medications is more straightforward than in chronic treatment facilities. The staff must document the need for the treatment without assuming that a declaration of incapacity is sufficient. The usual reasons in the emergency department are an immediate danger to self or others. Confronted with such a patient, emergency physicians should document the emergency nature of the treatment and not assume a patient is incompetent to refuse medication simply because that patient has been, or is being, committed. An involuntarily committed person may be capable of understanding the

risks and benefits of proposed treatment.

A review of consent and battery will reveal more of the matter's importance.[3] If there was no consent, then the institution and physicians may be liable for the results of the treatment, including the extrapyramidal side effects — even if the treatment was indicated, appropriate, and properly administered.

3

When the emergency physician found that hyperthyroidism might have been causing the patient's problem, the risk manager explained: "The reason no one is congratulating you is that we all feel terrible that we may have been missing the boat for years. Not to mention the fear that he may decide to sue us."

Not surprisingly, however, the patient's symptoms abated only slightly with treatment. Despite the new diagnosis, it was discovered that he had an underlying mental disorder exacerbated by the endocrinopathy. He is still brought into the emergency department occasionally and is still committed to the state facility for brief stays. Now, however, every physician in the department performs an adequate physical examination. The risk manager reviews all charts of committed patients for documentation of examination then sends copies of charts back to individual physicians with pointed questions: how do you know this patient didn't have . . . ? The nurses and physicians review these cases at monthly meetings. They are determined not to let these problems slip through again.

4

In *Tarasoff v Regents of the University of California*,[12] a young man articulated his hostility toward another student during counseling by a university psychologist. The psychologist tried to get the campus police involved, but they refused. When the student returned from out of the country, the patient shot her to death. The victim's family was allowed to sue the university; the state's supreme court held that the therapist had failed to warn, creating an affirmative duty to the third party, that is, a person outside the therapeutic relationship.

But in a similar California case, *McDowell v County of Alameda*,[13] the emergency department and hospital were held not to have a "special relationship" either to a victim or the assailant, who had been treated in the department. The emergency facility was dismissed from the case.

This last ruling is a result more predictable than that in *Tarasoff*, a 1976 case that is still reverberating down the corridors of precedent. In general, one person owes no duty to control another's conduct. Many authorities writing about *Tarasoff* have focused on the specificity of the threat — the victim was plainly identified to the therapist by the patient. This suggests that an impaired patient who makes a very specific threat, sufficient to allow the implication of a relationship between the emergency physician and intended victim, may trigger liability for the emergency department that releases him. In general, third-party liability has not yet become a major problem for emergency care providers, but the possibility remains real.

Key Points and Conclusion

- When clinical circumstances suggest that a patient has altered mental status, some effort to obtain additional information from someone other than the patient is often helpful. If the nearest relative is available, that person's formal consent to emergency care for the patient should be sought and documented if the patient allows information to be released.

- Patients with altered mental status must undergo periodic reassessments in the emergency department, and these must be documented.

- If a patient's condition is truly a medical emergency and there is doubt about the patient's mental competence or ability to give informed consent, emergency treatment should be provided.

- If a patient with altered mental status is to be discharged in the care of another person, a copy of the discharge instructions and other advice and warnings should be given to that person then documented in the chart.

- Discharge instructions, even when well documented, can be nullified as a malpractice defense if the patient could not understand what was said.

- If anything on a patient's chart raises the question of an abnormality in mental status, the question must be answered. Documentation must justify the physician's decisions.

References

1. Annas G. *The Rights of Doctors, Nurses, and Allied Health Professionals.* New York: Avon; 1981.

2. Kiscina SF. *Medical Law for the Attending Physician: A Case-Oriented Analysis.* Carbondale, Ill: Southern Illinois University Press; 1982.

3. American College of Legal Medicine. *Legal Medicine.* 3rd ed. St Louis: Mosby–Year Book; 1995.

4. Rozovsky FA: *Consent to Treatment: A Practical Guide.* Boston: Little, Brown & Co; 1984.

5. Mancini MR. *Emergency Care and the Law.* Gaithersburg, Md: Aspen Publishers; 1981.

6. Under review at the time of this publication's last edition, the US Supreme Court's holding that physician review was constitutionally sufficient seems to have reduced the level of litigation on this issue. *State of Washington v Harper*, 110 SCt 1028 (1990).

7. *Crouch v Most*, 432 P2d 250 (NM 1967). In discussing the emergency situation that nullified plaintiff's lack of informed consent claim, involving later gangrene and amputation of bitten fingers, the appellate court in this case said: " . . .[I]t would be most unusual for a doctor, with his patient who had just been bitten by a venomous snake, to calmly sit down and first fully discuss the various available methods of treating snake bite and the possible consequences, while the venom was being pumped through the patient's body."

8. *Health Care Law: A Practical Guide.* Matthew Bender; 1988.

9. Lewis SM. *Emergency Medicine Malpractice.* New York: Wiley Law Publications;1987:24.

10. *McKenna v St. Joseph Hospital*, RI, No. 87-285-Appeal, April 20, 1989. The McKenna case report above appeared in *Emergency Department Law*, 1989;1(7):1,5. It is reprinted as adapted with permission of the publisher, Business Publishers, Inc, 951 Pershing Drive, Silver Springs, MD 20910-4464. (800) 274-6737. Fax: (301) 589-8493. E-mail bpinews@bpinews.com and Web site www.bpinews.com.

11. *Nolen v Peterson and Wicks*, Ala Sup Ct, No. 87-446, January 13, 1989, rehearing denied, April 28, 1989. This case report and analysis appeared in a slightly different form in *Emergency Department Law*, 1989;(9). It is printed here with permission of the publisher, Business Publishers, Inc, 951 Pershing Drive, Silver Springs, MD 20910-4464. (800) 274-6737. Fax: (301) 589-8493. E-mail bpinews@bpinews.com and Web site www.bpinews.com.

12. *Tarasoff v Regents of the University of California*, 551 P2d 334 (1976).

13. *McDowell v County of Alameda*, 88 Cal App3d 321, 151 Cal Rptr 14 (1976).

Chapter 54

Use of Restraints

Hugh F. Hill III, MD, JD, FACEP, FCLM

Few of the common emergency department risk management issues can be so neatly delineated as when a patient's right to be free conflicts with preventing the patient from harming self or others. Some people would be shocked to learn that many emergency departments have at least one person in restraints every day. Often, people arrive so agitated or become so violent that no reflection or balancing is possible. For these situations, emergency departments must have a plan. Where the problem and the risk-benefit analysis are less obvious, emergency physicians must have legal definitions and an analytic framework to create a careful and well-documented response.

The need for and proper selection of restraints, either chemical or physical, are clinical issues. The medical-legal issues involve under what conditions the law allows this abrogation of personal autonomy and what requirements constitute proper documentation to justify either using restraint or deciding not to.

Case Studies

1

A 25-year-old woman with a history of mental illness is observed by her older sister saying repeatedly, "Jesus saves, Jesus saves," and striking herself on the chest. The sister calls 911, and the patient is admitted to the emergency department at 2:25 PM. The sister stays outside in the waiting room.

The patient admonishes the emergency department staff that they are not gods and attempts to stand on a cart. One staff member calls security, and others place the patient in five-point soft restraints. At 2:50 PM, the patient tells a nurse she is "all right now" and wants to go home. The emergency medicine resident on duty sees her at 3:10 PM and decided she is a danger to herself. His diagnosis is paranoid schizophrenic exacerbation. The emergency physician calls for a psychiatric consultation, but when the psychiatry resident arrives at 4:15 PM, the patient cannot be found. A short time later she wanders onto a busy street and begins shouting at cars and hitting them with her hands. One of the cars hits and kills her. The cause of death is listed as neck fracture and hemothorax.

An investigation of the incident suggests that the patient left shortly after 4:00 PM. The last nurses' note was written at 3:20 PM and indicated that the patient was resting quietly in full soft restraints. Entries in the hospital security officer's notebook indicate that she was seen leaving or being escorted from the main desk to a public bus at 4:07 PM.

Later, the patient's minor children successfully sue the hospital. The jury finds the hospital and its emergency department 100% at fault. The hospital appeals.

2

After a two-week hospitalization for depression, a woman is assigned to a physician for outpatient treatment. The physician is a psychiatry resident at a prominent academic medical center. A year later, he resigns. Four years later, the patient sues the medical center for multiple intentional torts. She claims that the physician had forced nonconsensual intercourse on her and threatened to commit her to a psychiatric hospital if she told anyone. The trial court throws out the case on the basis of the statute of limitations, and the patient appeals.

3

A 32-year-old woman with a long history of mental illness and drug abuse undergoes a tracheostomy. One evening during her hospital stay, she becomes agitated and knocks down the charge nurse. Seven staff members respond, and they restrain and medicate the patient.

Two hours later, the patient is partially released from the restraints so that she can eat, but she begins to tear at her tracheostomy site. She is allowed to walk around while in a straitjacket, but she harasses the staff. Later, the straitjacket is removed. She continues to bother staff and other patients and, at one point, disrobes and walks around nude until staff intervenes. At 5:30 AM, the patient urinates on the floor of the nursing station, so a nurse puts her back in her room. To get her back into restraints, the nurse kneels on the patient and gives her an injection.

About a half hour later, the nurse checks on the patient then runs out and calls code blue. CPR is unsuccessful, and the patient dies. An autopsy is performed and indicates that the patient had bruising on her neck and ligature marks on her wrists and ankles. An hepatic tear with bleeding was also discovered, but the medical examiner signed the case out as asphyxiation by mechanical compression.

4

A 43-year-old man is shouting and creating a disturbance outside a drugstore. A police officer calls 911, and the paramedics who respond place the patient on a stretcher and strap him in for transport to the emergency department.

When they get to the hospital, the patient becomes verbally abusive. The emergency physician comes to the stretcher but cannot interview the shouting patient, so she calls security to help transfer the patient to a gurney. She notes on the chart that the patient arrived in restraints, was possibly irrational, and would have to remain strapped down until she could investigate his situation.

As the physician approaches the patient, he begins shouting that he wants to call his lawyer. The physician puts her hand on the patient's arm and says: "I want to help you." The patient quiets down and she is able to get a partial history of what caused his outburst. She explains that she needs more information before he can be released, despite the patient's renewed protests.

The physician asks the nurses to check the patient every 15 minutes. She then calls the patient's family physician, the drug store clerk, the police officer at the scene, and the psychiatrist on call. The family physician says the patient has no prior psychiatric or drug history but is generally hot-tempered. The police do not return the call, and the drug store clerk refuses to give information unless the physician can tell him about the patient's status, despite the physician's explanations about confidentiality.

When the psychiatrist comes to the emergency department, he concludes that the patient can be released. He notes this evaluation and discharge decision on the records. The patient leaves, still shouting angrily at the emergency physician and staff for not allowing him to leave earlier. No one is surprised when, five months later, lawsuit notice papers are served on the emergency physician and the hospital, charging them with holding the patient against his will.

5

A 27-year-old woman comes to the emergency department for treatment of pain and burning on urination and vaginal discharge. When the emergency physician tells her she has a sexually transmitted disease, she becomes angry and starts shouting before the emergency physician can finish explaining that such a disease can have a long incubation period and appear much later after the initial infection. Unconsoled, the patient loudly voices her intention to do grievous bodily harm to her current sexual partner.

Out in the hallway, the nurse assisting in the pelvic examination approaches the physician. "She's really p.o.'d. I think she might do something to her boyfriend. Can't we restrain her until she calms down?" "I don't think we can," the emergency physician responds. "She's not mentally incapacitated, and even if she does threaten somebody, we can't strap her down unless she's got a mental illness."

"Well, I think intending to kill someone is a mental illness," the nurse says, just as the patient storms out of the examination room, pushes past the physician, and runs out the door.

The Medical-Legal Perspective

The use of restraints must be regarded as a significant intervention in the care of a patient. The state authorizes compulsory treatment in certain conditions, such as communicable diseases, on a comparable rationale: the patient's own welfare or that of the larger community.[1] Restricting the movement of patients creates the risk of liability for a claim of false imprisonment[2] (see Chapter 48, "Refusal of Care"). A broad sense of the means and meaning of restraint, whether leather restraints, drugs, hands, or even coercion, is helpful in reducing the potential for liability.

Restraints, as used in this context, do not include those devices designed to help a compliant or willing patient. Poseys and bed rails are generally a problem only when a patient falls out of bed or is otherwise injured because of them. If a patient who accepted restraint initially begins to object to it, the same legal analysis applies as in the initial application of restraints. For example, the drug overdose victim who is strapped down before narcotic antagonists are administered and who wakes up and wishes to be let go must be reassessed to determine the need and justification of restraints. The patient cannot simply be tied down for past transgressions but can be kept restrained if there is medical justification to do so.

Emergency department staff tend to take the use of restraints too lightly, probably because they have to use them daily. Restricting someone's movement is tantamount to imprisonment. Locking up or tying down a person is a major violation of that persons rights and as such requires serious justification and careful documentation.

A restrained patient has grounds to bring a lawsuit against the individuals and the institution responsible for the restraints and for false imprisonment. The documentation must explain, excuse, and defend the restraint. The legal definition of false imprisonment is the unlawful detention of one person by another, for any length of time, whereby the restrained individual is deprived of personal liberty. An older term sometimes still used is "unlawful detainer." Battery, which is an unpermitted touching, is a concomitant tort that can be another basis for lawsuit, stimulated by the same circumstances as false imprisonment.[3]

Today, a legal action for false imprisonment can be initiated for any unlawful restriction of an individual's movement. Thus, confinement to a particular place through threats of personal harm or harm to another person can be the basis of a civil action, even without locked doors or other physical restrictions.

As opposed to negligence, false imprisonment is viewed as an intentional tort, or wrong. Intentional wrongs necessarily involve an intended act of commission, in this situation, with the intent to keep the person from leaving, or with the intent to touch when not permitted. Negligence, on the other hand, can be found in a failure to do something, an act of omission. In general, intentional torts are unusual in a medical context. False imprisonment and battery, however, sometimes do appear in malpractice cases.

Three critical differences between negligence and intentional tort claims are in the required proofs. First, to win a lawsuit for false imprisonment or for other intentional torts, the plaintiff does not need to produce an expert witness because the standard of care is not an issue. In most cases, the medical decision to restrain is commented on by experts, but there is no technical requirement for an expert to say there was substandard care. A second difference is that no actual or physical injury or damages need to be shown. A plaintiff can sue for false imprisonment even though there was no monetary or physical harm. The third distinction is that injuries caused by the wrongful act do not need to be causally connected with any negligence. What would be acceptable adverse effects or complications of a procedure if the issue were negligence, such as bruising from the restraints, become compensable injuries when the claim is for intentional tort. Punitive damages are possible if a plaintiff wins such a case.

Health care providers sued for false imprisonment defend both affirmatively and by denying that the plaintiff has proved the case. The defense presents the reasons for the restraint and argues that the actions were lawful. The documentation on the medical record of every patient who is put in restraints, even temporarily, must include the reasons why the restraint was necessary and an indication that the patient was incompetent to refuse treatment (see Chapter 53, "Patients With Altered Mental Status"). A competent patient must not be touched without implying or giving explicit permission; if the patient is an immediate danger to self or others, the same behavior that indicates such danger usually indicates incapacity as well, or at least enough to justify initial restraint until further investigations.

Careful documentation should be used in every case that might possibly be described as restraint, constraint, limitation, or coercion. Staff will recognize the need for these notations when a patient is in "four-point leathers" but must also be alert for situations in which other means are used. For example, if an injection of a tranquilizer is administered to "quiet the patient down," an attorney can make it appear to be a restraint. If security is called to stand at a patient's bedside to make sure the patient does not get up, a false imprisonment claim is possible, even though no one lays hands on the patient. Older case law in this area reports lawsuits in which hospitals were accused of refusing to discharge inpatients because of their failure to pay the hospital bills.

Albeit unfairly so, a direct relationship exists between the outrageousness of the patient's conduct and the opportunity to characterize the physician's response as vindictive. An extremely provocative patient, especially one who is only verbally threatening, will be able to use that very behavior to suggest that the physician ordered restraints for reasons other than the patient's best interests. Rare case reports exist of physicians striking patients, and the courts' opinions discuss justification or lack thereof for the physician's actions. Although striking a patient can be justified only in the most extreme cases of self-defense or defense of others in the department, judicial analysis in these cases intimate the law's response to claims of vindictive restraint.[4]

Two cases in particular bring some focus to the issue. In one, a physician struck an obnoxious patient who was cursing in the presence of nurses. The court said malice could be implied from the act and allowed punitive damages. In the other, a physician slapped a 2-year-old child to get her to open her mouth so that he could extract his finger. He had been repairing a laceration to her tongue when she bit his finger and would not let go. The court allowed the physician's justification, explaining that it was defensive, not disciplinary. (Today, a better-informed plaintiff's attorney would argue that the physician failed to anticipate this common 2-year-old response.)

Liability for failure to restrain is the flip side of this dilemma. The need to make a decision whether to use restraints should alert the physician that the situation is high risk; the need for careful documentation is easily recognized. If a nurse suggests restraints, or the police bring a patient in because of bizarre behavior, or any incident occurs in which the physician decides not to order restraints or continue restraints ordered earlier when they might be indicated, the basis of that choice must be documented carefully. If a patient regains the requisite capacity to appreciate the hazards of refusing treatment and insists on leaving, that patient must be let go. Here, extraordinary documentation is needed to record the change in mental status that led to the patient's release. The better practice is to chart carefully even seemingly routine releases; once patients are discharged, their continued cooperation and behavior cannot be guaranteed.

Recognizing the benefits of restraints too late presents a different problem. A patient with minimal evidence of dangerousness who later becomes uncontrollable, risking or doing harm to self or others, raises an issue for subsequent reviewers: why wasn't the person restrained initially? Although a thorough analysis and documentation of the mental status of each patient is impractical and unnecessary, this risk can be managed. Medical records have great credibility in legal disputes. Without evidence to the contrary, they are generally assumed to be contemporaneous and accurate notes of the writer's perceptions. Notes written after some untoward episode carry less weight because of the inherent implication of self-protective bias. However, even these records are still useful, especially in the absence of other documentation.

If emergency physicians and nurses pay careful attention to possible false imprisonment claims, they can identify high-risk cases, alerting staff to document them carefully. The liability risk can be well managed with proper records that justify the use and continued maintenance of restraints.

Emergency department risk managers should have the following items on their checklists for reviewing charts of restrained patients:
- Indications justifying the use of restraints
- Means and safety measures used in administering or applying restraints
- Procedure notes or statements of no injuries to the patient
- Frequent checks on the patient who is restrained, for example, proper circulation in the extremities

Case Discussions

1

The hospital in this case, *Boles v Milwaukee County*,[5] defended itself on the basis of the Wisconsin civil commitment statute and public policy grounds. It claimed it had no authority to restrain the patient because her condition did not meet the criteria for involuntary commitment. In this state, a patient who is suspected of mental illness and who has not committed a crime cannot be involuntarily detained unless there is a "substantial probability" of physical harm to self or others, manifested by recent threats, acts, or omissions.

Although this state's language is similar to that of other states, it tends to be more restrictive in that it requires more certainty prior to commitment. The appeals court said that the issue was not determining whether the patient met the criteria for commitment, but whether the hospital had violated its duty of care. The opinion pointed out that the emergency physician requested continued restraint and nursing observation. The jury found that the emergency department failed to restrain or monitor the patient and thus violated the duty owed her and endangered her well-being.

The hospital also appealed on the grounds of public policy, claiming that the verdict put too great a burden on emergency departments in situations laden with conflicting duties. The appeals court also rejected this argument. The hospital could have anticipated that the patient would pursue a "course of her own self-destruction." The court attempted to limit the reach of its decision, however, by suggesting that its opinion in this case should not be extended to cases in which patients leaving the emergency department against medical advice are not mentally ill or are mentally ill but present no immediate danger to themselves or others. With one dissenting vote, the appeals court upheld the trial court verdict against the hospital.

The dissenting judge pointed out that the jury was never told about the severe limits on the hospital's authority to restrain the patient. The majority ruling effectively rejected the commitment statute as irrelevant and ignored the dilemma it presents emergency care providers who are caught between liability for releasing an impaired patient and liability for restraining a patient not yet committed. The dissenting judge said that, unless the patient met the commitment statute's criteria, she was free to go at any time. By holding the commitment statute's provisions irrelevant to the determination of the emergency department's duty, the appeals court was in effect holding that "there are circumstances where hospital personnel must violate the law in order to be free from negligence. This clearly is against public policy. It also places hospitals between the Scylla of tort liability for failure to detain and the Charybdis of tort liability for unwarranted detention. That, too, is something the law should not tolerate."[5]

Civil commitment is a definitive judgment, not a sliding scale; whether the patient meets commitment criteria is a definitive choice. Even if a patient needs only minimal restraint, the emergency department staff must still decide if the patient is so impaired as to present an acute danger to self or others. If not, the patient may walk out. If the danger exists, the patient must be protected and prevented from leaving. This does not mean that staff should be directed or even permitted to place themselves in jeopardy when handling these patients. Sometimes, the risk of injury to staff, the patient, or even other patients outweighs the risk of letting a violent patient leave.

The risk management principle in restraint situations is to interpret the commitment statute liberally to protect the patient. This is not to say, as some have maintained, that emergency physicians must treat the patient and let the consequences be damned. But if there is any ambiguity in the clinical situation, err on the side of paternalism — then document extensively and carefully. If a patient is kept restrained during or awaiting an evaluation, then, by reverse logic, there must have been a decision that the patient met the statute's criteria on the basis of available information. The chart should reflect this judgment. If the psychiatric consultant sees the patient and authorizes release, this does not necessarily mean that the earlier determination was in error, but was justified by what was known at that time.

The risk management lesson is basic and generally applicable: if restraints are to be used, they must be used properly, according to legal statutes and sound medical judgment. Alternative treatment options were not an issue in this case. The chart revealed what was needed and attempted; the problem was that the restraint orders were not carried out. Whatever is decided, the response must be thorough. If a patient needs restraints and observation, then something less than this approach can trigger liability. In general, if the physician or some other staff member departs from a course of treatment once initiated, there should be good, well-documented medical reasons on the chart. When the treatment plan is reversed or altered, the reasons for the change must be recorded. In an important sense, the standard of care is established by the initial course.[6]

2

The psychiatry resident had been forced to resign from the hospital staff because he falsified his credentials. Not only had he not graduated from Harvard Medical School, he was not even a physician.

The appellate court reversed the trial court ruling, holding that there was an issue as to whether the patient's mental condition should suspend the time limits of the statute. There were different terms in this state for the intentional torts and negligence claims, but both had expired, except for a mental disability excuse. The case was sent back for trial.[7]

Although this is not an emergency department case, it is cited here for two points. First, the statute of limitations can be set aside for patients whose mental disabilities are sufficient to excuse missing filing deadlines. This extends the department's liability beyond the statutory time limits for other cases. Thus, a patient's mental incapacity used to justify restraints can be used by an attorney to argue for deadline extension. Of course, this same argument presents a dilemma for the patient who attempts to argue that the restraints were unjustified.

Second, the threat made by the "psychiatrist" was a form of restraint. An emergency patient who allows treatment or even stays under protest following a threat of involuntary commitment is under restraint. This coercive oral restriction on movement is enough of a problem to warrant caution when informing the patient of alternatives in any informed consent or refusal counseling session, when such a possibility might be or become an option.

3

The nurse in this case was charged with manslaughter and criminally negligent homicide. Although a jury found the nurse guilty, in an unusual move, the trial judge overturned the verdict, saying: "I don't condone the conduct here and I was very upset by not only [the nurse's] conduct, but by the whole hospital's conduct." However, explained the judge, "I don't

think the prosecution proved there was any criminal responsibility."

The appeals court, with one dissenting opinion, reversed and reinstated the jury verdict. The required proof had been offered — that the nurse had recklessly caused the death of another person (second-degree manslaughter) and done so by consciously disregarding a substantial and unjustifiable risk (criminally negligent homicide). One dissenting appeals judge said: "That the action taken may have been insensitive does not make it criminal."[8]

All emergency departments get some altered mental status patients who are provocative and obnoxious. All emergency department personnel must deal with their own angry feelings provoked by such patients. The ideal of loving and caring kindness is difficult to maintain with a patient who is spitting or abusive. To the extent possible, staff actions must be done for the patient, not to the patient, and these actions must be carefully documented. The more abusive or difficult the patient's behavior, the more it can be made to appear that a staff member was taking revenge on the patient and not acting in the patient's best interests.

Whenever a patient requires forcible restraint, emergency staff should request enough assistance to do the job safely. Injuries are still possible, so documentation of the case must be clear and address the important points. Why were the restraints necessary? How many people came to help? Were any injuries noted? Were the names of other witnesses recorded?

4

The emergency physician was at first dismayed during her first meeting with the insurance company-selected attorney. She thought the case would be dropped because no experts would testify for the plaintiff. The lawyer explained that no expert was needed because the case was an intentional tort action, not negligence. The plaintiff's theory, he said, was that because the psychiatric consultant released the patient, he never should have been restrained. The release implied that an error had been made earlier.

The physician explained to the lawyer that she had made her judgment on the information she had at the time and did not think it wise to release the patient until she had a psychiatrist's opinion. "Are you saying," the lawyer asked, "that the patient had to be restrained, in your medical judgment, up until the time the psychiatrist was consulted?" The physician said yes and showed him her documentation to that effect. The lawyer called the insurance company while she was still in the office and told them to reduce the reserves because he was confident they could prevail.

Depositions were taken, and the plaintiff refused a nuisance value settlement offer. The defense attorney was worried when the drug store clerk and the police officer could cite only the patient's screaming as a basis for concern about his mental condition. However, the psychiatrist's deposition supported the use of restraints to protect the patient from potentially harming himself and others. In the psychiatrist's opinion, the emergency physician had exercised prudent medical judgment on the basis of the information available to her at the time.

Following this deposition, the litigation process came to a halt. The plaintiff's physician consultant examined the emergency department chart and could find no solid basis for bringing the case to trial. The plaintiff tried to renew settlement discussions, and when the defense refused, dropped the case.

5

After the patient stormed out of the department, the physician became worried about what the nurse had said and about the patient's threat. He decided to call the police and tell them about the patient's threat. Then, he remembered patient confidentiality. He called the hospital administrator, who quickly called the hospital's attorney. The physician gave the attorney a brief history of the incident concluded by saying, "Now I'm worried about what I should have done. What can I do now?"

The hospital's attorney reassured him. "Clearly, you couldn't hold her against her will, given what you've told me. You were right about that. But the police report is a different matter. The threat is to a specific, identifiable person, so I'm going to advise you to call the police. Be sure to write down the name of the officer who takes your report." After making the telephone call, the emergency physician never heard any more about the case.

Emergency department liability to third parties has been infrequent. Most cases hold no duty where there was no relationship. The few that have held for liability focus on the foreseeability of the harm that actually happens. States that do not limit liability to specific named victims of a patient's actions will limit on the basis

of a "zone of danger." There is no automatic protection from lawsuits for violating confidentiality when making reports to law enforcement, but the risk is difficult to estimate when balancing two unknowns. Where states have spoken on the subject, a privilege to report should be a reasonable inference.

Key Points and Conclusion

Logical consistency in the use of restraints must be reflected in the chart. If a restraint is used, the record must clearly show why it was needed. The fact of use alone is not enough.

The use of restraints has become a medical-legal "hot button." All hospitals now have, or should have, policies and procedures for emergency application of restraints. Most have their own forms for physicians or staff to use to document the initiation of restraints and patient reassessments. Compliance with all steps will prevent a *per se* violation of the hospital's established standard of care.

If restraint is used, it must be adequate. Better that too much physical restraint be applied, once the decision to restrain is made, unless the restraint itself becomes a source of injury. However, the same reasoning does not apply to chemical restraint. In these cases, appropriate dosage is important.

Physicians who want to partially restrain a patient should consider this course carefully. If the staff does not want to commit to adequate restraint, frequent patient reassessments, and careful documentation, then perhaps the patient should be released and the reasons for release recorded.

If restraints are removed, the physician should note the change in the patient's condition on the medical record that justified this action.

When police bring a patient for examination, such as drawing blood alcohol, emergency physicians and staff should remember that the patient's refusal can be used against him in subsequent criminal proceedings. The emergency physician, no matter how sympathetic to authorities, is not an employee of the state. If restraining the patient and forcibly drawing blood or performing some other examination risks injury to the patient or others, do not comply with the officer's request without considering the consequences. Some states have statutes promising immunity to emergency personnel who act on a police officer's request, but others do not.[9]

If the patient seems to have provoked the physician's anger, the physician should let someone else manage the case, if possible. If not, the physician must take care of the patient and safeguard the department, making every effort to focus on the patient's needs. Thorough documentation is required.

Emergency staff should not say or do anything, even in a humorous vein, that might be quoted out of context later to suggest that the patient deserved to be punished or that the restraints are part of an effort in behavioral modification. The staff must find a better tension release, one that does not offer ammunition to someone who might sue later.

After any event that might have been prevented by placing a patient in restraints, an accurately timed note reflecting the problem, response to it, and result of examination if the patient is still in the emergency department becomes an essential part of the record. Either on the record itself or in a separate report, the physician or staff should document the condition of the patient on arrival and lack of sufficient indicators of incapacity and/or dangerous behavior. Although not as reliable as a record made before the change in patient behavior, even this arguably self-serving note can be helpful in any subsequent inquiry.

References

1. Rozovsky FA. *Consent to Treatment: A Practical Guide.* Boston: Little, Brown & Co; 1984.

2. Mancini MR. *Emergency Care and the Law.* Gaithersburg, Md; Aspen Publishers; 1981.

3. George JE. *Law and Emergency Care.* St Louis: Mosby–Year Book; 1980.

4. Kiscina SF. *Medical Law for the Attending Physician: A Case-Oriented Analysis.* Carbondale, Ill: Southern Illinois University Press; 1982.

5. *Boles v Milwaukee County,* No. 88-1185 (Wis App May 11, 1989).

6. This case study and analysis appeared in *Emergency Department Law* 1989;1(12):1,5,6. It is reprinted as adapted with permission of the publisher, Business Publishers, Inc, 951 Pershing Drive, Silver Springs, MD 20910-4464. (800) 274-6737. Fax: (301) 589-8493. E-mail bpinews@bpinews.com and Web site www.bpinews.com. For a case holding no liability for injuries to the emergency department escapee where there was no basis for commitment or restraint, see *Torres v City of New York,* 396 NYS2d 34 (1977).

7. *Dunkley v Shoemate,* No. COA95-279 (NC Ct App January 2, 1996).

8. *People v Simon,* NY Sup Ct, No. 37633 (January 16, 1990). This case report and analysis above appeared in *Emergency Department Law* 1990;1(24):6. It is reprinted as adapted with permission of the publisher, Business Publishers, Inc, 951 Pershing Drive, Silver Springs, MD 20910-4464. (800) 274-6737. Fax: (301) 589-8493. E-mail bpinews@bpinews.com and Web site www.bpinews.com.

Chapter 55

Family Violence

Arthur R. Derse, MD, JD

Violence has been declared a national public health epidemic. Child abuse, domestic violence, and elder abuse, often referred to collectively as family violence, are on the rise.[1] Emergency physicians are on the front lines as more patients present with traumatic injuries resulting from these various forms of family violence. Emergency physicians may be familiar with their duty to detect child abuse and to comply with mandatory reporting laws. However, determining whether an injury is the result of child abuse and what level of suspicion requires reporting are difficult risk management issues. Emergency physicians may be even less familiar with the laws dealing with domestic violence and elder abuse and may be missing opportunities to diagnose these problems and to intervene before a patient is injured again or even killed.

Legal precedent and increased societal awareness of the devastating effects of family violence make the duty of diagnosing and reporting abuse part of the standard of care for all physicians. Increased knowledge of the medical-legal aspects of these forms of family violence can benefit patients and decrease liability from misdiagnosis and failure to report.

Epidemiology

In the United States, the number of children reported as abused or neglected increased by 50% from 1985 to 1993. In 1993, nearly three million children were reported to child protective services agencies as suspected victims of abuse or neglect.[2] More than half of these reports were substantiated after investigation by child protective agencies. As many as 5,000 children die annually as a result of abuse.[3] There is a disproportionate increase of reported child abuse and neglect cases in older children and adolescents. Adolescents experience maltreatment at rates equal to or exceeding those of younger children.[4]

More than 95% of adult victims of domestic abuse are women. Estimates of the number of female victims of partner violence run as high as four million each year.[5] Increasingly, a woman's killer is likely to be her partner. In one study,[6] more women in New York City were killed by their husbands or boyfriends than in robberies, disputes, sexual assaults, drug violence, random attacks, or any other crime in cases where the motive for murder was known.

Although statistics on elder abuse are less reliable, national estimates of reported incidence are as high as 186,000 cases a year.[7] State agencies charged with identifying, investigating, and preventing elder abuse have all reported increased caseloads over the past decade.[8]

Definitions

Family violence is defined as intentional intimidation; physical and/or sexual abuse; and battering of children, adults, or elders by a family member, intimate partner, or caretaker. It includes child abuse and neglect (sometimes referred to as child maltreatment), domestic abuse (also known as spouse abuse or partner violence), and elder abuse (or elder mistreatment).[9] Abuse and neglect of children and elders are often defined by state statute.

Child abuse, domestic abuse, and elder abuse have different characteristics but a similar theme: infliction of injury by one caretaker or family member on another family member. In any manifestation of family violence, sexual assault may accompany physical intimidation and violence.

Child Abuse and Neglect

The Child Abuse Prevention and Treatment Act of 1974,[10] which many states adopted into statutory law, defines an abused child as any unemancipated person under 18 years of age whose parent, immediate family member, or any person who is responsible for the child's welfare who resides in the same home as the child or who is an intimate of the child's parent does one or more of the following:

- Inflicts, causes to be inflicted, or allows to be inflicted on the child physical injury, by other than accidental means, that causes death, disfigurement, impairment of physical or emotional health, or loss or impairment of any bodily function.
- Creates a substantial risk of physical injury to the child, by other than accidental means, that would be likely to cause death, disfigurement, impairment of physical or emotional health, or loss or impairment of any bodily function.
- Commits or allows to be committed any sex offense against the child.
- Commits or allows to be committed an act or acts of torture on the child.
- Inflicts excessive corporal punishment.

A neglected child is any person under 18 years of age whose parent or other person responsible for the child's welfare does one or both of the following[11]:

- Withholds or denies nourishment or medically indicated treatment, including food or care, denied solely on the basis of the present or anticipated mental or physical impairment as determined by a physician acting alone or in consultation with other physicians.
- Otherwise does not provide the proper or necessary support, legally required education, or medical or other remedial care recognized by law as necessary for a child's well-being, including adequate food, clothing, and shelter.

Domestic Violence

Domestic violence, spouse abuse, partner abuse, and battering all refer to the victimization of a person with whom the abuser has or has had an intimate or romantic relationship.[12] Because there are few laws designed to address domestic violence, there is no generally accepted statutory definition.

Elder Abuse and Neglect

Abuse of older adults includes physical violence as well as psychological or emotional abuse. Elder abuse includes misappropriation of money and/or property, thefts of social security or pension checks, and the use of threats to enforce the signing or changing of a will or other legal documents. Neglect of the elderly is a caregiver's failure, whether intentional or unintentional, to meet the needs of a dependent elderly person. Various state agencies have different definitions of elder abuse. Connecticut, for example, defines abuse as "the willful infliction of physical pain, injury, or mental anguish, or willful deprivation by a caretaker of services necessary for physical and/or mental well being."[13,14]

Case Studies

1

A mother brings her 11-month-old daughter to the hospital for medical treatment. After examining her, the emergency physician diagnoses a comminuted spiral fracture of the right tibia and fibula. The mother has no explanation for the injury. The patient also has bruises over her entire back, superficial abrasions on other parts of her body, and a nondepressed linear fracture of the skull, which is in the process of healing. When approached, the child appears fearful and apprehensive. She is returned to the custody of her mother and her mother's boyfriend. Both have been physically abusing her, and the abuse continues. During one incident, she sustains traumatic blows to her right eye and back, puncture wounds over her left lower leg and across her back, severe bites on her face, and second- and third-degree burns on her left hand. She is then taken to a different physician and hospital, where her injuries are diagnosed as being the result of abuse. The incident is reported to the police and juvenile probation authorities, and she is taken into protective custody.

2

The mother of a 14-month-old girl takes her to a physician's office several times over a two-month period for treatment of a broken arm, a "wobbly demeanor," a swollen right temple and eye, and then swelling and bruising of both eyes. The physician does not know that the mother's boyfriend has been battering the child, who dies as a result of the next beating a few weeks later.

3

A mother discovers three red marks on the chest of her 1-month-old daughter and takes her to the emergency department. The mother is afraid that the child's father has struck her, but when she is questioned by the emergency physician, she says that the child has not been subjected to trauma. She asks whether the red marks might be bite marks made by another of her young children. The emergency physician orders no x-rays and prescribes a pain reliever for the bruises. One month later, the child is killed by her abusive father.

4

A physician diagnoses the condition of a child as malnutrition and reports the child's parents to the authorities for child abuse and neglect. After the child is placed in temporary foster care, it is discovered that the child has malabsorption syndrome and cirrhosis and fibrosis of the liver. The child is returned to the parents, who sue the physician and the hospital, alleging that the physician negligently diagnosed their child's malnutrition as child abuse and neglect.

5

A 1-month-old baby becomes ill and is taken to an emergency department for treatment. She had had fever and demonstrated symptoms consistent with seizures. She is transferred to another hospital, where the physician orders a head CT scan to determine the cause of the seizures. The scan reveals a diffuse subarachnoid hemorrhage. The report notes that "on the basis of this examination alone, the possibility of Battered Child Syndrome cannot be excluded." The physician notes that he is "obligated to pursue follow-up since it could be 'Shaken Baby Syndrome'," and he reports the case to social services. After an investigation, the baby is removed from her parents' home, and the father is charged with child abuse. The charges later prove to be unfounded, and the father sues the physician for negligent diagnosis and reporting.

Making the Diagnosis of Abuse and Neglect

Child Abuse

The single most important element in diagnosing child abuse is a history that is inconsistent with the apparent injury. Rarely is the injury itself pathognomonic. One of the most suspect circumstances is when a severely injured child presents without documentation of a serious accident. Other warning signs are apparent lack of parental concern, evidence of parental drug use, and previous emergency department visits for minor trauma. Soft tissue injuries are the most common manifestation of child abuse, followed by occult fractures, bites, and burns.

When child abuse is suspected, a skeletal survey should be obtained, including at least AP and lateral skull, AP and lateral chest, lateral views of the spine, and frontal views of the upper and lower extremities. Although long bone fractures are the most common fractures in child abuse cases, they are not the most specific identifiers. Metaphyseal fractures, which are usually the most specific for abuse, result from torsional forces when a child is grabbed, pulled, or twisted. Skull fractures are the second most frequently encountered fracture.[15] Head injuries account for most of the mortality and morbidity associated with child abuse.

Domestic Abuse

Emergency physicians are also apparently missing important indicators of partner violence. One study[16] showed that 30% of all injured women who presented to an emergency department acquired the injuries as a result of their partners' battering them. Another study[17] showed that 11.7% of women who presented to an emergency department for any reason were victims of domestic violence.

Approximately one in five battered women presenting to physicians will have sought medical attention for domestic abuse injuries 11 times before.[18] One abused woman presented to an emergency department seven times in 15 months with injuries that included broken bones and stab wounds. None of the physicians or nurses ever addressed the nature of the woman's injuries or asked about the possibility of domestic abuse. They simply treated each injury and sent her back home.[19]

It should be easier to diagnose domestic abuse than child abuse because an adult patient is capable of telling about the abuse in the history. Yet studies depict an appalling failure to diagnose domestic abuse, in part because of the patient's unwillingness to disclose the abuse and in part because emergency physicians do not always ask if the patient has been abused, even when they may suspect it. Possible indicators of domestic abuse include the following:

- Delay in seeking care
- A mechanism that does not fit the injury
- The patient claims to be "accident prone"
- Substance abuse by either the patient or partner
- History of the patient's children being abused
- Family stress
- Patient evasiveness
- Patient depression
- Adamant denial of even the possibility of abuse
- Minimizing injuries
- Demonstrating inappropriate responses
- Deferring to the partner's description of the injury mechanism

Typical findings in domestic abuse include facial injuries, breast or abdominal injuries, particularly during pregnancy, internal injuries, mid-arm injuries as a result of defensive posturing, injuries at various stages of healing, injuries to multiple sites, bites, and scald and cigarette burns. The risk of domestic abuse frequently escalates during pregnancy.[20]

Elder Abuse and Neglect

Characteristics of elder abuse are similar to those used to identify domestic abuse:

- Delay in seeking care for an injury
- Injury inconsistent with history
- Lacerations, bruises, and ecchymoses in various stages of healing
- Multiple fractures
- Scald and cigarette burns
- Conflicting injury reports by the patient and caregiver
- Patient inability to describe the injury

High-risk situations conducive to elder abuse include caregivers who have a history of alcohol or drug abuse, mental illness, stress, or problems controlling their tempers. A caregiver who depends on the elder for housing or money may be abusive. There is also risk when the elder's problems are progressive or unstable and exceed the caregiver's ability to cope.

Elder neglect may be most observable to prehospital care providers. Indicators of abuse include airless quarters, lack of food in the house, the patient being either locked in a room or placed in restraints when no one is home, dehydration, malnutrition, and the presence of bed sores.[21]

Duty to Report

Child Abuse

Every state has enacted statutes requiring that child abuse be reported to authorities. Many of the child abuse statutes were enacted soon after the Children's Bureau of the Department of Health, Education, and Welfare published a model statute in 1963. This statute required physicians to report suspected child abuse and made it a misdemeanor to fail knowingly and willfully to report it.

Statutes vary regarding the types of abuse or injuries subject to the reporting requirement. Some states require a report only when the injuries are "serious" or "severe." In other states, injuries must be reported if the physician thinks they have been caused by other than accidental means or are indicative of abuse or neglect. Most statutes require reporting when there is "reasonable cause to believe" or "reasonable suspicion" that abuse or neglect has occurred.[22]

All child abuse statutes provide immunity from civil liability for physicians who report suspected child abuse. Some require that the reporting be done in "good faith." This immunity extends to lawsuits for slander, libel, breach of confidentiality, and invasion of privacy.[22] For example, the law in one state reads as follows[23]:

> ...[Any . . . medical practitioner] . . . Who has knowledge of or observes a child in his or her professional capacity or within the scope of his or her employment whom he or she knows or reasonably suspects has been victim of child abuse shall report the known or suspected instance of child abuse to a child protective agency immediately or as soon as practically possible by telephone and shall prepare and send a written report thereof within 36 hours of receiving the information concerning the incident. No . . . medical practitioner who reports a known or suspected instance of child abuse shall be civilly or criminally liable for any report required or authorized by this article.[23]

The California statute gives physicians

immunity for reporting child abuse under all circumstances. An emergency physician reporting according to this statute is immune, whether the report is true or false, made in good faith or not.

Although California and a few other states grant absolute, unqualified immunity, most provide only limited immunity for "good faith" reporting.[24] "Good faith [e]ncompasses, among other things, an honest belief, the absence of malice and the absence of design to defraud or seek an unconscionable advantage."[22] A presumption of good faith is established by some statutes.[22]

One state statute requiring that the report be made in "good faith" reads as follows: "Any person . . . participating in good faith in the making of a report . . . shall be immune from any liability, civil or criminal, that results by reason of the [reporting]."[25] Immunity may also be expressly limited to those who have "reasonable cause" to suspect abuse or neglect. Although many states also provide misdemeanor criminal penalties for failure to report,[26] there have been no criminal prosecutions for this action.[27]

Elder Abuse

All states have passed legislation intended to curb elder abuse, and 42 states have adopted laws requiring health care professionals to report abuse or neglect to a state agency.[28] Additionally, Colorado, New York, and Wisconsin have voluntary reporting laws that state abuse "may be reported" instead of mandating it "shall be reported."[29] Despite these laws, surveys show that most emergency personnel are unaware of the laws and the need to report,[30] thus making intervention in and prevention of further abuse more difficult.

States have differing standards for immunity when physicians erroneously report child and elder abuse. For example, New Jersey grants absolute immunity for those who err in reporting child abuse but grant immunity to those who erroneously report elder abuse only if it is done in good faith.[31]

Domestic Abuse

In contrast to child and elder abuse, most states do not have reporting requirements for domestic abuse or the concomitant immunity provisions to protect physician reporters.[32] One state explicitly grants immunity and allows reporting at the discretion of the individual, but does not require the reporting of spousal abuse.[32]

Failure to Report

Courts do not agree about whether physicians who suspect or diagnose abuse and fail to report it should be held civilly liable for subsequent injuries a patient may suffer. However, the supreme courts in California and Arkansas found that a failure to report child abuse could be used to show negligence, which then resulted in foreseeable harm to the injured plaintiff. Thus, if the harm was foreseeable and the failure to report was the proximate cause of the harm, the defendant physician may be liable.

Patient Confidentiality

Child Abuse

Potential conflicts may arise between the physician's duty to report suspected child abuse and the physician-patient privilege. Most reporting statutes abrogate the physician-patient privilege to the extent that it conflicts with the reporting requirement.[22] Because all states have mandatory child abuse reporting requirements, abusive parents' desire for confidentiality will not affect the duty of the emergency physician to report.

Elder Abuse

Most states have mandatory reporting requirements that supersede the physician's duty to maintain confidentiality. A few states have permissive statutes, stating that the emergency physician may report the abuse but is not required to do so. In those states, emergency physicians must weigh the elder's potential benefit from the report (e.g., prevention of future harm) against any immediate harm or continued abuse that may occur if it is not reported.

Domestic Abuse

In many cases, the victim of domestic abuse will admit to being abused but will plead with the emergency physician not to report it. The police and the district attorney have a much more daunting task investigating and prosecuting when the victim is a reluctant witness against the abuser. Nevertheless, the emergency physician should document the historical and physical evidence of abuse and urge the patient to agree to reporting.

If the patient still asks that the abuse not be reported, the emergency physician should recommend counseling and may consider reporting the suspected abuse anyway. The risk to the patient from future abuse is great, and the patient is often dependent on her abuser. She may need support to admit that she is being abused. Once abuse is reported, there is risk of further abuse, but there is also risk in allowing abuse to continue unreported and unabated. If victims and physicians maintain a conspiracy of silence, the epidemic of abuse may continue to increase.

Victims of domestic abuse may need both counseling and shelter. Hospital social services departments and many police departments have trained staff to counsel victims who are willing to prosecute their abusers. A recent search of the literature uncovered no cases reported in which a domestic abuse victim successfully sued a physician for breach of confidentiality for reporting acknowledged abuse to the appropriate authorities.

On the other hand, some other authors have cautioned that spouses, partners, and other third parties, including the police, "should not be notified of an abuse diagnosis without the expressed consent of the patient," citing needs for patient autonomy and empowerment. These authors argue that, in contrast to policy in cases of suspected child abuse, "it is not evident . . . that mandatory reporting of domestic violence [by physicians] would contribute to the safety of battered women or would facilitate their access to appropriate resources."[12,33] Therefore, in the case of the patient who is unwilling to report, the emergency physician must carefully weigh patient confidentiality and autonomy against the likely benefits from reporting.

The situation is particularly vexing when an emergency physician strongly suspects domestic abuse and the victim denies it. When this problem occurs, a social worker or nurse specifically trained to address domestic abuse may be able to work with the victim in a nonthreatening way. In most states, emergency physicians do not have a mandatory duty to report abuse, and only a few states have immunity for good faith mistakes. Therefore, the harms of both disbelieving the patient and reporting the abuse in error would seem to outweigh the potential benefits of reporting, if the suspicion is correct.

Emergency physicians may be surprised to find little guidance in this area from their hospitals' policies. Since 1991, the Joint Commission on Accreditation of Healthcare Organizations has had a requirement that hospitals and their emergency departments have written policies and procedures, along with staff training that includes identifying, treating, gathering evidence, and reporting and referring victims of domestic violence. A study done by the Arizona Department of Health showed that only 30% of the emergency departments in that state had any such policies, and only one sixth of those were in total compliance with the requirement.[34] Emergency physicians should make sure their departments have policies pertaining to domestic violence and that all staff members are familiar with them.

Case Discussions

1

The plaintiff in this case claimed that the first physician failed to diagnose child abuse. The claim alleged that skull and long-bone x-rays would have confirmed abusive injury. The plaintiff also alleged that the physician had a duty to report the diagnosed abuse to prevent the child from further injury. The defendant physician argued that, although there may be a standard of care for the correct diagnosis and treatment of the child's injuries, the standard of care does not include identifying an injury as being the result of child abuse. Therefore, duty to treat the child did not include a duty to identify child abuse. The defendant argued that the later beating was a superseding cause of her injuries, thus relieving the physician of liability.

The California Supreme Court found for the plaintiff, holding that the standard of care requires physicians to be able to diagnose and treat a battered child. Additionally, if a diagnosis of child abuse is made, the failure to report it constitutes negligence. Finally, the court held that injuries caused by the parents after the physician's failure to diagnose and report were reasonably foreseeable. The defense of a superseding cause for the child's ultimate injuries could not be used to shield the defendant physician.[34]

2

In this case,[35] the mother's boyfriend was arrested, convicted of first-degree murder, and sentenced to life in prison. Representatives of the child's estate sued the physician for malpractice, alleging that she had fallen below the standard of care. If she had recognized the pattern of injuries and diagnosed child abuse, the plaintiff alleged, the child's death might have been prevented. An emergency physician testified as an expert witness against the defendant regarding the standard of care. The defendant argued that the failure to diagnose child abuse is not medical malpractice; that there was no evidence that making the diagnosis would have prevented the child's death; and that an emergency physician could not testify as to the standard of care for a family practitioner.

The trial court agreed with the defendant. However, the Arkansas Supreme Court reversed the decision, holding that medical practitioners could be found liable for failing to diagnose abuse. The court also stated that whether the diagnosis would have prevented the child's death was a question for the jury. Further, "the knowledge necessary to evaluate a potential child abuse situation is one that is basic to the science of medicine and is the same regardless of whether the physician had a family medicine practice or an emergency room practice."[35]

The court ordered a new trial, and the jury decided that the defendant should have diagnosed child abuse and notified authorities. The estate of the murdered child was awarded $200,000.[36]

In cases of child abuse that are more difficult to diagnose, some state statutes require that professionals evaluate the facts known to them in light of their training and experience to determine whether it is reasonable to suspect child abuse, thus establishing a duty to report. At least one court, however, has held that such a statute does not require health practitioners to elicit information not ordinarily obtained in the course of providing care or treatment.[37] Although the defense that there is no standard of care to diagnose child abuse failed in California and Arkansas, it has been used successfully in other jurisdictions.[38]

3

In *Cechman v Travis*,[39] the plaintiffs alleged that the physician failed to report suspected child abuse. The state's appeals court held that, although state statutes required reporting, no private cause of action was created by the statute. Thus, the state could impose sanctions for failure to report abuse, but the individual who was injured could not recover damages.

Other appellate courts have agreed that mandatory reporting statutes do not give rise to a private cause of action against a physician for failing to report child abuse.[40,41] Emergency physicians should either know their state's approach or should err on the side of diagnosing and reporting.

4

The plaintiff in *Maples v Siddiqui*[42] argued that the statutory immunity for good faith reporting of suspected child abuse or neglect should not protect a physician from liability for a report based on a negligent diagnosis. The state's supreme court rejected the argument and concluded that the legislature granted immunity with the understanding that a physician might be negligent and that to permit liability for mere negligence would discourage those who suspect abuse from reporting.[11,42]

This case is an example of blanket immunity for reporting. There is no need to show good faith. Plaintiffs in states where statutes do not require good faith reporting have an even higher hurdle to overcome when alleging negligence in diagnosis or reporting.

5

In this final case, *Hazlett v Evans*,[43] the plaintiffs argued that the physician clearly did not have reasonable cause to suspect child abuse, as the child's injuries were "the obvious result of birth trauma and that even a minimally trained pediatrician should have determined this." But the federal district court held that, even if the physician did not have reasonable cause, the physician was protected by statutory immunity. "[B]ecause doctors are required to report for fear of criminal charges in failing to do so, it is reasonable to conclude that the legislature felt a responsibility to ensure that if doctors reported a suspected case of child abuse which ultimately turned out to be unfounded, they would not be held liable for their misdiagnosis unless it was done with bad intent."[43]

This case applies the good faith standard. Because the plaintiffs alleged negligence and not bad faith in reporting, the court's application of the law resulted in essentially the same outcome as in *Maples*. Both cases reflect the legislative intent of setting the balance toward protecting children by allowing the possibility of error in diagnosing and reporting suspected abuse to far outweigh any harms that might come to the person erroneously accused of child abuse.

Courts have frequently questioned whether circumstances in particular cases were sufficient to establish a reasonable cause to suspect child abuse. They have also questioned whether a suspected child abuse report was submitted in good faith. Statutory immunity may depend on establishing reasonable cause, good faith, or both. Reasonable cause most often arises when litigants dispute whether a particular party had a duty to report suspected abuse. Frequently, the same set of facts establish both reasonable cause and good faith. Courts have held that the facts were sufficient to establish reasonable cause to suspect child abuse and/or good faith reporting when individuals who observed a child's injuries received either a dissatisfactory explanation or no explanation about the cause of injury from the child's parents. To date, no person identified by statute as a mandatory reporter has been denied statutory immunity for reporting suspected child abuse, as no lack of good faith or reasonable cause has been found in cases applying those requirements for immunity.[22]

Key Points and Conclusion

Emergency physicians will continue to encounter victims of family violence and must be prepared to diagnose accurately all forms of family violence, especially raising their threshold for suspecting domestic violence and elder abuse. The ability to diagnose the constellation of injuries that add up to abuse is increasingly seen as part of the standard of patient care.

Emergency physicians may be liable for failure to diagnose and report child abuse, elder abuse, and domestic abuse. All 50 states have laws mandating the reporting of child abuse and giving emergency physicians immunity for errors made while reporting in good faith, at a minimum. Many state laws also mandate the reporting of elder abuse, although many state statutes do not grant emergency physicians immunity for errors in reporting. The dangers of continued abuse to elders far outweigh the risk to emergency physicians for errors in reporting suspected cases.

Most states do not have statutes mandating the reporting of suspected cases of domestic abuse or granting immunity to physicians for errors in reporting. In the case of the patient who is unwilling to report an abuser, the emergency physician must carefully weigh the harms to patient confidentiality and autonomy against the likelihood of benefits from reporting.

Emergency physicians should become familiar with their state's laws regarding diagnosing and reporting all types of family violence.

Acknowledgment

The author wishes to thank Mary Olson of the Center for the Study of Bioethics for her editorial assistance. Portions of this chapter have been adapted from Derse AR: Family violence and the emergency physician: Legal and ethical considerations. *Emergency Department Legal Letter,* May 1997.

References

1. Koop CE, Lundberg GB. Violence in America: a public health emergency: time to bite the bullet back. *JAMA* 1992;267:3075-3076.

2. McCurdy K, Daro D. Current trends in child abuse reporting and fatalities: the results of the 1993 fifty state survey. National Committee to prevent child abuse. Chicago: National Center on Child Abuse Prevention Research; 1994, as cited by Alpert et al.

3. Meyers M, Bernier J. *Preventing Child Abuse: A Resource for Policy Makers and Advocates.* Boston: Massachusetts Committee for Children and Youth; 1987, as cited by Alpert et al.

4. Council on Scientific Affairs, American Medical Association. Adolescents as victims of family violence. *JAMA* 1993;270:1850-1856.

5. Bachman R, Saltzman LS. Violence against women: Estimates from the redesigned survey. US Dept of Justice, Office of Justice Programs, Bureau of Justice Statistics, NCJ-154348. Washington DC: Government Printing Office; August 1995, as cited by Alpert et al.

6. Belluck P. A woman's killer is likely to be her partner, a study finds. *The New York Times,* March 31, 1997.

7. Tatara T. Toward the development of estimates of the national incidence of reports of elder abuse based on currently available state data: an exploratory study. In: Filinson R, Ingman SR, eds. *Elder Abuse: Practice and Policy.* New York: Human Sciences Press; 1988:153-164, as cited by Alpert et al.

8. Tatara T. Understanding the nature and cope of domestic elder abuse with the use of state aggregate data: summaries of key findings of a national survey of state APS and aging agencies. *J Elder Abuse Neglect* 1993;5:35-57, as cited by Lachs MS, Pillemer K.

9. Alpert EJ, Cohen S, Sege RD. Family violence: an overview. *Acad Med* 1997;72:S3- S6.

10. Bergman GE. Evaluation and management of child abuse. In: Schwartz GR, ed. *Principles and Practice of Emergency Medicine.* 3rd ed. Baltimore: Williams & Wilkins; 1992:2536-2546.

11. Sullivan DJ. Child abuse. *1993-4 Yearbook of Law & Emergency Medicine.* River Forest, Ill: Physician's Law Review; 1994:29-32.

12. Council on Ethical and Judicial Affairs, American Medical Association. Physicians and domestic violence: ethical considerations. *JAMA* 1992;267:3190-3193.

13. Lachs MS, Pillemer K. Abuse and neglect of elderly persons. *N Engl J Med* 1995;332:437-443.

14. State of Connecticut. General Statutes. Chapter 319h. Section 17A-430.

15. Sheridan C, Mellick LB, Sherwin T. Recognizing child abuse and neglect: the role of the emergency physician. *Emerg Med Rep* 1993;14(8):67-74.

16. McLeer SV, Anwar R. A study of battered women presenting in an emergency department. *Am J Public Health* 1989;79:65-66.

17. Abbott J, Johnson R, Koziol-McLain J, et al. Domestic violence against women: Incidence and prevalence in an emergency department population. *JAMA* 1995;273:1763-1767.

18. Stark E, Flitcraft A, Zuckerman D, et al. Wife abuse in the medical setting: an introduction for health personnel. Washington, DC: Office of Domestic Violence; 1981. Monograph 7, as cited by Alpert et al.

19. Congdon TW. A medical student's perspective on education about domestic violence. *Acad Med* 1997;72:S7-S9.

20. deLahunta EA. Partner abuse: recognition, evaluation, and management of battered women in the emergency setting. *Emerg Med Rep* 1996;17(2):13-22.

21. Stewart C, Stewart C. Confronting the grim realities of elder abuse and neglect. *Emerg Med Rep* 1991;12(20):179-186.

22. 73 A.L.R.4th 782, §2.

23. Malpractice — Physician's Liability for Failure to Diagnose and Report Child Abuse. 23 Wayne L Rev 1187, 1191 (1977), as cited in McMenamin JP, Bigley GL. Children as patients. In: Sanbar SS, ed. *Legal Medicine*. St Louis: CV Mosby Co; 1995:475-487.

24. Cal. Penal Code §11166 (West 1992), as cited in as cited in Bisbing SB, McMenamin JP, Granville RL. Competency, capacity, immunity. In: Sanbar SS, ed. *Legal Medicine*. St Louis: CV Mosby Co; 1995:27-45.

25. Wisconsin Statutes §48.981(4) (1995-1996).

26. See, for example, *Cechman v Travis*, 414 SE2d 1282, 284 (Ga Ct App 1991) (in dicta), *cert denied*, (1992), as cited in McMenamin JP, Bigley GL. Children as patients. In: Sanbar SS, ed. *Legal Medicine*. St. Louis: CV Mosby Co; 1995:475-487.

27. McMenamin JP, Bigley GL. Children as patients. In: Sanbar SS, ed. *Legal Medicine*. St Louis: CV Mosby Co; 1995:475-487, updating Kohlman, Malpractice Liability for Failure to Report Child Abuse, 49 Cal St B J 118, 121 (1974).

28. Culhane C. Federal, state effort urged to prevent elder abuse. *Am Med News* July 21, 1989;18-19, as cited by Clark-Daniels CL, Daniels RS, Baumhover LA. Abuse and neglect of the elderly: are emergency department personnel aware of mandatory reporting laws? *Ann Emerg Med* 1990;19:970-977.

29. Brewer RA, Jones JS. Reporting elder abuse: limitations of statutes. *Ann Emerg Med* 1989;18:1217-1221.

30. Clark-Daniels CL, Daniels RS, Baumhover LA. Abuse and neglect of the elderly: are emergency department personnel aware of mandatory reporting laws? *Ann Emerg Med* 1990;19:970-977.

31. *Rubinstein v Baron*, 219 NJ Super 129, 529 A2d 1061 (1987).

32. Bisbing SB, McMenamin JP, Granville, RL. Competency, capacity, and immunity. In: Sanbar SS, ed. *Legal Medicine*. St Louis: CV Mosby Co; 1995:41-42.

33. Flitcraft AH. Violence, values, and gender. *JAMA* 1992;267:3194-3195.

34. Bedard L. Domestic violence can no longer be tolerated. *ACEP News*, October 1996:2.

35. *Estate of Laura Allison Fullbright v Joseph John Rank, Mary Ellen Robbins, and Rheeta Stecker, M.D.*, 323 Ark 390; 915 SW2d 262 (1996).

36. Doctor cited for malpractice after ignoring abuse. *American Medical News*, October 28,1996.

37. *David M. v Erie County Department of Human Services*, (1994) Ohio App LEXIS 2785 (6th Dist Ct App 1994).

38. *People v Stockton Pregnancy Control Medical Clinic, Inc.* (1988, 3rd Dist) Cal App 3d 225, 249 Cal Rptr 762.

39. *Cechman v Travis*, 202 Ga App 255, 414 SE2d 282 (1991)

40. *Valtakis v Putnam*, 504 NW2d 124 (Minn Ct App 1993).

41. *Marcelletti v Bathani*, 500 NW2d 124 (Mich Ct App 1993).

42. *Maples v Siddiqui*, 450 NW2d 529 (Iowa 1990).

43. *Hazlett v Evans*, 943 F Supp 785 (ED Ky 1996).

Chapter 56

Specific High-Risk Medical-Legal Issues

Gregory L. Henry, MD, FACEP

Although there is a large body of information on how to prevent malpractice lawsuits, very little research has been done on this issue specific to emergency medicine. There is, however, consensus among those who are active in emergency medicine risk management that liability situations are identifiable and, to a large part, preventable. No learned treatise can anticipate all the possible poor outcomes that might arise in the practice of emergency medicine, yet the major risk and loss areas can be identified within a 95% confidence level. Every legal action has its own character, but the same types of alleged breaches in standards of care happen so often that they have become predictable.

This chapter presents the physician and the hospital risk manager with a set of specific "do's and don'ts" for these high-risk situations. Emergency physicians will always have to make critical patient care decisions. Frequently, these decisions will involve choosing the lesser of two evils to minimize risk. The information in this chapter should help place the physician in the most reasonable position.

The scientific data supporting specific activities to improve patient outcome are voluminous. Because considerable specific medical-legal data are unpublished, many of the actions suggested in this chapter represent the general consensus of authors of this book, plus contributions from other practicing emergency physicians and attorneys who specialize in emergency medicine malpractice defense. Their collective wisdom is reflected in the case analyses and the key points.

Change of Shift

Case Study

One-half hour before the end of a shift, an emergency physician begins the workup of a patient who is a known alcoholic and frequent visitor to the emergency department. Initial evaluation reveals a patient who is intoxicated and somewhat belligerent. No other specific problems appear to exist, and the patient's only complaint is that his friends brought him to the emergency department because they thought he needed help. He does not view himself as needing medical attention.

Shortly after the examination, the patient falls asleep in the examining room. Vital signs at that time are normal. At the shift change, another emergency physician comes on duty and is told that the patient has already been evaluated. All that needs to be done, the first emergency physician says, is "wait for his blood alcohol level to drop and he wakes up, then you can discharge him."

Five hours later, when the patient wakes up and is ready to be discharged, the emergency physician orders a repeat blood alcohol test but does not reexamine him. He is discharged from the department. Four hours after discharge, the man is brought back by ambulance. He is in a coma and has right-sided weakness and a dilated left pupil. Despite rapid intervention, the patient dies as the result of a subdural hematoma. Both physicians are sued by the patient's family.

Analysis

Many physicians, risk managers, and attorneys consider change of shift to be an extremely dangerous time for patients. Normal vigilance is relaxed when a physician thinks a patient has already been evaluated properly by another physician. In this case, the patient suffered from the fact that no formal transfer of responsibility from one physician to the other took place, and no acknowledgment was given that the second physician had responsibility for the case and for reevaluating the patient. Subsequent examinations were not performed throughout the rest of the patient's stay, and he was discharged without any reevaluation.

The fundamental problem is that the second emergency physician accepted the initial diagnosis of alcohol intoxication at face value and did not reevaluate the patient prior to discharge. Certainly, intoxicated patients are notorious for having sustained other injuries. Because of this, they require reevaluation as the effects of alcohol are wearing off.

Change of shift lawsuits always involve several particularly thorny situations. First, two physicians are involved in this case, which may double the amount of insurance money the plaintiffs feel they should receive. Second, whenever two physicians are involved, the exact point at which one's responsibility ends and another's begins is often difficult to assess and may lead to bickering and in-fighting among professionals. Such in-fighting only strengthens the plaintiffs' case. The lack of documentation by the second emergency physician not only fails to support her contention that she had taken over the case, but also leaves all remembered findings or interactions in question.

Key Points

- Change of shift should not result in a lower standard of care for the patient. If a physician for some reason cannot stay to complete the workup, proper transfer of responsibility — and liability — needs to occur.
- The incoming physician needs to reassess the patient completely, establish priorities, monitor the patient's progress, and reevaluate and instruct the patient at the time of discharge. To assume that any of these things have been done by the first physician is to court disaster.
- The physician who discharges a patient should be the physician of record and as such, will bear the responsibility not only for the evaluation of the patient, but also for the reevaluations and the discharge program.
- The transfer of responsibility at the change of shift should be an orderly, formal process so that no patient or family member is ever in doubt about who is in charge of the patient's care and who will direct further therapy.

Return Visits

Case Study

A 32-year-old woman with back pain presents to the emergency department of a major metropolitan center at 10:00 PM. The emergency physician who examines her finds no neurologic abnormality, so he treats her for muscular strain with a muscle relaxant and codeine-containing analgesics. She is discharged to the care of her husband. The discharge instructions include strict bed rest for three days and a follow-up visit with a family practitioner.

At 10:00 AM the following day, the patient's back pain is somewhat worse, and she notes tingling in the buttocks bilaterally. She goes back to the emergency department for reevaluation. During the registration process, the triage nurse criticizes the patient for not giving the medication "a chance to work."

A different physician sees the patient and asks her about her symptoms. He reiterates that she needs bed rest and medication. Because he had observed the patient walking into the department, he decides not to perform specific neurologic testing. The patient is discharged again and instructed to rest in bed and take her medications.

Eight hours later, the patient loses control of her bladder and experiences tingling down both legs and difficulty walking. She is returned to the emergency department by ambulance, where neurologic evaluation indicates nerve compression. A myelogram reveals cauda equina syndrome secondary to a midline herniated disk. Neurosurgical consultation is obtained, but there is no surgical remedy. She is left with urinary incontinence, anesthesia in the buttocks and perineal area, and some mild leg weakness.

The patient and her family immediately bring legal action against the hospital for failure to recognize her worsening neurologic condition.

Analysis

The validity of return visits to the emergency department has been carefully studied. Traditionally, emergency department personnel have believed that such patients are abusing or misusing the emergency department. This perception is incorrect. The return visit patient suffers from the fact that some diagnosis has already been made — a diagnosis that may be wrong in up to 25% of these patients. Even if the diagnosis is correct, the course of the patient's illness is not running as predicted. Perhaps the follow-up instructions were not adequately explained to the patient. These facts, combined with the reality that getting into private physicians' offices may be difficult, constitute legitimate reasons for a patient to return to the emergency department.

From a risk management standpoint, the return visit to the emergency department is essentially the patient giving the hospital and the physicians a second chance to solve a problem. When these patients present, they should be seen as if they are completely new patients. Reassess the history, repeat the physical examination, and order any pertinent laboratory tests as if the patient is arriving for the first time. Do not be prejudiced by the initial visit and the initial diagnosis. Disease processes change with time. The first evaluation, although it may have been perfectly correct, does not always guarantee a proper diagnosis. To assume that the first evaluation revealed all problems is to deny the ever-changing nature of diseases and many injuries.

Similarly, a patient who is transferred from another hospital also should be considered as a totally new patient. The conservative course of action is for the emergency physician to work up transferred patients from the broadest possible perspective. Assume that, during the transfer interval, problems not initially appreciated may have developed. Transferred patients sometimes arrive in a different condition than initially "advertised," but it is no defense for the receiving hospital to say that it relied on the first hospital's evaluation to diagnose the case.

Key Points

- The patient who returns for a second visit or a patient who is transferred from another institution should be considered, for evaluation purposes, to be a new patient.
- It is perfectly reasonable to refer to a patient's earlier records, but the physician is obligated to take an independent history and to perform a physical examination as if the patient were presenting with the symptoms for the first time.
- The physician is obligated to review previous laboratory data and to repeat tests that may be relevant to the patient's care.
- The physician is obligated to review the entire treatment program on a return visit to make certain that the disease entity is progressing as expected and that the therapies previously recommended are adequate to meet the patient's current needs.

Private Patients

Case Study

A 54-year-old woman with known congestive heart failure presents to an emergency department complaining that, over the past two days, she has had mildly increasing shortness of breath. At the time of registration, she informs the clerk that her private physician sent her to the emergency department and that he will meet her there. Someone from the private physician's office calls to inform the emergency staff that he is on his way in to see "his patient." The patient is placed in a room and puts on a gown.

After approximately 15 minutes, the patient's shortness of breath increases to 40 breaths per minute and mild cyanosis is present. The private physician still has not arrived in the emergency department; the nurses administer oxygen. Forty minutes later, the patient suddenly begins foaming from her mouth and shows signs of pulmonary edema. She arrests just as the emergency physician is being called into the room by the nursing staff and just as the private physician arrives. Intubation is very difficult. Despite aggressive medical management, the patient suffers significant anoxia leading to brain injury. The family immediately files a lawsuit against the emergency physician. The private physician is not named in the legal action.

Analysis

Several principles of good risk management were violated in this case. Physicians do not "own" patients; patients choose their physicians. When patients present to the emergency department, they become the patients of the emergency physician. The emergency physician has an absolute obligation to be aware of any and all patients in the department and of their status.

The emergency nursing personnel have a similar duty to treat patients expeditiously and to inform the emergency physician of any patient whose condition is deteriorating. In situations such as this case, plaintiffs' attorneys generally contend that the emergency physician knew or should have known that a patient with a potentially serious illness was left essentially unattended by a physician in the department.

Theoretically, this case may also represent a violation of the Emergency Medical Treatment and Active Labor Act (EMTALA). The emergency department had the duty to perform a medical screening examination to determine if the patient had an emergency medical condition. The fact that a patient has an identified private physician does not relieve the emergency department staff of the obligation to assess the urgency of any situation. Emergency department staff never have any guarantee that a private physician will be immediately available or that the physician will be capable of handling an emergency situation.

Essentially, this patient received a lower standard of care precisely because she had an identified private physician. If she had presented without the expectation of seeing her own physician, her care would have been more expeditious, and an emergency physician would have been involved in the case from the start. Nothing short of a patient's informed refusal to be seen relieves the emergency physician of the responsibility of acting to treat emergencies within the department, no matter who patients may initially identify as their private physicians.

Key Points

- Private patients in the emergency department should be viewed as any other patients. They should be properly triaged, and emergency physicians should see them as they would any other patient until the private physician arrives and a proper transfer of responsibility has occurred.
- Emergency department policy should expressly state that patients in the department must be evaluated even when they are waiting for their private physicians.
- If the hospital wants to provide attending physicians with a place to meet their patients, such as a hospital clinic, it should be an area away from the emergency department, that is, one not covered by the federal EMTALA statute.

Patient Sent for Injections

Case Study

A 35-year-old man is sent to the emergency department of a medium-sized community hospital by his private physician to receive a combination shot of Demerol and Vistaril. The family physician has seen his patient in the past for severe headaches and feels comfortable ordering pain medication for him without reevaluating his condition. An order for this medication is taken by an emergency department nurse, and the patient is given the injection, with moderate relief of symptoms. He is then discharged in the care of his wife.

Two hours after discharge, the patient is found comatose by his wife and is returned to the emergency department by ambulance. A CT scan reveals a large subarachnoid hemorrhage. In the ensuing lawsuit, the wife brings action against not only the family physician, but also the emergency physician who was on duty when her husband received the injection.

Analysis

The plaintiff's attorney claimed that the hospital violated a considerable number of regulations in this case. Although it was the usual and customary procedure of the emergency department to honor physician requests for giving injections to their private patients, such an action is clearly in violation of several statutes. Notably, federal narcotics laws specifically prohibit giving narcotics to patients who have not been seen concurrently by a physician.

The plaintiff's attorney also claimed that, because the patient "presented to the emergency department" according to the EMTALA definition, the emergency department had an affirmative duty to provide a medical screening examination for the patient. After all, an emergency physician was on duty, and it was the standard of care for all other patients presenting to the department to receive an examination. Hospitals and medical staffs must understand that the emergency department has specific legal obligations to patients under federal statues. Previous customs do not override federal law.

Key Points

The Board of Directors of the American College of Emergency Physicians (ACEP) has gone on record with a policy against taking telephone orders from physicians to administer narcotics to their unexamined patients.[1] The following sections of the U.S. Code of Pharmaceuticals[2] also speak to this issue.

- **Schedule II substances** — Except when dispensed directly by a practitioner, other than a pharmacist, to an ultimate user, no controlled substance in Schedule II, which is a prescription drug as determined under the Federal Food, Drug, and Cosmetic Act, may be dispensed without the written prescription of a practitioner, except that in emergency situations, as prescribed by the Secretary by regulation after consultation with the Attorney General, such drug may be dispensed upon oral prescription in accordance with section 503(b) of that Act. Prescriptions shall be retained in conformity with the requirements of Section 827 of this title. No prescription for a controlled substance in Schedule II may be refilled.
- **Schedule III and IV substances** — Except when dispensed directly by a practitioner, other than a pharmacist, to an ultimate user, no controlled substance in Schedule III or IV, which is a prescription drug as determined under the Federal Food, Drug, and Cosmetic Act, may be dispensed without a written or oral prescription in conformity with section 503(b) of that Act. Such prescriptions may not be filled or refilled more than six months after the date thereof or be refilled more than five times after the date of the prescription unless renewed by the practitioner.
- **Schedule V substances** — No controlled substance in Schedule V, which is a drug, may be distributed or dispensed other than for a medical purpose.
- **Nonprescription drugs with abuse potential** — Whenever it appears to the Attorney General that a drug not considered to be a prescription drug under the Federal Food, Drug, and Cosmetic Act should be so considered because of its abuse potential, he shall so advise the Secretary and furnish to him all available data relevant thereto.

The following information is taken from a letter issued by the Houston Field Office of the Drug Enforcement Administration. It was written in response to inquiries concerning the ordering of controlled drugs from emergency department stocks by physicians' "orders" to the emergency department:

"The stock of drugs maintained in hospital emergency rooms or outpatient facilities is kept for use by or at the direction of physicians in the emergency room. Therefore, in order to receive such medication, a patient must be examined by a physician in the emergency room or outpatient facility, and the need for a particular controlled substance determined. It is not possible, under federal requirements for a physician to see a patient outside the emergency room setting or talk to him or her on the telephone and proceed to call the emergency room and order the administration of a stocked controlled substance upon the patient's arrival at the emergency facility.

"Section 829 of the U.S. Code provides that prescriptions must be utilized, except when controlled substances are dispensed directly by a practitioner, other than a pharmacist, to an ultimate user. It follows, of course, that only pharmacists can fill prescriptions. Hence, a physician cannot make an "order" or a prescription and expect it to be honored by hospital emergency rooms. The stock of the emergency room is part of the hospital stock and cannot be construed to be pharmacy stock.

"The options of a physician, in a case of this type, are as follows:

1. Administer or dispense drugs to the patient from his or her drug supplies.

2. Write a prescription to be filled by a pharmacy (including a hospital pharmacy) which is separate and distinct from the hospital emergency room stocks.

3. Send the patient to the emergency room for examination and the possible obtaining of whatever drugs that examination indicates from the emergency room stocks."

The Intoxicated Patient

Case Study

A 39-year-old alcoholic is brought to a community hospital emergency department by the police and left to "dry out." The patient is mildly obstreperous, refuses to be quiet or sit down, and paces. He finally agrees to sit on the bed but is not restrained. While left alone for a brief moment, he gets off the gurney, runs through the department, and assaults other patients. In his rage, he cuts a 4-year-old child with the glass from a broken IV bottle and seriously injures the child's mother. During the vicious attack, the patient also inadvertently cuts himself. He is finally subdued, treated, and taken to jail.

The family of the injured child and mother

files a lawsuit against the hospital and the emergency physician for failure to restrain a potentially dangerous patient. The patient himself brings action against the hospital and the emergency physician for his injuries. He alleges that if he had been properly restrained, he would not have assaulted the other patients.

Analysis

Whenever a patient with altered mental status or potentially altered mental status is in the emergency department, emergency personnel must properly assess that patient for dangerousness to self or others. There is no singular criterion on which such potential dangerousness is based. Clearly, it is the role of emergency personnel to document the mental status of the patient. Blood alcohol levels are rarely of use. The clinical correlation between a blood alcohol level and the patient's mental status is tenuous at best. Instead, it is the patient's behavior that should determine the need for protecting that person from harm and from harming staff and other patients. Even with a minimal level of alcohol intoxication, abnormal behavior can signal the presence of other drugs of abuse, prescription drugs, or organic disease causing the abnormal behavior. The anticipation of potential trouble needs to be reasonable, but clearly there are some patients in whom such trouble should be both anticipated and expected.

The allegations of the injured mother and child are understandable and supportable. The patient's behavior was abnormal and should have alerted the staff to take action. The fact that the patient was brought in by the police on a drunk and disorderly charge and with altered mental status should have been another red flag. The legal duty here is an extrapolation of duty to predicted but unknown third parties. Ordinary patients using the emergency department have a right to feel protected in such an environment. Failure of the staff to adequately restrain, thus placing them in line for significant injury, is problematic from a legal standpoint.

The allegations of the intoxicated patient are at first angering but no less predictable. He is claiming that a competent medical staff should have understood the potential threat he represented to himself and to others. As a criminal action, there is little legal basis for his argument because he became intoxicated voluntarily. However, a civil action related to patient restraint may have legitimate grounds. Once in the emergency department, patients are the responsibility of staff, not only for their proper examination and diagnosis, but also when substitute judgment is required due to altered mental status.

Key Points

- Emergency department patients with altered mental status become the responsibility of the emergency staff.
- Decisions to restrain should be based on patient behavior.
- Restraint requires specific orders with regard to type of restraint, length of restraint, and a program for reevaluation of the patient at intervals.
- The patient is not the only one at risk. Physicians, other staff members, other patients, and potentially the public at large are in danger if a patient is allowed to act in a diminished capacity mode.
- When in doubt, restrain. Restraints should be humane and limited, but patients should not be allowed to injure themselves or others.
- Reevaluation at intervals is important because, as the intoxicating substance wears off, the patient may qualify to be released from restraints.
- There is no law that prevents a patient from having two diseases. The intoxicated patient who is not improving may have organic disease (e.g., hypoglycemia, subdural hematoma). It is the obligation of the department to reevaluate patients and decide whether aggressive testing and intervention are necessary.
- In many states, intoxication is no longer a crime. Violent behavior and public endangerment, however, are still crimes. Patients who cannot be managed in the emergency department may require the intervention of police agencies.

References

1. Telephone Orders in the Emergency Department. ACEP Policy Statement, approved January 1997. To obtain a copy, call (800) 798-1822, touch 6, or go to www.acep.org.
2. Public Law 91-513, Title II §309, October 27, 1970, 84 Stat 1260. Schedules II, III, IV, and V, referred to in text, are set out in section 812 (c) of this title. The Federal Food, Drug, and Cosmetic Act, referred to in subsections (a), (b), and (d), June 25, 1938, c. 675, 52 Stat. 1040, as amended, classified generally to chapter 9 (section 301 et. seq.) of Title 21 USCA, Food and Drugs. Section 503(b) of that Act is classified to section 353(b) of Title 21.

Chapter 57

Specific High-Risk Clinical Presentations

Gregory L. Henry, MD, FACEP
James E. George, MD, JD, FACEP

The medical problems described in this chapter represent some of the more common troublesome cases encountered by emergency physicians and staff. The case studies and analyses provide guidelines for reducing the risk of liability for emergency physicians, emergency departments, and health care facilities.

Emergency Medicine Actuarial Studies

The first comprehensive emergency department actuarial studies were done by John T. Rogers, MD, FACS, FACOG, and reported in *Risk Management in Emergency Medicine*,[1] a book published by ACEP in 1985. Dr. Rogers reported the following findings:

- Failure to diagnose fractures represented 27% of all claims submitted and 13% of the total dollars paid.
- Failure to diagnose foreign bodies in a wound, 13% of claims, 4% of payments.
- Complications of lacerations, including tendon and nerve injuries, 13% of claims, 5% of payments.
- Failure to diagnose or failure to treat myocardial infarction, 10% of claims, 31% of payments.
- Failure to diagnose appendicitis, 4% of claims, 4% of payments.
- Failure to diagnose meningitis, 2% of claims, 15% of payments.
- Failure to diagnose ectopic pregnancy, 2% of claims, 8% of payments.

Another study[2] of closed claims from 1976 through 1984, which comprised more than 50 million patient visits, reported slightly different findings specific to total dollars lost to emergency medicine malpractice claims, as follows:

- Failure to diagnose or treat myocardial infarction, 19% of total dollars lost.
- Failure to diagnose or treat fractures, 14%.
- Failure to diagnose or treat meningitis, 9%.
- Improper management of wounds, 8%.
- Failure to diagnose or treat appendicitis, 5%.
- Failure to diagnose or treat ectopic pregnancy, 2%.

The findings of three other studies from the late 1980s and early 1990s are summarized in Table 1.

Chest Pain

Case Study 1

A 37-year-old man presents to an emergency department around midnight on a hot summer night. He is sweating profusely and says that he cannot sleep because of indigestion. The emergency physician evaluates the patient and orders an ECG and a single CPK, both of which are normal. The emergency physician diagnoses gastritis and discharges the patient. Four hours later, the patient is returned to the emergency department in full cardiac arrest. Autopsy reveals a large, fresh infarct.

Table 1

Summary of emergency medicine malpractice claims from closed claims data

	John D. Dunn, MD, loss run data from private claims analysis, 1989;1992[3]		Century American Insurance Company, closed claim analysis, June 1993[4]		Massachusetts College of Emergency Physicians, 1975-1993[3]	
	% of Claims	% of Dollars paid	% of Claims	% of Dollars paid	% of Claims	% of Dollars paid
Myocardial infarction	8%; 9.6%	22%; 33%	11%	17%	10%	25%
Wound care	5%; 5%	14%; 11%	18%	4%	19%	3%
Fractures			11%		17%	17%
Abdominal pain	4.1%	0.4%	12%	7%	10%	5%
Meningitis	5%; 1.4%	4%; 2%	4%	17%		
Spinal cord injury			3%	8%		
SAH/intracranial bleeding/stroke				6%	3%	6%

Analysis

Failure to diagnose and treat myocardial infarction is still the costliest high-risk area in emergency medicine malpractice. Up to 5% of all patients with acute myocardial infarction are mistakenly sent home.[6-8] As the collective data in Table 1 indicate,[3-5] missed myocardial infarction constitutes 8% to 11% of all malpractice claims against emergency physicians but accounts for as much as 33% of damages paid.

Most of the problems seen in the vast majority of these chest pain cases are associated with the emergency physician's failure to distinguish the atypical coronary chest pain that is not indicative of classic angina. This, in conjunction with an inadequately recorded history, forms the basis of most allegations of negligence. Close behind is the failure to recognize the limited diagnostic value of ECGs and cardiac enzymes.

The patient's history is paramount. Patients who have suspected acute ischemic heart disease based on their history should be treated as if they have a serious medical condition until proved otherwise. Although the ECG may be diagnostic in acute myocardial infarction, a normal ECG never rules out an infarction. Current literature indicates that as many as 50% of patients in acute myocardial infarction may initially have nondiagnostic ECGs.[9] Therefore, a history of heart condition should take precedence over ECG results.

The usefulness of the ECG in acute myocardial infarction is changing as the use of thrombolytic agents evolves. Clearly, emergency physicians are now being sued for failure or delay in starting thrombolytic therapy in an attempt to salvage myocardium and prevent arrhythmias. In the case of a clear-cut myocardial infarction in which the patient meets the criteria for administration of thrombolytic agents, the emergency physician should move quickly to obtain patient consent and begin thrombolytic therapy. If contacting a cardiologist or a family physician will create a significant time delay, the emergency physician should begin therapy.[10,11]

Cardiac enzymes are, in medical-legal terms, a major source of risk for emergency physicians. The total CPK is not specific for cardiac muscle and is certainly not sensitive enough to diagnose myocardial infarction in the emergency department. Even with the use of the myocardial band of CK (CK-MB), diagnosing a myocardial infarction can be difficult in its early stages. The CK-MB may not begin to rise for four to six hours after an infarction and will peak somewhere between 12 and 24 hours, followed by a return to normal at approximately 36 hours.[12] Therefore, to use the CPK level as evidence that no myocardial infarction is taking place is untenable. If the emergency physician considers a patient's condition serious enough to order one CPK, the patient should be admitted or placed in an observation unit and a second CPK ordered at the time when it would be expected to rise.

Key Points

- A missed diagnosis of myocardial infarction is the source of the most significant dollar loss in emergency medicine malpractice cases, constituting an estimated one third of all indemnity payments.
- Failure to elicit proper history and to recognize atypical forms of myocardial infarction may lead to a misdiagnosis.
- Up to 50% of ECGs may be normal in the early stages of a myocardial infarction.
- Enzyme testing is extremely unreliable in the early stages of a myocardial infarction, and results will not be positive in cases of unstable angina. If the emergency physician orders one CPK, the patient should be admitted or observed carefully and a second CPK ordered at the proper time interval.
- Chest pain that is not definitely musculoskeletal or related to a discernible infectious process should be considered myocardial or a pulmonary embolus until proved otherwise. The patient should be properly observed and reexamined until a diagnosis is obtained. Clinical suspicion is still the most important element in correctly diagnosing ischemic heart disease and acute myocardial infarction in its early stages. Nonspecific chest pain should be considered cardiac until proved otherwise.
- Chest pain presentations have all the elements that make a lawsuit a nightmare. The victims are usually younger and in high-earning potential years, have dependent children, and experience onset of the illness as a complete surprise.
- Emergency physicians should keep this "formula" in mind: new angina equals unstable angina equals admission and workup.
- No attending physician talking to the patient over the telephone can relieve the emergency physician of responsibility. If the

patient goes home and something goes wrong, the attending will always say: "If only they had told me."

Case Study 2

A 46-year-old woman with chest pain of several hours' duration presents to the emergency department of a general community hospital. An ECG is performed and there are ST segment elevations consistent with an anterior lateral myocardial infarction. The changes are recognized on both the automatic reading of the ECG and by the emergency physician. The patient and her husband are informed that she is most likely having a myocardial infarction. In utter disbelief, the family requests that the emergency physician contact a family friend who is a physician in another community. Telephone calls are made, but the physician is not immediately available.

Finally, three hours later, the physician and the family are able to speak with the family friend. Thrombolytic therapy is then initiated. The patient has a somewhat stormy course in the ICU and is found to have a significant decrease in ejection fraction as a result of the size of the infarct. The family brings legal action against the emergency physician, alleging that he did not state the case for thrombolytic therapy firmly enough. They claim that if they had understood the ramifications of receiving thrombolytic therapy, it could have been started earlier when it would have had more benefit.

Analysis

Failure to diagnose a myocardial infarction traditionally has been the primary basis of lawsuits in emergency medicine related to chest pain. A new avenue of attack is the concept that "time is muscle." Many therapeutic modalities have been proposed to lessen the effect of an ongoing myocardial infarct. The administration of aspirin and, although somewhat more controversial, heparin, has received considerable support.[13] Timely use of β-blockers has also had positive effects. Also controversial but still important are considerations of the use of medications such as magnesium and, when appropriate, calcium channel blockers.

The most widely discussed and time-dependent of these newer treatments is thrombolytic therapy. An incredibly large amount of time, effort, and money has gone into proving the efficacy of thrombolytic agents. The most important clinical trials are discussed in a broad range of medical literature and have finally come into perspective. Thrombolytic therapy appears to reduce mortality significantly at one year.[14] Therefore, it is essential to provide thrombolytic therapy in a timely manner in the emergency department.[15,16] There is also some suggestion that cardiac output is improved in those survivors. This information has been widely disseminated by the lay media. The public believes that we now have a medicine that will reverse or stop heart attacks in progress. The factual information is difficult to debate when a patient is in the emergency department.

There have been lawsuits based on allegations that an emergency physician did not forcefully put forward the case for thrombolytic agents or presented the information in such a way that it "frightened the patient" into not accepting a "lifesaving procedure."[17] Science seems to be secondary to emotion in these matters. Emergency physicians must recognize the strong public perception that a "wonder drug" exists. In a joint statement, the American Heart Association and the American College of Cardiology emphasize the fact that there should be no unreasonable delay in the administration of thrombolytic therapy when a patient meets the criteria.[18] These two organizations clearly do not require that the emergency physician receive some consultation or "permission" from another physician to begin therapy. Besides, there is overwhelming evidence that the drug is better administered sooner than later. The decision as to whether the patient meets the criteria and whether the drug should be administered needs to be made as quickly as possible. The door-to-needle time will be the subject of considerable discussion should litigation occur.

Key Point

- The use of newer chemical modalities, including thrombolytic therapy, should be evaluated early in a patient's presentation and, if they seem appropriate, should be started without undue delay.

Orthopedic Injuries

Case Study 1

A previously healthy 17-year-old boy presents to the emergency department of a community hospital complaining of pain in his right thumb and wrist area. The boy says that he fell while skiing and jammed his thumb into the planted ski pole, causing hyperextension stress to the thumb. The injury happened approximately 12 hours earlier, and now it is painful for him to move.

On examination, the patient has some swelling and tenderness along the navicular bone, the first metacarpal, and first metacarpophalangeal joint on the right hand. Because of the intensity of pain, significant range of motion testing is impossible. X-rays reveal no obvious fracture. The patient is given an ice band and Ace bandage and instructions to follow up with his family physician if the thumb is not completely normal in three weeks. Four weeks later, the patient presents to the emergency department with a nonunion of the scaphoid bone.

Case Study 2

A 27-year-old woman is brought to the emergency department four hours after suffering a severe inversion and rotation injury to the left ankle. The patient is complaining of extreme discomfort and is in too much pain to ambulate.

The patient is examined while sitting in a wheelchair in the hallway; the nurse has removed the sock and shoe and rolled up the pant leg. The physician records that the ankle is swollen, with tenderness over both the medial and lateral malleolus and pronounced swelling. Range of motion with stress cannot be tested because of excessive swelling. The emergency physician orders an x-ray of the ankle, which reveals no fracture. The patient is discharged home with an Ace bandage and crutches and instructed to begin activity in one week. The patient presents to the emergency department two weeks later with compartment syndrome.

Analysis

Orthopedic injuries represent another significant source of lawsuits in emergency medicine. The most common allegation is missed fracture, with missed dislocations and neurovascular injury as occasional sources. Fractures of the axial skeleton, which may be associated with severely disabling neurologic problems, can dramatically increase the total dollar amount of claims paid.

The principal areas in which the emergency physician may make a mistake are relatively few and can be prevented or mitigated. It is important that the emergency physician document the nature of an injury so that associated areas of injury may be suspected. For example, a patient who has suffered a rapid deceleration injury, such as jumping out of a window or falling off a ladder, that is significant enough to cause calcaneal fractures should be suspected of suffering spinal injury and should be adequately examined to rule this out. Similarly, a patient who has suffered enough trauma to fracture a femur should be considered a major multiple trauma victim and should undergo a complete examination. Assume that the patient is, at least to some degree, hypovolemic.

Along with the pattern of injury, take into consideration the patient's age. An elderly patient who has a painful thigh following a fall should be considered to have a broken hip until proved otherwise. Particularly with the very young and the very old, beware the patient who has lost function in an extremity. Emergency physicians frequently overestimate the value of an x-ray. A major error is thinking that one x-ray at any given point of time precludes the possibility of a fracture. It is always worthwhile for emergency physicians not only to read all their own x-rays, but also to understand that such x-rays may not show a fracture in its early stages.

Anticipatory guidance on the part of the emergency physician is essential to prevent unreasonable expectations and anger in a patient. Inform the patient that, although an obvious fracture cannot be seen, a hidden fracture can always exist. As a result, if the pain does not subside in a predictable manner, the patient needs to be reevaluated and may require further x-ray examination.

When a physician misses a fracture, the biggest problem is usually the patient's surprise and anger. If the emergency physician warns the patient of the possibility of a hidden fracture, then treats the injured extremity as if it were fractured and ensure appropriate follow-up, there generally is no harm or loss to the patient. Misinterpretation of an original x-ray is not, in and of itself, malpractice. If the patient's injury is splinted and treated as if it were fractured, there is no diminution in the standard of care and no opportunity for the injured patient to claim that further harm was done through the physician's failure to detect the injury earlier.

X-ray reporting systems are crucial if liability is to be reduced regarding orthopedic injuries. When the final report is received from radiology, all variances must be resolved by the emergency physician. The patient should be contacted and advised immediately, either to return for further treatment or to keep scheduled appointments. The physician needs to be highly suspicious of injury in those areas of the body where initial x-rays are difficult to interpret and do not routinely show recent fractures. The wrist, digits, feet, and legs may have hidden fractures that will be clearly visible in a repeat x-ray in 7 to 10 days. Specific follow-up should be planned for every patient. If an injury is not resolving in the usual time, consultation with the family physician or an orthopedic surgeon is indicated. All patients should be told when to seek further care so that they do not continue to injure a damaged extremity.

Failure to recognize neurovascular complications of fractures is a relatively rare cause of legal action but can be costly when proved. Severe fractures in the knee area should make the physician suspect concomitant subluxation and damage to the popliteal artery. Fractures in the lower leg should at least raise the suspicion of a vascular compartment syndrome. Even if this condition is not demonstrated clinically, the patient should be instructed to return for a follow-up reevaluation in a few days. In any case in which there is significant suspicion for compartment syndrome, orthopedic surgery should be notified for timely consultation. In all cases of suspected injury, it is difficult for the emergency physician to go wrong by properly splinting the injury, telling the patient to keep weight off the extremity, and instructing the patient to be reexamined in a few days.

Key Points

- There is no such diagnosis as "sprained wrist" in the emergency department. All such injuries should be treated as fractures until proved otherwise by splinting, repeat examination, and, if necessary, repeat x-ray.
- A "sprained thumb" can also be a disruption of the ulnar collateral ligament until proved otherwise. Such injuries should be properly splinted. These patients also should be referred for return visit or reevaluation by an orthopedic surgeon on a short-interval follow-up.
- Most acute injuries require immobilization of the joint above and the joint below. The emergency physician concerned enough about an injury to x-ray it should also splint it properly, both for comfort and for the possibility of hidden fracture.
- In all injury situations, expose the injured joint properly to conduct an adequate evaluation. This may include exposure of the joint immediately distal and proximal to the injury.

- Patients with knee injuries should not be examined in a wheelchair. They need to be undressed and placed on a gurney so that correct examination maneuvers can be performed.
- Traumatic knee injuries with effusions or any question of instability requires proper immobilization, non–weight-bearing, and immediate follow-up by an orthopedic surgeon.
- Suspect neurovascular injury in patients with major knee fractures.
- Lower leg fractures should raise the suspicion for anterior compartment syndrome. Proper follow-up is required.
- A carefully written emergency department chart should not only document inspection, palpation, and range of motion of the injured extremity and the joint above and below, but also address distal circulation, sensory examination, and motor testing.
- Whenever orthopedic injury is suspected, emergency physicians should take the following steps to protect patients and themselves: elevation, cold therapy, proper splinting, short-term reevaluation, and discussion with the patient about the possibility of hidden injuries.
- The Joint Commission on Accreditation of Healthcare Organizations requires that a system be in place to resolve all differences in x-ray interpretation between the emergency physician and the radiologist. This system must work each and every time to the patient's benefit.

Wounds and Lacerations

Case Study

A 28-year-old woman comes to the emergency department after she accidentally cuts the palm of her right hand on broken glass while opening a baby food jar. The bleeding has stopped, but the wound is still open. The patient's tetanus status is current. On examination, the physician finds no obvious problems. The wound is sutured. No infection ensues, and the patient has the sutures removed in seven days. Twelve days after the injury, the patient notices difficulty flexing the third finger of her right hand. One week later, when the problem still has not resolved, she returns to the emergency department. A diagnosis of flexor tendon laceration is made. An x-ray also reveals a 0.5x1 cm glass fragment in the wound.

Analysis

Lawsuits associated with wound care account for as much as 19% of all malpractice claims against emergency physicians.[5] The issues related to laceration lawsuits are few but common. Most are based on retained foreign body in the wound, missed tendon or nerve injury, and resulting infection. Lawsuits against emergency physicians over the appearance of a scar are extremely rare.

To reduce potential liability, emergency physicians must obtain a detailed history of the mechanism of wounds and laceration injuries. When that mechanism includes glass, the possibility of a retained foreign body should be considered. Because glass shows up on x-ray,[19,20] physicians should consider ordering an x-ray as a general rule in such cases. In puncture wounds, the possibility of a foreign body must likewise be entertained.[21]

Management of a foreign body or suspected foreign body depends on factors such as the nature, location, and size of the foreign body; the presence or absence of infection; and the location of the foreign body relative to pertinent structures. The important factor is to involve the patient in treatment and to make sure the patient understands the discussion of the risks and benefits of searching for foreign bodies. If large-scale exploration for foreign bodies is not to be carried out immediately, the physician should warn the patient that such an exploration may be required if infection or dysfunction occurs.

As a general rule, all foreign substances that have been injected into the body, such as high-pressure injection of grease, paint, or other hydrocarbons, should be considered medical emergencies. Injection injuries are almost always into the hand, and failure to act properly can result in increased disability. Organic foreign bodies, such as vegetation, wood, or animal spines, are highly reactive protein substances that generally require immediate removal.[22,23] Foreign bodies that are visible or superficial or which are already infected are also generally removed on the first visit. Foreign bodies adjacent to fractured bones also should be removed to reduce the risk of osteomyelitis.

Generally, nonreactive, nonorganic foreign bodies, such as steel shotgun pellets or copper BBs deep in tissue, generally can be left in place until they become an irritant. During exploration of wounds, have the patient move the involved extremity so that any tendons can be seen through their range of motion. A partially lacerated tendon may "hide" in the soft tissue until moved back to its original position at the time of the injury. Following exploration for foreign bodies and tendon injuries, make all reasonable efforts to reduce infection. Copious irrigation of wounds is advised. The emergency physician should inform all patients that up to 10% of all wounds become infected despite removal of foreign particles and proper irrigation, and that they should be sure to seek follow-up care.

Wounds caused by animal bites pose a particular problem. Although little evidence exists to suggest that dog bites require antibiotic prophylaxis, many experts recommend antibiotic therapy if the wound penetrates into deep tissue structures. Cat bites are seven times more infective than dog bites; *Pasteurella multocida* is the principal infective agent.[24] Antibiotic therapy is generally recommended for cat bite wounds. Human bites are considered more infective than cat bites and significantly more infective than dog bites. A careful history should be taken whenever a human bite is suspected. Consider lacerations over the knuckles to be caused by human bites until proved otherwise. When lacerations on the hand are declared or suspected to be human bites, search carefully for tooth fragments, injuries to tendons, and, most important, injury to the joints. Joint space involvement from a human bite is considered by some to be an emergency and may require consultation with hand or orthopedic surgery. Open exploration in the operating room may be necessary.

Key Points

- Wound care is associated with approximately 19% of all lawsuits in emergency medicine.
- Principal issues in these lawsuits are failure to detect a foreign body, failure to diagnose tendon or nerve injury, and failure to prevent resultant infection. Poor cosmetic results are rarely a cause for lawsuits in emergency medicine.
- Proper history-taking should include the mechanism of injury. Proper physical examination must include a search for any retained foreign bodies in the tissue. Tendon function should be documented by observation of movement and inspection of the wound.
- When a laceration is caused by broken glass, the emergency physician should consider

obtaining x-rays if the wound cannot be completely explored.

- Tendons should be observed through their range of motion.
- Foreign bodies should be detected; decisions on whether to remove them should be made on a case-by-case basis.
- Whenever a foreign body is suspected, tell the patient and explain the reasons for and against surgical exploration. Patients who have a potential foreign body should be instructed on how to watch for infection and to return for reexamination.
- Bite wounds are high risk for infection and require detailed explanation and follow-up instructions for the patient.
- In any suspicious wound, a repeat examination should occur within 48 hours.

Painful Scrotum

Case Study 1

A usually healthy 12-year-old boy is brought to the emergency department complaining of pain on the left side of his scrotum. He says that it started while he was playing soccer at school and that "it feels like someone kicked me in the groin." The boy is in moderate pain and vomits once while in the emergency department. On physical examination, the physician notes that the left testis is tender and somewhat larger than the right. The history, as recorded in the chart by the physician, reads: "Kicked in groin while playing soccer at school." The position of the testis, Doppler pulse in the testis, and factors to relieve pain are not listed.

The boy is discharged with a diagnosis of contusion to the testis and is told to use ice bags, rest, and Tylenol for pain. Instructions to the patient and the family indicate that, if the child is not better in two days, he should be seen by the family physician. The boy's pain continues. Following the physician's orders, the parents take the child to the pediatrician in two days, and the pediatrician immediately refers the child to a urologist. Surgery performed that day reveals a torsed, dead testis.

Analysis

The painful scrotum, especially in children, is one of the most challenging clinical problems faced by the emergency physician. The diagnosis emergency physicians, patients, and families fear most in the presentation of painful scrotum is that of testicular torsion. The challenge for

the emergency physician is that the diagnosis and treatment are extremely time-dependent.

Some experts say that torsion of the testis must be surgically repaired within two to four hours of onset if the testis is to be saved. On the other hand, testicular torsion can also become untwisted during the course of its manifestation and result in intermittent torsion. Intermittent torsion certainly adds minutes and perhaps hours to the time available for making a correct diagnosis and initiating surgical therapy.

Torsion may or may not be associated with testicular trauma. The presence of trauma does require a careful physical examination and thorough emergency department medical record documentation. In this case study, the emergency physician made a few disposition errors. First, for a contusion of the testis, the emergency physician should have instructed the patient and family to follow-up with a urologist the next day if the condition did not considerably improve. Second, the patient should not have been referred back to his family physician, because this referral created an additional delay in appropriate treatment. However, it is certainly appropriate to contact the family physician to discuss the disposition of the case and to agree on the selection of a urologist for follow-up care.

Third, it would have been helpful to have the time of the injury documented in the emergency department record, if in fact the child was actually kicked in the groin. This fact is not certain. The absence of trauma should heighten the suspicion of testicular torsion.

Some experts believe that it is essential to have a testicular scan performed before discharging a patient who has testicular pain in whom torsion is suspected. Still, there can be a number of false-negative scans. Other experts believe that such a patient should be seen in the emergency department as soon as possible. Some urologists would make the decision to operate based on the history and clinical findings alone without the need for a testicular scan. A certain number of testicular torsions will be misdiagnosed by any physician, including a urologist.

Case Study 2

A 5-year-old boy is brought to the emergency department of a busy urban hospital after complaining of pain in the scrotum for the past several hours. There is no previous history of illness or previous problems with the genitalia. No history of trauma is elicited, although the mother says the child had been playing outside. On physical examination, the child has normal vital signs and, except for some crying and complaints of pain, is generally normal.

Examination of the genitalia reveals that the child's scrotum is diffusely tender, more on the right than on the left. The urinalysis reveals 3 WBCs but no bacteria or crystals. The patient is diagnosed as having acute epididymitis and is discharged home on pain medication and antibiotics. Twenty-four hours later, the patient is seen by the family physician, who diagnoses testicular torsion.

Analysis

This case is interesting because epididymitis is an uncommon diagnosis in small children. There is a much higher level of suspicion for testicular torsion when presented with a diagnosis of epididymitis in a 5-year-old boy. The urinalysis in this case was really not helpful. There is no evidence to document the follow-up instructions given to the family by the emergency physician. This case would be much more defensible if the child had been seen in the emergency department in a timely manner by a consulting urologist. This is especially true in view of the fact that the complaint of pain in the scrotum had been going on for "several hours."

One could argue that testicular death would have already occurred because the patient had been experiencing symptoms for several hours before the emergency department visit. Therefore, timely referral to a urologist would have protected the emergency physician against any liability. Plaintiffs' attorneys often argue that the torsion may have become untwisted periodically during this time and might have resulted in a viable testis at the time of the initial visit to the emergency department.

Key Points

- Testicular torsion is a very difficult diagnosis to make. Some of these cases will be missed by any treating physician, including urologists. Therefore, torsion should be in the emergency physician's mind whenever a patient presents with a painful testis.
- Document the physical examination and the history thoroughly, along with the length of time the patient has experienced symptoms.
- If the emergency physician suspects the diagnosis of testicular torsion, obtain at least telephone consultation with the attending urologist as soon as possible. Then, decide whether to obtain a testicular scan.
- The emergency physician cannot force the urologist to come to the hospital. The urologist may choose to rely on the patient's history, physical examination by the emergency physician, and the results of the testicular scan. In any event, time is of the essence. This should always be in the forefront of the emergency physician's mind.
- A significant number of testicular scans are falsely negative, which means that a certain number of testicular torsions are going to be unavoidably missed. The emergency physician must involve the attending urologist in the diagnosis and treatment of suspected testicular torsion.
- Delays in testing can cause delays in treatment. If in doubt, surgical exploration is the most conservative route. Time delays can lead to castration by procrastination.
- The physical examination of any male with lower abdominal pain should be considered incomplete without examination of the genitalia. Testicular pain may present as diffuse lower abdominal pain, and without proper examination may be missed.

Major Trauma

Case Study

A 19-year-old man is involved in an altercation with the police, during which he is shot several times in the abdomen. EMS is called immediately, and the young man is transported to a local hospital designated to receive such cases. The EMTs properly radio the hospital and give them a clear assessment of the case, including the patient's hypotension and profuse bleeding.

On arrival at the emergency department, the emergency physician starts two large-bore IV lines, orders trauma blood work, including a crossmatch for blood, and calls the general surgeon. The general surgeon arrives 30 minutes later, and the patient is moved to the operating room. However, no anesthesia personnel are available, and another 35 minutes pass before they are able to start the surgery. The man dies on the operating table.

Analysis

This situation is a serious medical-legal problem for the receiving hospital. The facts clearly show that the EMTs radioed the hospital well in advance of their arrival and gave them a clear assessment of the patient's condition. Thus, the hospital and the emergency physician had clear knowledge that the patient was going to need emergency surgery. There is no indication that the emergency physician immediately called the surgeon or notified the operating room and anesthesia department that they would soon be receiving an emergency case.

When the patient arrived, the emergency physician apparently did everything right, except for the delay in notifying the surgeon and anesthesia personnel. This delay resulted in a loss of 30 minutes while they waited for the general surgeon's arrival and another 35 minutes for the arrival of anesthesia personnel. Given these circumstances, it is not surprising that the patient died on the table.

Could this death have been avoided? The only true answer to this question depends on the autopsy results. The patient's injuries might have been too severe for him to survive. Unfortunately, patients brought to major trauma centers in a timely manner often do not survive their traumatic injuries. On the other hand, the autopsy may show that the patient could have been saved by a more timely intervention within the "golden hour." If so, then the case may be indefensible.

A larger medical-legal problem than penetrating trauma is the more insidious clinical presentation of blunt trauma. In blunt trauma, the extent and nature of the injuries may not be apparent early on. When the injuries finally manifest themselves, which may be a matter of minutes or hours later, they often present in a catastrophic manner. In many cases, evaluation of blunt trauma requires CT scanning and other imaging modalities on an immediate basis.

Key Points

- Time is of the essence in major trauma cases. Many patients and families have heard about the "golden hour." The family of any patient whose trauma treatment is not successfully initiated within the "golden hour" is likely to ask for an explanation.
- It is critically important for the emergency physician and emergency department staff to advise the attending surgeon on call and the operating room and anesthesia staff of the imminent arrival of a trauma patient as soon as that information is available. Every minute counts. Clear delineation of responsibility for this activity needs to be formally stated in policy and procedure.
- Any emergency physician would be reluctant to call the attending surgeon and alert the operating room for a case that turns out not to require surgery. Nobody likes the embarrassment of having "cried wolf." Nonetheless, this embarrassment pales compared with the feelings of guilt and inadequacy that consume emergency physicians and staff when they do not call the surgeon or operating room early enough, or at all, and a patient dies as a result.
- No matter how badly injured or deformed a patient is, the basics are still the most important thing. Airway, breathing, cardiac status, fluid resuscitation, chest tubes if needed, immobilization, and early use of blood in significant hemorrhage are what makes the difference in a critically injured patient.
- Believe the vital signs. Abnormal signs mean that immediate action is needed.
- There is no reason to remove cervical-spinal immobilization equipment in the major trauma patient until the patient has been triaged, registered, and properly examined.
- Abnormal mental status should not be automatically ascribed to alcohol or drug abuse.
- Unstable trauma patients belong in the emergency department or the operating room, not in the x-ray suite for extended films.
- Rarely will a laboratory test result change initial clinical decision-making in the early management of trauma.
- In head trauma patients, the most common basis for legal action is the physician's failure to perform repeat examinations and to get the patient to surgery in time. A physician who suspects the patient may have a surgically correctable lesion should request a neurosurgeon immediately for consultation.

Obstetrics Emergencies

Case Study

A 32-year-old woman, otherwise healthy and eight months pregnant, is involved in an automobile collision in which she is the restrained front seat passenger. She sustains injuries to her legs, knees, forehead, and shoulder. There were no direct blows to the chest or abdomen, but she reports some soreness from the seat belt, which was around her waist. The patient is brought to the emergency department of a large hospital. After the history is obtained, she is examined by the emergency physician, who recognizes significant orthopedic injuries that require treatment. A fetal pulse measured by Doppler is 140 and strong.

During the emergency department evaluation, the patient is in the x-ray suite for imaging of a fractured tibia and fibula. The rest of the orthopedic injuries are soft tissue. The orthopedic surgery resident is called to cast the patient. During the casting procedure, the patient begins to have accelerating cramps in the lower abdomen. By the time the casting is complete, the cramps have increased and fetal pulse has dropped to 110. The obstetrics service is contacted, and the patient is evaluated in the emergency department then taken immediately to the operating room. A cesarean delivery is performed, and a normally formed but dead infant is delivered.

Analysis

This case presents a mystifying pattern. Information is not available regarding the specific time when the patient began to develop cramps in her lower abdomen during the casting procedure. Also, there is no indication of the time the orthopedic casting procedure ended, when it was noted that her cramping had increased. The facts reveal that fetal heart tones were documented to have dropped to 110. From that time forward, the patient's care was conducted properly. The obstetrics service was contacted immediately. The patient was evaluated in the emergency department and taken immediately to the operating room, where a cesarean delivery was performed. Unfortunately, the infant was stillborn.

There is no indication from these facts about the status of the placenta. There is insufficient information available to draw a conclusion about why the child died.

Key Points

- Time is of the essence when dealing with obstetrics emergencies. The fetal tolerance for intrauterine hypoxia is very limited. Emergency department records must be thorough in obstetrics emergencies.
- The biggest single error in this case was the failure to stop the orthopedic casting procedure when the patient first complained of cramps in the lower abdomen. Because her only abdominal complaint on arrival in the emergency department was some

"soreness" from the seat belt, her complaint of rapidly accelerating cramps in the lower abdomen was an important new development that required immediate assessment.

- Ultrasound is a key diagnostic tool that has an important role in the diagnosis and treatment of obstetric and gynecologic emergencies. Ultrasound provides information about fetal age and viability, status of the placenta, and other information helpful in determining whether ectopic pregnancy exists, a frequent emergency department diagnosis.
- Ultrasound should be available and used without hesitation. In this case, ultrasound might have been useful, although fetal death might have been unavoidable. If there is any information on autopsy pointing to the inevitability of fetal death despite earlier intervention, this may help make the case more defensible.
- Unilateral pelvic inflammatory disease is rare. In a pregnant patient, the physician should consider ectopic pregnancy as a possible or even more likely cause of a patient's symptoms.

Sexually Transmitted Diseases

Case Study

A 24-year-old man in good health presents to the emergency department complaining of burning on urination and urethral discharge. His history includes several sexual partners. Physical examination reveals a healthy male. General physical examination is normal; there are no regional nodes in the genital area. Testes are nontender, and the penis has no visible lesions. Milking of the urethra produces a thick yellow-green pus, which is positive for Gram-negative intracellular diplococci. The patient is treated with an injection of ceftriaxone and is placed on oral doxycycline. He is given instructions to see his family physician if not better in seven days. No cultures are taken.

One year later, the emergency physician is named in a lawsuit. A 19-year-old woman claims that she has severe pelvic inflammatory disease that resulted in an ectopic pregnancy with a complicated course and probably decreased fertility. There is no evidence that the emergency physician ever took a culture of the man's urethral discharge or that his condition was reported to the public health department. The woman bringing the lawsuit claims that this lack of proper follow-up prevented her from being notified of his condition and seeking treatment, which predisposed her to pelvic inflammatory disease, the ectopic pregnancy, subsequent medical therapy, and potential sterility.

Analysis

Sexually transmitted disease cases are of great concern to emergency physicians. The woman's allegation of negligence by the emergency physician involves the failure to culture the discharge and to report the case to the public health department. Whether it is customary to culture this type of discharge if a positive microscopic slide diagnosis is made for gonorrhea is questionable. The man was treated with appropriate antibiotics but should have been given other instructions to inform his sexual partners of his condition, not just "see your family physician if not better in seven days."

Specifically, the patient should have been told not to engage in any sexual activity until after he had been cleared by a urologist. The burden of follow-up care should have been placed on the patient to contact either the public health department or the urologist on call for follow-up care. If the patient fails to seek follow-up care, the responsibility should rest with him and those with whom he has sexual relations, rather than with the emergency physician.

One of the woman's allegations is absolutely true: the case should have been reported as a sexually transmitted disease to the appropriate public health authority. Although the language of many public health reporting laws requires the treating physician to notify the department of such cases, the customary practice in many emergency departments is for the hospital laboratory to make a timely report to the public health department. This is especially true because most culture test results and syphilis reports are not available for several days, and the emergency physician who performed the examination may not be on duty when the report becomes available. Therefore, the laboratory must have a mechanism in place for reporting positive culture test results to appropriate public health authorities on a timely basis. Unfortunately, the emergency physician still has some responsibility, at least in the eyes of the third-party sexual contact who filed the lawsuit.

Some facts are missing from this case. For example, the plaintiff claims that failure to report prevented her from being notified of the patient's condition and prevented her from seeking follow-up treatment. However, there is no information about whether the plaintiff was a sexual partner before or after the patient sought treatment in the emergency department. If her sexual contact with the patient occurred before he sought treatment, then there was no way to prevent her infection. If she were symptomatic in any way, she should have promptly sought treatment from her own physician. On the other hand, the burden and legal risk for the emergency physician are greater if the sexual contact occurred after the patient was treated. There would have been at least an opportunity to prevent further spread of this infection by reporting the case to the public health authorities and by instructing the patient not to engage in any additional sexual contact until he was cleared by a subsequent treating physician.

Key Points

- It is important to take all appropriate cultures in cases of suspected sexually transmitted disease. It may also be appropriate to do serum testing for syphilis exposure at the same time.
- Emergency physicians should refer all patients who have sexually transmitted disease to a urologist or a gynecologist or a primary care physician for appropriate follow-up treatment and advice. The burden to seek follow-up care should always be placed on patients, not only for their own good health, but also to relieve the emergency physician of any accusation of negligent failure to give appropriate follow-up care instructions. These referrals and instructions should be well documented in the emergency department record.
- All cases should be reported by the hospital laboratory in a timely manner to the appropriate public health authority as required by state and local laws.
- The emergency physician should be alert to the fact that sexually transmitted diseases affect more than one person and there may be some responsibility to these other parties. The risk of contracting HIV should also be discussed with these patients. They should be referred outside the emergency department for testing and follow-up counseling.
- When a sexually transmitted disease is suspected, the emergency physician has an obligation to warn the patient about the

possibility of contagion and advise the patient to contact any sexual partners so they can seek evaluation and treatment, if needed.

Eye Injuries

Case Study 1

A 31-year-old man in good health presents to an emergency department after having a motor vehicle collision. He had not been restrained and went forward, striking his face on the frame and windshield of the car. He did not lose consciousness but reports severe head pain and some decreased vision in the right eye.

On examination, the emergency physician finds no injuries of the trunk or limbs. The neck is supple and nontender. The face is swollen bilaterally with a considerable amount of ecchymosis lateral to the right eye. The extraocular movement of the eye seems normal, and there are no actual injuries to the eyeball itself. There is no hyphema; ophthalmoscopic examination is normal. Visual testing reveals scores of 20/20 in the left eye and 20/100 in the right eye. The patient does not wear corrective lenses. X-ray evaluation reveals a small crack in the lateral orbit of the right eye, with no other findings.

The emergency physician consults an ophthalmologist, who suggests that the patient come to his office the next day for examination. When the patient is examined 15 hours later, the light perception is gone from the right eye. Immediate CT scanning reveals a retro-orbital hematoma, which has compressed the cranial nerve. The emergency physician is sued for failure to obtain immediate consultation.

Analysis

This emergency physician will be difficult to defend. A key point here is that the patient presented with ocular trauma and a decreased visual acuity of 20/100 in the right eye. This visual acuity was probably abnormal for the patient because his left eye Snellen score was 20/20 and he did not wear corrective lenses. It may or may not be clinically relevant that the x-ray taken in the emergency department revealed a small crack in the lateral orbit of the right eye. Even if the x-ray had been normal, the fact remains that the patient sustained ocular trauma and had diminished visual acuity. These facts alone imply a significant degree of ocular injury for which treatment should not be delayed, even for a few hours.

The emergency physician did the right thing by calling the ophthalmologist and discussing the case with him. This call will help in his defense, depending on how thoroughly he documented the conversation in the emergency department record. As a general rule, the emergency physician should document more meticulously if the consulting physician is not being particularly helpful in treating the patient.

On the other hand, why did the ophthalmologist not come to the emergency department to see the patient? Emergency physicians should not allow consultants to talk them out of hands-on consultation when they genuinely believe it is necessary. If the consultant refuses to come to the department, the emergency physician should take this matter up with the head of the consultant's department or with the president of the medical staff. At the very least, the emergency physician should arrange for a consultation with an appropriate specialist if the first one called refuses to come in.

Case Study 2

A 45-year-old man is struck in the left eye by a ball while playing tennis. He reports seeing bright lights for a few minutes after the impact but now, other than pain and swelling, feels all right. Ophthalmologic testing reveals that the patient has normal vision in the eye. There is no hyphema, and the pupil works normally. Ophthalmoscopic examination reveals no obvious lesion. The patient is discharged with advice to use ice bags and rest.

The next day, the patient has flashes of light in the eye and describes a sensation similar to "a dark curtain or haze" descending over his vision. He returns to the emergency department and is referred to an ophthalmologist, who diagnoses a detached retina. Subsequently, the man sues the emergency physician.

Analysis

This case is a classic example of ocular trauma. Many of these patients develop a hyphema as well as a retinal detachment. The emergency physician probably could not have made the definitive diagnosis of detached retina at the time the patient was initially seen in the emergency department, but the facts of the case are highly suspicious of an early retinal detachment. The patient saw bright lights for a few minutes but was all right after that. An ophthalmologic examination was normal, with a normal pupil and no evidence of hyphema. Ophthalmoscopic examination revealed no obvious lesion.

The symptoms of detached retina did not develop until the next day. Therefore, it is doubtful that the patient will succeed in a claim that the first emergency physician deviated from accepted standards of diagnosis and treatment.

There also appears to be no significant delay in follow-up treatment. The patient promptly returned to the emergency department and was subsequently referred to an ophthalmologist. There is no evidence that the initial and subsequent emergency department treatments were inappropriate, and there is no reason to believe that there was a delay in referring the patient for definitive care.

Key Points

- Eye injuries can be difficult to treat in the emergency department and carry a high degree of liability risk. Damage is often permanent and involves an organ system that most people regard as more important than the other senses. Therefore, emergency physicians must approach these injuries with considerable suspicion that more damage may be involved than appears to be the case.
- Eye injuries, like any other clinical condition, should be handled carefully, and appropriate consultations should be obtained. If the attending ophthalmologist refuses to provide an appropriate consultation, document this fact and consult with a different ophthalmologist. If an ophthalmology consultation is not available, transfer the patient to a medical center that can conduct a thorough emergency ophthalmology examination.
- Above all, the goal in the treatment of eye injuries is to minimize complications resulting from delays in obtaining ophthalmology consultation. All calls made to consultants should be documented carefully in the emergency department record.
- Despite pain, the outpatient use of topical anesthetic agents should be discouraged when examining an injured eye.
- Vision is the function of the eye. No patient with an eye complaint should leave the emergency department until visual acuity is measured.
- Infections in or around the eye may be serious. Orbital cellulitis and retro-orbital infection should be treated as medical emergencies.
- Irrigation of chemical irritants should be rapidly performed, copious, and well documented.
- Patients with eye injuries that result in decreased vision should be warned of the possible alteration of depth perception and resultant blurring. This warning should include a specific warning not to drive, particularly if one eye is patched.
- Patients with acute diplopia who have a definitive cranial nerve or extraocular muscle lesion require neurologic and/or neurosurgical consultation.

Airway Obstruction

Case Study

A 3-year-old girl is brought to the emergency department by her mother, who says that the child is having difficulty breathing. According to the mother, the child has been ill for about eight hours and has gone from being afebrile to having a temperature of 103.5°F over the past few hours. The child also has developed difficult respirations and is now drooling saliva. There is no significant previous medical history; she is on no medications and has no allergies.

On physical examination, the temperature of 103.5°F is confirmed rectally; the heart rate is 152, and the respirations are 32 per minute with strider. The child is sitting forward, and a small amount of saliva is drooling from her mouth.

The emergency physician sends the child to the x-ray department for a lateral neck film. As she is being positioned by the radiology technician, the child develops extreme respiratory distress. The emergency physician brings the child back to the emergency department and, with repositioning, she becomes more relaxed.

The hospital has no ENT department, so the emergency physician arranges a transfer with a hospital 14 miles away. A respiratory therapist is sent with the team. On the way to the hospital, the child arrests and the respiratory therapist cannot secure an airway. The child is resuscitated at the receiving hospital but has already suffered severe brain damage.

Analysis

Airway is everything. There is a reason why it is first in the emergency ABCs: it is the one aspect of emergency medicine in which there is a direct correlation between action and outcome. In the case of this child, a small piece of plastic tubing running from the carina to the mouth would have made the difference between a brain-damaged child and one who is normal. In airway management, it is difficult to make rules that can be followed 100% of the time, but clearly the decision to intubate is a clinical one and not dependent merely on blood gases and x-rays.

The reason for sending this child for an x-ray is not clear. Sick patients belong in the emergency department or the operating room, not unattended in x-ray. There are no data to suggest that this patient's treatment would have changed based on x-ray findings. A child in respiratory distress who is unable to handle secretions requires airway management no matter what the cause.

The ability to secure an airway should be one of the hallmarks of the emergency physician. Airway equipment in the emergency department should be readily accessible, frequently checked, and familiar to all who must use it. Physicians must have the ability to perform oral tracheal and nasal tracheal intubation and the necessary materials to perform a surgical airway if the situation warrants.

The decision to transfer a child with an unstable and unsecured airway is questionable at best. Generally, it is better to establish airways in an emergency department where lighting, suction, and ancillary personnel are available. To expect someone who is minimally qualified in the procedure to control the problem in the back of a moving ambulance with poor lighting and inadequate backup is an invitation to a malpractice claim.

Nearly all medical-legal actions related to airway management are neurology cases. The outcome of a poor gas exchange is decreased oxygen to sensitive neuro-tissues. In adults, excluding cold water drownings, irreversible neurologic damage begins within four to five minutes of lack of gas exchange. In children, although the time frame is somewhat longer, lack of oxygen can be equally devastating.

The emergency physician, when confronted by such a case, has several options. Observe the child cautiously, giving supplemental oxygen, if possible. Call for backup from anesthesia and ENT if such help appears necessary. If it is not available, the emergency physician should establish the airway as best as possible by whatever technique it takes prior to transfer. Simple techniques, such as head-down positioning and use of the bag-valve-mask technique, may be adequate to ventilate such children.

Key Points

- Airway is everything no matter what the disease entity. Establishing an airway and proper air exchange should be the emergency physician's number one priority.
- Intubate liberally. Rarely will there be any medical-legal consequences of intubating too quickly if it is done in a reasonable and prudent manner.
- Patients in respiratory distress belong in the emergency department, not in the x-ray suite.
- Before transporting or admitting a patient, the physician must make certain that the airway is secure.
- Equipment for airway management must be immediately available, in good working order, and familiar to all who must use it.
- There is no skill more important for an emergency physician than rapid management of the airway.

Abdominal Pain

Case Study 1

A 32-year-old man in generally good health presents to an emergency department complaining of nausea, vomiting, and abdominal pain for the past 24 hours. He says that several of his children have had a similar problem recently. He has had no chills, cough, or upper respiratory tract symptoms or diarrhea or urinary tract symptoms. Past medical history is negative for allergies or operations. He is on no medications and is not under medical care for any problems.

On physical examination, the patient has a blood pressure of 150/90, a pulse rate of 110, respiratory rate of 20, and a temperature of 100°F. Examination of the head, ears, eyes, nose, neck, and throat are normal. The chest, lungs, and heart are within normal limits. Abdominal examination reveals diffuse tenderness with mild generalized guarding but no rebound. Bowel sounds are somewhat decreased but are present. No organomegaly or masses are noted. Rectal and genital examinations are not recorded on the chart.

The emergency physician diagnoses gastroenteritis. He tells the patient to take fluids, and he gives him Compazine suppositories for his nausea. He also instructs the patient to see his physician in three days if not well. The patient is discharged but continues to have discomfort. He returns to the hospital 24 hours later with a diagnosis of ruptured appendix.

Analysis

Abdominal pain comprises 4% to 12% of malpractice claims in emergency medicine and as much as 7% of dollars paid.[3-5] The classic elements that lead to a lawsuit are generally present. First, most abdominal pain cases involve young or relatively young people with long life expectancies and earning capacities. Second, patients are frequently given a benign diagnosis, such as gastroenteritis or cystitis. When the condition turns out to be more serious and they require an operation and a long convalescence, they are likely to express anger and disappointment. In the case presented, the patient gave no history of ever having had his appendix removed, so appendicitis should have been a consideration.

Third, a physician who fails to examine the genitalia and rectum in a patient with lower abdominal pain creates a potentially high-risk situation. Occasionally, an inguinal hernia or a testicular torsion will be felt in the nerve distribution that lies higher in the abdomen. Certainly, a patient with an inflamed appendix will have suspicious findings on rectal examination.

However, it is clearly not the standard of care to arrive at a definitive diagnosis in every patient who presents to the emergency department with abdominal pain. Although studies vary, it is generally considered that about half the time a specific diagnosis cannot be made on abdominal pain patients during a first-time emergency department visit. The principal medical-legal issues regarding abdominal pain patients are associated not only with the physical examination, but also with the follow-up instructions. A three-day time frame, as was given in this case, is too long in a patient whose condition is not improving. An 8- to 12-hour time frame seems more appropriate.

There is no definitive test for most abdominal complaints. The variability of tests and measures, such as WBC counts, urine findings, and x-rays, limits their value in most cases of generalized abdominal pain. The most significant error in this case is the diagnosis itself. Gastroenteritis as a diagnosis is not only nonspecific, but also dangerous. In the case presented, the patient clearly had no enteritis symptoms. Conveying to patients that they have "stomach flu" creates a false sense of security. The disposition of this patient should have included a discussion of the fact that signs and symptoms change and that reevaluation is required. There is no substitute for repeat examination to establish a direction for the patient's disease process.

A woman of reproductive age who has abdominal pain presents added diagnostic possibilities. Record a careful menstrual and reproduction history, as well as previous pelvic infections. Histories related to sexual activity are often variable and modified by the patient for a variety of reasons. A liberal policy of obtaining the 25-unit β-hCG pregnancy test should be adopted. It is one of the few tests where a positive finding clearly lays out a definitive course of evaluation and specific treatment.

Patients can handle honesty. Telling a patient that repeat examinations or further testing may be required and reassuring her that surgery is not necessary at that moment is not usually a problem. The extra few minutes spent educating the patient to these issues properly transfers the responsibility for follow-up care and immediate return to the emergency department to the patient.

Key Points

- Any patient with abdominal pain who has not had an appendectomy may have appendicitis.
- The possibility of pregnancy or ectopic pregnancy must be considered in all women of childbearing age who present with lower abdominal pain.
- The sexual histories patients give may not be related to pregnancy status. Patients may be reluctant to admit they are sexually active or that they have multiple partners.
- Gastroenteritis is the diagnosis that appears in more emergency department medical-legal cases than any other. Real diagnoses include meningitis, missed appendicitis, ectopic pregnancy, and inferior wall myocardial infarction.
- Laboratory tests are rarely of value in determining the presence or absence of an acute surgical disease process. Repeat evaluations and short-term follow-up are the keys to diagnosis in abdominal pain.
- Candor with patients about the course of their illnesses and the need for follow-up care can help them understand the time frame for the diagnostic process and minimize their emotional reactions. In elderly patients with abdominal pain,

abdominal aneurysm and mesenteric ischemia should always be considered.

Case Study 2

A 67-year-old man in generally excellent health presents to the emergency department with a three-hour history of lower abdominal and back pain. He has had some mild diarrhea and nausea but no vomiting. The pain seems to come more from the right side, radiate from the flank, and down toward the scrotum. The patient is currently on no medications and claims to never see a physician unless he is "desperately ill." Past medical history includes an appendectomy and herniorrhaphy.

On physical examination, the patient is awake and alert and in moderate to severe pain. He is mildly diaphoretic. Examinations of the heart and lungs are clear. Examination of the abdomen reveals diffuse tenderness but no guarding or rebound. Examination of the back reveals some nonspecific tenderness in costovertebral angle areas. The patient's blood pressure is 184/72 and pulse rate is 110. While in the department, the patient becomes more diaphoretic and has one diarrhea stool. Plain films of the abdomen show no signs of obstruction, and urinalysis detects just a few red cells and white cells.

The emergency physician treats the patient with Immodium and Demerol and considers the condition to be a form of gastroenteritis. The patient is discharged, only to return four hours later, dead from a dissecting abdominal aortic aneurysm.

Analysis

As the United States becomes an ever-aging society, the prevalence of aortic disease will continue to increase. The maxim of abdominal pain in the elderly is important to remember: severe abdominal pain in the elderly is always a problem and is seldom constipation. In this case, a stoic man presents with poorly localized abdominal symptoms, profound diaphoresis, and abnormal vital signs. The diagnosis of gastroenteritis is itself a red flag that there has been inadequate evaluation of the case. The patient in whom all of the elements do not fit requires rethinking.

Abdominal aortic aneurysm is often misdiagnosed as kidney stones, back strain, or gastroenteritis. The lethal nature of the disease process, combined with the ease of diagnosis with newer modalities makes this a particularly trouble-

some problem from a medical-legal standpoint. The emergency department should be able to perform or obtain ultrasound evaluation of the abdominal aorta on a timely basis so that this noninvasive yet extremely high sensitivity test can be used when there is significant suspicion.

Key Points

- When an older patient with nonspecific abdominal pain and pain out of proportion to the systems presents, take it seriously.
- Constipation as a diagnosis in an elderly patient with abdominal pain is rarely correct.

Headache

Case Study

A 27-year-old woman with a history of severe headaches presents to the emergency department with a three-hour history of throbbing bilateral pain worse on the right than on the left. She has vomited twice and says that she has never had a pain this severe before in her life. The patient has never had a workup for headache and is without medical problems; she is not pregnant and is not under a physician's care for any condition. She has had no previous surgeries or allergies and is on no medication. She denies any other neurologic symptoms.

On physical examination, the patient has a blood pressure of 150/90, a pulse rate of 80, a respiratory rate of 18, and a temperature of 97.8°F. Examination of the head, ears, eyes, nose, and throat reveals that the fundi are benign and there are no areas of tenderness over the head or face. The neck is recorded as supple. Heart, lung, and abdominal examinations are normal. The neurologic examination reveals that the patient is oriented to person, place, and time but is in significant pain. The cranial nerves are normal. Strength and sensation are normal, and the toes are down-going.

The emergency physician administers a narcotic analgesic, which dulls the pain but does not alleviate it. The patient is then taken for a CT scan to "rule out hemorrhage," as written on the requisition. Thirty minutes later, the patient returns from the x-ray department, and the reading on the CT scan is normal. The patient is discharged to the care of her family. She is returned to the emergency department in a coma 24 hours later. Lumbar puncture reveals blood in the subarachnoid space.

Analysis

Headaches in patients can become medical-legal headaches for physicians. These patients often suffer brain injury, which means costly lawsuits. Head pain in the emergency department should be considered no different than chest pain or abdominal pain. It is a legitimate medical emergency until proved otherwise. Subarachnoid hemorrhage generally arises from a congenital berry aneurysm of the circle of Willis. As a result, the incidence of subarachnoid hemorrhage and its resultant morbidity and mortality have remained constant despite advances in headache management.

To reduce risk, the emergency physician needs to adopt a specific philosophy when treating the headache patient, particularly if the pain is severe. That philosophy should be to suspect subarachnoid hemorrhage or meningitis until proved otherwise. Not all patients with headaches require CT scanning or lumbar puncture. If, however, there is adequate historical and physical data to prompt the physician to begin the workup of a specific problem, that workup should be performed properly.

In this case, the emergency physician ordered a CT scan to rule out subarachnoid hemorrhage. The limitations of the CT scan should be well understood; if one is ordered and is found to be negative, a lumbar puncture is imperative to rule out subarachnoid bleeding. If meningitis is suspected and there is to be any delay in obtaining a CT scan or lumbar puncture, antibiotics should be given empirically.

Headache sufferers, like patients with low back pain, are often treated as an annoyance by the emergency department staff. Severe head pain, like pain in any other part of the body, should be taken seriously. Proper evaluation is required each and every time the patient presents. A timely and sympathetic approach with the offer of medication frequently reassures the patient and allows for a supportive physician-patient interaction. Having had previous headaches is no protection against either subarachnoid hemorrhage or meningitis.

Key Points

- Emergency physicians should takes a serious approach to patients who present with the worst headaches of their lives. Head pain is a medical emergency, and the patient should be given the same attention as any other patient with a medical emergency.
- Patients who pass out with a headache should not be sent home, but kept for observation.
- If a CT scan is ordered to rule out hemorrhage and the CT scan is negative, then lumbar puncture should be performed as well.
- If meningitis is suspected, the physician should administer antibiotics right away, particularly if there may be a delay in performing tests.
- Neck findings in both meningitis and subarachnoid hemorrhage may be nonexistent or late-developing in the very young and the elderly.
- There is no reason to perform a lumbar puncture in the emergency department on a patient with focal findings with lateralized neurologic deficit.

Febrile Children

Case Study

An 8-week-old boy is brought to the emergency department by his mother, who says that he has been fussy and eating poorly. The mother says the child is not taking as much formula as usual. He has been urinating and having bowel movements but just seems less interested in eating. The mother relates no trauma, and the child otherwise had been well.

Physical examination reveals an awake 8-week-old child in acute distress. Rectal temperature is 101.8°F, pulse rate 142, respiratory rate 28; no blood pressure is obtained. The child's head, ears, eyes, nose, and throat are remarkable only for fluid in the nose, but the fontanel appears concave. The child's neck is supple, lungs are clear, and the heart has a normal-sized rhythm without murmur. The abdomen is soft, nontender, and nondistended. Genitalia appear normal. The skin is clear and somewhat dry with minimal tenting. Neurologically, the child has a normal startle response and can move all four extremities. No other parts of the neurologic examination are recorded.

Because it is late in the evening, the emergency physician decides to send the child home in the care of the mother, but on the off-chance of an infection, he starts the child on oral ampicillin. The mother is instructed to contact her physician in the next few days if the child is not doing well. The mother and child return to the emergency department the following evening. The child is flaccid and has a bulging fontanel. At that time, a diagnosis of meningitis is confirmed, and the child is transferred to a hospital with a pediatric ICU. On discharge, the child is left with profound hearing deficit, decreased vision, and generalized increased spasticity.

Analysis

Although meningitis represents, at the most, only 5% of emergency medicine malpractice claims, it accounts for up to 17% of the medical liability dollars expended.[3,4] Patients with a missed diagnosis of meningitis invariably have long hospitalizations and significant neurologic deficits that may require lifelong medical care. Certainly, earning capacity is decreased. The sympathy factor for such cases should never be underestimated.

In this case, several elements require emphasis. First, children are immunologically vulnerable during the first 12 weeks of life. An infected child less than 12 weeks of age may have an extremely difficult time generating the proper response to an invading organism. Classic findings, such as meningism and altered mental status, may be very deceptive in late findings. By the time the child has developed seizures and coma secondary to an infection, the process is already well on its way to causing significant neurologic impairment. Second, the mother's report of the child's inability to eat was not challenged in the emergency department. A child who can eat and appears alert can usually be handled on an outpatient basis.

Over the past 10 years, considerable efforts have been spent to analyze whether any laboratory tests are useful in the early diagnosis of the child with septicemia and meningitis. It has been repeatedly shown that the WBC count, the sedimentation rate, seroactive protein, the differential count, and serum electrolytes are useless. There is no better test to identify the child who requires workup than the physical examination conducted by an experienced physician. Because many of the factors required to diagnose meningitis are not present in extremely young children, those who are less than 8 weeks of age — and some would argue 12 weeks — who are febrile or who appear generally ill without specific focus of infection require a septic workup. Because extremely young children dehydrate rapidly in the face of infection, the ability to hold down fluids is critical.

Feeding the child in the emergency department not only helps reassure the parents, but also actually tests the ability of the child to function at home. Younger children may be fed bottles of electrolyte solution. In slightly older children, popsicles are an excellent indicator of the child's ability to feed. A child who will not take fluid in the department should be suspect for underlying illness. Children are much like adults, in that the diagnosis of gastroenteritis is a label often placed on patients who do not truly meet the criteria. Short-term follow-up is the only reasonable approach in the child who does not meet criteria for admission.

In this case, the mother claimed to have called the pediatrician the next morning, but a visit was not scheduled until late that afternoon. Children must not be allowed to fall between the cracks of the system. A proper safety net with repeat examination within 6 to 12 hours goes a long way in reassuring parents and in detecting disease that may not be evident on the first emergency department visit.

Key Points

- Infants less than 8 weeks of age with a fever require a septic workup.
- For children sent home, rapid follow-up either by a pediatrician or an emergency physician should be arranged.
- If meningitis is suspected, it must be treated immediately.
- If family circumstances could prevent the child from getting proper care, the physician should find some reason to admit the child.
- Feed children in the emergency department. The child who will take a popsicle and ask for a second one is rarely severely ill.

Pelvic Pain

Case Study

A 23-year-old woman presents to the emergency department with lower abdominal and pelvic pain and mild vaginal discharge. She relates a history of multiple sexual experiences and is concerned that she may have contracted a disease. She is having some generalized pain, more on the right side than the left. Past medical history includes an appendectomy, which was uneventful. The patient is generally in good health and has no allergies. On physical examination, the emergency physician finds that the abdomen is generally tender in both adnexa, much more on the right than the left. There is no rebound or guarding. The rectal examination is negative.

Pelvic examination reveals that the uterus is somewhat diffusely tender but not enlarged. The adnexa are tender, but much more so on the right side than on the left. There is a discharge; gonorrhea and *Chlamydia* cultures are taken. The emergency physician concludes that the patient has pelvic inflammatory disease. She is given Rocephin IM and doxycycline for 10 days. The pain is treated with a combination of Motrin and Vicodin.

Twenty-four hours later, the patient is brought back to the emergency department. The diagnosis is a ruptured ectopic pregnancy. Fluid resuscitation and immediate surgical intervention save the patient, but she has a stormy recovery. A lawsuit is filed against the emergency physician for failure to diagnose an ectopic pregnancy.

Analysis

Here is another emergency medicine maxim: the PID of "pelvic inflammatory disease" also stands for "pretty inadequate diagnosis." The possibility of a woman having both an active pregnancy and an infection is likely. The fact that this patient's pain was basically right-sided should have alerted the physician that some other problem existed. Bacterial infections of the genital tract should not be one-sided. The fact that the patient may or may not have a normal menstrual history is irrelevant. Studies have certainly shown that women are often inaccurate in describing their menstrual histories, and the variability of each individual with regard to menstrual bleeding is such that it is not of sufficient predictive value to avoid testing. The 25-unit β-hCG pregnancy test is universally available and is sensitive to the 99.8% level in most studies.[25,26] All women of childbearing age who present with lower abdominal pain should have a urine pregnancy test.

Key Points

- Menstrual histories in women are frequently inaccurate and are not sufficient to definitively rule out pregnancy.
- In women of reproductive age with lower abdominal pain, pregnancy should always be a consideration.

References

1. Rogers JT. *Risk Management in Emergency Medicine*. Dallas: American College of Emergency Physicians; 1985.
2. Personal communication from John D. Dunn, MD, JD, FACEP. Data courtesy of EPT Enterprises, Inc.
3. Personal communication from John D. Dunn, MD, JD, FACEP, based on private analysis of closed claims data from the Galtney Group, Houston, Texas, Health Care Insurance Services, and the Western Indemnity Insurance Company.
4. Personal communication from John D. Dunn, MD, JD, FACEP, based on a closed claim analysis performed by Century American Insurance Company.
5. Karcz A, Korn R, Burke MC, et al. Malpractice claims against emergency physicians in Massachusetts: 1975-1993. *Am J Emerg Med* 1996;14:341-345.
6. Goldman L. Acute chest pain: emergency room evaluation. *Hosp Pract* July 1986:94A.
7. Lee TH, Cook EF, Weisberg M, et al. Acute chest pain in the emergency room. Identification and examination of low-risk patients. *Arch Intern Med* 1985;145:65-69.
8. Lee TH, Rowan GW, Weisberg MC, et al. Clinical characteristics and natural history of patients with acute myocardial infarction sent home from the emergency room. *Am J Cardiol* 1987;60:219-224.
9. Hedges JR, Kobernick MS. Detection of myocardial ischemic/infarction in the emergency department patient with chest discomfort. *Emerg Med Clin North Am* 1988;6:317-340.
10. Brush JE Jr, Brand DA, Acampora D, et al. Use of the initial electrocardiogram to predict in-hospital complications of acute myocardial infarction. *N Engl J Med* 1985;312:1137-1141.
11. Miller DH, Kligfield P, Schreiber TL, et al. Relationship of prior myocardial infraction to false-positive electrocardiographic diagnosis of acute injury of patients with chest pain. *Arch Intern Med* 1987;147:257-261.
12. Nowakowski JF. Use of cardiac enzymes in the evaluation of acute chest pain. *Ann Emerg Med* 1986;15:354-360.
13. Hennekens CH, O'Donnell CJ, Ridker PM, et al. Current issues concerning thrombolytic therapy for acute myocardial infarction. *J Am Coll Cardiol* 1995;25(7Suppl):18S-22S.
14. Califf RM, White HD, van de Werf F, et al. One-year results from the global utilization of streptokinase and TPA for occluded coronary arteries (GUSTO-I) trial. *Circulation* 1996; 94:1233-1238.
15. The Emergency Department: Rapid Identification and Treatment of Patients with Acute Myocardial Infarction. National Heart Attack Alert Program Coordinating Committee. Sixty Minutes to Treatment Working Group. U.S. Department of Health and Human Services, Public Health Service, National Institutes of Health, Bethesda, MD. Publication No. 93-3278. September 1993.
16. Ryan TJ, Anderson JL, Antman EM, et al. ACC/AHA guidelines for the management of patients with acute myocardial infarction. A report of the American College of Cardiology/American Heart Association Task Force on Practice Guidelines (Committee on Management of Acute Myocardial Infarction). *J Am Coll Cardiol* 1996;28:1328-1428.
17. Henry G, Little N. Personal communication concerning malpractice cases in which they served as expert witnesses.
18. ACC/AHA guidelines for the early management of patients with acute myocardial infarction. A report of the American College of Cardiology/American Heart Association Task Force on Assessment of Diagnostic and Therapeutic Cardiovascular Procedures. *Circulation* 1990;82:664-707.
19. Lammers RL. Soft tissue foreign bodies. *Ann Emerg Med* 1988;17:1336-1347.
20. Tandberg D. Glass in the hand and foot. Will the x-ray show it? *JAMA* 1982;248:1872-1874.
21. Fitzgerald RH Jr, Cowan JD. Puncture wounds of the foot. *Orthop Clin North Am* 1975;6:965-972.
22. Smoot EC, Robson MC. Acute management of foreign body injuries of the hand. *Ann Emerg Med* 1983;12:434-437.
23. Lindsey D, Lindsey WE. Cactus spine injuries. *Am J Emerg Med* 1988;6:362-369.
24. Tintinalli JE, Ruiz E, Krome RL, eds. *Emergency Medicine: A Comprehensive Study Guide*. Fourth edition. New York: McGraw-Hill; 1996.
25. Stengel CL, Seaberg DC, MacLeod BA. Pregnancy in the emergency department. Risk factors and prevalence among all women. *Ann Emerg Med* 1994;24:697-700.
26. Norman RJ. When a positive pregnancy test isn't. *Med J Aust* 1991;154:718-719.

Chapter 58

The Appropriate Medical Screening Examination

Mark M. Moy, MD, MJ, FAAFP, FACEP

The term medical screening examination has taken on a new meaning and importance with the advent of the Emergency Medical Treatment and Active Labor Act, or EMTALA.[1] In the past, medical screening simply referred to quick, superficial, low-risk examinations for nonemergent conditions, such as might be performed for insurance physicals, employment physicals, and psychiatric admissions. Now the term is legally defined and carries with it a heightened level of duty under the requirements of federal law. The stakes are high. Providing an inappropriate medical screening examination can subject a physician to fines of up to $50,000 per violation and loss of participation in Medicare. A hospital can be penalized with similar fines, termination from Medicare participation, and civil lawsuits.

Emergency physicians must be sure that the medical screening examinations they perform are "appropriate" according to the law. However, complying with this EMTALA requirement is problematic. The specific elements of the appropriate medical screening examination have never been defined, and requirements of managed care plans often create conflict with the law.

The Law

EMTALA, known for many years as "COBRA," was passed in 1985 in response to a perceived practice of "dumping"[2] indigent patients from emergency departments. The appropriate medical screening examination[3] requirement of EMTALA is designed to ensure that hospitals create screening procedures that they apply to all persons who come to the emergency department for care regardless of their ability to pay. The law obligates a hospital to create standard emergency screening procedures based on that hospital's particular abilities and circumstances.

The law also requires that an appropriate medical screening examination must be provided to every patient who comes to the emergency department to determine if an emergency medical condition exists. According to EMTALA:

In the case of a hospital that has a hospital emergency department, if any individual (whether or not eligible for benefits under this subchapter) comes to the emergency department and a request is made on the individual's behalf for examination or treatment for a medical condition, the hospital must provide for an appropriate medical screening examination within the capability of the hospital's emergency department, including ancillary services routinely available to the emergency department, to determine whether or not an emergency medical condition (within the meaning of subsection (e)(1) of this section) exists.[4]

Who Does the Law Affect?

Any emergency physician who works in a hospital that participates in the Medicare program must provide a medical screening examination to any patient who presents requesting care.[3] This provision covers practically all hospitals in the United States, because virtually every hospital has entered into a Medicare provider agreement. Although the statute states: "In the case of a hospital that has a hospital emergency department,"[3] there is no absolute requirement that the hospital must have a formal emergency department. The statutory phrase "emergency department" is defined in regulations[5] as a hospital that offers services for any emergency medical condition. Physicians working in a hospital's urgent care or ambulatory care center, for example, are also obligated to comply with this EMTALA requirement.

The emergency physician must provide a medical screening examination to any patient who "comes to"[3] the emergency department. What exactly does this mean to the practicing physician? In *Johnson v University of Chicago Hospital*,[6] a child suffered a cardiopulmonary arrest at home and paramedics requested en route a transfer to the University of Chicago Hospital. The emergency nurse advised the paramedics by telemetry that the hospital was on "partial bypass" because of full occupancy of the pediatric ICU beds. The nurse instructed the paramedics to transport the child to a nearby hospital. The child was temporarily resuscitated but died after a second transfer to Cook County Hospital. Initially, the U.S. Court of Appeals for the 7th Circuit[7] ruled that mere telemetry contact with a hospital was equivalent to "coming to the emergency department," creating a duty by the University of Chicago to provide the medical screening examination. The Chicago area EMS system alarmingly responded with Amicus Curiae[8] from all the major trauma centers in Chicago, stressing that such a ruling would create havoc with the existing telemetry system. After reconsideration, the court reversed its own decision and ultimately ruled that the patient in *Johnson* never "came to" the emergency department, stating "for purposes of EMTALA, a hospital-operated telemetry system is distinct from that same hospital's emergency room."[9]

In 1994, the Health Care Financing Administration (HCFA) issued interim final regulations for the enforcement of EMTALA[10] to try to clarify the interpretation of this issue. The interpretation is codified in the Code of Federal Regulations[11] as follows:

> Comes to the emergency department means, with respect to an individual requesting examination or treatment, that the individual is on the hospital property (property includes ambulances owned

and operated by the hospital, even if the ambulance is not on hospital grounds). An individual in a non–hospital-owned ambulance on hospital property is considered to have come to the hospital's emergency department. An individual in a non–hospital-owned ambulance off hospital property is not considered to have come to the hospital's emergency department, even if a member of the ambulance staff contacts the hospital by telephone or telemetry communications and informs the hospital that they want to transport the individual to the hospital for examination and treatment. In such situations, the hospital may deny access if it is in "diversionary status," that is, it does not have the staff or facilities to accept any additional emergency patients. If, however, the ambulance staff disregards the hospital's instructions and transports the individual onto hospital property, the individual is considered to have come to the emergency department.[3]

What Makes an Examination 'Appropriate'?

Both the courts and the medical community have been confused as to what exactly constitutes an "appropriate" medical screening examination. The authors of the EMTALA legislation failed to define the phrase "appropriate medical screening examination" when they wrote the law, leaving the courts to define the phrase. In the early years of EMTALA, the courts interpreted the phrase to mean that a violation occurred when an inappropriate medical screening examination was performed as a result of economic or some other form of discrimination.

In *Cleland v Bronson Health Care Group, Inc. Hospital*,[12] a 15-year-old boy was treated in the emergency department for vomiting and abdominal cramps. He was released with a diagnosis of gastroenteritis. He actually had an intussusception, and the next day suffered a cardiac arrest and died. The parents sought legal action under EMTALA for failure to provide an appropriate medical screening examination. In 1990, the *Cleland* court stated that "a hospital that provides a substandard (by its standards) or nonexistent medical screening for any reason (including without limitation race, sex, politics, occupation, education, personal prejudice, drunkenness, spite, etc.) may be held liable under [EMTALA]."[13]

Currently, federal courts are in disagreement and have come to recognize that an inappropriate medical screening examination may occur even when there is no evidence of discrimination at all on the part of the treating physician. In *Gatewood v Washington Healthcare Corporation*,[14] a patient with chest pain was discharged from the emergency department after an ECG and chest x-ray were normal. He died the next morning of a myocardial infarction. The *Gatewood* court reasoned that, to violate EMTALA, the care merely needed to be substandard without requiring a bad motive. According to the *Gatewood* ruling:

a hospital fulfills the "appropriate medical screening" requirement when it conforms in its treatment of a particular patient to its standard screening procedures . . . any departure from standard screening procedures constitutes inappropriate screening in violation of [EMTALA]. The motive for such departure is not important to this analysis, which applies whenever and for whatever reason a patient is denied the same level of care provided others and guaranteed him or her by [EMTALA].[14]

The term appropriate as interpreted by the courts has evolved. Now, emergency departments are required to provide screening examinations uniformly to all patients in similar medical circumstances. In *Summers v Baptist Medical Center Arkadelphia*,[15] a patient was released without proper diagnosis of his vertebral, sternal, and rib fractures and bilateral hemopneumothoraces. The court in *Summers* held that "EMTALA requires hospitals to develop screening procedures that identify critical conditions and to apply the procedures uniformly to all patients. All patients complaining of the same problem or exhibiting the same symptoms must receive similar screening examinations from a given emergency room."[16]

A medical screening examination performed by a nonphysician, such as a nurse or a paramedic, may be appropriate. Any individual who is determined to be qualified by the hospital's policy and procedures or bylaws[17] may perform the screening examination. HCFA provided this ruling to accommodate rural primary care hospitals that do not always have physicians present in the hospital. HCFA does require that this designation of qualified screening personnel be set forth in a formal policy document that is approved by the hospital's board of directors. However, HCFA further states:

Although it is up to the hospital to determine under what circumstances a physician is required to perform an appropriate medical screening examination, that does not mean that HHS [Health and Human Services] must accept the hospital's determination of what circumstances require that the screening exam be performed by a physician.[18]

HCFA, therefore, can rule on a case-by-case determination and may not accept whom a hospital determines is qualified to perform the examination. Emergency physicians should recognize that they may ultimately share responsibility for any screening examination performed by a nonphysician in their departments.

On-call physicians are specifically included by HCFA as part of the ancillary services to be used by a hospital to provide an appropriate medical screening examination.[19] The emergency physician may require the services of an on-call specialist, such as an obstetrician, to provide the appropriate medical screening examination in order to determine if the patient has an emergency medical condition. In such a situation, the on-call physician has the same duty under EMTALA to provide the screening examination. EMTALA obligates the hospital to maintain and post in the emergency department a list of available on-call physicians.[20]

If the on-call physician fails or refuses to come to the emergency department within a reasonable period of time when notified by an emergency physician, then the on-call physician is potentially liable under EMTALA and may be fined or terminated from the Medicare program.[21] If the emergency physician has to transfer the patient because the on-call physician fails to provide care, EMTALA obligates the emergency physician to write on the transfer form the name and address of any on-call physician who fails to provide needed services to stabilize a patient.[22] Failure to do so may result in monetary penalties against the emergency physician.[22]

EMTALA also obligates the hospital to provide a medical screening examination "within [its] capabilities."[3] HCFA defines capability to include the expertise of the medical staff, beds and other hospital facilities, hospital services, and all diagnostic equipment. Capacity encompasses such things as numbers and availability of qualified staff, open beds, available equipment, and the hospital's past practices of accommodating additional patients in excess of its occupancy limits.[23] Hospitals need not expand their resources or offer more services, because EMTALA focuses only on existing capabilities. However, HCFA has taken a rigid position on capabilities of a transferring hospital as a way to prevent hospitals from searching for excuses to avoid providing the medical screening examination.

For example, if a hospital has the ability to stabilize a patient by delivering a baby through a normal vaginal delivery by an emergency physician or family physician then it must do so — even though it lacks an obstetrics department — rather than transfer the patient to another hospital. If the hospital has accommodated such patients in the past "by whatever means,"[23] including calling in additional staff, then "it has demonstrated the ability to provide services to patients in excess of its occupancy limit."[23] A hospital needs to search all of its resources in order to provide an appropriate medical screening examination as required by EMTALA.

Managed Care

Managed care has created direct conflicts with the federal requirement to provide every patient who presents to the emergency department with an appropriate medical screening examination. In *Correa v Hospital San Francisco*,[24] the patient presented to the emergency department with sweats, dizziness, and chest pain. After a two-hour wait and without any examination, the secretary referred Mrs. Correa to her insurance company's day clinic as required by her insurance rules. She suffered a cardiac arrest at the clinic and died. The jury awarded $700,000 for violation of EMTALA's medical screening examination requirement. The court ruled that "the Hospital's inaction here amounted to a deliberate denial of screening. EMTALA should be read to proscribe both actual and constructive dumping of patients."[24]

The conflict usually arises when a managed care organization refuses to authorize payment for care even after the patient has already arrived at the emergency department. Releasing the patient without an examination puts the emergency physician at risk of violating EMTALA, but insisting on an examination leaves the patient in the middle without a guarantee that the cost of the examination will be covered by insurance. The result of the conflict is tension

between managed care payers and emergency departments, as well as uncertainty among consumers about how and where to get emergency medical care and what will be covered.

With the increasing penetration of managed care into the health care market, both in private insurance and in Medicare and Medicaid programs, tension and uncertainty can only grow. Fortunately, many hospitals are creating innovative protocols in the emergency department in order to comply with the federally mandated medical screening examination and refer managed care patients without emergency medical conditions out of the emergency department.

The HCFA Task Force on EMTALA

At the time of this writing, HCFA is attempting to clarify the definition for appropriate medical screening examinations under EMTALA. In June 1996, HCFA convened a task force to review the interpretation and enforcement of EMTALA.[25] The task force presented a definition for an appropriate medical screening examination, as follows:

A medical screening examination (MSE) is the process required to reach, with reasonable clinical confidence, the point at which it can be determined whether a medical emergency does or does not exist. So long as a hospital applies, in a nondiscriminatory manner, a screening process that is reasonably calculated to determine whether an emergency medical condition exists, it has met its EMTALA obligations.

1. Depending on the patient's presenting symptoms, the MSE represents a spectrum ranging from a simple process involving only a brief history and physical examination to a complex process that also involves performing ancillary studies and procedures such as (but not limited to) lumbar punctures, clinical laboratory tests, CT scans, and/or diagnostic tests and procedures.

2. The clinical outcome of an individual's condition is not the basis for determining whether a screening was appropriate.

3. Triage is not equivalent to an MSE. Triage merely determines the "order" in which patients will be seen, not the presence or absence of an emergency medical condition.

4. A screening process is not the

equivalent of a clinical practice guideline.[25]

The "Interface with Managed Care" work group, a section of the EMTALA task force, was charged with clarifying the conflict between performing the medical screening examination and following managed care organization requirements. The work group arrived at a consensus on screening examinations, as follows:

> It is not appropriate for a hospital to request or a health plan to require prior authorization before the patient has received a medical screening exam to determine the presence or absence of an emergency medical condition or until an existing emergency medical condition has been stabilized. Once an emergency medical condition has been determined not to exist or the emergency medical condition has been stabilized, section 1867 [EMTALA] no longer applies and prior authorization for further services can be sought.[26]

Key Points and Conclusion

EMTALA has created a heightened duty for emergency physicians to provide a medical screening examination to every patient who arrives at the hospital. EMTALA attached significant monetary penalties to encourage emergency physicians to comply with this duty. Recent court cases show that the courts are viewing an appropriate medical screening examination, at a minimum, as one that is applied uniformly to all patients presenting with the same signs and symptoms.

The courts want every patient who comes to the emergency department requesting care to receive the same level of screening examination. Managed care organization denials of coverage for patients presenting to the emergency department come into direct conflict with EMTALA requirements. The HCFA task force, convened in 1996, should help reduce the tensions of this conflict. Individual hospitals are creating unique protocols to address this conflict. Perhaps a workable solution will evolve from these efforts. In the meantime, emergency physicians must make a conscious effort to provide appropriate medical screening examinations in a nondiscriminatory manner to all patients who present for treatment.

References

1. The Emergency Medical Treatment and Active Labor Act (EMTALA), also commonly known as COBRA (Consolidated Omnibus Budget Reconciliation Act), Pub. L. No. 99-272, Title IX, §9121(b), 100 Stat. 164 (codified as amended at 42 USC §1395dd).

2. "Patient dumping" refers to the practice of denying emergency medical care to patients who present to a hospital with inadequate insurance or no insurance and "dumping" them back on the streets without care or allow them to be transferred in an unstable medical condition to public "charity" hospitals. See HR Rep. No. 241(II), 99th Cong., 2nd Sess 27 (1986).

3. 42 USC §1395dd (a) (1995).

4. 42 USC §1395dd (a) (1995)

5. 42 CFR §489.24 (b) (1995).

6. *Johnson v University of Chicago Hospital*, 774 F Supp 510 (ND Ill 1991).

7. *Johnson v University of Chicago Hospital*, 1992 WL 259404, (No. 91-3587, 7th Cir Ill) October 7, 1992.

8. Amicus Curiae means, literally, friend of the court. A person with strong interest in or views on the subject matter of a lawsuit but not a party to it, may petition the court for permission to file a brief, ostensibly on behalf of a party but actually to suggest a rationale consistent with its own views. See Fed. R. App. P.29.

9. *Johnson v University of Chicago Hospital*, 982 F2d 230 (7th Cir 1992).

10. The Health Care Financing Administration (HCFA) is part of the Department of Health and Human Services (HHS). The Office of the Inspector General (OIG) is the investigative arm of the HHS entrusted with assessing civil penalties under the Act. See 42 CFR §1003.102 (1992).

11. The CFR is the annual cumulation of executive agency regulations published in the daily *Federal Register*, combined with regulations issued previously that are still in effect. The CFR contains the general body of regulatory laws governing practice and procedure before federal administrative agencies. *Black's Law Dictionary* 176 (Abr. 6th ed. 1991).

12. *Cleland v Bronson Health Care Group, Inc.*, 917 F2d 266 (6th Cir 1990), *Evitt v Univ. Heights Hospital*, 727 F Supp 495 (SD Ind 1989) (the court ruled that economic discrimination was necessary for an EMTALA violation), *Nichols v Eastbrook*, 741 F Supp 325, 330 (NH 1989) (finding that the congressional intent was "to provide some assurance that patients with emergency medical conditions will be examined and treated regardless of their financial resources"). *Bryant v Riddle Memorial Hospital*, 689 F Supp 490, 491 (ED Pa 1988) (stating that EMTALA was enacted in order to combat the growing problem of patient dumping).

13. *Cleland v Bronson Health Care Group, Inc.*, at 272.

14. *Gatewood v Washington Healthcare Corp.*, 933 F2d 1037 (DC Cir 1991).

15. *Summers v Baptist Medical Center Arkadelphia*, 69 F3d 902 (8th Cir. 1995), Also see, *Baber v Hospital Corp. of America*, 977 F2d 872 (4th Cir 1992) (The court concluded that "[a] hospital satisfies the requirements of [EMTALA] if its screening procedure is applied uniformly to all patients in similar medical circumstances."), *Collins v DePaul Hosp.*, 963 F2d 303 (10th Cir 1992) (The court states that the sole legal purpose of the medical screening examination is to determine whether an emergency medical condition exists: "Nothing more, nothing less"), *Power v Arlington Hosp. Ass'n.*, 42 F3d 851 (4th Cir) (The court stated that "there is nothing in the statute itself that requires proof of indigence, inability to pay, or any other improper motive on the part of a hospital as a prerequisite to [EMTALA].").

16. *Summers v Baptist Medical Center Arkadelphia*, at 904.

17. 42 CFR §482.55 (1995).

18. 59 *Federal Register* 32092 (1994) (to be codified at 42 CFR §489.24).

19. 59 *Federal Register* 32099 (1994).

20. 59 *Federal Register* 32100 (1994).

21. 59 *Federal Register* 32090 (1994) (codified at 42 CFR §489.24).

22. 42 CFR §489.24 (d)(2)(iii) (1995).

23. 59 *Federal Register* 32121 (1994).

24. *Correa v Hospital San Francisco*, 69 F3d 1184 (1st Cir 1995).

25. Memorandum from Larry A. Bedard, MD, FACEP, President ACEP, January 6, 1997.

26. Health Standards & Quality Bureau Interface with Managed Care Workgroup consensus paper on Managed Care/Emergency Department Issues Relating to COBRA/EMTALA, (Draft) (Emphasis added), revised November 19, 1996, from the "Interface with Managed Care" workgroup of HCFA's EMTALA task force as noted in note 13 above.

Chapter 59

Contracting With Managed Care Plans

Stephen J. Dresnick, MD, FACEP

With ever-increasing numbers of patients enrolling in managed care plans, emergency physicians must become well versed in the issues associated with managed care contracts. Although this topic does not immediately come to mind in a discussion of risk management, emergency physicians need to understand that a bad contract will expose them to financial as well as other risks.

Many hospitals pressure their emergency physicians to accept managed care contracts in the naive belief that the managed care organization (MCO) will direct more patients their way. This trend has resulted in the need for emergency physicians to get involved in negotiations with MCOs whether they are contracting directly with the company or through a hospital-sponsored physician-hospital organization or independent practice association. Whether an emergency physician contracts directly with a hospital, or a group is on independent billing, a firm grasp of the issues will help physicians enhance their practices.

Making the Decision to Contract With a Managed Care Organization

Every managed care plan promises to deliver more patients if the providers are willing to give a discount off their normal fees. Although the promise is not always fulfilled, most providers have been willing to grant a nominal discount. This agreement may result in reduced physician income unless additional patient volume offsets the reduction in charges. Ideally, no discounts should be granted unless there is additional patient volume. Unfortunately, this is hardly ever the case and usually is not practical.

So why do it? Emergency physicians contract with managed care plans either because their hospitals, as part of their contracts with the plans, require emergency physicians to belong, or because their hospital-physician group contracts stipulate that the groups will join any plans that the hospitals request.

Emergency physicians should also consider joining a particular plan when they determine that the plan either has or will become a dominant player in the local market. There may be political reasons to join a plan, for example, if it is sponsored by an employer that is a supporter of the hospital. In such cases, the employer may ask the hospital and the physician group to join the plan or else direct patients to another institution.

Another factor to consider is the financial viability of the plan. Physicians should not enter into complex agreements when all indications are that the plan is not financially sound.

Business History

Knowing the business history of the plan is helpful when negotiating a contract. The company's past dealings with other hospitals should alert physicians to specific areas that should be addressed. Gaining an in-depth knowledge of the principals or owners can reveal how they might deal with problems in the future. If the plan had difficulties in other markets, they might behave the same way again. If the company is publicly owned, this information should be contained in their annual filings with the Securities and Exchange Commission. If the plan is privately held, this information may be obtained through the state office of insurance. Beware of companies whose principals draw enormous salaries when the plans are losing money or whose senior managers who are divesting themselves of company stock. These actions may indicate that the company will not be around for the long term.

Have an accountant review the plan's financial statements to give a clear picture of the company's financial health. The accountant should pay particular attention to contingent liabilities, or liabilities that show up only in footnotes of the financial statements, for example, pending lawsuits. Such actions can be important if they are for nonpayment of fees to providers. If the plan does not appear to be in good financial health, the company may delay or even deny payment of claims. Although this fact alone may not be reason enough not to sign an agreement, it might cause the physician or group to seek better terms than would be offered otherwise.

Always check company references, particularly if the plan is new to the area. Before signing any agreement, insist on receiving copies of all available written materials, including marketing brochures and advertising materials. These documents will show what the company is telling patients and will help focus discussions. This material should be filed with the contract; it may be helpful in resolving future disputes.

Contract Issues

A contract is a written document that outlines the duties and responsibilities of the parties involved. A contract should address as many issues as possible, whether in the text of the agreement or as attachments. Physicians often are presented with contracts they do not read or refer to appropriate advisers to review. This practice inevitably creates a problem. When plan administrators suggest that a clause does not say what it appears to say, physicians must have the language clarified rather than rely on the company's oral assurances. In a court of law, oral commitments hold no weight when a written document exists. Contract language should be as specific as possible.

Contracts are two-way agreements and should address the rights and responsibilities of both parties. Obviously, managed care plan administrators will attempt to present a contract more favorable to them. Although many physicians accept these contracts at face value, they should always remember that all agreements are negotiable. Even the best written contract is only as good as the integrity of the parties involved.

Term

Any contract entered into with an MCO should have a specified term, or time that the contract is in force. If a contract does not have a set term, the MCO may have no responsibility to update the fees. If a fee schedule is to be used, physicians should insist that the contract term be for one year. This will ensure that the fee schedule will be updated, particularly when the contract states that if it is not renewed, the MCO is obligated to pay the physicians' usual and customary charges. Many MCOs will attempt to persuade physicians to sign "evergreen" contracts, which are simply contracts that remain in force until they are canceled. The company's rationale is that many physicians will not remember when the contract is up for renewal, and the MCO will not have to raise fees until forced to do so.

Termination

Physicians should insist on a provision that allows them to terminate their agreement without cause with reasonable notice, usually 90 to 120 days. They must be sure that the provision states exactly what the MCO will do once the contract is terminated, particularly in regard to payment of fees.

Fee Schedules

The fee schedule to be used is perhaps the most important aspect of any contract with a managed care plan. The contract should specify how the fee schedule is to be determined. When possible, the actual fee schedule should be attached as an exhibit to the contract.

If RBRVS is to be used as the fee schedule, specify the conversion factor for medical as well as surgical procedures. Because RBRVS updates usually come out in February or March, the contract should specify when the fee schedule will be updated and the manner in which the physicians will be notified of the update. When using RBRVS, the plan should specify the types of patients to which the contract applies. For example, applying a Medicare fee schedule to commercial patients usually results in a significant reduction in revenue.

The contract should also specify which coding system will be accepted, preferably CPT-4. Ideally, physician codes should be accepted at face value. If the physicians' charges cannot be accepted, the contract should specify the process by which the plan can change the codes. Whenever a change is made, the physician should receive notification, with a summary report provided quarterly. Although some room for interpretation of codes will still be available, physicians will usually have valid justification for their coding practices to limit their exposure to claims of fraudulent billing practices.

Hold Harmless Clauses

Hold harmless provisions mean that each party to the contract agrees to hold the other party harmless from its own acts of negligence or other errors and omissions. If the MCO requests a hold harmless clause from the physicians, the physicians should insist on a reciprocal hold harmless. This precaution becomes very important if the MCO is accused of negligence in adopting standards of care or in its case management and denial of services. However, physicians must not rely on a plan's denial of payment as a shield from liability for not providing patients with the care they feel is necessary.

Favored Nation

Favored nation clauses allow the plan to get the same discount off physicians' fees as the physicians offer to other plans. There may be extenuating circumstances that cause physicians to grant special discounts to a hospital, for example, for hospital employees. Physicians should be aware, however, that granting this same discount to other managed care plans could have disastrous results. They should carefully avoid such clauses. If a discount is given, the contract should also specify that it applies only to plan enrollees and may not be assigned or applied to patients who are not specifically enrolled in the contract plan.

Dispute Resolution

When possible, physicians should insist on arbitration to resolve disputes, as it is generally less expensive and can be accomplished in a shorter time. Arbitration should be applied to the entire contract, but particularly to disputes involving fee schedules and utilization review.

Amendments

All amendments to the contract should be written and agreed to by both parties. The contract should contain a detailed procedure for how amendments will be made and the notice needed. Physicians should not sign a contract that allows for unilateral amendment of the contract. Amendments will serve as a reason to review the entire contract, particularly its financial aspects.

Policies and Procedures

Regardless of the discount granted, the plan's policies and procedures will be critical in determining the physician-plan relationship. Therefore, physicians should carefully review them before signing an agreement. If possible, the policies and procedures should be incorporated into any agreement, either by reference (citing revision number or date) or as an attachment. Some important policies and procedures that should be considered are discussed here.

Eligibility

Any agreement should clearly outline to whom the agreement applies. As most MCOs have multiple products, for example, Medicare, Medicaid, and commercial, physicians should make sure that the agreement states to which of these groups, or others, the agreement should apply. This documentation is important when establishing fees, as the average physicians Medicare charge may be as much as 50% greater than the average charge for commercial enrollees. Documentation is also important when dealing with copayments and deductibles. Medicaid plans typically do not have either. If these issues are not specifically addressed, physicians may not be able to collect the additional money directly from commercial or Medicare patients.

Recently, some MCOs have entered into agreements with other plans to have the MCOs' rates tagged onto an existing agreement with the other company. Physicians should make sure that only members enrolled in the named plan are eligible for the fees outlined and that the contract applies only to a specific class of patients (e.g., Medicaid) unless each class is addressed separately.

Preauthorization

The issue of preauthorization has become one of the major problems physicians have when dealing with MCOs. In theory, the concept is meant to discourage inappropriate use of the emergency department. In reality, preauthorization is a confusing and, at times, contentious issue between physicians and MCOs. Emergency departments are mandated to provide medical screening examinations under the federal EMTALA statute. Therefore, emergency department staff must understand that preauthorization is never authorization to treat, but rather authorization to pay for treatment.

The contract should have a clause specifying that preauthorization is not necessary for examination and treatment mandated by federal and/or state law and regulations. This clause will not totally solve the problem, but it is an important first step. An additional clause of the contract that can address this situation is the agreement to a set fee for screening examinations or for patients who present with nonurgent conditions. It is preferable for emergency physicians to work with the plan to refer these patients back to their primary care physicians rather than fight continuously over whether they should present to the emergency department in the first place.

Billing Issues

Many plans require that claims be submitted within a defined period of time, usually 60 days. The longer the time period specified in the contract, the better for the physicians.

If there is a limited period for submission, there should also be a maximum time the plan has to pay claims. Ideally, the time to pay claims should lapse before the end of the submission period. This allows the billing office to review the files and resubmit claims within the allowable period of time. The contract should specify which form is to be used. HCFA-1500 forms usually will be accepted, as this is the standard billing form most physicians use. If the contract specifies another form, it may be a tactic to delay or even deny payment for services rendered.

Physicians should insist on the ability to bill the patient directly if the plan does not pay the claim for any reason. Most plans will attempt to insert language prohibiting physicians from billing their patients. If this restriction is in the contract and the plan does not pay because the claim was not submitted "in time," the physician may have no recourse. Similarly, physicians must have the ability to bill patients directly if the plan denies a claim because there was no preauthorization. Remember: preauthorization

is for payment, not for treatment. If a patient seeks treatment and receives it without preauthorization, the patient should be held responsible for the bill.

Many plan administrators will attempt to change the CPT code submitted by the physician. They usually downcode in order to pay less for the visit. If at all possible, the contract should be worded to prohibit this activity.

Fees

Most plan administrators will attempt to negotiate the lowest possible fees. Physicians must either become proficient in performing the analysis themselves or seek professional assistance in this area. When a plan offers a 20% discount, the issue is discount off what base amount. A 20% discount off a Medicare allowable may, in fact, equal a 40% to 50% discount off a physician's normal fees.

Grievances

Any agreement should have procedures for handling grievances. If at all possible, there should be a two-step grievance procedure. The first step should be an internal procedure and, at a minimum, should be a presentation of the grievance to the plan's medical director. The second step should be an external process for settling disputes that cannot be resolved through the internal grievance procedure. Depending on the state, arbitration is usually preferable to litigation because it is generally quicker and less expensive. Most plans will not readily agree to arbitration because they know that the expense of litigation often prevents physicians from filing a lawsuit.

Utilization Review

In many smaller plans, utilization review is conducted by the medical director, who may or may not have any experience in emergency medicine. The contract should state that any utilization review will be conducted by physicians of the same specialty. Although this provision does not always ensure a favorable review, it is usually a fairer process.

Credentialing

Credentialing of emergency physicians is unique and falls outside the normal procedures of many managed care plans. If the contract is with a group, physicians should insist that the hospital credentialing process is sufficient. If at all possible, any credentialing clause should be removed from the contract in its entirety. Emergency department patients will be seen by the physician on duty regardless of the status of that physician's credentials with the managed care plan. The contract should be focused on payment-related issues instead of physician credentials.

Covered and Excluded Services

Some plans define what is a covered or excluded service. This language should be examined carefully. Most plans are required to provide coverage for emergency services; however, they try to define what constitutes an emergency after the fact. When emergency services are listed, the definition of an emergency must be what a prudent layperson, having average medical knowledge, would consider as an emergency. Many states have already adopted "prudent layperson" definitions of emergency, and the contract should reflect such language.

Medical screening examinations conducted as the result of federal and/or state law should be considered covered services and specified in any contract. When possible, a negotiated fee should be included as part of the fee schedule.

Key Points and Conclusion

There are several key issues that physicians should be aware of when contracting with managed care plans. Although by no means all inclusive, the issues presented in this chapter should be reviewed prior to signing any contract. Physicians should have contracts carefully examined by qualified advisers before signing them.

Chapter 60

Managed Care in Emergency Medicine

Paul K. Bronston, MD, FACMQ, FACEP
Mark E. Reagan, Esq.

"… Anyone who challenges the prevailing orthodoxy finds himself silenced with surprising effectiveness." — George Orwell, in his unpublished preface to *Animal Farm*, 1945.

Managed care is now a reality in emergency departments and hospitals across the United States. But what is it? How will it affect patient care, the practice of emergency medicine, and liability risks? This chapter provides answers to these questions and explanations about the law as it relates to managed care. It also offers practical advice about how to handle the more difficult aspects of emergency medicine in a managed care environment.

Managed Care Defined

Managed care systems manage and coordinate the total health care needs of patients from preventive care to acute care to home health care, and so on. The goal of managed care systems is to provide quality health care in the most efficient and cost-effective manner.[1] To attain these goals, managed care systems typically do the following:

- Enter into contractual agreements with providers, both individuals and organizations, that contain financial incentives to provide quality health care and medically necessary treatment.
- Use a process known as "utilization review," "utilization management," or "resource management" to review proposed or continued treatment for its medical necessity.

- Require patients or providers to receive advance authorization (i.e., approval or certification) before receiving additional treatment.
- Use practice guidelines and criteria to standardize quality and cost-effective behavior by providers.
- Oversee providers' decisions by profiling their practices, issuing report cards to "grade" their performance, and, if necessary, removing them from the system altogether (typically known as "de-listing") because of substandard care provided and inefficient performance.
- Stress preventive care to decrease the need for care in the long run.

If well designed, each of these tools may be used to promote quality, timely access and appropriate delivery of health care in an efficient manner. However, in the current market-driven environment, if managed care systems are inappropriately designed and implemented, they will all too often focus on cost containment at the expense of quality. These cost-driven systems corrupt and create defectively designed managed care systems that serve to deny access to medically necessary care, inevitably produce bad outcomes, and create liability exposure.

The first of these tools and techniques involves the structuring of contractual relationships so that providers, in return for access to large pools of patients, will agree to accept discounted, or "per case," rates. These discounted arrangements typically are used by preferred provider organizations (PPOs), which are networks of contracted providers who have agreed to accept discounted rates, or by independent practice associations (IPAs), associations of physicians practicing in different offices who organize to negotiate with managed care systems to provide medical care for members of the plan.

Another type of "contractual" managed care includes the provider's receipt of monthly capitation payments, typically from health maintenance organizations (HMOs). Generally speaking, there are two types of capitated arrangements. In the first, providers agree to accept a monthly fee per patient in return for providing all specified care and treatment for a defined population without regard for the time, effort, or cost associated with providing such care. In the second, an emergency department may receive a fixed amount of money on a monthly basis in return for seeing all patients belonging to a capitated medical group who present to the department.

For both, there may be an additional agreement in which a certain portion of the monthly capitated fee is withheld and placed into a trust account held by the managed care system (known as a "risk pool"). This amount is then distributed back to the provider if the provider's resource usage (e.g., laboratory, radiology, and other diagnostic procedures; acute hospitalization admission rates; and prescription drug use) is within predetermined target rates. Likewise, providers may receive a bonus, depending on how their performance compares to the target rates.

In addition to these contractual tools and techniques, a quality managed care system focuses on assisting providers in effectively managing the care of their patients. They scrutinize provider treatment plans to ensure not only that care is cost-effective, but also that quality medical care is being provided. In discounted fee-for-service arrangements involving PPOs and IPAs, these activities, known as utilization review or resource management, are performed by reviewers who are employed by the PPO or IPA, or who contract with outside review organizations. In capitated arrangements, utilization management may be performed by reviewers directly affiliated with the HMO, or by designated primary care physicians (PCPs) or other "gatekeepers" within the medical group or IPA that has contracted with the HMO, the medical group's management service organization (MSO), or other similar entity.

Another tool used by managed care systems involves the use of practice guidelines. Credible practice guidelines are based on current medical-scientific information published in the peer-reviewed literature. Designed as a tool to assist physicians in medical decision-making, these guidelines are used by managed care systems to determine the appropriateness of treatment and monitor the provider's medical practices and use of medical resources, a practice known as profiling.

Although managed care has, at times, been able to rein in spiraling health care costs, many question whether patients and the practice of medicine by physicians are properly served in this type of environment. The answers to such questions involve the extent to which managed care systems intrude into the medical decision-making process and result in medical determinations that fall below the standard of care.

Patients can be well served in quality managed care systems through the following:
- Increased coordination of care between PCPs and specialists
- Increased use of preventive care
- Implementation of oversight review systems that help physicians make appropriate care and treatment decisions
- Application of efficient and effective technologies to improve patient management

On the other hand, "corrupt" managed care systems can produce difficulties in the following ways:
- Denying patient access to medically necessary care
- Loss of the traditional physician-patient relationship
- Failing to obtain accurate and timely reimbursement
- Failing to practice medicine within the legally required standard of care

Such systems merely operate to manage cost rather than quality of care.

As managed care expands into new markets serving Medicare, Medicaid, and Worker's Compensation patients, providers will undoubtedly struggle to balance the competing economic and quality interests so prevalent in health care today. Only through effective, credible oversight systems can such a balance, within existing legal requirements, be struck.

Emergency Medical Decision-Making in the Managed Care Environment

"… Uncomfortable truths travel with difficulty." — Primo Levi, in *The Drowned and the Saved*.

Sound emergency medical decision-making in a managed care environment must be based on a solid foundation, which includes the following:

- Well-accepted principles of clinical medical decision-making based on risk-benefit analysis.
- An understanding of how liability will be determined for malpractice and other new legal theories involving bad faith and false claims.
- Knowledge of how managed care systems use managed care tools and techniques, the parlance of managed care and how it relates to access to treatment and the standard of care.
- The appropriate development and use of practice guidelines.
- Principles of documenting the medical necessity of treatment.

Standard of Care

"… The hottest places in hell are reserved for those who, in a time of great moral crisis, maintain their neutrality." — Dante.

As with any profession, health care must have standards to guide practitioners and payers and to create accountability. Without recognized standards in medicine, there will be little uniformity in medical decision-making between and among providers and payers and, as a result, greater opportunity for fraud, manipulation, overutilization of medical resources, and poor medical practice. Sound medical practice demands that there be reasonable and credible benchmarks so that appropriate medical care can be judged. The challenge in establishing a medical standard is that the practice of medicine is not an exact science, and uniform tools for measurement are not always available or applicable. Also, medicine is frequently changing as new developments and technologies are recognized.

Credible medical decision-making must include two elements: the exercise of clinical judgment; and current scientific data published in recognized peer-reviewed literature. The practice of medicine can neither be limited to blind adherence to a predetermined protocol or guideline[2] nor be based exclusively on clinical judgment.

To be reasonable, medical standards must contain both the science (objective) and art (subjective) elements that reflect a minimally acceptable range of care and treatment. A defective benchmark that is accepted and implemented will cause a physician's decision-making to be judged incorrectly, and all oversight systems (utilization review, medical quality management, physician profiling) set up to encourage adherence to this defective benchmark will also be invalid.[3-6]

The recognized benchmark in the medical-legal community is called the standard of care. The standard legal definition of the term standard of care is "that degree of care and skill which is ordinarily employed by the profession generally, under similar conditions and in like surrounding circumstances."[7] Although this term has been a source of much controversy in the medical field, it is the accepted standard by which liability for medical malpractice is determined. It also has been successful in increasing quality and decreasing variability among providers and payers in which neither overutilization nor underutilization of medical resources is accepted. The Institute of Medicine (IOM) and the American College of Medical Quality (ACMQ) define quality as "the degree to which health care systems, services and supplies for individuals and populations, consistent with the current professional standards of care, increase the likelihood for positive health outcomes."[6,8-11]

In the health care industry today, the standard of care is largely being determined and measured by national rather than by local standards. Under a national standard, both providers and managed care systems presumably will be held to more uniform criteria and will no longer be able to justify their actions using local provider or payer practices. Similarly, these standards are clinical in nature and are not defined by physician reviewers or managers not directly involved in direct patient care.

In establishing the standard of care, recognized practice guidelines may be of assistance. However, such guidelines by themselves do not set the standard of care and are not substitutes for the clinical judgment of practitioners. Guidelines are never to be used to tell physicians what to do, but only to assist them in medical decision-making. This principle has been recognized by the courts as well as by the Department of Quality Assurance of the

American Medical Association, the ACMQ, and the Agency for Health Care Policy and Research (AHCPR) of the federal government.[6,12-14]

In sum, the standard of care is the case-specific analytical process that produces a clinical benchmark that reflects the art and science of medicine and holds providers and managed care systems accountable in determining exposure to liability.[7,9] It is defined on a national and clinical basis rather than a local provider community or payer review basis.[15] Because the process of medical decision-making is a combination of objective and subjective elements, practice guidelines alone do not establish the standard of care. However, they may be important in contributing to the national standard.

New Legal Theories

Bad faith and false claims, two legal theories recently applied to managed care systems, could significantly affect the liability exposure of emergency physicians. Bad faith occurs when defective review systems prevent access to timely quality medical care, resulting in the denial of contractually guaranteed health care plan benefits to its members. False claims occur when a provider submits a bill for reimbursement of medical services in which either no care was provided or the care was substandard. The federal government will prosecute providers who submit false claims. The federal government also has recently taken the position that it considers substandard care equal to no care at all.

These two legal theories may result in large financial penalties that can be applied directly against the emergency physician. Traditional medical malpractice insurance does not cover these penalties.

Medical Necessity

Medical necessity is the term payers use to describe whether medical care is appropriate. This terminology is used for medical care that is requested (preauthorization), being provided (concurrent review), or has already been provided to a patient (retrospective review). If a particular form of treatment is determined to be medically necessary and is covered by the patient's health plan or benefit package, the payer must pay for or provide the treatment.[16]

The benchmark used to determine medical necessity is the standard of care. Allowing payers to define medical necessity allows them essentially to define their own standard of care. This is not defensible and leads to poor quality of care and inappropriate medical resource consumption.

Payers must make medical necessity determinations in a manner consistent with the clinical standard of care that reflects both the art and science of medicine.[15] As a result, the payer must ensure the following:

- The decisionmaker conducting the review is qualified to make treatment or coverage decisions by having the experience, education, and training to render clinical judgments.[17]
- The information provided is sufficient to make a determination pursuant to the standard of care.[2,17]
- The objective elements used to assist in determining medical necessity, that is, the practice guidelines, are supported by sound, objective science.[6]
- The ultimate determination falls within the clinical standard of care practiced in the national community of medicine.[2-4,6,17,18]

Payers may use nurse reviewers to approve treatments, but they may not deny treatment requests.[6,18] Medical review determinations that deny or limit proposed treatment plans must reflect the medical decisions of "peers," that is, other physicians, who adhere to the clinical standard of care.

There are only three types of medical necessity determinations that a physician reviewer can make:

- The reviewer has enough information based on the applicable standard of care to certify medical necessity.
- The reviewer has enough information based on the applicable standard of care not to certify medical necessity.
- The reviewer does not have enough information to be able to make a determination of medical necessity based on the applicable standard of care.

A managed care system cannot make a claim that a medical service is not medically necessary based on lack of information. Instead, it must seek to obtain such information.[2,6,17,18]

Practice Guidelines

"… Logic is the Beginning of Wisdom, Not the End." — Spock, in *Star Trek VI*.

For the purpose of this discussion, the term "practice guidelines" encompasses practice guidelines (also known as practice parameters), clinical pathways, and criteria. Some health care professionals believe that there are differences among them, but the underlying principles concerning their development, application, and use are the same.

Practice guidelines represent a synthesis of current scientific, peer-reviewed literature presented in a user-friendly format, such as an outline or decision-making trees. To be legitimate as a tool to enhance medical decision-making, practice guidelines must be developed appropriately, applied correctly, and used by physicians who have the clinical expertise, training, and experience to incorporate them in clinical decision-making consistent with the standard of care.[6,12,13]

Appropriate Development. There are national standards for the appropriate development of practice guidelines established by the American Medical Association (AMA), the ACMQ, and the AHCPR.[6,12] These standards include the use of appropriate methodology and panels of objective, board-certified, clinically practicing medical experts and are updated annually. Practice guidelines must be based on sound scientific research findings and professional literature and must reflect the standard of care practiced in the national clinical community of medicine.

There have been instances in which an organization has used medical experts in the development of practice guidelines only to have these experts' work inappropriately edited by a medical director or an administrator in the final development stage. As a result, the ACMQ requires that physicians who develop practice guidelines sign their names and date the particular guideline as evidence of their participation and support for the final version.

Many health care entities would prefer to keep their practice guidelines confidential. To promote the credibility of these guidelines, a number of organizations, such as the American Accreditation Health Care Commission (AAHCC) (formerly the Utilization Review Accreditation Commission [URAC]), require that guidelines be made public for peer review. Similarly, if such guidelines are used to deny requested care, a number of states as well as the AAHCC and the ACMQ mandate that they be provided on request.

Applied Correctly. If practice guidelines are to be useful in standard of care clinical decision-making, in either direct patient care or in reviewing a physician's performance, they must be used appropriately. Practice guidelines do not equal the standard of care. It is inappropriate for any provider or payer to base any medical decision, whether providing direct clinical patient care or reviewing the necessity of such care (for certification of treatment, reimbursement, or profiling a physician), exclusively on a guideline.[2,6,17-20]

In the clinical setting, practice guidelines should be looked on as a tool that can help a physician in standard of care medical decision-making. In the peer review setting, they should be looked at as a screening tool that may help physician reviewers identify substandard practice. When a physician falls outside a norm in the screening process, this does not necessarily mean that the physician has violated any standard of care. In fact, if physicians are adhering to the standard of care, they will be deviating from practice guidelines at times simply because it is impossible for any practice guideline to be relevant for all clinical situations and patients. Therefore, physician profiling cannot be performed based on practice guidelines. It must be performed on a case-by-case basis based on the standard of care and conducted by clinical peers.

Use by Appropriate Medical Personnel. Physician reviewers or gatekeepers must adhere to the same analytical process in determining the clinical standard of care in medical decision-making as those who actually care for patients. A physician who is reviewing the care of another physician must have the clinical background, based on education, training, and experience, to formulate standard of care medical benchmarks that would be appropriate for a particular patient given the information the physician had at the time of treatment.[2,3,6,17,18]

For example, it would be inappropriate to have a dermatologist review a cardiac bypass case. The dermatologist does not have the clinical judgment required to formulate standard of care medical decisions and render a medical review decision because the clinical situation is outside a dermatologist's clinical expertise.

Documentation

Documentation is essential to the continuous quality improvement (CQI) process and ensures communication among medical personnel. Appropriate documentation of the pertinent facts and outcomes of a case demonstrates the analytical assessment process involved in medical decision-making. Documentation also justifies a physician's ordering of tests, admissions, and level of care to hospitals in addition to determining patient stability for the purpose of transfer.

Third-party payers will base their reimbursement and profiling of physicians on the detailed and appropriate recording of medical information in the chart.[6] Hence, documentation is essential to demonstrate to managed care organizations that emergency physicians are practicing efficient, cost-effective, quality medical care. Documentation of medical necessity based on the standard of care is one of the keys to the successful practice of emergency medicine in a managed care environment.

The Medical-Legal Perspective

"... The fact that you and your unlamented brother killed from institutional and patriotic ambush doesn't mean you're killers — it only means you're cowards." — Nikko Hel (Nicholai Alexandrovich) from *Shibumi*.

The principal risk management issue for emergency physicians in a managed care environment is to what degree the various tools and techniques used by managed care systems affect medical decision-making. Because of this, emergency physicians must be keenly aware of the legal requirements surrounding the medical decision-making process.

Historical Perspective

Managed care became an integral part of the health care system as a result of spiraling costs and the desire by employers to control such costs. To meet these goals, managed care systems ultimately received approval from the courts, although resisted by providers, not only to review the medical necessity of treatment retrospectively, but also to do so prospectively and concurrently, thereby influencing access to treatment.

Once managed care tools began to be used in the health care marketplace, the economic incentives for these plans to deny payment or certification for, and therefore access to, care began to affect the medical decisions made by practitioners. To deal with these incentives, courts began applying the legal duties required to be met by health professionals and institutions, that is, the "standard of care," to payers and all those individuals and entities participating in managed care. Thus, regardless of whether a decision is made by a treating physician or by a reviewer performing utilization review or credentialing, the recognized principle is the same: the determination must meet the clinical standard of care.

Medical Malpractice Versus Bad Faith

When the traditional legal principles of medical decision-making were extended to encompass managed care systems, the legal liability exposure of medical decision-making by corrupted managed care review systems increased dramatically. Although the traditional medical malpractice case focused merely on whether the provision of care (or lack of care) was negligent, the principle of bad faith meant that claims focused on defective review systems that prevented timely access to quality medical care.

Cost-savings components of managed care systems were designed to eliminate excess financial risk for health insurers and HMOs. The claims and remedies traditionally available against insurance companies for insurance bad faith have also been applied to managed care. Bad faith claims against managed care systems (including HMOs) and insurance companies are based on the principle that the system/insurer unreasonably withheld medical benefits based on faulty medical review decision-making that was not based on the standard of care.

Bad faith will be found when managed care systems unreasonably withhold contractually guaranteed medical benefits by a faulty review decision that results from one or more of the following:

- Failure to adhere to the clinical standard of care
- A poorly qualified reviewer
- Blind adherence to practice guidelines without the exercise of clinical judgment
- Financial incentives to deny necessary care
- Arbitrary or capricious decision-making

As a result, in addition to an award of the contractual benefits that were withheld, the successful plaintiff may also recover monetary damages for pain and suffering and mental distress. If a jury determines that defendants acted with the intent to harm a patient or without concern for the patient's well-being or rights (referred to as "conscious disregard"), these defendants can be assessed punitive damages. Punitive awards can reach the multimillion-dollar level and are not covered by insurance in most states. Most states do not allow managed care systems or providers, including emergency physicians, to be indemnified (i.e., shielded against liability by another person or entity who agrees to be responsible) for such awards.

Under current law, all participants in the health care delivery system who use managed care tools and techniques are exposed to potential liability for bad faith. Both providers and reviewers need to be keenly aware of these risks as well as their responsibilities when working within such systems.

Representative Case Law

"... A lawyer's either a social engineer or a parasite on society." — Charles Hamilton Houston, an African-American attorney born in 1895, who pioneered the idea of using the Constitution to promote racial justice. Attended Harvard Law School, doctorate in 1923, dean of Howard Law School, brilliant trial lawyer and special lawyer to NAACP.

Although the decisions of state courts are not necessarily binding in other states, they are likely indicators of what other courts would do. The following cases serve as a foundation for appropriate standards of medical review (Appendix 2). If managed care systems are found to have altered or influenced the decision-making process of emergency physicians such that the standard of care is not adhered to and a bad outcome results, the physician is exposed to traditional malpractice. However, if the physician is seen by the court as acting as part of or participating in the managed care system, that physician could also be exposed to bad faith liability. This liability (with accompanying exposure to largely uninsurable awards of punitive damages) is potentially far beyond that contemplated in a garden-variety medical malpractice action.

Economic incentives to promote efficient delivery of care should not result in withholding medically necessary care. Many managed care plans have effective review systems that promote quality medical care, not just cost-effective care. In a managed care environment, this distinction is of critical importance to the emergency physician.

Hughes v Blue Cross of Northern California.[3] Defendant Blue Cross's utilization management program retrospectively denied the Hughes family's claim for payment for psychiatric services provided to their troubled son associated with his suicidal tendencies. The Hughes family claimed that Blue Cross had caused them to lose $16,500 in contractual benefits and unspecified emotional distress. They also sought an award of punitive damages based on Blue Cross's alleged bad faith. Blue Cross argued that the medical care was not wrongfully denied, and the case proceeded to trial.

The evidence presented at trial demonstrated that the decision to deny the claim was made by a Blue Cross physician reviewer, who devoted on average approximately eight minutes to the review of every claim and did not have the requisite qualifications to make standard of care determinations regarding the presence or absence of medical necessity for the claim. The jury awarded the plaintiffs $1.2 million in damages, of which approximately $800,000 was awarded in punitive damages. Blue Cross appealed. The California Court of Appeals upheld the jury's verdict. The court stated that the retrospective decision-making by the Blue Cross physician reviewer failed to meet the clinical standard of care as it was practiced in the community.

By recognizing that even retrospective decision-making will be judged by the same clinical standards as those governing medical treatment, the *Hughes* decision is particularly significant. The court's decision also demonstrates that any managed care system and those who practice within it and make decisions that significantly deviate from the clinical standard of care may be exposed to significant liability. In addition, the court stated that health insurance companies and managed care systems are responsible for obtaining all necessary medical information before they are able to deny medical necessity. Denials based on lack of information are not defensible.

Wickline v State of California.[4] Medi-Cal (California's Medicaid system) beneficiary Lois Wickline claimed that she suffered damages from the loss of her leg as a result of being denied medical services by a utilization review conducted by Medi-Cal. The review determined that her continued stay in the hospital was no longer medically necessary. She prevailed at the trial court level.

The California Court of Appeals reversed the trial court judgment on the grounds that the Medi-Cal review did not adversely affect her treatment, because her attending physician also agreed that the discharge was medically appropriate. However, the court stated that cost-containment programs can result in liability if they are defectively structured or implemented. Moreover, it found that cost-containment review systems cannot operate to corrupt the judgment of treating physicians and that medical review must conform to the standard of care.

Wilson v Blue Cross of Southern California.[5] The parents of decedent Howard Wilson, a Blue Cross insured, sought damages against two Blue

Cross plans and a utilization review organization that was hired to review Mr.Wilson's psychiatric hospitalization stay concurrently. The plaintiffs claimed that Mr.Wilson's discharge from the psychiatric hospital resulted in his suicide and was the result of a defective utilization review that was both unauthorized and involved unqualified physician reviewers who made decisions outside the standard of care. The plaintiffs also alleged that the review process fell below the standard of care in medical decision-making as practiced in the clinical community.

The trial court dismissed the case, stating that the failure of Mr. Wilson's attending physician to appeal the original review decision barred this action. The court of appeals reversed the decision, stating that, when a review decision is a substantial factor in a discharge that is below the standard of care and produces harm, the utilization review organization and the insurers can still be held liable for the discharge even if the appeal mechanism was not accessed.

After the appellate court decision, the case went to trial. During trial, the utilization review company settled for a confidential amount. The jury ultimately found that one of the Blue Cross plans had breached Mr. Wilson's insurance contract as a result of the utilization review performed by its agent. It also held that the review was performed in bad faith. However, it found that the Blue Cross plan did not intend to harm Mr. Wilson nor did it consciously disregard his rights. As a result, punitive damages were not awarded because the jury accepted Blue Cross's claim that it was not allegedly aware of the utilization review company's practices at the time of the review.

Fox v Health Net.[21] The family of Nelene Fox, a patient with advanced breast cancer, brought a contract and bad faith action against HMO Health Net based on the HMO's denial of a preauthorization request for high-dose chemotherapy with an autologous bone marrow transplant. After the denial, Mrs. Fox raised the funds for the procedure on her own after six months, ultimately had the procedure, and subsequently succumbed to cancer.

At trial, the plaintiffs presented evidence that the HMO had commissioned a study that concluded that this form of treatment was efficacious and not experimental. In addition, the plaintiffs presented evidence that the HMO had approved a similar procedure for one of its own employees who had a similar condition. Based on this evidence, the plaintiffs argued that Health Net's medical necessity determination was arbitrary and capricious.

The plaintiffs also submitted evidence that the HMO's medical director, who had no clinical expertise in breast cancer and was acting in the role of physician gatekeeper, was provided financial incentives to deny prior preauthorizations and had engaged in attempting to pressure physicians not to seek preauthorizations for expensive procedures. The plaintiffs also presented evidence that the medical director had attempted to do so in Mrs. Fox's case.

At trial, the jury found that Health Net had breached its health care service contract with Mrs. Fox and had committed bad faith in denying her preauthorization request by making a defective medical necessity review determination. It awarded the plaintiffs $2 million in compensatory damages based on the breach of contract and emotional distress and $87 million in punitive damages. The case was subsequently settled for a confidential amount prior to appeal.

Lowry v Henry Mayo Newhall Memorial Hospital.[2] The plaintiffs brought a wrongful death and malpractice action against an emergency physician who unsuccessfully attempted to resuscitate an inpatient after she sustained a cardiac arrest. The plaintiffs alleged that the defendant was negligent because his patient care and treatment deviated from the American Heart Association's ACLS guidelines. In upholding the trial court's judgment for the defendant, the court of appeals indicated that the provider's failure to adhere to ACLS guidelines did not *per se* establish liability in the case. Rather, it stated that the guideline could be deviated from without liability.

Although not a managed care case, this case illustrates that, although practice guidelines may be tools to enhance medical decision-making, they do not set the standard of care. Further, the particular clinical facts and the physician's clinical judgment applied from case to case will prevail.

Muse v Charter Hospital of Winston-Salem, Inc.[22] The parents of Joseph Muse, a psychiatric inpatient, brought an action against Charter Hospital for wrongful death and interfering with the decedent's relationship with his physician based on his discharge from the hospital after his insurance benefits expired, after which he committed suicide. The plaintiffs alleged that the hospital had a policy and practice of discharging patients when their insurance benefits expired regardless of their medical and psychiatric condition. The parents included in the lawsuit their son's physician who settled immediately.

At trial, the plaintiffs presented evidence that, when their son's benefits expired, his physician immediately planned for his discharge and ultimately placed him in a county outpatient mental health program. Mr. Muse never attended the outpatient program. The plaintiffs also presented evidence from hospital staff members that it was hospital policy to instruct physicians to discharge patients based on their inability to pay regardless of their medical condition.

The jury found the hospital liable for wrongful death and interfering with the decedent's relationship with his physician. It awarded $1 million in compensatory damages and $2 million in punitive damages against the hospital. It awarded $4 million in additional punitive damages against the hospital's parent corporation.

Hand v Tavera.[23] Mr. and Mrs. Hand brought a medical malpractice case against Dr. Tavera, a physician who acted as an on-call gatekeeper for Humana Health Plan. Dr. Tavera denied an emergency physician's request to admit Mr. Hand to the hospital, and the patient subsequently suffered a stroke. Reversing the trial court's dismissal of the action, the Texas Court of Appeals found that the contractual relationship between Dr. Tavera and Humana established a physician-patient relationship between Mr. Hand and the physician. As a result, the Hands could pursue a medical malpractice case against Dr. Tavera.

In finding the existence of a physician-patient relationship of gatekeepers, the appellate court held that: ". . . when the health-care plan's insured shows up at a participating hospital emergency room, and the plan's doctor on call is consulted about treatment or admission, there is a physician-patient relationship between the doctor and the insured."

Utilization Review and Preauthorization

Utilization Review

"... Sometimes the public good must outweigh private gain." — Teddy Roosevelt.

Utilization review/management is an oversight system used to eliminate overutilization. Sometimes utilization review is carried out without concern for potential liability exposure or its effect on medical quality. Because utilization review inevitably affects both quality and risk

management, this system must foster and ensure quality.[24]

Utilization review and management of emergency department patients typically begins at the time preauthorization is sought and continues until the patient is either admitted or transferred to another hospital or discharged. Such review consists of determinations of medical necessity for care, treatment rendered in the emergency department, and any recommendations for additional testing or admission to the hospital or stability of the patient to be transferred.

The key in setting up an appropriate utilization management program in an emergency department is to link it to medical quality and risk management, with all decisions based on the standard of care. Any practice guidelines used in medical decision-making must be developed and applied appropriately. Established guidelines are available through the AMA's Directory of Practice Parameters and DATTA Program, as well as from AHCPR.

The AAHCC, the National Committee For Quality Assurance (NCQA), and the Health Care Financing Administration (HCFA) have established standards regarding the review process. These certifying bodies have the authority to decertify organizations that do not follow minimum requirements of oversight review. A number of states have also adopted review standards. All emergency departments should obtain these review standards annually to assess whether their review activities comply.

These organizations will review and investigate complaints and take appropriate action. Many states do not allow utilization review firms to operate without AAHCC certification. Likewise, several states will not license HMOs without NCQA certification. Increasing numbers of employers will not do business with managed care systems that do not have such certifications.

Preauthorization

Increasingly, HMOs are requiring hospitals to obtain preauthorization before administering emergency treatment. Many HMOs have written contracts with their gatekeepers or PCPs in which they are financially responsible for the emergency department workup if the patient does not have a true emergency. This obviously creates undue financial pressures on gatekeepers to deny medically necessary emergency department workups and treatment. Regardless of the nature of such agreements, federal law mandates that an appropriate medical screening examination cannot be delayed for the purpose of determining payer status. The American College of Emergency Physicians (ACEP) policy suggests that an emergency physician should perform the screening examinations. In the event a physician is not physically present in the emergency department 24 hours a day, the examination may be performed by properly trained ancillary personnel according to written policies and procedures.[25]

If the emergency physician and the gatekeeper disagree as to the necessity of treatment, the emergency physician must always adhere to the standard of care. The emergency physician must also document the conversation with the gatekeeper about why the patient meets medical necessity based on the applicable standard of care for examination and then provide workup and treatment based on the initial patient complaint and not what the ultimate diagnosis or disposition may be.

Physicians must appropriately communicate and document the "medical necessity based on the standard of care" regarding treatment decisions. The ability to communicate using managed care terminology and link this to standard of care medical decision-making is essential. It is the key to obtaining certification for services, obtaining appropriate reimbursement, and preventing negative profiling of emergency physicians. Emergency physicians must insist that only qualified medical personnel, such as clinically matched physician advisers, make review determinations concerning their patients. Nonphysicians or unqualified physician gatekeepers should not deny medical necessity requests made by emergency physicians.[3,18]

Financial Incentives That Influence Medical Decision-Making

The most prevalent contractual tools used by managed care systems include discounted fee-for-service and *per diem* rates, capitation, risk-pooling, and bonus incentive programs. Whether these programs can be structured and implemented in a manner that does not compromise quality patient care is controversial. A poorly designed or implemented program that is not balanced by systems that promote quality of care will corrupt the medical decision-making and negatively affect patient care, thus increasing liability risk to providers.

Discounted Fee-for-Service and Per Diem Rates

The most common managed care arrangements in emergency medicine are those that either provide for discounted fee-for-service reimbursement or establish a "per-visit" flat fee. These arrangements lower reimbursement per patient but are designed to make up for it with higher patient volume. Because these arrangements do not create the same pressures to deny access to medically necessary care, they are probably the safest from a liability perspective.

Discounted fee-for-service contracts will be financially viable only if sufficient volume is generated, so emergency physicians should have clear expectations as to the anticipated patient volume. Providers also should have a good idea what volume to expect when negotiating a per-visit fee agreement. Global per-visit fees, which may consist of both hospital and provider reimbursement can be a disincentive for physicians to provide all medically necessary care and treatment because the same fee will be paid regardless of the actual utilization. However, as with other forms of contractual managed care, the practitioner should disregard the financial aspects of these contracts and ensure that the medical services meet the clinical standard of care.

Capitation and Risk-Pooling

Capitation is an agreement by a provider to accept a certain fixed amount per patient per month without regard to utilization of medical resources or how often the patient receives treatment. In return for these prepaid amounts, the provider is required to provide covered services to those patients.

Some portion of capitated payments may be initially withheld and distributed later if the provider complies with quotas for the costs of workup and treatment. The funds that are withheld are often placed in a "risk pool." Risk pools typically focus on use of resources related to overall cost of care and treatment and the costs associated with acute hospitalization, tests, procedures, and prescription drugs. After a specified period of time, the provider's history of spending on tests, procedures, and treatment is compared against target spending limits. Based on how the provider did compared to target costs, the provider may receive a distribution from the funds placed in the risk pool.

The use of capitation and risk pools creates a

powerful incentive to use resources efficiently in the care and treatment of patients. On the other hand, they may create undue pressure to underutilize resources for financial reasons and thereby compromise the standard of care. Providers must resist yielding to this economic pressure and continue to make medical decisions within the standard of care.

There are several ways in which providers can alleviate some of the financial pressures that can increase exposure to liability. The first key component is understanding and applying sound business judgment in the analysis of the financial impact of such agreements. For example, before entering into a contractual arrangement, the provider must know whether the reimbursement formula is realistic given the demographics of the covered patients and the associated revenue.

Second, the purchase of "stop loss" insurance, which sets a cap on the financial risk of providing care and treatment in return for capitated rates, can provide a buffer against undue economic pressure. This type of coverage should be available through the managed care system or purchased independently.

Third, extending the time frames by which risk pools are to be calculated and grouping multiple practitioners within risk pools may foster a team spirit about efficiency without putting too much economic pressure on any one physician-patient encounter in the hospital.

Bonus Incentive Programs

A managed care organization may also create a bonus incentive program to contracted emergency providers and reviewers and gatekeepers based on specified criteria. Under these programs, as with capitation and risk-pooling, providers, reviewers, and gatekeepers are rewarded with additional compensation for meeting certain target utilization rates. Incentive programs that focus exclusively on resource use may place even greater economic pressure on providers, reviewers, and gatekeepers and have the potential to corrupt the medical decision-making process.

To reduce some of this economic pressure, some managed care organizations build in customer satisfaction, rudimentary outcomes information, and administrative compliance as additional criteria for awarding bonus incentives. As the collection and processing of health information become more sophisticated and

outcomes measurement possibly more predictable, the ultimate goal is to move bonus incentive programs away from resource use and toward quality indicators. For the time being, however, resource use seems to be the predominant factor. Regardless, emergency physicians should not make medical decisions based on the financial ramifications of incentive programs. As always, medical decisions must be based on the standard of care. Emergency physicians should avoid participating in these bonus programs.

Other Contractual Issues

The terms of the managed care arrangements entered into by emergency medicine providers have never been so important from a risk management perspective. These contracts will, among other things, determine the following:

- How patients will be able to gain access to covered care.
- Whether a provider can deliver services not covered by the HMO by billing the patient directly.
- The scope of contractual rights and responsibilities when managed care systems declare bankruptcy or go out of business.
- Who bears the responsibility for costs resulting from disputes between payers.

Regulating Utilization

Most managed care agreements require providers to comply with the managed care system's utilization review program. However, not all agreements make utilization review part of the contract. Instead, some merely incorporate these materials by reference. A few agreements state that the utilization review program can be changed by the managed care system without agreement from the provider. Before signing any managed care agreement, providers must be able to review and understand the utilization review program and ensure that it can be amended only by mutual agreement.

At a minimum, the provider must understand how to obtain authorizations for treatment or reimbursement for care by gatekeepers and how to appeal denials. The program should provide for immediate appeal and ensure that the appeal reviewer is from the appropriate medical specialty and was not involved in the initial review. Providers should consider not signing a managed care agreement unless it provides for these minimal protections.

Direct Billing for Noncovered Charges

Some managed care contracts prohibit providers from offering to managed care patients services that are not covered and, with the exception of collection of copayments, from billing patients directly for such services. Such contractual provisions put physicians in a very difficult position. For example, when a procedure or test is medically necessary and not a covered benefit of the health plan, the physician will not be able to provide it and collect for the service. To overcome this dilemma, providers should ensure that their managed care contracts allow billing for medically necessary services that are not covered by the HMO. Also, there should be a system in place to resolve any billing disputes among the managed care organization, provider, and patient.

Managed Care Bankruptcy, Patient Abandonment, and Unpaid Bills

Many managed care contracts have provisions that, in the event of contract termination, the responsibilities of the managed care system and the provider will continue for some limited period of time. This provision exists so that patient care will not be disrupted while appropriate arrangements are being made for the payer and alternative providers to assume responsibility. These provisions protect providers by allowing them to continue to be reimbursed and protect patients by preventing abandonment.

Unfortunately, these provisions often do not cover situations where the managed care system becomes insolvent and can no longer pay its bills. In this circumstance, the provider has a responsibility not to abandon patients even when reimbursement is unavailable. The best protection against this situation is for providers to scrutinize the fiscal health of the managed care systems with which they do business. This is difficult to do. At a minimum, providers should ensure that the contract between payer and patient and between payer and provider allows direct billing. A provider in this situation should continue to provide medically necessary care to the patient while looking for alternative health resources for the patient. In the event of bankruptcy, the provider will have to look to the bankruptcy trustee for reimbursement.

Even if the contract with the HMO permits direct billing, the provider must raise the issue with patients concerning direct reimbursement. However, the emergency medicine provider must always meet the requirements of the Emergency Medical Treatment and Active Labor Act (EMTALA) and never abandon a patient who has no alternative means of care.

Claims Disputes

Inevitably, at some point during the course of a contractual arrangement with a managed care system, a provider will have a dispute over the reimbursement of claims. The costs associated with such disputes can be significant. As a result, providers should seek to include in managed care contracts provisions that require the system to reimburse them for the costs associated with seeking claims payment when they are successful in their efforts. Not only does such a provision offer a way to recover such costs, it also motivates the managed care system to be more objective in denying claims.

Present and Future Trends

Gag Clauses

Some managed care contracts include so-called "gag" clauses that regulate the content of conversations between the provider and the patient. Some forbid provider criticism of the managed care organization. Some direct the provider not to discuss aspects of coverage under the patient's benefit plan. Others seek to prohibit discussion of medical options that are not covered under the terms of the patient's benefit plan. Several states have passed laws forbidding the use of gag clauses that limit discussion of pertinent medical considerations between the physician and patient. In other states, providers have brought legal action to contest these contractual provisions.

Regardless of the existence of a state law forbidding gag causes, the physician should never limit discussion with a patient based on a contractual agreement with a managed care organization. Even in states where there is not an "anti-gag clause," contractual provisions that interfere with the physician-patient relationship are not enforceable.[26]

No physician should sign a contract that contains any contractual provision that seeks to inhibit speech between the provider and patient to dictate medical decisions below the standard of care. If a practitioner complies with a gag clause and fails to inform a patient of a risk or potential course of treatment, the practitioner increases the potential for exposure to malpractice and bad faith liability.

Telephone Advice and Telephone Triage

"… I only did enough to assuage my conscience, but not enough to rock the boat." — Christian Bernard, South African heart surgeon, commenting on his behavior toward his government's policy on apartheid.

In the present environment, payers are concerned about patients using emergency departments inappropriately or using health care facilities that they have not contracted with for discounted rates. As a result, there are marketplace pressures to direct patients away from emergency departments and toward contracted health care facilities, such as clinics, urgent care centers, or physician offices.

One of the ways payers attempt to redirect patients is through telephone triage. There are different names for these services — "help line," "triage line," "advice line" — but they all represent an attempt to have health care personnel make a medical decision over the telephone and direct patients to certain health care centers.

On the surface, this type of system may not appear to compromise care. For example, it may help limit overutilization. It may reassure a panicky patient that he is in no immediate danger. However, telephone advice is considered to be a medical decision and will be measured against the standard of care. Even a so-called telephone triage decision is still considered a medical decision that entails an assessment and diagnosis.[23,27,28] Often, a patient will speak either to a nonphysician who uses a guideline to make medical decisions or a physician who does not know the patient and who may not be qualified to deal with the patient's medical problems. Sometimes, patients do not give accurate information to the health care provider on the other end of the telephone.

The biggest problem with telephone triage, however, is that the provider cannot perform a physical examination over the telephone and cannot determine whether the patient has a legitimate medical emergency. ACEP and a number of states now define a medical emergency as a medical condition of recent onset and severity that would lead a prudent layperson, possessing an average knowledge of medicine and health, to believe that urgent and/or unscheduled medical care is required.[29] As a result of all of these deficiencies, the provider lacks essential information needed to perform appropriate standard of care medical decision-making.

Emergency physicians should resist the temptation to be involved with telephone triage systems that focus on limiting access to medically necessary services. They are not medically ethical and cannot adhere to the standard of care of appropriate medical decision-making. Participation in these types of systems exposes physicians to significant liability in the area of medical malpractice and bad faith, including punitive damages, if patients are denied medically necessary care.[29]

Paramedic Triage

Another trend is paramedic triage. Here, too, the goal is laudable: direct the patient to the appropriate contracted health care facility. However, these systems, if contracted between payers and ambulance services or emergency department base stations, may be based on defective criteria or financial incentives to the providers to make diagnoses and prescribe treatment that is below the applicable standard of care. This includes triage decisions to direct patients to contracted facilities rather than to the nearest emergency department according to the standard of care. Emergency physicians, in their positions of leadership in EMS systems, should work to stop these practices and continue to exert their control and medical direction.

Medicaid, Medicare, and Worker's Compensation

As the advent of managed care has generally decreased the rate of growth in health care spending in the private group health sector, the tools and techniques are increasingly being used in other areas of the health care system. In Medicaid, Medicare, and Worker's Compensation, there has been a strong drive to direct patients into managed care systems. This trend will continue, at least in the short term. Each of these aspects of the health care system is unique, and the introduction of managed care may have additional consequences for patients.

Medicaid. Medicaid populations are increasingly being moved into managed care systems. Similarly, managed care organizations are increasingly competing for capitated Medicaid contracts. As in the private commercial market, managed care organizations, largely HMOs, contract with individual providers, PPOs, and IPAs to serve these patient populations.

Providers participating in Medicaid managed care should keep in mind a number of important considerations. First, the level of service made available to a Medicaid beneficiary may not differ from that offered to other patients in the managed care plan. The standard of care is the same for all patients regardless of their source of payment.

Second, managed care patients are often confused about the terms of coverage and use emergency services when not medically necessary. This will be the case even more with Medicaid patients. As a result, there is a greater potential for payment denials by Medicaid managed care plans. Medicaid patients may need to be educated about how managed care will work for them. Emergency departments may have to provide written information to these patients regarding the appropriate use of emergency medical resources (Appendix 3).

Third, most patients would not be able to pay for significant health care expenses without insurance. This is particularly the case with Medicaid beneficiaries. If preauthorizations for medically necessary care are denied, these patients may become discouraged and confused about the appropriate use of emergency care. They may believe that the HMO's initial denial will ultimately result in nonpayment for medical treatment. Through appropriate patient and physician education in the appeals process and detailed documentation of the medical necessity of emergency department visits based on the standard of care, this potentially difficult scenario can be prevented.

Fourth, Medicaid beneficiaries historically have not complied with managed care requirements, such as seeing or calling their PCPs before seeking treatment in the emergency department. Emergency physicians may find that patients enrolled in one Medicaid managed care plan come to the emergency department of a hospital not participating in that plan as an alternative to primary care. Regardless of the patients' insurance status, under EMTALA, the emergency physician still has a responsibility to assess and stabilize patients before discharging them from the emergency department. In fact, an increasing number of states require managed care plans to pay for medically necessary emergency services based on the patient's complaint as mandated by EMTALA, regardless of whether the facility has a contract with the managed care system.

Fifth, there has been at least one instance in which the U.S. Attorney has sought to apply federal criminal false claims charges against a provider alleged to have given substandard care.[30] This law prohibits the submission of bills for medical services that were not actually provided to Medicare or Medicaid patients. The criminal penalties associated with false claims action are severe, including treble damages for funds wrongfully paid, civil penalties from $5,000 to $10,000 for each false claim (bill) submitted, attorneys' fees, and the provider's and HMO's expulsion from the Medicaid and Medicare programs. Under the false claims statute, whistle-blowers may confidentially report a false claim to the Department of Justice and share in up to one third of all monies recovered. Any whistle-blower who is retaliated against is entitled to double back pay, interest, attorneys' fees, general and punitive damages, and reinstatement.

One potential application of this theory to emergency medicine practice is when an HMO instructs an emergency physician to transfer a Medicare or Medicaid HMO patient inappropriately, perform an incomplete examination or treatment, or in some other way provide substandard care. Any attempt by the HMO or provider to receive reimbursement from the federal government for this type of care could be determined to be a false claim. Liability insurance policies typically do not provide coverage for this type of criminal wrongdoing.

Medicare. As Medicare moves toward managed care, its predominantly elderly patient population will need additional direction and reassurance to learn how to work through the system. Also, Medicare managed care providers will need a thorough understanding of geriatrics and the process of aging.

With respect to medical necessity denials and appeals, Medicare managed care plans, particularly HMOs, and their contracted providers will be subject to different rules compared to individual and group health plans. For example, an appeal of a negative medical necessity determination by a Medicare HMO will be decided ultimately by a federal administrative law judge. HCFA is in the process of drafting regulations for the appeals process.

The rules are also different with respect to financial disincentives to provide care and treatment. Recently, HCFA published regulations concerning the financial risk that providers, such as emergency physicians, may assume by contracting with managed care plans, for example, to provide care and treatment to Medicare beneficiaries. These regulations require, among other things, that providers obtain "stop loss" protection whenever a physician or group is at "substantial financial risk."[31] This requirement is designed to alleviate the financial pressure for physicians who contract with managed care systems to provide care and treatment to Medicare patients.

At the time HCFA published these regulations, it was facing a national class action lawsuit based on its alleged failure to police Medicare HMOs. In that case, *Grijalva v Shalala*,[32] a federal district court judge issued an injunction against HCFA, requiring it to force Medicare HMOs to exceed federally mandated criteria with respect to appeals of denied authorizations. Medicare HMOs now must explain to Medicare enrollees the reasons for denials and how to appeal effectively, and expedite review of the decision on appeal if requested.

The practical effect of this ruling is to allow the enrollee to remain hospitalized at least until the expedited review process is completed. As such, this decision allows emergency departments to appeal adverse medical necessity determinations that affect Medicare HMO enrollees.

In the wake of the *Grijalva* decision, HCFA is rewriting regulations to expedite appeals for urgently needed care and to require HMOs to give the federal government more information about the number and kinds of grievances it receives. The new rules may be announced sometime in late 1997 or 1998.[33]

In late 1996, the 9th Circuit Court of Appeals held that an HMO and an MSO could be liable for the wrongful death of a Medicare enrollee. In that case, *Ardary v Aetna Health Plans*,[34] the HMO and MSO unsuccessfully argued that the exclusive remedies of the Medicare Act foreclosed the ability of the plaintiffs to bring a wrongful death action. Although *Ardary* is the only current appellate case to address this principle, it is particularly significant for the conclusion. That is, regardless of whether the enrollee is a Medicare participant, the HMO and its agents are still accountable for the outcome of defective and substandard medical decision-making.

Based on these developments, it is fair to assume that in the future managed care organizations and their providers participating in Medicare managed care will continue to be subject to additional requirements not present with group or individually purchased health plans. As in the Medicaid program, providers and HMOs in Medicare managed care programs may be exposed to false claims actions for providing substandard care if they withhold medically necessary care and treatment.

Worker's Compensation. To integrate Worker's Compensation into the managed care environment and exercise more control over worker health care, providers must understand the following:

- Occupational medicine
- How employers and Worker's Compensation insurers make medical decisions
- Appeals mechanisms to resolve disputes
- State reporting requirements
- Disability criteria
- Modified work issues
- Psychological ramifications of workplace injuries, symptom exaggeration, and incentives regarding secondary gain

First, in the group health setting, some services, such as testing, are considered not medically necessary. In the Worker's Compensation area, however, providers may be pressured to provide these services in an attempt to get an employee to return to work sooner, or to obtain objective evidence that the worker is not injured. The incentives in Worker's Compensation are materially different than those in other aspects of the health care system. Providers must have a working knowledge of occupational medicine in structuring a Worker's Compensation managed care system. Likewise, because medical treatment is more expensive than disability costs in some instances, providers may be discouraged from giving injured workers necessary treatment.

Second, in Worker's Compensation systems, claims adjusters with no medical training have traditionally made determinations about the medical necessity of care and treatment. Although this may have been the practice when workers could simply receive treatment on credit, it is not acceptable standard of care medical decision-making to have nonphysicians making such decisions. This practice will no longer be tolerated in an environment where access to care is tightly controlled by managed care systems. As the law governing medical decision-making has been uniformly applied to all participants in the health care system, only qualified, medically trained practitioners may function as reviewers. Accordingly, emergency physicians must ask about the qualifications of any reviewer, particularly when treating an injured worker. An emergency physician should never accept a medical review decision by a nonphysician and should always insist on speaking to a qualified physician reviewer.

Third, in many states, a Worker's Compensation appeals board, or its equivalent, may exist to adjudicate disputes. Appeal mechanisms may or may not be available under state law. Emergency physicians should know their states' requirements as applied to Worker's Compensation and the use of managed care techniques. Fourth, emergency physicians are likely to be familiar with some Worker's Compensation reporting requirements, for example, physician's first report of occupational injury. Development of a state-based managed Workers' Compensation system may require additional reporting requirements.

Outcome Data and Physician Profiling

"... There are three types of lies: lies, damn lies and statistics." — Mark Twain.

The health care marketplace is demanding tools that can be used to judge the performance of providers in delivering quality medical care in a cost-effective and efficient manner.

Performance-based profiles, or report cards, are being used either to augment or supplant the traditional case-by-case peer review process. The theory behind performance-based profiling is that it can detect trends where physicians may be deviating from certain norms, such as length of hospital stay or the number of tests ordered for certain complaints.

Similarly, outcome data are being touted by some health care professionals and managed care systems as a panacea for the problems associated with assessing and comparing providers' performances. However, the current state of the art of physician profiling using outcome data is fraught with difficulties, including the following:

- Severity adjusting, for example, coexisting illnesses, compliance, patient socioeconomic status, home support, preventive services, baseline functional status.
- The qualifications of personnel who extract the data, as there is no current acceptable, standardized methodology for handling such data.
- When, where, and how the data are obtained. Without complete and accurate data, it is impossible to assess physicians' competence or to compare their performance accurately with other physicians.

Managed care systems and hospitals are increasingly accepting outcome data as a tool to judge performance and formulate report cards on physicians. There is a growing industry marketing computer software to third-party payers that claims to use legitimate profiling systems to produce meaningful and credible report cards. The real danger is that these profile systems may be defective or geared only to measuring costs, not quality of patient care. These systems may not be severity adjusted (if indeed it is possible to severity adjust) and may not take into consideration changing standards of care. They also may not take into consideration physician support services or the lack thereof, may use inappropriate methodology and inadequately developed databases to generate their norms, or may be otherwise defective. For example, data collected geographically instead of nationally would be defective, as would be data collected from Medicare or Medicaid patients then extrapolated to other groups of patients.

Data collected over a period of years that do not reflect changing and current standards of care may be another problem. To adhere to the changing applicable standard of care, physicians may need to order more expensive tests or eliminate or limit expensive testing. Legitimate physician variability and clinical judgment may not be permitted or encouraged.[35] Hospitals or managed care organizations may use cost-oriented report card systems to determine which physicians or physician groups are hired, fired, or disciplined or to decide which reimbursement claims are paid.

Providers must understand the limits of these new profiling systems and how they may be misused, especially if outcome data are used to justify provider termination. As such, the topic should be discussed when negotiating a contract with a managed care system. For example, some providers may wish to negotiate provisions that state that there will be no negative repercussions against a physician for a "bad report card" generated by these systems without due process and objective, case-by-case peer review.

Again, appropriate documentation in the patient's chart, justifying the physician's workup by documenting the medical necessity of care, is a key element in any future hearing or litigation (Appendix 4). Physicians should insist in any hearing that a case-by-case analysis be conducted and that a qualified reviewer examine the charts for adherence to the standard of care.

In certain situations, physicians may need to remind the HMO about its exposure to bad faith liability (and punitive damages awards) if it uses outcome data to pressure emergency physicians to deny patients access to timely, medically necessary care.

Notwithstanding the above, outcome data can be used legitimately as a screening tool. When a physician's practice patterns are found to deviate significantly from a legitimately developed norm, such a system could trigger a more in-depth, case-by-case, peer-reviewed analysis. However, if one jumps directly from outcome data to report cards without case-by-case peer review, the report card process may be defective and may either give the impression that a physician is more or less competent than he or she really is. Outcome data could also discourage physicians from doing an adequate workup or from treating severely ill patients for fear of having a report card that shows high medical resource utilization.

Key Points and Conclusions

"… The law is never settled until it is right. It is never right until it is just." — Unknown.

"… Never doubt that a small group of thoughtful committed citizens can change the world. Indeed, it's the only thing that ever has." — Margaret Mead.

As the nature of health care is changing, so is the liability exposure. There are tremendous marketplace forces putting pressure on emergency physicians. These forces demand quality medical care delivered in an efficient and cost-effective manner. On the other hand, these same forces at times endanger emergency physicians by placing them in untenable positions in which they may compromise patient care. The ultimate goal of the marketplace to produce cost-effective and quality medical care is laudable. Specific tools currently being used and embraced by the marketplace, such as physician profiling, economic credentialing, telephone triaging, substituting guidelines for a physician's clinical judgment, and the use of financial incentives, may not deliver efficient or quality health care.

On the other hand, review systems set up appropriately to encourage and assist physicians to adhere to a national standard of care create the opportunity to produce a higher quality of care that is both more efficient and more cost-effective. The challenges that face not only emergency medicine, but also the whole of medicine, are to have the courage to recognize what effective systems we are able to develop, use, and participate in versus identifying defective systems that must be eliminated.

References

1. *Defining Managed Care.* Seattle: Group Health Cooperative of Puget Sound; April 1993.

2. *Lowry v Henry Mayo Newhall Memorial Hospital,* 185 Cal App 3d 188 (1986).

3. *Hughes v Blue Cross of Northern California,* 215 Cal App 3d 832; 263 Cal Rptr 850 (1989).

4. *Wickline v State of California,* 192 Cal App 3d 1630, 239 Cal Rptr 810 (1986).

5. *Wilson v Blue Cross of Southern California,* 222 Cal App 3d 660, 271 Cal Rptr 876 (1990).

6. American College of Medical Quality. Ethical policies. *Focus Newsletter.* Bethesda, Md. 1996;2(1):1.

7. 61 *Am Jur* 2d Physicians and Surgeons, §110.

8. Lohr KN, ed. *Medicare: A Strategy for Quality Assurance.* Washington, DC: National Academy Press; 1990.

9. Mattson MR, ed. *Manual of Psychiatric Quality Assurance.* Washington, DC: American Psychiatric Press; 1992.

10. American Medical Association Council on Long Range Planning and Development in cooperation with the Council on Constitution and Bylaws, and the Council on Ethical and Judicial Affairs. *Policy Compendium of the American Medical Association.* Chicago: American Medical Association; 1995.

11. *Compendium of AAFP Positions on Selected Health Issues.* Kansas City, Mo: American Academy of Family Physicians; 1994-1995.

12. American Medical Association Specialty Society Practice Parameters Partnerships and Practice Parameter Forum. *Attributes to Guide the Development of Practice Parameters.* Chicago: Office of Quality Assurance and Medical Review of the American Medical Association; 1994.

13. *Implementing Practice Parameters on the Local/State/Regional Level.* Chicago: Office of Quality Assurance and Medical Review of the American Medical Association; 1994.

14. Agency for Health Care Policy and Research (AHCPR), Rockville, Md, 1997. www.ahcpr.gov.

15. Reagan ME. Medical review and the practice of medicine. *Focus Newsletter.* Bethesda, Md: American College of Medical Quality;1995; 5(1):6.

16. Health Insurance Association of America. *Code of Ethics.* Washington, DC: Health Insurance Association of America; September 1995.

17. *An Overview of NCQA Standards.* Washington, DC: National Committee for Quality Assurance; 1996.

18. National Utilization Review Standards of the American Accreditation Health Care Commission, formerly the Utilization Review Accreditation Commission; April 1994.

19. *Health Care Management Guidelines.* Seattle: Milliman & Robertson; 1994, 1996. www.milliman-hmg.com.

20. Utilization Review Regulations. *DWC Newsline.* San Francisco: Division of Worker's Compensation, State of California, July 24, 1995; Bulletin 95-11. www.dir.ca.gov/dir/workers'_compensation/dwc/dwc_newsline.html.

21. *Fox v Health Net,* Riverside Super Ct Case No. 219692.

22. *Muse v Charter Hospital of Winston-Salem, Inc.,* 452 SE2d 589, aff'd 464 SE2d 44 (1995).

23. *Hand v Tavera,* 864 SW2d 678 (1993).

24. *Utilization Review, Information on External Review Organizations.* Washington, DC: United States General Accounting Office (GAO); November 1992.

25. Medical Staff Responsibility for Emergency Department Patients. ACEP Policy Statement, approved June 1993. To obtain a copy call (800) 798-1822, touch 6, or go to www.acep.org.

26. *Humana Medical Plan, Inc. v Jacobson,* 614 So2d 520 (1992).

27. *Gilinsky v Indelicato,* 894 F Supp 86 (ED NY 1995).

28. *Miller v Sullivan,* 214 AD2d 822, 625 NYS2d 102 (1995).

29. Providing Telephone Advice From the Emergency Department. ACEP Policy Statement, approved August 1995. To obtain a copy, call (800) 798-1822, touch 6, or go to www.acep.org.

30. *United States v Tucker House, et al,* US District Court for the Eastern District of Pennsylvania.

31. 42 CFR §417.479.

32. *Grijalva v Shalala,* 946 F Supp 747 (D Ariz 1996).

33. Feds to Rewrite Medicare Rules. *AP Online,* November 6, 1996.

34. *Ardary v Aetna Health Plans,* 98 F3d 496 (9th Cir 1996).

35. Kassirer JP. The use and abuse of practice profiles. *N Engl J Med* 1994;330:634-636.

Appendix 1

Organizations you should know about

American College of Medical Quality (ACMQ)
(301) 365-3570; (800) 924-2149
- Recognized by the AMA as the specialty of physicians who have expertise in quality assurance and utilization review.
- Has a seat on the House of Delegates to the AMA.
- Certified by the Accreditation Council for Continuing Medical Education to issue CME credit for its lectures.
- Produces national standards for the medical review process.

Agency for Health Care Policy and Research (AHCPR)
(800) 358-9295
- Created by Congress in 1989.
- Purpose is research, data development, and other activities to increase quality, improve appropriateness of health care, increase effectiveness of health care, and increase access to health care.
- Key issues are cost, access, quality, and improving medical practice.
- Part of the public health care service of the U.S. Department of Health and Human Services.
- Has no enforcement capabilities.
- Works closely with the IOM.
- Involved in patient outcomes research.
- Provides patient brochures regarding questions to ask physicians, but does not tell patients what to do.
- Produces national clinical practice guidelines.

National Committee for Quality Assurance (NCQA)
(202) 628-5788
- Surveys and accredits all managed care organizations.
- An independent nonprofit institution.
- Has reviewed more than 150 managed care organizations.
- Provides certification for managed care organizations that many corporations require before contracting with these groups.

American Accreditation Health Care Commission (AAHCC), formerly known as Utilization Review Accreditation Committee (URAC)
(202) 296-0120
- A trade organization.
- Formed by private utilization review firms.
- Certifies utilization review organizations.

American Association of Health Plans (AAHP), formerly known as American Managed Care and Review Association (AMCRA)
(202) 778-3200
- A trade organization.
- Represents the interests of managed care organizations (more than 500 HMOs, PPOs, IPAs), involving 250,000 physicians and 25 million covered patients.

American Health Quality Association (AHQA), formerly known as American Peer Review Association (AMPRA)
(202) 331-5790
- A trade organization for the Medicare peer review organizations, now known as quality improvement organizations.

Juran Institute
(203) 761-1719
- A leading source of training and consulting for total quality management in the health care industry.
- Provides workshops, strategies, literature, training materials, videos.

The Diagnostic and Therapeutic Technology Assessment Project of the AMA (DATTA)
(800) 621-8335
- Provides evaluation of the safety and effectiveness of drugs, devices, and procedures.
- Started in 1982 by the AMA.
- Uses experts nominated by AMA councils, deans of medical schools, state medical societies, and national specialty societies represented in the AMA's House of Delegates.
- Undergoes extensive national peer review.

American Accreditation Program, Inc. (AAPI)
(703) 255-1200
- Credentials PPOs for quality, utilization, management, etc.
- Established January 1990.
- Funded solely by accreditation fees.

Appendix 2

Significant health care law

Hughes v Blue Cross of Northern California, **215 Cal App 3d 832;263 Cal Rptr 850 (Nov 1989).***

The medical decision-making process and reimbursements based on medical necessity must reflect a clinical standard of care practiced within the community. Third-party payers are the ones "responsible" for obtaining all relevant information before the payer can make a negative determination of medical necessity. Punitive damages are based not simply on poor judgment, but on the theory that the defective review process of oversight mechanism was rooted in established company practice.

Wickline v State of California, **192 Cal App 3d 1630; 239 Cal Rptr 810 (July 1986).***

Medical review must conform to the standard of care. Cost containment mechanisms must not corrupt medical judgment. Third-party payers can be held legally accountable when inappropriate medical decisions are made secondary to defects of the review process.

Wilson v Blue Cross of Southern California, **222 Cal App 3d 660; 271 Cal Rptr 876 (July 1990).***

Private medical review organizations can be liable for bad outcomes even if appeal mechanism is not used.

Lowry v Henry Mayo New Hall Memorial Hospital, **185 Cal App 3d 188 (1986).***

Standard of care exceeds practice parameters/criteria/guidelines as the ultimate benchmark in determining appropriate medical decision-making. A practice parameter does not equal the standard of care and is only to be considered as a guideline in helping a provider or reviewer make clinical or review decisions.

Corcoran v United Health Care, Inc., **965 F2d 1321 (5th Cir 1992).**

Defective medical review may be protected in group health cases covered under ERISA regulations.

Boyd v Albert Einstein Medical Center, **377 Pa Super 609, 547 A2d 1229 (1988).**

Gatekeeper and HMO can be held liable for patient's wrongful death.

Raglin v HMO Illinois, Inc., **230 Ill App 3d 642, 595 NE2d 153 (1992).***

HMO cannot be held vicariously liable for a physician's malpractice when the HMO did not control the physician's activities.

Chase v Independent Practice Association, Inc., **31 Mass App Ct 661, 583 NE2d 251 (1991).***

IPA was not vicariously liable for physician's malpractice.

Nazay v Miller, **949 F2d 1323 (3rd Cir 1991).***

Patient's failure to comply with utilization management procedures can result in financial penalties.

Weaver v Phoenix Home Life Mutual Insurance Co., **990 F2d 154 (4th Cir 1993).***

Basis for adverse utilization management decisions must be disclosed to patient.

Fox v Health Net, **Riverside County Superior Court (12/28/93).**

Defective medical decision-making process resulted in punitive damages against managed care organization.

Elam v College Park Hospital, **132 Cal App 3d 332.***

If a hospital and physician do not have an employer-employee relationship, the hospital can still be held accountable for the physician's negligent acts if the hospital was negligent in the selection and credentialing of the physician.

Darling v Charleston Community Memorial Hospital, **33 Ill 2d 326, 211 NE2d 253.**

Hospitals have direct corporate liability for acts of physician negligence.

Ferguson v New England Mutual Life Insurance Co., **196 Ill App 3d 766 (1990).***

Physician held financially liable for incorrect insurance benefit interpretation for a patient.

Muse v Charter Hospital of Winston-Salem, Inc., 452 SE2d 589, aff'd 464 SE2d 44 (1995).*

Psychiatric hospital fined $7 million in compensatory and punitive damages after the court found that the hospital pressured a physician to discharge his patient, based on financial ramifications to the hospital.

United States v Tucker House

Application of federal false claims (billing) law against a provider for giving inadequate (substandard) quality of care without any billing irregularities. Federal government's position suggests that inadequate provision of one or more categories of care may become tantamount to a failure to provide any care whatsoever. *Qui tam* (whistle-blower) provision of the False Claims Act may stimulate more false claims acts.

Grijalva v Shalala, 946 F Supp 747 (D Az 1996).

Medicare HMOs must ensure beneficiaries due process by providing sufficient information and assistance with appeals.

Ardary v Aetna Health Plan, 98 F3d 496 (9th Cir 1996).

Wrongful death action against Medicare HMO not preempted by Medicare Act.

* Appellate court decisions

Appendix 3

Sample informed rights of patients in the emergency department

(Addressograph)   (Date)

In accordance with federal law, the medical personnel in the emergency department at
_____ Medical Center have performed a medical screening examination to determine whether your medical condition is stable or constitutes an emergency. This has been done
before contacting your insurance company, or "payer" (HMO, insurer, utilization review organization,
etc.).

After informing your payer of your medical condition (at _____AM/PM), _____,
representing the payer, has stated his/her belief that, at this time, your condition is stable and that
further emergency department assessment and/or treatment is not medically necessary at this facility (or that your payer will retrospectively review whether your visit to the emergency department was
medically necessary). This may mean that your payer may not reimburse the emergency department
or the emergency physicians for their charges (screening examination, other treatment). You could be
held ultimately responsible for part or all of the medical bill.

If you (we) disagree with your payer's initial assessment of your condition and that your presenting
complaints require a screening examination based on the applicable standard of care at this emergency department and that further treatment is required, then it is within your legal rights to appeal
to your payer and, if necessary, to the appropriate Department of Consumer Affairs, the Insurance
Commissioner of the State of _____, and _____
(your state's agency that regulates the payer).

If you so desire and request further medical treatment at this facility, we will be happy to accommodate you. However, you may be ultimately responsible for the hospital and physician fees if your
payer determines that the emergency department workup and treatment are not medically necessary
and will not pay for part or all of the emergency department medical bill.

Having read the above and signed, you understand that you have had a medical screening examination (and stabilization where necessary). If you decide to leave our facility now, it will represent an
informed decision by you to do so.

_____   _____
Signature of patient or responsible party   Date and time

_____   _____
Signature of witness and title   Date and time

Appendix 4

Sample emergency medicine review discussion letter

This letter is to be used when discussing the medical necessity of medical services that require pre-certification, concurrent review, reimbursement, or retrospective review. It is also used when an emergency physician has been unfairly profiled (deselected/negative report card) as a result of alleged overutilization of medical resources.

(Emergency Department's Letterhead)

(Date)

To Whom It May Concern:

This letter serves to discuss the medical care and treatment of a patient, Ms./r._____, during his/her emergency department visit of_____(date). I appreciate your concern about the inappropriate use of medical services and supplies. I can assure you that the _____ Emergency Medical Group is also concerned about appropriate medical quality of care delivered in an efficient and cost-effective manner.

In this particular case, however, there was medical necessity for _____ *(place here all that is applicable: admission, nontransfer, use of labs, x-rays, procedures, screening examination, etc.)* based on the applicable standard of care and federal law regarding the assessment, stabilization, and transfer (defined by HCFA as movement of a patient, including discharge) of patients. If this medically necessary care had not been rendered, the quality of patient care would have suffered, with possible resulting injury to the patient, a poor outcome, and a violation of the standard of care.

This letter contains additional information you will want to consider in making your definitive decision of medical necessity. This information reflects the appropriate medical decision-making of the emergency physician. The history and information available to the emergency physician at the time the patient first presented to the emergency department were as follows: *(Details of the patient's presentation, time and date of treatment, and the information available or lacking, such as a patient who was a poor historian or did not have his medications, lack of a medical chart, PMD not available for data-gathering).*

_____

_____

_____

_____

_____

_____

_____

_____

If you do not believe this additional information establishes medical necessity based on the applicable standard of care, please provide me/us with your written detailed clinical rationale, supported by scientific, evidence-based medical information, along with the name and specialty of the physician who reviewed this case and whether the person is board certified.

In conclusion, I would appreciate a review of this particular case by a board-certified, clinically practicing, specialty-matched, currently licensed physician who will make the review decision based on the applicable clinical standard of care and appropriate federal law. This would meet the medical review standards of nationally recognized review organizations (AAHCC and NCQA), ACMQ, applicable state and federal regulatory policies and statutes, and recent court decisions *(select from Hughes v Blue Cross of Northern California, Wickline v State of California, Wilson v Blue Cross of Southern California, and Muse v Charter Hospital of Winston-Salem, Inc., or other applicable authority).*

(*Use the following only as a last resort:*) If your review organization cannot meet the above review standards and you continue to deny medically necessary emergency department services, we will have to refer your organization and the reviewers to the above agencies, along with the appropriate documentation. I trust that this will not be necessary, and the medical review will be conducted along the lines outlined above.

Index

I

illiteracy, and communication barriers, 32-33

image, of emergency physicians, 9-13

immunity
  from antitrust law, 259-260
  and Good Samaritan statutes, 234-235
  in peer review, 59-60, 180-181, 183-186
  for review bodies, 60-61

incident reports, 309-311
  and confidentiality, 309
  and credentialing, 310
  preventing discovery, 310-311

infection control, 97-106 (see also
  environmental risks; facility design)
  airborne transmission, 98-99
  and biohazards, 102
  bloodborne infection, needlesticks, 99-102
  education, communication for, 102
  and facility design, 99
  and hepatitis B exposure, 103, 105
  and HIV exposure, 103
  medical-legal issues, 105
  potential for infection, 98
  universal precautions, 102-103

information management, 111-116
  amended x-rays, 111-114
  and automation, 115-116
  laboratory follow-up, 114

informed consent, 203-209
  and communication barriers, 30
  duty to obtain, 206
  granting consent, 207
  and liability, 207-208
  medical-legal issues, 204-205
  and medical records, 296-297
  and refusal of care, 400-401
  and rules of evidence, 247-248
  and standards of disclosure, 205-206
  types of, 205

in-house emergencies, 313-319
  documentation of, 317
  and insurance coverage, 316-317
  responsibility for patient care, 314-316

injections, as high-risk issue, 472-473

insurance (see liability insurance)

interpretation services, 31-32

intoxicated patient, as high-risk clinical
  presentation, 473-474

J

Jehovah's Witnesses, and refusal of care, 407-408

Johnson v University of Chicago Hospitals, 357, 437, 496

Joint Commission on Accreditation of
  Healthcare Organizations (JCAHO)
  and adverse patient occurrences, 311
  clinical practice guidelines, 120, 123
  and disaster preparedness, 108
  and emergency medical record
    requirements, 296
  and orientation, 38
  and patient rights, 31
  and peer review, 179, 190-191

joint defense, 136

joint and several liability, 147-151
  common law theory of, 147
  effects of on case management, 150
  impact on insurance limits, 150-151
  medical-legal issues, 148
  and state statutes, 149-150

L

language, and communication barriers, 31-32

latex, as environmental risk, 90-91

left without being seen (LWBS), 399, 405-406, 424-425

left without treatment (LWOT), 399, 405-406, 424-425

liability insurance (see also malpractice
  lawsuits; settlement, theories of)
  and clinical practice guidelines, 123-126
  definitions, 131-132
  insured's consent-to-settle right, 136-137
  joint, several liability, 147-151
  and joint defense, 136
  negligence versus responsibility, 135-136
  NPDB effect on, 137-138
  and settlement, 139-145

living wills, 409-410, 436

*Lowry v Henry Mayo Newhall Memorial
  Hospital,* 514, 527

M

major trauma, as high-risk clinical
  presentation, 483-484

malpractice lawsuits, risk (see also civil law;
  criminal law; liability insurance; settlement,
  theories of)
  and altered medical records, 285-286
  and civil commitment, 221-222
  and civil law, 153-164
  and clinical practice guidelines, 124-125
  defined, 154